T0304308

Essays in Econometrics

This book, and its companion volume in the Econometric Society Monographs series (ESM No. 33), present a collection of papers by Clive W. J. Granger. His contributions to economics and econometrics, many of them seminal, span more than four decades and touch on all aspects of time series analysis. The papers assembled in this volume explore topics in spectral analysis, seasonality, nonlinearity, methodology, and forecasting. Those in the companion volume investigate themes in causality, integration and cointegration, and long memory. The two volumes contain the original articles as well as an introduction written by the editors.

Eric Ghysels is Edward M. Bernstein Professor of Economics and Professor of Finance at the University of North Carolina, Chapel Hill. He previously taught at the University of Montreal and Pennsylvania State University. Professor Ghysels's main research interests are time series econometrics and finance. He has served on the editorial boards of several academic journals and has published more than sixty articles in leading economics, finance, and statistics journals.

Norman R. Swanson is Associate Professor of Economics at Texas A&M University and formerly taught at Pennsylvania State University. He received his doctorate at the University of California, San Diego, where he studied theoretical, financial, and macroeconometrics under Clive Granger's tutelage. Professor Swanson is an associate editor for numerous academic journals and is the author of more than thirty refereed articles and research papers.

Mark W. Watson is Professor of Economics and Public Affairs at the Woodrow Wilson School, Princeton University. He previously served on the faculties of Harvard and Northwestern Universities and as associate editor of *Econometrica*, the *Journal of Monetary Economics*, and the *Journal of Applied Econometrics* and currently is a Research Associate of the National Bureau of Economic Research (NBER) and consultant at the Federal Reserve Bank of Richmond. Professor Watson is currently a Fellow of the Econometric Society and holds research grants from NBER and the National Science Foundation.

Econometric Society Monographs No. 32

Editors:
Peter Hammond, Stanford University
Alberto Holly, University of Lausanne

The Econometric Society is an international society for the advancement of economic theory in relation to statistics and mathematics. The Econometric Society Monograph Series is designed to promote the publication of original research contributions of high quality in mathematical economics and theoretical and applied econometrics.

CLIVE WILLIAM JOHN GRANGER

Essays in Econometrics
Collected Papers of Clive W. J. Granger

Volume I: Spectral Analysis, Seasonality, Nonlinearity, Methodology, and Forecasting

Edited by

Eric Ghysels
University of North Carolina at Chapel Hill

Norman R. Swanson
Texas A&M University

Mark W. Watson
Princeton University

CAMBRIDGE
UNIVERSITY PRESS

CAMBRIDGE
UNIVERSITY PRESS

32 Avenue of the Americas, New York NY 10013-2473, USA

Cambridge University Press is part of the University of Cambridge.

It furthers the University's mission by disseminating knowledge in the pursuit of education, learning and research at the highest international levels of excellence.

www.cambridge.org
Information on this title: www.cambridge.org/9780521772976

First published 2001

A catalogue record for this publication is available from the British Library

Library of Congress Cataloguing in Publication data
Granger, C. W. J. (Clive William John), 1934–
    Essays in econometrics: collected papers of Clive W. J. Granger / edited by Eric Ghysels, Norman R. Swanson, Mark W. Watson.
        p.   cm. – (Econometric Society monographs; v. 32)
    Contents: v. 1. Spectral analysis, seasonality, nonlinearity, methodology, and forecasting – v. 2. Causality, integration and cointegration, and long memory.
        ISBN 0-521-79697-0 (set : pbk.) – ISBN 0-521-77297-4 (v. 1) – ISBN 0-521-77496-9 (v. 1 : pbk.) – ISBN 0-521-79207-X (v. 2) – ISBN 0-521-79649-0 (v. 2 : pbk.)
        1. Econometrics.   I. Title: Collected papers of Clive W. J. Granger.   II. Ghysels, Eric, 1956–   III. Swanson, Norman R. (Norman Rasmus), 1964–   IV. Watson, Mark W. V. Title.   VI. Series.

HB139.G69   2001
330´.01´5195–dc21   00-034306

ISBN 978-0-521-77297-6 Hardback
ISBN 978-0-521-77496-3 Paperback

To Clive W. J. Granger:
Mentor, Colleague, and Friend.
We are honored to present this selection
of his research papers.

E. G.
N. R. S.
M. W. W.

Contents

Acknowledgments

Grateful acknowledgment is made to the following publishers and sources for permission to reprint the articles cited here.

ACADEMIC PRESS

"Non-Linear Time Series Modeling," with A. Andersen, *Applied Time Series Analysis*, edited by David F. Findley, 1978, Academic Press, New York, 25–38.
"Time Series Analysis of Error Correction Models," with A. A. Weiss, in *Studies in Econometrics: Time Series and Multivariate Statistics*, edited by S. Karlin, T. Amemiya, and L. A. Goodman, Academic Press, New York, 1983, 255–78.

AMERICAN STATISTICAL ASSOCIATION

"Is Seasonal Adjustment a Linear or Nonlinear Data-Filtering Process?" with E. Ghysels and P. L. Siklos, *Journal of Business and Economic Statistics*, 14, 1996, 374–86.
"Semiparametric Estimates of the Relation Between Weather and Electricity Sales," with R. F. Engle, J. Rice, and A. Weiss, *Journal of the American Statistical Association*, 81, 1986, 310–20.
"Estimation of Common Long-Memory Components in Cointegrated Systems," with J. Gonzalo, *Journal of Business and Economic Statistics*, 13, 1995, 27–35.

BLACKWELL PUBLISHERS

"Time Series Modeling and Interpretation," with M. J. Morris, *Journal of the Royal Statistical Society, Series A*, 139, 1976, 246–57.
"Forecasting Transformed Series," with P. Newbold, *Journal of the Royal Statistical Society, Series B*, 38, 1976, 189–203.

"Developments in the Study of Cointegrated Economic Variables," *Oxford Bulletin of Economics and Statistics*, 48, 1986, 213–28.

"Separation in Cointegrated Systems and Persistent-Transitory Decompositions," with N. Haldrup, *Oxford Bulletin of Economics and Statistics*, 59, 1997, 449–64.

"Nonlinear Transformations of Integrated Time Series," with J. Hallman, *Journal of Time Series Analysis*, 12, 1991, 207–24.

"Long Memory Series with Attractors," with J. Hallman, *Oxford Bulletin of Economics and Statistics*, 53, 1991, 11–26.

"Further Developments in the Study of Cointegrated Variables," with N. R. Swanson, *Oxford Bulletin of Economics and Statistics*, 58, 1996, 374–86.

"An Introduction to Long-Memory Time Series Models and Fractional Differencing," with R. Joyeux, *Journal of Time Series Analysis*, 1, 1980, 15–29.

BUREAU OF THE CENSUS

"Seasonality: Causation, Interpretation and Implications," in *Seasonal Analysis of Economic Time Series*, Economic Research Report, ER-1, edited by A. Zellner, 1979, Bureau of the Census, 33–46.

"Forecasting White Noise," in *Applied Time Series Analysis of Economic Data*, Proceedings of the Conference on Applied Time Series Analysis of Economic Data, October 1981, edited by A. Zellner, U.S. Department of Commerce, Bureau of the Census, Government Printing Office, 1983, 308–14.

CAMBRIDGE UNIVERSITY PRESS

"The ET Interview: Professor Clive Granger," *Econometric Theory*, 13, 1997, 253–303.

"Implications of Aggregation with Common Factors," *Econometric Theory*, 3, 1987, 208–22.

CHARTERED INSTITUTION OF WATER AND ENVIRONMENTAL MANAGEMENT

"Estimating the Probability of Flooding on a Tidal River," *Journal of the Institution of Water Engineers*, 13, 1959, 165–74.

THE ECONOMETRICS SOCIETY

"The Typical Spectral Shape of an Economic Variable," *Econometrica*, 34, 1966, 150–61.

"Modeling Nonlinear Relationships Between Extended-Memory Variables," *Econometrica*, 63, 1995, 265–79.

"Near Normality and Some Econometric Models," *Econometrica*, 47, 1979, 781–4.

"Investigating Causal Relations by Econometric Models and Cross-Spectral Methods," *Econometrica*, 37, 1969, 424–38. Reprinted in *Rational Expectations*, edited by T. Sargent and R. Lucas, 1981, University of Minnesota Press, Minneapolis.

"Advertising and Aggregate Consumption: An Analysis of Causality," with R. Ashley and R. Schmalensee, *Econometrica*, 48, 1980, 1149–67.

"Co-Integration and Error-Correction: Representation, Estimation and Testing," with R. Engle, *Econometrica*, 55, 1987, 251–76.

ELSEVIER

"Testing for Neglected Nonlinearity in Time Series Models: A Comparison of Neural Network Methods and Alternative Tests," with T.-H. Lee and H. White, *Journal of Econometrics*, 56, 1993, 269–90.

"On The Invertibility of Time Series Models," with A. Andersen, *Stochastic Processes and Their Applications*, 8, 1978, 87–92.

"Comments on the Evaluation of Policy Models," with M. Deutsch, *Journal of Policy Modeling*, 14, 1992, 397–416.

"Invited Review: Combining Forecasts – Twenty Years Later," *Journal of Forecasting*, 8, 1989, 167–73.

"The Combination of Forecasts Using Changing Weights," with M. Deutsch and T. Teräsvirta, *International Journal of Forecasting*, 10, 1994, 47–57.

"Short-Run Forecasts of Electricity Loads and Peaks," with R. Ramanathan, R. F. Engle, F. Vahid-Araghi, and C. Brace, *International Journal of Forecasting*, 13, 1997, 161–74.

"Some Recent Developments in a Concept of Causality," *Journal of Econometrics*, 39, 1988, 199–211.

"Spurious Regressions in Econometrics," with P. Newbold, *Journal of Econometrics*, 2, 1974, 111–20.

"Some Properties of Time Series Data and Their Use in Econometric Model Specification," *Journal of Econometrics*, 16, 1981, 121–30.

"Seasonal Integration and Cointegration," with S. Hylleberg, R. F. Engle, and B. S. Yoo, *Journal of Econometrics*, 44, 1990, 215–38.

"Long-Memory Relationships and the Aggregation of Dynamic Models," *Journal of Econometrics*, 14, 1980, 227–38.

"A Long Memory Property of Stock Market Returns and a New Model," with Z. Ding and R. F. Engle, *Journal of Empirical Finance*, 1, 1993, 83–106.

FEDERAL RESERVE BANK OF MINNEAPOLIS

"The Time Series Approach to Econometric Model Building," with P. Newbold, in *New Methods in Business Cycle Research*, edited by C. Sims, 1977, Federal Reserve Bank of Minneapolis.

HELBING AND LICHTENHAHN VERLAG

"Spectral Analysis of New York Stock Market Prices," with O. Morgenstern, *Kyklos*, 16, 1963, 1–27. Reprinted in *Random Character of Stock Market Prices*, edited by P. H. Cootner, 1964, MIT Press, Cambridge, MA.

JOHN WILEY & SONS, LTD.

"Using the Correlation Exponent to Decide Whether an Economic Series Is Chaotic," with T. Liu and W. P. Heller, *Journal of Applied Econometrics*, 7, 1992, S25–40. Reprinted in *Nonlinear Dynamics, Chaos, and Econometrics*, edited by M. H. Pesaran and S. M. Potter, 1993, Wiley, Chichester.

"Can We Improve the Perceived Quality of Economic Forecasts?" *Journal of Applied Econometrics*, 11, 1996, 455–73.

MACMILLAN PUBLISHERS, LTD.

"Prediction with a Generalized Cost of Error Function," *Operational Research Quarterly*, 20, 1969, 199–207.

"The Combination of Forecasts, Using Changing Weights," with M. Deutsch and T. Teräsvirta, *International Journal of Forecasting*, 10, 1994, 45–57.

MIT PRESS

"Testing for Causality: A Personal Viewpoint," *Journal of Economic Dynamics and Control*, 2, 1980, 329–52.

"A Cointegration Analysis of Treasury Bill Yields," with A. D. Hall and H. M. Anderson, *Review of Economics and Statistics*, 74, 1992, 116–26.

"Spectral Analysis of New York Stock Market Prices," with O. Morgenstern, *Kyklos*, 16, 1963, 1–27. Reprinted in *Random Character of Stock Market Prices*, edited by P. H. Cootner, 1964, MIT Press, Cambridge, MA.

TAYLOR & FRANCIS, LTD.

"Some Comments on the Evaluation of Economic Forecasts," with P. Newbold, *Applied Economics*, 5, 1973, 35–47.

Contributors

A. Andersen
Department of Economic Statistics
University of Sydney
Sydney
Australia

H. M. Anderson
Department of Econometrics
Monash University
Australia

R. Ashley
University of California, San Diego
La Jolla, CA
U.S.A.

J. M. Bates
Bramcote
Nottingham
United Kingdom

C. Brace
Puget Sound Power and Light Company
Bellevue, WA
U.S.A.

M. Deutsch
Department of Economics
University of California, San Diego
La Jolla, CA
U.S.A.

Z. Ding
Frank Russell Company
Tacoma, WA
U.S.A.

R. F. Engle
Department of Economics
University of California, San Diego
La Jolla, CA
U.S.A.

E. Ghysels
Department of Economics
University of North Carolina at Chapel
  Hill
Chapel Hill, NC
U.S.A.

J. Gonzalo
Department of Economics
University Carlos III
Madrid
Spain

C. W. J. Granger
Department of Economics
University of California, San Diego
La Jolla, CA 92093

N. Haldrup
Department of Economics
University of Aarhus
Aarhus
Denmark

A. D. Hall
School of Finance and Economics
University of Technology
Sydney
Australia

J. Hallman
Federal Reserve Board
Washington, DC
U.S.A.

W. P. Heller
Department of Economics
University of California, San Diego
La Jolla, CA
U.S.A.

S. Hylleberg
Department of Economics
University of Aarhus
Aarhus
Denmark

R. Joyeux
School of Economics and Financial
    Studies
Macquarie University
Sydney
Australia

T.-H. Lee
Department of Economics
University of California, Riverside
Riverside, CA
U.S.A.

T. Lui
Department of Economics
Ball State University
Muncie, IN
U.S.A.

O. Morgenstern (deceased)
Princeton University
Princeton, NJ
U.S.A.

M. J. Morris
University of East Anglia
United Kingdom

P. Newbold
Department of Economics
Nottingham University
Nottingham
United Kingdom

P. C. B. Phillips
Cowles Foundation for Research in
    Economics
Yale University
New Haven, CT
U.S.A.

R. Ramanathan
Department of Economics
University of California, San Diego
La Jolla, CA
U.S.A.

J. Rice
Department of Statistics
University of California, Berkeley
Berkeley, CA
U.S.A.

R. Schmalensee
Sloan School of Management
Massachusetts Institute of Technology
Cambridge, MA
U.S.A.

P. L. Siklos
Department of Economics
Wilfrid Laurier University
Waterloo, Ontario
Canada

N. R. Swanson
Department of Economics
Texas A&M University
College Station, TX
U.S.A.

T. Teräsvirta
School of Finance and Economics
University of Technology
Sydney
Australia

F. Vahid-Araghi
Department of Econometrics
Monash University
Australia

M. Watson
Department of Economics
Princeton University
Princeton, NJ
U.S.A.

A. A. Weiss
Department of Economics
University of Southern California
Los Angeles, CA
U.S.A.

H. White
Department of Economics
University of California, San Diego
La Jolla, CA
U.S.A.

B. S. Yoo
Yonsei University
Seoul
South Korea

Introduction
Volume I

At the beginning of the twentieth century, there was very little fundamental theory of time series analysis and surely very few economic time
series data. Autoregressive models and moving average models were
introduced more or less simultaneously and independently by the British
statistician Yule (1921, 1926, 1927) and the Russian statistician Slutsky
(1927). The mathematical foundations of stationary stochastic processes
were developed by Wold (1938), Kolmogorov (1933, 1941a, 1941b),
Khintchine (1934), and Mann and Wald (1943). Thus, modern time series
analysis is a mere eight decades old. Clive W. J. Granger has been
working in the field for nearly half of its young life. His ideas and insights
have had a fundamental impact on statistics, econometrics, and dynamic
economic theory.

Granger summarized his research activity in a recent ET Interview
(Phillips 1997), which appears as the first reprint in this volume, by
saying, "I plant a lot of seeds, a few of them come up, and most of them
do not." Many of the seeds that he planted now stand tall and majestic
like the Torrey Pines along the California coastline just north of the
University of California, San Diego, campus in La Jolla, where he has
been an economics faculty member since 1974. Phillips notes in the ET
Interview that "It is now virtually impossible to do empirical work in
time series econometrics without using some of his [Granger's] methods
or being influenced by some of his ideas." Indeed, applied time series
econometricians come across at least one of his path-breaking ideas
almost on a daily basis. For example, many of his contributions in the
areas of spectral analysis, long memory, causality, forecasting, spurious
regression, and cointegration are seminal. His influence on the profession continues with no apparent signs of abatement.

SPECTRAL METHODS

In his ET Interview, Granger explains that early in his career he was
confronted with many applied statistical issues from various disciplines

because he was the only statistician on the campus of the University of Nottingham, where he completed his PhD in statistics and served as lecturer for a number of years. This led to his first publications, which were not in the field of economics. Indeed, the first reprint in Volume II of this set contains one of his first published works, a paper in the field of hydrology. Granger's first influential work in time series econometrics emerged from his research with Michio Hatanaka. Both were working under the supervision of Oskar Morgenstern at Princeton and were guided by John Tukey. Cramér (1942) had developed the spectral decomposition of weakly stationary processes, and the 1950s and early 1960s were marked by intense research efforts devoted to spectral analysis. Many prominent scholars of the time, including Milton Friedman, John von Neumann, and Oskar Morgenstern, saw much promise in the application of Fourier analysis to economic data. In 1964, Princeton University Press published a monograph by Granger and Hatanaka, which was the first systematic and rigorous treatment of spectral analysis in the field of economic time series. Spectral methods have the appealing feature that they do not require the specification of a model but instead follow directly from the assumption of stationarity. Interestingly, more than three decades after its initial publication, the book remains a basic reference in the field.

The work of Granger and Hatanaka was influential in many dimensions. The notion of business cycle fluctuations had been elaborately discussed in the context of time series analysis for some time. Spectral analysis provided new tools and yielded fundamental new insights into this phenomenon. Today, macroeconomists often refer to business cycle *frequencies*, and a primary starting point for the analysis of business cycles is still the application of frequency domain methods. In fact, advanced textbooks in macroeconomics, such as Sargent (1987), devote an entire chapter to spectral analysis. The dominant feature of the spectrum of most economic time series is that most of the power is at the lower frequencies. There is no single pronounced business cycle peak; instead, there are a wide number of moderately sized peaks over a large range of cycles between four and eight years in length. Granger (1966) dubbed this shape the "typical spectral shape" of an economic variable. A predecessor to Granger's 1966 paper entitled "The Typical Spectral Shape of an Economic Variable" is his joint paper with Morgenstern published in 1963, which is entitled "Spectral Analysis of New York Stock Market Prices." Both papers are representative of Granger's work in the area of spectral analysis and are reproduced as the first set of papers following the ET Interview.

The paper with Morgenstern took a fresh look at the random walk hypothesis for stock prices, which had been advanced by the French mathematician M. L. Bachelier (1900). Granger and Morgenstern estimated spectra of return series of several major indices of stocks listed on the New York Stock Exchange. They showed that business cycle and seasonal variations were unimportant for return series, as in every case the spectrum was roughly flat at almost all frequencies. However, they also documented evidence that did not support the random walk model. In particular, they found that very long-run movements were not adequately explained by the model. This is interesting because the random walk hypothesis was associated with definitions of efficiency of financial markets for many years (e.g., see the classic work of Samuelson 1965 and Fama 1970). The Granger and Morgenstern paper is part of a very important set of empirical papers written during the early part of the 1960s, which followed the early work of Cowles (1933). Other related papers include Alexander (1961, 1964), Cootner (1964), Fama (1965), Mandelbrot (1963), and Working (1960). Today, the long-term predictability of asset returns is a well-established empirical stylized fact, and research in the area remains very active (e.g., see Campbell, Lo, and MacKinlay 1997 for recent references).

SEASONALITY

Seasonal fluctuations were also readily recognized from the spectrum, and the effect of seasonal adjustment on economic data was therefore straightforward to characterize. Nerlove (1964, 1965) used spectral techniques to analyze the effects of various seasonal adjustment procedures. His approach was to compute spectra of unadjusted and adjusted series and to examine the cross spectrum of the two series. Nerlove's work took advantage of the techniques Granger and Hatanaka had so carefully laid out in their monograph. Since then, many papers that improve these techniques have been written. They apply the techniques to the study of seasonal cycles and the design of seasonal adjustment filters. For example, many significant insights have been gained by viewing seasonal adjustment procedures as optimal linear signal extraction filters (e.g., see Hannan 1967; Cleveland and Tiao 1976; Pierce 1979; and Bell 1984, among others). At the same time, there has been a perpetual debate about the merits of seasonal adjustment, and since the creation of the X-11 program, many improvements have been made and alternative procedures have been suggested. The Census X-11 program was the product of several decades of research. Its development was begun in the early 1930s by researchers at the National Bureau of Economic Research (NBER) (see, for example, Macaulay 1931), and it emerged as a fully operational procedure in the mid 1960s, in large part due to the work by Julius Shiskin and his collaborators at the U.S. Bureau of the Census (see Shiskin et al. 1967). During the 1960s and 1970s, numerous papers were written on the topic of seasonality, including important papers by Sims (1974) and Wallis (1974). Granger's (1979) paper, "Seasonality: Causation,

Interpretation and Implications," is the first of two papers on the topic of seasonality included in this volume. It was written for a major conference on seasonality, which took place in the late 1970s, and appeared in a book edited by Zellner (1979). In this paper, he asks the pointed question, "Why adjust?" and gives a very balanced view of the merits and drawbacks of seasonal adjustment. The paper remains one of the best reflections on the issue of seasonality and seasonal adjustment. The second paper in this subsection, "Is Seasonal Adjustment a Linear or a Nonlinear Data-Filtering Process?," written with Ghysels and Siklos (1996), also deals with a pointed question that was initially posed by Young (1968). The question is: Are seasonal adjustment procedures (approximately) linear data transformations? The answer to this question touches on many fundamental issues, such as the treatment of seasonality in regression (cf. Sims 1974; Wallis 1974) and the theory of seasonal adjustment. The paper shows that the widely applied X-11 program is a highly nonlinear filter.

NONLINEARITY

The book by Box and Jenkins (1970) pushed time series analysis into a central role in economics. At the time of its publication, the theory of stationary linear time series processes was well understood, as evidenced by the flurry of textbooks written during the late 1960s and the 1970s, such as Anderson (1971), Fuller (1976), Granger and Newbold (1977), Hannan (1970), Nerlove et al. (1979), and Priestley (1981). However, many areas of time series analysis fell beyond the scope of linear stationary processes and were not well understood. These areas included nonstationarity and long memory (covered in Volume II) and nonlinear models. Four papers on nonlinearity in time series analysis are reproduced in Volume I and are representative of Granger's important work in this area. Because the class of nonlinear models is virtually without bound, one is left with the choice of either letting the data speak (and suffering the obvious dangers of overfitting) or relying on economic theory to yield the functional form of nonlinear economic relationships. Unfortunately, most economic theories provide only partial descriptions, with blanks that need to be filled in by exploratory statistical techniques. The papers in this section address the statistical foundations of nonlinear modeling and some of the classical debates in the literature of nonlinear modeling.

The first paper, "Non-Linear Time Series Modeling," describes the statistical underpinnings of a particular class of nonlinear models. This paper by Granger and Andersen predates their joint monograph on bilinear models (Granger and Andersen 1978). This class of models is not as popular today as it once was, although bilinear models are connected in interesting ways to models of more recent vintage, such as the class of ARCH models introduced by Engle (1982). One of the classical debates in the literature on nonlinear models pertains to the use of deterministic versus stochastic processes to describe economic phenomenon. Granger has written quite extensively on the subject of chaos (a class of deterministic models) and has expressed some strong views on its use in economics, characterizing the theory of chaos as fascinating mathematics but not of practical relevance in econometrics (see Granger 1992, 1994). Liu, Granger, and Heller (1992), in the included paper entitled "Using the Correlation Exponent to Decide Whether an Economic Series Is Chaotic," study the statistical properties of two tests designed to distinguish deterministic time series from stochastic white noise. The tests are the Grassberger-Procacia correlation exponent test and the Brock, Dechert, and Scheinkman test. Along the same lines, Lee, White, and Granger (1993), in the paper entitled "Testing for Neglected Nonlinearity in Time Series Models" examine a battery of tests for nonlinearity. Both papers are similar in that they consider basic questions of nonlinear modeling and provide useful and practical answers.

The fourth paper in this section, "Modeling Nonlinear Relationships Between Extended-Memory Variables," is the Fisher-Schultz lecture delivered at the 1993 European Meetings of the Econometric Society in Uppsala. The lecture coincided with the publication of the book by Granger and Teräsvirta (1993) on modeling nonlinear economic relationships. This book is unique in the area because it combines a rich collection of topics ranging from testing for linearity, chaos, and long memory to aggregation effects and forecasting. In his Fisher-Schultz lecture, Granger addresses the difficult area of nonlinear modeling of nonstationary processes. The paper shows that the standard classification of $I(0)$ and $I(1)$ processes in linear models is not sufficient for nonlinear functions. This observation also applies to fractional integration. As is typical, Granger makes suggestions for new areas of research, advancing the notions of short memory in mean and extended memory, and relates these ideas to earlier concepts of mixing conditions, as discussed for instance in McLeish (1978), Gallant and White (1988), and Davidson (1994). At this point, it is too early to tell whether any of these will give us the guidance toward building a unified theory of nonlinear nonstationary processes.

The final paper in this section is entitled "Semiparametric Estimates of the Relation Between Weather and Electricity Sales." This paper with Engle, Rice, and Weiss is a classic contribution to the nonparamentric and semiparametric literature and stands out as the first application of semiparametric modeling techniques to economics (previous work had been done on testing). Other early work includes Robinson (1988) and

Stock (1989). Recent advances in the area are discussed in Bierens (1990), Delgado and Robinson (1992), Granger and Teräsvirta (1993), Härdle (1990), Li (1998), Linton and Neilson (1995), and Teräsvirta, Tjostheim, and Granger (1994), to name but a few. In this classic paper, Granger and his coauthors use semiparametric models, which include a linear part and a nonparametric cubic spline function to model electricity demand. The variable that they use in the nonparametric part of their model is temperature, which is known to have an important nonlinear effect on demand.

METHODOLOGY

The title of this subsection could cover most of Granger's work; however, we use it to discuss a set of six important papers that do not fit elsewhere. The first paper is Granger and Morris's 1976 paper "Time Series Modeling and Interpretation." This is a classic in the literatures on aggregation and measurement error. The paper contains an important theorem on the time series properties of the sum of two independent series, say ARMA(p,m) + ARMA(q,n), and considers a number of special cases of practical interest, like the sum of an AR(p) and a white noise process. A key insight in the paper is that complicated time series models might arise from aggregation. The paper also contains the seeds of Granger's later paper (Granger 1987) on aggregation with common factors, which is discussed later.

The next paper, Granger and Anderson's "On the Invertibility of Time Series Models," also deals with a fundamental issue in time series. Invertibility is a familiar concept in linear models. When interpreted mechanically, invertibility refers to conditions that allow the inverse of a lag polynomial to be expressed in positive powers of the backshift operator. More fundamentally, it is a set of conditions that allows the set of shocks driving a stochastic process to be recovered from current and lagged realizations of the observed data. In linear models, the set of conditions is the same, but in nonlinear models they are not. Granger and Anderson make this point, propose the relevant definition of invertibility appropriate for both linear and nonlinear models, and discuss conditions that ensure invertibility for some specific examples.

The third paper in this section is Granger's "Near Normality and Some Econometric Models." This paper contains exact small sample versions of the central limit theorem. Granger's result is really quite amazing: Suppose x and y are two independent and identically distributed (i.i.d.) random variables and let z be a linear combination of x and y. Then the distribution of z is closer to the normal than the distribution of x and y (where the notion of "closer" is defined in terms of cumulants of the random variables). The univariate version of this result is contained in Granger (1977), and the multivariate generalization is given in the paper included here. The theorem in this paper shows that a bivariate process formed by a weighted sum of bivariate vectors whose components are i.i.d. is generally nearer-normal than its constituents, and the components of the vector will be nearer-uncorrelated.

The fourth paper, "The Time Series Approach to Econometric Model Building," is a paper joint with Paul Newbold. It was published in 1977, a time when the merits of Box-Jenkins-style time series analysis versus classical econometric methods were being debated among econometricians. Zellner and Palm (1974) is a classic paper in the area. Both papers tried to combine the insights of the Box-Jenkins approach with the structural approach to simultaneous equations modeling advocated by the Cowles Foundation. The combination of time series techniques with macroeconomic modeling received so much attention in the 1970s that it probably seems a natural approach to econometricians trained over the last two decades. Work by Sims (1980) on vector autoregression (VAR) models, the rational expectations approach in econometrics pursued by Hansen and Sargent (1980), and numerous other papers are clearly a result of and in various ways a synthesis of this debate. Of much more recent vintage is the next paper in this subsection, entitled: "Comments on the Evaluation of Policy Models," joint with Deutsch (1992). In this paper, the authors advocate the use of rigorous econometric analysis when constructing and evaluating policy models and note that this approach has been largely neglected both by policy makers and by econometricians.

The final paper in this section is Granger's 1987 paper, "Implications of Aggregation with Common Factors." This paper concerns the classic problem of aggregation of microeconomic relationships into aggregate relationships. The paper deals almost exclusively with linear microeconomic models so that answers to the standard aggregation questions are transparent. (For example, the aggregate relationship is linear, with coefficients representing averages of the coefficients across the micorpopulation.) The important lessons from this paper don't deal with these questions but rather with the implications of approximate aggregation. Specifically, Granger postulates a microeconomic environment in which individuals' actions are explained by both idiosyncratic and common factors. Idiosyncratic factors are the most important variables explaining the microeconomic data, but these factors are averaged out when the microrelations are aggregated so that the aggregated data depend almost entirely on the common factors. Because the common factors are not very important for the microdata, an econometrician using microdata could quite easily decide that these factors are not important and not include them in the micromodel. In this case, the aggregate model constructed from the estimated micromodel would be very misspecified. Because macroeconomists are now beginning to rely on microdatasets in their empirical work, this is a timely lesson.

FORECASTING

By the time this book is published, Granger will be in his sixth decade of active research in the area of forecasting.[1] In essence, forecasting is based on the integration of three tasks: model specification and construction, model estimation and testing, and model evaluation and selection. Granger has contributed extensively in all three, including classics in the areas of forecast evaluation, forecast combination, data transformation, aggregation, seasonality and forecasting, and causality and forecasting. Some of these are reproduced in this section.[2]

One of Granger's earliest works on forecasting serves as a starting point for this section of Volume I. This is his 1959 paper, "Estimating the Probability of Flooding on a Tidal River," which could serve as the benchmark example in a modern cost-benefit analysis text because the focus is on predicting the number of floods per century that can be expected on a tidal stretch. This paper builds on earlier work by Gumbel (1958), where estimates for nontidal flood plains are provided. The paper illustrates the multidisciplinary flavor of much of Granger's work.

The second paper in this section is entitled "Prediction with a Generalized Cost of Error Function" (1969). This fundamental contribution highlights the restrictive nature of quadratic cost functions and notes that practical economic and management problems may call instead for the use of nonquadratic and possibly nonsymmetric loss functions. Granger illuminates the potential need for such generalized cost functions and proposes an appropriate methodology for implementing such functions. For example, the paper discusses the importance of adding a bias term to predictors, a notion that is particularly important for model selection. This subject continues to receive considerable attention in economics (see, for example, Christoffersen and Diebold 1996, 1997; Hoffman and Rasche 1996; Leitch and Tanner 1991; Lin and Tsay 1996; Pesaran and

---

[1] His first published paper in the field was in the prestigious *Astrophysical Journal* in 1957 and was entitled "A Statistical Model for Sunspot Activity."

[2] A small sample of important papers not included in this section are Granger (1957, 1967); Granger, Kamstra, and White (1989); Granger, King, and White (1995); Granger and Sin (1997); Granger and Nelson (1979); and Granger and Thompson (1987). In addition, Granger has written seven books on the subject, including *Spectral Analysis of Economic Time Series* (1964, joint with M. Hatanaka), *Predictability of Stock Market Prices* (1970, joint with O. Morgenstern), *Speculation, Hedging and Forecasts of Commodity Prices* (1970, joint with W. C. Labys), *Trading in Commodities* (1974), *Forecasting Economic Time Series* (1977, joint with P. Newbold), *Forecasting in Business and Economics* (1980), and *Modeling Nonlinear Dynamic Relationships* (1993, joint with T. Teräsvirta). All these books are rich with ideas. For example, Granger and Newbold (1977) discuss a test for choosing between two competing forecasting models based on an evaluation of prediction errors. Recent papers in the area that propose tests similar in design and purpose to that discussed by Granger and Newbold include Corradi, Swanson, and Olivetti (1999); Diebold and Mariano (1995); Fair and Shiller (1990); Kolb and Stekler (1993); Meese and Rogoff (1988); Mizrach (1991); West (1996); and White (1999).

Timmerman 1992, 1994; Swanson and White 1995, 1997; Weiss 1996). A related and subsequent paper entitled "Some Comments on the Evaluation of Economic Forecasts" (1983, joint with Newbold) is the third paper in this section. In this paper, generalized cost functions are elucidated, forecast model selection tests are outlined, and forecast efficiency in the sense of Mincer and Zarnowitz (1969) is discussed. The main focus of the paper, however, is the assertion that satisfactory tests of model performance should require that a "best" model produce forecasts, which cannot be improved upon by combination with (multivariate) Box-Jenkins-type forecasts. This notion is a precursor to so-called forecast encompassing and is related to Granger's ideas about forecast combination, a subject to which we now turn our attention.

Three papers in this section focus on forecast combination, a subject that was introduced in the 1969 Granger and Bates paper, "The Combination of Forecasts." This paper shows that the combination of two separate sets of airline passenger forecasts yield predictions that mean-square-error dominate each of the original sets of forecasts. That combined forecasts yield equal or smaller error variance is shown in an appendix to the paper. This insight has led to hundreds of subsequent papers, many of which concentrate on characterizing data-generating processes for which this feature holds, and many of which generalize the framework of Granger and Bates. A rather extensive review of the literature in this area is given in Clemen (1989) (although many papers have been subsequently published). The combination literature also touches on issues such as structural change, loss function design, model misspecification and selection, and forecast evaluation tests. These topics are all discussed in the two related papers that we include in this section – namely, "Invited Review: Combining Forecasts – Twenty Years Later," (1989) and "The Combination of Forecasts Using Changing Weights" (1994, joint with M. Deutsch and T. Teräsvirta). The former paper has a title that is self explanatory, while the latter considers changing weights associated with the estimation of switching and smooth transition regression models – two types of nonlinear models that are currently receiving considerable attention.

The literature on data transformation in econometrics is extensive, and it is perhaps not surprising that one of the early forays in the area is Granger and Newbold's "Forecasting Transformed Series" (1976). In this paper, general autocovariance structures are derived for a broad class of stationary Gaussian processes, which are transformed via some function that can be expanded by using Hermite polynomials. In addition, Granger and Newbold point out that the Box and Cox (1964) transformation often yields variables that are "near-normal," for example, making subsequent analysis more straightforward. (A more recent paper in this area, which is included in Volume II, is Granger and Hallman 1991). The sixth paper in this part of Volume I is entitled "Forecasting

White Noise" (1983). Here Granger illustrates the potential empirical pitfalls associated with loose interpretation of theoretical results. His main illustration focuses on the commonly believed fallacy that: "The objective of time series analysis is to find a filter which, when applied to the series being considered, results in white noise." Clearly such a statement is oversimplistic, and Granger illustrates this by considering three different types of white noise, and blending in causality, data transformation, Markov chains, deterministic chaos, nonlinear models, and time-varying parameter models.

The penultimate paper in this section, "Can We Improve the Perceived Quality of Economic Forecasts?" (1996), focuses on some of the fundamental issues currently confronting forecasters. In particular, Granger espouses on what sorts of loss functions we should be using, what sorts of information and information sets may be useful, and how forecasts can be improved in quality and presentation (for example, by using 50% rather than 95% confidence intervals). The paper is dedicated to the path-breaking book by Box and Jenkins (1970) and is a lucid piece that is meant to encourage discussion among practitioners of the art. The final paper in Volume I is entitled "Short-Run Forecasts of Electricity Loads and Peaks" (1997) and is meant to provide the reader of this volume with an example of how to correctly use current forecasting methodology in economics. In this piece, Ramanathan, Engle, Granger, Vahid-Araghi, and Brace implement a short-run forecasting model of hourly electrical utility system loads, focusing on model design, estimation, and evaluation.

Volume II

CAUSALITY

Granger's contributions to the study of causality and causal relationships in economics are without a doubt among some of his most well known. One reason for this may be the importance in so many fields of research of answering questions of the sort: What will happen to Y if X falls? Another reason is that Granger's answers to these questions are elegant mathematically and simple to apply empirically. Causality had been considered in economics before Granger's 1969 paper entitled "Investigating Causal Relations by Econometric Models and Cross-Spectral

Methods" (see, for example, Granger 1963; Granger and Hatanaka 1964; Hosoya 1977; Orcutt 1952; Simon 1953; Wiener 1956). In addition, papers on the concept of causality and on causality testing also appeared (and continue to appear) after Granger's classic work (see, for example, Dolado and Lütkepohl 1994; Geweke 1982; Geweke et al. 1983; Granger and Lin 1994; Hoover 1993; Sims 1972; Swanson and Granger 1997; Toda and Phillips 1993, 1994; Toda and Yamamoto 1995; Zellner 1979, to name but a very few). However, Granger's 1969 paper is a cornerstone of modern empirical causality analysis and testing. For this reason, Volume II begins with his 1969 contribution. In the paper, Granger uses cross-spectral methods as well as simple bivariate time series models to formalize and to illustrate a simple, appealing, and testable notion of causality. Much of his insight is gathered in formal definitions of causality, feedback, instantaneous causality, and causality lag. These four definitions have formed the basis for virtually all the research in the area in the last thirty years and will probably do so for the next thirty years. His first definition says that "... Y_t causes X_t if we are able to better predict X_t using all available information than if the information apart from Y_t had been used" (Granger 1969, p. 428). It is, thus, not surprising that many forecasting papers *post* Granger (1969) have used the "Granger causality test" as a basic tool for model specification. It is also not surprising that economic theories are often compared and evaluated using Granger causality tests. In the paper, Granger also introduces the important concept of instantaneous causality and stresses how crucial sampling frequency and aggregation are, for example. All this is done within the framework of recently introduced (into economics by Granger and Hatanaka 1964) techniques of spectral analysis.

The next paper in this part of Volume II, "Testing for Causality: A Personal Viewpoint" (1980), contains a number of important additional contributions that build on Granger (1969) and outlines further directions for modern time series analysis (many of which have subsequently been adopted by the profession). The paper begins by axiomatizing a concept of causality. This leads to a formal probabilistic interpretation of Granger (1969), in terms of conditional distribution functions, which is easily operationalized to include universal versus *not* universal information sets (for example, "data inadequacies"), and thus leads to causality tests based on conditional expectation and/or variance, for example. In addition, Granger discusses the philosophical notion of causality and the roots of his initial interest and knowledge in the area. His discussion culminates with careful characterizations of so-called instantaneous and spurious causality. Finally, Granger emphasizes the use of post-sample data to confirm causal relationships found via in-sample Wald and Lagrange multiplier tests.

Continuing with his methodological contributions, the third paper, "Some Recent Developments in a Concept of Causality" (1986), shows that if two $I(1)$ series are cointegrated, then there must be Granger causation in at least one direction. He also discusses the use of causality tests for policy evaluation and revisits the issue of instantaneous causality, noting that three obvious explanations for apparent instantaneous causality are that: (i) variables react without any measurable time delay, (ii) the time interval over which data are collected is too large to capture causal relations properly, or that temporal aggregation leads to apparent instantaneous causation, and (iii) the information set is incomplete, thus leading to apparent instantaneous causality. It is argued that (ii) and (iii) are more plausible, and examples are provided. This section closes with a frequently cited empirical investigation entitled "Advertising and Aggregate Consumption: An Analysis of Causality" (1980). The paper is meant to provide the reader with an example of how to correctly use the concept of causality in economics. In this piece, Ashley, Granger, and Schmalensee stress the importance of out-of-sample forecasting performance in the evaluation of alternative causal systems and provide interesting evidence that advertising does not cause consumption but that consumption may cause advertising.

INTEGRATION AND COINTEGRATION

Granger's "typical spectral shape" implies that most economic time series are dominated by low-frequency variability. Because this variability can be modeled by a unit root in a series' autoregressive polynomial, the typical spectral shape provides the empirical motivation for work on integrated, long memory, and cointegrated processes. Granger's contributions in this area are usefully organized into four categories. The first contains research focused on the implications of this low-frequency variability for standard econometric methods, and the Granger and Newbold work on spurious regressions is the most notable contribution in this category. The second includes Granger's research on linear time series models that explain the joint behavior of low-frequency components for a system of economic time series. His development of the idea of cointegration stands out here. The third category contains both empirical contributions and detailed statistical issues arising in cointegrated systems (like "trend" estimation). Finally, the fourth category contains his research on extending cointegration in time-invariant linear systems to nonlinear and time-varying systems. Papers representing his work in each of these categories are included in this section of Volume II.

The first paper in this section is the classic 1974 Granger and Newbold paper "Spurious Regressions in Econometrics," which contains what is arguably the most influential Monte Carlo study in econometrics. (The closest competitor that comes to our mind is the experiment reported in Slutsky 1927.) The Granger-Newbold paper shows that linear regressions involving statistically *independent*, but highly persistent random variables will often produce large "t-statistics" and sample R^2s. The results reported in this paper showed that serial correlation in the regression error together with serial correlation in the regressor have disastrous effects on the usual procedures of statistical inference. The basic result was known (Yule 1926), but the particulars of Granger and Newbold's experiments were dramatic and unexpected. Indeed, in his ET Interview, Granger reminisces about giving a seminar on the topic at the London School of Economics (LSE), where some of the most sophisticated time-series econometricians of the time found the Granger-Newbold results incredible and suggested that he check his computer code. The paper had a profound impact on empirical work because, for example, researchers could no longer ignore low Durbin-Watson statistics. One of the most insightful observations in the paper is that, when considering the regression $y = x\beta + \varepsilon$, the null hypothesis $\beta = 0$ implies that ε has the same serial properties as y, so that it makes little sense constructing a t-statistic for this null hypothesis without worrying about serial correlation. The basic insight that both sides of an equation must have the same time series properties shows up repeatedly in Granger's work and forms the basis of what he calls "consistency" in his later work.

The Granger-Newbold spurious regression paper touched off a fertile debate on how serial correlation should be handled in regression models. Motivated by the typical spectral shape together with the likelihood of spurious regressions in levels regressions, Granger and Newbold suggested that applied researchers specify regressions using the first-differences of economic time series. This advice met with skepticism. There was an uneasy feeling that even though first-differencing would guard against the spurious regression problem, it would also eliminate the dominant low-frequency components of economic time series, and it was the interaction of these components that researchers wanted to measure with regression analysis. In this sense, first-differencing threw the baby out with the bath water. Hendry and Mizon (1978) provided a constructive response to the Granger-Newbold spurious regression challenge with the suggestion that time series regression models be specified as autoregressive distributed lags in levels (that is, $a(B)y_t = c(B)x_t + \varepsilon_t$). In this specification, the first-difference restriction could be viewed a common factor of $(1 - B)$ in the $a(B)$ and $c(B)$ lag polynomials, and this restriction could be investigated empirically. These autoregressive distributed lag models could also be rewritten in error-correction form, which highlighted their implied relationship between the levels of the series (useful references for this includes Sargan 1964; Hendry, Pagan, and Sargan 1981; and Hendry 1995).

This debate led to Granger's formalization of cointegration (see ET Interview, page 274). His ideas on the topic were first exposited in his 1981 paper "Some Properties of Time Series Data and Their Use in

Econometric Model Specification," which is included as the second paper in this section of Volume II. The paper begins with a discussion of consistency between the two sides of the previously mentioned equation. Thus, if $y = x\beta + \varepsilon$ and x contains important seasonal variation and ε is white noise that is unrelated to x, then y must also contain important seasonal variation. The paper is most notable for its discussion of consistency in regards to the order of integration of the variables and the development of "co-integration," which appears in Section 4 of the paper. (As it turns out, the term was used so much in the next five years that by the mid-1980s the hyphen had largely disappeared and co-integration became cointegration.) The relationship between error-correction models and cointegration is mentioned, and it is noted that two cointegrated variables have a unit long-run correlation. The paper probably contains Granger's most prescient statements. For example, in discussing the "special case" of the autoregressive distributed lag that gives rise to a cointegrating relation, he states: "Although it may appear to be very special, it also seems to be potentially important." And after giving some examples of cointegrated variables, he writes: "It might be interesting to undertake a wide-spread study to find out which pairs of economic variables are co-integrated."

Granger expanded on his cointegration ideas in his 1983 paper "Time Series Analysis of Error Correction Models" with Weiss, which is included as the third paper in this section. This paper makes three important contributions. First, it further explores the link between error-correction models and cointegration (focusing primarily on bivariate models). Second, it introduces methods for testing for cointegration. These include the residual-based tests developed in more detail in Engle and Granger's later paper and the tests that were analyzed several years later by Horvath and Watson (1995). The paper does not tackle the unit-root distribution problems that arise in the tests (more on this later) and instead suggests practical "identification" procedures analogous to those used in Box-Jenkins model building. The final contribution of the paper is an application of cointegration to three classic economic relations, each of which was studied in more detail by later researchers using "modern" cointegration methods. The first application considered employee income and national income (in logarithms) and, thus, focused on labor's share of national income, one of the "Great Ratios" investigated earlier by Kosobud and Klein (1961) using other statistical methods. The second application considered money and nominal income, where Granger and Weiss found little evidence supporting cointegration. Later researchers added nominal interest rates to this system, producing a long-run money demand relation, and found stronger evidence of cointegration (Baba, Hendry, and Star 1992; Hoffman and Rasche 1991; Stock and Watson 1993). The third application considered the trivariate system of nominal wages, prices, and productivity, which was studied in more detail a decade later by Campbell and Rissman (1994).

The now-classic reference on cointegration, Engle and Granger's "Co-Integration and Error-Correction: Representation, Estimation and Testing," is included as the fourth paper in this section. This paper is so well known that, literally, it needs no introduction. The paper includes "Granger's Representation Theorem," which carefully lays out the connection between moving average and vector error correction representations for cointegrated models involving $I(1)$ variables. It highlights the nonstandard statistical inference issues that arise in cointegrated models including unit roots and unidentified parameters. Small sample critical values for residual-based cointegration tests are given, and asymptotically efficient estimators for $I(0)$ parameters are developed (subsequently known as Engle-Granger two-step estimators). The paper also contains a short, but serious, empirical section investigating cointegration between consumption and income, long-term and short-term interest rates, and money and nominal income.

Granger's 1986 "Developments in the Study of Cointegrated Economic Variables" is the next entry in the section and summarizes the progress made during the first five years of research on the topic. Representation theory for $I(1)$ processes was well understood by this time, and several implications had been noted, perhaps the most surprising was the relationship between cointegration and causality discussed in the last subsection. (If x and y are cointegrated, then either x must Granger-cause y or the converse, and thus cointegration of asset prices is at odds with the martingale property.) Work had begun on the representation theory for $I(2)$ processes (Johansen 1988a; Yoo 1987). Inference techniques were still in their infancy, but great strides would be made in the subsequent five years. A set of stylized cointegration facts was developing (consumption and income are cointegrated, money and nominal interest rates are not, for example). The paper ends with some new ideas on cointegration in nonlinear models and in models with time-varying coefficients. This is an area that has not attracted a lot of attention (a notable exception being Balke and Fomby 1997), primarily because of the difficult problems in statistical inference.

Cointegration is one of those rare ideas in econometrics that had an immediate effect on empirical work. It crystallized a notion that earlier researchers had tried to convey as, for example, "true regressions" (Frisch 1934), low-frequency regressions (Engle 1974), or the most predictable canonical variables from a system (Box and Tiao 1977). There is now an enormous body of empirical work utilizing Granger's cointegration framework. Some of the early work was descriptive in nature (asking, like Granger and Weiss, whether a set of variables appeared to be cointegrated), but it soon became apparent that cointegration was an implication of important economic theories, and this insight allowed researchers to test separately both the long-run and short-run implications of the specific theories. For example, Campbell and Shiller (1987) and Campbell (1987) showed that cointegration was an implication of rational expectations versions of present value relations, making the concept immediately germane to a large number of applications including the permanent income model of consumption, the term structure of interest rates, money demand, and asset price determination, for example. The connection with error correction models meant that cointegration was easily incorporated into vector autoregressions, and researchers exploited this restriction to help solve the identification problem in these models (see Blanchard and Quah 1989; King et al. 1991, for example).

Development of empirical work went hand in hand with development of inference procedures that extended the results for univariate autoregressions with unit roots to vector systems (for example, see Chan and Wei 1987; Phillips and Durlauf 1986). Much of this work was focused directly on the issues raised by Granger in the papers reproduced here. For example, Phillips (1986) used these new techniques to help explain the Granger-Newbold spurious regression results. Stock (1987) derived the limiting distribution of least squares estimators of cointegrating vectors, showing that the estimated coefficients were T-consistent. Phillips and Ouliaris (1990) derived asymptotic distributions of residual-based tests for cointegration. Using the vector error-correction model, Johansen (1988b) and Ahn and Reinsel (1990) developed Gaussian maximum likelihood estimators and derived the asymptotic properties of the estimators. Johansen (1988b) derived likelihood-based tests for cointegration. Many refinements of these procedures followed during the late 1980s and early 1990s (Phillips 1991; Saikkonen 1991; Stock and Watson 1993, to list a few examples from a very long list of contributions), and by the mid 1990s a rather complete guide to specification, estimation, and testing in cointegrated models appeared in textbooks such as Hamilton (1994) and Hendry (1995).

During this period, Granger and others were extending his cointegration analysis in important directions. One particularly useful extension focused on seasonality, and we include Hylleberg, Engle, Granger, and Yoo's "Seasonal Integration and Cointegration," as the next paper in this section. A common approach to univariate modeling of seasonal series is to remove the seasonal and trend components by taking seasonal differences. For example, for quarterly data, this involves filtering the data using $(1 - B^4)$. This operation explicitly incorporates $(1 - B^4)$ into the series' autoregressive polynomial and implies that the autoregression will contain four unit roots: two real roots associated with frequencies 0 and π and a complex conjugate pair associated with frequency $\pi/2$. Standard cointegration and unit-root techniques focus only on the zero-frequency unit root; the Hyllberg et al. paper discusses the complications that arise from the remaining three unit roots. Specifically, the paper develops tests for unit roots and seasonal cointegration at frequencies other than zero. This is done in a clever way by first expanding the autoregressive polynomial in a partial fraction expansion with terms associated with each of the unit roots. This simplifies the testing problem because it makes it possible to apply standard regression-based tests to filtered versions of the series. This paper has led to the so-called HEGY approach of testing for seasonal roots separately. It has been extended in several ways notably by Ghysels et al. (1994) who built joint tests, such as testing for the presence of all seasonal unit roots, based on the HEGY regressions.

Many of Granger's papers include empirical examples of the proposed techniques, but only occasionally is the empirical analysis the heart of the paper. One notable exception is "A Cointegration Analysis of Treasury Bill Yields," with Hall and Anderson, which is included as the sixth paper in this section. The framework for the paper is the familiar expectations theory of the term structure. There are two novelties: first, the analysis is carried out using a large number of series (that is, twelve series), and second, the temporal stability of the cointegrating relation is investigated. The key conclusion is that interest-rate spreads on 1–12 month U.S. Treasury Bills appear to be $I(0)$ except during the turbulent 1979–82 time period.

A natural way to think about cointegrated systems is in terms of underlying, but unobserved, persistent, and transitory components. The persistent factors capture the long-memory or low-frequency variability in the observed series, and the transitory factors explain the shorter memory or high-frequency variation. In many situations, the persistent components correspond to interesting economic concepts ("trend" or "permanent" income, aggregate productivity, "core" inflation, and so on) Thus, an important question is how to estimate these components from the observed time series, and this is difficult because there is no unique way to carry out the decomposition. One popular decomposition associates the persistent component with the long-run forecasts in the observed series and the transitory component with the corresponding residual (Beveridge and Nelson 1981). This approach has limitations: notably the persistent component is, by construction, a martingale, and the innovations in the persistent and the transitory components are correlated. In the next two papers included in this section, Granger takes up this issue. The first paper, "Estimation of Common Long-Memory Components in Cointegrated Systems," was written with Gonzalo. They propose a decomposition that has two important characteristics: first, both components are a function only of the current values of the series, and second, innovations in the persistent components are uncorrelated with the innovations in the transitory component. In the second paper,

"Separation in Cointegrated Systems and Persistent-Transitory Decompositions" (with N. Haldrup), Granger takes up the issue of estimation of these components in large systems. The key question is whether the components might be computed separately for groups of series so that the components could then be analyzed separately without having to model the entire system of variables. Granger and Haldrup present conditions under which this is possible. Unfortunately the conditions are quite stringent so that few simplifications surface for applied researchers.

The final three papers in this section focus on nonlinear generalizations of cointegration. The first two of these are joint works with Hallman. In "Nonlinear Transformations of Integrated Time Series," Granger and Hallman begin with integrated and cointegrated variables and ask whether nonlinear functions of the series will also appear to be integrated and cointegrated. The problem is complex, and few analytic results are possible. However, the paper includes several approximations and simulations that are quite informative. One of the most interesting results in the paper is a simulation that suggests that Dickey-Fuller tests applied to the ranks of Gaussian random walks have well-behaved limiting distributions. This is important, of course, because statistics based on ranks are invariant to all monotonic transformations applied to the data. In their second paper, "Long Memory Series with Attractors," Granger and Halman discuss nonlinear *attractors* (alternatively $I(0)$ nonlinear functions of stochastically trending variables) and experiment with semiparametric methods for estimating these nonlinear functions. The last paper, "Further Developments in the Study of Cointegrated Variables," with Swanson is a fitting end to this section. It is one of Granger's "seed" papers – overflowing with ideas and, as stated in the first paragraph, raising "more questions than it solves." Specifically, the paper not only discusses time-varying parameter models for cointegration and their implications for time variation in vector error-correction models, how nonlinear cointegrated models can arise as solutions to nonlinear optimization problems, and models for nonlinear leading indicator analysis but also contains a nonlinear empirical generalization of the analysis in King et al. (1991). No doubt, over the next decade, a few of these seeds will germinate and create their own areas of active research.

LONG MEMORY

Even though integrated variables have been widely used in empirical work, they represent a fairly narrow class of models capable of generating Granger's typical spectral shape. In particular, it has been noted that autocorrelation functions of many time series exhibit a slow hyperbolic decay rate. This phenomenon, called long memory or sometimes also called long-range dependence, is observed in geophysical data, such as river flow data (see Hurst 1951, 1956; Lawrence and Kottegoda 1977) and in climatological series (see Hipel and McLeod 1978a, 1978b;

Mandelbrot and Wallis 1968) as well as in economic time series (Adelman 1965; Mandelbrot 1963). In two important papers, Granger extends these processes to provide more flexible low-frequency or long-memory behavior by considering $I(d)$ processes with noninteger values of d. The first of these papers, Granger and Joyeux's (1980) "An Introduction to Long-Memory Time Series Models and Fractional Differencing," is related to earlier work by Mandelbrot and Van Ness (1968) describing fractional Brownian motion. Granger and Joyeux begin by introducing the $I(d)$ process $(1 - B)^d y_t = \varepsilon_t$ for noninteger d. They show that the process is covariance stationary when $d < \frac{1}{2}$ and derive the autocorrelations and spectrum of the process. Interestingly, the autocorrelations die out at a rate τ^{2d-1} for large τ showing that the process has a much longer memory than stationary finite-order ARMA processes (whose autocorrelations die out at rate $\rho\tau$ where $|\rho| < 1$). In the second of these papers, "Long Memory Relationships and the Aggregation of Dynamic Models," Granger shows how this long-memory process can be generated by a large number of heterogenous AR(1) processes. This aggregation work continues to intrigue researchers, as evidenced by recent extensions by Lippi and Zaffaroni (1999).

Empirical work investigating long-memory processes was initially hindered by a lack of statistical methods for estimation and testing, but methods now have been developed that are applicable in fairly general settings (for example, see Robinson 1994, 1995; Lobato and Robinson 1998). In addition, early empirical work in macroeconomics and finance found little convincing evidence of long memory (see Lo 1991, for example). However, a new flurry of empirical work has found strong evidence for long memory in the *absolute value* of asset returns. One of the most important empirical contributions is the paper by Ding, Granger, and Engle, "A Long Memory Property of the Stock Market Returns and a New Model," which is included as the last paper in this section. Using daily data on S&P 500 stock returns from 1928 to 1991, this paper reports autocorrelations of the absolute values of returns that die out very slowly and remain significantly greater than zero beyond lags of 100 periods. This finding seems to have become a stylized fact in empirical finance (see Andersen and Bollerslev 1998; Lobato and Savin 1998) and serves as the empirical motivation for a large number of recent papers.

REFERENCES

Adelman, I., 1965, Long Cycles: Fact or Artifact? *American Economic Review*, 55, 444–63.
Ahn, S. K., and G. C. Reinsel, 1990, Estimation of Partially Nonstationary Autoregressive Models, *Journal of the American Statistical Association*, 85, 813–23.

Alexander, S., 1961, Price Movements in Speculative Markets: Trends or Random Walks, *Industrial Management Review*, 2, 7–26.

1964, "Price Movements in Speculative Markets: Trends or Random Walks, No. 2," in P. Cootner, ed., *The Random Character of Stock Market Prices*, Massachusetts Institute of Technology Press, Cambridge, MA.

Andersen, T., and T. Bollerslev, 1998, Heterogeneous Information Arrivals and Return Volatility Dynamics: Uncovering the Long-run in High Frequency Returns, *Journal of Finance*, 52, 975–1005.

Anderson, T. W., 1971, *The Statistical Analysis of Time Series*, New York: Wiley.

Baba, Y., D. F. Hendry, and R. M. Star, 1992, The Demand for M1 in the U.S.A., 1960–1988, *Review of Economic Studies*, 59, 25–61.

Bachelier, L., 1900, Theory of Speculation, in P. Cootner, ed., *The Random Character of Stock Market Prices*, Cambridge, MA: Massachusetts Institute of Technology Press, 1964; Reprint.

Balke, N., and T. B. Fomby, 1997, Threshold Cointegration, *International Economic Review*, 38, No. 3, 627–45.

Bell, W. R., 1984, Signal Extraction for Nonstationary Time Series, *The Annals of Statistics*, 12, 646–64.

Beveridge, S., and C. R. Nelson, 1981, A New Approach to Decomposition of Time Series into Permanent and Tansitory Components with Particular Attention to Measurement of the "Business Cycle," *Journal of Monetary Economics*, 7, 151–74.

Bierens, H., 1990, Model-free Asymptotically Best Forecasting of Stationary Economic Time Series, *Econometric Theory*, 6, 348–83.

Blanchard, O. J., and D. Quah, 1989, The Dynamic Effects of Aggregate Demand and Supply Disturbances, *American Economic Review*, 79, 655–73.

Box, G. E. P., and D. R. Cox, 1964, An Analysis of Transformations, *Journal of the Royal Statistical Society Series B*, 26, 211–43.

Box, G. E. P., and G. M. Jenkins, 1970, *Time Series Analysis, Forecasting and Control*, San Fransisco: Holden Day.

Box, G. E. P., and G. Tiao, 1977, A Canonical Analysis of Multiple Time Series, *Biometrika*, 64, 355–65.

Burns, A. F., and W. C. Mitchell, 1947, *Measuring Business Cycles*, New York: National Bureau of Economic Research.

Campbell, J. Y., 1987, Does Saving Anticipate Declining Labor Income, *Econometrica*, 55, 1249–73.

Campbell, J. Y., A. W. Lo, and A. C. McKinlay, 1997, *The Econometrics of Financial Markets*, Princeton, NJ: Princeton University Press.

Campbell, J. Y., and R. J. Shiller, 1987, Cointegration and Tests of the Present Value Models, *Journal of Political Economy*, 95, 1062–88. Reprinted in R. F. Engle and C. W. J. Granger, eds., *Long-Run Economic Relationships, Readings in Cointegration*, Oxford, Oxford University Press.

Chan, N. H., and C. Z. Wei, 1987, Limiting Distributions of Least Squares Estimators of Unstable Autoregressive Processes, *The Annals of Statistics*, 16, 367–401.

Christoffersen, P., and F. X. Diebold, 1996, Further Results on Forecasting and Model Selection Under Asymmetric Loss, *Journal of Applied Econometrics*, 11, 651–72.

1997, Optimal Prediction Under Asymmetric Loss, *Econometric Theory*, 13, 808–17.

Clemen, R. T., 1989, Combining Forecasts: A Review and Annotated Bibliography, *International Journal of Forecasting*, 5, 559–83.

Cleveland, W. P., and G. C. Tiao, 1976, Decomposition of Seasonal Time Series: A Model for the X-11 Program, *Journal of the American Statistical Association*, 71, 581–7.

Cootner, P. ed., 1964, *The Random Character of Stock Market Prices*, Massachusetts Institute of Technology Press, Cambridge, MA.

Corradi, V., N. R. Swanson, and C. Olivetti, 1999, Predictive Ability With Cointegrated Variables, Working Paper, Texas A&M University.

Cowles, A., 1933, Can Stock Market Forecasters Forecast?, *Econometrica*, 1, 309–24.

1960, A Revision of Previous Conclusions Regarding Stock Price Behavior, *Econometrica*, 28, 909–15.

Cramér, H., 1942, On Harmonic Analysis of Certain Function Spaces, *Arkiv. Mat. Astron. Fysik*, 28B, No. 12, 1–7.

Davidson, J., 1994, *Stochastic Limit Theory*, Oxford: Oxford University Press.

Delgado, M. A., and P. M. Robinson, 1992, Nonparametric and Semiparametric Methods for Economic Research, *Journal of Economic Surveys*, 6, 201–49.

Diebold, F. X., and R. S. Mariano, 1995, Comparing Predictive Accuracy, *Journal of Business and Economic Statistics*, 13, 253–63.

Dolado, J. J., and H. Lütkepohl, 1994, Making Wald Tests Work for Cointegrated VAR Systems, *Econometric Reviews*.

Engle, R. F., 1974, Band Spectrum Regression, *International Economic Review*, 15, 1–11.

1982, Autoregressive Conditional Heteroskedasticity with Estimates of UK Inflation, *Econometrica*, 50, 987–1007.

Fair, R. C., and R. J. Shiller, 1990, Comparing Information in Forecasts from Econometric Models, *American Economic Review*, 80, 375–89.

Fama, E., 1965, The Behavior of Stock Market Prices, *Journal of Business*, 38, 34–105.

1970, Efficient Capital Markets: A Review of Theory and Empirical Work, *Journal of Finance*, 25, 383–417.

Frisch, R., 1934, *Statistical Confluence Analysis by Means of Complete Regressions Systems*, Oslo: Universitets, Økonomiske Institut.

Fuller, W. A., 1976, *Introduction to Statistical Time Series*, New York: John Wiley.

Gallant, A. R., and H. White, 1988, *A Unified Theory of Estimation and Inference for Nonlinear Dynamics Models*, New York: Basil Blackwell.

Geweke, J., 1982, Measures of Linear Dependence and Feedback Between Time Series, *Journal of the American Statistical Association*, 77, 304–24.

Geweke, J., R. Meese, and W. Dent, 1983, Comparing Alternative Tests of Causality in Temporal Systems, *Journal of Econometrics*, 21, 161–94.

Ghysels, E., C. W. J. Granger, and P. L. Siklos, 1996, Is Seasonal Adjustment a Linear or Nonlinear Data-Filtering Process? *Journal of Business and Economic Statistics*, 14, 374–86.

Ghysels, E., H. S. Lee, and J. Noh, 1994, Testing for Unit Roots in Seasonal Time-Series – Some Theoretical Extensions and a Monte Carlo Investigation, *Journal of Econometrics*, 62, 415–42.

Granger, C. W. J., 1957, A Statistical Model for Sunspot Activity, *The Astrophysical Journal*, 126, 152–8.

1963, Economic Processes Involving Feedback, *Information and Control*, 6, 28–48.

1966, The Typical Spectral Shape of an Economic Variable, *Econometrica*, 34, 150–61.

1967, Simple Trend-Fitting for Long-Range Forecasting, *Management Decision*, Spring, 29–34.

1974, *Trading in Commodities*, Cambridge, England: Woodhead-Faulkner.

1977, Tendency Towards Normality of Linear Combinations of Random Variables, *Metrika*, 23, 237–48.

1979, Seasonality: Causation, Interpretation and Implications, in A. Zellner, ed., *Seasonal Analysis of Economic Time Series*, Economic Research Report, ER-1, Bureau of the Census 1979.

1980, *Forecasting in Business and Economics*, San Diego: Academic Press.

Granger, C. W. J., 1992, Comment on Two Papers Concerning Chaos and Statistics by S. Chatterjee and M. Ylmaz and by M. Berliner, *Statistical Science*, 7, 69–122.

1994, Is Chaotic Economic Theory Relevant for Economics? *Journal of International and Comparative Economics*, forthcoming.

Granger, C. W. J., and A. P. Andersen, 1978, *An Introduction to Bilinear Time Series Models*, Göttingen: Vandenhoeck and Ruprecht.

Granger, C. W. J., and M. Hatanaka, 1964, *Spectral Analysis of Economic Time Series*, Princeton, NJ: Princeton University Press.

Granger, C. W. J., M. Kamstra, and H. White, 1989, Interval Forecasting: An Analysis Based Upon ARCH-Quantile Estimators, *Journal of Econometrics*, 40, 87–96.

1995, Comments of Testing Economic Theories and the Use of Model Selection Criteria, *Journal of Econometrics*, 67, 173–87.

Granger, C. W. J., and W. C. Labys, 1970, *Speculation, Hedging and Forecasts of Commodity Prices*, Lexington, MA: Heath and Company.

Granger, C. W. J., and J.-L. Lin, 1994, Causality in the Long-Run, *Econometric Theory*, 11, 530–6.

Granger, C. W. J., and O. Morgenstern, 1963, Spectral Analysis of New York Stock Market Prices, *Kyklos*, 16, 1–27. Reprinted in P. H. Cootner, ed., *Random Character of Stock Market Prices*, Cambridge, MA: MIT Press, 1964.

1970, *Predictability of Stock Market Prices*, Lexington, MA: Heath and Company.

Granger, C. W. J., and M. Morris, 1976, Time Series Modeling and Interpretation, *Journal of the Royal Statistical Society Series A*, 139, 246–57.

Granger, C. W. J., and H. L. Nelson, 1979, Experience with Using the Box-Cox Transformation When Forecasting Economic Time Series, *Journal of Econometrics*, 9, 57–69.

Granger, C. W. J., and P. Newbold, 1977, *Forecasting Economic Time Series*, New York: Academic Press.

1977, *Forecasting Economic Time Series*, 1st ed., San Diego: Academic Press.

Granger, C. W. J., and C.-Y. Sin, 1997, Estimating and Forecasting Quantiles with Asymmetric Least Squares, Working Paper, University of California, San Diego.

Granger, C. W. J., and T. Teräsvirta, 1993, *Modeling Nonlinear Dynamic Relationships*, Oxford: Oxford University Press.

Granger, C. W. J., and P. Thompson, 1987, Predictive Consequences of Using Conditioning on Causal Variables, *Economic Theory*, 3, 150–2.

Gumbel, D., 1958, Statistical theory of Floods and Droughts, *Journal I.W.E.*, 12, 157–67.

Hamilton, J. D., 1994, *Time Series Analysis*, Princeton, NJ: Princeton University Press.

Hannan, E. J., 1967, Measurement of a Wandering Signal Amid Noise, *Journal of Applied Probability*, 4, 90–102.

1970, *Multiple Time Series*, New York: Wiley.

Hansen, L. P., and T. J. Sargent, 1980, Formulating and Estimating Dynamic Linear Rational Expectations Models, *Journal of Economic Dynamics and Control*, 2, No. 1, 7–46.

Härdle, W., 1990, *Applied Nonparametric Regression*, Cambridge: Cambridge University Press.

Hendry, D. F., 1995, *Dynamic Econometrics*, Oxford, England: Oxford University Press.

Hendry, D. F., and G. E. Mizon, 1978, Serial Correlation as a Convenient Simplification, Not a Nuisance: A Comment on a Study of the Demand For Money by the Bank of England, *Economic Journal*, 88, 549–63.

Hendry, D. F., A. R. Pagan, and J. D. Sargan, 1984, Dynamic Specification, Chapter 18, in M. D. Intriligator and Z. Griliches, eds., *Handbook of Econometrics, Vol. II*, Amsterdam: North Holland.

Hipel, K. W., and A. I. McLeod, 1978a, Preservation of the Rescaled Adjusted Range, 2: Simulation Studies Using Box-Jenkins Models, *Water Resources Research*, 14, 509–16.

1978b, Preservation of the Rescaled Adjusted Range, 3: Fractional Gaussian Noise Algorithms, *Water Resources Research*, 14, 517–18.

Hoffman, D. L., and R. H. Rasche, 1991, Long-Run Income and Interest Elasticities of Money Demand in the United States, *Review of Economics and Statistics*, 73, 665–74.

1996, Assessing Forecast Performance in a Cointegrated System, *Journal of Applied Econometrics*, 11, 495–517.

Hoover, K. D., 1993, Causality and Temporal Order in Macroeconomics or Why Even Economists Don't Know How to Get Causes from Probabilities, *British Journal for the Philosophy of Science*, December.

Horvath, M. T. K., and M. W. Watson, 1995, Testing for Cointegration When Some of the Cointegrating Vectors are Prespecified, *Econometric Theory*, 11, No. 5, 952–84.

Hosoya, Y., 1977, On the Granger Condition for Non-Causality, *Econometrica*, 45, 1735–6.

Hurst, H. E., 1951, Long-term Storage Capacity of Reservoirs, *Transactions of the American Society of Civil Engineers*, 116, 770–99.

1956, Methods of Using Long Term Storage in Reservoirs, *Proceedings of the Institute of Civil Engineers*, 1, 519–43.

Ignacio, N., N. Labato, and P. M. Robinson, 1998, A Nonparametric Test for $I(0)$, *Review of Economic Studies*, 65, 475–95.

Johansen, S. 1988a, The Mathematical Structure of Error Correction Models, in N. U. Prabhu, ed., *Contemporary Mathematics, Vol. 80: Structural*

Inference for Stochastic Processes, Providence, RI: American Mathematical Society.

1988b, Statistical Analysis of Cointegrating Vectors, *Journal of Economic Dynamics and Control*, 12, 231–54.

Khintchine, A. 1934, Korrelationstheorie der Stationare Stochastischen Processe, *Math Annual*, 109, 604–15.

King, R., C. I. Plosser, J. H. Stock, and M. W. Watson, 1991, Stochastic Trends and Economic Fluctuations, *American Economic Review*, 81, No. 4, 819–40.

Kolb, R. A., and H. O. Stekler, 1993, Are Economic Forecasts Significantly Better Than Naive Predictions? An Appropriate Test, *International Journal of Forecasting*, 9, 117–20.

Kolmogorov, A. N., 1933, Grundbegriffe der Wahrscheinlichkeitrechnung, *Ergebnisse der Mathematik*. Published in English in 1950 as *Foundations of the Theory of Probability*, Bronx, NY: Chelsea.

1941a, Stationary Sequences in Hilbert Space (Russian) *Bull. Math. Univ. Moscow*, 2, No. 6, 40.

1941b, Interpolation und Extrapolation von Stationaren Zufalligen Folgen [Russian, German summary], *Bull. Acad. Sci. U.R.S.S. Ser. Math.*, 5, 3–14.

Kosobud, R., and L. Klein, 1961, Some Econometrics of Growth: Great Ratios of Economics, *Quarterly Journal of Economics*, 25, 173–98.

Lawrence, A. J., and N. T. Kottegoda, 1977, Stochastic Modeling of River Flow Time Series, *Journal of the Royal Statistical Society Series A*, 140, 1–47.

Lee, T.-H., H. White, and C. W. J. Granger, 1993, Testing for Neglected Nonlinearity in Time Series Models: A Comparison of Neural Network Methods and Alternative Tests, *Journal of Econometrics*, 56, 269–90.

Leitch, G., and J. E. Tanner, 1991, Economic Forecast Evaluation: Profits Versus the Conventional Error Measures, *American Economic Review*, 81, 580–90.

Li, Q., 1998, Efficient Estimation of Additive Partially Linear Models, *International Economic Review*, forthcoming.

Lin, J.-L., and R. S. Tsay, 1996, Co-integration Constraint and Forecasting: An Empirical Examination, *Journal of Applied Econometrics*, 11, 519–38.

Linton, O., and J. P. Neilson, 1995, A Kernal Method of Estimating Structured Nonparametric Regression Based on Marginal Integration, *Biometrika*, 82, 91 100.

Lippi, M., and P. Zaffaroni, 1999, Contemporaneous Aggregation of Linear Dynamic Models in Large Economies, Mimeo, Universita La Sapienza and Banca d'Italia.

Liu, T., C. W. J. Granger, and W. Heller, 1992, Using the Correlation Exponent to Decide whether an Economic Series Is Chaotic, *Journal of Applied Econometrics*, 7S, 525–40. Reprinted in M. H. Pesaran and S. M. Potter, eds., *Nonlinear Dynamics, Chaos, and Econometrics*, Chichester: Wiley.

Lo, A., 1991, Long-Term Memory in Stock Prices, *Econometrica*, 59, 1279–313.

Lobato, I., and P. M. Robinson, 1998, A Nonparametric Test for $I(0)$, *Review of Economic Studies*, 65, 475–95.

Lobato, I., and N. E. Savin, 1998, Real and Spurious Long-Memory Properties of Stock-Market Data, *Journal of Business and Economic Statistics*, 16, No. 3, 261–7.

Lütkepohl, H., 1991, *Introduction to Multiple Time Series Analysis*, New York: Springer-Verlag.

Macauley, F. R., 1931, *The Smoothing of Time Series*, New York, NY: National Bureau of Economic Research.

Mandelbrot, B., 1963, The Variation of Certain Speculative Prices, *Journal of Business*, 36, 394–419.

Mandelbrot, B. B., and J. W. Van Ness, 1968, Fractional Brownian Motions, Fractional Brownian Noises and Applications, *SIAM Review*, 10, 422–37.

Mandelbrot, B. B., and J. Wallis, 1968, Noah, Joseph and Operational Hydrology, *Water Resources Research*, 4, 909–18.

Mann, H. B., and A. Wald, 1943, On the Statistical Treatment of Linear Stochastic Difference Equations, *Econometrica*, 11, 173–220.

McLeish, D. L., 1978, A Maximal Inequality and Dependent Strong Laws, *Annals of Probability*, 3, 829–39.

Meese, R. A., and K. Rogoff, 1983, Empirical Exchange Rate Models of the Seventies: Do They Fit Out of Sample, *Journal of International Economics*, 14, 3–24.

Mincer, J., and V. Zarnowitz, 1969, The Evaluation of Economic Forecasts, in *Economic Forecasts and Expectations*, J. Mincer, ed., New York: National Bureau of Economic Research.

Mizrach, B., 1991, Forecast Comparison in L_2, Working Paper, Rutgers University.

Nerlove, M., 1964, Spectral Analysis of Seasonal Adjustment Procedures, *Econometrica*, 32, 241–86.

1965, A Comparison of a Modified Hannan and the BLS Seasonal Adjustment Filters, *Journal of the American Statistical Association*, 60, 442–91.

Nerlove, M., D. Grether, and J. Carvalho, 1979, *Analysis of Economic Time Series – A Synthesis*, New York: Academic Press.

Orcutt, G. H., 1952, Actions, Consequences and Causal Relations, *Review of Economics and Statistics*, 34, 305–13.

Pesaran, M. H., and A. G. Timmerman, 1992, A Simple Nonparametric Test of Predictive Performance, *Journal of Business and Economic Statistics*, 10, 461–5.

1994, A Generalization of the Nonparametric Henriksson-Merton Test of Market Timing, *Economics Letters*, 44, 1–7.

Phillips, P. C. B., 1986, Understanding Spurious Regressions in Econometrics, *Journal of Econometrics*, 33, No. 3, 311–40.

1991, Optimal Inference in Cointegrated Systems, *Econometrica*, 59, 283–306.

1997, ET Interview: Clive Granger, *Econometric Theory*, 13, 253–304.

Phillips, P. C. B., and S. N. Durlauf, 1986, Multiple Time Series Regression with Integrated Processes, *Review of Economic Studies*, 53, No. 4, 473–96.

Phillips, P. C. B., and S. Ouliaris, 1990, Asymptotic Properties of Residual Based Tests for Cointegration, *Econometrica*, 58, No. 1, 165–93.

Pierce, D. A., 1979, Signal Extraction Error in Nonstationary Time Series, *The Annals of Statistics*, 7, 1303–20.

Priestley, M. B., 1981, *Spectral Analysis and Time Series*, New York: Academic Press.

Rissman, E., and J. Campbell, 1994, Long-run Labor Market Dynamics and Short-run Inflation, *Economic Perspectives*.

Robinson, P. M., 1988, Root N-consistent Semiparametric Regression, *Econometrica*, 56, 931–54.

1994, Semiparametric Analysis of Long Memory Time Series, *The Annals of Statistics*, 22, 515–39.

1995, Gaussian Semiparametric Estimation of Long Range Dependence, *The Annals of Statistics*, 23, 1630–61.

Saikkonen, P., 1991, Asymptotically Efficient Estimation of Cointegrating Regressions, *Econometric Theory*, 7, 1–21.

Samuelson, P., 1965, Proof that Properly Anticipated Prices Fluctuate Randomly, *Industrial Management Review*, 6, 41–9.

Sargan, J. D., 1964, Wages and Prices in the United Kingdom: A Study in Econometric Methodology, in P. E. Hart, G. Mills, and J. N. Whittaker, eds., *Econometric Analysis of National Economic Planning*, London: Butterworths.

Sargent, T. J., 1987, *Macroeconomic Theory*, 2nd ed., New York: Academic Press.

Shiskin, J., A. H. Young, and J. C. Musgrave, 1967, The X-11 Variant of the Census Method II Seasonal Adjustment Program, Technical Paper 15, U.S. Bureau of the Census, Washington, DC.

Simon, H. A., 1953, Causal Ordering and Identifiability, in W. C. Hood and T. C. Koopmans, eds., *Studies in Econometric Method*, Cowles Commission Monograph 14, New York.

Sims, C. A., 1972, Money, Income, and Causality, *American Economic Review*, 62, 540–52.

1974, Seasonality in Regression, *Journal of the American Statistical Association*, 69, 618–26.

1980, Macroeconomics and Reality, *Econometrica*, 48, No. 1, 1–48.

Slutzky, E. 1927, The Summation of Random Causes as the Source of Cyclic Processes, *Econometrica*, 5, 105–46, 1937. Translated from the earlier paper of the same title in *Problems of Economic Conditions*, Moscow: Cojuncture Institute.

Stock, J. H., 1987, Asymptotic Properties of Least Squares Estimators of Cointegrating Vectors, *Econometrica*, 55, 1035–56.

1989, Nonparametric Policy Analysis, *Journal of the American Statistical Association*, 84, 567–75.

Stock, J. H., and M. W. Watson, 1993, A Simple Estimator of Cointegrating Vectors in Higher Order Integrated Systems, *Econometrica*, 61, No. 4, 783–820.

Swanson, N. R., and C. W. J. Granger, 1997, Impulse Response Functions Based on a Causal Approach to Residual Orthogonalization in Vector Autoregression, *Journal of the American Statistical Association*, 92, 357–67.

Swanson, N. R., and H. White, 1995, A Model Selection Approach to Assessing the Information in the Term Structure Using Linear Models and Artificial Neural Networks, *Journal of Business and Economic Statistics*, 13, 265–75.

1997, A Model Selection Approach to Real-Time Macroeconomic Forecasting Using Linear Models and Artificial Neural Networks, *Review of Economics and Statistics*, 79, 540–50.

Teräsvirta T., D. Tjostheim, and C. W. J. Granger, 1994, Aspects of Modeling Nonlinear Time Series, in *Handbook of Econometrics, Vol. IV*, Amsterdam: Elsevier.

Toda, H. Y., and P. C. B. Phillips, 1993, Vector Autoregressions and Causality, *Econometrica*, 61, 1367–93.

1994, Vector Autoregression and Causality: A Theoretical Overview and Simulation Study, *Econometric Reviews*, 13, 259–85.

Toda, H. Y., and T. Yamamoto, 1995, Statistical Inference in Vector Autoregressions with Possibly Integrated Processes, *Journal of Econometrics*, 66, 225–50.

Wallis, K. F. 1974, Seasonal Adjustment and Relations between Variables, *Journal of the American Statistical Association*, 69, 18–32.

Wiener, N., 1956, The Theory of Prediction, in E. F. Beckenback, ed., *Modern Mathematics for Engineers, Series 1*.

Weiss, A. A., 1996, Estimating Time Series Models Using the Relevant Cost Function, *Journal of Applied Econometrics*, 11, 539–60.

Wold, H., 1938, *A Study in the Analysis of Stationary Time Series*, Stockholm: Almqvist and Wiksell.

Working, H., 1960, Note on the Correlation of First Differences of Averages in a Random Chain, *Econometrica*, 28, 916–18.

Yoo, B. S., 1987, *Co-integrated Time Series Structure*, Ph.D. Dissertation, UCSD.

Young, A. H., 1968, Linear Approximations to the Census and BLS Seasonal Adjustment Methods, *Journal of the American Statistical Association*, 63, 445–71.

Yule, G. U., 1921, On the Time-Correlation Problem, with Especial Reference to the Variate Difference Correlation Method, *Journal of the Royal Statistical Society*, 84, 497–526.

1926, Why Do We Sometimes Get Nonsense Correlations Between Time Series? A Study in Sampling and the Nature of Time Series, *Journal of the Royal Statistical Society*, 89, 1–64.

1927, On a Method of Investigating Periodicities in Disturbed Series, with Special Reference to Wolfer's Sunspot Numbers, *Philosophical Transactions*, 226A.

Zellner, A., 1979, Causality and Econometrics, in K. Brunner and A. H. Meltzer, eds., *Three Aspects of Policy and Policymaking*, Carnegie-Rochester Conference Series, Vol. 10, Amsterdam: North Holland.

Zellner, A., and F. Palm, 1974, Time Series Analysis and Simultaneous Equation Econometric Models, *Journal of Econometrics*, 2, 17–54.

CHAPTER 1

The ET Interview:
Professor Clive Granger
Peter C. B. Phillips

Since the 1960's, Clive Granger has been one of our most influential scholars in time series econometrics. His writings encompass all of the major developments over the last 30 years, and he is personally responsible for some of the most exciting ideas and methods of analysis that have occurred during this time. It is now virtually impossible to do empirical work in time series econometrics without using some of his methods or being influenced by his ideas. In the last decade, the explosion of interest in cointegration is alone a striking testimony to the effect that his ideas have had on our discipline. For several decades, his work on causality, spurious regression, and spectral analysis have had profound and lasting influence. Most scholars would deem it the accomplishment of a lifetime if their work were to have the impact of a single one of these contributions. To have had repeated instances of such extraordinarily influential research is surely testimony to Clive Granger's special talent as a researcher and writer.

Possibly the most defining characteristic of Granger's work is his concern for the empirical relevance of his ideas. In a typical Granger paper, this message comes through in a powerful way, and it serves as a useful reminder to us all that ideas truly do come first in research and that mathematical niceties can indeed come later in the successful development of interesting new econometric methods. Another hallmark of the Granger style is the accessibility of his work, which stems from his unusually rich capacity to write highly readable papers and books, some of which have gone on to become citation classics. These demonstrable successes in communication show us the vital role that good writing plays in the transmission of scientific knowledge.

Like many Englishmen, Clive Granger loves to travel. He is a familiar face and a regular invited speaker at conferences in econometrics, time series, and forecasting throughout the world. Wherever he goes, he

Econometric Theory 13, 1997, 253–303.

is greeted by former students and welcomed by admirers of his research. It seems fitting, therefore, that the interview that follows was recorded away from his home in March 1996 at Texas A&M University, where we attended a conference on time series analysis hosted by the Department of Statistics. We met again in Rio de Janeiro in August 1996, at the Latin American Meetings of the Econometric Society, and concluded a penultimate version of the transcript while enjoying a further opportunity to talk econometrics and time series. Clive Granger's research has been an inspiration to us all, and it is a pleasure and honor to present this conversation with him to a wider audience.

Welcome Clive. Thank you for agreeing to do this interview. In the first part of the interview, I would like to cover your educational background and some of the highlights of your career. Can you start by telling us about your early intellectual interests – at school and at home.

I cannot say I was especially distinguished at anything, except mathematics. I was always relatively good at mathematics compared to my peers. This got me promotion in school and advancement to grammar school in Britain, which was important in those days, and then eventually to university. Otherwise, I had very wide interests, but nothing that I would say was worth recording.

Which grammar schools did you attend?

I attended two. They were the Cambridgeshire High School, just outside Cambridge, and West Bridgford Grammar School in Nottingham.

At school, were you already thinking about a career later in life?

I always wanted to use my mathematics, but not to be a pure mathematician. My hope was to find an area of applied mathematics that was going to be helpful or useful in some sense. I felt that pure mathematics in itself was rather sterile, being interesting, but not directly useful to people. I considered a variety of possible application areas and my first thought was meteorology. At high school on one occasion, we all had to stand up and announce what our future career was going to be. In those days I stuttered a bit, and I stood up and I tried to say meteorology and I could not say the "m," so I said statistician because at least I could say the word. That switched me into becoming a statistician, so stuttering partly determined my future career.

Almost a self-fulfilling prophecy.

Exactly.

When you went on to university, did you start studying statistics immediately or did that come later?

No, when I was applying to universities, I was looking at statistics departments and, of course, mathematics with statistics. Nottingham University, at that time, was just starting up the first-ever joint degree in economics and mathematics, and that struck me as a very interesting application. It was brand new in those days in Britain. And so I applied, even though Nottingham was my home town, and it was always thought a good idea to go away to another city. I liked the description of the degree because it mixed two things – one thing I thought I could do, and one thing I thought was going to be interesting, economics, and I liked very much the people there in Nottingham. They did not get too many applicants the first year, so I think that got me into that degree rather easily. So, I went to Nottingham to enter that joint degree, but at the end of the first year, the Math Department persuaded me to switch over to mathematics but to concentrate on statistics. My idea always was to go back and at some point try to finish off the economics part of the joint degree, but I never did that formally. Then, when I finished my math degree at Nottingham, I did a Ph.D. in statistics, but always with the idea of doing statistics that was useful in economics.

Did they have a statistics unit within the Mathematics Department at Nottingham?

No.

Just some people who were interested in statistics?

Yes. There were a couple of people there who taught statistics, but they were really pure mathematicians, just doing service teaching. And there was one pure mathematician, Raymond Pitt, the professor, who was an extremely good probability theorist. So between them, I got a rather formal training in statistics, with no applications of any kind.

So you went into this line of study thinking that there would be a strong connection with applications, but ended up being more of a mathematician by the time you had finished.

Right.

After you completed your degree, you had to steer yourself into applications. Were you able to do any reading in economics during the degree? I presume you did a few courses in economics as you went along?

Yes, but the way it was structured I could only do economics in the first year. That was rather frustrating, because the economists, though I held them in very high repute, were not very mathematical. Their discussions were always in words, which I would then try to rephrase mathematically, but that was not always that easy, because they did not always understand what I was trying to say and what they were trying to say did not always translate very clearly, in my opinion. In the first year, as a mathematician, I had trouble understanding the economists.

So looking back now, what do you think the major influences were on you during your university education?

I think I got a very sound, pure mathematics training, but I kept alive the interest in learning more about economics and applying mathematics and statistics in economics. The economists there were convinced that the future in economics lay in the mathematical and quantitative side of the subject, even though they themselves were not trained in that area. The head of the department at Nottingham, Brian Tew, was a brilliant economist, a specialist in banking and macroeconomics, who was not mathematically trained at all. He was not a believer in much of macrotheory and held the hope of new results coming from quantitative studies, particularly econometrics. That is why he encouraged me always to come back to economics and to apply new techniques to that area.

They must have thought very highly of you as a student to make the move of appointing you to a lectureship before you had finished your Ph.D. How did that come about?

That was a time when the British universities were expanding very rapidly, and getting an appointment was not particularly difficult. Nottingham had a new position in mathematics that they advertised, and they asked me whether I would apply, even though at that time I was only in my first year as a graduate student. I was lucky to get this opportunity, but I could hardly say no to my professor in that circumstance. They wanted me really to pad out the list of people to choose among. It turned out that they only had two applicants; the other one was much better qualified than I was but somehow managed to irritate the Appointments Committee, and so they selected me. Thus, I was appointed to be a lecturer, totally unqualified in my opinion, particularly compared to today's new appointments in universities. But it was just a chance event because of the high growth rate of British universities at that time.

So you completed your thesis and lectured in mathematics at the same time.

Right.

What sort of teaching assignments did you have in the early years?

As I was the only statistician, or official statistician, in the university, I was supposed to do service teaching for the Mathematics Department. This I did and taught in mathematics and for any other group who needed statistics courses. The only people who actually wanted a service course was economics, which I provided. The problem initially was that I knew all about Borel sets and things from my own learning of statistics from Cramér, but I did not know how to form a variance from data. I mean, I literally had never done that when I first started teaching, so I had to learn real statistics as I went along. I also taught a geometry course and various general courses in math for engineers and service courses of that type. But the best thing about my position there was that I was the only statistician on campus. Faculty from all kinds of areas would come to me with their statistical problems. I would have people from the History Department, the English Department, Chemistry, Psychology, and it was terrific training for a young statistician to be given data from all kinds of different places and be asked to help analyze it. I learned a lot, just from being forced to read things and think about a whole diverse type of problems with different kinds of data sets. I think that now people, on the whole, do not get that kind of training.

> *That does sound unusual. Statistics departments now service those needs with a group of people rather than just one person. So you encountered many different types of data in this work, not just time series, which was the main type of data in economics in those days.*

Yes.

> *Did you manage to maintain contact with the Economics Department during this time?*

Yes, although I actually published things in areas other than economics at that time, material that arose from some of this consulting work.

> *I gather from what you said a few moments ago that one of the main books that influenced you was Harald Cramér's* Mathematical Methods of Statistics?

Yes, that was the book that we used for our course work in probability and statistics.

> *Did you have to read it cover to cover?*

Pretty well, because my teacher was extremely strong on measure theory, as that was his major area for research at one time.

> *After you had been at Nottingham for a few years, you got an opportunity to go to Princeton. Would you tell us about this?*

There were some scholarships available to people from Britain and, in fact, also Australia, to go to the States, called the Harkness Scholarships of the Commonwealth Fund. They were fairly competitive, but I was lucky enough to get one. What they did was allow you to go to the States for a year or even two years, to choose wherever you wanted to go to and just do nothing but research for a period. They also gave you money to travel around the States and you had to guarantee to go back to your own country for several years afterwards. The idea was to get promising people from these countries to go to the USA, to understand the country better, and then go back to tell other people about, from inside as it were, what life was like in the U.S. and the way the country thought about things and did things. So I wrote to various places in the U.S., saying I had this scholarship and can I come and do some research. I got just two positive responses, one was from the Cowles Commission at Yale and one was from Princeton, from Oscar Morgenstern. Morgenstern said, "Come and join our time series project." As that sounded very promising, I decided to do that. I went to Princeton and the time series project turned out to be Michio Hatanaka and myself. But we were to study under John Tukey about spectral analysis. John Tukey had developed univariate and bivariate spectral analysis, and Oscar Morgenstern had been told by Von Neumann some years previously that Fourier methods should be used in economics, and Oscar had always wanted to have a project that used Fourier methods. Tukey had agreed to supervise a couple of people in Morgenstern's group in these methods and so Michio and I were the people designated to be taught these new methods. That was an extremely rewarding experience. I have tremendous admiration for John Tukey, intellectually and personally. We were taught in a very unconventional way. John Tukey was always unconventional in anything that he did. We would meet once a week and we would use real data, and he would just tell us to do a certain computation on this data. Michio, who knew more about computing than I did, would program and do the computation, and I would try and write down the mathematics of what we were doing. The next week, John Tukey would interpret the results we got from the computation and then tell us to do something else, the next computation. And so over a period, we built up this experience of working with data and interpreting it. At the same time, I was working out mathematically what we were actually doing, which John was not explaining.

How remarkable.

It was a very interesting way to learn.

It sounds like a team of rocket scientists, with the head scientist telling the juniors what to do and the juniors then trying to decipher what the instructions meant.

Exactly.

That style of directing research is not used much these days, at least in economics or econometrics.

Well, I think it would not work for every group of people, but John was very good. I would show him the mathematics and he would agree with me eventually, but the problem in the end came out that we wanted to publish this because it was all very new, particularly the bispectrum or cross-spectrum, but John Tukey was too busy to actually publish his work, so he just allowed us to publish it. That is how the book came out. We did refer to him, obviously, as the originator of all of this area, but we could not wait for him to publish, because it still would not have appeared. I do not think that he has ever published his work in this field.

That, in itself, is rather extraordinary, isn't it?

Yes.

The Princeton project was an interesting example of successful coordination between people in mathematics and economics departments.

There were a variety of skills that happened to mix fairly nicely in this case. Michio was a very good economist as well as a good statistician. We all got along together very well. We did not actually learn much about economics, in a sense, from the particular example we were working on, but we learned a lot about spectral analysis. Then, from that, we could move on to do other experiments and other applications.

A fascinating synergy – bringing people together with different skills from different parts of the world to achieve something that would not have been done otherwise. The Cowles Commission was very good at doing this sort of thing in the 40's and early 50's. Did Cowles offer you anything interesting as an alternative?

No, they just said you are welcome to come.

So, after Princeton you went back to Nottingham. Was that a little deflating after having been over in the U.S., working on this exciting research project?

Well, Morgenstern was very nice to me, and I had worked very hard at Princeton for him. I had done everything he had asked me to do, and, of course, I was benefiting from it, enjoying it and so on. He invited me back every summer for three years, and so I did not lose the link with Princeton. Because of that, Morgenstern and I wrote a book together on the stock market, plus some articles. So it was not as though I was cut off from America; I kept sòmething of a link for a period with both places. I would spend a year in Nottingham lecturing and then come back to summer in Princeton, which was not physically all that pleasant, but intellectually it was great, and Michio was there still. If in fact, he was permanently present there.

So that lent some continuity to the project. Did Michio ever get over to see you in Nottingham?

No.

After getting back to Nottingham, did you find it to be a "lower energy" environment than Princeton?

At Nottingham I was the only person – the only statistician or econometrician there – and so there was almost no one to talk to. I could do my own work, and read and so on, but at Princeton there were just dozens of people to talk to. David Brillinger was there at that time, as were a number of really good econometricians, some students of Tukey, all of whom were worthwhile for me to interact with, as well as faculty, like Dick Quandt. There were many people around, including the game theorists.

There was one rather exciting episode that was not really related to econometrics. I do not quite remember the year, but this was the year when the American President was going to meet with the Russian President for the first time in many years. Morgenstern was an advisor to Eisenhower on game theory, and so he came roaring into the department one day saying, "You have got to learn something about bargaining theory. No one knows anything about bargaining theory [at least to this point in time]. So drop everything you are doing." He called in everybody "to sit down and do nothing but think about bargaining theory for two weeks, because we must tell the President what to do when he meets the Russian President to bargain. Because he has few ideas from a scientific viewpoint." And so it was rather fun, and we had some really good game theorists in town, Kuhn and so on. I think Dick Quandt was also involved. We just had these continuously running seminars discussing what bargaining was about. It was really exciting because you felt that if we did something, it might have an impact on world history at some point.

Rather like the Manhattan Project.

That's right.

So, did anything come out of it?

No, because the U2 plane incident happened, and then the meeting was canceled. In my opinion, we did not discover all that much about bargaining theory. We got a few basic principles, that sort of thing; we did not get anything very deep. But it was exciting. It was different from what we had been doing.

Very different. Back in England in the 1960's, some important things were happening in econometrics, especially at the London School of Economics (LSE). You were physically distant from London, but did you have any contact with the group there?

From my perspective, the main activity was indeed at the LSE. It was rather an insider-outsider thing. I was very much an outsider, as I was not really included in their activities. I would hear about them, and I would occasionally see something from them. I knew a lot of the people at the LSE, such as Bill Phillips, Jim Durbin; and Denis Sargan, and later I knew Ken Wallis and David Hendry. But I was never a close member of that group.

At that stage, they had not started the regular Econometric Study Group meetings in the U.K., which did help to bring people in econometrics together. They started around the time I went to England in 1971. Given the separation, did you feel it was a disadvantage being outside London?

No, I wished I was part of the group in some ways, because then I would feel more accepted. But, on the other hand, I think there was some advantage to not being part of the group.

Maintaining your own research agenda and working independently?

Yes. I remember one instance where Paul Newbold and I had done some work on spurious regression, a Monte Carlo study, and I gave a talk about it at the LSE. It was met with total disbelief. Their reaction was that we must have gotten the Monte Carlo wrong – we must have done the programming incorrectly. I feel that if I had been part of the LSE group, they might well have persuaded me not to have done that research at that point.

I wish I had been there at that time! A fascinating story.

Later they became quite strong supporters of that point.

Indeed.

It shows how when people are so convinced that they are right that they have difficulty accepting the ideas of another person who holds a different opinion.

I remember that there was a strong negativism about the Box-Jenkins methodology at the LSE at that time. It was apparent at several of the Econometric Study Group meetings held there. Whereas up at Essex, there was a great deal of support for Box-Jenkins modeling methods – we had seminars on it in the statistics group with Chris

Winsten and others. Around that time, in 1974, you moved to UC San Diego. Would you like to tell us how this transition came about?

While I was at Princeton, one of my friends there was Dan Orr, who was a graduate student at the time. Eventually, he became the head of the department at San Diego, UC of San Diego, and he invited us out for a six-month visit. We really liked the place, liked it physically and liked the people very much. Then a couple of years later, he offered me a position there. At that time, I was getting rather fed up with England for various reasons. I had been at the same university at Nottingham for all my career. I had been an undergraduate and a graduate and had stayed on up to full professor in the same university, which is really not that good of an idea, I think. If it were not for Princeton, I would have been totally inbred. Also, the British economy was starting to go bad at that point. So I just felt the need for a change of scene. If you are going to move, you can move 6,000 miles as easily as 60, really. I mean, once you have packed up, it is not that much different. So we decided to go to San Diego for five years and see if we liked it. If we did not like it, we would return to Britain. Well, after five years, there were no jobs in Britain. The British economy had really gone bad and there was no choice to make. We were happy in San Diego at that point, and there was no alternative, so we stayed on.

But then, five years or so later, a lot of academics were leaving Britain.

Yes, exactly. When I left Nottingham, I made two forecasts: one was that the British economy would do less well than the U.S. economy, and the second was there would be better weather in San Diego than in Nottingham. Both forecasts turned out to be perfectly correct. So I was happy about them.

So you were not at all apprehensive about making this big international move?

Well, as we had visited for six months, we pretty well knew what we were getting into, because we knew the place and we knew the people. And we had good friends there. We were a bit apprehensive about some things. The children were more worried than we were, in a sense. As far as academic life was concerned, it clearly was going to be an improvement, I think, over Nottingham, but I was sorry to leave Paul Newbold. He and I were getting along very well and being very productive. Paul actually came to San Diego for the first year with me when I first went to San Diego. Yes, looking back, there were some difficulties in transition. But you have to make some adjustments sometimes.

Were your children in junior, middle, or high school at that time?

I think they were only ages 6 and 10.

That is probably a good stage to be moving with children.

Yes, my daughter was 6, so she moved okay. My son certainly had problems. He was worried about whether he would fit into the new environment.

San Diego has now turned into a first-rate department with a world-class econometrics unit. What was it like when you arrived? Can you give us some thoughts on what has happened in the interim?

Yes, when I arrived it was very quiet in econometrics. John Hooper was there, who did not publish very much and was not active in research at all. There were other people there who knew some econometrics but were not active in the area. So I was not going to a place that was strong in econometrics in the slightest. The group got built up by accident, in a sense. Rob Engle joined us because he and I were on a committee together for a conference in Washington, and because he happened to be looking for a position he just asked me if I knew of somewhere that was looking for an econometrician, and I said, "Yes, we are." He came out. We liked him. He liked us and joined us, and that was a terrific appointment. Then, Hal White came out as a visitor and again he liked the place very much, and just asked if there was a position. Again, we were delighted to say yes. And so that, again, was a terrific appointment. So neither of them were planned. This was not really empire building in the sense that somebody had a plan and an ambition to build a group. It just happened.

So destiny determined all these appointments, including your own. In a sense, they were almost incidental.

Yes, I think the fact that the faculty has stayed together has been more work than getting things together in the first place. It is clear that there have been offers for people to move and there have been counteroffers at San Diego, but the department has been very supportive of the group, and so people have been content to stay. They have been happy enough in San Diego and the salary differences are not that much between other offers and San Diego. And so the fact that we have managed to keep together has been one of the major reasons that the group looked so strong. There has not been much movement around. Stability, I think, is important.

And there has been growth and new strength in other areas. You now have Jim Hamilton, for example.

Absolutely, another very good appointment.

So, looking back over your career in England and the U.S., how would you characterize the main differences between the U.S. and the U.K. systems?

The U.K. system is self-stifling. The more research you do, the more administration you get to do, because as you get promoted in Britain the more committees you are put on and the less time you have to do research. Whereas in the States, there is much more time to do research over the whole year. Not only do we have teaching assistants to mark our scripts for us, which is a big help, but we also have research assistants to help us do some of our computing and data collection or whatever. I can spend a lot more time doing research in the States than I could in Britain. There are also more colleagues to talk to in an American university than in a British university. In a British university, you are lucky to have one other good person. In Nottingham, for years, I had nobody. Then I had Paul Newbold, which was like night and day. Having at least one good person to talk to was just terrific. In San Diego, I have several good people to talk to all the time, plus visitors. The one negative thing, I think, in the U.S. as compared to Great Britain, is that, in my experience in Britain, it is easier to talk to people from lots of different disciplines over lunch, in meetings and different committees. We would meet and talk about their problems or other intellectual matters. I do not find I do this in San Diego. Most departments do not interact very much. Whether that is just San Diego, I do not know, because I do not have enough experience in other universities in the State. But it seems to be a pity. I had expected when I went to San Diego that I would continue to be involved with people in other departments, but there is no cross-disciplinary discussion. I think that universities will suffer from that.

Is this also the case with the statistics group at San Diego? Have they been interested in fostering links with the econometrics group?

I think that it is a purely personal matter, depending on who happens to be in the group at the time. We have had people in the group there who have been very anxious to link up and do things jointly and other people who have not. The statistics group there has changed over the years. There is no overall plan of any kind.

Sometimes students can help to bring departments together. If there are good students in the mathematics and statistics departments who are interested in applications in other areas like economics, that can bring faculty together if only through joint thesis advising. Have you had any examples like this is San Diego, students coming over from statistics and mathematics?

I have been on several Ph.D. committees in the Math Department, but they are all extremely technical probabilistic-type Ph.D.'s, and I can hardly understand even what the topic is, let alone the details of the thesis.

Let's move on now to your own research. I want to start by asking you the unanswerable question that I think everyone would like me to ask. That is, what is the key to your own success in writing highly readable and influential papers over so many years?

I would claim to try and do research that other people find useful. And I think if I have any ability, it is a good taste in finding topics that I can make a contribution to and that other people then find interesting.

> *Some people would call it a nose for the right problem. Do you feel that instinct operating as you are thinking about problems to work on or areas to work in?*

I am usually working on several problems at once. I mean, I always have lots of things that I am thinking about and I will often drop topics that I do not think other people will find interesting. Even though I might find something fairly interesting myself, I just do not do it because I have a preference for topics that will have an impact somewhere. This goes back to my original idea of doing applicable work as opposed to just things to work on.

> *So, this is a theme that you have maintained from the time you were a student at university.*

Yes. I do not know why.

> *Is it personally satisfying to feel that you are still following much the same trajectory in your research?*

Yes, it gives you a kind of focus on things, a viewpoint that allows you to make decisions.

> *In the same general vein, what do you find interesting or impressive about other people's work?*

I find that if I can understand what the purpose of the research is, a simplicity of statement, and if the point being made is very clear cut, a simple point, then I am impressed by that. I do not mind whether there is a lot of technique or not in the paper. I am ambivalent about that. What I really want to see at the beginning is a statement about what is being done and why and that there is some sort of clear result to which I will say, "Well, that is really interesting." That impresses me. I do not like papers that are really complicated and that, in the end, have conclusions that are very complicated. Then it is too difficult for me to work out whether there is anything in there, anything that is worth having.

> *This is partly a matter of communication and partly a matter of the real objectives behind research. When you are looking for topics to work on yourself, do you have a hunch about whether or not something is going to work out?*

Yes, in fact, often with a lot of the ideas I have, already I have got some intuition about what the final result is going to look like, even before I start doing any mathematics or writing anything down. It does not always work out that way, but usually I know what the shape of the article is going to be before I start. And, from that, I think that I can sell it or not sell it, or work out whether it is interesting to other people. Quite a lot of the topics I work on have arisen from some applied area. So in a sense, if you solve something, you know that group is going to be interested in the topic. Sort of a ready-made audience for a solution. But, then again, I think, most people do not want very complicated answers to their questions. If you can tell them a nice simple answer, if there is a simple answer, then that is what they want.

> *Yes, I think that comes over clearly in empirical research. People like ordinary least-squares regression, vector autoregression, techniques like this that are easily used and understood. A lot of your papers emphasize ideas and concepts, and although they have technical derivations in them, you do not ever really dwell on the mathematics. You seem to want to get through to the useable end-product as quickly as possible. Another feature of your papers is that you have a clear desire to communicate what you are doing. Do you feel that that comes naturally or is that something that you work hard to achieve in your writing?*

I think it is something that I do think about when I am writing, but I also think that the British educational system does teach you to write fairly well compared to some other educational systems.

> *Not to mention any in particular?*

Exactly. Certainly, in England, I was forced to write an essay at university every week for a year or two, so you just get quite good at writing essays, and that is relevant for writing down fairly clear conclusions. That is not unimportant.

> *Scientific communication is difficult partly because it is so multifaceted. There are technical concepts, the mathematical development, all the working processes, the empirical calculations, and then the conclusions. Often, people are encouraged to emphasize the theorems, the derivations, the technical novelty, as distinct from the useable results. I do not want to dwell too long on this point, but I do think that this is one feature that distinguishes your work from others. If you can offer any more insights on your writing, then I think it will be valuable to people.*

Partly it is my limitation on technique. My math is okay, but it is not terrific. I do not do a lot of high-powered mathematics, because, in a sense, I am not that comfortable with it. I can follow it, but I do not necessarily want to develop it or to bring new mathematics to an area that is already well developed. I have enough mathematics to survive in what I am doing. I typically want to get an idea across, and so I am much more inclined to do it in terms of simple bivariate cases, and then say we can clearly generalize this, and let someone else do that. Because once people have got the idea, their generalization is not all that difficult and you often do not learn all that much from a generalization. I think it is the first idea that matters. That is what I am trying to get across.

> *Do you find that it is useful to stand back from your work and take a long, hard look at it? Or, to think in general terms about where you are going rather than the minutiae of working it all out? For example, with cointegration, there are clearly a lot of details that need to be worked out. Even the Granger representation theorem is not a trivial thing to resolve. Is thinking about what you are producing and where you are going important to you?*

No, I just rely on intuition. I just feel there is a result there, and I try to get most of the result myself and I am comfortable with presenting that and then letting other people do it properly. I would say that I try and get an idea and then I develop it a little bit and when the mathematics gets too difficult, I get out and let someone else proceed with it. That is true with the work on causality, for example. The causality idea is a very simple idea, but it can be put in a much more mathematical and technical framework, as now has been done by several people. Now, whether or not we learn much from all that technical stuff is a different matter.

> *In mathematics and statistics, some people find that they get a lot of false starts, spend a lot of time doing something, and nothing comes of it. Have you found that in your work?*

Yes, I was thinking of this the other day. I plant lots of seeds, a few of them come up, and most of them do not. So, all the time, I have lots of little ideas I am working on or thinking about, and some I find that I am not going to get anywhere with, and so I just drop them. And others seem very promising and I will dig into those much deeper, read more, and try and find things that are relevant for it. I do not often get a long way into a subject and then have to drop it. I typically find out pretty quickly if I am getting out of my depth, or if it is not looking very promising.

> *Do you have any projects that you have been working on or thinking about for long periods of time like 25 or 30 years and you still have not solved, that kind of thing?*

No, no, I drop things.

Let's talk about methodology. As you know, methodology has been a big topic in econometrics now for a decade or more at conferences and in the literature. Where do you see us going on this?

Let me just talk about time series for a moment. In time series, we are getting swamped with different alternative models we can fit. We have got hundreds of different sorts of nonlinear models, for example. We have dozens of different variations of ARCH model, and so on, as well as long-memory and short-memory models. Putting it all together, we have got so many different models now that we have to have a methodology of deciding which part of this group to aim at and use. That is a problem. And, as we get more computing power and more data, that is going to become more of a problem, not less of problem, because more and more models are potentially useable in a data set. What we are seeing now is different people who have different favorites just using those favorite models on their data and saying, "Look guys, it works," and not doing comparisons. The one advantage we have in time series is that we can do postsample analysis. We can compare models using forecasting ability as a criteria, because we can make forecasts and then compare them to actual observations. So, I think, in forecasting and in the time series area, provided the postsample is generated by the same type of mechanism as the sample itself, we do have a pretty clear way of comparing models and evaluating alternatives. Now, let us say this is either not available or has not been used in other areas of econometrics. For example, you do not see the same methodology used in panel data work or in cross-section analyses. I think that the methodology in these areas is in less good shape than in time series, because they do not have a proper evaluation technique. So, there are obviously many problems in methodology in time series, but at least we do have, in my opinion, a reasonable way of deciding between models.

So you see big differences between microeconometrics and time series econometrics in terms of the capability to compare and evaluate different models?

Yes, the criticism that I put to microeconometricians is that they do not phrase their output in terms of errors from a decision-making mechanism. They do not say that they are trying to generate a number that is going into a decision and the decision mechanism will lead to an error, and there is a cost to such errors and that we can compare different models with the cost of the error. I am not saying it is easy to do, I am just saying they are not even thinking in those terms. But we do think in those terms in forecasting and are hopefully learning by so doing.

Of course, time series analysts have been working for 25 years on model determination criteria, and we now know a great deal about

these criteria in a time series context. Do you favor a classical statis-
tical approach to this, or do you see some advantages in the Bayesian
paradigms here?

I have always told Arnold Zellner I am not a Bayesian because I lack self-confidence. That is, you have to have enough self-confidence to have a specific prior on things, and I do not think I know enough about things to have a specific prior. I may have a general prior on some things. I think that a good Bayesian, that is, a Bayesian who picks a prior that has some value to it, is better than a non-Bayesian. And a bad Bayesian who has a prior that is wrong is worse than a non-Bayesian, and I have seen examples of both. What I do not know is how do I know which is which before we evaluate the outcome.

Let's talk more about your personal research now. You have already
told us something about the history of spectral analysis. Is there any-
thing more you would like to say about this? For example, in the 50's
and 60's, economists were very concerned in macroeconomics about
business cycles and, no doubt, that was one of the driving forces
behind getting into the frequency domain approach.

Well, I think it was. But Oscar Morgenstern was not greatly involved with business cycles at the time, and it was not emphasized to us when we were doing it. John Tukey certainly was not thinking about business cycles. He was thinking about any kind of important frequency band. We were certainly trying to get away from narrow peaks in the spectrum. We were thinking about important regions of the spectrum. So we were not thinking about pure cycles, which some engineers emphasize. We were thinking about whether or not some band was important. Initially, the work we mostly did involved interest rates, exchange rates, and stock market prices. We certainly looked for a business cycle band and seasonal bands and so on, but we were not specifically looking at the business cycle. And, once we got to the cross-spectrum, then we did look at the business cycle particularly, because we considered leading indicators. One way to decide whether or not the indicator was leading was to look at the effect of the phase diagram around the business cycle frequencies. But, I think the business cycle was not the driving force in that. It was really to see whether the decomposition was going to be useful in some way for interpreting economic data.

So what would you say was the main empirical outcome of your work
at this stage?

Well, the typical spectral shape was the first thing that came out. Whenever we did a spectrum it looked sort of the same shape, and I felt that was interesting, but dull.

Your paper on the typical spectral shape was published later, wasn't it? It came out after the book.

Yes, that was because *Econometrica* kept it for four years. After two years, I think, the editor said to me, "It has still not been refereed yet. We think it must be okay, so we will publish it."

This paper created the first stylized fact in spectral analysis. Some authors have been trying to create a second stylized fact by looking at the spectrum of differenced series. Have you seen any of this work?

No. I always felt that the cross-spectrum was more important than the spectrum, because of the typical spectrum shape. Potentially, we are always interested in relationships in economics rather than univariate series, and the cross-spectrum has much richer interpretations. But it turned out, I think, that the cross-spectrum is not that easy to interpret because of the potential feedback in models.

Which connects to issues of causality, a second area where you worked that has had a huge impact on the subject, particularly empirical work. Would you like to tell us about the origins of your work on causality?

It was because of the cross-spectrum. I was trying to interpret the phase diagram. I realized that I needed to know whether or not one series affected the other or whether or not there was a bidirectional relationship. The interpretation of the phase diagram mattered, whether or not there was a one-way relationship or a two-way relationship, so I needed a causality-type definition and test. I attempted to invent such a definition, and was having difficulties in doing that. I had a friend at Nottingham called Andre Gabor, whom I was working with, and his brother was Dennis Gabor, who was at Imperial College and who won the Nobel Prize in physics for holography. A very nice man and a brilliant physicist. I had dinner with him, Dennis Gabor, one night and he said to me that there is a definition of causality in a paper by Norbert Wiener, and he gave me a reference. I looked up this paper and I could not find this definition in the paper. But I had such high respect for Dennis Gabor that I kept reading and reading this paper until eventually I found that there was a definition in it. What was misleading to me was that there was a section of the paper with the word causality in the heading of the section, but the definition was in a later section of the paper. Anyway, the definition there was the one that is now called Granger causality or Granger noncausality. That is what I used in the spectral analysis book to disentangle the bivariate relationship of empirical series and therefore reinterpret the phrase diagram. As I thought that this was an important concept, I published it separately in a journal called *Information and Control*. That article was pretty well ignored, so I published another article in

Econometrica on this definition, which again was ignored, until Chris Sims came along with an application of that definition that was very controversial because he was discussing a relationship between money and income and came out with a conclusion that did not suit some people. Then, a lot of attention was given to the definition. So it was the application that made the definition well known. Part of the defense of the people who did not like the conclusion of Chris Sims's paper was that this was not real causality, this was only Granger causality. So they kept using the phrase Granger causality, everywhere in their writings, which I thought was inefficient, but it made my name very prominent.

> *Yes, it certainly attracted an enormous amount of attention. How do you feel now about causality? Do you feel that the operational definition that we have is the right one and the one that we should be staying with, or do you have some further thoughts on it now?*

I feel that it is still the best pragmatic definition – operational definition. I feel that when we get to a universally accepted definition of causation, if that ever should occur, I imagine that this will be part of it but not necessarily all of it. I think there are more things that need to go in than just this pragmatic part. The philosophers who have been thinking about causation for thousands of years initially did not like this definition very much, but in recent years several books on philosophy have discussed it in a much more positive way, not saying that it is right, but also saying that it is not wrong. I view that as supporting my position that it is probably a component of what eventually will be a definition of causation that is sound. But, all I am worrying about is just a statistical definition that we can go out and apply. Now, whether we use the word causation or not, I do not care much in a sense. It is just a word that I used at that stage, and I used it because Wiener had used it. And, if he can use it, so can I.

> *It could easily have been predictability.*

Yes, exactly.

> *Are you happy with the mechanisms that people use to test causality? I think that this is surely one of the reasons that it has been so successful, that people can build VAR's and do causality tests on subblocks of the coefficients so easily.*

No, I am not happy about it.

> *What would you like to see people doing?*

The definition is a predictability test, not a test of fit, and so the fact that your model fits in-sample does not mean it is going to forecast out of sample. The test that I push is that you actually build in-sample models with or without the possible variable, so you have two models, and then you ask which model actually forecasts the better out of sample, using a comparison of forecasts test. That is a true test of the forecasting ability of the models and the definition is the forecasting definition.

> *Do you have any recommendations about the forecast horizon to be used and precisely how to mount the test?*

Yes, I use a one-step horizon, that is always a problem and you could discuss that, and there is always the cost function. Again, we can use least squares, but that is not necessarily the right cost function. There are several different tests of how to compare forecasts. There is a test that Lehmann suggested that is quite efficient and easy to use. It is in the Granger–Newbold book and there are better versions of that test that have appeared more recently, and are rather more complicated, but there are several tests available to compare forecasts.

> *That is typically not what people do. People still regularly use VAR's for testing causality.*

I have written a couple of papers saying that I do not like that – for example in the *Journal of Economic Dynamics and Control* in 1980 [5–9] – and another on advertising and consumption, with Ashley and Schmalensee – in *Econometrica*, also in 1980 [60]. Perhaps people do not read those parts of my papers.

> *Hopefully, this will direct attention to that work. Can we now talk about spurious regressions? You mentioned earlier how you spoke about the paper at the LSE and it got a rather hostile reception. How did your thinking emerge on that paper?*

That arose just because Paul Newbold was trained by George Box and was an expert in Box–Jenkins techniques. We were just thinking it through. In the Box–Jenkins way of thinking about things and the balancing in equations, you cannot usually have two $I(1)$ variables and the residuals be $I(0)$. So we realized that there could be a problem, that would explain some of the things that we were seeing. We were worried that so many papers were being written in which the Durbin–Watson statistic was not being reported, and if it was reported then it was extremely low. The R^2 was high, Durbin–Watson's were low and we were worried about what that meant. And so we thought that this was an interesting problem and so we tried a Monte Carlo study, a very small Monte Carlo for these days.

> *But, probably one of the most influential Monte Carlo studies of all time.*

It certainly made a structural change in the literature regarding the way people reported their results, anyway.

*Yes, there was a big subsequent debate in England about economet-
ric reporting and about the conduct of empirical research that led
eventually to the notion that it was necessary to report an army of
diagnostic statistics to accompany each regression. The spurious
regression paper gave rise to the alternative idea that if regression
equations are in balance, then something must be happening in order
to annihilate the integrated nature of the series. The idea of cointegration. Would you like to talk now about this idea and how your
thinking evolved in this direction?*

That was through a discussion with David Hendry. I do not remember where
it took place now, but he was saying that he had a case where he had two
$I(1)$ variables, but their differences was $I(0)$, and I said that is not possible,
speaking as a theorist. He said he thought it was. So I went away to prove I
was right, and I managed to prove that he was right. Once I realized that this
was possible, then I immediately saw how it was related to the formulation
of an error correction model and their balancing. So, in a sense, all the main
results of cointegration came together within a few minutes. I mean, without
any proof, at least not any deep proof, I just sort of saw what was needed.
The common stochastic trend was an immediate consequence of what I
wrote down. That is the basic way of viewing cointegration, and it just came
from this discussion. Then I had to go away and prove it. That was another
thing. But I could see immediately what the main results were going to be.

*To a certain extent, it must have been clear to many people that this
balancing of successful regression equations with trending data must
hold. Econometricians had long been running regressions in levels
that were clearly nonstationary, yet moving together in some general
sense, and the residuals from these regressions, when plotted, clearly
looked stationary.*

Yet. It is one of these things that, once it was pointed out to people, all kinds
of other things made sense, and I think that is why it was accepted so readily.

An idea whose time had come, essentially.

I think it fit in also with economic theory ideas to some extent, such as
equilibrium in macroeconomics. I am not actually pushing the equilibrium
interpretation very strongly, but it sort of fits in with the ideas that
macroeconomists have. I think macroeconomists at the time were so des-
perate for something else to do, and cointegration fitted in very well with
what they needed. It explained all kinds of different regressions that you saw
people getting results for. It is also one of the few things that I have done
that is largely uncontroversial. In a sense, it is uncontroversial because
people have accepted it uncritically, and I think there are things about it
which can be criticized, and I have even tried to do that in some writings.

But people have just sort of taken the whole thing and run with it. It certainly has been influential.

> *It is such an enormously useable apparatus. I believe that Box and Jenkins had a lot to do with this, because prior to Box and Jenkins we just extracted deterministic trends from series by regression and then used conventional time series procedures on what was expected to be stationary residual components. Now, we think about there being an additional element in the data – stochastic trends – and we need to take this component into account in empirical regressions. In a way, this line of thinking would not have emerged if it had not been for the Box–Jenkins emphasis on differencing the data. You noticed that unless something special was going on, regressions with undifferenced data would be spurious.*

Right.

> *This seems to be a case where pinpointing a concept, and naming it, can be very important. It brings together previous thinking in a creative synergy, something that would not otherwise have occurred.*

I think you are right. This is a case where the pure time series literature and the pure economics literature came together very nicely to help each other. So, someone brought up on pure econometrics in those days would not have taken over the Box–Jenkins ideas. You needed people who were trained in both areas to see that, to see what they got from bringing them together.

> *So, if it had not been for the economics community worrying about this issue, how long do you think it would have been before statisticians invented cointegration?*

Actually, I am really impressed by how statisticians do invent things before they are applied, so I just do not know the answer to that. I mean, you see all kinds of things, like some of the nonlinear methods, being developed before they are used anywhere. Still I wouldn't be surprised, for example, if statisticians had cointegration in some of their data, but they did not know about it, and they did not look for it.

> *The Box–Jenkins methodology was essentially univariate, and there had been no successful attempt to extend it to the multivariate case, partly because one simply cannot eyeball matrices of correlations. Because this literature persisted as univariate, I think it was more difficult for the idea of cointegration to emerge from it.*

Yes, although I believe it is mentioned in some early papers by Box and others.

Let's talk about long-memory models, which are now a big subject, especially with regard to stochastic volatility modeling. You wrote an important paper with Roselyn Joyeux on long-memory models in 1980. There has been a tremendous amount of subsequent work. Would you like to talk about some of the developments?

I think that is a fairly interesting class of models. And, for a long time, I did not work on the area after the first paper or two, because I did not think there were any good examples in economics. Some people suggested they had found examples, but I was not convinced. But, recently we have gotten some extremely good examples for long memory by using daily returns from speculative markets and they have significantly positive autocorrelations at lags up to 2,000, very clear evidence, unbelievable. And we find this for many different speculative markets, commodity markets, stock markets, interest rates, and so on. There are obviously a number of different models, all of which produce this same long-memory property. And what I would hope to see next is some more general discussion about alternative models that have this property and then how to distinguish between them. We should not just say that, because the data has a certain property and the model has a certain property that the model therefore generated that data. We can often find several models that have the same property. So I suspect that the next stage in this area is going to be comparing alternative models, not just fractionally integrated models, which are the ones that statisticians mostly look at right now. I think some of the other models might actually be more interesting and make more economic sense than the fractionally integrated model.

What models do you have in mind?

Well, there are some switching regime models that will do it. Some duration models that will do it. William Park at North Carolina has a duration model in which you have shocks coming from a certain distribution, and when they occur they have a duration attached to them. So they persist for a number of time periods. You can get for a particular survival probability distribution some long-memory processes from these duration models. So it is like having a news sequence to the stock market, but some news lasts only a few hours. Other news lasts several days. And some news may last a month. And if you have the right distribution for the length of the survival of the news, you can actually get a long-memory process out of it. It is a nice paper.

Yes, I have seen it. It is a cute idea. Again, it depends on a statistical artifact. Here there is a heavy-tailed distribution generating regimes that can have very long duration and these are the source of the long memory. It certainly is another way of looking at it. Your original idea was to use aggregation.

Yes.

Economics has yet to contribute any useful ideas to the formulation of models that might be appropriate for long memory in stochastic volatility. I think we would benefit enormously if there were some relevant economic model.

I agree totally. One of the differences between models is that forecasting will be different. I would like to have a theory if possible.

A purely statistical theory that relies on the arrival of heavy-tailed shocks in determining duration and consequently memory may not be very useful in practice, say, in forecasting.

Well, it might be possible to look at how many shocks there were in the last period. I have done it for the MA(1) case and have found there is a slight improvement in forecastability. You can sometimes work out whether there had been a shock that had lived in the previous time period and work out whether another shock could have lived this time. You get a different forecasting situation.

Another of your major interests over the years has been nonlinearity, which, again, is now a very active field. Some economists, for instance, have been working on deterministic nonlinear models, and you have worked a lot on bilinear stochastic models. How do you see this subject emerging in the next few years?

I think bilinear models are not going to have much future. I do not see much evidence of them helping forecasting, for example. Bilinear modeling is a nice example of a way to generate nonlinearity, where we can also work the mathematics out. I think that it is a good example for classrooms and textbooks. Bilinearity is also useful in working out the powers of certain tests of nonlinearity and linearity, because many tests of linearity have bad power against it, so it turns out. So it gives an example of the limitations of certain tests of linearity. I happen to be a strong disbeliever of chaos in economics, I should add. I have never seen any evidence of chaos occurring in economics. But I think there has been a great deal of misinterpretation of the evidence they think they have for chaos. I believe that there is a lot of nonlinearity in economics at the microlevel, but I do not see that we get much of that left at the macrolevel, after aggregation, temporal, and cross-sectional. There is not much nonlinearity after aggregation. I think we should look for nonlinearities and am pleased we do that. I do not myself have much hope in achieving very much using aggregate macro-nonlinear models. Interest rates, I think, are an exception, because these are already a strict aggregate. We can find nonlinearities there. I expect the area where we are going to have the most nonlinearity is in financial data. There we have a good chance of picking up something interesting.

We now have a proliferation of different approaches in modeling nonlinearity. We have partial linear models, semiparametric models, general nonparametrics, neural net models, and wavelet methods, just to mention a few. Do you have any instincts as to which of these are ultimately going to be the most valuable?

My impression is that they probably are going to fit data quite accurately but not necessarily going to be of much help in postsample work. I keep going back to the methodology question of evaluating a model by its post-sample properties. I have only run one very small experiment, so I am giving too much weight to my own personal experience. We generated some data with nonlinearities and the simple models picked them up very well and then forecast quite nicely out of sample. But then we ran some data with no non-linearities in it and still found a similar pattern, that is, the method overfitted in-sample and then forecast very badly out of sample. So my worry is that simple measures of fit are not going to be a very good way to judge whether or not these methods are finding anything in-sample, and thus postsample evaluation is going to be critical to these techniques. Hal White had convinced me from some experiments he has done that the neural net is a very good way to approximate the nonlinearity in-sample. The problem is that we cannot interpret any of the coefficients we get from any of these models. There is no relationship to any economic theory from those coefficients to anything that we started with. I think what they are mostly useful for is saying, yes, there is some nonlinearity in the data that appears to be of this type. We should go back and work out where is it coming from, what does it mean, and so forth.

Overfitting has always been a problem. One can get a model that looks very good within sample, but when you try to project with it the good sample period fit affects forecasts in a deleterious way. Over-fitting also affects inference, because of the downward bias in the regression error sum of squares. Time series analysts believe that you need good model determination methods in order to resolve these issues. In this case, the nonlinear factors have to perform well enough to warrant their inclusion in the model. We need mechanisms like these to narrow down a wide class of possible alternatives. Do you think that these methods should be used systematically in nonlinear models?

I have not seen many examples yet. If people are finding good forecasting results in the stock market, they would not actually be showing them to me, so I do not know quite whether I am getting a biased sample of evidence.

If they are successful, we will know about it eventually.

Yes. We have got to do it anyway, so whatever the arguments are, it is important to use these techniques on our data to see what we find.

How far do you think we have come with regard to economic forecasting in the last two decades?

I suspect that we have not improved very much. It is possible that the economy itself has got slightly more difficult to forecast, and it is possible that economic data have deteriorated in quality too. So, if the measurement error has increased, then our forecasts are going to deteriorate. I think we can probably look at certain areas and say we may be better at forecasting inflation than we were or something like that, so there are some areas where we have improved. But other areas are extremely difficult to forecast, like interest rates. I think that we are not using the evidence from a cross-section of forecasters effectively. That is, if there are lots of forecasters using different techniques, and they are all doing equally badly, or equally well, that tells us something. I do not know how to phrase that correctly, but, somehow, if there are people who are basing their forecasts totally on economic theory and others are basing their forecasts totally on ad hoc methods and other people are basing their forecasts on Box-Jenkins methods, and they are all presenting forecasts of equal quality, not necessarily the same forecasts, that tells us something about the economy, and we have never used that information properly, in my opinion. Not only could we combine these in some way, but maybe there is something to learn about the economy from the success or otherwise of different techniques being applied to the data set.

> *We do know that all of the models that we are using are wrong. So, if a group of forecasts from very different models and heuristic methods are all very similar, then it suggests that all those procedures may be missing out much the same thing, perhaps some critically important data. In this case, there may be some hope of improving forecasts by bringing in new data.*

Yes, it is always possible.

> *Like continuous data recording of some form, or the pooling of micro and macro data.*

Sure. Yes, perhaps replacing series that are explanatory series but slow in being recorded with other series that are more frequently recorded. For example, rather than wait for exports that come in two months late, use some customs data that are available weekly or something. There are things like this that you can do to improve that quality of forecasts, but I also think there are a certain amount of things we are missing in improving quality. I do not see at the moment where there is a big breakthrough to be made. I think we can improve forecasts by doing small things, but at the moment I do not see how to take a big step.

> *Your idea of combining forecasts has met with pretty much uniform approval. It seems to work because if both models are wrong some*

convex combination of them may do a little better. Do you have more thoughts on this, where this idea may be taking us?

Not really. Usually, using optimum weights does not much improve over using suboptimum weights on that combination. We tried using some non-linear combinations and we did not find that that helped much either. I am surprised people have not worried more about multistep forecast combining. Almost all the work has been on one-step forecast. The other thing I would like to see done, and I have not tried this myself, is to combine forecast intervals. If people provide forecast intervals, how do you combine those to get a combined forecast interval?

Modeling trends is also important in this context, and you have written on this topic also. Would you like to share some of your thoughts with us on this subject?

It has always intrigued me that for many macroseries the trend is clearly the most important component of the series, even though we do not know how to define trend, strictly speaking. But it is also the component that we analyze the least. For a long time we just stuck in a linear trend or some simplistic deterministic trend, and I have always felt that this was a very rich, unexplored area of time series modeling. In a sense, you have got to get that bit right to get the rest of the modeling right, because misspecification at one point always leads to overanalysis of other points. I think one can have quite complicated, say, nonlinear, stochastic trends but that is a very underdeveloped area still. I believe this is an area that will be developed in the next few years.

Yes, the trend-generating mechanism of accumulating shocks is essentially a linear operation. One can envisage some richly interesting alternative possibilities, but finding the right mathematics to do the analysis is always a major obstacle, isn't it?

Well, the growth processes in stochastic process theory are fairly well developed and they are quite general.

Have demographers or others been working on nonlinear stochastic mechanisms for growth do you know?

I think they have rather specific models.

Trending mechanisms in economics that are presently used seem to be so simplistic. Ultimately they boil down to the accumulation of technology shocks and demographic changes, don't they?

Yes.

So we have an impoverished class of economic models and econo-metric models to address trends. This is an irony given that, as you said, the trend is the most important visible feature of the series.

Exactly.

Over your career you have worked on a huge variety of topics. Is there any topic that you have not yet worked on that you would like to work on in the future?

The area that I want to think about is the whole evaluation process – both in econometrics and in economics generally. I want to know how people evaluate the theory and how people evaluate a technique and how to value the model. And I suspect that we are going to need to do that properly to understand whether we are making progress, whether we are developing in the right direction at all. I think that a lot of literature is losing the viewpoint that we are here to learn about the actual economy. They are playing games when they write papers. I would like to see consideration of what the objective of a piece of work is and then a statement about whether that objective has been achieved. By stating an objective, you would eventually be able to evaluate whether that objective has been reached or not in a paper, or in the model. We just need to have more thought about proper evaluation procedures, which may be tied to questions about utility functions and cost functions and many other things. There are a lot of threads out there that can be drawn together into a more general way of thinking about evaluation.

There is an accountability issue here, isn't there, about one's own personal research and that of a community of researchers. In some respects it was resolved under older regimes like the one that you were involved in at Princeton and in the early Cowles Commission program of research. There, a research director took responsibility for a research program, ensured that it was kept on track, and attracted people in to pursue a certain set of objectives and research goals. That does not seem to happen so much these days, does it?

I agree.

So do you think that this organizational feature is a factor in the problems that we have been talking about?

Absolutely. And, in fact, I go beyond that. I wish that the economics profession would be challenged to solve a real problem occasionally. The analogy I would use is how Kennedy challenged the scientific community to put an American on the moon by a certain date at a certain cost. That was a specific challenge to solve all kinds of problems like control theory problems and rocket theory problems and so forth, to be done within specific time and cost constraints. And they achieved it. Now, there was enormous benefit to the economy and the world of technology from so doing. I do not know whether the economic profession could succeed in such a challenge. Someone should think of an appropriate challenge to the economics profession. For example, although I am not actually pushing this as the right question, to lower black teenage unemployment by 20% in the next eight years. One might ask how that should be and could be achieved. That is a question that the economics profession, and perhaps sociologists, could get together and reach a conclusion about. In other words, ask, can we solve a problem that is a major problem in American society? If we cannot do it, then that is a reflection on the quality of the economics profession. Whatever the outcome, that would be an interesting project for the whole profession.

> *This is a fascinating thought. When Kennedy put forward the challenge to the nation to reach the moon by 1970 it had enormous positive externalities to society, even though the cost was gigantic. As I see it, the leaders of the profession have to bear this responsibility. Do you have any thoughts about mobilizing the leaders or elders of the profession to give some directive such as the one you have just mentioned?*

No, I do not have any hope that they have any interest in doing that. I suspect that they are fully satisfied with the present situation. I do not see why they would find it relevant to enter such a hazardous procedure.

> *The democratic world may be governed by majority, but it is pushed along by minorities. In the past, there have been visionary people in our intellectual community, like Ragnar Frisch, who set forth challenges to the profession and moved us forward in entrepreneurial ways.*

Global warming is an example now of this type of challenge, but the challenge is not specific. There is a lot of money being put into research on global warming, but there is no problem to be solved that we are being given. We have simply been told to do research on global warming.

> *Econometrics, as we all know, has now grown into an enormous subject, reaching into every field of economics and assimilating advances in computing capability in extraordinary ways. This makes designing a teaching program and a course sequence in econometrics complex and difficult. How have you been meeting this challenge at San Diego?*

At the undergraduate level we have not done anything special. Our students are all quite well trained in mathematics and computing, so we just get them to do a number of statistics courses that we call econometrics, which includes one hands-on practical course. These courses are not compulsory, but they are strongly advised. At the graduate level, we have five compulsory econometrics courses, although one of those is linear algebra, which is a necessary background course. And then we have two or three advanced econometrics electives, so a student who want to concentrate on econometrics has a lot of courses that he or she can take over a period of two or three years. Even then, we do not cover all the topics by any means. It depends on who is available and what we are willing to teach that year.

Do you have any mechanism of ensuring that the fundamentals are covered in the mainline courses, say, by laying out a core curriculum?

Yes, the five compulsory courses include linear algebra and then a basic course in probability and statistics. Then there are three rather standard econometrics courses: first of all, regression and then simultaneous equations; then, an asymptotics course that Hal White gives; an inference course; and then I or Rob Engle do a time series course. Right now, every student has to do an empirical project and around that there are some lectures given by someone who does microeconometrics. There is thought of another elective just on microeconometrics. This is not currently being offered but it is planned.

Do you have any general philosophy about the education of graduate students in econometrics?

We are so busy teaching them techniques and proofs that they do not really see enough applications and data. Many of them would benefit, I suspect, by working with the techniques and with empirical applications of the techniques. I think they learn an awful lot from doing it at the same time. We do not do enough of it.

What are your own favorite courses to teach and how do you integrate this type of philosophy into your own teaching?

Well, one of my undergraduate courses is on business and economic forecasting. We talk about leading indicators and the recent forecasts of the economy that have come from macromodels and so on, so I just discuss topical things with them. I also make then do a real-time forecasting exercise, so that at the beginning of the quarter they start to forecast something for the end of the quarter, of their own choice, and at the end of the quarter they can compare how well their forecasts correspond with what actually happened. They actually do learn from performing a real forecasting exercise. I may say they get more from that than they get from the course, actually, because they are forced to think about actual forecasting. Another course I do is on economic demographics and population growth, which I do as an applied econometrics course. The students really enjoy that because there are a lot of surprising facts about the size and growth of populations, interaction between different aspects in populations, and so on. I discuss a number of recent empirical studies relating population and economics, the effects of birth rates on wage rates, and such. There are all kinds of inter-relationships that you can find, and there are some nice examples to talk about. I do not give that course every year, just occasionally. At the graduate level, I teach an advanced time series course, but I do not do much practical work in it. I discuss certain results, but there is not enough time to do more. Ten weeks is not really enough to cover all macro–time series analysis these days. And then I do some advanced topics courses, but they vary from year to year, depending on what I have been working on recently, and so the topic can change. I do not do as much for graduate students in practical terms as I would like to.

> *There is a lesson from your undergraduate teaching experience that students, and maybe researchers too, often perform better and learn more when their backs are against the wall and they have to deliver. In the case of your undergraduate course, this was by means of enforced practical forecasting experience.*

They also think that they understand something, but when they have to actually do it, they realize that they do not understand it as well as they thought they did, and that may make them understand it better.

> *It is one thing to say that you can get a man to the moon; it is an entirely different matter to accomplish it.*

Exactly, yes.

> *That leaves us with thesis advising. You have done a great deal of advising since you have been at San Diego. Can you tell us about that experience?*

Yes, we have a good steady flow of pretty good students and some very good students, and I enjoy most of the supervision. I learned something from Oscar Morgenstern when I was at Princeton. I see every one of my students every week at a regular time for a short period of 20 minutes or half an hour. This way it forces them to come in and show me what they have done over the last week. If they have done nothing, they have to come in and say that they have done nothing. Most of them are too embarrassed to say that, so they always have done something. That is just good training for them, to have done something every week, despite all of the other work that they have to do, and just keep on producing. This is the key element that accumulates to something worthwhile at the end of the quarter, and, on the whole, they like that. Also, the fact that I limit their time means that they make best use of it, so that they come prepared usually and have some questions and they do not want to miss the meeting and so on. It is a discipline on them and on me.

I think they benefit more than by having a sort of vague arrangement of drop-in-when-you-want-to type of statement. I do give them things to read before the meeting sometimes, and we discuss things. And, of course, if they give me papers I will read them. And then, occasionally, for some special occasion, I will see them other times.

> *That sounds like a very workable system, similar to the one that I use. I believe thesis students really do need structure. It is no good saying you are going to see them from time to time and leaving it to them to call in and report.*

Exactly.

> *What general advice do you have for graduate students coming into economics and thinking about doing econometrics?*

I am firm in the belief that they must remember that the objective of all these exercises is to learn about the actual economy. And that they should study real data along with the theory. I have always found I learn a lot from looking at data and trying methods out on data. Again, when a method that should work doesn't, you have to ask why it did not work. So you go back and find out why and sometimes that improves the method a lot. It is this interaction between theory and application that I think generates better research.

> *This is the keep-your-feet-on-the-ground part of their education.*

Yes.

> *What about reading? You have mentioned books that were impor-tant to you. Do you think that it is important to make sure that gaps in students' learning are filled by pointing them to literature that they may not yet have read?*

Yes, I am always doing that. I am trying to keep up with journal articles and books that I am aware of and I am always lending my books out to gradu-ate students. I think one of the main jobs of a supervisor is to be aware of what students should be reading, because they have little idea where to start. The whole search procedure to them is just a mass of material, whereas we on the whole are experienced enough to know how to filter that material out into the good and the not-so-good. I spend quite a lot of time looking up things and being aware of good papers and interesting articles and books, and then telling my students about them.

> *Do you want to talk about books that have influenced you, like the Davis book?*

Yes. The reason I first did work in time series analysis was that I had decided to do a Ph.D. in the area of statistics that was going to be relevant for economics. As I knew just enough that most economic data was time series back in the mid-1950's, I went to the library and there was only one book there on economic times series. This was by H. T. Davis, *A Course on Economic Time Series*. It is a Cowles Commission book. From this fact, that this was the only book, I knew that there must be something that I could do, as it seemed to be a wide open field. Davis had written in 1942 or thereabouts, the early 1940's. That was why I choose the area of economic time series to study. Now it turned out that the Davis book was a very advanced book for the early 1940's. It had the beginning of spectral analysis in it for one thing, plus some quite interesting work on autocorrelations. It was an excellent book for its age and one that does not get sufficient credit. So that certainly was important to me in those days. I mean, then there were just a few econometrics books out and most had no time series in them. It was certainly before Box and Jenkins, so there really was not a great deal else to read at that time.

> *There was the book by Maurice Bartlett on stochastic processes. This gives a very readable introduction to stochastic processes but, in fact, is mainly about time series. Apparently, this book had a major impact on the education of many British statisticians and did so even prior to its publication because Bartlett's notes were widely available in Britain long before the book appeared in 1955. There was another time series book, by Quenouille, called* Multiple Time Series, *that appeared around 1958. It was a short book, but had a great deal in it.*

Yes, I thought that was way advanced, well ahead of its time, as well. That was before Box and Jenkins, and it had a lot of material on multivariate time series. It was fascinating. It also had the jackknife in it, but it was not called by that name.

> *The next important book on time series was a little book that had a big impact – Peter Whittle's book on prediction and regulation.*

That was an interesting book, but annoying because he would get to a certain point and then would not go to the next logical step. So, for example, in his book, he never proved that one-step forecast errors were white noise, which strikes me as one of the major properties of optimum forecasts.

> *That raises the big question of what models you should be using for multiperiod forecasts. Do you have any thoughts on that? Whether you should be using different models for multiperiod ahead forecasts from one-period ahead forecasts?*

I have come to the conclusion that for nonlinear models, we should build different models for each horizon. I do not see building a one-step nonlinear model and then trying to iterate that out to multistage, because you will just have misspecified the models. Even if you do not misspecify the multistep model, forecasts are difficult to find, but with the misspecified one-step model you know you are going to get awful forecasts in the multistep. So, I would rather build a different nonlinear model for each step, and then use these to forecast. The linear case is less clear, whether there is an advantage to building one-step and then just keep iterating out or whether to build different models for each one. I do not really hold a position on that.

I have found in some of my practical work that if you use model selection in multiperiod ahead forecasts you might include some trends or lags that you would not have included if you were just looking one-period ahead. Coming back to Peter Whittle's book, I wonder whether he felt that just doing the Wold decomposition was enough to make the point about one-step forecast errors being uncorrelated.

Yes, I suppose so.

Let's move on to talk about some other matters. Would you like to describe a typical working day scenario to us? Do you work at home, in the office, or both? How you carry your work back and forth, that sort of thing?

I live very near campus, but I drive in. I go into work fairly early, by eight usually, and I do my best work in the morning on campus. I am more awake in the mornings than in the afternoons. I always have a rest after lunch, about half an hour, something again I learned from Oscar Morgenstern. In the afternoon, I usually do some sort of office work or administration, whatever I need to do. And I try to put an hour aside to do some sort of exercise, so I go for a walk in the winter in the park or on the beach. In summer, I body surf, not every day, but most days. In the evenings I do a couple of hours of refereeing or just reading things or papers that people have given me to look at, not deep work, but things that have to be done. I am in the habit of never working on a Saturday. I feel that I need one day a week that I do not think about anything academic. On Sundays, I do not have any real sort of regular agenda. I often do things on Sunday, but I usually work at home.

What form does your rest take at lunchtime? You said that Morgenstern set an example there for you.

I actually have a chair that I can sleep in, a tip-back chair.

Do you turn the telephone off?

Yes, and a sign on my door saying, "Go away," or something.

Can you nap for an hour?

Half an hour, yes. Twenty minutes sometimes.

Winston Churchill used to do that.

I know. I once asked a doctor about it, and he said it is a good idea. If your body says it needs it, then do it. And I really feel a lot better in the afternoon by having done it. I do not see any social reason why we should not do it. If other people let you do it, then do it.

We have covered a lot of ground already. But I think there are one or two important matters left. For instance, what directions would you like to see the econometrics profession take in the next decade?

It is clear that panel data work is going to become more and more important and then I think it will bring together different parts of present-day econometrics in a useful way. We need to rethink the way we are analyzing panels now to incorporate that new panels which have long time series aspects to them. I think that would be exciting. I would like to see much more use of relevant economic theory in model building. Some of this we have been talking about in the econometrics profession for thirty years. I am worried by the fact that the Econometric Society includes both economic theorists and econometricians and that in their meetings the two sides never talk – or virtually never talk. There are very few joint sessions involving both theorists and econometricians. The econometricians keep asking for fully formulated dynamic models, and we do not get them properly specified and so we are forced to go back to building our models using ad hoc techniques. There is plenty to do in terms of improving the quality of the research and the quality of the models in econometrics. Whether that will happen, I am not so sure.

I wonder if the NSF could devise some scheme whereby, instead of giving individual researchers money, they went back to a system in which they supported a group of researchers and insisted on there being complementarity in the group so that it involved both theorists and econometricians. These groups would have to design a coherent research program that would be evaluated for support. If there was enough money involved, then presumably there would be sufficient incentive for research teams to get together, much the same way as the original Cowles Commission researches did or the Princeton team did, to design longer term projects that set some real goals and challenges in economics and econometrics and force some interaction between theorists and econometricians.

I think that would be a good idea. There has been a slight move in the direction of trying to bring econometrics groups and statistics groups together. I am not sure how successful that has been. We tried to put in for some of these grants, but they were trying to solve multiple problems. They were not for specific problems, they were for large problem areas really. And they also wanted a lot of teaching and conferences organized and efforts to include minorities, so there were a lot of other things involved – baggage in a sense – going along with the general idea of a team work. They did not seem quite ready to specify closely enough what was wanted.

> *The NBER has tried over many years to sponsor activities that are of a much more specific nature and, in doing so, has brought together smaller groups of researchers for conferences. But I do not think that you see much of this carrying over into research programs, which is what happened in earlier eras like that at Princeton, Yale, and Chicago. I think that the profession as a whole would benefit greatly from this.*

Yes, so do I.

> *Because Americans often respond best to financial incentives, it seems to me that the only way to get this going in North America is to organize it formally through the funding institutions, like the NSF.*

It is happening a little bit in Europe. There are a couple of places that have groups studying nonlinear methods – for example, at Cambridge and at Aarhus. They have visitors come for periods to link in with the local people. Whether it is going to work, I do not know, but there are attempts to have a common interest. But, again, I think these could be focused more sharply. Nonlinearity is still too wide an area.

> *Looking back over all of your own work, what personal favorites do you have among your papers and the topics that you have written on?*

I am going to mention two that we have not talked about, which I really enjoyed doing. One was on aggregation, an area where I have always found results that were both surprising and easy to get, which is a combination that I really appreciate. One paper appeared in *ET*. The results suggested that micromodeling could miss a feature that, when you aggregate up to the macrolevel, became the dominant feature, and this could explain why sometimes the microtheory did not help the macrotheory. That work has been rather ignored until recently, and there are now workers in Italy and Belgium using it. It was just one of these papers where you get the idea, and you can sit down and write it in a few days, really enjoy doing it, and then it gets published. The other area I enjoyed working on was some years ago at Nottingham, where we did some pricing research in supermarkets. We actually got permission in some supermarkets to change the prices on the shelves of certain goods and observed how demand changed. We could plot demand curves of these commodities and then fit various functions to these demand curves. What I enjoyed about it was that generating your own data somehow is more interesting than just reading data that comes off a computer tape, because you really see how it was done and what the problems were. You knew everything about that data set. I can recommend to people occasionally that they consider just going and asking someone for data or find their own data set. I feel that economists are not inclined to do that now. Economists do not ever think in terms of that type of real-life experiment. I am not sure that is true, but that is my impression.

> *They had a similar scheme at Essex University in the late 1960's and early 1970's in the university shop. The economists came in and were allowed to set up a differential pricing scheme according to the time of day, to try to encourage people not to shop at rush hour. Apparently, the consumers hated it because of the time delays in purchasing. Perhaps, it would work better now in these days of scanners and computerized pricing.*

We also once helped with an electricity time-of-day pricing scheme. It was an experiment done on the East Coast, but we were involved in analyzing the data, and that was also interesting. That was where they were trying to increase off-load demand for electricity by changing the time-of-day price of electricity. That worked very well, and people did not seem to mind that particularly. Because you could heat your pool at off-peak hours and there were no problems essentially, just maybe some planning. Yes, I think it is rather fun organizing a survey and organizing experiments sometimes.

> *They do this extensively in many of the other social sciences.*

There are other experimental economists who do experiments within labs, which is also interesting work, but I feel that the real world is also particularly good for experiments. It is not all that expensive to do. You just need to go out and find someone who will let you do it.

> *Just a thought about the presentation of data. Have you thought of other ways of presenting data rather than simply as graphical time series? Some thoughts come to mind that include audio as well as visual effects and color video graphics. With modern computing technology, some of these possibilities present themselves and I think that, on the whole, as a profession, we are generally a little bit behind the times in this respect. Do you have any thoughts on this?*

Certainly in time varying parameter models we could make some good video images. No, I have not done it.

> *Some experimental economists have been using audio effects to reveal data, as well as visual imaging. As market trades occur and prices go up, they change the pitch of the sound that records the transaction. It is really remarkable to me that the ear can pick up changes, subtle changes, that you might not notice so much on a graph.*

No, I have not done that.

One final question. What is there left to accomplish after having done so much and having written so many papers over the years?

I have not got many plans. I have got a couple of books I want to write, but they are in their early days yet. I am currently working on a project modeling the deforestation process in the Amazon, based on a large panel data set. That has been very interesting because the data set, although it is mostly of good quality, still has lots of problems. It is inherently difficult to measure anything in a place like the Amazon, and this is on fairly large areas. So we have to do all kinds of robust estimation. I really learned quite a bit about data handling from that project, and we are applying for some more funds to continue work on this. If successful, that will be my project in the next couple of years, and then once I have started on panels I might as well continue on them as that is a worthwhile new area for me.

Thank you very much, Clive.

Thank you.

PUBLICATIONS OF CLIVE W. J. GRANGER

BOOKS

1964

1. With M. Hatanaka. *Spectral Analysis of Economic Time Series.* Princeton, New Jersey: Princeton University Press. (French translation, *Analyze spectrale des series temporelles en economie*, Dunod, Paris, 1969.) Designated a "Citation Classic" by the publishers of *Citation Review*, 1986.

1970

2. With O. Morgenstern. *Predictability of Stock Market Prices.* Lexington, Massachusetts: Health.
3. With W. C. Labys. *Speculation, Hedging and Forecasts of Commodity Prices.* Lexington, Massachusetts: Heath. (Japanese edition, 1976).

1974

4. Editor and author of three chapters. *Trading in Commodities.* Cambridge, England: Woodhead-Faulkner, in association with *Investors*

Chronicle. (Republished in *Getting Started in London Commodities*, Investor Publications, London, 1975; third edition, 1980; fourth edition, 1983).

1977

5. With P. Newbold. *Forecasting Economic Time Series.* San Diego: Academic Press. (Second edition, 1986.)

1978

6. With A. P. Andersen. *An Introduction to Bilinear Time Series Models.* Gottingen: Vandenhoeck & Ruprect.

1980

7. *Forecasting in Business and Economics.* New York: Academic Press. (Second edition, 1989; Chinese translation, 1993; Japanese translation, 1994.)

1990

8. *Modeling Economics Series: Readings in Econometric Methodology.* Oxford: Oxford University Press.

1991

9. Edited with R. Engle. *Long Run Economic Relationships: Readings in Cointegration.* Oxford: Oxford University Press.

1993

10. With T. Teräsvirta. *Modeling Nonlinear Dynamic Relationships.* Oxford: Oxford University Press.

PAPERS

TIME SERIES ANALYSIS AND FORECASTING

1957

11. A statistical model for sunspot activity. *Astrophysical Journal* 126, 152–158.

1961

12. First report of the Princeton economic time series project. *L'Industria*, 194–206.

1963

13. Economic processes involving feedback. *Information and Control* 6, 28–48.
14. The effect of varying month-length on the analysis of economic time series. *L'Industria*, 41–53.
15. A quick test for serial correlation suitable for use with non-stationary time series. *Journal of the American Statistical Association* 58, 728–736.

1966

16. The typical spectral shape of an economic variable. *Econometrica* 34, 150–161.

1967

17. New techniques for analyzing economic time series and their place in econometrics. In M. Shubik (ed.), *Essays in Mathematical Economics (in Honor of Oskar Morgenstern)*. Princeton, New Jersey: Princeton University Press.
18. Simple trend-fitting for long-range forecasting. *Management Decision* Spring, 29–34.
19. With C. M. Elliott. A fresh look at wheat prices and markets in the eighteenth century. *Economic History Review* 20, 357–365.

1968

20. With A. O. Hughes. Spectral analysis of short series – A simulation study. *Journal of the Royal Statistical Society, Series A* 131, 83–99.
21. With H. Rees. Spectral analysis of the term structure of interest rates. *Review of Economic Studies* 35, 67–76.

1969

22. With J. Bates. The combination of forecasts. *Operational Research Quarterly* 20, 451–468.
23. Prediction with a generalized cost of error function. *Operational Research Quarterly* 20, 199–207.
24. Spatial data and time series analysis. In A. J. Scott (ed.), *Studies in Regional Science*. London: Pion.
25. Testing for causality and feedback. *Econometrica* 37, 424–438. (Reprinted in *Rational Expectations*, R. E. Lucas & T. Sargent (eds.), University of Minnesota Press, Minneapolis, 1981.)

1971

26. With A. O. Hughes. A new look at some old data: The Beveridge wheat price series. *Journal of the Royal Statistical Society, Series A* 19, 413–428.

1972

27. Random variables in time and space. In *Proceedings of the ARPUD 70 Conference on Regional Planning*. Dortmund. (In German.)
28. With D. Orr. Infinite variance and research strategy in time series analysis. *Journal of the American Statistical Association* 67, 275–285.

1973

29. Causality, model building and control: Some comments. In *Proceedings of the IEEE Conference on Dynamic Modeling and Control of National Economics*, pp. 343–355. London: Institute of Electrical Engineers.
30. With P. Newbold. Evaluation of forecasts. *Applied Economics* 5, 35–47.
31. Statistical forecasting – A survey. *Surrey Paper in Economics*, No. 9, January 1973.

1974

32. With P. Newbold. Experience with statistical forecasting and with combining forecasts. *Journal of the Royal Statistical Society* 137, 131–165.
33. On the properties of forecasts used in optimal economic policy decision. *Journal of Public Economics* 2, 347–356.
34. With P. Newbold. Spurious regressions in econometrics. *Journal of Econometrics* 2, 111–120.

1975

35. Aspects of the analysis and interpretation of temporal and spatial data. *The Statistician* 24, 189–203.
36. With P. Newbold. Forecasting economic series – The Atheist's viewpoint. In G. A. Renton (ed.), *Modeling the Economy*, pp. 131–147. London: Heinemann.

1976

37. With P. Newbold. Forecasting transformed variables. *Journal of the Royal Statistical Society, Series B* 38, 189–203.
38. With M. Morris. Time series modeling and interpretation. *Journal of the Royal Statistical Society, Series A* 139, 246–257.

39. With P. Newbold. The use of R^2 to determine the appropriate transformation of regression variables. *Journal of Econometrics* 4, 205–210.

1977

40. Comment on "Relationship – and the Lack Thereof – between Economic Time Series, with Special Reference to Money and Interest Rates," by David A. Pierce. *Journal of the American Statistical Association* 22–23.
41. With P. Newbold. Identification of two-way causal models. In M. Intriligator (ed.), *Frontiers of Quantitative Economics*, vol. III, pp. 337–360. Amsterdam: North-Holland.
42. With P. Newbold. The time-series approach to econometric model building. In *New Methods in Business Cycle Research*, pp. 7–22. Minneapolis: Federal Reserve Bank.

1978

43. Forecasting Input–Output Tables Using Matrix Time Series Analysis. Working paper, Statistics Department, Australian National University, Canberra.
44. Some new time series models. In *Proceedings of the SIMS conference: Time Series and Ecological Processes.* Philadelphia: SIAM.
45. On the synthesis of time series and econometric models. In D. Brillinger & G. Tiao (eds.), *Directions in Time Series*, pp. 149–167. Ames, Iowa: Institute of Mathematical Statistics.
46. With A. P. Andersen. On the invertibility of time series models. *Stochastic Processes and Their Applications*, 87–92.
47. With A. Andersen. Non-linear time series modeling. In D. F. Findley (ed.), *Applied Time Series Analysis*, pp. 25–38. New York: Academic Press.

1979

48. Nearer normality and some econometric models. *Econometrica* 47, 781–784.
49. New classes of time-series models. *The Statistician* 27, 237–253.
50. Seasonality: Causation, interpretation and implications. In A. Zellner (ed.), *Seasonal Analysis of Economic Time Series*, pp. 33–40. Economic Research Report ER-1, Bureau of the Census.
51. Some recent developments in forecasting techniques and strategy. In O. Anderson (ed.), *Proceedings of the Institute of Statisticians Cambridge Forecasting Conference: Forecasting.* Amsterdam: North-Holland.
52. With R. Ashley. Time series analysis of residuals from the St. Louis model. *Journal of Macroeconomics* 1, 373–394.

53. With A. Anderson, R. Engle, & R. Ramanathan. Residential load curves and time-of-day pricing. *Journal of Econometrics* 9, 13–32.
54. With R. Engle, A. Mitchem, & R. Ramanathan. Some problems in the estimation of daily load curves and shapes. In *Proceedings of the EPRI Conference.*
55. With H. L. Nelson. Experience with using the Box-Cox transformation when forecasting economic time series. *Journal of Econometrics* 9, 57–69.

1980

56. Long-memory relationships and the aggregation of dynamic models. *Journal of Econometrics* 14, 227–238.
57. Some comments on "The Role of Time Series Analysis in Econometrics." In J. Kmenta & J. B. Ramsey (eds.), *Evaluation of Econometric Models*, pp. 339–341. New York: Academic Press.
58. "Spectral Analysis" entry. In *Handworterbuch der Mathematischen.* Berlin: Gabler. Wirtshaftswissenschaften, vol. II. (In German.)
59. Testing for causality, a personal viewpoint. *Journal of Economic Dynamics and Control* 2, 329–352.
60. With R. Ashley & R. Schmalensee. Advertising and aggregate consumption: An analysis of causality. *Econometrica* 48, 1149–1168.
61. With R. Joyeux. An introduction to long-memory time series. *Journal of Time Series Analysis* 1, 15–30.

1981

62. The comparison of time series and econometric forecasting strategies. In J. Kmenta & J. B. Ramsey (eds.), *Large Scale Macro-Econometric Models, Theory and Practice*, pp. 123–128. Amsterdam: North-Holland.
63. Some properties of time series data and their use in econometric model specification. *Journal of Econometrics* 16 (supplement, *Annals of Econometrics*, edited by G. S. Maddala), 121–130.

1982

64. Acronyms in time series analysis (ATSA). *Journal of Time Series Analysis* 3, 103–107.

1983

65. Comments on "The Econometric Analysis of Economic Time Series," by Hendry and Richard. *International Statistical Review* 51, 151–153.

66. Forecasting white noise. In A. Zellner (ed.), *Applied Time Series Analysis of Economic Data*, pp. 308–314. Washington, D.C.: U.S. Government Printing Office.
67. Generating mechanisms, models and causality. In W. Hildenbrand (ed.), *Advances in Econometrics*. New York: Cambridge University Press.
68. With A. Weiss. Time series analysis of error-correction model. In S. Karlin, T. Amemiya, & L. A. Goodman (eds.), *Studies in Econometrics, Time Series and Multivariate Statistics, in honor of T. W. Anderson*, pp. 255–278. New York: Academic Press.

1984

69. With R. Engle. Applications of spectral analysis in econometrics. In D. Brillinger & P. R. Krishnaiah (eds.), *Handbook of Statistics*, vol. 3: *Time Series and Frequency Domain*, pp. 93–109. Amsterdam: North-Holland.
70. With R. Engle & D. Kraft. Combining competing forecasts of inflation using a bivariate ARCH model. *Journal of Economic Dynamics and Control* 8, 151–165.
71. With F. Huynh, A. Escribano, & C. Mustafa. Computer investigation of some non-linear time series models. In *Proceedings of the Conference on Computer Science and Statistics*. Amsterdam: North-Holland.
72. Edited with R. Ramanathan. Improved methods of combining forecasting. *Journal of Forecasting* 3, 197–204.
73. With K. Train, P. Ignelzi, R. Engle, & R. Ramanathan. The billing cycle and weather variables in models of electricity sales. *Energy* 9, 1061–1067.
74. With M. Watson. Time series and spectral methods in econometrics. In Z. Griliches & M. D. Intriligator (eds.), *Handbook of Econometrics*, vol. 2, pp. 980–1022. Amsterdam: North-Holland.
75. With A. Weiss. Rational Autoregressive Models. Working paper, University of California at San Diego.

1985

76. With R. Ramanathan & R. Engle. Two-step modeling for short term forecasting. In D. W. Bunn & E. D. Farmer (eds.), *Comparative Models for Electrical Load Forecasting*, pp. 131–158. New York: Wiley and Sons. (Russian translation, 1988).
77. With R. Ramanathan, R. Engle, J. Price, P. Ignelzi, & K. Train. Weather normalization of electricity sales. In *Proceedings of the EPRI Dallas Conference, "Short-Run Load Forecasting."* EPRI publication FA-4080.

78. With R. Robins & R. Engle. Wholesale and retail prices: Bivariate time series modeling with forecastable error variances. In E. Kuh & R. Belsley (eds.), *Model Reliability*, pp. 1–16. Cambridge, Massachusetts": MIT Press.

1986

79. Developments in the study of co-integrated economic variables. *Oxford Bulletin of Economics and Statistics* 48, 213–228. (Special issue on economic modeling with co-integrated variables.)
80. With R. Engle, J. Rice, & A. Weiss. Semi-parametric estimates of the relation between weather and electricity demand. *Journal of the American Statistical Association* 81, 310–320.
81. With J. Horowitz & H. White. The California Energy Data Bank. UERG California Energy Studies report, Berkeley.

1987

82. Are economic variables really integrated of order one? In I. B. MacNeill & G. J. Umphrey (eds.), *Time Series and Econometric Modeling*, pp. 207–218. Dordrecht: D. Reidel Publishing.
83. Four essays for the *New Palgrave Dictionary of Economics*, J. Eatwell, M. Milgate, & P. Newman (eds.). London: Macmillan (Causal inference, vol. 1, pp. 380–382; Forecasting, vol. 2, pp. 396–398; Spectral analysis, vol. 4, pp. 435–437; Spurious regressions, vol. 4, pp. 444–445).
84. Implications of aggregation with common factors. *Econometric Theory* 3, 208–222.
85. With R. Engle. Dynamic model specification with equilibrium constraints: Co-integration and error-correction. *Econometrica* 55, 251–276.
86. With C.-M. Kuan, M. Mattson, & H. White. Trends in unit energy consumption: The performance of end-use models. *Energy* 14, 943–960.
87. With P. Thomson. Predictive consequences of using conditioning on causal variables. *Economic Theory* 3, 150–152.

1988

88. Causality, cointegration and control. *Journal of Economic Dynamics and Control* 12 (2/3), 551–560.
89. Causality testing in a decision science. In B. Skyrms & W. K. Harper (eds.), *Causation, Change and Credence*, pp. 3–22. Dordrecht: Kluwer Publishers.
90. Comments on econometric methodology. *Economic Record* 64, 327–330.

91. Introduction to Stochastic Process Having Equilibria as Simple Attractors: The Markov Case. Working paper 86-20, University of California at San Diego, Economics Department.
92. Models that generate trends. *Journal of Time Series Analysis* 9, 329–343.
93. Some recent developments in a concept of causality. *Journal of Econometrics* 39, 199–212.
94. Where are the controversies in econometric methodology? In *Modeling Economic Series*, introductory chapter. Summary given at the Econometrics Workshop, Camp Arrowhead, 1988.
95. With R. Engle. Econometric forecasting – A brief survey of current and future techniques. In K. Land & S. Schneider (eds.), *Forecasting in the Social and Natural Sciences*, pp. 117–140. Dordrecht: D. Reidel Publishing.

1989

96. Combining forecasts – Twenty years later. *Journal of Forecasting* 8, 167–174. (Special issue on combining forecasts.)
97. With R. Engle & J. Hallman. Combining short and long-run forecasts: An application of seasoned co-integration to monthly electricity sales forecasting. *Journal of Econometrics* 40, 45–62.
98. With T.-H. Lee. Investigation of production, sales and inventory relationship using multicointegration and nonsymmetric error correction models. *Journal of Applied Econometrics* 4, S145–S159.
99. With H. White & M. Kamstra. Interval forecasting: An analysis based upon ARCH-quantile estimators. *Journal of Econometrics* 40, 87–96.

1990

100. Aggregation of time series variables – A survey. In T. Barker & H. Pesaran (eds.), *Disaggregation in Econometric Modeling*, pp. 17–34. London: Routledge.
101. Some recent generalizations of cointegration and the analysis of long-run relationship. *Cauernos Economics (Madrid)* 44, 43–52. (Translated into Spanish.)
102. With R. Engle, S. Hylleberg, & S. Yoo. Seasonal integration and co-integration. *Journal of Econometrics* 44, 215–238.
103. With T. H. Lee. Multicointegration. In T. Fomby (ed.), *Advances in Econometrics*, vol. 8, pp. 17–84. Greenwich, Connecticut: JAI Press.
104. With H. Urlig. Reasonable extreme bounds. *Journal of Econometrics* 44, 159–170.

1991

105. Developments in the nonlinear analysis of economic series. *Scandinavian Journal of Economics* 93, 263–276.
106. Reducing self-interest and improving the relevance of economics research. In D. Prawitz, E. Skyms, & P. Westershal (eds.), *Proceedings of the 9th International Conference of Logic, Methodology and Philosophy of Science, Uppsala, Sweden*, pp. 763–788. Amsterdam: Elsevier.
107. Time series econometrics. In D. Greenaway et al. (eds.), *Companion to Contemporary Economic Thought*, pp. 559–573. London: Routledge.
108. With J. Hallman. Long memory processes with attractors. *Oxford Bulletin of Economics and Statistics* 53, 11–26.
109. With J. Hallman. Nonlinear transformations of integrated time series. *Journal of Time Series Analysis* 12, 207–224.
110. With H. S. Lee. An introduction to time-varying parameter cointegration. In P. Hackl & A. Westlund (eds.) *Economic Structural Changes*, pp. 139–158. New York: Springer-Verlag.

1992

111. Evaluating economic theory. *Journal of Econometrics* 51, 3–5. (Guest editorial.)
112. Forecasting stock market prices – Lessons for forecasters. *International Journal of Forecasting* 8, 3–13.
113. Comments on two papers concerning Chaos and Statistics by Chatterjee and Yilmarz and by Berliner. *Statistical Science* 7, 69–122.
114. With M. Deutsch. Comments on the evaluation of policy models. *Journal of Policy Modeling* 14, 497–516. (Reprinted in *Testing Exogeneity*, edited by N. R. Ericsson & J. S. Irons, Oxford University Press, Oxford, 1995.)
115. With T. Teräsvirta. Experiments in modeling relationships between nonlinear time series. In M. Casdagli & S. Eubank (eds.), *Nonlinear Modeling and Forecasting*, pp. 189–198. Redwood City, California: Addison-Wesley.
116. With A. D. Hall & H. Anderson. Treasury bill curves and cointegration. *Review of Economics and Statistics* 74, 116–126.
117. With T. Liu & W. Heller. Using the correlation exponent to decide if an economic series is chaotic. *Journal of Applied Econometrics* 7S, 525–540. (Reprinted in *Nonlinear Dynamics, Chaos, and Econometrics*, edited by M. H. Peseran & S. M. Potter, J. Wiley, Chichester, 1993.)

1993

118. Comment on "The Limitations of Comparing Mean Square Forecast Errors," by M. P. Clements and D. F. Hendry. *Journal of Forecasting* 12, 651–652.
119. Comment on "Testing for Common Features" by R. F. Engle & Sharon Kozicki. *Journal of Business and Economic Statistics* 11, 384–385.
120. Implications of seeing economic variables through an aggregation window, *Ricerche Economiche* 47, 269–279.
121. Overview of forecasting in economics. In A. Weigend & N. Gershenfeld (ed.), *Time Series Prediction: Predicting the Future and Understanding the Past: A Comparison of Approaches*, pp. 529–538. Reading, Massachusetts: Addison-Wesley.
122. Positively related processes and cointegration. In T. Subba Rao (ed.), *Developments in Time Series Analysis: Book in Honor of Professor M. B. Priestley*, pp. 3–8. London: Chapman and Hall.
123. Strategies for modeling nonlinear time series relationships. *Economic Record* 60, 233–238.
124. What are we learning about the long-run? *Economic Journal* 103, 307–317.
125. With Z. Ding & R. Engle. A long memory property of stock market returns and a new model. *Journal of Empirical Finance* 1, 83–106
126. With R. Engle, S. Hylleberg, & H. S. Lee. Seasonal cointegration: The Japanese consumption function, 1961.1–1987.4. *Journal of Econometrics* 55, 275–298.
127. With L. Ermini. Some generalizations of the algebra of I(1) processes. *Journal of Econometrics* 58, 369–384.
128. With T. Konishi & V. Ramey. Stochastic trends and short-run relationships between financial variables and real activity.
129. With T.-H. Lee. The effect of aggregation on nonlinearity. In R. Mariano (ed.), *Advances in Statistical Analysis and Statistical Computing*, vol. 3. Greenwich, Connecticut: JAI Press.
130. With T.-H. Lee & H. White. Testing for neglected nonlinearity in time series models: A comparison of neural network methods and alternative tests. *Journal of Econometrics*, 56, 269–290.
131. With T. Teräsvirta & H. Anderson. Modeling non-linearity over the business cycle. In J. Stock & M. Watson (eds.), *Business Cycles, Indicators, and Forecasting*, pp. 311–325. National Bureau of Economic Research. Chicago: University of Chicago Press.
132. With T. Teräsvirta & C.-F. Lin. The power of the neural network linearity test. *Journal of Time Series Analysis* 14, 209–220.

1994

133. Is chaotic economic theory relevant for economics? A review essay. *Journal of International and Comparative Economics* 3, 139–145.
134. Some comments on empirical investigations involving cointegration. *Econometric Review* 32, 345–350.
135. Some recent textbooks in econometrics. *Journal of Economic Literature* 32, 115–122. (Book review.)
136. With M. Deutsch & T. Teräsvirta. The combination of forecasts using changing weights. *International Journal of Forecasting* 10, 47–57.
137. With T. Inoue & N. Morin. Non-linear stochastic trends. *Journal of Econometrics*.
138. With J.-L. Lin. Forecasting from non-linear models in practice. *Journal of Forecasting* 13, 1–10.
139. With J.-L. Lin. Using the mutual information coefficient to identify lags in non-linear models. *Journal of Time Series Analysis* 15, 371–384.

1995

140. Non-linear relationships between extended memory series. *Econometrica* 63, 265–279.
141. With J. Gonzalo. Estimation of common long-memory components in cointegrated systems. *Journal of Business and Economic Statistics* 13, 27–36.
142. With M. King & H. White. Comments on testing economic theories and the use of model selection criteria. *Journal of Econometrics* 67, 173–188.
143. With J.-L. Lin. Causality in the long run. *Econometric Theory* 11, 530–536.
144. With P. Siklos. Systemic sampling, temporal aggregation, seasonal adjustment and cointegration. *Journal of Econometrics* 66, 357–369.
145. With T. Teräsvirta & D. Tjøstheim. Nonlinear time series. In R. Engle & D. McFadden (eds.), *Handbook of Econometrics*, vol. 4. Amsterdam: North-Holland.

1996

146. Comments on Determining Causal Ordering in Economics" by S. LeRoy. In K. D. Hooper (ed.), *Macroeconomics: Developments, Tensions, and Prospects*, pp. 229–233. Boston: Kluwer Publisher.
147. With Z. Ding. Modeling volatility persistence of speculative returns. *Journal of Econometrics* 73, 185–216.

148. With Z. Ding. Varieties of long-memory models. *Journal of Econometrics* 73, 61–78. (Special issue on long-memory models.)
149. With N. Swanson. Further developments in the study of cointegrated variables. *Oxford Bulletin of Economics and Statistics* 58, 537–554.
150. Can we improve the perceived quality of economic forecasts? *Applied Econometrics* 11, 455–474.
151. With Z. Ding. Some properties of absolute return. An alternative measure of risk. *Annales d'Economie et de Statistique* 40, 67–92.

Forthcoming

152. "Granger Causality" entry. In *Encyclopedia of Economic Methodology*. Dordrecht: Edward Elgar Publishers.
153. With J.-L. Lin. Conjugate processes.
154. With D. Weinhold. Testing for causality in panels. In *Proceedings of the Conference of Analysis of Panal Data*.
155. On modeling the long run in applied economics. *Economic Journal*.

Submitted

156. "Cointegration" entry. In *Encyclopedia of Statistical Sciences*.
157. "Hierarchical Subjects."
158. With Z. Ding. Stylized facts on the temporal and distributional properties of daily data from speculative markets. *International Journal of Economics*.
159. With R. Engle, R. Ramanathan, F. Vahid-Arraghi, & C. Brace. Short-run forecasts of electricity loads and peaks.
160. With A. Escribano. Investigating the relationship between gold and silver prices.
161. With E. Ghysels, & P. Siklos. Is seasonal adjustment a linear or nonlinear data filtering process? *Journal of Business and Economics Statistics*.
162. With S. Grossbard-Shechtman. The baby boom and time trends in female labor force participation.
163. With N. Hyung, & Y. Jeon. Stochastic fractional unit root processes. Volume in honor of E. J. Hannan.
164. With T. Konishi. Separation in cointegrated systems.
165. With C.-Y. Sin. Estimating and forecasting quantiles with asymmetric least squares. *Journal of Econometrics*.
166. With N. Swanson. Impulse response functions based on a causal approach to residual orthogonalization in VAR'S.
167. With N. Swanson. Stochastic unit root processes.

1961

168. With A. Gabor. On the price consciousness of consumers. *Applied Statistics* 10, 170–188.

1964

169. With A. Gabor. Price sensitivity of the consumer. *Journal of Advertising Research* 4, 40–44. (Reprinted in *Readings in Marketing Research*, edited by K. Cox, New York, 1967.)

1965

170. With A. Gabor. Price as an indicator of quality. *Scientific Business* August, 43–70.
171. With A. Gabor. The pricing of new products. *Scientific Business* August, 3–12.

1969

172. With A. Gabor. The attitude of the consumer to prices. In B. Taylor & G. Wills (eds.) *Pricing Strategy*, pp. 132–151. London: Staples.
173. With A. P. Sowter & A. Gabor. The influence of price differences on brand shares and switching. *British Journal of Marketing* Winter, 223–230.

1970

174. With A. Gabor & A. P. Sowter. Real and hypothetical shop situations in market research. *Journal of Marketing Research* 7, 355–359.

1971

175. With A. P. Sowter & A. Gabor. Comments on "Psychophysics of Prices." *Journal of Marketing Research* 8.
176. With A. P. Sowter & A. Gabor. The effect of price on choice: A theoretical and empirical investigation. *Applied Economics* 3, 167–182.

1972

177. With A. Billson. Consumers' attitude to package size and price: Report on an experiment. *Journal of Marketing Research* 9.
178. With A. Gabor. Ownership and acquisition of consumer durables. *European Journal of Marketing* 6 (4), 234–248.

1973

179. With A. Gabor. Developing an effective pricing policy. In L. W. Rodger (ed.), *Marketing Concepts and Strategies in the Next Decade*, pp. 171–194. London: Cassell.

1977

180. Technical appendix. In A. Gabor (ed.) *Pricing – Principles and Practice*, pp. 325–336. London: Heinemann Press. (French edition, 1981; second edition, 1985; Japanese edition, 1987.)

Note: All of the papers co-authored with A. Gabor were reprinted in the volume *Pricing Decisions* 17 (8), 1979, of *Management Decision*.

SPECULATIVE MARKETS AND THEORY OF FINANCE

1964

181. With M. D. Godfrey & O. Morgenstern. The random-walk hypothesis of stock market behavior. *Kyklos* 17, 1–30. (Reprinted in *Frontiers of Investment Analysis*, 2nd ed., edited by E. Bruce Fredrikson, Intext Educational Publisher, 1971.)

182. With O. Morgenstern. Spectral analysis of New York stock market prices. *Kyklos* 16, 1–27. (Reprinted in *Random Character of Stock Market Prices*, edited by P. H. Cootner, MIT Press, Cambridge, Massachusetts, 1964.)

1968

183. Some aspects of the random-walk model of stock market prices. *International Economic Review* 9.

1970

184. What the random walk model does NOT say. *Financial Analysis Journal* May–June. (Reprinted in *Investment Analysis and Portfolio Management*, edited by B. Taylor, Elek Books, London, 1970.)

1971

185. The interdependence of stock prices around the world: Is it a myth? *Money Manager* July–August, 25–27.

1972

186. Empirical studies in capital markets: A survey. In G. Szego & K. Shell (eds.), *Mathematical Methods in Investment and Finance*. Amsterdam: North–Holland.

187. Prediction of stock market prices. *Bulletin of Institute of Mathematics and Its Applications.*
188. Random walk, market model and relative strength – A synthesis. In *Proceedings of the Conference Mathematics in the Stock Market.* Organized by the Institute of Mathematics and Its Applications.
189. With N. A. Niarchos. The gold sovereign market in Greece – An unusual speculative market. *Journal of Finance* 27, 1127–1135.

1975

190. Some consequences of the valuation model when expectations are taken to be optimum forecasts. *Journal of Finance* 30, 135–145.
191. A survey of empirical studies in capital markets. In E. J. Elton & M. Gruber (eds.), *International Capital Markets*, pp. 3–36. North-Holland. (Updated version of Granger, in *Mathematical Methods in Investment and Finance*, edited by G. Szego & K. Shell, 1972).

Note: These two publications in this section are reprinted in *Selected Economic Writing of Oscar Morgenstern*, edited by A. Schotter, New York University Press, New York, 1976.

1993

192. Forecasting stock market prices. Public lecture, issued by Fundacion BBr, Madrid, Spain.

STATISTICAL THEORY AND APPLIED STATISTICS

1959

193. Estimating the probability of flooding on a tidal river. *Journal of the Institution of Water Engineers* 13, 165–174.

1963

194. The teaching of mathematics to students of economics both at school and university. *Economics* 3.

1964

195. With M. Craft. The prediction of future behavior of psychopaths from past and present data. Proceedings of the First International Congress of Social Psychiatry, London, 1964.
196. With M. Craft & G. Stephenson. A controlled trial of authoritarian and self-government regimes with adolescent psychopaths. *American Journal of Orthopsychiatry* 34, 543–554.

197. With M. Craft & G. Stephenson. The relationship between severity of personality disorder and certain adverse childhood influences. *British Journal of Psychiatry* 110, 392–396.

1968

198. With H. Neave. A quick test for slippage. *Journal of the International Institute of Statistics.*
199. With H. Neave. Two-sample tests for differences in mean – Results of a simulation study. *Technometrics* 10, 509–522.

1977

200. Tendency towards normality of linear combinations of random variables. *Metrika* 23, 237–248.

PART ONE

SPECTRAL ANALYSIS

Spectral Analysis of New York Stock Market Prices*[1]

Clive W. J. Granger and Oskar Morgenstern

Summary

New York stock price series are analyzed by a new statistical technique. It is found that short-run movements of the series obey the simple random walk hypothesis proposed by earlier writers, but that the long-run components are of greater importance than suggested by this hypothesis. The seasonal variation and the "business-cycle" components are shown to be of little or no importance and a surprisingly small connection was found between the amount of stocks sold and the stock price series.

1. THE RANDOM WALK HYPOTHESIS

The stock market is an institution of considerable interest to the public at large and of real importance to students of a nation's economy. The variables which make up a stock market may not directly affect the mechanism of the economy but they certainly influence the psychological climate within which the economy works. To the extent to which the movements of the economy directly affect the stock market, a feedback situation occurs, although there are reasons to suspect that the strength of the feedback is not strong. The stock market produces large amounts of high quality data derived from well-understood variables. Despite these facts, the stock market has attracted surprisingly little study by professional economists or statisticians. It is interesting to note that CARL MENGER is reported to have made careful studies of the Vienna stock market before, in 1871, developing the concept of marginal utility and his theory of prices. Later, the French mathematician, M. L. BACHELIER,

* Kyklos, 16, 1963, 1–27. Reprinted in *The Random Character of Stock Market Prices*, edited by P. H. Cootner, M.I.T. Press, 1964.
[1] This work, done at the Econometric Research Program of Princeton University, was supported by a grant from the National Science Foundation.

published his *Théorie de la Spéculation* (1900) in which the random character of stock price movements was derived. While strictly theoretical studies are rare, the stock market having been largely neglected in the development of price theory, there exist, of course, descriptive works, too numerous to mention. Of theoretical-statistical works, first reference has to be made to the highly significant studies by A. COWLES.[2] In the last few years, however, a number of studies have appeared: KENDALL,[3] ALEXANDER,[4] COOTNER,[5] OSBORNE[6] etc., chiefly concentrating on the weekly price movements either of particular stocks or of the over-all market.

In this paper we restrict ourselves as do most of the above mentioned authors to prices of the New York Stock Exchange and, strictly speaking, our results apply only to this sample. There is, however, little likelihood that stock markets in other countries will behave very differently. Nevertheless studies of other markets are indicated. The various authors, though starting from different viewpoints and developing slightly different hypotheses, have been surprisingly consistent in their general conclusions, which are that these price series can be represented by a very simple model: If x_t is the (discrete) price series the model suggested is that the first differences of this series appear to be purely random; in symbols

$$x_t - x_{t-1} = \varepsilon_t$$

where ε_t has mean zero and is uncorrelated with ε_{t-k}, all $k \neq 0$.[7] (Henceforth, series such as ε_t will be called "white noise".) This model has been called a "random walk" model and, although this designation is not entirely correct as steps of an unequal length are allowable this term will be used to describe the model throughout this paper. Thus, if the model is correct, the series will proceed by a sequence of unconnected steps, starting each time from the previous value of the series.

---

[2] A. COWLES and H. E. JONES, "Some A Posteriori Probabilities in Stock Market Action", *Econometrica*, Vol. 5, 1937, pp. 280–294.
   A. COWLES and H. E. JONES, "A Revision of Previous Conclusions Regarding Stock Price Behaviour", *Econometrica*, Vol. 28, 1960, pp. 909–915.
[3] M. G. KENDALL, "The Analysis of Economic Time Series – Part I: Prices", *J. Royal Stat. Soc.* (Series A), Vol. 96, 1953, pp. 11–25.
[4] S. ALEXANDER, "Price Movements in Speculative Markets: Trends or Random Walks", *Industrial Management Review*, Vol. 2, 1961, pp. 7–26.
[5] P. H. COOTNER, "Stock Prices: Random vs. Systematic Changes," *Industrial Management Review*, Vol. 3, 1962, pp. 24–45.
[6] M. F. M. OSBORNE, "Brownian Motion in the Stock Market", *Operations Research*, Vol. 7, 1959, pp. 145–173.
   M. F. M. OSBORNE, "Periodic Structure in the Brownian Motion of Stock Prices", *Operations Research*, Vol. 10, 1962, pp. 345–379.
[7] In some of the above-mentioned papers, the series x_t was transformed first, e.g. OSBORNE considers log x_t. The need for such transformations is discussed in Appendix A.

The phenomenon of a random walk of prices will arise if a large number of people are continually predicting price and use as their best predictive model that the price at the next moment of time is the same as the present value, the time units between readings being minutes, hours, days or even possibly weeks. The model based on this observation appears to fit the data extremely well and COOTNER properly finishes his paper with this remark: "If their (stock price series) behavior is more complicated than the random walk model suggests, it will take more sophisticated statistical testing to discover it." It is one of the objects of the present paper to suggest such a sophisticated method. We shall show that, although the random walk model does appear to fit the data very well, there are certain prominent long-run features of the variables which are not explained by this model.

Further objects of the present paper are to promote the idea that stock market data (and particularly stock exchange "folk-lore") should be investigated by rigorous methods and that the most appropriate statistical techniques to be used in such an investigation are the recently developed spectral methods. These have already been used with considerable success in other fields of research and, although they have required considerable adaptation and improvement before being entirely applicable to economic series we contend that spectral analysis has now reached a stage of development where it can be used with some confidence on economic series. A group of workers at the Econometrics Research Program of Princeton University has been studying these methods with particular reference to economics and the results so far achieved are shortly to be published in book form.[8] Only a few of the manifold methods are used in this paper.

The series analyzed by us for this investigation were various Securities and Exchange Commission's (SEC) weekly price series (1939–1961), monthly price series for six US companies (1946–1960), weekly price series together with the weekly turnover of their stocks for two further companies (1957–1961), the Standard and Poor common stock price index (monthly, 1915–1961) and the Dow-Jones Index 1915–1961. (Full details may be found in Appendix B.)

In the next section, a brief, non-mathematical description of the ideas underlying spectral methods is given and this is followed by an account of the more important results achieved by these methods when applied to data drawn from the New York Stock Exchange. The various

---

[8] *Analysis of Economic Time Series* by C. W. J. GRANGER, in association with M. HATANAKA, Princeton University Press (1963). Particular chapters of this reference will henceforth be denoted by GRANGER, *op. cit.*, Chapter 9, etc. The general philosophy underlying these studies is described in O. MORGENSTERN: "A New Look at Economic Time Series Analysis", in H. HEGELAND (ed.) *Money, Growth and Methodology*, in honor of J. Akerman, Lund 1961, pp. 261–272.

technical problems that arise during this work are described in *Appendix A* and a full list of the series so far analyzed together with the major results are given in *Appendix B*.

2. SPECTRAL METHODS

Consider a discrete time series having neither trend in mean, trend in variance nor trend in correlation between the present value and any past value. Such a series, which we will call stationary, essentially has the property that the underlying laws which generate it are invariant over time. Since A. SCHUSTER'S work of the beginning of this century, it has been realized that a finite stationary series can be represented by a finite number of Fourier-terms and an infinite series can be represented by a countably infinite number of such terms. Only in the last twenty years has it been suggested that results, both more general and more rigorously established, may be achieved by using a more general representation.

It may be useful to illustrate this idea by using an analogy between an ordinary statistical variable (such as height of a given population) and the Fourier-representation of a stationary series.[9] A term which first needs to be defined is "frequency" which is proportional to the inverse of the well understood concept of "period". Thus, if a component has a period of k weeks, when weekly data are being used, this component will have the frequency $2\pi/k$.

Just as it is not generally assumed that a statistical variable has only a finite number of possible values (as would a variable with a binomial distribution) or a countably infinite number of possible values (as would a variable with a Poisson-distribution), there is no good reason why a series need be represented by a finite or a countably infinite number of frequencies in the Fourier-representation. Greater generality is achieved by allowing the statistical variable to take all possible values (as is the case when a variable is normally distributed). Similarly we achieve greater generality by using all frequencies in the Fourier-representation of the series. The extra degree of generality involved is exactly that of moving from an infinite series to an integral over the whole real line.

When considering a statistical variable we are usually interested in the probability of some event. If the variable X is distributed normally, then the probability that X equals some given constant is zero, but the probability that it lies in some given interval is nonzero. By suitably choosing the intervals we are able to define the useful frequency function $f(x)$ by using

$$f(x)dx = \text{Prob}\,(x \le X \le x + dx).$$

---

[9] It is hoped that this analogy is not confusing; the type of statistical variable envisaged is an independent sample and the fact that the time series is itself a statistical variable is not here taken into account.

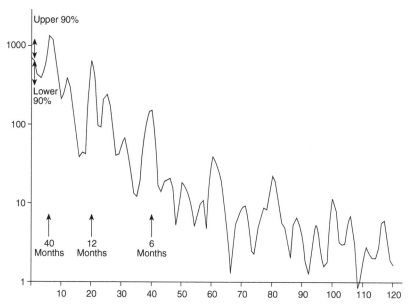

Figure 2.1. Power Spectrum of New York Commercial Paper Rate 1876–1914.

In practice, we are unable to estimate $f(x)$ for all x as only a finite amount of data is available and so we use the histogram as an estimate.

When considering the Fourier-representation of a time series we are most interested in the contribution that some particular frequency component makes to the over-all variance. In the most general representation of the series (using a Fourier-integral rather than a Fourier-series) no *one* frequency contributes any finite amount to the variance but the *set* of all frequencies lying in some *interval* will contribute a positive amount. If the frequency band $(\omega, \omega + d\omega)$ contributes $f(\omega)d\omega$ to the total variance, we call the function $f(\omega)$ the *power spectrum of the series*. Just as in the case of the frequency function, we are unable to estimate $f(\omega)$ for every ω and therefore we have to form estimates of $f(\omega)$ over a set of frequency bands. A large value of estimated $f(\omega)$ indicates that the frequencies of this band are of particular importance as they contribute a large amount of the total variance.

Figure 2.1 shows the logarithm of the estimated spectrum (at 120 frequency points) of the monthly New York commercial paper rate series for the period 1876–1914.[10] This series was chosen as an illustration as it

---

[10] This important short-term interest rate series is fully discussed in OSKAR MORGENSTERN: *International Financial Transactions and Business Cycles*, Princeton, 1959. The 90 percent confidence bands are of constant width about the estimated spectrum. Their size is shown at zero frequency.

was found to contain cycles of a conventional type (40 months) and an important but not overpowering annual (seasonal) component. We note that the bands centered on components with periods of 40 and 12 months are of particular importance, together with the harmonics of the annual component. The first of these bands contributes 40 percent of the variance, the annual component contributes 17 percent.

The spectrum of an independent sequence of terms (i.e. white noise) is a horizontal line parallel to the x-axis over the complete frequency range $(0, \pi)$. But economic series frequently have spectra of this shape:

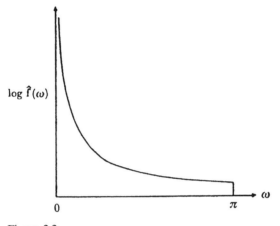

Figure 2.2.

Such a spectral shape can be interpreted as implying that the longer the period of the component the larger is its amplitude. This is not particularly surprising as in the past many cycles have been seen by economists in their data and if such "cycles" had not been of obvious importance they would have been indistinguishable from the ever-present background noise.

The section of the power spectrum of most interest to economists is the low-frequency range, within which all the "long-run" components are concentrated. Unfortunately, this range is also the most difficult to deal with. Any trend in mean in the series will give the zero frequency band a large value and, due to the estimation methods used, this large value will be inclined also to raise the values of the neighboring frequency bands. (This effect is known as "leakage".) Thus, before the low frequencies can be studied, a trend in mean would have to be removed. Various methods are available[11] but a long, equal-weight moving average of the series subtracted from the series is both convenient and easily appreciated. A second problem connected with the

---

[11] See GRANGER, *op. cit.*, Chapter 8.

low-frequency bands is the fact that one requires several repetitions of a periodic component before its amplitude can be estimated at all accurately.

Interpretation of the terms "low-frequency" or "long-run" depend both upon the length of the available data and the time-interval used. A component that is extremely long-run in a series of 700 pieces of weekly data is only moderately so in a series of monthly data of comparable length. It is for this reason that we can say nothing about the business-cycle component of the Securities and Exchange Commission's weekly price series even though we used data for more than a thousand weeks, but in our analysis of the monthly Standard and Poor price series, which was shorter but covered a longer period of time, information about this component could be extracted. Oscillations with periods comparable in length with the length of series available will then be grouped with "trend" when spectral methods are used.

The existence of a trend in mean is only one way in which a time-series can show its non-stationary character and is the easiest of all to deal with. Trends in variance or in underlying structure also invariably occur in economics and these cannot be entirely removed. As spectral methods assume series to be stationary and as virtually no economic series are stationary it would seem that spectral methods are not appropriate for use in economics. However, a number of studies at Princeton, both theoretical and experimental, indicate that as long as the underlying structure of the series is not changing quickly with time, spectral analysis may be used with confidence.[12]

This result also holds true when *cross-spectral* methods are used. Whereas a power-spectrum, by an extension of the classical analysis of variance, analyzes a single series, cross-spectral methods investigate the relationship between a pair of series.

It has been explained above that a series may be decomposed into a (possibly infinite) number of frequency bands. Let us call the jth band λ_{jt}, so that the sum of these terms over j will be the original series. As the time series is itself a statistical variable, so all the λ_{jt}'s will be statistical variables and it is an interesting property of a stationary series that λ_{jt} and λ_{kt} are uncorrelated, where $k \neq j$.

If now we consider two series X_t, Y_t and decompose each into corresponding components $\lambda_{jt}(x)$ and $\lambda_{jt}(y)$ then, if both series are stationary, $\lambda_{jt}(x)$ and $\lambda_{kt}(y)$ will be uncorrelated. Thus, the two series are connected only via the correlation between the corresponding frequency bands $\lambda_{jt}(x)$ and $\lambda_{jt}(y)$. These correlations need not be the same for all pairs of frequencies, there being no reason why two long-run components need be as highly correlated as two short-run components of a given pair of time series. The diagram which plots the square of these correlations

---

[12] This work is described in GRANGER, *op. cit.*, Chapter 9, and methods of analyzing non-stationary series are introduced in GRANGER, *op. cit.*, Chapter 10.

against frequency is known as the *coherence-diagram*.[13] Similarly, it is possible that one of any pair of corresponding frequency bands will be time lagged to the other, but again this time-lag need not be the same for all pairs of frequencies. Indeed, it seems likely that if one series is inherently lagged to the other, then the long-run components will have a longer lag than do the short-run components. Such lags may be estimated directly from a diagram known as the *phase-diagram*. It should be clear that use of such methods allow very complex relationships to be discovered and interpreted in a useful way.

An example of such a relationship was found when the cross-spectra were estimated between the monthly New York call money rate and the New York commercial paper rate for the period 1876 to 1914. It was found that all components of the former were leading the corresponding components of the latter, but that the lead was *proportional* to the period for each pair. Thus, the long-run components of the call money rate were leading the long-run components of the commercial paper rate by an amount that was larger than the corresponding lead for the short-run components.

Spectral methods are not necessarily easy to use, but we shall illustrate their power and value in the next section by discussing results on stock market data.

3.   RESULTS OF THE ANALYSIS

Our first consideration was to test if the random walk model appeared to fit the price data without any transformations. We ignored any trend in variance (see Appendix A) and estimated the spectrum of the first difference of various of the major indices of the Securities and Exchange Commission. In every case the resulting spectrum was very flat over the whole frequency range, apart from a few exceptional frequencies which will be discussed later. Figure 2.3 shows a typical resulting spectrum, that of the first difference of the SEC composite weekly stock price index for the period January 7, 1939 to September 29, 1961. The initial result was that the simple random walk model fits the data very well as very few points are outside the 95 percent confidence limits.

However, there are various important implications about series generated by such a model. The theoretically significant one that the resulting variance is infinite need not concern us in practice, as explained in Appendix A. The fact that the simple random walk model tells us little about the long-run (low-frequency) properties of the series is more important. This is easily seen by noting that if X_t is a series obeying the random walk model and Y_t is a second series defined by

$$Y_t = X_t + a \cos \omega t$$

[13] *Figure 2.7* shows such diagrams.

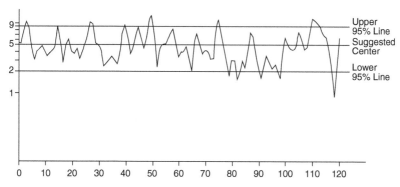

Figure 2.3. Power Spectrum of SEC Composite Weekly Stock Price Index 1939–1961.

then we have

$$X_t - X_{t-1} = \varepsilon_t$$

and

$$Y_t - Y_{t-1} = b \cos[\omega t + \Theta] + \varepsilon_t,$$

where

$$b^2 = 2a^2(1 - \cos\omega)$$

and

$$\tan\Theta = \frac{\sin\omega}{1 - \cos\omega}.$$

Thus, if ω is small, b will be small and the first differences of the two series X_t, Y_t are virtually indistinguishable although the latter contains a (possibly) important long-run component. As an example, with weekly data if the frequency ω corresponds to periods of 28 weeks or 62 weeks, then the ratio of b^2 to a^2 will be 5 percent and 1 percent respectively.

To test whether the original stock price series contain long-run components of greater importance than the random walk hypothesis implies, the spectra for the original series were estimated after trend had been removed by the use of two long simple moving averages of lengths 104 and 78 weeks. It is necessary to remove the trend in mean first in order to ensure that no "leakage of power" has occurred from the zero frequency band to neighboring bands. The effect on the spectrum of applying such moving averages is to multiply it by a known function (described in Appendix A). When the spectrum is estimated at 156 points, the function's value is zero at the first point, it reduces the size of the next three points, but the remaining frequency bands are not appreciably affected.

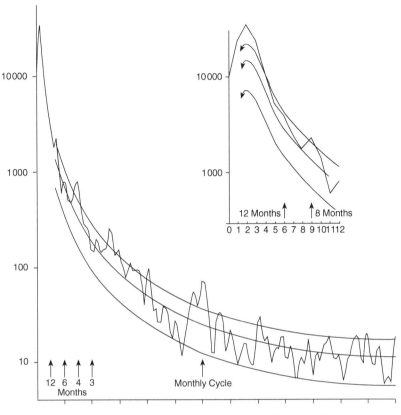

Figure 2.4. Power Spectrum of Composite Weekly SEC Index.

Figure 2.4 shows the estimated spectrum of the weekly SEC composite price index for the same period as before. Superimposed upon the estimated spectrum is the expected spectrum if the random walk hypothesis were true, taking into account the effect of applying the moving averages, together with the 90 percent "confidence bands" appropriate to this hypothesis. The insert in Fig. 2.4 shows an expanded version of the important section of the figure, involving the first twelve frequency bands. It is seen that for the large majority of the frequency bands, the random walk model is upheld; but the first, second and third bands are significantly greater than the model would lead us to expect. In fact, for all six of the major SEC indices (composite, manufacturing, transportation, utility, mining and trade, finance and services) the second and third bands are significantly larger than would be expected from the model and the first, fourth and fifth are consistently above the expected spectrum. It thus seems that the model, although extremely successful in explaining most of the spectral shape, does not adequately explain the strong long run

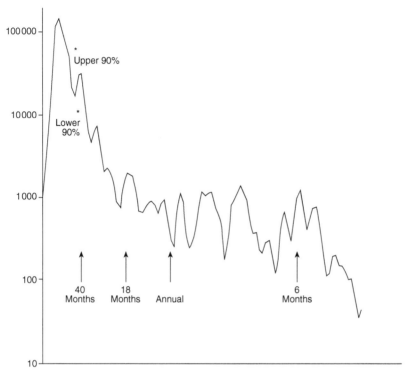

Figure 2.5. Power Spectrum of Standard and Poor Series 1875–1952.

(24 months or more) components of the series. Nothing definite can be said about the business cycle component of these series as they cover too short a time-span.

However, by using the monthly *Standard and Poor* common stock price index for the period October 1875 to March 1952 and the monthly Dow-Jones stock price index for the years 1915 to 1958, we were able to investigate the business cycle component more closely. Figure 2.5 shows the estimated power spectrum of the Standard and Poor series after an important trend in mean has been removed by using moving averages of lengths 80 and 36. (The spectrum was estimated at 240 frequency bands but only the first 100 are shown.) A small peak at 40 months can be seen but it is not statistically significant as a smooth curve can easily be inserted between the 90 percent confidence bands of the estimated spectrum in this area. Even after trend removal, this peak only accounts for slightly less than 10 percent of the total remaining variance. Thus, the component corresponding to the American business cycle of approximately 40 months, although noticeable, is not of particular importance and is much less important than components with periods of five years or more.

Power spectra were estimated for the Standard and Poor index over each of the periods 1875–1896, 1896–1917, 1917–1934 and 1934–1956. Although each one of these periods is too short to give definite information about the 40-month cycle, the eight-month component was invariably of some importance, this being a harmonic of the business cycle.[14]

The estimated spectra of the *Dow-Jones* stock price series were similar to those of the Standard and Poor index and thus provide confirmation of the accuracy of these results. The analysis of this index produces no additional information in this connection.

Certain other frequencies are also consistently outside the confidence bands but they are only those bands corresponding to a monthly variation and to the second and third harmonics of an annual (seasonal) component. In the spectrum shown, neither of the two peaks corresponding to four months and one month account for more than one-third of one percent of the total variance of the series not already explained by the random-walk hypothesis. Therefore it seems extremly unlikely that either of the "cycles" could be profitably exploited by investors. For no series so far studied has there been a significant twelve month component, although in several of them its harmonics have been just visible, yet it is commonly assumed that the New York stock market possesses a significant seasonal movement (e.g. the "summer rise"). (Further details can be found in Appendix B.)

The estimated coherence and phase diagrams between the various SEC stock price indices produced few novel results. The full details are given in Appendix B but the more noteworthy results can be summarized by the following figure:

Figure 2.6.

A strong connection (coherence generally high) is denoted by ⟷ and a moderately strong connection is denoted by ↔. The coherence diagram between the stock price indices for Manufacturing and Transportation is shown in the upper half of Figure 2.7. The Utilities index appears to be unrelated to the other four major subsections of the composite index shown in the table above. The indices for durables and non-durables are strongly connected, but the index for the Radio and

---

[14] It should be noted that a good clue to possibly important long-run components which, due to the shortness of the data, do not stand out in the estimated spectrum, is provided when harmonics of this component have some importance.

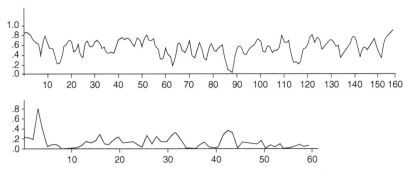

Figure 2.7. Upper part: Coherence of Stock Price Indices of Manufacturing and Transportation. Lower part: Coherence of SEC Composite Price Index and Volume of Turnover of Stocks.

Television section of durables have no connection with the motor manufacturers' section; neither has the rail transport index with the air transport index. *In no case is there any indication of one series leading another.*

Results which are more surprising arise from the coherence diagrams between certain weekly price series and the corresponding *volume of sales* of stocks. The lower section of Figure 2.7 shows the coherence between the SEC composite price index and the over-all volume of turnover of stocks of the New York Stock Exchange for the same period. The coherence is seen to be extremely low. Only at the third frequency point could one reject the hypothesis that the true coherence is zero with any worthwhile confidence. The exceptional frequency (corresponding to a period of 40 weeks) appears to correspond to no known phenomena and we suggest on the basis of our present knowledge that it is spurious. However, as spectral analysis is applied to more and more areas of the economy it is possible that other series also exhibit unexplained characteristics which, if taken together, may give rise to a new meaningful interpretation. The coherence diagrams between the weekly closing prices and the turnover of stocks for the two companies so considered (General Electric Corporation and Idaho Power) were also low for all frequencies, including the third, which was large in Figure 2.6.

The *phase diagrams* contain little worthwhile information as the corresponding coherences are very low, but there is a slight tendency to oscillate about the value π. These results seem to indicate that, at least in the short-run, and for the normal day-to-day or week-to-week workings of the stock exchange the movements in the amount of stock sold are unconnected with movements in price. It might be argued that the first-difference of price should have been correlated to the volume sold; but the connection cannot be large between these series and still give a low coherence. This statement, of course, says nothing about exceptional price movements or of *trends* in either series, it being a comment on the normal oscillations of the series. Perhaps this result concerning the volume of sales is not surprising when the previous result is recalled, i.e., that in the very short run prices can be well represented by a random walk model. This follows, since in the short run the direction of price changes cannot be predicted and so stocks cannot be profitably sold on such predictions. We realize that professional stock exchange operators may from time to time have special knowledge of particular movements and so may make a profit using this knowledge, such as when a stock-broker influences large numbers of his customers to buy a particular stock. But this section of the market is clearly a small one.

We finally mention some results by M. HATANAKA to be published else-where[15] concerning the question of whether stock price indices provide useful leading business cycle indicators. The coherence diagram, between the monthly Standard and Poor Index with Industrial Production for the period 1919–1956 and between the same index and bank clearing for 1875–1956, are both generally low. The phase-diagrams suggest that the stock price index has leads of $1\frac{1}{4}$ months and 2 months respectively in the relevant frequency bands.

The whole problem of studying business-cycle indicators is bedeviled with the vagueness of the concept of the business cycle movement of the economy and the huge inaccuracies known to exist in many series used to indicate the cycles.[16] HATANAKA's study did not need to use the extremely vague notion of "turning-points" but the significance of the leads is still small, particularly as the coherences found were small, indicating that the stock price indices are poor indicators. It is as though the whole stock exchange were continually predicting the long-run movements of the economy and about 55 percent of these predictions were actually correct. This cannot be considered to be a very impressive record of prediction.

The results of this study show, we believe, some of the power of spec-tral analysis. This new statistical method is still under active develop-ment. In application to fields other than economics it has shown that it can discover cycles of obscure phenomena hidden in a great deal of background noise. If in the case of its application to the stock market no commonly assumed strong "cycles" have been found, this is then an indi-cation that such cycles have no reality.[17] Once one gets used to thinking in terms of frequencies, the interpretation of the results will become

[15] GRANGER, *op. cit.*, Chapter 12.
[16] See OSKAR MORGENSTERN: *On the Accuracy of Economic Observations*, Princeton Uni-versity Press, 1950, a completely revised and enlarged edition being in press.
[17] In the face of the new evidence one of us feels that he has to modify earlier statements made about the alleged existence, duration and interaction of stock market "cycles". These statements were made on the strength of the determination of such "specific cycles" by the National Bureau of Economic Research, but the existence of such cycles is not supported by the present findings. They are probably spurious. Clearly many of the consequences drawn also have to go overboard. Cf. O. MORGENSTERN: *International Financial Transactions, op. cit.*

rather natural for economics. The present investigation being a pilot study, and the methods used still being capable of extension, suggest that our findings may be considered to be preliminary.[18] Yet we feel that the dominant features of stock market behavior have been illuminated.

Finally there is an interest to say a few words about the implications of our findings for investment behavior. To the extent that stock prices perform random walks the short term investor engages in a fair gamble, which is slightly better than playing roulette,[19] since that game is biased in favor of the bank. For the long term investor, i.e., one who invests at the very minimum for a year, the problem is to identify the phases of the different long-run components of the over-all movement of the market. The evidence of "cycles" obtained in our studies is so weak that "cyclical investment" is at best only marginally worthwhile. Even this small margin will rapidly disappear as it is being made use of. The extreme weakness of the seasonal component is an example of a cycle which has been practically removed by utilizing the opportunities it seemed to offer.

APPENDIX A

Some Technical Considerations

A stochastic process X_t is stationary, in the wide sense, if

$$E[X_t] = m, \quad E[(X_t - m)(X_{t-\tau} - m)] = \mu_\tau \quad \text{for all } t.$$

The power spectrum of such a series, $f(\omega)$, is defined by

$$\mu_\tau = \int_{-\pi}^{\pi} e^{i\tau\omega} f(\omega) d\omega.$$

Let a set of stochastic processes $\{X_t(k)\}$ be given with a corresponding set of power spectra $\{f(\omega, k)\}$, then if a non-stationary process Y_t is defined by

$$Y_t = X_t(t)$$

we may call $f(\omega, t)$ the instantaneous spectrum of Y_t at time t. Provided that $f(\omega, t)$ changes slowly with time, it may be shown that if one estimates the spectrum of Y_t as though it were a stationary series, one is actually estimating (approximately)

$$\frac{1}{n} \sum_{t=1}^{n} f(\omega, t),$$

---

[18] An interesting open problem is to see whether individual stocks (rather than indices) exhibit runs.

[19] That is, without considering costs of purchases and sales.

where n is the length of data available. Thus, if a series has a slowly trending variance but no trend in mean, the effect on the estimated spectrum will merely be a scale factor. It is for this reason that spectral methods could be used directly on the stock price series without transformations such as the logarithmic transformations. Such transformations are, of course, sensible if the utility function attached to the price of the variable being considered is proportional to the (trending) mean price. However, over the relatively short period used in the analysis, any trend in variance was not of particular importance in the method used.

Trends in mean are, of course, of greater importance, especially when the low frequencies are being particularly studied. The moving-average method of trend removal used on the SEC series was to apply two moving averages of lengths 104 and 78 and then subtract the resulting series from the original series. The effect is to multiply the spectrum of the series by

$$[1 - a(\omega, 104) \cdot a(\omega, 78)]^2$$

where

$$a(\omega, m) = \frac{\sin(m\omega/2)}{m\sin(\omega/2)}.$$

If a series is generated by a random walk model

$$X_t - X_{t-1} = \varepsilon_t$$

where ε_t is white noise, it will have power spectrum

$$f_x(\omega) = \frac{k}{2(1 - \cos\omega)},$$

where

$$k = \frac{\sigma_\varepsilon^2}{2\pi}.$$

We note that an alternative representation for such a series is

$$X_t = \sum_{j=0}^{\infty} \varepsilon_{t-j}$$

and thus, in theory, the variance of X_t is infinite. This also follows from the fact that

$$\int_{-\pi}^{\pi} f_x(\omega) d\omega = \infty.$$

However

$$\int_D f_x(\omega)\,d\omega < \infty,$$

where D is the complete segment of the real line $(-\pi, \pi)$ excluding the narrow band $(-\delta, \delta)$ centered at zero, for any $\delta > 0$. Thus, if $F[\ ]$ is a filter which has a continuous transfer function $a(\omega)$ such that

$$\frac{a(\omega)}{1 - \cos\omega}$$

has a finite value at $\omega = 0$, then the process $F[X_t]$ has finite variance and can be analyzed by spectral methods. The fact that we know the series X_t only over a finite length of time is essentially equivalent to such a filter.

Processes generated by the Markov model

$$X_t - aX_{t-1} = \varepsilon_t,$$

where ε_t is white noise, have very similarly shaped spectra, except for very low frequencies, when the parameter a takes any value between 0.8 and 1.1. Thus, although the value $a = 1$, giving a random walk model, is acceptable from an economic point of view, the methods presented in the paper do not prove that this is the correct value. We thus conclude that the infinite variance aspect of the random walk model need not overduly concern us.

The spectral estimating method used throughout was the Tukey-Hanning estimate as described in Granger, *op. cit.*, Chapter 4. The associated estimating lags mentioned in the following appendix are the number of frequency bands for which the spectrum was estimated. Thus, if m lags were used, the kth frequency band begins at frequency $\pi k/m$.

APPENDIX B

Description of Series Analyzed

The various stock market series analyzed for this study are listed below, together with the major results.

Power Spectra

In describing the estimated power spectra, the following abbreviations are used:

(i) *Shape of spectrum:* U = "usual" shape, as described in section 2 above; U* = "usual" shape, except that some or all of the lower frequencies are less prominent than usual.

(ii) *Annual harmonics visible:* If any of the annual harmonics are visible, these are noted. $\alpha = 12$ months, $\beta = 6$ months, $\gamma = 4$ months, $\delta = 3$ months.

(iii) *Prominent frequencies:* Frequency bands which are particularly prominent, other than connected with the annual component, are listed. M = monthly component, E = eight month component.

Cross Spectra

In describing the coherence diagrams, the following terms are used:

(i) Very high: Many coherence values above 0.95
(ii) High: Some coherence values above 0.8, most above 0.5
(iii) Moderate: Most coherence values between 0.6 and 0.3
(iv) Low: Few coherence values above 0.4
(v) Very Low: Majority of values below 0.25

Phase Diagrams: These attempt to discover whether one series is leading another. If no such lead is found the abbreviation N is used, if the diagram contains little or no useful information (due, usually, to low coherence) the abbreviation L is used.

I. Stock Price Indices, Securities and Exchange Commission,
Indices of Weekly Closing Prices of Common Stocks on the New York Stock Exchange,
January 7, 1939 to September 29, 1961

Trend adjustment by use of two moving averages of lengths 104, 78
1957–1959 = 100

Original number of data = 1,182
Number after trend adjustment = 1,002
Estimating Lags = 156

POWER SPECTRA	Shape of Spectrum	Annual Harmonics Visible	Prominent Frequencies
1. *Composite* – 300 stocks in 32 industrial groups	U	β	M, E
2. *Manufacturing*	U	β, γ	M, E
3. *Durable Goods Manufacturing*	U	γ	M, E
4. *Radio, Television and Communications Equipment*	U	–	M, E
5. *Motor Vehicle Manufacturing*	U	γ, δ	M
6. *Non-Durable Goods Manufacturing*	U*	–	M, E
7. *Transportation*	U	–	M, E
8. *Railroad*	U	–	M, E
9. *Air Transportation*	U	–	E
10. *Utilities*	U	δ	–
11. *Trade, Finance and Service*	U	–	M
12. *Mining*	U	–	M, E

CROSS SPECTRA			Coherence	Phase
Composite Index	with	Manufacturing	Very High	N
		Transportation	High	N
		Utilities	Moderate	N
		Trade	High	N
		Mining	Moderate	N
Manufacturing	with	Durable	Very High	N
		Non-Durable	Very High	N
		Transportation	Moderate to High	N
		Utilities	Low	N
		Trade, Finance and Service	Moderate	N
		Mining	Moderate	N
Durable	with	Non-Durable	High	N
		Radio, Television and Communication Equipment	Moderate	N
		Motor Vehicle	High	N
Radio, Television and Communication Equipment	with	Motor Vehicle	Moderate	N
Transportation	with	Railroad	Very High	N
		Air Transportation	Low	N
		Mining	Low	N
Railroad	with	Air Transportation	Low	N
Utilities	with	Mining	Very Low	N
Trade, Finance and Service	with	Mining	Low	N

II. Stock Prices of Six Large US Companies, Monthly:
January 1946 to December 1960

Average of low and high prices for each month
Original number of data = 180
Estimating lags = 60

POWER SPECTRA	Shape	Annual Harmonics Visible	Prominent Frequencies
1. American Tobacco	U	–	–
2. General Foods	U	δ	–
3. American Can	U*	δ	E
4. Woolworth	U	δ	–
5. Chrysler	U	–	E
6. US Steel	U*	–	E

CROSS SPECTRA			Coherence	Phase
American Tobacco	with	General Foods	High	N
		American Can	Mixed	U
		Woolworth	High	N
		Chrysler	Moderate	N
		US Steel	High	N

CROSS SPECTRA			Coherence	Phase
General Foods	with	American Can	Mixed	L
		Woolworth	High	N
		Chrysler	High	N
		US Steel	High	N
American Can	with	Woolworth	Mixed	L
		Chrysler	Mixed	L
		US Steel	Mixed	L
Woolworth	with	Chrysler	Mixed	L
		US Steel	Large	N
Chrysler	with	US Steel	Mixed	N

III. Standard and Poor Common Stock Price Index,
Industrials, Rails and Utilities, Monthly, 1875–1956

Industrial production index, monthly, 1919–1956
Trend adjusted by moving averages of lengths 80, 36
Estimating lags = 60, except where specified

POWER SPECTRA	Shape	Annual Harmonics	Prominent Frequencies
1. October 1875 to March 1952 (estimating lags: 240)	U	β	Slight 40 month, E
2. October 1875 to October 1896	U	β, γ	Slight 10 month
3. October 1875 to October 1917	U	–	–
4. October 1896 to October 1917	U	–	–
5. October 1917 to March 1952	U	β	E
6. October 1917 to March 1934 (estimating lags: 40)	U*	β	E
7. March 1934 to March 1952 (estimating lags: 40)	U	–	E
8. Industrial Production Index (estimating lags: 120)	U	$\alpha, \beta, \gamma, \delta$	–

CROSS SPECTRA

Estimating lags = 120

	Coherence	Phase
1. Standard and Poor Index with Industrial Production Index 1919–1956	Low with occasional moderates	Some evidence of a $1\frac{1}{4}$ month lead in low frequencies
2. Standard and Poor Index with Bank Clearings, 1875–1956	As above	As above, but lead of 2 month

(Stock prices lead in both cases.)

IV. Dow-Jones Industrial Stock Price Index, Monthly, January 1915 to June 1961
(20 stocks through September 1928, 30 thereafter)

POWER SPECTRA	Shape	Annual Harmonics	Prominent Frequencies
1. 1915–1958 (estimating lags: 120)	U	–	E
2. 1915–1934 (estimating lags: 60)	U	β	–
3. 1935–1957 (estimating lags: 60)	U	–	E

V. Price and Volume Data

Weekly data, January 1957 to December 1961
SEC composite price index, over-all volume of sales during week
Closing price and volume of sales of stocks of two firms:
General Electric Corporation, Idaho Power

POWER SPECTRA	Shape	Annual Harmonics Visible	Prominent Frequencies
1. Composite price index	U	β	M
2. Over-all volume series	U*	–	–
3. GEC closing prices	U	–	M
4. Volume of GEC stocks sold	U*	β	M
5. Idaho Power closing prices	U	–	–
6. Volume of Idaho Power stocks sold	Special shape requiring further investigation	–	–

CROSS SPECTRA		Coherence	Phase
1. Composite price index	with over-all volume series	Very Low	L
2. GEC closing prices	with GEC volume	Very Low	L
3. Idaho Power closing prices	with Idaho Power	Very Low	L

The Typical Spectral Shape of an Economic Variable*

C. W. J. Granger

In recent years, a number of power spectra have been estimated from economic data and the majority have been found to be of a similar shape. A number of implications of this shape are discussed, particular attention being paid to the reality of business cycles, stability and control problems, and model building.

1. INTRODUCTION

DURING THE past four or five years a fairly large number of power spectra have been estimated using economic data.[1] It might thus be an appropriate time to review the results obtained and to ask if the advent of spectral methods has thrown any light on the basic characteristics of economic variables. The almost unanimous result of these investigations is that the vast majority of economic variables, after removal of any trend in mean and seasonal components, have similarly shaped power spectra, the typical shape being as in Figure 3.1.

It is the purpose of this paper to illustrate this result and to discuss briefly its implications both for economic theory in general and for economic model building in particular.

It is not, of course, suggested that every economic time series produce such spectra nor that nothing else is discernable from the estimated spectra other than this simple shape. Nevertheless, the fact that such a shape arises in the majority of cases does suggest that there are certain general, overall implications for economics, and, possibly, that the estimation of power spectra alone is unlikely to be a productive technique. Cross spectral methods which, in the author's opinion, are likely to prove more important and which attempt to discover and explain the rela-

---

* Prepared under the auspices of National Science Foundation Grant GP-82.
[1] In addition to his own work, the author is familiar with the calculations by J. Cunnyngham, D. Fand, M. Godfrey, M. Hatanaka, M. Nerlove, E. Parzen, and M. Suzuki.

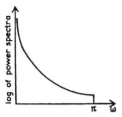

Figure 3.1. Typical spectral shape.

tionships between economic variables, will not be considered in this paper.[2]

Spectral methods are based upon the idea of the decomposition of a stochastic process into a (possibly non-finite) number of orthogonal components, each of which is associated with a "frequency." Such a decomposition is always possible for processes that are "covariance stationary," i.e., have variances and autocovariances independent of real time. The power spectrum records the contribution of the components belonging to a given frequency band to the total variance of the process. If a band contributes a large proportion of the total variance it may be considered to be important compared to a band which contributes a smaller amount to be variance. As the introduction, interpretation, and estimation of power spectra have been dealt with in detail elsewhere,[3] it is not considered necessary to expand on these subjects further in this paper. It must be emphasized that spectral methods do not require the specification of a model but follow directly from the assumption of stationarity.[4]

2.   EXAMPLES OF ESTIMATED SPECTRA

A number of power spectra of economic series displaying the "typical shape" have been published. Nerlove (1964) shows the estimated spectra for the Federal Reserve Board index of industrial production (U.S.A., monthly, March, 1920 – September, 1960, seasonally adjusted), federally inspected hog slaughter and cattle slaughter (monthly, January, 1907 – December, 1960) and various U.S. employment series (monthly, July, 1947 or 1948 – December, 1961, both original series and seasonally adjusted). Cunnyngham (1963) has estimated spectra for the wholesale commodity price index (monthly, 1908–1960) and money supply (monthly, 1908–1960). It has been found that price series from the

[2] For a description of cross-spectral methods and other generalizations see [3].
[3] See [3] or Nerlove [8].
[4] In fact, spectral methods can provide useful results for wider classes of process but description of these processes lies outside the scope of this paper.

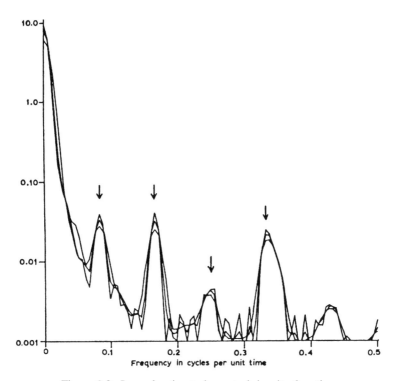

Figure 3.2. Log of estimated spectral density functions.

New York stock market produce the typical shape. Diagrams illustrating this may be found in Granger and Morgenstern (1963) and in Chapter 4 of Granger and Hatanaka (1964).

There also exist many unpublished estimated spectra. In the course of his studies of business cycle indicators, Granger and Hatanaka (1964), Chapter 12, and (1963) has estimated the spectra of twenty-two important economic series, the large majority of which display the typical shape. Unpublished studies by Godfrey, Parzen, and Suzuki provide further examples.

It must be emphasized that many of these series contained important seasonal components so that the "typical shape" had added to it peaks at frequencies corresponding to a period of 12 months and its harmonics.

Figure 3.2 provides an example of a "typical" spectral shape with peaks corresponding to the seasonal component. It shows the logarithm of the estimated power spectrum for United States bank clearing data (monthly, 1875–1958) from which an exponential linear trend ($\exp(a + bt)$) has been estimated and subtracted. Despite this trend-removal procedure, considerable power remains at very low frequencies. In this example, roughly 99 per cent of the total power lies in the frequency band $(0, 2\pi/40)$ which illustrates the extreme subtlety of the analysis one attempts in measuring the power spectrum at higher frequencies. The fact that it is usually possible to obtain a good estimate at all frequencies illustrates the considerable power of the available estimating procedures. The diagram shows the spectral estimates using the Parzen window and with 60, 80, and 90 lags. The consistent shape of the estimated spectrum using these different lags implies that the shape found may be accepted as being realistic with some confidence.

3.   THE PROBLEM OF TREND

The most noticeable characteristic of the typical spectral shape is the over-powering importance of the low frequency components. The majority of economic time series contain important trends in mean, and it is known that such trends raise the value of the power spectrum at the low frequencies. One must thus ask if the "typical shape" is not largely due to these trends.

Before inquiring further into this possibility, one must first decide upon a definition of trend. A definition which is generally acceptable is not obvious, it being remembered that we have no reason to suppose that the trend in mean can be well approximated by a simple polynominal or exponential expression or even that it will be monotonic. It is clear that a curve that would be considered as a "trend" in a short series would not be so considered if the series were longer. An example of this would be temperature readings gathered every minute for four hours during the day. The known daily fluctuation would appear as a trend in such data but would not be considered as trend if the data were available for a period of three months (in which case the annual fluctuation would appear as trend). Thus the definition is likely to depend on the amount of data (n) available. In this paper "trend in mean" will be defined as comprising all frequency components with frequency equal to or less than $2\pi/n$, i.e., all components with wave length equal to or greater than the length of the series. Although, of course, this definition is to a certain extent arbitrary, it is precise and does appear to include the intuitive meaning of trend given by the majority of users of time series methods.

This definition of trend does not allow us to answer in the negative the question stated in the first paragraph of this section. The reason for this is that if the spectrum of a series containing a trend in mean is estimated directly, the resulting shape is likely to be the typical shape due to a characteristic of the estimation procedure known as leakage. If the true spectrum contains an important peak at some frequency, not only will the value of the estimated spectrum at neighboring frequency bands be raised, but up to 3 per cent of the value of the peak may also be found in the estimated value at other nearby frequency bands. This leakage, although it is a small percentage of the large value at the peak, may nevertheless introduce overwhelming biases in the estimates of the

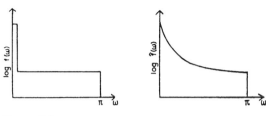

Figure 3.3.

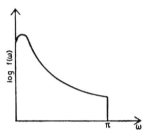

Figure 3.4.

spectrum at these frequencies. As the component we have called trend
will usually contribute by far the largest proportion of the total variance
of the series, the value of the spectrum at the zero frequency band ($0 \leq \omega \leq \pi/2m$, if m lags used in the spectral estimating procedure) will be large
and the leakage effect will make it likely that the estimated spectrum will
be quickly but smoothly decreasing for the next few frequency bands.

Thus, suppose for instance that a series is constructed as the sum of
white noise[5] and an important but very long cycle (with period longer
than the length of the series). The theoretical spectrum will be as in
Figure 3.3 but the leakage effect will produce an estimated spectrum as
shown in this figure, on the right.

It follows from this that if one estimates the power spectrum of an
economic series containing an important trends, a "typical shape" spectral estimate is likely to result. The important point about the typical
shape, however, is that it still appears even if trend in mean is removed.
Suppose that the trend is removed by either a filter or regression method.
It is known that such methods will both effectively remove a trend in
mean and that the spectrum of the residual will be (almost) unbiased for
all frequencies except for very low frequencies which, in general, will
lose power. In the investigations cited above, it is found that the power
spectrum of the residual is basically of the form shown in Figure 3.4, i.e.,

---

[5] A series is called white noise if the covariance between the value at time t and the value
at time s is zero for all $t \neq s$.

of the typical shape apart from the loss of power at the low frequencies. Moreover, the same basic shape is found *regardless of the length of data available*, the size of the truncation point used in the estimation procedure, or the trend removal method used. For very long series (such as pig iron production or monthly bank clearing data for the U.S., for which over a thousand recordings are available) the trend-removal techniques need affect only extremely low frequencies and the indication is consistently that the logarithm of the power spectrum increases montonically as frequency decreases for frequency bands lower than that corresponding to a 12-month period.

It is, of course, possible that the typical shape does reach an absolute peak at some low frequency; but if this is so, the peak must be at an extremely low frequency as no evidence of such a turning point has been found in studies of long series.

Studies in which the pre-whitening technique have been used, which decreases the bias due to leakage, support this finding (e.g., Nerlove (1964)) as do analyses of data that contain no apparent trend in mean (e.g., New York Commercial Paper Rate, monthly, 1876–1914, see [1964, Chapter 4] and (1963)).

It must thus be concluded that the typical spectral shape of an economic series is as illustrated in Figure 1 and that any possible trend in mean will only accentuate this shape.

4.   INTERPRETATION: BUSINESS CYCLES

The existence of a typical spectral shape suggests the following law (stated in nonrigorous but familiar terms):

The long-term fluctuations in economic variables, if decomposed into frequency components, are such that the amplitudes of the components decrease smoothly with decreasing period.[6]

One may care to associate the frequency components with various "cycles" suggested as existing in economic series by some economists prior to the Second World War, such as the Kondratieff long wave (40 to 60 years), Kuznets long wave (20 to 30 years), the building cycle (15 to 20 years), minor or Kitchin cycle (2 to 4 years), and so forth. In this case the law suggests that the amplitude of the Kondratieff long wave is greater than the amplitude of the Kuznets long wave which is greater than the amplitude of the building cycle and so on.[7] The law also indicates, however, that the spectrum does not consist of a series of peaks of decreasing size corresponding to each of the above cycles but is rather

---

[6] It might be possible to restate the law as "events which affect the economy for a long period are more important than those which affect it only for a short time."

[7] If this were not the case, it is doubtful if such fluctuations could have been "seen." Thus, the existence of this early work in business cycles can be interpreted as an early discovery of this part of the "law."

a smooth, decreasing curve with no (significant) peaks corresponding to periods longer than 12 months.

It has, of course, long been realized that those cycles are not strictly periodic fluctuations that would correspond to jumps in the spectral distribution function but that they should be interpreted as important frequency bands. The evidence of estimated power spectra is that the peaks corresponding to these bands do, in fact, blend together to form a smooth, continuous curve. If this is the case, it might well be asked why certain fluctuations have been picked out as being of special importance, particularly the minor business cycle of roughly 30 to 50 months duration. To discuss this we first need to consider the likely properties of a sample from a process possessing a spectrum of the typical shape.

The most obvious property of such a sample would probably be a visual long-term fluctuation which would not be in any way periodic. The fluctuation need not be visible at all moments of time and would, of course, be somewhat blurred by the high frequency and seasonal components.[8] The estimated power spectrum would have essentially the correct shape but would usually also contain a number of peaks and troughs about the true spectral shape. A different sample from the same process would produce a similar estimated spectrum but with the peaks and troughs at different frequencies. This "sampling error" is due to the fact that the samples are only of finite length. The peaks found in the estimated spectra should not, of course, be significant. Suppose now that a sample is such that the most visible peak is found in the power spectrum at a frequency corresponding to 63 months, for example. In this case it appears likely that if one looks at the data with the intention of finding a cycle, the cycle one will "find" is one with a period near 63 months. In a sense, the sample does contain such a cycle but it will be only a transient feature as it is unlikely to occur in the next stretch of data from the process.

The estimated spectra for a number of economic series do, in fact, contain peaks at a frequency corresponding to roughly 40 months. Examples of such a series are certain pre-First World War short-term interest rates (illustrated in Granger and Hatanaka (1964), Chapter 4 and in Hatanaka (1963) and stock price indices (illustrated in (1963)). As Hatanaka (1963) points out, however, similar small peaks may be found in the logarithm of other economic series such as bank clearings and pig iron production. The reason for the logarithm of the series being required to find the peaks is that these series usually contain an important trend in variance, the effect of which is to blur any small peak in the spectrum. Taking the logarithm of the series, providing it is positive, moves any

---

[8] It would be theoretically possible to find the mean length of the long-term fluctuation but it seems doubtful if this would prove to be a useful concept.

trend in variance into a trend in mean, which may be removed by the usual methods.[9]

The peaks found at or near 40 months are never statistically significant and the evidence available indicates that they are more pronounced prior to 1914. The fact that the same peak occurs in several series might appear to add to the statistical significance but actually is only a reflection of the fact that most economic series follow the long-term fluctuations of the economy as a whole.

The fact that such a peak is found in long series could, of course, indicate that this is a true and permanent characteristic of the economy. The evidence, however, is not sufficiently strong for the rejection of the simple hypothesis that the true underlying spectrum is smooth and so does not contain a peak near 40 months. In any case, the size of the peak found in practice indicates that it is of little importance compared to neighboring frequency bands in terms of its contribution of the total variance of the series and so no evidence has been found that particular attention should be paid to this or any other frequency band.

5.   DESCRIPTION: MODEL FITTING

Consider a process having the typical spectral shape. If we define a filter $F_\alpha(\ )$ to be such that an input of series X_t is transformed into an output series Y_t where Y_t obeys the equation

$$Y_t - \alpha Y_{t-1} = X_t,$$

it seems certain that a good representation of our process will be $F_\alpha(\varepsilon_t)$ or $F_\alpha[F_{\alpha'}(\varepsilon_t)]$ where ε_t is white noise and α and α' have values in the range $\frac{1}{2} \le \alpha, \alpha' \le 1$. For example, first order autoregressive schemes were fitted to the following series with results as indicated:

		estimated α
(1)	Various stock price series (see (1963))	0.98
(2)	Manufacturer's inventory (1924–1955)	0.98
(3)	Bank clearings	0.95
	Logarithm of bank clearings	0.97
(4)	Lay-off rate (1930–1958)	0.78
(5)	Average work week (1932–1958)	0.97

(the first three series are trend-adjusted, the latter two were not).

The results by Ames and Reiter (1961), Orcutt (1948), and unpublished results by Parzen concerning the fitting of autoregressive schemes

[9] It is proved in [3] that if the standard deviation of the series is small compared to the mean, the spectrum of the original series is similar in shape to the spectrum of the logarithm of the series.

to economic data further confirm the above suggestion. The main implication is that economic processes are almost unstable.

It must also be emphasized that these results do not preclude the possibility that the processes are best fitted by an explosive autoregressive
model.

Quenouille [(1948), p. 58] points out that the simple explosive Markov
process

$$Y_t - \beta Y_{t-1} = \varepsilon_t, \quad \beta > 1$$

may be viewed as the sum of two components X_t and Z_t, where

$$Y_t = X_t + Z_t,$$

$$X_t - \beta^{-1} X_{t-1} = \eta_t,$$

and

$$Z_t = Z_0 \beta^t.$$

Here ε_t and η_t are both white noises.

Thus, suppose the true model is an explosive autoregressive scheme
with parameter $\beta = 1.05$, for example. Then, after trend removal the
residual may be represented as the output of the filter $F_\alpha(\eta_t)$ with $\alpha = 0.95$.
The process of first removing the trend in mean and then analyzing the
residual is essentially based upon the assumption that the trend is being
generated by a different mechanism than is generating the residual.

As, however, many economic series have an exponential trend in
mean and a typical spectral shape, it is not clear that the two mechanisms
are unconnected. It is quite possible, in fact, that the trend contains useful
information about the rest of the process and in such a case this information should be used.

It has not been felt worthwhile to attempt to fit such schemes to a
large number of economic variables. This is because one must first
remove efficiently any seasonal component and because of the important inaccuracies contained in the majority of economic data which tend
to introduce possibly important biases into the estimates. Nerlove (1964)
has discussed the first of these problems and has indicated that some of
the methods currently used would certainly spoil the estimate. For a complete description of the second problem see Morgenstern (1963).

6. IMPLICATIONS FOR MODEL BUILDING

Let us first investigate the very simple accelerator multiplier model:

$$C_t = cY_{t-1} + \varepsilon_t',$$

$$I_t = v(Y_t - Y_{t-1}) + \eta_t',$$

$$Y_t = C_t + I_t,$$

where C is consumption, Y is national income, I is investment, and it is assumed that ε_t' and η_t' are both white noise processes.

Rearranging, we have

$$Y_t - \alpha Y_{t-1} = \varepsilon_t,$$

$$C_t - \alpha C_{t-1} = \eta_t,$$

$$I_t - \alpha I_{t-1} = \varepsilon_t - \eta_t,$$

where $(1 - v)\varepsilon_t = \varepsilon_t' + \eta_t', \eta_t = \varepsilon_t' + \varepsilon_{t-1}' + \dfrac{c}{1-v}(\varepsilon_{t-1}' + \eta_t')$ and $\alpha = \dfrac{v-c}{v-1}$.

Y_t, C_t, and I_t may each be considered as outputs of the filter $F_\alpha(\ )$ but with different inputs. The power spectra of Y_t and C_t are

$$f_Y(\omega) = \frac{f_\varepsilon(\omega)}{2(1 - \alpha \cos \omega)},$$

$$f_C(\omega) = \frac{f_\eta(\omega)}{2(1 - \alpha \cos \omega)}.$$

It should be noted that if α is near one, the term $(1 - \alpha\cos\omega)$ will be dominating the values of $f_Y(\omega)$ and $f_C(\omega)$ for low frequencies and thus the typical shape will arise. It is, perhaps, interesting to record the value of α for various suggested "realistic" values for the accelerator and the multiplier.

Values of $\alpha = (v - c)/(v - 1)$ for realistic combinations of c and v

$c \backslash^v$	2	3	4
$\frac{1}{3}$	—	1.33	1.22
$\frac{1}{2}$	—	1.25	1.17
$\frac{2}{3}$	1.33	1.17	1.11
$\frac{3}{4}$	1.25	1.12	1.08
$\frac{4}{5}$	1.2	1.10	1.07

Thus, this simple model suggests that an explosive autoregressive scheme is appropriate and spectra of typical shape will certainly be forthcoming.

Reasoning similar to the above may be used to obtain a more general result suggesting a reason for the typical shape being obtained in practice. Let U be the shift operator such that $UX_t = X_{t-1}$. Consider the vector of exogenous variables $X' = (X_1, X_2, \dots, X_n)$ and suppose that X_t obeys the matrix autoregressive scheme

$$P(U)X_t = Q(U)Y_t + \varepsilon_t$$

where Y_t is a $1 \times q$ vector ($q \leq m$) of endogenous variables, ε_t is a $1 \times m$ white noise vector, and $P(U), Q(U)$ are $m \times m$ and $m \times q$ matrices, respectively, each element of which is a polynomial in U.

Thus, we may write (providing the inverse of P exists)

$$X_t = P^{-1}(U)Q(U)Y_t + P^{-1}\varepsilon_t = \frac{L(U)}{|P(U)|}Y_t + \frac{K(U)}{|P(U)|}\varepsilon_t.$$

The power spectrum for each component of X_t may be derived from this formula, but it should be noted that each of the power spectra will have a denominator term which is the square of the modulus of the determinant $|P(e^{i\omega})|$. Thus, if the determinant $|P(z)|$ has a root (or roots) near $z = 1$ (corresponding to $\omega = 0$), this denominator is likely to dominate the value of the power spectra at low frequencies. If the modulus of the determinant is not small for other values of ω, the resulting spectrum is likely to be typical, i.e., high valued at low frequencies and lower valued at other frequencies. The spectra of the components of X_t (possibly after trend removal) may vary in details but their basic shapes will be similar.

An implication of the existence of a typical spectral shape is that if a model is constructed involving economic variables, one aspect of deciding if it is reasonable is to inquire whether the power spectra derived from the model has the typical shape. An example of a simple model that does have this property is Klein's model (1950). As noted by Theil and Boot (1962), "this model describes the American economy as a system which is close to instability and, in fact, leaves the question of stability open."

7.   IMPLICATIONS FOR CONTROL

It has been suggested above that it might be possible to describe many economic variables in terms of one of either of two simple models:[10]
   (i) an explosive scheme

$$X_t - \alpha X_{t-1} = \varepsilon_t,$$

with α greater than but near 1 (say $1 < \alpha \leq 1.4$), or
   (ii) X_t = trend in mean + Y_t where

$$X_t - \alpha Y_{t-1} = \varepsilon_t,$$

with α less than but near 1 (say $0.7 \leq \alpha < 1$).

It was pointed out that spectral methods alone are unable to distinguish between these two models. The essential difference between them is that in (i) both the trend in mean and the long-term fluctuations of the

---

[10] The models are stated in terms of first-order autoregressive schemes. It is easily seen that the arguments still follow if higher-order schemes had been used.

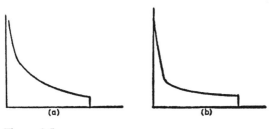

Figure 3.5.

variables are generated by the same mechanism, whereas in (ii) they need not be.

One of the possible aspects of controlling an economy might be stated as an attempt to smooth out the long-term fluctuations without affecting the (upward) trend. In spectral terms this could be described diagramatically by moving from a variable with spectral shape *a* to one with spectral shape *b* (see Figure 3.5), i.e., removing power in the "business cycle" band without removing power at zero frequency.

If model (i) were the correct representation it might be difficult to achieve this change without slowing down the trend. If model (ii) were correct the effect of applying such control might be to make the variable less stable, resulting in more violent, very long-term fluctuations. Either of these two effects would probably be considered undesirable. It is seen that the effect of such a control policy will be to make the process become nearer to being a random walk. The implication of this would seem to be that for a method of control to be really appropriate for use, it must be capable of controlling the whole of the low-frequency component of the variable and not just one section of this component. Thus, for instance, it can be argued that one should not use a "stop-go" policy similar to that used by the British government in recent years without at the same time implementing long-term policies that help to control the trend element. It is clear that more precise statements cannot be made on this subject using this approach without further information about the true inter-relationship between the trend and long-fluctuation elements of important economic variables.

REFERENCES

AMES, E., AND S. REITER: "Distribution of Correlation Coefficients in Economic Time Series," *Journal of the American Statistical Association*, Vol. 56 (1961), pp. 637–656.

CUNNYNGHAM, J.: "Spectral Analysis of Economic Time Series," Working Paper No. 16, U.S. Department of Commerce, Bureau of the Census, 1963, New York.

GRANGER, C. W. J., AND M. HATANAKA: *Spectral Analysis of Economic Time Series*, Princeton, 1964.

GRANGER, C. W. J., AND O. MORGENSTERN: "Spectral Analysis of Stock Market Prices," *Kyklos*, Vol. 16 (1963), pp. 1–27.

HATANAKA, M.: "A Spectral Analysis of Business Cycle Indicators: Lead-lag in Terms of All Time Points," Econometric Research Program, Princeton Research Memorandum No. 53, 1963.

KLEIN, L. R.: *Economic Fluctuations in the U.S.*, 1921–1941, New York, 1950.

MORGENSTERN, O.: *On the Accuracy of Economic Observations*, Second edition, Princeton, 1963.

NERLOVE, M.: "Spectral Analysis of Seasonal Adjustment Procedures," *Econometrica*, Vol. 32 (1964), pp. 241–286.

ORCUTT, G. H.: "A Study of the Autoregressive Nature of the Time Series Used for Tinbergen's Model of the Economic System of the United States, 1919–1932," *Journal of the Royal Statistical Society*, Vol. B10 (1948), pp. 1–45.

QUENOUILLE, M. H.: *Multivariate Time Series Analysis*, London, 1957.

THEIL, H., AND J. C. G. BOOT: "The Final Form of Econometric Equation systems," *Review of the International Statistical Institute*, Vol. 30 (1962), pp. 136–152.

PART TWO

SEASONALITY

CHAPTER 4

Seasonality: Causation, Interpretation, and Implications*

Clive W. J. Granger**

1. CAUSES OF SEASONALITY

It is a very well-known fact that many economic series display seasonality; that is, they have an observable component consisting of a fairly constant shape repeated every 12 months. This component is often treated as being so easily explained that neither an exact definition nor an explanation of its origins is required. It is the objective of this paper to suggest that ignoring consideration of causation can lead to imprecise or improper definitions of seasonality and consequently to misunderstanding of why series require seasonal adjustment, to improper criteria for a good method of adjustment and to have implications for the evaluation of the effects of adjustment both on a single series and when relating two or more series. These considerations do not necessarily lead to better practical methods of adjustment, but they should lead to a better understanding of how to interpret time series and econometric analysis involving seasonal components and seasonally adjusted series. The only other author, prior to this conference, who emphasizes causation of seasonals appears to be BarOn (1973).

There are at least four, not totally distinct, classes of causes of seasonal fluctuations in economic data. These classes are discussed in the following sections.

1.1   Calendar

The timing of certain public holidays, such as Christmas and Easter, clearly affects some series, particularly those related to production. Many series are recorded over calendar months, and, as the number of working days varies considerably from one month to another in a predetermined way, this will cause a seasonal movement in flow variables, such as

* *Seasonal Analysis of Economic Time Series, Economic Research Report, ER-1*, Bureau of the Census, edited by A. Zellner, 1979, 33–46.
** *Research supported, in part, by NSF Grant Soc. 74/12243.*

imports or production. This working-day problem could also lead to spurious correlations between otherwise unrelated series, as I have discussed elsewhere (Granger, 1963).

1.2   Timing Decisions

The timing of school vacations, ending of university sessions, payment of company dividends, and choice of the end of a tax year or accounting period are all examples of decisions made by individuals or institutions that cause important seasonal effects, since these events are inclined to occur at similar times each year. They are generally deterministic or pre-announced and are decisions that produce very pronounced seasonal components in series such as employment rates. These timing decisions are generally not necessarily tied to any particular time in the year but, by tradition, have become so.

1.3   Weather

Actual changes in temperature, rainfall, and other weather variables have direct effects on various economic series, such as those concerned with agricultural production, construction, and transportation, and consequent indirect effects on other series. It could be argued that this cause is the true seasonal, being itself a consequence of the annual movement of the earth's axis which leads to the seasons. Other natural causes can be important, such as the seasonal fluctuations in the abundance of fish, as discussed by Crutchfield and Zellner in their book *Economic Aspects of the Pacific Halibut Fishery* (U.S. Govt. Printing Office, 1963).

1.4   Expectation

The expectation of a seasonal pattern in a variable can cause an actual seasonal in that or some other variable, since expectations can lead to plans that then ensure seasonality. Examples are toy production in expectation of a sales peak during the Christmas period, the closing down of certain vacation facilities immediately after Labor Day in expectation of a decline in demand for these facilities, and the expectation of bad weather in New Jersey in January may mean that few plans are made for new house construction during that month. People choose their vacation destinations on the expectation of weather conditions rather than on the actual situation. Without the expectation-planning aspect, the seasonal pattern may still occur but might be of a different shape or nature. An extreme example is that of British egg prices in the early sixties. The eggs were produced almost entirely by battery hens, who had no idea of the seasons as they existed in a closely controlled, stable environment, and, thus, production could be made steady throughout the year. The egg prices were fixed by the Egg Marketing Board who, on being asked why the prices contained a strong seasonal element, replied that "the housewives expect it." The seasonal in egg prices vanished soon after the enquiry was made. Expectations may arise, because it has been noted that the series being considered has, in the past, contained a seasonal, or because it is observed that acknowledged causal series have a seasonal component.

These four groups may be thought of as basic causes. They are not always easily distinguishable, may often merge together, and the list of basic causes may not be complete. Some series may have seasonal components which are only indirectly due to these basic causes. Weather may cause a seasonal in grape production that then causes a seasonal in grape prices, for example. For many series, the actual causation of a seasonal may be due to a complicated mix of many factors or reasons, due to the direct impact of basic causes and many indirect impacts via other economic variables. Even if only a single basic cause is operating, the causal function need not be a simple one and could involve both a variety of lags and nonlinear terms. Two fairly obvious examples follow.

The first example is the impact on a production series of a public holiday, such as Christmas, might be simply modelled as production = $g_t h_t$, where g_t is a stochastic production series on working-day t, and h_t is a dummy variable, taking the value 1 on nonholidays and 0 on holidays. Thus, the initial impact of the advent of Christmas involves a multiplicative seasonal. However, this model is clearly too simple to be an acceptable approximation of the true situation. If there is spare capacity, the occurrence of the Christmas vacation can be allowed for in the production scheduling by increasing production in working days around the vacation, giving both expectations and a delayed effect. The extent to which this planning occurs will depend partly on the state of the economy, or the order book, and on current production levels, or unused capacity of the factory. Thus, the actual seasonal effect may depend on the level of the economic variable being considered and possibly also on other variables.

A second example is the effect of rainfall on a crop, such as outdoor tomatoes grown in California. Early, plentiful rainfall could bring on a good crop, provided it is not followed by further heavy rainfall in the next 2 months to the exclusion of sufficient sun. Thus, the rain provides both a distributed lag effect and also an accumulation effect on the quality, quantity, and timing of the actual crop.

Two important conclusions can be reached from such considerations: (1) The causes of the seasonal will vary greatly from one series to another, and, therefore, the seasonal components can be expected to have differing properties, and (2) the seasonal components cannot be assumed to be deterministic, i.e., perfectly predictable. Although it would be interesting and perhaps worthwhile to perform a causal analysis of the seasonal component for every major economic series, this task would be both difficult and expensive. Nevertheless, it would be unreasonable to assume that all seasonal components are generated by the same type of simple model, and this must be acknowledged when attempting to seasonally adjust a series. Even though some of the basic causes can be thought of as deterministic series (the calendar and timing decisions, for example), there is certainly no reason to suppose that they will lead to deterministic seasonal components, since the reaction to these causes need not be deterministic. The other basic causes, weather and expectations, are not deterministic and cannot lead to deterministic seasonals. Although an assumption of a deterministic seasonal component may have some value, this value is usually very limited and leads to techniques that are capable of improvement. Implications of these conclusions for seasonal models will be discussed in the section "Seasonal Models."

The consideration of causation also throws doubt on the idea of the seasonal being simply either an additive or a multiplicative component, as will also be discussed in the section "Seasonal Models."

Before turning to the problem of how to define seasonality, it is worthwhile considering briefly the types of economic series that are clearly seasonal and those that are not. For purposes of illustration, consider just those series that the U.S. Department of Commerce decides are in need of seasonal adjustment and those that apparently have no such need. The types of series that are adjusted are generally those concerned with production, sales, inventories, personal income and consumption, government receipts and expenditures, profits, unemployment rates, and imports and exports. Series not seasonally adjusted include prices (other than farm and food prices), interest rates, exchange rates, index of consumer sentiment, new orders (manufacturing), liquid liabilities to foreigners, and U.S. official reserve assets. If it is possible to generalize about such a wide range of variables, it seems that those needing adjustment are usually variables requiring planning or long-range decisionmaking, whereas the nonadjusted series are typically those that can quickly change in value and, thus, require only a stream of short-run decisions.

If one tries to write down the main causes of seasonal components in the first group of variables, I think that it is easily seen that the proper specification of these causes is not a simple task and that this problem needs to be tackled by empirical analysis as much as by introspection.

2.   DEFINITION

It is impossible to proceed further without a reasonably precise definition of seasonality, although it is remarkable how many papers discuss the topic without consideration of definition. The belief is, presumably, that the seasonal component is so simple and obvious that it hardly needs a formal definition. Nevertheless, to sensibly discuss such topics, as the objectives of seasonal adjustment or the evaluation of actual methods of adjustment, a formal definition is required. It is obvious that this definition should not be based on a specific model, since this model may not properly reflect reality, nor should it rely on the outcome of a particular method of adjustment, since the method may not be ideal, and it also becomes difficult to evaluate that particular method. These limitations, together with the fact that the most obvious feature of a seasonal component is its repetitiveness over a 12-month period, strongly suggest that a definition can be most naturally stated in the frequency domain, since spectral methods investigate particular frequencies and are essentially model-free.

Let X_t be a stochastic generating process and $x_t, t = 1, \ldots, n$ be a time series generated by this process. X_t and x_t might be considered to correspond to a random variable and a sample respectively in classical statistical terminology. For the moment, X_t will be assumed to be stationary, although this assumption will later be relaxed. Let $f(\omega)$ be the power spectrum of X_t and $\hat{f}(\omega)$, the estimated spectrum derived from the observed x_t. Define the seasonal frequencies to be $\omega_s k, k = 1, 2, \ldots, [N/2]$, where

$$\omega_s = \frac{2\pi}{N}$$

N is the number of observations of the series taken in a 12-month period, and $[N/2]$ is the largest integer less than $N/2$. For ease of exposition, the case of monthly recorded data will be considered almost exclusively in what follows, so that the seasonal frequencies are just $2\pi k/12$; $k = 1, 2, \ldots, 6$. Further, define the set of seasonal frequency bands to be

$$\omega_s(\delta) = \{\omega \ in \ (\omega_s k - \delta, \omega_s k + \delta), k = 1, \ldots, 5, (\omega_s 6 - \delta, \pi)\}$$

and so consists of all frequencies within δ of the seasonal frequencies.

2.1   Definition 1

The process X_t is said to have property S if $f(\omega)$ has peaks within $\omega_s(\delta)$ for some small $\delta > 0$.

2.2   Definition 2

The series x_t is said to apparently have property S if $\hat{f}(\omega)$ has peaks in $\omega_s(\delta)$ for some small $\delta > 0$.

A process with property S will be called a process with seasonal component. This definition closely resembles that proposed by Nerlove (1964) in an important paper on seasonal adjustment.

2.3   Definition 3

A process S_t is said to be strongly seasonal if the power contained in $\omega_s(\delta)$ almost equals the total power, for some appropriate, small δ. This can be stated more formally as

$$\int_{\omega_s(\delta)} f(\omega)\,d\omega \bigg/ \int_0^{\pi} f(\omega)d\omega = \lambda(\delta)$$

where $\lambda(\delta)$ is near 1. Thus, the variance due to the seasonal band frequencies is nearly equal to the total variance of the process S_t. It follows that $f(\omega)$ is relatively small for ω in the region not $-\omega_s(\delta)$, compared to ω in the region $\omega_s(\delta)$. The choice of δ is unfortunately arbitrary and has to be left to the individual analyst. It can be strongly argued that the need for allowing the seasonal component to be nondeterministic implies that it is not correct to take $\delta = 0$. If $\lambda(0)$ is some positive quantity, then the seasonal does contain a deterministic component, but, given just a finite amount of data, this hypothesis cannot be tested against the alternative $\lambda(\delta) > 0$ for some small positive δ, which allows also a nondeterministic seasonal component.

The assumption of stationarity in these definitions is too restrictive for our needs. Although the spectrum is strictly based on this assumption, the problem can be removed in the case of actual data analysis if in the definitions one replaces the estimated spectrum by the pseudospectrum (1967). The pseudospectrum is essentially the spectrum estimated by the computer as though the data were stationary. It can also be loosely thought of as the average of a time-changing spectrum. If this way out is taken, peaks in the pseudospectrum at the seasonal frequency bands will indicate that the series did have property S for at least some of the time span considered.

3.   SEASONAL MODELS

There are many time series models that generate data with property S. Some examples follow, using the notation that X_t is a process with property S, Y_t is a process without property S, and S_t is a strongly seasonal process. The additive seasonal models then take the form

$$X_t = Y_t + S_t$$

where Y_t is a unrestricted nonseasonal series. Various forms for S_t have been suggested.

3.1   Model 1

S_t is perfectly periodic so that $S_t = S_{t-12}$. Thus, S_t can always be represented by

$$S_t = \sum_{j=1}^{6} a_j \cos(\omega_s jt + \Theta_j)$$

or by

$$S_t = \sum_{j=1}^{12} a'_j d_j$$

where $d_j = 1$ is j^{th} month of the year
$\quad\quad = 0$ in all other months.

In this model, S_t is deterministic.

3.2   Model 2

S_t is almost periodic, so that

$$S_t = \sum_{j=1}^{6} a_{j,t} \cos(\omega_s jt - \Theta_{j,t})$$

where a_{jt}, Θ_{jt} are slowly time-varying and can either be assumed to be deterministic functions of time, such as $a_{jt} = exp(\alpha_j t)$, or they can be considered to be stochastic processes with spectra dominated by low-frequency components. If S_t is perfectly periodic, as in model 1, its theoretical spectrum will be zero, except at the seasonal frequencies, whereas, if S_t is almost periodic, its spectrum will be almost zero outside of the frequency band $\omega_s(\delta)$ where the size of δ will depend on the rate at which a_{jt}, Θ_{jt} change in value.

3.3   Model 3

S_t is a strongly seasonal process. For example, S_t could be a multiple of a filtered version of an observed strongly seasonal causal series, such as a weather series. Equally, S_t may be generated by a simple ARMA model with coefficients such that the resulting process is strongly seasonal. An example S_t generated by

$$S_t = 0.9S_{t-12} + \eta_t + 0.6\eta_{t-1}$$

where η_t is white noise, as considered by Grether and Nerlove (1970). The weather series just considered might also be considered to be generated by such a model, but presumably the η_t could then be estimated by analysis of causal series. If the causal series has not been identified, the S_t component might be thought of as unobservable, meaning that the η_t cannot be directly observed or estimated from data. These problems are further considered in the next section.

3.4   Model 4

In multiplicative models, where

$$X_t = Y_t \cdot S_t$$

and Y_t is constrained to be positive, S_t can be taken to be generated by any of the previous models, plus a constant to ensure that it is positive. These models seem to be suggested to allow for the apparently observed fact that the amplitude of the seasonal component increases in size as does the level of X_t. An assumption of a multiplicative model is an attractive one as the application of a logarithmic transformation to the data produces an additive seasonal model. However, although attractive, this assumption is not necessarily realistic, since the amplitude of S_t may be trending in the same direction as is X_t but not proportionately. Other transformations may be appropriate or much more general classes of models should perhaps be considered.

3.5   Model 5

Harmonic processes form a very general class of the nonstationary processes, which allow the amplitude of one frequency component, such as the seasonal, to be correlated with that of another component, such as the low-frequency component corresponding to business cycles. In the frequency domain, such processes have the representation.

$$X_t = \int_{-\pi}^{\pi} e^{it} dz(\omega)$$

where

$$E\left[dz(\omega)\overline{dz(\lambda)}\right] = d^2 F(\omega, \lambda), \text{ all } \omega, \lambda$$

$d^2 F(\omega, \lambda)$ is the bivariate spectral function, and its values are in a sense dominated by values along the main diagonal $\omega = \lambda$. If $d^2 F(\omega, \omega) = f(\omega) d\omega$ and $f(\omega)$ has peaks at the seasonal frequency bands, the harmonic process will be said to have property S. Stationary processes, the almost-periodic model 2 and the smoothly changing class of nonstationary processes considered by Priestley (1965), are usually members of the class of harmonic processes. Unfortunately, much of this class has not been studied empirically and no specific set of time-domain models have been identified that represent the majority of the class.

3.6   Model 6

Adaptive models are any models that take a white noise series and, by the choice of an appropriate filter, produce a series where property S is clearly an appropriate model. The class of such models, suggested by Box and Jenkins (1960), has received the most attention recently and can be represented by

$$\frac{\alpha_s(B^s)(1-B^s)^{d_s} X_t}{b_s(B^s)} = Y_t$$

where B is the backward operator, $s = 12$ for monthly data, a, b are polynomials in B^s and Y_t does not have property S and is usually taken to be ARIMA. The only values of d_s required for economic data seem to be 0 or 1, and, typically, a series with property S is assumed to have $d_s = 1$. They are called adaptive models, as the seasonal can change shape in an unspecified way and still belong to the class. Other adaptive models have also been suggested, but they are generally special cases of the Box-Jenkins model. It has been suggested that a very simple form of the model, such as

$$(1-\lambda B^{12})Y_t = \varepsilon_t$$

where ε_t is white noise and λ is near one, cannot be used to represent real data. The reason given is that the estimated spectrum of real series, with property S, has peaks of very unequal heights, whereas the theoretical spectrum, generated by the simple model, has peaks of almost equal heights at the seasonal frequencies. Although the theory is correct, in practice, a series generated by the simple model can produce almost any seasonal spectral shape depending on the starting values used. Thus, the full model consists of the generating equation, plus the 12 starting values. It is clearly important to fit the model to a series whose first year is in some way typical in terms of its season shape.

This list of models, producing series with property S, is merely an illustrative one and does not pretend to be complete. However, it is sufficient to show the wide variety of models available and how inappropriate it is just to assume that some single model is the correct one and then to base subsequent analysis on this chosen model, without performing any confirmatory analysis or diagnostic checking. In practice, given a limited amount of data from a single series, it may be impossible to distinguish between various models. This suggests that a good method of seasonal adjustment must be fairly robust against various types of generating models. However, it does not follow that it is sufficient to assume the correctness of a simple model, such as a deterministic Model 1, and to adjust using a method designed to deal with such a model. Although a complicated, stochastic model might be well approximated by a deterministic model, in some sense over time periods, to use the simple model can lead to important problems when a sophisticated analysis is undertaken. It is similar to saying that a random walk with drift can be approximated by a linear-trend function and then using this function to forecast future values of economic variables (or their logarithms). Although such forecasts may not be disastrously bad in the short run, they can be easily improved upon.

4.   DECOMPOSITION

A great deal of the academic literature dealing with seasonal problems is based on the idea that a seasonal series can always be represented by

$$X_t = Y_t + S_t$$

this is possibly after a logarithmic transformation, where Y_t does not have property S, and S_t is strongly seasonal. It is often further assumed that the two components Y_t and S_t are uncorrelated. This idea is so basic that it needs very careful consideration. At one level, it might be thought to be clearly true, given the assumption that Y_t is stationary. Let $X_t(\omega_s(\delta))$ be the summation of all of the frequency components of X_t over the frequency set $w_s(\delta)$ and let $X_t^e = X_t - X_t(\omega_s(\delta))$; then S_t can be associated with $X_t(\omega_s(\delta))$ and Y_t with X_t^e. S_t will necessarily be strongly seasonal, Y_t will not have property S, and S_t, Y_t are uncorrelated.

However, this solution to the decomposition problem is not a generally acceptable one, since X_t^e does not have the kind of properties that are usually required, at least implicitly, for the nonseasonal component Y_t. This component is almost inevitably taken to be a typical kind of series, generated, for instance, by a nonseasonal ARIMA process and, thus, to have a smooth spectrum with neither peaks nor dips at seasonal frequencies. On the other hand, X_t^e has a spectrum which takes zero values at the seasonal frequency band $\omega_s(\delta)$. The equivalent requirement, placed on S_t for the decomposition to be acceptable, is that it contributes the peaks to the spectrum at the seasonal frequencies but not the total power at these frequency bands. If this requirement is not imposed, a series without property S, such as a white noise, would have a seasonal decomposition into X_t^e and $X_t(\omega_s(\delta))$.

To illustrate the consequent difficulties that arise concerning seasonal decomposition from these considerations, suppose that Y_t is generated by

$$a(B)Y_t = b(B)\varepsilon_t$$

and S_t by

$$a_s(B)S_t = b_s(B)_{\eta t}$$

where ε_t, η_t are two white-noise or innovation series, a and b are chosen so that the spectrum of Y_t has no peaks at seasonal frequencies, and a_s, b_s are such that the spectrum of S_t has virtually no power outside the seasonal frequency band $\omega_s(\delta)$ for some small δ. If ε_t and η_t are uncorrelated, the spectrum of X is the sum of the spectra for Y and S. However, if the only data available for analysis are a sample from X, then Y_t and

S_t are unobservable components; it follows that there is no unique decomposition of X_t into Y_t plus S_t. Coefficients of a and b can be chosen so that $f_y(\omega)$ has a slight dip at $\omega = 2\pi/12$, and the coefficients of a_s, b_s are altered so that $f_x(\omega)$ remains unchanged. Only by imposing very stringent conditions, of a rather arbitrary kind, on the shape of $f_y(\omega)$ around the frequencies in $\omega_s(\delta)$, can a unique decomposition be achieved, and one rarely has a strong a priori knowledge about the series to impose such conditions.

The situation becomes clearer if S_t is a filtered version of a causal series, such as monthly rainfall R_t. Suppose

$$S_t = c(B)R_t$$

and

$$R_t = \frac{b_s^*(B)}{a_s(B)}\eta_t$$

where a_s, b_s^*, and c are all polynomials in B. It then follows that $b_s(B) = b_s^*(B) \cdot c(B)$. By analysis of R_t, the η_t series can, in principle, be estimated, and, by the joint analysis of R_t and X_t, the seasonal component S_t can be isolated, hence also Y_t. It is then seen that, at least intrinsically, the use of causal knowledge can allow a unique seasonal decomposition that cannot be achieved without the use of this knowledge.

It is interesting to relate the decomposition model with that employed by Box and Jenkins, discussed as Model 6. Using the notation introduced at the start of this section,

$$X_t = Y_t + S_t = \frac{b(B)}{a(B)}\varepsilon_t + \frac{b_s(B)}{a_s(B)}\eta$$

so

$$a_s(B)a(B)X_t = b(B)a_s(B)\varepsilon_t + a(B)b_s(B)_\eta$$

The righthand side is the sum of two uncorrelated moving averages and, consequently, can always be represented by $d(B)\theta_t$, where $d(B)$ is a polynomial in B of limited order, and θ_t is a white noise. Typically, θ_t is a very complicated amalgam of the two component white noises ε_t, η_t. (For proof, see Granger and Morris (1976).) Thus, a Box-Jenkins-type model is achieved but with the driving series θ_t involving η_t, which is the driving series of the seasonal component S_t. If one analyzes X_t by building a single-series Box-Jenkins model, it will be virtually impossible to pick out Y_t and S_t. By the use of partial fractions, one might be able to obtain a decomposition of the form

$$X_t = A_s(B)\theta_t + A(B)\theta_t$$

where $A_s(B)\theta_t$ is strongly seasonal, but now both the seasonal and the nonseasonal components are driven by the some innovation series θ_t. The two components clearly will not be independent.

It is probably true to say that the requirement that a series be decomposed into seasonal and nonseasonal parts has the implicit idea that the two parts have their own separate, nonoverlapping sets of causes. It is these different causes that ensure the two parts are uncorrelated and, in fact, independent and also provide one reason for seasonally adjusting. However, using a single series, it is seen that the seasonal decomposition is very difficult and perhaps impossible to achieve, provided the seasonal component is taken to be stochastic, which is essential. The only sure way of achieving the required decomposition is by a full-scale causal analysis of one or another of the components, which may not always be practical. In later sections, a method of adjustment that uses the past values of the series to be adjusted will be called an autoadjustment method, whereas, if the past values of seasonal causal series are also used, the method will be called a causal adjustment.

5.   WHY ADJUST?

The seasonal components of economic series are singled out for very particular attention. Why should this be so, and why is so much effort expended on trying to remove this component? Presumably, the seasonal is treated in this fashion, because it is economically unimportant, being dull, superficially easily explained, and easy to forecast but, at the same time, being statistically important in that it is a major contributor to the total variance of many series. The presence of the seasonal could be said to obscure movements in other components of greater economic significance. Such statements contain a number of value judgments and, thus, should not be accepted uncritically. It can certainly be stated that, when considering the level of an economic variable, the low frequency components, often incorrectly labelled the "trend-cycle components," are usually both statistically and economically important. They are statistically important, because they contribute the major part of the total variance, as the typical spectral results and the usefulness of integrated (ARIMA) models indicates. The economic importance arises from the difficulty found in predicting at least the turning points in the low-frequency components and the continual attempts by central governments to control this component, at least for GNP, employment, price, and similar series. Because of their dual importance, it is desirable to view this component as clearly as possible and, thus, the interference from the season should be removed. This argument can be taken further and leads to the suggestion that only the low-frequency component is of real economic importance and, thus, all other components should be removed. This is easily achieved by applying a low-band pass filter to the series.

However, if one's aim is not merely to look up the business cycle component but to analyze the whole series, this viewpoint is rather too extreme.

I think that it is true to say that, for most statistically unsophisticated users of economic data, such as most journalists, politicians, and upper business management, the preference for seasonally adjusted data is so that they can more clearly see the position of local trends or the place on the business cycle. It is certainly true that for any series containing a strong seasonal, it is very difficult to observe these local trends without seasonal adjustment. As these users are an important group, there is clearly a powerful reason for providing seasonally adjusted data.

For rather more sophisticated users who wish to analyze one or more economic series, without using supersophisticated and very costly approaches, it also makes sense to have adjusted data available. If one is forecasting, for instance, it may be a good strategy to build a forecasting model on the adjusted series, possibly using simple causal techniques such as regression, and then to add a forecast of the seasonal component to achieve an overall forecast. Similarly, if the relationship between a pair of economic variables is to be analyzed, it is obviously possible to obtain a spurious relationship if the two series contain important seasonals. By using adjusted series, one possible source of spurious relationships is removed. The kinds of users I am thinking of here are economists or econometricians employed by corporations, government departments or financial institutions.

There are obviously sound reasons for attempting to produce carefully adjusted series, but there are equally good reasons for the unadjusted series to also be made equally available. For very sophisticated analysis, an unadjusted series may well be preferred, but, more importantly, many users need to know the seasonal component. Firms having seasonal fluctuations in demand for their products, for example, may need to make decisions based largely on the seasonal component. The Federal Reserve System is certainly concerned with seasonal monetary matters, and a local government may try to partially control seasonal fluctuations in unemployment. Many other examples are possible. Only by having both the adjusted and the unadjusted data available can these potential users gain the maximum benefit from all of the effort that goes into collecting the information.

It is seen that alternative users may have different reasons for requiring adjusted series. I believe that it is important for econometricians and others who analyze economic data to state clearly why they want their data seasonally adjusted and what kind of properties they expect the adjusted series to possess, since these views may be helpful in deciding how best to adjust.

It is not completely clear why the central government should place most of its control effort on the long swings in the economy and yet make little attempt to control the seasonal. Perhaps, people prefer having seasonal components in the economy rather than not having them because of the generally surprise-free variety of experience provided. One wonders if, when a group of astronauts go on a 20-year trip through space, their enclosed environment will be given an artificial seasonal.

6.   OVERVIEW OF ADJUSTMENT METHODS

There is certainly no lack of suggested methods for seasonal adjustment; dozens already exist, and others are continuously being proposed. It would be inappropriate to attempt to review even the major properties or objectives of all of these methods in this paper. There are, however, certain features of the methods actually used that deserve emphasis. I think that it is fair to say that virtually all of the methods are automatic ones in that essentially the same procedure is used on any series given as an input to the computer rather than being individually redesigned for each series. Secondly, all of the methods are based on the past values of the series being adjusted and not on the values taken by other series. That is, they are auto-adjustment methods rather than causal adjustment.

The two basic approaches involve regression techniques, using seasonal dummy variables or cosine functions and filtering methods, designed to isolate a major part of the seasonal frequency component. These two approaches are not unrelated, and, with an assumption of stationarity, the theoretical properties of these methods can be derived from some well-known theory, the easiest interpretation coming from the effects of linear filters on a spectrum. However, most of the more widely used methods of adjustment are not perfectly equivalent to a linear filter for two reasons that are much emphasized by those applied statisticians, usually in government service, who are most concerned with the mechanics of the adjustments and with the production of adjusted series. These reasons are the strong belief that the seasonal pattern is often time-varying to a significant degree and the concern that an occasional aberrant observation, or outlier, may have an unfortunate effect on the adjusted values over the following few years. In attempting to counteract these apparently observed properties of real data, to which academic writers have generally paid little attention, nonlinear filters or data-specific methods of adjustment have been devised. The properties of these methods cannot usually be determined by currently available theory. As a simple illustration of a method devised to allow for these affects, suppose that the estimate of the seasonal component next January is taken to be the average January figure over the last n years. To allow for the possibility of a changing pattern n has to be kept small, say $n = 5$, and, to allow for the possibility of outliers rather than simply averaging over the last five January values, one could reject the smallest and largest of these five values and average the rest. If changing seasonals and outliers are important, as has been suggested, there are clear benefits in adapting methods to take these problems into account, but if they are not really important, the extra costs involved in the performance of the adjustment method may outweigh the benefits, as will be discussed in the section "Effects of Adjustment in Practice." It would be interesting to see evidence on the frequency of occurrence and importance of evolving seasonal patterns and outliers, since this would be helpful in evaluating methods of adjustment. Some methods would be badly affected by these data properties but others much less so. For example, techniques based on the adaptive models in Model 6., including those associated with Box and Jenkins, cope very well with changing seasonal patterns, if the change is not too rapid, but are very badly thrown out by outliers or extraordinary data values.

The question of how to deal with outliers clearly exemplifies the basic differences between the auto- and causal-adjustment approaches. Just suppose that a series can be decomposed as

$$X_t = Y_t + S_t$$

where Y_t does not have property S, S_t is strongly seasonal, and S_t can be fully explained in terms of known and recorded weather variables. If an exceptionally severe winter occurs, then, since it cannot be explained by past values of X_t, any auto-adjustment technique will have to consider the difference between the exceptional value of X_t and its value predicted from the past as noise. A causal adjustment technique, if based on the correct structural equation will automatically take the exceptional value into account and there will be no residual problems for later years. Now, the outlier is not noise but an integral part of the seasonal and is dealt with accordingly. It is quite clear that the causal-adjustment approach is superior as the exceptional winter is not just noise but correctly considered part of the seasonal, since such winters only occur in the winter months! The other popular cause of outliers, strikes, and particularly dock strikes, have similar properties, since the preponderance of strikes has a seasonal pattern, with few strikes starting in the United States in December and the next few months than at other times in the year. Thus, to consider strike effects as completely noise to the system ignores the fact that this "noise" has property S.

A further problem of considerable practical importance concerns the question of how to adjust up to the present. If one is adjusting historical data, it is generally thought to be very desirable that important components, such as the business cycle are not lagged as a result of the adjustment. If a linear filtering method of adjustment is used, so that

$$x_t^a = \sum_{j=-m}^{m} a_j x_{t-j}$$

with $\Sigma \alpha_j = 1$, the no-lagging property can be achieved by taking $\alpha_j = \alpha_{-j}$. However, as t approaches the present time n, the use of such a symmetric filter is not possible, as the filter involves values of the series that have not yet occurred. One method of proceeding is to alter the parameters of the filter as t gets near n. A simple example is the following filter applied to quarterly data:

$$x_t^a = 1/4[1/2x_{t+2} + x_{t+1} + x_t + x_{t-1} + 1/2x_{t-2}]$$

but if $t = n - 1$

$$x_{n-1}^a = 1/4[3/2x_n + x_{n-1} + x_{n-2} + 1/2x_{n-3}]$$

and, if $t = n$

$$x_n^a = 1/4[5/2x_n + x_{n-1} + 1/2x_{n-1}]$$

It is seen that the filter is here rolled-up, with the weight attached to an unobserved value being given to the latest available figure. The effects of doing this are to remove only part of the seasonal, even if the seasonal is perfectly periodic and deterministic, and to induce lags in non-seasonal components. The seasonal is not properly removed because if in the above example the $n - 1$ filter weights were used at all times on a series with property S then the adjusted series will still usually have this property. As an example of the lags induced, if the series to be adjusted contained a cycle of period 40 months, the x_{n-1} will contain this component lagged approximately 0.4 months, and, in x_n, it will be lagged 1.5 months. Thus, if the component peaked at time n, this peak would not be observed until time $n + 1$, using quarterly data or n plus 1.5 months if more regularly observed data were available but this particular quarterly filter were used. Methods of adjustment that adapt as the time point approaches the present will generally have this property of inducing varying lags in the most recent data. This is potentially a very annoying feature given that in a policymaking situation this most recent data is by far the most important and if one is model-building it would probably usually be preferred that the model best fits the most recent data. This is certainly true for forecasting purposes. A further unfortunate side effect of using techniques that introduce varying lags in the most recent data is that it then becomes inappropriate to compare the most recent adjusted figure with the adjusted figure for twelve months earlier, to calculate an annual rate of change, for example. The fact that different lags are involved effectively means that the change is being calculated over a period shorter than 1 year.

An alternative approach is to use nonsymmetric filters but with constant coefficients. A simple example would be

$$x_t^a = x_t - x_{t-12}$$

This method always introduces a lag of approximately 6 months to the business-cycle components, but, at least, this is a constant lag and no unnecessary nonstationarity is introduced into the data. Incidentally, any method of adjustment that subtracts from x_t, a measure of seasonal estimated from data at least 1 year old, will introduce a lag of at least 6 months into low-frequency components.

A method of adjustment that has few problems with outliers, adjusting up to the present or changing seasonal shape can be constructed, at least in principle, by identifying causal series for the seasonal component. Suppose that, as before

$$X_t = Y_t + S_t$$

where S_t is strongly seasonal, Y_t does not have property S, and that analysis suggests that

$$S_t = \alpha_0 + \alpha_1 R_t + \alpha_2 R_{t-1} + \eta_t$$

where R_t is a monthly rainfall series, η_t is white noise and α_0, α_1 and α_2 are coefficients that have been carefully estimated. It follows that the seasonal component can be estimated directly from the observed values of the R_t series and up to the most recent time period. Such a method would have to be based on individual analysis of each series to be adjusted and may well prove impractical and too difficult or costly to implement in most cases. A slightly less satisfactory method would be to replace the causal series by a leading indicator of the seasonal. I know of no attempts to construct such leading indicators, although methods devised for the business cycle could be appropriate.

7.   CRITERIA FOR EVALUATION

If, as suggested in the section "Decomposition," it is often difficult to identify completely a seasonal component, it is clearly going to be difficult to evaluate a method of adjustment. It is insufficient to say that the adjusted series should consist just of the nonseasonal component, if this component cannot be identified. I would like to suggest that there are three highly desirable properties that, ideally, one would like a method of adjustment to possess, plus a set of desirable but not totally necessary properties. The first of the highly desirable properties is that there should be no change-of-scale effect. If x_t is the raw series and x_t^a the adjusted series, then refer to property 1.

7.1   Property 1

$(cx_t + d)^a = cx_t^a + d$ where c, d are constants. It thus follows that if one is adjusting a temperature series, for example, it is of no consequence whether the temperature is measured in degrees centigrade or fahrenheit. The second highly desirable property described in property 2.

7.2   Property 2

x_t^a should not have property S. As property S was defined in terms of spectral shape, it means that property 2 can only be tested by looking at the estimated spectrum of x_t^a; this spectrum should have no peaks at seasonal frequencies. It is almost as important that one has property 2′.

Property 2′

x_t^a should not have property anti-S, which is just an unnecessarily formal way of saying that the estimated spectrum of x_t^a should not have dips at seasonal frequencies, since this would imply that part of the nonseasonal component has also been removed. Property 2 was a criterion used by Nerlove (1964) in an early spectral study of adjustment methods.

It is not necessary to emphasize property 2′ further, since it is subsumed in the next property. Assume that $x_t = y_t + S_t$, where S_t is the seasonal component and further suppose that S_t can be fully identified, then it is highly desirable that one has property 3.

7.3   Property 3

Coherence $(x_t^a, y_t) = 1$ and phase $(x_t^a, y_t) = 0$, at all frequencies which essentially says that x_t^a and y_t are identical apart from scale effects. This property can only be investigated if S_t or y_t are known, which will be true if x_t is a constructed, simulated series or if S_t has been identified by use of a causal series analysis. Property 3 is stated in the form given, because, by looking at the estimated coherence and phase functions between x_t^a and y_t, the extent to which the property does not hold can be evaluated. Godfrey and Karreman (1967) applied this criterion to a wide variety of simulated series and various methods of adjustments. Some of their conclusions will be discussed in the next section. Their results prove why it is easier to evaluate the break-down of property 3, using spectral methods, than it would by using correlation (x_t^a, y_{t-k}) for various k, for example. It is usually pointless to look at the cross-spectrum between x_t and x_t^a as if x_t contains a strong, stochastic seasonal component; the cross-spectrum will not be interpretable at the seasonal frequency bands and leakage will spoil estimates of this function at other frequencies unless a very long series is available. It thus follows that one cannot evaluate a method of adjustment on property 3 given only the raw data of a real economic variable and the adjusted series. Simulation is the only easy method of investigating property 3. A corollary of this property is property 3′.

Property 3′

$(y_t)^a \simeq y_t$ if y_t is nonseasonal, so that adjustment of a series with no seasonal should ideally leave the series unchanged. The combination of properties 2 and 3′ gives us property 3″.

Property 3″

$(x_t^a)^a \simeq x_t^a$ so that a second application of the adjustment procedure should not have any important effect. An appropriate way of studying this is to use the estimated cross-spectrum between x_t^a and $(x_t^a)^a$ that can be obtained directly from real data. Although not an ideal way to check on property 3, it might well provide a useful test that is quite easy to conduct.

Turning now to properties that are desirable but not completely necessary, the first is that the adjusted series and the estimated seasonal component are unrelated, which may formally be stated as property 4.

7.4   Property 4

$$\mathrm{corr}(x_t - x_t^a, x_{t-k}^a) = 0, \quad \text{all } k \text{ or}$$
$$\text{cross-spectrum } (x_t^a, x_t) = \text{spectrum } x_t^a$$

The desirability of this property relates to the idea discussed in the section "Decomposition" that the seasonal and nonseasonal components have separate and distinct causes and, thus, should be unrelated. However, as model 5 suggests, there is no clear-cut reason why the real world should have this property. A number of writers have discussed this property without mentioning the empirical problems that arise when trying to test it. If the adjustment procedure is at all successful, $x_t - x_t^a$ will be highly seasonal and x_t^a, virtually or totally nonseasonal. A method based on a simple correlation or regression between such a pair of series will be biased towards accepting the null hypothesis of no relationship just as a regression between two highly seasonal series or two trending series is biased towards finding significant relationships, as illustrated by Granger and Newbold (1974). It follows that property 4 cannot be effectively tested using estimated correlations when the amount of data available is limited. The correct way to test is to find filters separately for each of x_t^a and $x_t - x_t^a$ that reduce these series to white noises and then to estimate correlations between these residual white-noise series. This is in fact a test of the hypothesis that the two series, x_t^a and $x_t - x_t^a$, have different causes, as shown by Pierce and Haugh (1975) and by Granger and Newbold (1977).

A further property that has been suggested as being desirable is that of summability in property 5.

7.5   Property 5

$(x_{1t} + x_{2t})^a = x_{1t}^a + x_{2t}^a$, but this does restrict the adjustment methods to being linear filters, I suspect, and this is a rather severe restriction. Lovell (1963) has a very interesting theorem stating that if property 5 holds and also $(x_{1t}x_{2t})^a = x_{1t}^a x_{2t}^a$, then either $x_t^a = x_t$ or $x_t^a = 0$, so that it is unrealistic to ask that a method of adjustment has both of these properties.

A requirement placed on adjusted series by some government statisticians is a consistency of sums over a calendar year, which may be proposed as property 6.

7.6   Property 6

$\Sigma x_t = \Sigma x_t^a$ where the sums are over the months in a calendar year. This property is based on the belief that the sum of S_t, over a 12-month period, should be zero, which follows from the idea that S_t is purely periodic and deterministic, an idea that was earlier suggested should be rejected. The property is politically motivated and is arbitrary in nature, since, if one strictly believed S_t to be purely periodic, then the property should hold for every consecutive 12-month period, but to require this would remove virtually all of the available degrees of freedom and no relevant x_t^a could be found. It might be more reasonable to ask that property 6 holds approximately true, which would, in any case, follow from property 3, and to leave it at that. It is my strong opinion that property 3 is the most important one, although it has been little discussed except by Godfrey and Karreman, due to the difficulty in testing it on actual data.

It will be seen that what is meant in this paper by a good adjustment method is one that removes a seasonal component without seriously altering the nonseasonal component. There also exist various methods which merely try to remove the seasonal but make no claims about not altering the nonseasonal. The application of seasonal filters in the Box-Jenkins approach is such a method. They suggest a method of producing a series without property S and which produces a known effect on the nonseasonal part of the series that can be allowed for in later analysis. A simple example is the use of a twelfth-difference, so that

$$Z_t = x_t - x_{t-12}$$

If x_t contains a strong seasonal, then Z_t will contain, at most, a much weaker seasonal, but the model now to be built on the nonseasonal component has become more complicated. The use of such methods can be considered as one stage in the process of finding a model that reduces the series to white noise, which has been found to be an important technique for building single and multipe series forecasting models. (See Granger and Newbold (1977).) However, such topics are too far away from the main theme to be discussed in this paper.

8. EFFECTS OF ADJUSTMENT IN PRACTICE

It would be inappropriate to try to survey all of the work on the evaluation of actual methods of adjustment, but since spectral methods have been emphasized in the previous section, a brief review of three papers using this approach will be given. Nerlove (1964) used an adjustment method, devised by the Bureau of Labor Statistics (BLS), on a variety of economic series and compared the spectra of the raw and the adjusted series. It was found that the spectrum of the adjusted series frequently contained dips at the seasonal frequency bands so that, in a sense, the method was taking too much out of the raw series at these frequencies. In a later paper, Rosenblatt (1968) presented spectral evidence that more recent methods of adjustment devised by the BLS and the Census Bureau had overcome this problem. Nevertheless, there do appear to be some occasions even now when the spectral seasonal dips problem arises, as it is sometimes noted when Box-Jenkins model building, that the twelfth autocorrelation coefficient of an adjusted series is significantly nonzero and negative.

Property 3 was tested by Godfrey and Karreman (1967) by adding a constant or time-varying seasonal term to an autoregressive series to form a raw series. This raw series was then adjusted by four different methods. Amongst other quantities, the cross-spectrum between the autoregressive series, being the original nonseasonal component, and the adjusted series, the eventual estimate of this component, was estimated and the coherence and phase diagrams displayed in their figures 6.Om.1, $m = 2$, (1), 10. The spectra of the autoregressive and the adjusted series were also compared. It was generally found that the coherence was near one for the low frequencies, that is those up to the lowest seasonal frequency, and the phase was near zero over this band. For other frequencies, the coherence was not near one and was often rather small and the phase was generally near zero but not consistently so. The power spectrum of the adjusted series was generally of a similar shape but lay above that of the autoregressive series. These results suggest that the important business cycle and low-frequency component was generally little affected by the adjustment method, but the higher frequency components were greatly affected, either having an extra high-frequency component added or part of the original high-frequency component being lost and replaced by a component induced by the method of adjustment. Symbolically, one could illustrate these results by

$$x_t = y_t + S_t$$

$$y_t = y_t^h + y_t^H$$

$$x_t^a = \left(x_t^a\right)^h + \left(x_t^a\right)^H$$

where h indicates a low-frequency component and H, the remaining higher frequency component. Then y_t^h and $(x_t^a)^h$ are virtually identical, but y_t^H and $(x_t^a)^H$ are only imperfectly correlated, and $(x_t)^H$ has a higher variance than y_t^H. Thus, the methods tested by Godfrey and Karreman do not have property 3, except at low frequencies. It seems that little would have been lost by just applying a low-band pass filter to x_t and using that as the adjusted series, particularly since the actual adjusted series are effectively just the original low-frequency component plus an added nonoriginal hash term. The test of property 3 has proved to be both a stringent one and also to point out important failings with adjustment methods.

The zero phase observation, which corresponds to a zero lag, arises partly because the adjustment used was on historical data, and no attempt was made to adjust to the present.

Both Nerlove and Rosenblatt present the cross-spectra between x_t and x_t^a. It has been argued in the previous section that, with limited amounts of data, these figures are difficult to interpret, but the estimates shown do agree in form with the suggested interpretation of the Godfrey and Karreman results.

9.   RELATING PAIRS OF ADJUSTED SERIES

Suppose that two stationary series, X_{1t}, X_{2t}, are each made up of two components

$$X_{1t} = Y_{1t} + S_{1t}$$

$$X_{2t} = Y_{2t} + S_{2t}$$

where Y_{1t}, Y_{2t} do not have property S, and S_{1t}, S_{2t} are stochastic, strongly seasonal series. There are numerous possible interrelationships between the two X series, for example, Y_{1t} may be causing Y_{2t}, but S_{1t}, S_{2t} are interrelated in a feedback (two-way causal) manner. The effect of seasonal adjustment on the analysis of such relationships have not been studied thoroughly, although both Sims (1974) and Wallis (1974) have recently considered in some detail the case where Y_{1t} causes Y_{2t}, and S_{1t}, S_{2t} are possibly interrelated.

If S_{1t}, S_{2t} are important components, then it is clear that even if they are not strictly related, so that they do not have any causes in common, it is virtually impossible to analyze properly the relationship between X_{1t}, X_{2t} without using a seasonal adjustment procedure. This is because S_{1t} and S_{2t} will certainly appear to be correlated, with the maximum correlation between S_{1t} and $S_{2,t-k}$ where k is the average distance between the seasonal peaks of the two series. Such spurious relationships are disturbing, and thus an adjustment is required. There are three ways that the seasonal can be allowed for, either by using auto-adjustments on both observed series X_{1t} and X_{2t} or by using individual causal-adjustments on each of these series or by building a bivariate model interrelating the X's but including in the model relevant seasonal-causal series. The third of these procedures is probably preferable and the use of seasonal dummy variables in a model is an inefficient attempt to use this approach. The method that is almost invariantly used is the first, involving auto-adjustment. Unfortunately, this can lead to difficulties in finding the correct relationship between the Y series, as Wallis (1974) and Sims (1974) show, particularly if an insufficiently sophisticated method of analysis is used, such as a simple distributed lag.

One aspect not apparently previously emphasized is that spurious relations may be found if autoadjustment is used in the case where the Y series are unrelated, but the S series are related. Suppose that the economically important components are Y_{1t} and Y_{2t}, but, in fact, these series are independent. The economic analyst would presumably want the adjusted series to be unrelated in any analysis that he performs. However, in theory, this will not occur if S_{1t}, S_{2t} are correlated, and an autoadjustment is used. This is easily seen in spectral terms by noting that the coherence function is the correct one to measure relatedness between a pair of series, that the coherence between X_{1t} and X_{2t} will be the same as that between S_{1t} and S_{2t}, which is assumed to be nonzero, that all autoadjustment techniques correspond exactly or approximately to a linear filter, and that the coherence function is unaltered by using different linear filters on the pair of series involved.

Although this proof is completely general, it is interesting to illustrate this result, using a particular Box-Jenkins modeling approach. Suppose that Y_{1t}, Y_{2t} are independent white-noise series, denoted by

$$Y_{1t} = \varepsilon_{1t}, \ Y_{2t} = \varepsilon_{2t}$$

and that S_{1t}, S_{2t} are generated by

$$S_{1t} = \alpha S_{1,t-12} + \theta_t$$
$$S_{2t} = \beta S_{2,t-12} + \phi_t$$

where monthly data is considered, θ_t and ϕ_t are zero-mean white-noise series with

$$E[\phi_t \theta_{t-k}] = C \quad k = 0$$
$$= O \quad k \neq 0$$

It follows that

$$(1 - \alpha B^{12})X_{1t} = (1 - \alpha B^{12})\varepsilon_{1t} + \theta_t$$

and from consideration of the autocovariance sequence of the lefthand side, this becomes

$$(1 - \alpha B^{12})X_{1t} = (1 - \alpha' B^{12})\varepsilon_{1t}'$$

where ε'_{1t} is a white-noise series and α' is given by

$$\frac{\alpha'}{1+(\alpha')^2}=\frac{\alpha}{(1+\alpha^2)\sigma_1^2+\sigma_\theta^2}$$

where σ_1^2 = variance (ε_{1t}). Thus, applying the filter $(1-\alpha B^{12})/(1-\alpha' B^{12})$ to X_{1t} results in a series without property S, in fact, to a white-noise series. There is a similar filter which reduced X_{21} to the white-noise series ε'_{2t}.

A little further algebra shows that

$$E[\varepsilon'_{1t}\varepsilon'_{2,t-12k}]=\frac{C}{1-\alpha'\beta^1}(\alpha')^k \quad \text{if} \quad k\geq 0$$

$$=\frac{C}{1-\alpha'\beta^1}(\beta')^k \quad \text{if} \quad k\leq 0$$

and $E[\varepsilon'_{1t}\varepsilon_{2,t-s}] = 0$ if $S \neq 12k$, k an integer. Thus, the cross-correlogram between the series with seasonal removed, by a Box-Jenkins modeling approach, is not zero but is seasonal in nature due to the relationship between the original components. In fact, a feedback relationship is indicated.

It should be clear that autoadjustment of series can lead to results that are not interpretable in terms of the usual view of a decomposition of a series into seasonal and nonseasonal, with the first part being removed by the adjustment procedure.

10. CONCLUSIONS

By considering the causation of seasonal components, one reaches the conclusions that it is incorrect to believe that the seasonal component is deterministic, that a complete decomposition into seasonal and nonseasonal components is possible by analyzing only the past of the series and that autoadjustment methods do remove the seasonal part, and this can lead to relationships being found between series that are in some sense spurious. Because of these conclusions, most autoadjustment methods cannot be completely evaluated when applied to actual data rather than to simulated or constructed data. An alternate technique is to identify seasonal causal series and to build a structural model using these series so that the seasonal component of the series to be adjusted is estimated from the past of this series and past and present terms of the causal series. Potential advantages of this approach are that the same method of adjusting is used on historical data and also up to the most recently available piece of data, the seasonal might be totally removed so the relationship between a pair of adjusted series is more easily analyzed, and the question of how to deal with outliers becomes of much less importance. In practice, a complete causal analysis is not easy to perform, and the inherent costs may not allow this approach to be used very frequently. It is also not completely clear how a causal analysis would be conducted, although possibilities include demodulation techniques, band-pass spectral analysis,[1] or the causal filtering method suggested by Box and Jenkins (1960), used, and generalized by Granger and Newbold (1977). In this latter approach, a filter is found which reduces the causal white noise, the same filter is then applied to the series being adjusted, and this filtered series regressed on the causal white-noise series, both lagged and unlagged. Some of these approaches will be investigated at a later time.

Many problems have not here been considered, including such practical ones as how to adjust a ratio of two series that is to appear in some model – does one take the ratio and then adjust, or adjust and then take the ratio? The latter seems to be recommended, but this would depend on the underlying theory being invoked that suggests the use of a ratio. A particularly important problem that has not been discussed is how to distinguish between additive and multiplicative seasonal effects, the use of instantaneously transformed series and the causes of nonadditive effects. These questions will be examined at another time.

REFERENCES

BarOn, Raphel R. V. *Analysis of Seasonality and Trends in Statistical Series.* Vol. 1: *Methodology, Causes and Effects of Seasonality.* Technical Publication No. 39. Jerusalem: Israel Central Bureau of Statistics, 1973.

Box, George E. P., and Jenkins, G. M. *Time Series Analysis: Forecasting and Control.* San Francisco: Holden–Day, Inc., 1960.

Godfrey, Michael D., and Karreman, H. "A Spectrum Analysis of Seasonal Adjustment." In *Essays in Mathematical Economics in Honor of Oskar Morgenstern.* Edited by M. Shubik. Princeton, N.J.: Princeton University Press, 1967.

Granger, Clive W. J. "The Effect of Varying Month–Length on the Analysis of Economic Time Series," *L'Industrie,* 1963, pp. 41–53.

"Testing for Casuality and Feedback." *Econometrica* 37 (1969): 424–438.

and Morris, Michael. "Time Series Modeling and Interpretation." *Journal of the Royal Statistical Society,* ser. A, 138 (1976).

and Newbold, Paul. "Spurious Regressions in Econometrics." *Journal of Econometrics* 2 (1974): 111–120.

and Newbold, Paul. *Forecasting Economic Time Series,* San Diego: Academic Press, March 1977.

Grether, David M., and Nerlove, Marc. "Some Properties of 'Optimal' Seasonal Adjustment." *Econometrica* 38 (1970): 682–703.

Hatanaka, Michio, and Suzuki, M. "A Theory of the Pseudospectrum and Its Applications to Non–Stationary Dynamic Econometric Models," In *Essays*

---

[1] See, for example, the paper by Engle included in this working paper.

in Mathematical Economics in Honor of Oskar Morgenstein. Edited by M. Shubik. Princeton, N.J.: Princeton University Press, 1967.

Lovell, Michael C. "Seasonal Adjustment of Economic Time Series and Multiple Regression Analysis." *Journal of the American Statistical Association* 58 (December 1963): 993–1010.

Nerlove, Marc. "Spectral Analysis of Seasonal Adjustment Procedures." *Econometrica* 32 (July 1964): 241–286.

Pierce, David A., and Haugh, L. D. *The Assessment and Detection of Causality in Temporal Systems*. Technical Report No. 83. Gainsville, Fla.: University of Florida. Department of Statistics, 1975.

Priestley, Michael B. "Evolutionary Spectra and Non–Stationary Processes." *Journal of the Royal Statistical Society*, ser. B, 27 (1965): 204–237.

Rosenblatt, Harry M. "Spectral Evaluation of the BLS and Census Revised Seasonal Adjustment Procedures." *Journal of the American Statistical Association* 63 (June 1968): 472–501.

Sims, Christopher A. "Seasonality in Regression." *Journal of the American Statistical Association* 69 (September 1974): 618–626.

Wallis, Kenneth F. "Seasonal Adjustment and Relations Between Variables." *Journal of the American Statistical Association* 69 (March 1974): 18–31.

CHAPTER 5

Is Seasonal Adjustment a Linear or Nonlinear Data-Filtering Process?*

Eric Ghysels, Clive W. J. Granger, and Pierre L. Siklos**

We investigate whether seasonal-adjustment procedures are, at least approximately, linear data transformations. This question was initially addressed by Young and is important with respect to many issues including estimation of regression models with seasonally adjusted data. We focus on the X-11 program and rely on simulation evidence, involving linear unobserved component autoregressive integrated moving average models. We define a set of properties for the adequacy of a linear approximation to a seasonal-adjustment filter. These properties are examined through statistical tests. Next, we study the effect of X-11 seasonal adjustment on regression statistics assessing the statistical significance of the relationship between economic variables. Several empirical results involving economic data are also reported.

Keywords: Aggregation; Cointegration; Nonlinearity; Regression; X-11 filter.

The question of whether seasonal-adjustment procedures are, at least approximately, linear data transformations is essential for several reasons. First, much of what is known about seasonal adjustment and estimation of regression models rests on the assumption that the process of removing seasonality can be adequately presented as a linear (two-sided and symmetric) filter applied to the raw data. For instance, Sims (1974, 1993), Wallis (1974), Ghysels and Perron (1993), and Hansen and Sargent (1993), among others, examined the effect of filtering on estimating parameters or hypothesis testing. Naturally, the linearity of the filter is assumed because any nonlinear filter would make the problem analytically intractable. Second, the theoretical discussions regarding seasonal adjustment revolve around a linear representation. Indeed, for

* *Journal of Business and Economic Statistics*, 14, 1996, 374–386.
** *Editor's Note*: This article is the 1995 *JBES* Invited Address given at the Joint Statistical Meetings, Orlando, Florida, August 11, 1995.

more than three decades, seasonal adjustment has been portrayed in the context of spectral-domain representations. See, for instance, Hannan (1963), Granger and Hatanaka (1964), Nerlove (1964), and Godfrey and Karreman (1963), among others. The frequency-domain analysis led to the formulation of seasonal adjustment as a signal-extraction problem in a linear unobserved component autoregressive integrated moving average (henceforth UCARIMA) framework, in which the emerging optimal minimum mean squared error filters are linear.

The theory of signal extraction involving nonstationary processes, which will be the case covered here, was developed by Hannan (1967), Sobel (1967), Cleveland and Tiao (1976), Pierce (1979), Bell (1984), Burridge and Wallis (1988), and Maravall (1988). As a result, the widely used X-11 Census method, and its later developments like X-11 ARIMA, X-12 and REGARIMA (regression and ARIMA), have been examined to determine which UCARIMA model would generate an optimal linear signal-extraction filter similar to X-11 and its variants. Moreover, the few attempts that were made to model formally the operations of a statistical agency on the data-generating process (DGP) of economic time series – as did Sargent (1989), for example – adopted the linear filtering paradigm. Finally, whenever nonlinearities in time series are discussed, the possibility that such nonlinearities may be (partly) produced by seasonal adjustment is never seriously entertained.

Several authors have examined the linear representation of the X-11 program, notably Young (1968), Wallis (1974), Bell (1992), and Ghysels and Perron (1993). Young (1968) investigated the question of whether the linear filter was an adequate approximation and found it to be a reasonable proxy to the operations of the actual program. This result was, to a certain extent, a basic motivation as to why the linear filter representation was extensively used in the literature. The main objective of our article is to reexamine the question posed by Young. We come to quite the opposite conclusion – namely, that the standard seasonal-adjustment procedure is far from being a linear data-filtering process. We reached a different conclusion, primarily because we took advantage of several advances in the analysis of time series, developed over the last two decades, and the leaps in the computational power of computers that enabled us to conduct simulations that could not be easily implemented before. We rely both on artificially simulated data and on actual series published by the U.S. Census Bureau to address the question of interest. In Section 1, we first discuss the attributes of the X-11 program that might be the source of nonlinear features. In Section 2, we propose several properties that allow us to assess whether the actual program can be adequately presented by a linear filter. For instance, in the context of a linear UCARIMA, we expect the nonseasonal $I(1)$ component and its X-11 extraction to be cointegrated and the extraction error to be a linear process. Finally, the difference between the unadjusted series filtered with the linear filter and the X-11 adjusted series should not be nonlinearly predictable. Through a combination of simulations and statistical hypotheses, we verify these properties for a large class of model specifications. Finally, we propose to reexamine the effect of X-11 filtering in linear regression models and study whether spurious relationships are produced by the nonlinearities. In Section 3, we report the results from the simulations and for a large class of data published by the U.S. Census Bureau. Section 4 concludes the article.

1. ON POTENTIAL SOURCES OF NONLINEARITY IN THE X-11 PROGRAM

In this section, we will identify features contained in the X-11 program that may be sources of nonlinearity [see Shiskin, Young, and Musgrave (1967) for details]. Because the program is almost exclusively applied to monthly data, we cover exclusively that case and ignore the quarterly program. In a first subsection, we describe the different versions of the X-11 program. This aspect is important because the operations potentially inducing nonlinearity in the data transformations differ from one version to another. Individual subsections are devoted to the different features we need to highlight – (1) multiplicative versus additive, (2) outlier detection, (3) moving average filter selection, and (4) aggregation.

1.1   The Decompositions

One must distinguish between two versions of the X-11 program. One is called the additive version and is based on the following decomposition:

$$X_t \equiv TC_t + S_t + TD_t + H_t + I_t, \tag{1.1}$$

where X_t is the observed process and TC_t is the trend-cycle component, S_t is the seasonal, and TD_t and H_t are, respectively, the trading-day and holiday components. Finally, I_t in (1.1) is the irregular component. The second version is called the multiplicative version and is based on the decomposition

$$X_t \equiv TC_t \times S_t \times TD_t \times H_t \times I_t. \tag{1.2}$$

There would be no need to distinguish between the two versions if a logarithmic transformation applied to (1.2) would amount to applying the additive version of the program. Unfortunately, that is not the case because the multiplicative version has features that are distinct from the additive one. These will be discussed shortly. It may be noted parenthetically that one sometimes refers to the log-additive version of X-11 when the additive version is applied to the logarithmic transformation of the data.

The first of several parts in both procedures deals with trading-day and holiday adjustments. Typically, one relies on regression-based methods involving the number of days in a week, and so forth, as regressors. Because a linear regression model is used, we will not explore this aspect of the program any further. Neither the simulations nor the empirical investigation consider effects related to TD_t or H_t. In our empirical analysis, we considered several series in which no trading-day and holiday effects appear to be significant. The extraction of the TC_t, S_t, and I_t components will be of more interest for our purposes. These components are not estimated with regression-based methods but instead are extracted via a set of moving average (MA) filters. This is the most important part of the X-11 program. Although it consists of a series of MA filters, it is important to note that the same set of filters is not necessarily applied to a series through time. Hence, the filter weights may be viewed as time varying. In addition, both the additive and multiplicative X-11 procedures are designed to identify extreme values, or so-called outliers, and replace them one by one by attenuated replacement values. These two features – namely, the scheme determining the selection of MA filters and the outlier corrections – make the application of the additive procedure different from the default option linear variant of the program.

Two other features, specific to the multiplicative version, are also a potential source of significant nonlinearity. First, despite the multiplicative structure of the decomposition in (1.2), the program equates the 12-month *sums* of the seasonally adjusted and unadjusted data rather than their products. Second, the multiplicative version of the X-11 program also involves arithmetic means rather than geometric mean operations.

Because the filters in the X-11 program are two sided, one must also deal with the fact that, at each end of the sample, the symmetric filters need to be replaced by asymmetric ones due to lack of observations. This feature is also a deviation from the default option linear filter, but it will not be considered in our simulation design, as will be discussed in Section 2.

1.2   Multiplicative Versus Additive

The bulk of economic time series handled by the U.S. Bureau of the Census and the U.S. Bureau of Labor Statistics are adjusted with the multiplicative version of the program. Only a small portion are treated with the additive version, apparently around 1% of the 3,000 series covered by the two aforementioned agencies. The Federal Reserve uses the additive version more frequently because of the nature of the time series it treats. Roughly 20% of the 400 or so series it deals with are additively adjusted. Young (1968, p. 449) described the nonlinear features of the multiplicative version, emphasizing the complications and departures of (log-) linearity due to the equating of the 12-month sums of the seasonally adjusted and unadjusted data and the use of arithmetic moving averages instead of geometric ones. Young (1968, p. 446) justified the presence of the former feature in the multiplicative X-11 program arguing that "traditionally, economists have not wanted to give up ... (the condition of equating sums) ... just to obtain a linear model ... the desire to present seasonally adjusted series in which annual totals rather than products are unchanged." In the remainder of the article, we keep in mind the distinguishing features of the additive and multiplicative X-11 programs.

1.3   Outlier Detections

The treatment of extremes, or outliers, is a key element in seasonal-adjustment programs like X-11. Because this feature is fundamentally the same for the additive and multiplicative versions, we will discuss it using the former as an example. The X-11 program produces a first estimate of the seasonal and irregular components $S_t + I_t$ via a 13-term MA filter trend-cycle estimator. Seasonal factors are obtained from this preliminary estimate using a weighted five-term MA. At this point, the program has obtained a first-pass estimate of the irregular component process $\{I_t\}$. The scheme to detect outliers is activated at this stage. First, a moving five-year standard deviation of the estimated I_t process is computed. Hence, extractions of I_t will be evaluated against a standard-error estimate only involving the surrounding five years – that is, 60 observations in a monthly setting. We shall denote the standard error applicable to I_t as $\sigma_t^{(1)}$, where the superscript indicates that one has obtained a first estimate. The standard error is reestimated after removing any observations on I_t such that $|I_t| > 2.5\sigma_t^{(1)}$, yielding a second estimate $\sigma_t^{(2)}$, where the number of observations entering the second estimate is random. The second-round estimated standard error $\sigma_t^{(2)}$ is used to clear the $S_t + I_t$ process from outlier or influential observations. The rules followed to purge the process can be described as follows:

1. A weighting function w_t is defined as

$$w_t = \begin{cases} 1 & \text{if } 0 \le |I_t| \le 1.5\sigma_t^{(2)} \\ 2.5 - |I_t|/\sigma_t^{(2)} & \text{if } 1.5\sigma_t^{(2)} < |I_t| \le 2.5\sigma_t^{(2)} \\ 0 & \text{if } |I_t| > 2.5\sigma_t^{(2)} \end{cases} \tag{1.3}$$

2. $S_t + I_t$ is replaced by an average of its weighted value and the two nearest following full-weighted $S + I$'s if

$$w_t < 1. \tag{1.4}$$

The criterion in (1.4) is used to replace any perceived outlier by the smoothed nearest neighbor estimate. The 1.5 and 2.5 values in (1.3), setting the benchmarks of the weighting function, play, of course, a key role besides the two-step standard-error estimate $\sigma_t^{(2)}$ described earlier. The (1.3)–(1.4) scheme is, however, entirely based on rules of thumb and not so easy to rationalize. The value of $1.5\sigma_t^{(2)}$ in (1.3) that sets off the correction scheme because it determines whether $w_t < 1$, is quite tight.

1.4   Moving Average Filter Selection

We will continue with the additive version of the program again for the sake of discussion. The seasonal plus irregular components modified through (1.3)–(1.4) will be denoted $(S_t + I_t)$. The series is used to compute a new set of seasonal factors that are applied to the original raw series, yielding a first estimate of the seasonally adjusted series, which we shall denote X_{1t}^{SA}. Obviously, if the outlier correction procedure were turned off, then $S_t + I_t$ would be used to compute the seasonal factors and, as a result, different estimates of seasonally adjusted series would already be obtained at this stage. The X-11 procedure continues with a second and final iteration of seasonal adjustment. As a first step in this second stage, one extracts again the trend-cycle component by applying a 13-term Henderson MA filter to the seasonally adjusted X_{1t}^{SA} series. [The design of Henderson MA filters is described in the works covering the linear X-11 approximation; formulas for the Henderson filter weights were also given by Macaulay (1931) and Gouriéroux and Monfort (1990).] The trend-cycle component estimate obtained at this point will be denoted $TC_t^{(1)}$. The MA filter-selection scheme now comes into play. To describe the scheme, let us define two average percentage changes: μ_{1t} is the average absolute month-to-month change of $(X_{1t}^{SA} - TC_t^{(1)})$, and μ_{2t} is the average absolute month-to-month change of $TC_t^{(1)}$. The averages are updated as new raw data are added to the sample and are therefore made time varying. The filter selection scheme can then be formulated as follows:

1. Apply 9-term Henderson MA if

$$\mu_{1t} < .99\mu_{2t}. \tag{1.5}$$

2. Apply 13-term Henderson MA if

$$.99\mu_{2t} \leq \mu_{1t} < 3.5\mu_{2t}. \tag{1.6}$$

3. Apply 23-term Henderson MA if

$$3.5\mu_{2t} \leq \mu_{1t}. \tag{1.7}$$

The Henderson MA filter thus selected is reapplied to X_{1t}^{SA} to yield a second estimate $TC_t^{(2)}$. This yields a new estimate of the seasonal and irregular component. The program then repeats the process of estimating a standard error $\sigma_t^{(i)} i = 1, 2$ and proceeds with a second application of the outlier correction process described in (1.3) and (1.4).

1.5   Aggregation

So far, we have highlighted the two distinct features that represent the possible causes of nonlinearity and/or time variation in the actual X-11 filtering process. Another source of nonlinearity also needs to be highlighted, however. It is not related to the intrinsic operational rules of the program but rather to the modus operandi of its application to several series. Indeed, seasonal-adjustment procedures are quite often applied to disaggregated series, like narrowly defined industrial sectors or components of monetary aggregates, and the output is then aggregated to produce a seasonally adjusted aggregate. Obviously, the separate decomposition (1.1) for two series, say X_t and Y_t, is not the same as the decomposition for a Z_t process defined as $Z_t \equiv X_t + Y_t$. The question of whether seasonal adjustment should precede or follow aggregation was discussed by Geweke (1978) and was recently reexamined by Ghysels (in press). When the seasonal-adjustment process is linear and uniform, then aggregation and seasonal adjustments are interchangeable. Another potential source of nonlinearity is introduced, however, when seasonal adjustment and aggregation are not interchangeable and one applies the procedure to disaggregated series with only the aggregated series available to the public. In practice, this setup is quite common. We therefore included in our simulation design a setup similar to the effect of aggregation combined with seasonal adjustment. This issue was, of course, studied separately. We first investigated the potential source of nonlinearity produced by the internal design of X-11.

2.   A SIMULATION STUDY

The effect of filtering on the statistical properties of time series and properties of estimators in linear regression models and cointegration tests is reasonably well understood when the adjustments are performed with a linear filter. The seminal articles by Sims (1974) and Wallis (1974) justified the routine use of seasonally adjusted series in linear regression models. Their result – namely, that linear regressions with filtered series yield consistent estimators – together with the more recent developments by Hansen and Sargent (1993), Ghysels and Perron (1993), Sims (1993), Ericsson, Hendry, and Tran (1994), and Ghysels and Lieberman (in press), all rely on the key assumption that the filter is linear and uniformly applied to all series (and also in certain cases that it is two-sided and symmetric like the linear X-11 filter). In dealing with the question of potential nonlinearities in the actual X-11 procedure, we have to give up the elegance of econometric theory because there is no longer an explicit and easy characterization of the operations of the filter. The key question then is whether the features described in Section 1 intervene to a degree that the linear filter can no longer be viewed as an adequate representation of the adjustment procedure in practice. A subsidiary question is to find out what effects are produced by the actual procedure if in fact the linear approximation is inadequate. The only way to address these questions is through simulations.

Unfortunately, the question of the simulation design is not simply one of a judicious choice of DGP's. It is first and foremost a question about what we characterize as departures from a linear filter and how these are measured. We settled for a design centered on two broad topics that follow certain established traditions in the literature. First, we define a set of desirable properties that any filtering procedure should have to ensure that the linear approximation is adequate. This part of the design follows a tradition in the time series statistics literature concerned with defining properties that seasonal-adjustment procedures ought to have [see, for instance, Bell and Hillmer (1984) for discussion and references]. Second, we also focus on questions that have a tradition rooted in the econometrics literature, particularly as established since Sims (1974) and Wallis (1974). Here we are not so much concerned with univariate filtering but rather with the measurement of relationships among economic time series through linear regression analysis. Young (1968) did not examine nonlinearities through simulated data. Hence, we cannot really make any direct comparison with his study. He took three test series – U.S. imports from 1948 to 1965, unemployed men from 1950 to 1964, and carbon steel production from 1947 until 1964 – and reported a very detailed study of the seasonal factors produced by the X-11 method and its linear version. We take advantage of advances on two fronts, (1) an incredible leap in the computational power of computers and (2) progress in the theory of time series analysis. Like Young, we will also study real data except that our analysis of actual series will only be complcmcntary to the simulation results to verify the similarities between the two.

Examining (statistical) properties of adjustment procedures and studying regression output will require, in both cases, generating data that subsequently are filtered with a linear filter and the X-11 adjustment program. We will therefore devote a first subsection to the description of the DGP's. A second subsection deals with the properties of linear approximations, and a third subsection covers seasonal adjustment and regression analysis. A final and fourth subsection deals with technical notes regarding the simulations.

2.1   The Data-Generating Processes

We generated data from a set of linear UCARIMA models, with Gaussian innovations. Each process consisted of two components, including one exhibiting seasonal characteristics. Let the X_t process consist of two components,

$$X_t = X_t^{NS} + X_t^S, \qquad (2.1)$$

where X_t^{NS} represents a nonseasonal process and X_t^S displays seasonal characteristics. Obviously, Equation (2.1) is adapted to the additive decomposition (1.1). The multiplicative one will be discussed later. The first component in (2.1) has the following structure:

$$(1 - L)X_t^{NS} = (1 - \alpha_{NS}L)\varepsilon_t^{NS} \qquad (2.2)$$

with ε_t^{NS} iid $N(0, \sigma_{NS}^2)$ and where α_{NS} is the MA parameter. The process is chosen to be I(1) and invertible, determined only by two parameters – namely, α_{NS} and σ_{NS}^2. The (monthly) seasonal component has the following structure:

$$(1 + L + \ldots + L^{11})X_t^S = (1 - \alpha_S L^{12})\varepsilon_t^S \qquad (2.3)$$

with ε_t^S again iid $N(0, \sigma_S^2)$. Here also two parameters determine the process. Obviously, the data generated have neither trading-day nor holiday effects, nor is there an explicit distinction made between the TC_t and I_t components appearing in (1.1). This simplification was done purposely. Indeed, it is well known that the decomposition of a time series into a trend cycle, a seasonal, and irregular components is not unique. Hence, it is not clear at the outset that if we were to define a structure for X_t^{NS} as the sum of two components, TC_t and I_t, the X-11 program would select exactly that same decomposition. For similar reasons, it is not clear that the X-11 procedure will identify S_t as exactly equal to X_t^S. Consequently, we must view our design as one in which four parameters are selected to form an X_t time series with the stochastic structure

$$(1 - L^{12})X_t = \psi_x(L)\varepsilon_t, \qquad (2.4)$$

where ε_t is iid $N(0, \sigma_x^2)$ and

$$\sigma_x^2\psi_x(z)\psi_x(z^{-1}) \equiv \sigma_S^2[(1 + z + \ldots + z^{11})(1 + z^{-1} + \ldots + z^{-11})$$
$$\times (1 - \alpha_S z^{12})(1 - \alpha_S z^{-12})]$$
$$+ \sigma_{NS}^2[(1 - z)(1 - z^{-1})(1 - \alpha_{NS} z)(1 - \alpha_{NS} z^{-1})].$$

The additive version of the X-11 program will operate on the time series X_t and choose a decomposition $TC_t + S_t + I_t$. Theoretically, this decomposition is defined by taking the maximal variance of the irregular component [see Bell and Hillmer (1984) or Hotta (1989) for further discussion].

In Section 2.4, we will provide further technical details regarding parameter values, starting values and sample sizes. Before leaving the subject, however, we would like to conclude with a few words regarding the

Table 5.1. *Data-generating processes*

Cases	α_{NS}	α_S	Cases	α_{NS}	α_S
1/17/33	.0	.0	9/25/41	.0	.5
2/18/34	−.5	.0	10/26/42	−.5	.5
3/19/35	.5	.0	11/27/43	.5	.5
4/20/36	.9	.0	12/28/44	.9	.5
5/21/37	.0	−.5	13/29/45	.0	.9
6/22/38	−.5	−.5	14/30/46	−.5	.9
7/23/39	.5	−.5	15/31/47	.5	.9
8/24/40	.9	−.5	16/32/48	.9	.9

Note: Cases 1–16: $\sigma_{NS} = \sigma_S = 1$ with zero starting values; cases 17–32: $\sigma_{NS} = 1$, $\sigma_S = 3$ with zero starting values; cases 33–48: $\text{var}(1 - L)X_t^{NS}/\text{var}(1 + L + \ldots + L^{11})X_t^S = .1$ with quarterly mean shift starting values described in 2.4.3

multiplicative decomposition. The same steps as described in (2.1) through (2.4) were followed except that the generated series were viewed as the logarithmic transformation of the series of interest. Hence, $\exp(X_t) = \exp(X_t^{NS})\exp(X_t^S)$ was computed before applying the multiplicative X-11 program.

2.2   Properties of Linear Approximations

The design of seasonal-adjustment filters is typically motivated on the basis of a set of desirable properties that the procedure ideally should exhibit. Most often, these theoretical discussions revolve around a linear representation. In reality however, as we noted in Section 1, there are many potential sources of nonlinearity. This raises the question of which properties one would like to advance so that the linear filter approximation is reasonably adequate. The purpose of this section is to exploit certain properties of the *linear* X-11 filter that will allow us to predict what will happen if the actual procedure were approximately linear. Let us denote the seasonally adjusted series, using the linear X-11 filter, as

$$X_t^{LSA} \equiv \Theta_{X-11}^L(L)X_t,\qquad(2.5)$$

where the linear polynomial lag operator represents the X-11 filter. It has been shown that the linear filter includes the $(1 + L + \ldots L^{11})$ operator (e.g., see Bell 1992). Moreover, the filter has the property that $\Theta_{X-11}^L(1) = 1$ (see Ghysels and Perron 1993), implying that it will leave the zero-frequency unit root in the X_t process unaffected when the process follows the specification described in Section 2.1.

The purpose now is to identify a set of properties that would hold if X-11 were linear and to associate with those properties statistical tests that can be conducted either with simulated data, with real data, or with both.

We will first consider a class of relatively weak conditions applicable to simulated data; in particular we know the following:

PROPERTY 1L: The X_t^{NS} and X_t^{LSA} processes are cointegrated.

Obviously, we would also like the actual X-11 procedure to yield an estimate of the nonseasonal component that is cointegrated with X_t^{NS}. Suppose that we denote X_t^{SA} as the seasonally adjusted series using the actual X-11 procedure. Then the following property should also hold:

PROPERTY 1X: The X_t^{NS} and X_t^{SA} processes are cointegrated.

Failure of Property 1X to hold is an indication of inconsistencies when the actual X-11 program is applied to the data. Some caution is necessary, however, with the use of cointegration arguments. In principle, one should not expect cointegration properties possessed by the linear approximation to X-11 to translate *exactly* to the X-11 program itself. Indeed, cointegration is defined as two series being exactly I(1) and for which there is an exact (though not necessarily unique) linear relationship cancelling the zero-frequency unit roots. In our context, it is perhaps more appropriate to interpret cointegration as a property that we expect to hold *approximately* for the X-11 adjusted data when the filter approaches its linear version.

A second property is much stronger because it is borrowed directly from the theoretical linear signal-extraction framework in which we know that the extraction error defined as

$$\delta_t^{LSA} \equiv X_t^{NS} - X_t^{LSA} \equiv \left[1 - \Theta_{X-11}^L(L)\right]X_t^{NS} - \Theta_{X-11}^L(L)X_t^S \qquad (2.6)$$

will also be a linear process. Moreover, because $\Theta_{X-11}^L(1)$ and X_t^S do not have a zero-frequency unit root, it follows that δ_t^{LSA} is stationary. This yields a second property of interest:

PROPERTY 2L: The extraction-error process δ_t^{LSA} is linear and stationary.

It will be interesting, once again, to investigate whether a similar property holds for the X-11 program. Let δ_t^{SA} be the extraction-error process defined as in (2.6) yet involving X_t^{SA} instead of X_t^{LSA}. We are then interested in the following:

PROPERTY 2X: The extraction-error process δ_t^{SA} is linear and stationary.

Again, if this property fails to hold this is an indication that there are significant departures from linearity. So far, we have examined properties that are only applicable to simulated series because they involve the unobserved component series. Clearly, instead of comparing X_t^{NS} with X_t^{LSA} and X_t^{SA}, respectively, it is also useful to analyze X_t^{LSA} and X_t^{SA} in terms of cointegration and linearity. This yields two additional properties:

PROPERTY 3: The X_t^{LSA} and X_t^{SA} processes are cointegrated.
PROPERTY 4: The $(X_t^{LSA} - X_t^{SA})$ process is linear and stationary.

The latter is simply a combination of Properties 2L and 2X, since $X_t^{LSA} - X_t^{SA} \equiv \delta_t^{LSA} - \delta_t^{SA}$. Likewise, the former is a consequence of Properties 1X and 1L. Properties 3 and 4 are relatively straightforward to implement both with actual and simulated series.

The properties discussed so far pertain to the possible sources of non-linearity associated with the internal operations of the program discussed in Section 1. At the end of Section 1, it was noted that the combination of seasonal adjustment and aggregation can also be a source of nonlinear features. To investigate this aspect of the problem, we included in the simulation design a second process, called Y_t, with the same stochastic properties as the X_t process. Note though that, although Y_t is a replica of X_t in terms of laws of motion, its path is generated by an independent realization of the innovation processes for the unobserved components, which will be denoted by analogy, Y_t^{NS} and Y_t^S. We also define the Y_t^{LSA} and Y_t^{SA} processes to describe extractions. The process of ultimate interest for our purposes will be the Z_t process defined as $Z_t \equiv X_t + Y_t$. Given the nature of aggregation, we restrict our attention to the additive version of the X-11 program. Hence, Z_t consists of two components – namely, $Z_t^S \equiv X_t^S + Y_t^S$. For the linear X-11 filter, one can unambiguously define the Z_t^{LSA} process because summation and linear filtering are interchangeable. For the X-11 procedure, however, one must distinguish between two potentially different outcomes. If seasonal adjustment is performed on the Z_t process using the X-11 program, then the outcome will be denoted Z_t^{SAA}. The second superscript A indicates that the aggregated series was adjusted. Conversely, if X_t and Y_t are adjusted separately, then $Z_t^{SAD} \equiv X_t^{SA} + Y_t^{SA}$. We could investigate Properties 1–4, again, using the Z_t process and its extractions. This, to a certain extent, would be repetitive, except that the stochastic properties of the Z_t process would differ from those of X_t in each case. Instead of repeating such analysis, we will instead focus exclusively on the aggregation effects. In particular, we will be interested in the following properties:

PROPERTY 5: The Z_t^{SAA} and Z_t^{SAD} processes are cointegrated.
PROPERTY 6: The $(Z_t^{SAA} - Z_t^{SAD})$ process is linear and stationary.

Both properties follow naturally from arguments similar to those used to formulate Properties 3 and 4.

2.3   Linear Regression and Filtering

Ultimately, economists are interested in understanding the comovements between economic time series. Until the work of Sims (1974) and Wallis (1974), discussions regarding seasonal adjustment were mostly centered on a single economic series. We now have some strong results regarding (linear) filtering and seasonality in (linear) regression models. To date there has been no attempt to assess how fragile this finding is when faced with the practical and routine application of the X-11 procedure. In this section, we describe how our simulation design attempts to shed light on this relatively simple and fundamental question.

We propose to look at the linear regression model

$$y_t^i = \beta_0 + \beta_1 x_t^i + \varepsilon_t^i, \tag{2.7}$$

where $i = NS, LSA$, and SA and where y_t^{NS} and x_t^{NS} are *independently* generated processes mean 0 so that $\beta_0 = \beta_1 = 0$ in our simulations. For the additive version of the X-11 program, the processes appearing in the regression model (2.7) were defined as follows:

$$y_t^i = (1-L)Y_t^i \quad \text{and} \quad x_t^i = (1-L)X_t^i \tag{2.8}$$

for $i = NS, LSA$, and SA, but for the multiplicative version it was

$$y_t^i = (1-L)\log Y_t^i \quad \text{and} \quad x_t^i = (1-L)\log X_t^i. \tag{2.9}$$

To tackle immediately the most practical question, we focus on testing the null hypothesis $\beta_1 = 0$; that is, we examine how spurious relationships can emerge from departures from linear filtering in a linear regression model. Obviously, because the error process in Equation (2.7) will not be iid, we need to correct for the serial dependence. This will be done in the now-established tradition among econometricians by using nonparametric procedures often referred to as heteroscedastic and autocorrelation-consistent estimators for the variance of the residual process. The details are described in Section 2.4. To conclude, we would like to note that to simplify the design, we will adopt a strategy similar to the one used in the construction of the aggregate process Z_t described in Section 2.2. In particular, the series X_t and Y_t used to run the regression in (2.7) will be independent draws from the same process structure.

2.4   Technical Details

Several technical details need to be explained regarding the actual simulation setup. We will, in particular, describe the choice of parameter values to generate the data. Next, we will explain how we conducted the statistical inference regarding the properties described in Section 2.2. Then, we turn our attention to the specifics about the linear regression model of Section 2.3. Finally, we conclude with some information about the software used in the computations.

2.4.1. Parameters, DGP's, and Sample Sizes. We have tried to cover a reasonably wide class of processes. A total of 48 cases were considered – that is, 16 model configurations with three different settings for the innovation variances σ_{NS}^2 and σ_S^2. The parameter settings appear in Table 5.1. All data series were generated independently.

We first considered what will be called equal variance cases, which correspond to $\sigma_{NS}^2 = \sigma_S^2 = 1$ in cases 1–16. The "large" standard-error cases 17–32 were chosen with σ_S three times larger and hence a nine-times-larger variance; that is, $\sigma_{NS}^2 = 1$ and $\sigma_S^2 = 9$. The innovation variances in cases 33–48 were set in a different way. By fixing σ_S^2 and σ_{NS}^2 and varying the MA parameters, we actually do not directly control the variances of the unobserved component series. Hence, to have a more direct control on the process features, we fixed the ratio $\text{var}(1 - L)X_t^{NS}/\text{var}(1 + L + \ldots + L^{11})X_t^S$. Many empirical estimates of UCARIMA reported in the literature yield values for this ratio ranging from about .01 to .2 (e.g., see Bell and Hillmer 1984; Nerlove, Grether, and Carvalho 1979, chap. X). We took the ratio to be equal to .1. Besides controlling the parameters, we also set the starting values, which will be discussed in Section 2.4.3.

2.4.2. Test Statistics. In Section 2.2, we formulated several properties that we expect to hold if no significant nonlinearities occur in the X-11 program. We now turn our attention to the analysis of these properties via statistical hypothesis testing. The null hypothesis of the test statistics will correspond to a situation in which a property of interest holds whenever it relates to linearity and stationarity conditions – that is, Properties 2L, 2X, 4, and 5. Because of the structure of cointegration tests, the situation will be slightly different with such tests. Indeed, the null hypothesis will correspond to a lack of cointegration, and hence Properties 1L, 1X, 3, and 5 will be violated. The testing procedures proposed by Engle and Granger (1987) and Johansen (1991) were used to test the cointegration hypothesis. Because both procedures are by now widely known and applied, we refrain here from formally representing the tests. Instead, in the remainder of this section, we shall focus on the tests for nonlinearity in time series and conclude with observations regarding the *t* statistics in the linear regression model.

Obviously, there are many tests for nonlinearity in time series. The size and power properties against specific alternatives have been the subject of several Monte Carlo studies, including, most recently, that of Lee, White, and Granger (1993). With 48 series and several properties to investigate, we were forced to make a very selective choice. Tests proposed by Tsay (1986, 1989) and Luukkonen, Saikkonan, and Teräsvirta

Table 5.2. *Monte Carlo simulations t statistics in linear regression model*

| | Additive X-11 | | | | | | Multiplicative X-11 | | | | | |
| | Small sample | | | Large sample | | | Small sample | | | Large sample | | |
Cases	T	L	X	T	L	X	T	L	X	T	L	X
17	18.0	20.0	47.4	7.2	8.6	50.8	17.2	20.0	51.0	6.8	8.6	59.6
18	17.6	24.0	43.8	5.4	9.8	54.8	17.2	24.0	44.4	6.4	9.8	52.0
19	18.0	17.8	44.6	5.6	6.8	52.2	15.2	17.8	39.4	6.8	6.8	43.8
20	14.4	19.6	55.2	7.0	9.4	59.6	20.8	19.6	55.4	8.8	9.4	56.6
21	18.0	15.2	56.4	6.0	7.2	60.8	19.2	15.2	58.2	5.6	7.2	64.2
22	18.0	16.2	53.6	4.6	7.6	63.2	14.4	16.2	53.2	5.8	7.6	52.2
23	18.0	15.6	54.0	5.4	6.8	57.6	16.6	15.6	53.0	7.0	6.8	53.0
24	15.8	20.6	55.2	7.8	8.6	57.8	18.8	20.6	57.6	7.4	8.6	66.2
25	15.2	22.4	53.4	8.0	8.2	59.4	16.4	22.4	58.4	5.2	8.2	63.4
26	16.8	21.4	50.4	7.6	13.2	57.6	16.2	21.4	50.8	5.6	13.2	57.8
27	20.2	26.2	50.2	6.0	9.6	55.6	16.2	26.2	45.8	8.6	9.6	50.0
28	14.6	23.2	49.0	7.2	11.2	55.8	16.6	23.2	51.0	8.8	11.2	58.8
29	17.3	21.3	48.8	6.8	10.1	54.1	16.6	19.2	48.0	7.1	10.0	60.1
30	16.1	19.2	49.9	6.5	9.1	51.3	15.1	18.1	49.1	6.1	8.1	53.1
31	15.8	18.1	49.1	6.1	8.5	50.0	14.8	17.3	47.6	5.9	6.8	51.2
32	14.1	17.3	51.2	5.8	9.3	47.8	31.0	39.2	65.8	5.6	9.0	62.4
33	22.6	21.0	32.2	7.4	7.9	6.4	17.5	28.8	32.8	8.8	8.7	9.8
34	26.9	25.1	36.8	10.4	8.9	9.8	27.8	26.1	37.8	7.2	7.1	10.0
35	24.3	23.8	31.4	9.2	8.1	6.4	24.9	26.3	31.2	9.4	8.8	11.0
36	25.5	26.1	37.4	9.4	10.5	7.8	24.2	25.1	39.0	9.6	8.7	11.0
37	22.2	23.4	35.8	8.8	11.1	11.0	26.7	25.9	34.8	7.6	7.5	10.6
38	22.3	22.1	34.2	7.2	8.3	7.8	25.4	25.9	39.0	10.2	10.1	14.0
39	26.9	26.3	35.2	9.8	9.9	9.8	23.5	24.3	35.6	6.6	6.8	12.8
40	30.6	31.4	35.8	8.0	7.9	11.0	23.6	24.9	39.6	6.6	7.3	15.8
41	24.2	25.1	32.6	6.4	7.5	8.2	24.4	25.3	34.6	9.8	9.0	12.8
42	22.9	21.0	40.4	8.6	8.1	9.0	25.9	26.1	37.8	7.6	8.3	13.6
43	24.9	26.1	37.0	8.2	9.0	12.4	26.4	27.8	36.0	8.6	8.1	12.2
44	25.3	23.8	34.6	8.0	8.5	9.8	24.4	25.3	40.0	10.8	9.2	10.2
45	24.0	25.1	40.0	8.0	8.8	9.8	24.3	25.1	38.2	9.4	9.0	12.2
46	24.0	23.8	37.0	6.4	7.5	9.8	24.2	25.2	37.0	9.0	9.8	11.7
47	23.4	22.2	31.6	10.6	10.0	10.6	25.8	26.1	33.2	6.8	6.7	7.2
48	27.8	26.0	36.4	8.2	8.1	9.4	21.8	22.5	32.6	8.0	8.1	13.4

Note: The rejection rates correspond to the 5% nominal size tests. T stands for "true," L for "linear," and X for "X-11". Entries to the table are rejection rates of the null hypothesis $\beta_1 = 0$ in Regression (2.7).

(1988) were used in our investigation. Tests in this class are all designed according to a unifying principle; namely, they are all of the same form and yield an F test.

The first step in all F-type tests consists of extracting a linear structure via an $AR(p)$ model. Let the fitted value be denoted $\hat{x}_t$ and the residual $\hat{a}_t$, while the original series is denoted x_t. Obviously, x_t will be a stand-in series for any of the series involved in testing the properties of interest formulated in the preceding section. The second step consists of regressing $\hat{a}_t$ onto p lags of x_t, a constant, and a set of nonlinear functions of past realizations of the x_t process. This operation yields a residual denoted $\hat{e}_t$. Finally, an F test is computed from the sum of squared residuals obtained from both regressions. The tests differ in terms of the choice of nonlinear functionals used to form the regression producing the $\hat{e}_t$ residuals. Tsay (1986) proposed to use the $\{x_{t-1}^2, x_{t-1}x_{t-2}, \ldots, x_{t-1}x_{t-p}, x_{t-2}^2, x_{t-2}x_{t-3}, \ldots, x_{t-p}^2\}$ regressors. Luukkonen et al. (1988) added cubic terms to Tsay's test – namely, $\{x_{t-1}^3, \ldots, x_{t-p}^3\}$. Finally, the second test proposed by Tsay (1989) is designed to test linearity against threshold nonlinearity, exponential nonlinearity, and bilinearity. The fact that the test is designed against threshold nonlinearity may be of value because the outlier-detection schemes described in Section 1 may result in threshold behavior of the linearly filtered versus X-11 filtered series. To conduct the test, one selects a threshold lag, say, x_{t-d}. Again, an AR(p) regression is fit to compute normalized predictive residuals $\hat{e}_t$ similar to a cumulative sum test. Then one regresses $\hat{e}_t$ onto p lags of x_t, a constant, the regressor sets $\{x_{t-1}\hat{e}_{t-1}, \ldots, x_{t-p}\hat{e}_{t-p}\}$, $\{\hat{e}_{t-1}\hat{e}_{t-2}, \ldots, \hat{e}_{t-p}\hat{e}_{t-p-1}\}$, $\{x_{t-1}\exp(-x_{t-1}^2/\gamma\}, G(z_{t-d}), x_{t-1}G(z_{t-d})\}$, where $\gamma = \max|x_{t-1}|$ and $z_{t-d} = (x_{t-d} - \bar{x}_d)/S_d$ with $\bar{x}_d$ and S_d being the sample mean and standard deviation of x_{t-d} and $G(\cdot)$ the cdf of the standard normal distribution. One proceeds in the same manner as in the other two F tests. In all of our computations, we let $p = 12$ and $d = 1$ and 2.

We now turn our attention to the regression model. Because the series in Equation (2.7) were generated independently, we are interested in testing the null hypothesis $\beta_1 = 0$ knowing that the errors are not iid. We followed the customary practice in econometrics of dealing with the temporal dependence in the residuals via a nonparametric estimator. The weights were those of the Bartlett window using 12 lags in the small sample and 24 in the large one [see Andrews (1991) for a more elaborate discussion].

2.4.3. The Monte Carlo Simulations and X-11 Procedure. The original creators of the X-11 procedure probably never meant it to be inserted in a Monte Carlo simulation. The program is structured to be used on a case-by-case basis, leaving many choices open to the discretion of the user. It would be impossible to simulate this elaborate day-to-day implementation of the procedure in dozens of statistical agencies around the globe. These so-called "judgmental corrections" are omnipresent and are most probably going to aggravate rather than attenuate the nonlinearities we will investigate. In our article, we aimed to apply the X-11 procedure without any active intervention on the part of the user. Doing otherwise, at least in a Monte Carlo setup, would simply be impossible. All calculations were done with the SAS version 6.01 PROC X-11 procedure. The number of replications was 500, which is low by the usual standards, but the X-11 program was not available to us in a convenient format to construct a computationally efficient simulation setup. Even a stripped-down version of the X-11 program would still be very demanding in terms of central processing unit time. For the regression model, we investigated both a "small" sample which amounted to 10 years of monthly data – that is, 120 observations – and a "large" sample – 83 years, or 996 data points to be more precise. The properties 1L, 1X, and 3 were also studied via Monte Carlo. The tests associated with the other properties were not investigated via a Monte Carlo experiment because it was simply beyond our computational resources to do so. In such cases, we considered a single large sample. Although we created samples of 120 monthly observations and 996 data points, we actually simulated longer samples that were shortened at both ends. This was done primarily for two reasons, (1) to be able to compute the two-sided linear filter estimates requiring data points beyond the actual sample and (2) because we wanted to a certain degree to reduce the effect of starting values. Because all the time series generated are nonstationary, we have to be careful regarding the effect of starting values. In a sense, the question of starting values is quite closely related to many of the questions regarding nonlinearities in X-11. There is, however, no obvious choice for these values. This implies a certain degree of arbitrariness in dealing with the problem. First of all, as noted before, we took 10 years of pre-sample data points. In cases 1–32, all components started at zero initial values. The cases 32–48 had nonzero starting values. We took a quarterly seasonal pattern as starting values. For the additive version, all months of the first three quarters of the year took a value −1, and the months of the fourth quarter took a starting value of 3. For the multiplicative version, we set the arithmetic mean of the seasonal factors equal to 1 (which is what X-11 assumes) with a fourth quarter factor of 1.5 and the three other quarters .8333. These values appear reasonable, given the other parameter settings and empirical findings. One has to keep in mind though that picking starting values is not straightforward and is subject to a fair amount of arbitrariness.

3. SIMULATION AND EMPIRICAL RESULTS

We have identified a set of properties and regression statistics. In this section, we summarize the findings of the simulation study and we complement them with empirical evidence drawn from actual economic time series. A first subsection is devoted to the regression results obtained from simulated data. In the next subsection, we describe the results pertaining to the properties of a linear approximation described in Section 2.2. Section 3.3 concludes with a summary of the empirical evidence.

3.1   Seasonal Filtering and Linear Regression

We turn our attention first to an important question, which without any doubt is the most relevant for econometric practitioners: Are there spurious statistical relationships in linear regression models due to the nonlinear features in seasonal adjustment? We have conducted a Monte Carlo simulation study of the distribution of the t statistic in Regression (2.7). There are 48 cases for the DGP and for each case, two filters (additive and multiplicative), as well as large- and small-sample distributions for three regression t statistics associated with (1) the true unobserved components, (2) the linearly filtered data, and (3) X-11. Hence, we have a total of 576 distributions. The first is labeled "T" for "true" when the unobserved component series are used, a second is labeled "L" for "linear" when the series are linearly filtered, and a third is labeled "X" for "X-11." The results are reported in Table 5.2. Cases 1–16 are omitted from the table because they are quite similar to cases 17–32 appearing in Table 1.

Because of the nonparametric correction of the residual variance estimator, the statistic is distributed as $\chi^2(1)$. Let us first focus on the top panel of Table 2 covering cases 17–32. The results in Table 5.2 show that there are clearly some minor size distortions because the 5% critical value does not yield a 5% rejection rate but instead a higher one in many cases. The size distortion issue is not our main concern here, of course. In particular, it is interesting that, although the true and linear regressions have very different dependencies across their residuals, one observes that they have quite similar tail behavior. In contrast, the tail behavior of the X-11 distribution in small samples almost always dominates that of the two others. The results in the top panel show that the rejections in the X columns are much higher than in the two other columns and that the true and linear cases are often very close. Moreover, the multiplicative filter often, though not always, leads to a higher rejection rate than the additive linear decomposition filter. For the X column, in large samples and using the multiplicative filter, the rejection rates range from 43.8% to 64.2%, but the T column ranges from 5.2% to 8.8% and the L column from 6.8% to 13%. The results for the additive filter are equally dramatic for the X column because rejection rates range from 47.8% to 63.2%. Finally, the rejection rates drop significantly from small to large samples in the T and L cases, but often they do not drop much in comparison with the X-11 filter.

Let us now turn our attention to the bottom part of Table 5.2 which covers cases 33–48. The differences between the top and bottom panels are the nonzero starting values and the characterization of the innovation variances. The order of magnitude of rejection rates for the additive filter T and L "small-sample" columns are slightly higher in the bottom panel compared to the top one. In contrast, the rejection rates for the X column are lower but the spurious rejections due to filtering remain prominent. The large-sample cases are different, however. Indeed, unlike in the top panel, we observe a considerable drop in rejection rates for the X column. They still remain slightly higher but the large margin of the top panel disappeared. For the multiplicative X-11 filter, we have quantitatively similar results except that the rejection rates for large-sample X column increase slightly, showing again though in a less dramatic fashion the spurious rejection effect.

3.2   Simulation Evidence on Properties of Linear Approximation

We shall first report the results regarding cointegration tests and then proceed with the tests for nonlinearity. It was noted in Section 2.4 that properties 1L, 1X, and 3 were investigated via Monte Carlo simulations, whereas the other properties were studied only via a single large sample. Table 3 summarizes the cointegration tests for the first 32 model specifications for each of the three properties examined via Monte Carlo. Unlike the regression results, cases 33–48 yielded results similar to cases 17–32 and were therefore omitted. The table contains the small- and large-sample results for the additive and multiplicative filters. A lag length of 24 was selected and a constant and trend were included in all the test regressions. The "small" and "large" variance cases were grouped because the simulated results were roughly the same, and we only report the former of the two. Whenever the null hypothesis is rejected, we find supporting evidence for the property of interest. The table reports rejection rates, hence the stronger the rejections the better. The tests have a nominal size of 5% although we do not, as before, adjust the rejection rates for potential size distortions that might occur. Let us first focus on the top panel of Table 3 covering cases 1–16. In large samples, Property 1L holds, which is reassuring because we reject almost all the time the null hypothesis that X_t^{NS} and X_t^{LSA} are not cointegrated. This is true for the additive and multiplicative version of the program. When we turn to the large-sample behavior of the property 1X, we observe a considerable drop of rejection rates compared with 1L. This result holds even slightly more with the multiplicative filter. Both properties combined yield Property 3. It is not surprising therefore to find that this property often does not hold either. This first result illustrates quite clearly the impact in large samples of the nonlinear features that were described in Section 1. The lower panel of Table 5.3 shows results for cases 17–32 similar to those in the top panel, although it appears that with the mixed variance processes the cointegration tests appear not as powerful, judging on the basis of property 1L. The qualitative results for cases 17–32 are quite similar, however.

Let us turn now to the small-sample cases in Table 5.3. Here, the results are fairly inconclusive. They seem to reflect more the deficiencies in cointegration testing than anything else. Hence, with sample sizes

Table 5.3. *Monte Carlo simulations of Engle-Granger cointegration tests for Properties 1L, 1X, and 3*

	Additive X-11						Multipicative X-11					
	Small sample			Large sample			Small sample			Large sample		
Cases	1L	1X	3	1L	1X	3	1L	1X	3	1L	1X	3
1	52.0	49.4	54.2	96.0	69.8	69.4	49.4	36.0	39.0	96.0	71.2	68.0
2	54.8	50.8	51.8	96.0	71.0	70.2	56.4	37.2	35.6	62.6	45.6	42.2
3	52.4	50.2	52.6	93.0	68.0	65.6	54.8	38.4	38.2	63.4	50.4	45.2
4	54.6	54.0	54.4	95.8	65.0	63.4	54.6	42.0	40.6	60.4	55.4	50.6
5	57.6	48.8	52.8	95.4	69.4	66.8	52.8	36.4	36.8	62.8	48.8	46.6
6	67.4	51.8	57.4	95.6	66.0	67.4	48.4	37.0	37.0	58.6	47.4	42.6
7	51.0	51.4	51.0	96.8	68.0	67.8	53.8	41.6	39.4	61.4	50.2	43.0
8	57.0	50.6	52.8	95.8	69.6	66.0	52.4	37.2	35.2	56.4	49.6	46.4
9	58.0	50.4	49.8	84.8	67.4	67.2	55.8	44.0	42.0	61.4	48.6	46.4
10	54.2	54.6	52.8	82.0	65.4	64.0	56.6	38.0	39.2	60.2	45.2	43.0
11	56.8	48.8	50.8	83.6	64.8	64.2	47.4	39.6	38.8	56.8	47.8	45.4
12	56.8	53.4	52.4	86.6	70.4	67.0	53.0	46.4	47.8	61.6	52.2	45.8
13	55.6	53.2	54.8	85.4	68.0	67.2	53.6	40.0	31.0	63.0	49.4	45.4
14	55.6	52.4	52.6	85.4	64.4	65.6	55.8	37.0	36.8	58.2	44.8	40.8
15	52.1	54.2	54.6	86.0	68.4	66.0	57.0	45.4	35.8	62.2	49.0	45.2
16	53.2	50.4	49.8	84.2	67.0	62.6	56.4	45.2	41.8	60.4	51.8	46.4
17	59.6	55.6	50.6	34.6	39.6	35.6	69.6	67.2	65.0	34.6	46.4	41.2
18	61.2	61.0	52.2	32.2	43.0	37.6	66.4	66.4	67.2	62.4	56.6	60.0
19	58.0	59.0	52.0	31.4	41.8	35.0	67.0	63.6	63.8	51.8	51.4	56.4
20	56.6	56.0	54.0	31.2	41.6	38.8	62.4	62.8	62.4	57.2	49.6	52.8
21	59.0	59.8	50.6	32.8	43.0	36.0	65.6	65.6	65.8	51.4	52.6	53.8
22	57.0	61.4	53.2	31.6	41.2	36.8	71.6	66.4	66.2	54.8	53.2	59.4
23	56.4	56.6	50.0	28.6	44.2	37.0	68.0	61.2	62.2	52.8	52.6	58.4
24	58.0	55.2	48.4	29.8	41.8	36.0	70.0	68.8	68.4	51.2	50.4	54.0
25	56.6	62.2	55.6	27.6	45.8	39.0	64.0	53.4	63.2	55.0	53.0	55.6
26	49.0	56.0	52.6	29.2	46.2	40.0	66.8	66.0	63.8	60.2	58.2	58.8
27	54.2	59.8	47.8	28.0	44.8	36.6	64.4	61.4	62.6	52.8	54.4	56.4
28	52.4	59.2	53.2	27.0	42.8	36.4	67.0	55.6	55.2	52.8	51.0	55.2
29	51.8	57.0	50.6	26.0	43.2	36.4	63.4	62.0	61.2	55.2	52.6	58.0
30	53.6	56.4	51.0	27.2	47.2	37.6	67.2	65.8	65.6	57.6	56.4	59.4
31	53.4	57.8	49.6	28.8	43.8	38.4	62.2	56.2	56.2	49.0	52.0	54.4
32	51.4	58.6	51.4	27.0	43.0	35.8	61.2	60.4	61.8	45.6	50.4	56.4

Note: Entries to the table are rejections of the null hypothesis of cointegration using Engle-Granger tests (see also Table 5.2).

often used in econometric applications, it appears that nonlinear filters may result in spurious results, but the statistical properties of cointegration tests are equally cumbersome. Obviously, there is an important message in this. Indeed, as we get more powerful cointegration tests and/or larger samples, we expect the "large-sample" properties to become more relevant. We now turn to Property 5, which is no longer investigated via Monte Carlo nor, as noted in Section 1, is related to the internal modus operandi of the program. We found rather strong results, which we summarize here without reporting them in a table. In fact, it was found that aggregation adds a potentially important source of non-linearity to the data-adjustment process because less than a third of the 48 cases studied yielded a cointegration relationship between Z_t^{SAA} and Z_t^{SAD}. Clearly, all the potential sources of nonlinearity in Z_t^{SA}, X_t^{SA}, and Y_t^{SA} combined make it quite likely that the linear approximation will not be adequate in the sense that seasonal adjustment and aggregation are not interchangeable.

Next, we turn our attention to tests for nonlinearity. Strictly speaking, the distribution theory for such tests applies to stationary time series only. Therefore, we have limited our analysis to the cases in which cointegrating relationships were found and ignored all other cases. To keep matters simple, however, we focused on all the small-variance cases – that is, models 1–16 – and deleted individual cases that, according to the initial cointegration tests related to Properties 1L and 1X, did not support the cointegration hypothesis. Consequently, Tables 5.4–5.6 contain some missing values that correspond to the position where the hypothesis of no cointegration could not be rejected. Hence, conditional on having found cointegration, we investigate the stronger nonlinear properties.

For the sake of simplicity, we use *Ori-F* for Tsay's (1986) original test, *Aug-F* for the Luukkonen et al. (1988) test, and *New-F* for Tsay's (1989) threshold test. The null hypothesis of linearity is almost always rejected for Properties 4 and 6, regardless of the test statistic and model specification. Both properties are quite important because they have an empirical content; that is, they involve series that can be constructed from data. The results for properties 2L and 2X are mixed and depend on the test being used. For Property 2L, we should not find nonlinearity and depend on the test being used. For Property 2L, we should not find nonlinearity, and indeed most often we do not, but size distortions seem to be present in quite a few cases. For Property 2X, we also find a mixture of results. It is interesting to note, however, that, whenever we do not reject the null for Property 2L and hence there is no size distortion, we tend to reject the null of linearity for Property 2X.

3.3 An Empirical Investigation

To conclude, an empirical investigation is reported that is meant to match the simulations of Section 3.2. In particular, we investigated Properties 3, 4, 5, and 6 with actual data. The data do not involve corrections for trading-day variations and holidays. Hence, we tried to have the data conform to some of the assumptions made in the simulation experiments. A total of 39 series were investigated with some of the series being aggregates of several series. According to our information, they

Table 5.4. *Summary of Tsay Ori-F tests for nonlinearities – additive decomposition*

Property								Cases								
	1	2	3	4	5	6	7	8	9	10	11	12	13	14	15	16
2L	.19	.09	.00	.35	.42	.28	.06	.92	.20	.08	.71	.34	.65	.53	.19	.15
2X	.02	.21	.35	.00	.41	.10	.88	.17	.36	.05	—	—	.16	—	.04	.04
4	.00	.00	.00	.00	.00	.00	.00	.01	.00	—	.02	.00	—	—	.01	.00
6	.00	—	.00	.04	.61	.00	—	.01	—	—	—	.08	—	—	—	.00

Table 5.5. *Summary of Luukkonen et al. Aug-F tests for nonlinearities – additive decomposition*

Property								Cases								
	1	2	3	4	5	6	7	8	9	10	11	12	13	14	15	16
2L	.11	.21	.00	.11	.27	.58	.05	.50	.33	.17	.48	.43	.52	.51	.20	.32
2X	.03	.33	.08	.00	.15	.28	.58	.08	.28	.04	—	—	.02	—	.04	.00
4	.00	.00	.00	.00	.00	.00	.00	.00	.00	—	.00	.00	—	—	.00	.00
6	.00	—	.00	.03	.05	.10	—	.01	—	—	—	.03	—	—	—	.00

Table 5.6. *Summary of Tsay New-F tests for nonlinearities – additive decomposition*

Property								Cases								
	1	2	3	4	5	6	7	8	9	10	11	12	13	14	15	16
2L	.89	.64	.00	.63	.11	.97	.14	.04	.34	.09	.07	.08	.78	.48	.44	.21
2X	.32	.07	.04	.16	.06	.40	.20	.16	.35	.09	—	—	.16	—	.00	.00
4	.00	.00	.00	.01	.95	.46	.17	.41	.00	—	.02	.00	—	—	.02	.14
6	.00	—	.01	.22	.01	.45	—	.10	—	—	—	.01	—	—	—	.00

are all treated with the multiplicative X-11 program. The aggregate series were included to address the empirical evidence regarding Properties 4 and 6. To construct X_t^{LSA} in each case, we used the two-sided symmetric filter applied to the logs of unadjusted data. Obviously, because of the number of leads and lags, a fair number of data points were lost at each end of the sample of unadjusted data. As a result, the data covered 10 to 15 years of monthly time series. For X_t^{SA}, we took the officially adjusted series provided by the U.S. Census Bureau or Federal Reserve (for monetary data). This may be considered as deviation from the simulation in which the SAS X-11 procedure was used. It was noted that in practice there are often judgmental corrections made to the X-11 output. Such interventions probably enforce rather then weaken nonlinearity.

Table 5.7 summarizes the results of the Engle–Granger cointegration tests applied to X_t^{SA} and X_t^{LSA} for each of the 39 series listed. The BR, NBR, and TR series are borrowed, nonborrowed, and total reserve series of the U.S. money supply. The BA extension is a break-adjusted version of those series. All other series are drawn from the U.S. Census Industry Division, including industrial production (IP), finished goods inventories (FI), work in progress (WI) for several two-digit standard industrial classification (SIC) industries, and finally, total inventories (TI) for five subcategories of the SIC 20 sector (food). In all cases, the aggregates denoted TOT were also considered. Quite often, we do not reject the null hypothesis, implying that X_t^{LSA} and X_t^{SA} are not cointegrated. In 17 out of the 39 cases, or almost 50%, we find no cointegration at 10%, and in 21 out of the 39 cases, we find no cointegration at 5%.

The empirical evidence with respect to the other properties – that is, nonlinearity of $X_t^{LSA} - X_t^{SA}$ and properties regarding Z_t^{SAD} and Z_t^{SAA} are not reported in a table because they are relatively easy to summarize. All $X_t^{LSA} - X_t^{SA}$ series were found to have nonlinearities. The rejections of the null hypothesis were very strong without any exception. Of course, unlike the case of the simulated data that are by construction linear, an important caveat must be made regarding the interpretation of empirical results. Indeed, the individual series or any combination of them may very well be nonlinear at the outset. For the TRBA, TR, FITOT, IPTOT, WITOT, and TI20TOT series, we analyzed the nonlinearities via cointegration properties 5 and 6 because they involved a combination of aggregation and seasonal adjustment. We found no cointegration and evidence of nonlinearity, though evidence regarding the latter is difficult to interpret because of lack of cointegration, of course.

4. CONCLUSION

This article probably raises more questions than it actually answers. There is indeed more research to be done on the topics that were dis-

Table 5.7. *Summary of cointegration test statistics (Property 3)*

	Series	Engle-Granger procedure	Lag length		Series	Engle-Granger procedure	Lag length
1.	BRBA	-4.96^+	(15)	21.	IP34	-3.26	(12)
2.	BR	-4.96^+	(15)	22.	IP36	$-3.67°$	(12)
3.	NBRBA	$-3.97*$	(13)	23.	IP37	-6.08^+	(11)
4.	NBR	-1.85	(1)	24.	IPTOT	-4.80^+	(11)
5.	TRBA	-4.89^+	(15)	25.	W120	-3.55	(11)
6.	TR	-0.15	(11)	26.	W129	-4.59^+	(12)
7.	F120	$-3.81°$	(12)	27.	W130	$-4.19*$	(12)
8.	F129	-3.02	(12)	28.	W132	-3.33	(11)
9.	F130	-4.83^+	(12)	29.	W133	$-4.28*$	(12)
10.	F132	-3.52	(12)	30.	W134	$-3.94*$	(11)
11.	F133	$-4.00*$	(12)	31.	W136	-5.45^+	(12)
12.	F134	-3.36	(12)	32.	W137	$-4.93*$	(12)
13.	F136	-4.05	(12)	33.	WITOT	$-4.00*$	(12)
14.	F137	-3.51	(12)	34.	T120A	-1.66	(2)
15.	FITOT	-4.51^+	(12)	35.	T120B	-1.71	(12)
16.	IP20	$-3.56°$	(11)	36.	T120C	-1.70	(2)
17.	IP29	$-4.08*$	(12)	37.	T120D	$-3.77°$	(9)
18.	IP30	-4.66^+	(12)	38.	T120E	-2.21	(10)
19.	IP32	-3.07	(11)	39.	T120TOT	-2.42	(1)
20.	IP33	-3.41	(12)				

Note: * signifies rejection of the null at the 5% level, + at the 1% level, ° at the 10% level. Series 1–6 are based on a lag length of 15 months; series 7–39 on a 12-month lag. Lag lengths were chosen on the basis of Schwert's (1987) criterion $[12(T/100)^{.25}$, where T = number of observations]. BR: borrowed reserves; BA: break adjusted; NB: nonborrowed reserves; TR: total reserves; FI: finished goods inventories; TOT: total of all two-digit SIC industries listed; IP: industrial production; WI: work in progress; TI: total inventories of 5 three-digit industries 20A, B, C, D, E; T120TOT: total of five industries listed.

cussed here. The issue of seasonality will never really easily be resolved and keeps intriguing generations of time series econometricians and statisticians. A quarter of a century after Young's article was written addressing serious questions regarding the linearity of adjustment procedures, we find ourselves with the same question, having reached a different answer.

ACKNOWLEDGMENTS

We have benefited from invaluable and insightful comments and suggestions from Bill Bell and the staff of the Statistical Research Bureau of the U.S. Bureau of the Census, in particular Brian Monsell. Without

out implicating them in any remaining errors, they helped us uncover a mistake in a previous draft of our article regarding invariance properties of the X-11 program. We also benefited from the comments of Catherine Bac, David Findley, Svend Hylleberg, Ken Wallis, Mark Watson, and three reviewers, who helped increase greatly the quality of our article. Early versions were presented at the 1994 European Meeting of the Econometric Society in Maastricht, the 1995 Winter Meetings of the Econometric Society in Washington, D.C., the Séminaire Malinvaud (INSEE, Paris) and at the University of Nottingham. We thank all the participants for their comments. This article came about initially as the first author and the second and third started independently similar yet complementary research. We would like to thank Ruey Tsay for kindly providing us with the Nonlinear Time Series (NTS) software program. The first author would especially like to thank Don Andrews, who initiated his interest in the subject of this article, and to acknowledge the financial support of the Natural Science and Engineering Research Council of Canada and the Fonds pour la Formation de Chercheurs et l'Aide de la Recherche of Québec.

REFERENCES

Andrews, D. W. K. (1991), "Heteroskedasticity and Autocorrelation Consistent Covariance Matrix Estimation," *Econometrica*, 59, 817–858.

Bell, W. R. (1984), "Signal Extraction for Nonstationary Time Series," *The Annals of Statistics*, 13, 646–664.

——— (1992), "On Some Properties of X-11 Symmetric Linear Filters," unpublished document, Statistical Research Division, U.S. Bureau of the Census.

Bell, W. R., and Hillmer, S. C. (1984), "Issues Involved With the Seasonal Adjustment of Economic Time Series," *Journal of Business & Economic Statistics*, 2, 526–534.

Burridge, P., and Wallis, K. F. (1988), "Prediction Theory for Autoregressive Moving Average Processes," *Econometric Reviews*, 7, 65–95.

Cleveland, W. P., and Tiao, G. C. (1976), "Decomposition of Seasonal Time Series: A Model for the X-11 Program," *Journal of the American Statistical Association*, 71, 581–587.

Engle, R. F., and Granger, C. W. J. (1987), "Cointegration and Error Correction: Representation, Estimation and Testing," *Econometrica*, 55, 251–276.

Ericsson, W. R., Hendry, D. F., and Tran, H. A. (1994), "Cointegration Seasonality, Encompassing, and the Demand for Money in the United Kingdom," in *Nonstationary Time Series Analysis and Cointegration*, ed. C. P. Hargreaves, Ocford, U.K.: Ocford University Press, pp. 179–224.

Geweke, J. (1978), "The Temporal and Sectorial Aggregation of Seasonally Adjusted Time Series," in *Seasonal Analysis of Economic Time Series*, ed. A. Zellner, Washington, DC: U.S. Bureau of the Census, pp. 411–427.

Ghysels, E. (in press), "Seasonal Adjustment and Other Data Transformations," *Journal of Business & Economic Statistics*, 15.

Ghysels, E., and Lieberman, O. (in press), "Dynamic Regression and Filtered Data Series: A Laplace Approcimation to the Effects of Filtering in Small Samples." *Econometric Theory*, 12.

Ghysels, E., and Perron, P. (1993), "The Effect of Seasonal Adjustment Filters and Tests for a Unit Root," *Journal of Econometrics*, 55, 57–98.

Godfrey, M. D., and Karreman, H. F. (1967), "A Spectrum Analysis of Seasonal Adjustment," in *Essays in Mathematical Economics, in Honor of Oskar Morgenstern*, ed. M. Shubik, Princeton, NJ: Princeton University Press.

Gouriéroux, C., and Monfort, A. (1990), *Séries temporelles et modèles dynamiques*, Paris: Economica.

Granger, C. W. J., and Hatanaka, M. (1964), *Spectral Analysis of Economic Time Series*, Princeton, NJ: Princeton University Press.

Hannan, E. (1963), "The Estimation of the Seasonal Variation in Economic Time Series," *Journal of the American Statistical Association*, 58, 31–44.

   (1967), "Measurement of a Wandering Signal Amid Noise," *Journal of Applied Probability*, 4, 90–102.

Hansen, L. P., and Sargent, T. J. (1993), "Seasonality and Approximation Errors in Rational Expectations Models," *Journal of Econometrics*, 55, 21–56.

Hotta, L. K. (1989), "Identification of Unobserved Component Models," *Journal of Time Series Analysis*, 10, 259–270.

Johansen, S. (1991), "Estimation and Hypothesis Testing of Cointegrating Vectors in Gaussian Vector Autoregressive Models," *Econometrica*, 59, 1551–1580.

Lee, T. H., White, H., and Granger, C. W. J. (1993), "Testing for Neglected Nonlinearity in Time Series Models," *Journal of Econometrics*, 56, 269–290.

Luukkonen, R., Saikkonen, P., and Teräsvirta, T. (1988), "Testing Linearity Against Smooth Transition Autoregressive Models," *Biometrika*, 75, 491–499.

Macaulay, F. R. (1931), *The Smoothing of Time Series*, New York: National Bureau of Economic Research.

Maravall, A. (1988), "A Note on Minimum Mean Squared Error Estimation of Signals With Unit Roots," *Journal of Economic Dynamics and Control*, 12, 589–593.

Nerlove, M. (1964), "Spectral Analysis of Seasonal Adjustment Procedures," *Econometrica*, 32, 241–286.

Nerlove, M., Grether, D. M., and Carvalho, J. L. (1979), *Analysis of Economic Time Series*, New York: Academic Press.

Pierce, D. A. (1979), "Signal Extraction Error in Nonstationary Time Series," *The Annals of Statistics*, 7, 1303–1320.

Sargent, T. J. (1989), "Two Models of Measurement and the Investment Accelerator," *Journal of Political Economy*, 97, 251–287.

Schwert, G. W. (1987), "Effects of Model Specification on Tests for Unit Roots in Macroeconomic Data," *Journal of Monetary Economics*, 20, 73–103.

Shiskin, J., Young, A. H., and Musgrave, J. C. (1967), "The X-11 Variant of the Census Method II Seasonal Adjustment Program," Technical Paper 15, U.S. Bureau of the Census, Washington DC.

Sims, C. A. (1974), "Seasonality in Regression," *Journal of the American Statistical Association*, 69, 618–626.

(1993), "Rational Expectations Modeling With Seasonally Adjusted Data," *Journal of Econometrics*, 55, 9–20.

Sobel, E. L. (1967), "Prediction of a Noise-Distorted Multivariate Non-Stationary Signal," *Journal of Applied Probability*, 4, 330–342.

Tsay, R. S. (1986), "Nonlinearity Tests for Time Series," *Biometrika*, 13, 461–466.

(1989), "Testing and Modeling Threshold Autoregressive Processes," *Journal of the American Statistical Association*, 82, 590–604.

Wallis, K. F. (1974), "Seasonal Adjustment and Relations Between Variables," *Journal of the American Statistical Association*, 69, 18–32.

Young, A. H. (1968), "Linear Approximations to the Census and BLS Seasonal Adjustment Methods," *Journal of the American Statistical Association*, 63, 445–471.

PART THREE

NONLINEARITY

CHAPTER 6

Non-Linear Time Series Modeling*
C. W. J. Granger and A. Andersen

1. NON-LINEAR MODELS

Single-series time-series models have been analyzed and used for a very long time and it is hardly necessary to defend further consideration of them. Their use in providing forecasts for comparison with alternative techniques is justification enough if any is needed. The traditional search has been for a class of models that can be analyzed with reasonable ease yet are sufficiently general to be able to well approximate most series that arise in the real world. The class of models considered by Box and Jenkins (1970) known as the integrated mixed autoregressive, moving average or ARIMA models, have this property and have been used with considerable success in many scientific fields, including economic forecasting. It is natural to ask if there exists a more general class of models that will provide a yet better fit to reality. The obvious directions to go are to consider either models with time-varying parameters or non-linear models. This investigation is more concerned with the second of these possibilities.

When considering single-series non-linear models, it seems obvious to start with forms such as

$$x_t = h(x_{t-1}) + \varepsilon_t \tag{1.1}$$

where $h(\ )$ is some function, and ε_t is a white noise series. Wiener (1958), for example, suggests that the function $h(\ )$ should be a polynomial. However, even simple models such as

$$x_t = ax_{t-1}^2 + \varepsilon_t \tag{1.2}$$

are almost invariably highly explosive unless a is very small and the distribution of ε_t is truncated and very limited in extent. As actual economic series are not generally explosive, such models seem to be of limited value. If in (1.1) the function h is chosen so that

* *Applied Times Series Analysis*, edited by David F. Findley, Academic Press, 1978, 25–38.

$$|h(x)| < |x|$$

then stationary series can occur, but this seems to be a restriction that is not easily explained or readily interpreted in economic terms. For example, if $h(x) = \sin x$, then a stationary model is achieved but it has very little intuitive appeal. Thus, models of form (1.1) and the obvious generalizations do not appear to be a profitable class to consider.

Nelson and Van Ness (1973) have considered a somewhat related class of models of the form

$$x_t = \alpha y_{t-1} + \beta y_{t-1}^2 + \gamma y_{t-2} + \delta y_{t-2}^2 + \ldots + \varepsilon_t \qquad (1.3)$$

where y_t is a "driving" or "causal" stationary series generated, say, by

$$y_t = \sum_{j=1}^{p} a_j y_{t-j} + \eta_t. \qquad (1.4)$$

Thus, y_t is generated by a linear model and x_t by a non-linear function of past y's. However, the method of analysis proposed by Nelson and Van Ness specifically excludes the use of non-linear terms of past x's on the right-hand side of (1.3) or of linear terms of past x's on the right-hand side of (1.4). These limitations again seem to be unnecessarily restrictive in the eyes of a time-series analyst, who generally expects to start explaining x_t from past x_t, so this class of models does not seem to be the natural extension of the Box-Jenkins class.

A further related class of models can be called generalized moving average models, an example being

$$x_t = \varepsilon_t + \alpha \varepsilon_{t-1} + \beta \varepsilon_{t-1}^2 + \gamma \varepsilon_{t-2} \varepsilon_{t-1} + \ldots \qquad (1.5)$$

where ε_t is a white noise series. Although similar in form to the models just considered, these are very different when analysis is attempted, since the y_t's are taken to be observed in (1.3) but the ε's in (1.5) are not directly observed. To estimate ε_t even with the α, β, γ, etc., given, one would have to invert (1.5), that is solve ε_t in terms of past and present x_t. Although not necessarily impossible, such invertibility will be difficult to establish. We delay an exact definition of the invertibility of a non-linear model until a later paper. An appropriate definition seems to be: if a model is completely known and estimates $\hat{\varepsilon}_t$ of the residuals ε_t are obtained by using a set of assumed starting values and solving the iterative equation, then the model is said to be invertible if

$$\mathrm{plim}\ \hat{\varepsilon}_t = \varepsilon_t$$

whatever (sensible) set of starting values are used. If models such as (1.5) are invertible, then the series generated may have interesting properties. For example, suppose x_t is formed by

$$x_t = \varepsilon_t + \beta \varepsilon_{t-1}^2$$

where ε_t is a Gaussian zero-mean white noise, then

$$E(x_t) = 0$$

and

$$\text{corr}(x_t, x_{t-\tau}) = 0 \quad \text{all } \tau \neq 0,$$

so that x_t will appear to be white noise if just covariances are considered even though it is *potentially* forecastable from its own past, although in a non-linear fashion. However, it may be shown that this model is never invertible, for any non-zero value of β, and so in practice it cannot be used for forecasting.

One further class of non-linear models that have been considered, by Granger and Newbold (1976a) for example, involves taking an instantaneous transform $y_t = g(x_t)$ of the original data x_t and then building a linear model on the y_t's. Again, this is a very restrictive class of non-linear models and there is considerable difficulty in the proper choice of the function $g(\ )$. These models are further considered in the next section.

The other class of models considered in this paper in any detail is one that we believe might be sufficiently non-linear to pick up part of any real non-linearity in the system but are still in a form for which analysis is possible. These *bilinear* models are linear both in the x_t's and in the innovation series ε_t, an example being

$$x_t = \beta x_{t-1} \varepsilon_{t-1} + \varepsilon_t.$$

There has been some interest in such models, and their continuous time counterparts, by control engineers in recent years; a good survey of the results achieved in the field is given by Bruni, Di Pillo, and Koch (1974). However, we know of no previous work discussing the statistical or time series aspects of these models.

2. INSTANTANEOUS DATA TRANSFORMATIONS

It has become common practice amongst econometricians to build models not on their raw data, X_t, but rather on instantaneously transformed data $Y_t = T(X_t)$. By far the most usual transformation is the logarithmic although there has recently been considerable interest in using the transformation suggested by Box and Cox,

$$Y_t = \frac{(X_t + m)^\theta - 1}{\theta}. \tag{2.1}$$

Here m is a constant chosen to ensure that $X_t + m$ is positive and θ is the main transformation parameter. The main advantage of the Box-Cox transformations is that they include the linear ($\theta = 1$) and logarithmic ($\theta = 0$) as special cases. The usual stated reason for making such transformations is to produce models with homogeneous error terms. In the single series forecasting context, the question that has to be asked is – are superior forecasts produced for the original series X_t from model building on the Y_t's. It has been suggested that superior forecasts do frequently occur.

For whatever reason, instantaneous transformations are often used in practice, and it is important to study the time-series properties of the resulting series and also the question of how to forecast X_{n+h} given that one only has available a model for $Y_t = T(X_t)$, where $T(\ )$ is the transformation used. These questions have been considered in some detail by Granger and Newbold (1976a) and so only the main results will be presented here, largely without proof.

Let X_t be a stationary, Gaussian series with mean μ, variance σ^2 and autocorrelation sequence

$$\operatorname{corr}(X_t, X_{t-\tau}) = \rho_\tau.$$

Set

$$Z_t = \frac{X_t - \mu}{\sigma}$$

so that $Z_t, Z_{t-\tau}$ will be jointly distributed as bivariate Normal with zero means, unit variance and correlation ρ_τ. Consider an instantaneous transformation of the form

$$Y_t = T(Z_t)$$

where $T(\ )$ can be expanded in terms of Hermite polynomials in the form:

$$T(Z) = \sum_{j=0}^{m} \alpha_j H_j(Z) \tag{2.2}$$

and where m can be infinite. The jth Hermite polynomial $H_j(Z)$ is a polynomial in Z of order j with, for example, $H_0(Z) = 1$, $H_1(Z) = Z$, $H_2(Z) = Z^2 - 1$, $H_3(Z) = Z^3 - 3Z$, and so forth. If X and Y are Normally distributed random variables with zero means, unit variances and correlation ρ, these polynomials have the important orthogonal properties

$$\left. \begin{array}{ll} E[H_n(X)H_k(X)] = 0 & n \neq k \\ \qquad\qquad\qquad = n! & n = k \end{array} \right\} \tag{2.3}$$

and

$$\left. \begin{array}{ll} E[H_n(X)H_k(Y)] = 0 & n \neq k \\ \qquad\qquad\qquad = \rho_n^n! & n = k \end{array} \right\} \tag{2.4}$$

Using these properties, it is easy to show that $E(Y_t) = \alpha_0$ and

$$\operatorname{cov}(Y_t, Y_{t-\tau}) = \sum_{j=1}^{m} \alpha_j^2 j! \rho_\tau^j.$$

Thus, the linear properties of the transformed series can be determined. It follows, for example, that if

$$Y_t = a + bX_t + cX_t^2 \tag{2.5}$$

then

$$\text{cov}(Y_t, Y_{t-\tau}) = (b + 2c\mu)^2 \sigma^2 \rho_\tau + 2c^2 \sigma^2 \rho_\tau^2$$

and if

$$Y_t = \exp(X_t)$$

then

$$\text{cov}(Y_t, Y_{t-\tau}) = \exp(2\mu + \sigma^2)(\exp(\sigma^2 \rho_\tau) - 1).$$

Further, if X_t is MA(q), Y_t has autocovariances appropriate for MA(q), but if X_t is AR(p) and Y_t is given by (2.5), then its autocovariances correspond to a mixed ARMA $(1/2\, p(p + 3), 1/2\, p(p + 1))$ process.

It may also be shown that if X_t is an integrated ARIMA $(p, 1, q)$ process then Y_t will also be such that its first differences can be modelled as an ARMA process.

If X_t is Gaussian, or is at least assumed to have this property, and a model has been formed for it, then standing at time n an optimum forecast, $f_{n,h}$ of X_{n+h} can be easily formed by classical methods as have been discussed in Chapters 4 and 5 of Granger and Newbold (1976b), and it will be linear in $X_{n-j}, j \geq 0$. Suppose, however, that X_{n+h} is not the quantity for which a forecast is required, but rather

$$Y_{n+h} = T\left(\frac{X_{n+h} - \mu}{\sigma}\right)$$

needs to be forecast. An example would be an economist who has built a model for log price but actually wants to forecast-price. The optimum forecast of Y_{n+h} under a least-squares criterion is given by

$$g_{n,h}^{(1)} = E[Y_{n+h}|I_n]$$

where I_n is the information set $X_{n-j}, j \geq 0$. As Y_{n+h} is a function of a Gaussian variable, it can be shown that this optimum, generally non-linear, forecast is given by

$$g_{n,h}^{(1)} = \sum_{j=0}^{m} \alpha_j A^j H_j(P)$$

where

$$A = (1 - s^2(h)/\sigma^2)^{1/2}; \quad P = (f_{n,h} - \mu)/(\sigma^2 - s^2(h))^{1/2},$$

$f_{n,h}$ is the optimum forecast of X_{n+h} and $S^2(h)$ is the variance of $(X_{n+h} - f_{n,h})$.

Define as a measure of forecastability of a series Y_t, having finite variance, using a given information set, the quantity

$$R_{h,y}^2 = \frac{\mathrm{var}(f_{n,h}^{(y)})}{\mathrm{var}(y_{n+h})}$$

where $f_{n,h}^{(y)}$ is the optimum forecast of Y_{n+h}, possibly a non-linear forecast, based on the information set and using a least-squares criterion. Clearly, the nearer this quantity is to unity, the more forecastable is the series. It may be shown that any non-linear instantaneous transformation of a Gaussian process X_t is always less forecastable than X_t, provided X_t is not simply a white noise series.

As an example, suppose that X_t has $\mu = 0$ and $\sigma = 1$ and is Gaussian, but that a forecast is required of

$$Y_{n+h} = \exp(X_{n+h}).$$

This would correspond to the example given earlier where X_t is log price and Y_t is price. Let, as before, $f_{n,h}^{(x)}$ be the optimum forecast of X_{n+h} using $I_n : X_{n-j}, j \geq 0$ and $S^2(h)$ be the variance of the h-step forecast error of X_{n+h}. The optimum forecast of Y_{n+h} is then given by

$$R_{n,h}^{(1)} = \exp(f_{n,h}^{(x)} + 1/2\,s^2(h)).$$

The usual naive forecast is

$$R_{n,h}^{(2)} = \exp(f_{n,h}^{(x)})$$

which is seen to be biased and, naturally, to lead to a higher expected squared error. In this case, it is fairly easily shown that

$$R_{h,y}^2 = e^{-s^2(h)}$$

and of course

$$R_{h,x}^2 = 1 - s^2(h).$$

At first sight, these results seem both very general and potentially very useful. Provided an instantaneous transformation can be found that turns the original series X_t into a Gaussian series Y_t, the usual model building techniques can be applied to Y_t, forecasts derived for Y_t and thus optimum forecasts for X_t. The forecasts for X_t so derived might well be expected to be better than those from a linear model fitted directly to the X_t series. The main problems with this approach are the choice of an appropriate transformation and the heavy reliance placed on the normality of the transformed series. Some unpublished results by H. Nelson (1976) at the University of California, San Diego, have suggested that the Box-Cox transformation, with the optimal value of θ, by no means achieves normality and does not generally produce superior forecasts of the original series compared to using a linear model.

It is possible that a different class of transformation would produce better results, but there is no inherent reason why the type of non-linearity that occurs in the real world can be captured by using linear models of transformed series. We believe that the bilinear class of models, to be discussed in the remainder of this paper, has greater potential.

3. INTRODUCTION TO BILINEAR MODELS

As was mentioned in the first section, the class of bilinear models has some features which are interesting in themselves and which also may be useful to the time series analyst. The general Bilinear Autoregressive Moving Average model of order (p, q, Q, P), BARMA (p, q, Q, P), is of the form

$$X_t = \sum_{j=1}^{p} \alpha_j X_{t-j} + \sum_{i=0}^{q} \theta_i \varepsilon_{t-i} + \sum_{k=0}^{Q} \sum_{\ell=0}^{P} \beta_{k\ell} \varepsilon_{t-k} X_{t-\ell}, \tag{3.1}$$

where $\theta_0 = 1$.

It may be noted that the model (3.1) is a simplification of the general non-linear model, with the property of linearity in the X variables and the ε variables separately, but not in both. At this point, it is convenient to give names to several subclasses of the general model.

Firstly, if $p = 0$, the model is said to be homogeneous in the output, which if $q = 0$, one has homogeneity in the input. The models to be considered in this paper are homogeneous in both variables. That is, (3.1) reduces to

$$X_t = \sum_{k=0}^{Q} \sum_{\ell=1}^{P} \beta_{k\ell} \varepsilon_{t-k} X_{t-\ell} + \varepsilon_t. \tag{3.2}$$

Let B be the $((Q + 1) \times P)$ matrix of the β coefficients. If $\beta_{ij} = 0$ for all $j < i$, the model is called superdiagonal. Here, the multiplicative terms with non-zero coefficients are such that the input factor ε_{t-i} occurs after the output factor X_{t-j}, so that these two terms are independent. Correspondingly, the model is subdiagonal if $\beta_{ij} = 0$ for all $j \geq i$ and is said to be diagonal if $\beta_{ij} = 0$ for all $i \neq j$. The superdiagonal models are the easiest to analyze but are not necessarily the most realistic. The restriction $\beta_{0j} = 0$ for all j gives models of particular interest, as they can always be solved in the form

$$X_t = \varepsilon_t + H(\varepsilon_{t-1}, \varepsilon_{t-2}, \ldots)$$

where $H(\ )$ is some non-linear function. This means that if the model is invertible, forecasting is particularly easy.

Before proceeding to analyze some special cases, it is interesting to ask if bilinear models can arise from the linear models with which econometricians and time series analysts are more familiar. To a certain extent they can, as the following examples show:

(a) Suppose that a true rate of return for a series X_t is generated by an MA(1) model, so that

$$\frac{X_t - X_{t-1}}{X_{t-1}} = \varepsilon_t + b\varepsilon_{t-1}$$

then, this may be written

$$X_t = X_{t-1} + \varepsilon_t X_{t-1} + b\varepsilon_{t-1}X_{t-1}$$

which is already in a bilinear model form. If now one cannot observe X_t directly but only with additive noise, so that the available data are

$$Y_t = X_t + \eta_t,$$

then a non-homogeneous bilinear model for Y_t becomes appropriate and analysis of the rate of return series for Y_t may be less appropriate.

(b) If a pair of series is related by the model

$$X_t = a + bY_t + cX_{t-1} \varepsilon_t$$

$$\log Y_t = \alpha\log Y_{t-1} + \log \eta_t$$

so that one equation is linear, and the second is log-linear, then if one only has data for X_t, this will appear to be generated by

$$(X_t - a - cX_{t-1} - \varepsilon_t) = (X_{t-1} - a - cX_{t-2} - \varepsilon_{t-1})^\alpha b^{1-\alpha}\eta_t.$$

Approximating the term on the right-hand side that is raised to the power α by the first few terms (linear and cross-product) of a Taylor expansion will again produce a model of a bilinear type, or at least one that will analyze like a bilinear model rather than a linear one.

(c) If a series X_t is generated by

$$X_t = \text{expectation of } X_t \text{ made at time } t - 1 + \varepsilon_t$$

and if these expectations are a function of the most recent data available at time $t - 1$, that is X_{t-1} and ε_{t-1}, the previous expectation error, of the form

$$\text{expectation} = g(X_{t-1}, \varepsilon_{t-1}),$$

there is no overpowering reason to suppose that this function will be linear. One way of picking up at least part of this non-linearity is to use the approximation

$$g(X, \varepsilon) = AX + CX\varepsilon + D\varepsilon$$

which then gives a bilinear model for the series X_t.

A number of examples have been given by Mohler (1973) of how bilinear models, often multivariate, can arise in a variety of fields, but particularly in a control theory context. The continuous time version of bilinear models arise from consideration of the stochastic difference equations, see for example Brockett (1975).

However, these examples of how bilinear models can arise are not necessarily completely convincing to time-series analysts. Our major reasons for considering these models are largely pragmatic; they do offer a class of models that are potentially capable of analysis, that may pick up part of any non-linearity in the data and thus could suggest improved methods of forecasting and also indicate model mis-specification if a linear model has been used. As will be shown in the following sections, bilinear models have interesting properties which can match known properties of real data. This is true both of the distributional properties of the data generated by these models and also the covariance properties. The present techniques of time series analysis concentrate on interpretation of the autocovariance sequence, which we shall term COVA. It is shown in the following sections that such analysis can be misleading, for example, a series that is white noise according to COVA may well be forecastable from its own past, although obviously not in a linear fashion. The fact that such possibilities exist is clearly sufficient reason for bilinear models to be worth considering.

4. PARTICULAR CASE 1: A DIAGONAL MODEL

The model discussed in this section is the diagonal BARMA $(0, 0, 1, 1)$ model, with $\beta_{01} = 0$ and $\{\varepsilon_t\}$ a sequence of independent, identically distributed Normal $(0, \sigma^2)$ random variables. The model chosen has a particularly simple form and some interesting properties. The assumption of normality in the inputs is vital for some results, and may be ignored for others, although the assumption of independence for the ε_t sequence is always required. It will be stated whenever the normality assumption may be ignored. The distribution of ε_t will always be taken to be symmetric.

The model is written

$$X_t = \beta_{11} X_{t-1} \varepsilon_{t-1} + \varepsilon_t. \tag{4.1}$$

In what follows it is convenient to use the notation $\lambda = \beta_{11} \sigma$.

We have given the details with proofs of the properties of this model elsewhere (Andersen and Granger (1976)) and so here only list the most interesting of these properties.

1. If $|\lambda| < 1$, the process is stationary.
2. The autocorrelation structure of the process is the same as for a moving average of order one, so that $\rho_k \equiv \text{corr}(X_t, X_{t-k}) = 0, k > 1$.

3. ρ_1 increases with $\lambda > 0$ up to a maximum value of 0.155 at $\lambda = 0.6$ but then decreases.
4. The model is certainly invertible up to $|\lambda| < 0.6$ and is clearly not invertible beyond $|\lambda| > 0.707$, but the issue is less clear-cut for intermediate values of λ.
5. The distribution of X_t is generally skewed and is non-normal. Its third moment increases with $\lambda > 0$ taking a maximum at $\lambda = 0.8$ and decreasing thereafter. The fourth moment does not exist for $\lambda > 0.75$ and for any non-zero λ some higher moments do not exist.

The complicated fashion in which the properties of this bilinear model varies with λ contrasts sharply with the simple properties of MA(1) and AR(1) models.

If data are actually generated by such a model, they will be identified by ordinary linear, COVA analysis as MA(1) but if it is then forecast using this MA(1) model rather than by the true model, considerable forecasting loss results. For example, if var$(\varepsilon_t) = 1$ and $\lambda = \beta = 0.55$, the error variance from the MA(1) model is nearly double that from using the true model. However, it should be asked how one could identify if one's data actually do come from an MA(1) model or the suggested bilinear model. One way of doing this is to examine the autocorrelations of X_t^2, as using the results of the previous section it can be shown that if X_t is MA(1), then so will be X_t^2, but it can also be shown that if X_t is bilinear of form (4.1), then the autocorrelations of X_t^2 are the same as for an ARMA(1, 1) model. Thus, identification is possible, in principle.

5.   PARTICULAR CASE 2: WHITE NOISE MODELS

Now consider the model

$$X_t = \alpha X_{t-2}\varepsilon_{t-1} + \varepsilon_t \tag{5.1}$$

where ε_t is Gaussian, zero-mean white noise. This is a particular example of a superdiagonal model. The process is stationary if $|\alpha\sigma| < 1$ where $\sigma^2 = $ var(ε_t) and has the autocorrelation structure of a white noise process, so that

$$\text{corr}(X_t, X_{t-k}) = 0, \quad \text{all } k \neq 0.$$

It is thus possible that a COVA analysis has suggested that some series, such as the residuals of a Box-Jenkins model-fitting procedure, are white noise, but that in reality they are generated by a model such as (5.1). This has very clear consequences for forecasting. The "white noise" property suggests that the series cannot be forecast from its own past, whereas if actually given by (5.1) it can be so forecast, although in a non-linear fashion. Identification between the white noise and bilinear models can again be achieved by looking at the autocorrelations of X_t^2, which will be as for a white noise process if X_t is really white noise but as for an ARMA (2, 1) model if X_t is generated by (5.1).

We have found by experience with both real and simulated data that there is no particular difficulty in estimating the parameter of models such as (5.1), using a non-linear, search procedure.

As an example of this work, a bilinear model similar to (5.1) was fitted to the residuals obtained from a linear Box-Jenkins model. The complete details of the identification and estimation are given in Andersen and Granger (1976). The final result was that the variance of the residuals was decreased. More importantly though, the variance of the one step ahead forecast errors, in a period not used for estimation, was reduced by eight percent. This suggests a useful improvement over the usual naive forecasts.

REFERENCES

Andersen, A. P. and C. W. J. Granger, (1976), "Introduction to Bilinear Time Series Models," Department of Economics Discussion Paper 76-5, University of California, San Diego.

Box, G. E. P. and G. M. Jenkins, (1970), *Time Series Analysis, Forecasting and Control*, San Francisco: Holden Day.

Brockett, R. W., (1975), "Parametrically Stochastic Linear Differential Equation," Mimeo: Harvard University, Department of Control Engineering.

Bruni, C., G. DiPillo, and G. Koch, (1974), "Bilinear Systems: An Appealing Class of 'Nearly Linear' Systems in Theory and Applications," *IEEE, 4*, August, 1974.

Granger, C. W. J. and P. Newbold, (1976a), "Forecasting Transformed Series," *J. R. Statist. Soc. B, 38*.

   (1976b), *Forecasting Economic Time Series*, to be published by Academic Press.

Johnson, N. L., E. Nixon, and D. E. Amos, "Table of Percentage Points of Pearson Curves, for given $\sqrt{\beta_1}$ and $\sqrt{\beta_2}$, Expressed in Standard Measure," *Biometrika, 50*, 3 and 4.

Mohler, R. R., (1973), *Bilinear Control Processes (with Applications to Engineering, Ecology and Medicine)*, Academic Press: New York.

Nelson, J. Z. and J. W. Van Ness, (1973), "Formulation of a Nonlinear Predictor," *Technometrics*, 15, 1–12.

Nelson, H., (1976), unpublished Ph.D. thesis, University of California, San Diego.

Wiener, N., (1958), *Nonlinear Problems in Random Theory*, Technology Press of Massachusetts Institute of Technology, Clapman & Hall.

CHAPTER 7

Using the Correlation Exponent to Decide Whether an Economic Series is Chaotic*

T. Lui C. W. J. Granger, and W. P. Heller

'In Roman mythology, the god Chaos is the father of the god Time'
> Robert Graves, *I Claudius* – Arthur Barker, London, 1934

Summary

We consider two ways of distinguishing deterministic time-series from stochastic white noise; the Grassberger–Procaccia correlation exponent test and the Brock, Dechert, Scheinkman (or BDS) test. Using simulated data to test the power of these tests, the correlation exponent test can distinguish white noise from chaos. It cannot distinguish white noise from chaos mixed with a small amount of white noise. With i.i.d. as the null, the BDS correctly rejects the null when the data are deterministic chaos. Although the BDS test may also reject the null even when the data are stochastic, it may be useful in distinguishing between linear and nonlinear stochastic processes.

1. INTRODUCTION

Econometricians and applied economists often take the viewpoint that unforecastable shocks and innovations continually bombard the actual economy. In other words, the economy is essentially stochastic in nature. By contrast, some models in the economic theory literature (e.g. Grandmont, 1985) suggest that an essential nonlinearity in real economic forces permits deterministic time-series to have the appearance

* *Journal of Applied Econometrics*, 7, 1992, S25–S40. Reprinted in *Nonlinear Dynamics, Chaos, and Econometrics*, edited by M. H. Pesaran and S. M. Potter, J. Wiley, Chichester.

of chaos. It is our purpose here to examine some of the tests that have been proposed to resolve the issue. The choice is whether the economy is better modelled as (1) essentially linear in structure with significant stochastic elements, or (2) having a nonlinear structure with insignificant stochastic forces or (3) having a clear nonlinear structure but with significant stochastic shocks. Much of the chaos literature only discusses the first two of these three possibilities. Our results cast doubt on the hope that stochastic shocks can be reduced to insignificance in nonlinear models when doing empirical work.

In applied economic models it is common practice for the unforecastable shocks to an economy to be equated to the residuals of a specification. Assume that the shocks are independent and identically distributed (or i.i.d., for short). Further, assume the existence of second moments. Necessary conditions for a series x_t to be i.i.d. are: (1) that the mean and variance of x_t are constant, and (2) autocovariances $\text{cov}(x_t, x_{t-k})$ are all zero for all $k \neq 0$. These are called the "white noise conditions", and a series that has them is called white noise. Clearly an i.i.d. series is a white noise but not necessarily vice-versa, although a Gaussian white noise is i.i.d. It is well known that non-i.i.d. processes can have the white noise properties; see the examples in Granger (1983).

Some deterministic processes can also have white noise properties. Many find this observation interesting, and even surprising. A chaotic deterministic process is often characterized by its non-periodic trajectory. In particular, some chaos has first and second moment properties (means, variances and covariances) that are the same as a stochastic process. If these properties are the same as white noise, the process will be called here "white chaos". An example of such a process is the tent map, where it is generated by:

$$x_t = a^{-1}x_{t-1}, \qquad \text{if } 0 \leq x_{t-1} < a$$
$$= (1-a)^{-1}(1-x_{t-1}), \quad \text{if } a \leq x_{t-1} \leq 1. \qquad (1)$$

Sakai and Tokumaru (1980) show that the autocorrelations for the tent map are the same as that of some first-order autoregressive process. Especially when the constant a is near to 0.5, the autocorrelations for tent map are close to that of an i.i.d. process.

Time-series data from the "logistic map" have similar properties. The logistic map is given by:

$$x_t = 4x_{t-1}(1-x_{t-1}) \qquad (2)$$

with some suitable starting value x_0 in the range (0, 1). Table 7.1 shows the estimated autocorrelations and partial autocorrelations for a tent map and logistic map. The autocorrelations for x_t are all small and

Table 7.1. *Autocorrelation and partial autocorrelation function for the tent map and logistic map*

	The original series				The squares of observations			
	Tent map estimated		Logistic map estimated		Tent map estimated		Logistic map estimated	
Lag	ACF	PACF	ACF	PACF	ACF	PACF	ACF	PACF
1	0.001	0.001	0.016	0.016	−0.215*	−0.215*	−0.221*	−0.221*
2	−0.006	−0.006	0.006	0.006	−0.058*	−0.110*	0.001	−0.050*
3	−0.012	−0.012	0.004	0.004	−0.024	−0.066*	0.001	−0.009
4	0.001	0.001	0.006	0.006	−0.000	−0.030*	0.005	0.004
5	0.004	0.003	−0.001	−0.001	0.005	−0.008	0.004	0.007
6	−0.008	−0.008	−0.025	−0.025	−0.008	−0.013	−0.026*	−0.025
7	−0.003	−0.003	0.003	0.004	−0.003	−0.009	0.010	−0.000
8	0.006	0.006	−0.003	−0.002	0.009	0.004	−0.003	−0.002
9	−0.006	−0.007	−0.002	−0.002	−0.008	−0.007	−0.004	−0.005
10	0.003	0.003	0.012	0.012	0.006	0.004	0.014	0.012

Note: The initial value is 0.1 and 6,000 observations are generated. The first 100 observations are truncated. For the tent map, the constant a in (1) is 0.49999. Asterisks indicate significant lags.

insignificantly different from zero, indicating that these series have at least the dynamic part of the white noise properties. However, x_t is clearly not i.i.d., as x_t is generated from a nonlinear deterministic process. Surveys of the relevance of chaos in economics can be found in Frank and Stengos (1988) and Brock and Sayers (1988).

2.   CORRELATION EXPONENT TABLES

The existence of deterministic white chaos raises the question of how one can distinguish between it and a true stochastic white noise, such as an i.i.d. series. One possibility is to use a statistic known as the "correlation exponent". Let $\{x_t\}$ be a univariate time series. Define first the "correlation integral" as

$$C(\varepsilon) = \lim_{N \to \infty} \frac{1}{N^2} \{\text{number of pairs } (i, j) \text{ such that } |x_i - x_j| < \varepsilon\} \quad (3)$$

Thus, all pairs of values of the series are compared and those within ε of each other are counted; they are then normalized by the number of all possible pairs N^2. The limit is taken as N grows large.

Intuitively, $C(\varepsilon)$ measures the probability that any particular pair in the time-series is close. Suppose that for small values of ε, $C(\varepsilon)$ grows exponentially at the rate υ:

$$C(\varepsilon) \approx \varepsilon^{\upsilon} \tag{4}$$

The symbol υ is the above-mentioned correlation exponent; it is also called the "correlation dimension". Grassberger and Procaccia (1983) show that the correlation exponent is bounded above by the Hausdorff dimension and information dimension.

These dimensions are measures of the local structure of fractal attractors. For some chaotic process the dimension of the attractors is fractional. Notice that the correlation exponent is used not only for distinguishing white chaos from stochastic white noise, but also for distinguishing the low-dimensional chaos from high-dimensional stochastic process.

A generalization is needed to obtain a useful set of statistics. Let $X_{t,m}$ be the vector of m consecutive terms $(x_t, x_{t+1}, \ldots, x_{t+m-1})$. Define the correlation integral as:

$$C_m(\varepsilon) = \lim_{N \to \infty} N^{-2} \{\text{number of pairs } (i, j) \text{ such that each}$$
$$\text{corresponding component of } X_{i,m}$$
$$\text{and is } X_{j,m} \text{less than } \varepsilon \text{ apart}\}. \tag{5}$$

Thus, for each $X_{i,m}$ all other lengths of m of the series are compared to it. If $X_{i,m}$ and $X_{j,m}$ are ε close to each other, then they are counted. Similarly, for small values of ε, $C_m(\varepsilon)$ grows exponentially at the rate υ_m:

$$C_m(\upsilon) \approx \varepsilon^{\upsilon_m} \tag{6}$$

The length m is called the "embedding dimension". By properly choosing m, the correlation exponent υ of a deterministic white chaotic process can be numerically measured by υ_m provided $m > \upsilon$. Grassberger and Procaccia (1983) give some numeral values of υ_m with different m values for logistic map and Hénon map.

However, it is easily seen that, for stochastic white noise, $\upsilon_m = m$ for all m. If the correlation exponent υ is very large (so that one has a high-dimensional chaotic process), then it will be very difficult to estimate υ without an enormous amount of data. It is also true that it is difficult to distinguish high-dimensional chaos from stochastic white noise by just looking at estimates of υ_m. The length of economic time-series is usually short by comparison with the physical sciences, and this fact diminishes the usefulness for macroeconomics of statistics based on the correlation exponent. For choosing the proper sample size, refer to the paper by Smith (1992a). The correlation exponent, υ_m can be approximated by

$$\hat{\upsilon}_m = \lim_{\varepsilon \to 0} \frac{d \log(C_m(\varepsilon))}{d \log(\varepsilon)}. \tag{7}$$

There are several empirical ways of estimating the correlation exponent. For example, ordinary linear regression is used by Denker and Keller

(1986) and by Scheinkman and Lebanon (1989); generalized least-square is used by Cutler (1991); and the random coefficient regression is used by Ramsey and Yuan (1989). In the regression method a set of $\log C_m(\varepsilon)$ and $\log \varepsilon$ are obtained from the data series by "properly" choosing some values of ε. It is obvious that the choice of the range of ε is arbitrary and subjective. Brock and Baek (1991) also note this point.

The other type of estimation of the correlation exponent is the regression-free method. The typical examples are the point estimator presented in this paper and the binomial estimator used by Smith (1992a,b). Because of the similarity between these two estimators a comparison will be made in the following. More extensive references for these estimations of correlation exponent can be found in papers listed above.

The point estimator is defined by

$$v_{m,j} = \frac{\log(C_m(\varepsilon_j)) - \log(C_m(\varepsilon_{j+1}))}{\log(\varepsilon_j) - \log(\varepsilon_{j+1})}, \tag{8}$$

where ε_j and ε_{j+1} are constants greater than zero and less than 1. That is $\varepsilon_j = \phi^j$ with $0 < \phi < 1$, $j \geq 1$, and $C_m(\varepsilon_j)$ is the correlation integral defined by (5). Notice that $v_{m,j}$ is the point elasticity of $C_m(\varepsilon)$ on ε. In the following empirical work the minimum of the sample will be subtracted from each observation and then divided by the sample range. Hence, the transformed observations will take a value between zero and one. This ensures that the distance between any two points of $\{x_t\}$ is less than one. Thus the constant ε_j can also be restricted within the range of zero and one, and the possible range of ε is objectively given. As shown in (4) and (6), the correlation exponent can be observed only when ε is small enough. Let $\varepsilon_j = \phi^j$, for $0 < \phi < 1$ and $j \geq 1$. Then the correlation exponent is related to the value of $v_{m,j}$ for sufficiently large j.

The point estimator is also used by Brock and Baek (1991). They derived the statistical property of this estimator under the assumption that x_t is i.i.d. However, this statistical property cannot apply to low-dimensional chaos. When statistical inference for chaos is conducted, the statistic should be based on an assumption of low information dimension. Also, hypothesis testing based on the x_t being i.i.d. cannot be used for testing the difference between deterministic chaos and a stochastic process. This is because the rejection of the null is caused by dependence among the x_t. Our section on the BDS test will give details of this argument.

The assumptions on x_t can be relaxed from i.i.d. towards some degree of mixing (as in Denker and Keller, 1986 and Hiemstra, 1992). But the derived statistics are still not appropriate for statistical inference and hypothesis testing for chaos. Any statistic based on the null of stochastic x_t, instead of more general assumptions, will give the estimate $v_m = m$.

If the statistic is used for low-dimensional chaos, which has $v_m = v$ and $v < m$, the statistical inference will be incorrect and the conclusion from the hypothesis testing is ambiguous. Furthermore, the correlation exponent is only approximated for ε close to zero. Any statistic based on the correlation exponent needs to consider this point.

Smith (1992b) defines his binomial estimator with this in mind. He uses the independence assumption in a different way. In his estimator for correlation exponent, independence is applied to the inter-point distance. If there are N data points for x_t, then there are $N(N-1)/2$ inter-point distances. The "independent distance hypothesis" (IDH) implies that these inter-point distances are independent when $\varepsilon \to 0$ (Theiler, 1990). This IDH is different from an independence assumption on x_t, and it avoids the problems of $v_m = m$ if x_t is assumed to be stochastic. Let N_j be the number of inter-point distances less than ε_j, where $\varepsilon_j = \varepsilon_0 \phi^j$ for $j \geq 0$ and $0 < \phi < 1$. Based on IDH, Smith's binomial estimator is

$$\tilde{v}_m = \frac{\log\left(\sum_{j=0}^{K} N_{j+1}\right) - \log\left(\sum_{j=0}^{K-1} N_j\right)}{\log \phi} \tag{9}$$

For sufficiently large N, equation (5) implies that

$$C(\varepsilon_j) = \frac{N_j}{[N(N-1)/2]}$$

and

$$\tilde{v}_m = \frac{\log\left(\sum_{j=0}^{K} C(\varepsilon_{j+1})\right) - \log\left(\sum_{j=0}^{K-1} C(\varepsilon_j)\right)}{\log \varepsilon_{j+1} - \log \varepsilon_j} \tag{10}$$

An alternative estimator for the correlation exponent used by Smith (1992a) is

$$\tilde{\tilde{v}}_m = \frac{\frac{1}{K} \sum_{j=1}^{K} (\log N_j - \log N_{j-1})}{\log \phi} \tag{11}$$

It is equivalent to

$$\tilde{\tilde{v}}_m = \frac{1}{K} \sum_{j=1}^{K} \left(\frac{\log C(\varepsilon_j) - (\log C(\varepsilon_{j-1}))}{\log \varepsilon_j - \log \varepsilon_{j-1}}\right) \tag{12}$$

which is the average of the point estimator in (8) for some range values of ε_j. The following simulation shows the properties of the point estimator and consequentially it also provides some of the properties of the binomial estimator $\tilde{\tilde{v}}_m$.

Table 7.2. *Correlation exponents for logistic map*

| | Sample size = 500 | | | | | | Sample size = 5,900 | | | | | |
| | m | | | | | | m | | | | | |
j	1	2	3	4	5	10	1	2	3	4	5	10
16	0.78	0.96	1.05	1.00	0.95	0.80	0.76	0.89	0.97	1.02	1.14	2.16
17	0.66	0.82	0.84	0.88	0.96	1.27	0.77	0.90	0.97	1.01	1.11	1.41
18	0.66	0.80	0.78	0.84	0.91	0.80	0.77	0.90	0.97	1.00	1.08	1.32
19	0.74	0.86	0.85	0.87	0.98	2.17	0.79	0.90	0.96	0.99	1.05	1.39
20	0.77	0.90	0.92	1.02	1.12	0.76	0.78	0.90	0.96	0.98	1.02	1.19
21	0.82	0.88	0.95	0.92	0.92	0.73	0.78	0.89	0.94	0.97	0.99	1.18
22	0.77	0.89	0.90	0.94	0.96	0.79	0.78	0.89	0.95	0.98	1.02	1.33
23	0.73	0.84	0.87	0.88	0.82	0.53	0.77	0.89	0.94	0.97	1.00	1.38
24	0.86	0.89	0.93	0.92	0.90	1.04	0.78	0.88	0.93	0.97	0.99	1.22
25	0.81	0.89	0.94	0.93	0.86	0.50	0.80	0.91	0.97	1.00	1.03	1.15
26	0.81	0.95	0.99	1.01	0.93	0.39	0.81	0.91	0.96	0.99	1.02	1.05
27	0.77	0.83	0.90	0.91	0.87	0.84	0.80	0.89	0.95	0.98	1.00	1.12
28	0.79	0.81	0.86	0.87	0.83	0.45	0.80	0.88	0.94	0.96	0.99	1.14
29	0.81	0.81	0.87	0.88	0.88	0.97	0.80	0.88	0.94	0.97	0.97	1.22
30	0.74	0.88	1.00	0.98	0.97	1.08	0.81	0.89	0.95	0.98	0.98	1.11
31	0.74	0.85	0.93	1.02	1.16	0.79	0.82	0.90	0.95	0.98	0.99	0.98
32	0.68	0.79	0.83	0.80	0.82	0.86	0.82	0.90	0.95	0.97	0.98	0.98
33	0.83	0.89	1.02	1.06	0.88	0.23	0.83	0.91	0.96	0.97	0.98	1.10
34	0.83	0.93	0.99	1.06	0.81	0.00	0.82	0.90	0.95	0.98	0.96	0.95
35	0.81	0.85	0.84	0.86	0.97	0.47	0.83	0.90	0.94	0.97	0.95	1.01
36	0.77	0.86	0.84	0.71	0.87	1.59	0.82	0.89	0.93	0.95	0.94	0.94
37	0.88	0.83	0.82	0.93	0.97	0.90	0.82	0.89	0.94	0.96	0.94	1.01
38	0.88	0.95	0.93	0.89	0.78	0.00	0.85	0.92	0.96	0.98	0.99	1.02
39	0.87	0.90	0.96	0.94	0.82	1.00	0.86	0.91	0.96	0.96	0.98	1.08
40	0.74	0.80	0.81	0.78	0.90	1.94	0.83	0.91	0.97	0.99	1.05	1.20

Note: Each column represents different embedding dimension m and each row shows different value of j such that $\varepsilon_j = 0.9^j$. Each cell is the point estimate of the correlation exponent, $v_{m,j}$, as defined in (8).

Table 7.2 shows the point estimates of the correlation exponent, $v_{m,j}$, for six values of the embedding dimension m and 25 epsilon values. The table uses data from the logistic map with sample sizes of 500 and 5,900. For most macroeconomic series, 500 is a large but plausible sample size (approximately 40 years of monthly data). A sample of 5,900 observations is large compared to most economic time-series. However, financial data are often of this size (20 years of week-day daily price data). The data are chaotic and known to have a true correlation dimension of one. Thus, for $m \geq 2$ and small ε_j (or large j), where $\varepsilon_j = 0.9^j$, the figures in the table should all equal one if the sample size is large enough. Using the larger sample of 5,900 observations the values are indeed near one

Table 7.3. *Correlation exponents for Gaussian white noise*

| | Sample size = 500 | | | | | | Sample size = 5,900 | | | | | |
| | m | | | | | | m | | | | | |
j	1	2	3	4	5	10	1	2	3	4	5	10
16	0.78	1.56	2.34	3.13	3.91	7.49	0.66	1.32	1.97	2.63	3.30	6.61
17	0.83	1.67	2.47	3.25	4.01	9.95	0.72	1.43	2.15	2.86	3.58	7.21
18	0.88	1.80	2.76	3.74	4.73	9.79	0.76	1.52	2.28	3.04	3.81	7.61
19	0.89	1.82	2.75	3.61	4.26	5.79	0.80	1.61	2.41	3.22	4.03	8.15
20	0.88	1.75	2.62	3.46	4.39	9.70	0.84	1.68	2.52	3.35	4.20	8.43
21	0.90	1.83	2.68	3.38	3.89	10.43	0.87	1.73	2.60	3.46	4.33	8.51
22	0.95	1.86	2.87	3.87	5.17	3.85	0.89	1.78	2.67	3.55	4.43	8.46
23	0.96	1.91	2.93	4.01	4.96	—	0.91	1.83	2.75	3.67	4.60	9.43
24	0.96	1.90	2.90	3.64	4.33	—	0.93	1.86	2.79	3.73	4.69	9.24
25	0.99	1.95	2.91	3.71	4.55	—	0.94	1.88	2.81	3.76	4.69	10.61
26	0.99	2.01	2.81	4.19	5.22	—	0.95	1.90	2.85	3.79	4.75	7.14
27	0.99	2.06	3.12	3.88	4.59	—	0.96	1.92	2.87	3.79	4.67	8.84
28	0.99	1.89	2.64	3.56	2.99	—	0.97	1.94	2.91	3.85	4.86	5.88
29	0.99	2.05	3.08	5.06	8.52	—	0.97	1.95	2.93	3.93	4.94	11.89
30	0.99	1.99	3.04	4.33	5.75	—	0.98	1.97	2.95	3.92	4.98	—
31	0.99	2.13	2.88	4.17	1.73	—	0.98	1.97	2.95	3.90	4.88	—
32	0.94	1.82	2.73	4.01	4.85	—	0.99	1.98	2.97	4.00	5.23	—
33	1.00	2.07	3.14	6.09	3.85	—	0.99	1.98	3.01	4.11	5.32	—
34	0.99	1.94	2.73	3.39	6.58	—	0.99	1.99	2.92	3.88	4.95	—
35	0.96	1.83	2.46	0.00	—	—	0.99	1.97	2.93	4.00	5.53	—
36	0.96	1.82	2.69	8.04	—	—	0.99	1.98	2.98	4.00	5.62	—
37	0.96	1.97	2.08	3.85	—	—	0.99	1.98	2.93	3.87	4.81	—
38	0.97	1.84	2.67	0.00	—	—	1.00	1.97	2.94	4.00	5.37	—
39	0.95	2.26	2.99	6.58	—	—	0.99	1.98	2.91	3.85	2.86	—
40	1.00	1.71	1.94	0.00	—	—	1.00	2.02	3.03	4.15	5.38	—

Note: See footnote in Table 2.

for $2 \le m \le 5$ and small epsilon, or $j > 20$. There does appear to be a slight downward bias, with most values under 1.0.

The estimate is less reliable for $m = 10$. Using a much smaller sample of 500 observations, this general pattern is the same but with higher variability. Looking at the table for $m > 1$ and small enough epsilon (or large j) gives ample visual evidence that the quantity being estimated is close to unity. It is stable as m goes from 2 to 5. This result if consistent with those of Grassberger and Procaccia (1983). In particular, they also found that v_m is underestimated when $m = 1$.

These results are thus encouraging, as tables such as these do give the correct pattern if the data are truly chaotic. The same results were found with data from the Hénon map, but these are not shown. Table 7.3 shows the same results for "stochastic" Gaussian white noise series, of sample sizes 500 and 5,900 respectively. Theory suggests that these estimates should equal m and thus should take the value 1, 2, 3, 4, 5 and 10 in the columns. The pattern in these tables is as predicted by the theory for small enough epsilon, say $j > 25$. Note that there is a fairly consistent downward bias in the calculated dimension. The results from the correlation exponent tables are rather similar to those from the regression approach, such as Ramsey and Yuan (1990).

Interpretation of this type of "ocular econometrics" is not easy. One has to be selective as to which parts of the table are emphasized. Statistical inference is needed for more accurate conclusions. Brook and Baek (1991) and Smith (1991a,b) give statistical properties for the correlation exponent. The simulations as shown in Tables II and III reveal an important message on the empirical use of the correlation exponent. The choice of epsilon is important. Different ranges of epsilon may give different conclusions. Further, distinguishing stochastic white noise from white chaos based on the correlation exponent is only valid for small epsilon. Brook and Baek (1991) have similar and intensive simulations on point estimates for Gaussian white noise. It should be noticed that their statistic is for all epsilon and not only for small epsilon, as is required for the definition of the correlation exponent.

Smith (1992b) has a simulation for the binomial estimates of low-dimension chaos. It is clear from Table II that the quality of binomial estimates is related to the range of epsilon chosen. In addition, the reliability in estimating the correlation exponent varies with the sample size and the embedding dimension. Ramsey and Yuan (1989) and Ramsey, Sayers, and Rothman (1990) also recognize this point.

It follows that a chaotic series can be distinguished if it has a fairly low correlation dimension, say five or less. Random number generators on computers typically have at least this dimension. Brock (1986) reports a dimension of approximately 11 for the Gauss random number generator. It is also true that it is difficult to distinguish high-dimensional chaos from stochastic white noise just by looking at estimates of v_m. For more on choosing the proper sample sizes and embedding dimensions, refer to the papers by Smith (1992a,b), Sugihara and May (1990), and Cheng and Tong (1992).

Statistical inference on chaos is a difficult task, and it is not easy to solve all the issues at the same time. When using statistics based on the correlation exponent for chaos, one must bear in mind their limitations. The point estimate tables indicate that it may be possible to distinguish a low-dimensional chaotic process from a truly stochastic i.i.d. process. Operationally, a "stochastic process" here is a high-dimensional chaotic process, such as the random number generators used in this experiment.

To be useful with economic data these techniques must cope with added, independent "measurement error". With this in mind, data were formed

Table 7.4. *Correlation exponents for logistic map with additive white noise (sample size = 5,900)*

j	$\sigma^2 = 0.3, S = 0.4$			$\sigma^2 = 0.1, S = 1.2$			$\sigma^2 = 0.01, S = 12$			$\sigma^2 = 0.001, S = 120$		
	m			**m**			**m**			**m**		
	1	3	5	1	3	5	1	3	5	1	3	5
4	0.01	0.02	0.03	0.01	0.03	0.06	0.21	0.64	1.07	0.65	2.27	3.59
8	0.13	0.40	0.66	0.21	0.64	1.08	0.67	2.02	3.46	0.69	1.40	1.83
12	0.45	1.34	2.24	0.56	1.66	2.76	0.73	1.38	1.99	0.71	1.03	1.43
16	0.72	2.15	3.57	0.79	2.30	3.80	0.80	1.49	2.10	0.76	1.01	1.18
20	0.87	2.61	4.33	0.90	2.65	4.39	0.88	2.01	3.12	0.79	1.07	1.21
24	0.94	2.83	4.74	0.96	2.85	4.72	0.94	2.50	4.03	0.84	1.39	1.78
28	0.98	2.89	4.75	0.98	2.92	4.83	0.97	2.75	4.74	0.90	1.96	2.94
32	0.99	2.98	5.03	0.99	3.00	4.90	0.98	2.85	4.72	0.95	2.45	3.95
36	0.99	3.00	5.04	1.00	2.95	4.91	1.00	2.96	5.00	0.98	2.76	4.62
40	1.00	3.11	9.16	1.00	2.92	5.31	1.00	3.02	5.46	0.99	2.82	5.39

Note: The variance of the logistic map is about 0.12 and σ^2 is the variance of the white noise. S = (variance of logistic map/variance of noise), i.e. "signal/noise ratio". See also footnote in Table II. Only partials of j are shown in this table.

$$z_t = x_t + \sigma\varepsilon_t \tag{13}$$

where x_t is white chaos generated by the logistic map as in (2), ε_t is i.i.d. Gaussian white noise and σ^2 is varied to produce four alternative "signal to noise ratio" (S). We show the results in Table 7.4 for various signal to noise ratios.

The point estimates for the correlation exponent are shown only for $m = 1, 3, 5$ and for a reduced set of epsilon. Note that if the data were pure white chaos, the numbers should be approximately equal (to one) for each m value. For the majority of the table the estimates increase approximately proportionally to m, suggesting that the data are stochastic. Only for the largest S values and for a narrow range of epsilon values ($10 \le j \le 20$, say) does the estimate seem to be approximately constant. Smith (1992b) also gives estimators of the correlation exponent and variance of noise for the chaos with additive noise. From Table IV it is found that his estimators are sensitive to the range of epsilon chosen.

In a sense the correlation technique is working too well, since the true data-generating mechanism does contain a stochastic (or high-dimensional) element, ε_t. This is what is "seen" by the point estimates. The low-dimensional deterministic chaos component, x_t, is totally missed, even when it has a much larger variance than the noise. It may well be that when deterministic chaos is present in economic data, it can be

Table 7.5. *Correlation exponents for daily IBM and S&P 500 rate of returns (from 2 July 1962 to 31 December 1985 with 5903 observations)*

| | IBM daily returns | | | | | | S&P 500 daily returns | | | | | |
| | m | | | | | | m | | | | | |
j	1	2	3	4	5	10	1	2	3	4	5	10
16	0.20	0.38	0.55	0.72	0.87	1.56	0.33	0.63	0.89	1.14	1.36	2.27
17	0.26	0.50	0.72	0.94	1.14	2.04	0.40	0.75	1.07	1.37	1.64	2.71
18	0.33	0.63	0.91	1.18	1.43	2.56	0.46	0.87	1.24	1.59	1.90	3.13
19	0.39	0.76	1.10	1.43	1.73	3.09	0.52	0.99	1.42	1.81	2.17	3.54
20	0.46	0.90	1.31	1.68	2.05	3.63	0.58	1.10	1.58	2.03	2.43	3.93
21	0.53	1.03	1.49	1.93	2.35	4.17	0.63	1.21	1.74	2.23	2.68	4.30
22	0.59	1.15	1.68	2.18	2.65	4.75	0.69	1.32	1.90	2.43	2.91	4.63
23	0.65	1.27	1.85	2.40	2.93	5.26	0.73	1.41	2.03	2.61	3.13	4.97
24	0.70	1.37	2.00	2.60	3.18	5.79	0.77	1.49	2.16	2.77	3.33	5.32
25	0.74	1.46	2.14	2.78	3.41	6.27	0.81	1.57	2.27	2.92	3.51	5.65
26	0.79	1.55	2.28	2.98	3.66	6.77	0.84	1.63	2.37	3.07	3.69	5.94
27	0.83	1.63	2.40	3.14	3.86	7.22	0.87	1.69	2.45	3.16	3.82	6.44
28	0.85	1.69	2.49	3.26	4.02	7.68	0.89	1.74	2.53	3.28	3.96	6.59
29	0.88	1.74	2.58	3.39	4.19	8.08	0.91	1.78	2.60	3.39	4.12	7.00
30	0.89	1.76	2.61	3.44	4.27	8.44	0.93	1.82	2.67	3.49	4.25	6.93
31	0.92	1.82	2.70	3.56	4.42	8.81	0.94	1.86	2.72	3.56	4.35	7.81
32	0.93	1.85	2.76	3.65	4.52	8.56	0.95	1.88	2.77	3.63	4.47	8.37
33	0.95	1.89	2.83	3.74	4.62	9.54	0.96	1.89	2.80	3.69	4.56	7.67
34	0.96	1.91	2.86	3.82	4.82	9.10	0.97	1.92	2.84	3.74	4.60	7.60
35	0.97	1.93	2.88	3.82	4.79	9.84	0.98	1.94	2.88	3.79	4.75	11.00
36	0.96	1.90	2.84	3.79	4.78	14.62	0.98	1.95	2.90	3.82	4.71	7.75
37	0.99	1.98	2.97	3.98	5.04	10.43	0.98	1.94	2.90	3.84	4.75	7.09
38	0.96	1.92	2.87	3.77	4.85	—	0.99	1.96	2.91	3.81	4.74	10.43
39	0.98	1.96	2.90	3.89	4.89	—	0.99	1.98	2.93	3.95	4.79	—
40	0.98	1.96	2.94	3.86	4.94	—	0.99	1.98	2.92	3.84	4.81	—

Note: See footnote in Table 2.

found only if it contains very little measurement error. Further, the generating process must be of low correlation dimension for detection to take place.

A possible source of such data is stock market prices. Two series were used: daily rates of returns for IBM and the Standard and Poor 500 stock index, for the period 2 July 1962 to 31 December 1985, giving 5,903 observations. The autocorrelations for both series were uniformly very small and generally insignificant, as predicted by efficient market theory. Table 7.5 shows the point estimates for the IBM returns and S&P 500 returns. The patterns of the estimates for these two returns are extremely similar. Values were small for larger epsilon. Further, for small enough epsilon, the estimates are seen to increase approximately with m, but again with a downward bias. The pattern is consistent either with these returns being a stochastic white noise or being chaotic with a true correlation dimension of around six. To distinguish between these alternatives higher m values would have to be used. This would require a much larger sample size. These stock price series are not low-dimensional chaos, according to this technique. Other studies involving aggregate and individual stock market time-series confirm this experience (Scheinkman and LeBaron, 1989).

3.   THE BDS TEST

Looking for patterns in tables may be useful, but as different people may reach different conclusions it is preferable to have a formal test with no subjectivity. Brook and Baek (1991) describe the statistical properties of the point estimator for the correlation exponent under the i.i.d. assumption for x_t. We are interested in how well it detects the presence of chaos. Since the point estimator for the correlation exponent is equal to the point elasticity of the correlation integral, Brock and Baek's statistic is derived from a statistic using the correlation integral. Such a statistic was developed by Brock, Dechert and Scheinkman (1987) (henceforth BDS). We examine the properties of the BDS statistic here, yielding some insight into the statistic proposed by Brock and Baek. A good discussion of a BDS application can be found in Brock and Sayers (1988).

Using the correlation integral $C_m(\varepsilon)$ defined in (5), the BDS test statistic is

$$S(m, \varepsilon) = C_m(\varepsilon) - [C_1(\varepsilon)]^m \tag{14}$$

The null hypothesis is

$$H_0 : x_t \text{ is i.i.d.} \tag{15}$$

and it is shown that for large samples under the null, $S(m, \varepsilon)$ is asymptotically distributed as normal, i.e.

$$S(m, \varepsilon) \sim N(o, q) \tag{16}$$

where q is a complicated expression depending on m, ε, and sample size.

If a series is linear but has autocorrelation, then the test should reject the null. In practice the BDS test statistic is applied to the residuals of a fitted linear model. The model specification is constructed first and then tested to see if the fitted model gives i.i.d. residuals. BDS (1987) show that asymptotically, (16) still applies when residuals are used, so that there is no "nuisance parameter" problem. However, it was pointed out by Brock et al. (1991a) that the BDS test is not free of the nuisance parameter problem if heteroscedastic errors are involved. Since BDS is being used here as a test for stochastic or deterministic nonlinearity, it is necessary to remove linear components of the series before applying the test. To do this in practice, an AR(p) model is built for x_t, using some criteria such as AIC or BIC[1] to select the order p of the model. The test is then applied to the residuals of this linear fitting procedure.

Recall that the test is constructed using a null of i.i.d., and that rejection of the null does not imply chaos. The test may well have good power against other alternatives, such as stochastic nonlinear processes. Nevertheless, if the linear component has been properly removed, rejection of the null does correspond to presence of "nonlinearity" in the data, however defined.

Lee, White and Granger (1990) have compared the BDS with several other tests of nonlinearity for a variety of univariate nonlinear processes. They find that it often has good power, but does less well than some of the other tests. However, the test used there had an embedding dimension of $m = 2$ and just a single epsilon value. Other simulations, such as Hsieh and LeBaron (1991) and Hsieh (1991), also show the size and power of BDS test for some nonlinear models. We study here how the BDS test is affected by other values of m and how sensitive it is to the choice of epsilon. Also, it is essential to look at the BDS test properties when epsilon values are small, where it is the only relevant range for the testing of chaos. Then it can also be applied to the statistical properties of the point estimator used by Brock and Baek (1991).

The following experiment was conducted. A series of length 200 is generated by some mechanism. As the BDS test is not affected by the norm used in calculating the correlation integral, each observation can be transformed within the range $(0, 1)$ as above. The BDS test is then applied and the null rejected or not, and this procedure repeated 1,000 times. The tables show the percentage of rejections with given significance levels for m = 2, 3, and 4, and for epsilon values $\varepsilon_j = 0.8^j$, with $j = 1, 2, 4, 6, 8$ and 10. Small j values correspond to large epsilons, and this is a range of no relevance for testing chaos.

To check if the critical values used in the test (which are based on the asymptotic theorem) are unbiased, the experiment was first run in the case where the null hypothesis was correct. Machine-generated random numbers from a Gaussian distribution were used. These numbers were random shuffled to reduce any hidden non-randomness in the data. Both sets of data produced similar results, and just those for the shuffled data are shown. Table 7.6 shows the size of the BDS test for various significance levels.

For columns with significance level $\alpha = 0.05$, for example, if the asymptotic critical values were correct, the proportion of times the null hypothesis is rejected should be 5 per cent of the time. The approximate

---

[1] I.e., Akaike's Information Criterion and the Bayesian Information Criterion, respectively.

Table 7.6. *Size of BDS test for shuffled pseudo-random numbers*

| | α = 1% | | | α = 2.5% | | | α = 5% | | | α = 10% | | |
| | m | | | m | | | m | | | m | | |
j	2	3	4	2	3	4	2	3	4	2	3	4
1	0.878	0.821	0.819	0.893	0.848	0.832	0.910	0.868	0.849	0.931	0.884	0.867
2	0.157	0.207	0.268	0.225	0.284	0.331	0.315	0.374	0.430	0.421	0.480	0.514
4	0.033	0.033	0.034	0.056	0.059	0.060	0.085	0.094	0.105	0.154	0.166	0.181
6	0.016	0.018	0.015	0.041	0.033	0.034	0.067	0.059	0.067	0.118	0.116	0.112
8	0.017	0.019	0.016	0.045	0.032	0.050	0.072	0.072	0.075	0.126	0.128	0.131
10	0.041	0.059	0.078	0.070	0.086	0.124	0.111	0.139	0.169	0.184	0.207	0.240

Note: Four significance levels (α), 0.01, 0.25, 0.05 and 0.10, are used for the BDS statistic, $S(m, \varepsilon_j)$, with different embedding dimension m and different epsilons, $\varepsilon_j = 0.8^j$. The pseudo-random numbers are generated from Fortran subroutine, IMSL. Each observation in the replication is randomly chosen from an array of 100 dimension. The numbers in this array are randomly generated from pseudo-normal numbers and the position of the array being chosen is randomly decided by pseudo-uniform random numbers.

95 per cent region is 0.037–0.063. The values are seen consistently biased towards too frequent rejection of H_0 with a sample size of 200.[2]

However, in most cases, with $j = 6$ and $j = 8$, the values are not badly biased. With the other values of j the critical values are so biased that they are unusable. This is not surprising. When low j values (i.e. larger epsilon values) are considered, most of the pairwise distances in (5) will be smaller than epsilon. Clearly, when epsilon is small (e.g. $j = 10$), few pairs are within an epsilon distance. In either case it is not easy to find the independence based on the relationship of $C_m(\varepsilon) = C_1(\varepsilon)^m$. It will be more likely that $C_m(\varepsilon)$ is close to $C_1(\varepsilon)$ instead of $C_1(\varepsilon)^m$. Hence $S(m, \varepsilon)$ should not have mean zero and the null hypothesis is easily rejected. The results are seen to vary little as m goes from 2 to 4. Although values are shown for all j with the other experiments, only for $j = 6$ and 8 are sensible interpretations and comments about power possible.

Further experiments are conducted for the testing i.i.d. of the fitted residuals. Table 7.7 shows the size and power of the BDS test based on fitted residuals using 5 per cent significance level. Applying the BDS test to the residuals from a linear fitted model of autoregressive order 1 and 2, gives the size of the test. As shown in the upper part of Table 7.7, the size is similar to the random numbers case. The power of the test is examined by applying the test to: (1) a moving average model, (2) two

---

[2] Hsieh and LeBaron (1988) and Brock, Hsieh and LeBaron (1991b) find that the BDS test does not have good finite sample properties. The size of the test can be improved by increasing the sample size.

Table 7.7. *Size and power of BDS test for residuals*

j	m 1	2	3	m 1	2	3	m 1	2	3	m 1	2	3
	AR(1)			AR(2)			MA(2)			NLSIGN		
1	0.931	0.885	0.885	0.916	0.892	0.877	0.909	0.860	0.864	0.886	0.845	0.840
2	0.350	0.413	0.439	0.338	0.405	0.442	0.344	0.436	0.448	0.310	0.374	0.394
4	0.086	0.092	0.099	0.098	0.106	0.107	0.100	0.126	0.130	0.102	0.119	0.108
6	0.061	0.058	0.057	0.061	0.068	0.079	0.073	0.094	0.089	0.059	0.073	0.075
8	0.070	0.064	0.078	0.063	0.079	0.100	0.092	0.095	0.116	0.070	0.123	0.162
10	0.107	0.124	0.157	0.102	0.124	0.155	0.132	0.158	0.266	0.113	0.205	0.311
	Logistic map			Tent map			Bilinear			BLMA		
1	1.000	0.985	0.887	0.776	0.872	0.847	0.969	0.907	0.911	0.975	0.931	0.934
2	0.955	0.961	0.978	0.999	0.802	0.592	0.546	0.584	0.579	0.393	0.391	0.400
4	1.000	1.000	1.000	1.000	1.000	0.985	0.878	0.920	0.917	0.675	0.725	0.717
6	1.000	1.000	1.000	1.000	1.000	1.000	0.988	0.996	0.995	0.971	0.988	0.990
8	1.000	1.000	1.000	1.000	1.000	1.000	0.987	0.997	0.996	0.992	0.996	0.996
10	1.000	1.000	1.000	1.000	1.000	1.000	0.981	0.993	0.991	0.986	0.997	0.996
	NLMAI			NLAR			TAR			NLMA2		
1	0.969	0.925	0.902	0.942	0.910	0.906	0.896	0.853	0.861	0.894	0.824	0.832
2	0.405	0.480	0.518	0.381	0.486	0.516	0.325	0.408	0.453	0.375	0.426	0.442
4	0.080	0.120	0.150	0.082	0.100	0.103	0.187	0.185	0.182	0.371	0.464	0.455
6	0.081	0.165	0.194	0.126	0.171	0.209	0.145	0.134	0.132	0.328	0.435	0.436
8	0.075	0.170	0.234	0.242	0.372	0.489	0.195	0.168	0.168	0.285	0.402	0.414
10	0.065	0.182	0.245	0.417	0.711	0.914	0.464	0.443	0.391	0.273	0.400	0.420

Note: The residuals from first-order autoregressive regression for AR(1), NLSIGN, Bilinear, NLAR, and TAR models are derived for the BDS statistic $S(m, \varepsilon_j)$, $\varepsilon_j = 0.8^j$. For AR(2), MA(2), BLMA, NLMA1, and NLMA2 models, the residuals are derived from the second-order autoregressive regression. In case of chaos, the BDS test is applied to the original series. The numbers show the percentage rejections in 1000 replications with 5 per cent significance level.

white chaos series and (3) seven nonlinear stochastic processes. In the white chaos case, no linear regression is needed before applying the BDS test.

The test works very well for a fairly small sample size with true chaotic series, in that the null is rejected uniformly for smaller epsilon values. Using data from the logistic map which is chaos data, the BDS test rejected the null with a probability of 1.0 for all j values, $j \geq 4$. Similar results were found with chaotic data generated by the tent map.

The experiments for nonlinear stochastic process are divided into two groups. For the first group the BDS test has very good power. The BDS test rejects the null hypothesis of i.i.d. more than 90 per cent of replica-tions. The results are shown in the centre part of Table VII along with the results on white chaos. The models in this group are bilinear (BL) and bilinear moving average (BLMA) models, which are

$$\text{(BL)} \qquad x_t = 0.7x_{t-1}\varepsilon_{t-2} + \varepsilon_t \qquad\qquad (17)$$

$$\text{(BLMA)} \quad x_t = 0.4x_{t-1} - 0.3x_{t-2} + 0.5x_{t-1}\varepsilon_{t-1} + 0.8\varepsilon_{t-1} + \varepsilon_t \qquad (18)$$

For the second group the BDS test has power smaller than 50 per cent. This means that the BDS test does not easily detect these types of non-linearity. The models are the nonlinear sign model (NLSIGN), two non-linear moving average models (NLMA1 and NLMA2), rational nonlinear autoregressive model (NLAR), and threshold autoregressive model (TAR), which have the following forms:

$$\text{(NLSIGN)} \quad x_t = \text{SIGN}(x_{t-1}) + \varepsilon_t, \ \text{SIGN}(x) = 1, 0,$$
$$\text{or } -1, \text{ if } x < 0, = 0, > 0 \qquad (19)$$

$$\text{(NLMA1)} \quad x_t = \varepsilon_t - 0.4\varepsilon_{t-1} + 0.3\varepsilon_{t-2} + 0.5\varepsilon_t\varepsilon_{t-2} \qquad (20)$$

$$\text{(NLAR)} \qquad x_t = \frac{0.7\,|x_{t-1}|}{2 + |x_{t-1}|} + \varepsilon_t \qquad (21)$$

$$\text{(TAR)} \qquad x_t = 0.9x_{t-1} + \varepsilon_t \text{ if } |x_{t-1}| \le 1$$
$$= -0.3x_{t-1} + \varepsilon_t \text{ if } |x_{t-1}| > 1 \qquad (22)$$

$$\text{(NLMA2)} \quad x_t = \varepsilon_t - 0.3\varepsilon_{t-1} + 0.2\varepsilon_{t-2} + 0.4\varepsilon_{t-1}\varepsilon_{t-2} - 0.25\varepsilon_{t-2}^2 \quad (23)$$

Table 7.7 shows that the BDS test has the greatest power on the bilin-ear model. It rejects the null hypothesis of i.i.d. more than 90 per cent replications. But the BDS test has the least power on the nonlinear sign model. Actually, the residuals are seen to be i.i.d. by the BDS test. For the other four models the power for the NLMA1 model is slightly higher than nonlinear sign model, and the highest power is found for the NLMA2 model. The power of these four models is shown in the lower part of Table 7.7. The low power of NLMA1 and NLMA2 may be because of the heteroscedastic errors.

As noted before, the figures for $j = 1, 2$ and 10 are based on a biased significance level and so should be discounted. The power is seen to vary widely with the type of nonlinearity that is present, as is found to occur with other tests of nonlinearity. There is a general pattern of increasing power as j increases and as m increases, but this does not happen in all cases. It does seem that the choice of epsilon is critical in obtaining a satisfactory test, and that this is more important than the choice of the embedding dimension. Furthermore, the "correct" range of epsilon for BDS test may or may not coincide with the range of small epsilon required for the definition of low-dimensional chaos. Other simulations, such as Hsieh and LeBaron (1988), Hsieh (1991), Brock *et al.* (1991a) and Brock, Hsieh, and LeBaron (1991b) also show the size and power of BDS test for some nonlinear models. Those results are rather similar with what has been found here. The BDS test may be useful in distinguishing linear stochastic process from nonlinear stochastic process. It cannot be used alone for distinguishing between deterministic chaos and stochastic process. In addition to the problem of choosing proper epsilon, rejection of the i.i.d. null hypothesis may be caused by dependence among x_t or stochastic nonlinearity in x_t.

4. CONCLUSIONS

Our specific results include the following:

1. Some deterministic systems behave like white noise (Table 7.1).
2. The correlation exponent technique can be used to distinguish these systems (Table 7.2) from stochastic white noise (Table 7.3).
3. The correlation exponent does not work very well in uncovering even a low-dimensional deterministic process when stochastic noise is present (Table 7.4).
4. Real economic data fail to exhibit low-dimensional chaos (e.g. Table 7.5).
5. A BDS test for stochastic white noise correctly rejects a null of white noise when the series deterministically generated, but rejected the null too often in cases where the data came from essentially stochastic sources (Table 7.6).
6. The BDS test has power to reject the stochastic nonlinearity. But its power varies as models differ (Table 7.7). BDS correctly rejected the i.i.d. null if the data came from bilinear processes, but had less power when series came from threshold autoregressive or nonlinear, moving-average processes. It had no power for the nonlinear sign model or the NLAR.
7. For empirical work, both the correlation exponent and the BDS test require a great deal of care in choosing epsilon, see Tables 7.2–4 and Table 7.7.

Our results are consistent with current practice in the economic literature. Any economy is in theory essentially nonlinear in nature with complex interactions among many variables of economic significance. However, at the current state of the art there is no good way to capture the richness of these models in testable form. At the level of applied works the models are linearized and the corresponding error terms modelled as residuals. The question remains: Do we live in an essentially linear economic world with unforecastable events exogenous to the model? Pragmatism dictates that we continue to develop better estimation methods for a world having both nonlinear interactions and unforecastable shocks.

Some general speculative remarks can be made about the difficulties of distinguishing between chaotic and stochastic processes. There are several tests, such as BDS, with stochastic white noise as the null. If the null is rejected with prewhitened data, then nonlinearity can be accepted. However, the theory is still lacking for making the choice between stochastic and deterministic. This lacuna follows from our observation that, so far as we are aware, there is no statistical test with deterministic chaos as its null hypothesis.

A common fallacy in many fields using time-series data is that: "The data-generating process G has property P; if our data has property P it is because they are generated by process G." Naturally, this is logically correct only if P characterizes G. That the data are consistent with G does not rule out other models of the universe. It is vital for researchers working with time-series to have a statistic that completely characterizes chaotic processes.

One can certainly argue that statistical tests are not the proper way to detect deterministic processes. In this view, evidence of "strange attractors", say, is convincing enough. However, the sample sizes available from economic time-series data are not large enough to provide such evidence. New techniques that could cope with small sample sizes are needed here as well. We are led to the conclusion that probabilistic methods are for the time being the most appropriate technique for analysing economic time-series data. We suspect that this conclusion also applies to much data where chaos has been "found" in the behavioural sciences, biology, health sciences and education.

ACKNOWLEDGEMENT

The work of C. W. J. Granger was partially supported by NFS Grant SES 89-02950.

REFERENCES

Brock, W. A. (1986), "Distinguishing random and deterministic systems", *Journal of Economic Theory*, 40, 168–195.

Brock, W. A., and E. G. Baek (1991), "Some theory of statistical inference for nonlinear science", *Review of Economic Studies*, 58, 697–716.

Brock, W. A., and C. L. Sayers (1988), "Is the business cycle characterized by deterministic chaos?", *Journal of Monetary Economics*, 22, 71–90.

Brock, W. A., W. D. Dechert, and J. A. Scheinkman (1987), "A test of independence based on the correlation dimension", SSRI Working Paper No. 8702. Department of Economics, University of Wisconsin–Madison.

Brock, W. A., W. D. Dechert, J. A. Scheinkman, and B. LeBaron (1991a), "A test of independence based on the correlation dimension", Department of Economics, University of Wisconsin–Madison.

Brock, W., D. Hsieh, and B. LeBaron (1991b), *Nonlinear Dynamics, Chaos and Instability*. MIT Press, Cambridge, MA.

Cheng, B., and H. Tong (1992), "Consistent nonparametric order determination and chaos", *Journal of Royal Statistical Society B*, 54 (in press).

Cutler, C. (1991), "Some results on the behavior and estimation of the fractal dimensions of distributions on attractors", *Journal of Statistical Physics*, 62, 651–708.

Denker, G., and G. Keller (1986), "Rigorous statistical procedures for data from dynamical systems", *Journal of Statistical Physics*, 44, 67–93.

Frank, M., and T. Stengos (1988), "Chaotic dynamics in economic time systems", *Journal of Economic Surveys*, 2, 103–134.

Grandmont, J. (1985), "On endogenous competitive business cycles", *Econometrica*, 53, 995–1045.

Granger, C. W. J. (1983), "Forecasting white noise", In A. Zellner (ed.), *Applied Time Series Analysis of Economic Data*, US Department of Commerce, Bureau of the Census, Washington, DC.

Grassberger, P., and I. Procaccia (1983), "Measuring the strangeness of strange attractors", *Physica*, 9D, 189–208.

Hiemstra, C. (1992), "Detection and description of nonlinear dynamics: using correlation integral based estimators", Department of Economics, Loyola College, Baltimore, January.

Hsieh, D. A. (1991), "Chaos and nonlinear dynamics: application to financial markets", *Journal of Finance*, 46(5), 1839–1877.

Hsieh, D. A., and B. LeBaron (1988), "Finite sample properties of the BDS statistic", University of Chicago and University of Wisconsin–Madison.

Lee, T. W., H. White, and C. W. J. Granger (1990), "Testing for neglected nonlinearity in time series: a comparison of neural network methods and alternative tests", Working Paper, Economics Department, University of California, San Diego.

Ramsey, J., and H. Yuan (1989), "Bias and error bias in dimension calculation and their evaluation in some simple models", *Physical Letters A*, 134, 287–297.

(1990), "The statistical properties of dimension calculations using small data sets", *Nonlinearity*, 3, 155–176.

Ramsey, J. B., C. L. Sayers, and P. Rothman (1990), "The statistical properties of dimension calculations using small data sets: some economic applications", *International Economic Review*, 31(4), 991–1020.

Sakai, H., and H. Tokumaru (1980), "Autocorrelations of a certain chaos", *IEEE Transactions on Acoustics, Speech, and Signal Processing*, ASSP-28(5), 588–590.

Scheinkman, J., and B. LeBaron (1989), "Nonlinear dynamics and stock returns", *Journal of Business*, 62, 311–337.

Smith, R. L. (1992a), "Optimal estimation of fractal dimension", in M. Casdagli and S. Eubank (eds), *nonlinear Modeling and Forecasting*, SFI Studies in the Science of Complexity, Proceeding, Vol. 12. Addison-Wesley, Reading, MA (in press).

Smith, R. L. (1992b), "Estimating dimension in noisy chaotic time series", *Journal of Royal Statistical Society B*, 54, 329–352.

Sugihara, G., and R. M. May (1990), "Nonlinear forecasting as a way of distinguishing chaos from measurement error in time series", *Nature*, 344, 734–741.

Theiler, J. (1990). "Statistical precision of dimension estimators", *Physical Review A*, 41, 3038–3051.

Testing for Neglected Nonlinearity in Time Series Models***

A Comparison of Neural Network Methods and Alternative Tests

Tae-Hwy Lee, Halbert White, and
Clive W.J. Granger

In this paper a new test, the neural network test for neglected nonlinearity, is compared with the Keenan test, the Tsay test, the White dynamic information matrix test, the McLeod–Li test, the Ramsey RESET test, the Brock–Dechert–Scheinkman test, and the Bispectrum test. The neural network test is based on the approximating ability of neural network modeling techniques recently developed by cognitive scientists. This test is a Lagrange multiplier test that statistically determines whether adding 'hidden units' to the linear network would be advantageous. The performance of the tests is compared using a variety of nonlinear artificial series including bilinear, threshold autoregressive, and nonlinear moving average models, and the tests are applied to actual economic time series. The relative performance of the neural network test is encouraging. Our results suggest that it can play a valuable role in evaluating model adequacy. The neural network test has proper size and good power, and many of the economic series tested exhibit potential nonlinearities.

1. INTRODUCTION

Specification and estimation of linear time series models are well-established procedures, based on ARIMA univariate models or VAR or VARMAX multivariate models. However, economic theory frequently suggests nonlinear relationships between variables, and many economists appear to believe that the economic system is nonlinear. It is thus interesting to test whether or not a single economic series or group of

* *Journal of Econometrics*, 56 (1993), 269–290.

** We would like to acknowledge the helpfulness of Tung Liu who allowed us use of his results on the BDS test, and thank the referees and editors for numerous helpful suggestions. We retain responsibility for any remaining errors. White's research was supported by NSF grant SES-8921382.

series appears to be generated by a linear model against the alternative that they are nonlinearly related. There are many tests presently available to do this. This paper considers a 'neural network' test recently proposed by White (1989b), and compares its performance with several alternative tests using a Monte Carlo study.

It is important to be precise about the meaning of the word 'linearity'. Throughout, we focus on a property best described as 'linearity in conditional mean'. Let $\{Z_t\}$ be a stochastic process, and partition Z_t as $Z_t = (y_t, X_t')'$, where (for simplicity) y_t is a scalar and X_t is a $k \times 1$ vector. X_t may (but need not necessarily) contain a constant and lagged values of y_t. The process $\{y_t\}$ is *linear in mean conditional on* X_t if

$$P[E(y_t|X_t) = X_t'\theta^*] = 1 \quad \text{for some} \quad \theta^* \in \mathbb{R}^k.$$

Thus, a process exhibiting autoregressive conditional heteroskedasticity (ARCH) [Engle (1982)] may nevertheless exhibit linearity of this sort because ARCH does not refer to the conditional mean. Our focus is appropriate whenever we are concerned with the adequacy of linear models for forecasting.

The alternative of interest is that y_t is not linear in mean conditional on X_t, so that

$$P[E(y_t|X_t) = X_t'\theta] < 1 \quad \text{for all} \quad \theta \in \mathbb{R}^k.$$

When the alternative is true, a linear model is said to suffer from 'neglected nonlinearity'.

Most of the tests treated here have as a first step the extraction of linear structure by the use of an estimated filter. Typically, an AR(p) model is fitted to the series and the test then applied to the estimated residuals. To automate this procedure a particular value of p is used in the simulations, usually $p = 1$ or 2, but when dealing with actual data we shall choose p using the SIC criterion leading to consistent choice of p [Hannan (1980)].

Several tests involve regressing linear model residuals on specific functions of X_t, chosen to capture essential features of possible nonlinearities; the null hypothesis is rejected if these functions of X_t are significantly correlated with the residual. When the null is rejected, the implied alternative model may provide forecasts superior to those from the linear model. These forecasts need not be optimal, merely better. Tests not based on models that imply such forecasts are the McLeod–Li test (based on the autocorrelation of the squared residuals), the Brock–Dechert–Scheinkman test (BDS) (arising from consideration of chaotic processes), and the Bispectrum test. As not all tests are based on alternative forecasting models, we have not considered the relative forecasting abilities of the linear and implied alternative models, although this should be informative and may be considered in further work.

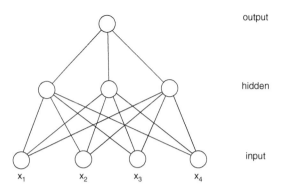

Figure 8.1. Single hidden layer feedforward network

2.   THE NEURAL NETWORK TEST

Cognitive scientists have recently introduced a class of 'neural network' models inspired by certain features of the way in which information is processed in the brain. An accessible treatment is given by Rumelhart, Hinton, and Williams (1986). A leading model is the 'single hidden layer feedforward network', depicted in Fig. 8.1. In this network, input units ('sensors') send signals x_i, $i = 1, \ldots, k$, along links ('connections') that attenuate or amplify the original signals by a factor γ_{ji} ('weights' or 'connection strengths'). The intermediate or 'hidden' processing unit j 'sees' signals $x_i\gamma_{ji}$, $i = 1, \ldots, k$, and processes these in some characteristic, typically simple way. Commonly, the hidden units sum the arriving signals [yielding $\tilde{x}'\gamma_j$, where $\tilde{x} = (1, x_1, \ldots, x_k)'$, $\gamma_j \equiv (\gamma_{j0}, \gamma_{j1}, \ldots, \gamma_{jk})'$] and then produce an output 'activation' $\psi(\tilde{x}'\gamma_j)$, where the 'activation function' ψ is a given nonlinear mapping from $\mathbb{R}$ to $\mathbb{R}$. Often, ψ is a cumulative distribution function (c.d.f.), such as the logistic, $\psi(\lambda) = (1 + e^{-\lambda})^{-1}$, $\lambda \in \mathbb{R}$. Hidden unit signals $\psi(\tilde{x}'\gamma_j)$, $j = 1, \ldots, q$, then pass to the output, which sums what it sees to produce an output

$$f(x, \delta) = \beta_0 + \sum_{j=1}^{q} \beta_j \psi(\tilde{x}'\gamma_j), \quad q \in \mathbb{N}, \qquad (2.1)$$

where $\beta_0, \ldots, \beta_q$ are hidden to output weights and $\delta = (\beta_0, \ldots, \beta_q, \gamma_1', \ldots, \gamma_q')'$. For convenience and without loss of generality, we suppose that the output unit performs no further transformations.

As discussed by White (1989a, 1990), functions defined by (2.1) belong to a family of flexible functional forms indexed by ψ and q. Hornik, Stinchcombe, and White (1989, 1990) and Stinchcombe and White (1989) – among others – have shown that for wide classes of nonlinear functions ψ, functions of the form (2.1) can provide arbitrarily accurate approximations to arbitrary functions in a variety of normed function spaces (e.g., continuous functions on a compact set with the uniform norm, functions in L_p space, and functions in Sobolev spaces with Sobolev norm), provided that q is sufficiently large. Thus, functions of the form (2.1) are capable of approximating an arbitrary nonlinear mapping. Considerable practical experience shows that when the mapping is fairly smooth, tractable values for q can provide quite good approximations. For example, Lapedes and Farber (1987) well approximated the deterministic chaos of the logistic map using five hidden units, while Gallant and White (1992) well approximated the Mackey–Glass chaos with five hidden units.

Similar approximation-theoretic issues arise in the context of projection pursuit [Friedman and Stuetzle (1981), Diaconis and Shahshahani (1984), Huber (1985), Jones (1991)]. In fact, (2.1) can be viewed as a restricted projection pursuit function in which the functions ψ are given a priori. In standard projection pursuit, ψ may differ for each term (replace ψ with ψ_j) and one must estimate the ψ_j.

The neural network test for neglected nonlinearity uses a single hidden layer network augmented by connections from input to output. Network output o is then

$$o = \tilde{x}'\theta + \sum_{j=1}^{q} \beta_j \psi(\tilde{x}'\gamma_j).$$

When the null hypothesis of linearity is true, i.e.,

$$H_0: \quad P[E(y_t | X_t) = \tilde{X}_t'\theta^*] = 1 \quad \text{for some } \theta^*,$$

then optimal network weights β_j, say β_j^*, are zero, $j = 1, \ldots, q$, yielding an 'affine network'. The neural network test for neglected nonlinearity tests the hypothesis $\beta_j^* = 0, j = 1, \ldots, q$, for particular choice of q and γ_j. The test will have power whenever $\sum_{j=1}^{q} \beta_j \psi(\tilde{x}'\gamma_j)$ is capable of extracting structure from $e_t^* = y_t - \tilde{X}_t'\theta^*$. [Under the alternative, θ^* is the parameter vector of the optimal linear least squares approximation to $E(y_t | X_t)$.] Recent theoretical work of Stinchcombe and White (1991) suggests that when ψ is the logistic c.d.f., the terms $\psi(\tilde{x}'\gamma_j)$ are generically (in γ_j) able to extract such structure.

Implementing the test as a Lagrange multiplier test leads to testing

$$H_0': \quad E(\Psi_t, e_t^*) = 0 \quad \text{vs} \quad H_a': \quad E(\Psi_t, e_t^*) \neq 0,$$

where $\Psi_t \equiv (\psi(\tilde{X}_t'\Gamma_1), \ldots, \psi(\tilde{X}_t'\Gamma_q))'$, and $\Gamma = (\Gamma_1, \ldots, \Gamma_q)$ is chosen a priori, independently of the random sequence $\{X_t\}$, for given $q \in \mathbb{N}$. We call Ψ_t the 'phantom hidden unit activations'. As in Bierens (1987) and Bierens and Hartog (1988), we shall choose Γ at random. An analysis for Γ chosen to maximize departures of $E(\Psi_t e_t^*)$ from zero (with $q = 1$, say) can be carried out along the lines of Bierens (1990), but is beyond the scope of the present work.

In constructing the test, we replace e_t^* with estimated residuals $\hat{e}_t = y_t - \tilde{X}_t'\hat{\theta}$, with $\hat{\theta}$ obtained by least squares. This leads to a statistic of the form

$$M_n = \left(n^{-1/2}\sum_{t=1}^{n}\Psi_t\hat{e}_t\right)'\hat{W}_n^{-1}\left(n^{-1/2}\sum_{t=1}^{n}\Psi_t\hat{e}_t\right),$$

where $\hat{W}_n$ is a consistent estimator of $W^* = \text{var}(n^{-1/2}\sum_{t=1}^{n}\Psi_t e_t^*)$. Standard asymptotic arguments lead to the conclusion $M_n \xrightarrow{d} \chi^2(q)$ as $n \rightarrow \infty$ under H_0.

Two practical difficulties may be noted: 1) Elements of Ψ_t tend to be collinear with X_t and with themselves. 2) Computation of $\hat{W}_n$ can be tedious. These can be remedied by 1) conducting the test using $q^* < q$ principal components of Ψ_t not collinear with X_t, denoted Ψ_t^*, and 2) using an equivalent test statistic that avoids explicit computation of $\hat{W}_n$,

$$nR^2 \xrightarrow{d} \chi^2(q^*),$$

where R^2 is the uncentered squared multiple correlation from a standard linear regression of $\hat{e}_t$ on $\Psi_t^*, \tilde{X}_t$.

3.   ALTERNATIVE TESTS

In every case an $AR(p)$ model is first fitted to the data and nonlinearity tested for the residuals. In fact any linear model could first be used.

3.1   The Keenan, Tsay, and Ramsey RESET Tests

Let y_t be series of interest and let $X_t = (y_{t-1}, \ldots, y_{t-p})'$ be used to explain y_t. (An obvious generalization allows X_t to include other explanatory variables.) In performing the tests, p and any other contents of X_t have to be determined by the user.

The first step of these tests is linear regression of y_t on $\tilde{X}_t$, producing an estimate $\hat{\theta}$, a forecast $f_t = \tilde{X}_t'\hat{\theta}$, and estimated residuals $\hat{e}_t = y_t - \tilde{X}_t'\hat{\theta}$.

Keenan (1985) introduced a test based on the correlation of $\hat{e}_t$ with f_t^2. The Keenan test essentially asks if the squared forecast has any additional forecasting ability, and so tests directly for departures from linearity in mean.

The test of Tsay (1986) has a similar form to the Keenan test, but tests the possibility of improving forecasts by including $p(p + 1)/2$ cross-product terms of the components of X_t, of the form $y_{t-j}y_{t-k}, k \geq j, j, k = 1, \ldots, p$. The test is again directly designed to test for departures from linearity in mean.

The RESET test proposed by Ramsey (1969) generalizes the Keenan test in a different way. Using the polynomials in f_t we can postulate an alternative model of the form

$$y_t = \tilde{X}'_t\theta + a_2 f_t^2 + \ldots + a_k f_t^k + v_t \quad \text{for some} \quad k \geq 2.$$

The null hypothesis is H_0: $a_2 = \ldots = a_k = 0$. Denoting $\hat{e} = (\hat{e}_1, \ldots, \hat{e}_n)'$ and $\hat{v} = (\hat{v}_1, \ldots, \hat{v}_n)'$, the test statistic is RESET $= [(\hat{e}'\hat{e} - \hat{v}'\hat{v})/(k-1)]/[\hat{v}'\hat{v}/(n-k)]$, which is approximately $F(k-1, n-k)$ when H_0 is true.

As for the neural network tests, collinearity can be avoided by forming the principal components of $(f_t^2, \ldots, f_t^k)$, choosing the $p^* < (k-1)$ largest (except the first principal component so as not to be collinear with $\tilde{X}_t$), and then regressing y_t on these and $\tilde{X}_t$, giving the residual $\hat{u}_t$. The test statistic is $RESET1 = [(\hat{e}'\hat{e} - \hat{u}'\hat{u})/p^*]/[\hat{u}'\hat{u}/(n-k)]$, which is $F(p^*, n-k)$ when H_0 is true.

A Lagrange multiplier version of the test is obtained by regressing $\hat{e}_t$ on $\tilde{X}_t$ and $f_t^2, \ldots, f_t^k$ to get an R^2 statistic. Under regularity conditions nR^2 is asymptotically distributed as $\chi^2(k-1)$ under the null. Again, forming the principal components of $(f_t^2, \ldots, f_t^k)$, choosing the p^* largest, and then regressing $\hat{e}_t$ on these and $\tilde{X}_t$, also gives an R^2 statistic. Under regularity conditions, the statistic $RESET2 = nR^2$ is distributed as $\chi^2(p^*)$ for n large, under H_0. For this test both k and p^* have to be selected by the user. The RESET tests are sensitive primarily to departures from linearity in mean.

3.2   The White Dynamic Information Matrix Test

White (1987, 1992) proposed a specification test for dynamic (time series) models, based on the covariance of conditional score functions. For the normal linear model

$$y_t = \tilde{X}'_t\theta + e_t, \quad e_t \sim N(0, \sigma^2),$$

the log-likelihood is

$$\log f_t(x_t, \theta, \sigma) = \text{constant} - \log\sigma - (y_t - \tilde{X}'_t\theta)^2 / 2\sigma^2.$$

With $u_t = (y_t - \tilde{X}'_t\theta)/\sigma$, the conditional score function is

$$s_t(X_t, \theta, \sigma) \equiv \nabla \log f_t(X_t, \theta, \sigma) = \sigma^{-1}(u_t, u_t X'_t, u_t^2 - 1)',$$

where ∇ is the gradient operator with respect to θ and σ. Denoting $s_t^* = s_t(X_t, \theta^*, \sigma^*)$, correct specification implies $E(s_t^*) = 0$ and $E(s_t^* s_\tau^{*\prime}) = 0$, $t = 1, 2, \ldots, \tau = 1, \ldots, t$. The dynamic information matrix test can be based on the indicator $m_t = S \text{ vec } s_t s'_{t-1}$, where S is a nonstochastic selection matrix focusing attention on particular forms of possible misspecification.

Denoting $\hat{s}_t = s_t(X_t, \hat{\theta}, \hat{s})$ and $\hat{m}_t = S \text{ vec } \hat{s}_t \hat{s}'_{t-1}$, where $\hat{\theta}$ and $\hat{\sigma}$ are the quasi-maximum likelihood estimators (QMLEs), the following versions of the test statistic can be formed: 1) $WHITE1 = n\hat{\mu}'_n \hat{J}_n^{-1} \hat{\mu}_n$ where $\hat{\mu}_n = n^{-1}\Sigma_{t=1}^n \hat{m}_t$, $\hat{J}_n = n^{-1}\Sigma \hat{m}_t \hat{m}'_t - (n^{-1}\Sigma \hat{m}_t \hat{s}'_t)[n^{-1}\Sigma \hat{s}_t \hat{s}'_t]^{-1}(n^{-1}\Sigma \hat{s}_t \hat{m}'_t)$; 2) $WHITE2 = nR^2$, where R^2 is the (constant unadjusted) squared multiple correlation coefficient of the regression of the constant unity on the explanatory variables $\hat{m}_t$, $\hat{s}_t$; 3) $WHITE3 = nR^2$ where R^2 is the (constant unadjusted) squared multiple correlation coefficient from the regression of $\hat{u}_t = (y_t - \tilde{X}_t'\hat{\theta})/\hat{\sigma}$ on $\tilde{X}_t$ and $\hat{k}_t$, with $\hat{k}_t$ being defined from $\hat{m}_t = \hat{k}_t\hat{u}_t'$. Under H_0, $WHITE1$, $WHITE2$, and $WHITE3$ all have the $\chi^2(q)$ distribution asymptotically, where q is the dimension of m_t. These tests will be sensitive to departures from linearity in mean to the extent that these departures induce autocorrelation in s_t^*. Other misspecifications resulting in such autocorrelations will also be detected.

3.3   The McLeod and Li Test

It was noted in Granger and Andersen (1978) that for a linear stationary process

$$\text{corr}(y_t^2, y_{t-k}^2) = [\text{corr}(y_t, y_{t-k})]^2 \quad \text{for all} \quad k,$$

and so departures from this would indicate nonlinearity. McLeod and Li (1983) use the squared residuals from a linear model and apply a standard Box–Ljung Portmanteau test for serial correlation. This test is sensitive to departures from linearity in mean that result in apparent ARCH structure; ARCH itself will also be detected.

3.4   The BDS Test

Whilst conducting research on tests for chaos, Brock, Dechert, and Scheinkman (1986) derived a test appropriate for detecting general stochastic nonlinearity. For a series y_t, define
$$C_m(\varepsilon) = n^{-2} \text{ [number of pairs } (i, j) \text{ such that}$$

$$|y_i - y_j| < \varepsilon, |y_{i+1} - y_{j+1}| < \varepsilon, \ldots, |y_{i+m-1} - y_{j+m1}| < \varepsilon],$$

so that $y_i, \ldots, y_{i+m-1}$ and $y_j, \ldots, y_{j+m-1}$ are two segments of the series of length m, such that all corresponding pairs of points differ from each other by size ε. The test statistic is $BDS = n^{1/2}[C_m(\varepsilon) - C_1(\varepsilon)^m]$. Under the null hypothesis that the series is independently and identically distributed, BDS is asymptotically normally distributed with zero mean and a known complicated variance. The test is interesting because it arises from very different considerations than the others. For our implementation, y_t is replaced by the linear model estimated residuals. The BDS test will be sensitive to departures from linearity in mean, but may also have power against series linear in mean with ARCH.

3.5   The Bispectrum Test

Following earlier work by Subba Rao and Gabr (1980, 1984), a test based on the bispectrum was suggested by Hinich (1982) and Ashley, Patterson, and Hinich (1986). If $\{y_t\}$ is a zero mean stationary series, it can be expressed as $y_t = \sum_{i=0}^{\infty} a_i \varepsilon_{t-i}$, where $\{\varepsilon_t\}$ is purely random and the weights $\{a_i\}$ are fixed. Define the second- and third-order autocovariances by $c(h) = E[y_{t+h}y_t]$ and $c(h, k) = E[y_{t+h}y_{t+k}y_t]$, and write their corresponding Fourier transforms (the power spectrum and power bispectrum) as $S(\omega) = \sum_h c(h)\exp(-2\pi i\omega h)$ and $B(\omega_1, \omega_2) = \sum_{h,k} c(h, k)\exp(-2\pi i(\omega_1 h + \omega_2 k))$. It can be shown that

$$\frac{|B(\omega_1, \omega_2)|^2}{S(\omega_1)S(\omega_2)S(\omega_1 + \omega_2)} = \frac{\mu_3^2}{\sigma_\varepsilon^6} \quad \text{for all} \quad (\omega_1, \omega_2),$$

where $\sigma_\varepsilon^2 = E\varepsilon_t^2$ and $\mu_3 = E\varepsilon_t^3$. The square root of this is called the skewness of $\{y_t\}$. The fact that the skewness of such a time series is independent of (ω_1, ω_2) is used to test nonlinearity. The test statistic of Hinich (1982) is based on the interquartile range of the estimated ratio of the skewness over a set of frequency pairs, (ω_1, ω_2). This proved to be too expensive to use in the Monte Carlo simulation but was used in section 6. We thank the authors of this test for providing the software to perform the test. In our implementation y_t is again replaced by the linear model estimated residual. The Bispectrum test is sensitive to departures from linearity in mean, but will also detect ARCH.

4. THE SIMULATION DESIGN

Two blocks of univariate series were generated from models chosen to represent a variety of stable nonlinear situations. Throughout $\varepsilon_t \sim N(0, 1)$ is a white noise series.

4.1 Block1

(i) Autoregressive (AR)

$$y_t = 0.6y_{t-1} + \varepsilon_t,$$

a representative linear model.

(ii) Bilinear (BL)

$$y_t = 0.7y_{t-1}\varepsilon_{t-2} + \varepsilon_t,$$

a bilinear model having the same covariance properties as a white noise; see Granger and Andersen (1978).

(iii) Threshold autoregressive (TAR)

$$\begin{aligned} y_t &= 0.9y_{t-1} + \varepsilon_t \quad \text{for} \quad |y_{t-1}| \le 1, \\ &= -0.3y_{t-1} + \varepsilon_t \quad \text{for} \quad |y_{t-1}| > 1, \end{aligned}$$

an example considered by Tong (1983).

(iv) Sign autoregressive (SGN)

$$y_t = \text{sgn}(y_t - 1) + \varepsilon_t,$$

where sgn(x) = 1 if $x > 0$, = 0 if $x = 0$, = −1 if $x < 0$. This is a particular form of nonlinear autoregression (NLAR).

(v) Nonlinear autoregressive (NAR)

$$y_t = (0.7|y_t - 1|)/(|y_t - 1| + 2) + \varepsilon_t,$$

another NLAR model, closely related to a class of models known as rational NLAR.

The models of the second block have been used in previous papers on nonlinear testing, particularly by Keenan (1985), Tsay (1986), Ashley, Patterson and Hinich (1986), and Chan and Tong (1986), and so are included to allow comparison with these studies.

4.2   Block2

(1) MA (2) (Model1)

$$y_t = \varepsilon_t - 0.4\varepsilon_{t-1} + 0.3\varepsilon_{t-2},$$

(2) Heteroskedastic MA (2) (Model2)

$$y_t = \varepsilon_t - 0.4\varepsilon_{t-1} + 0.3\varepsilon_{t-2} + 0.5\varepsilon_t\varepsilon_{t-2},$$

where the forecastable part of y_t is linear and the final product term introduces heteroskedasticity.

(3) Nonlinear MA (Model3)

$$y_t = \varepsilon_t - 0.3\varepsilon_{t-1} + 0.2\varepsilon_{t-2} + 0.4\varepsilon_{t-1}\varepsilon_{t-2} - 0.25\varepsilon_{t-2}^2,$$

where the final two terms give a nonlinear MA model that is typically noninvertible.

(4) AR (2) (Model4)

$$y_t = 0.4y_{t-1} - 0.3y_{t-2} + \varepsilon_t,$$

a stationary linear AR model.

(5) Bilinear AR (Model5)

$$y_t = 0.4y_{t-1} - 0.3y_{t-2} + 0.5y_{t-1}\varepsilon_{t-1} + \varepsilon_t,$$

a model containing both linear and bilinear terms.

(6) Bilinear ARMA (Model6)

$$y_t = 0.4y_{t-1} - 0.3y_{t-2} + 0.5y_{t-1}\varepsilon_{t-1} + 0.8\varepsilon_{t-1} + \varepsilon_t.$$

It is seen that three linear models are included for purposes of comparison. Data were generated with sample sizes 50, 100, and 200.

1,000 replications were used to obtain estimates of power. In a few sample cases the plot of y_t against y_{t-1} was constructed. It was generally true that there was no obvious nonlinearity visible, except possibly for the SGN autoregressive series.

All of the tests can be generalized in fairly obvious ways to consider nonlinear relationships between pairs of series. As part of an initial exploration of this situation, two nonlinearly related pairs of series were also generated.

4.3   Bivariate Models

SQ

$$y_t = x_t^2 + \varepsilon_t,$$

EXP

$$y_t = \exp(x_t) + \varepsilon_t,$$

where $x_t = 0.6x_{t-1} + e_t$, ε_t and e_t are independent, $\varepsilon_t \sim N(0, v)$ and $e_t \sim N(0, 1)$ white noises. Three different values for the variance of ε_t were used, $v = 1, 25, 400$. Plots of y_t against x_t with $v = 1$ clearly showed a nonlinear relationship, but this was no longer clear when $v = 400$.

For all the simulations except for TSAY2, the information set is $X_t = y_{t-1}$ for Block1, $X_t = (y_{t-1}, y_{t-2})'$ for Block2, and $X_t = x_t$ for the bivariate models. For the TSAY2 test, $X_t = (y_{t-1}, y_{t-2}, y_{t-3}, y_{t-4}, y_{t-5})'$ for Block1 and Block2 and $X_t = (x_t, x_{t-1}, x_{t-2}, x_{t-3}, x_{t-4})'$ for bivariate models.

In performing neural network tests the logistic c.d.f. $\psi(\lambda) = [1 + \exp(-\lambda)]^{-1}$ is used. The input to hidden unit weights Γ_{ji} were randomly generated from the uniform distribution on $[-2, 2]$. The variables y_t, X_t have been rescaled onto $[0, 1]$. We choose $q = 10$ for NEURAL1 and $q = 20$ for NEURAL2. We use $q^* = 2$ largest principal components (excluding the first principal component) for the Block1 and bivariate models and $q^* = 3$ for the Block2 models.

For the White dynamic information matrix tests, appropriate choice of S gives

$$m_t' = \sigma^{-2}(u_t u_{t-1}, X_t u_t u_{t-1}, X_{t-1} u_t u_{t-1}, X_t X_{t-1} u_t u_{t-1}),$$

where $X_t = y_{t-1}$ for Block1, $X_t = (y_{t-1}, y_{t-2})'$ for Block2, and $X_t = x_t$ for the bivariate models, so that $q = 4$ for the Block1 and bivariate models and $q = 8$ for the Block2 models.

We choose 20 degrees of freedom for the McLeod and Li tests, and $k = 5, p^* = 1$ in RESET1 and RESET2 for every model.

5.   RESULTS OF THE SIMULATION

Critical values for the various tests were constructed using both the asymptotic theory and by simulation using a linear model. For Block1

Table 8.1. *Critical values (5%) for Block1 models*[a]

Test	n = 50	n = 100	n = 200
NEURAL1	5.52	5.40	5.58
	(5.99)	(5.99)	(5.99)
NEURAL2	5.52	5.45	5.65
	(5.99)	(5.99)	(5.99)
KEENAN	3.09	3.28	3.67
	(4.05)	(3.94)	(3.84)
TSAY1	3.16	3.32	3.69
	(4.05)	(3.94)	(3.84)
TSAY2	2.50	2.02	1.88
	(2.03)	(1.80)	(1.67)
WHITE1	9.95	9.15	8.92
	(9.49)	(9.49)	(9.49)
WHITE2	11.84	10.82	10.02
	(9.49)	(9.49)	(9.49)
WHITE3	9.01	9.24	9.34
	(9.49)	(9.49)	(9.49)
MCLEOD	31.14	31.42	31.67
	(31.41)	(31.41)	(31.41)
RESET1	3.01	3.19	3.59
	(4.06)	(3.94)	(3.84)
RESET2	3.05	3.11	3.39
	(3.84)	(3.84)	(3.84)

[a] The first number in each cell is the simulated critical value from AR(1), $y_t = 0.6y_{t-1} + \varepsilon_t$, with 6,000 replications, and the second number in parentheses in the asymptotic critical value.

the AR(1) (Model (i)) was used and for Block2 the AR(2) (Model4) was used, for sample sizes 50, 100, and 200, and with 6,000 replications. The bivariate models used the AR(1) values. 10%, 5%, 2.5%, and 1% critical values were constructed for each test, but to conserve space only 5% values are reported.

Tables 8.1 and 8.2 show the 5% critical values simulated for sample sizes 50, 100, and 200, and the asymptotic values.

Table 8.3 illustrates the stability of the 5% critical values using 6,000 simulations. 5% critical values were obtained from each of the AR(1) models $x_t = \phi x_{t-1} + \varepsilon_t$, with ϕ taking the values −0.9, −0.6, −0.3, 0.0, 0.3, 0.6, and 0.9, for sample size $n = 100$. Again, with this sample size, 1,000 replications of the AR(1) model with $\phi = 0.6$ were constructed, and the tests applied with the critical values obtained from the previous simulation. The 'power' or percent rejection in each case is shown in table 3. Thus the table 8.1 at the top left means that data from an AR(1) with $\phi = 0.6$ led to rejection of the linearity null hypothesis on 4.2% of occasions by the NEURAL1 test using the critical value obtained from the AR(1)

Table 8.2. *Critical values (5%) for Block2 models[a]*

Test	n = 50	n = 100	n = 200
NEURAL1	7.72	7.47	7.98
	(7.81)	(7.81)	(7.81)
NEURAL2	7.74	7.52	7.85
	(7.81)	(7.81)	(7.81)
KEENAN	3.70	3.84	4.00
	(4.06)	(3.94)	(3.84)
TSAY1	2.84	2.63	2.69
	(2.82)	(2.70)	(2.60)
TSAY2	2.23	1.86	1.74
	(2.03)	(1.80)	(1.67)
WHITE1	23.45	18.58	16.90
	(15.51)	(15.51)	(15.51)
WHITE2	19.36	17.42	16.74
	(15.51)	(15.51)	(15.51)
WHITE3	14.98	14.86	15.49
	(15.51)	(15.51)	(15.51)
MCLEOD	31.41	31.29	31.19
	(31.41)	(31.41)	(31.41)
RESET1	3.49	3.77	3.92
	(4.06)	(3.94)	(3.84)
RESET2	3.57	3.71	3.82
	(3.84)	(3.84)	(3.84)

[a] The first number in each cell is the simulated critical value from Model4, $y_t = 0.4y_{t-1} - 0.3y_{t-2} + \varepsilon_t$, with 6,000 replications, and the second number in parentheses is the asymptotic critical value.

Table 8.3. *Size of tests and similarity[a]*

Test	−0.9	−0.6	−0.3	0.0	0.3	0.6	0.9	Asymp.
NEURAL1	4.2	4.2	4.0	4.9	4.8	5.6	4.0	4.2
NEURAL2	4.2	4.1	4.1	4.8	4.7	5.6	3.5	4.0
KEENAN	3.0	3.5	3.5	3.5	4.0	5.1	8.9	3.1
TSAY1	3.0	3.5	3.5	3.5	4.0	5.1	8.9	3.2
TSAY2	8.0	7.4	7.6	9.6	7.8	6.1	5.1	10.1
WHITE1	2.5	3.0	5.3	4.5	5.4	4.1	2.4	3.6
WHITE2	4.5	4.1	4.9	4.5	4.2	4.1	3.6	7.4
WHITE3	4.0	4.0	4.7	4.4	5.1	4.1	3.9	3.8
MCLEOD	4.4	4.4	4.4	4.4	4.4	4.4	4.7	4.4
RESET1	3.7	3.7	3.7	3.7	4.1	5.0	4.9	3.5
RESET2	3.9	3.7	3.6	3.6	3.7	5.2	5.9	3.6

[a] (1) Each column shows the power (%) for AR(1) $y_t = 0.6y_{t-1} + \varepsilon_t$, using the 5% critical values simulated with $y_t = \phi y_{t-1} + \varepsilon_t$, $\phi = -0.9, -0.6, -0.3, 0.0, 0.3, 0.6, 0.9$. The last column shows the power for the AR(1) using 5% asymptotic critical values. (2) 95% confidence interval of the observed size is (3.6, 6.4), since if the true size is s the observed size follows the (asymptotic) normal distribution with mean s and variance $s(1 - s)/1,000$. (3) Sample size = 100, replications = 1,000.

Table 8.4. *Power for Block1 and bivariate models*[a]

Test	AR	BL	TAR	SGN	NAR	SQ	EXP
NEURAL1	5.2	58.0	79.8	98.9	20.4	100.0	100.0
	(4.5)	(55.6)	(77.2)	(98.6)	(18.3)	(100.0)	(100.0)
NEURAL2	5.4	57.1	80.7	99.3	19.9	100.0	100.0
	(4.4)	(55.5)	(78.3)	(98.7)	(17.9)	(100.0)	(100.0)
KEENAN	4.7	39.3	4.2	15.0	23.8	100.0	100.0
	(4.2)	(38.1)	(3.9)	(13.8)	(21.8)	(100.0)	(100.0)
TSAY1	4.7	39.3	4.2	15.0	23.8	100.0	100.0
	(4.3)	(38.2)	(3.9)	(13.9)	(21.8)	(100.0)	(100.0)
TSAY2	4.8	47.7	2.7	5.2	2.8	66.9	36.2
	(8.4)	(55.5)	(5.2)	(8.4)	(5.4)	(72.8)	(42.8)
WHITE1	5.2	97.5	4.1	7.7	4.5	75.5	71.1
	(3.2)	(96.8)	(3.0)	(5.9)	(3.2)	(71.5)	(66.4)
WHITE2	5.8	95.9	5.9	12.8	5.7	67.0	62.7
	(7.0)	(96.8)	(7.4)	(14.3)	(7.4)	(70.5)	(66.2)
WHITE3	5.5	99.5	4.2	12.1	5.5	79.5	60.0
	(5.2)	(99.4)	(3.9)	(11.7)	(5.1)	(78.9)	(59.6)
MCLEOD	4.6	90.2	5.0	3.8	4.8	23.0	15.0
	(4.9)	(90.3)	(5.2)	(3.9)	(5.0)	(23.2)	(15.0)
RESET1	5.0	38.5	6.1	32.3	23.5	96.0	61.2
	(3.9)	(36.0)	(5.1)	(30.3)	(21.3)	(95.9)	(58.7)
RESET2	5.2	40.2	7.0	32.7	26.2	95.4	59.5
	(3.4)	(36.2)	(5.3)	(29.5)	(22.1)	(95.2)	(56.0)
BDS	(6.1)	(98.8)	(14.5)	(12.6)	(5.9)	(70.6)	(49.6)

[a] Power using 5% critical value simulated with AR(1) model is shown (except for BDS test), and power using 5% asymptotic critical value is shown in parentheses. Sample size = 200, replications = 1000. The results for BDS test in Liu (1990) with embedding dimension $m = 2$ and $\varepsilon = (0.8)^6$ are reported here. The series were divided by the range of the data before applying the BDS tests.

model with $\phi = -0.9$. With 1,000 replications, the 95% confidence intervals of these powers (sizes) around the hoped for value of 5%, is 3.6 to 6.4%. The final column shows the rejection percentage of H_0 using the asymptotic 5% critical values. Virtually all of the neural network test results lie in the 95% confidence interval for size, as do all of the values in the column when $\phi = 0.6$. However, some tests do not perform satisfactorily, particularly the KEENAN, TSAY1, TSAY2, and WHITE1 tests, suggesting either that the critical values are not stable across simulation models or that the asymptotic theory is not appropriate with a sample size of 100. Because of its complexity, the BDS test was not calculated in this particular exercise.

Table 8.4 shows the power of the tests using the Block1 models plus the bivariate models with $v = 1$ and with sample size $n = 200$. The first number is the power using the 5% critical value from the simulation of the AR(1) model with $\phi = 0.6$ and below it, in parentheses, is the power

Table 8.5. *Power for Block2 models[a]*

Test	Model1	Model2	Model3	Model4	Model5	Model6
NEURAL1	5.0	17.2	98.1	5.8	94.2	85.8
	(5.3)	(18.1)	(98.4)	(6.2)	(94.5)	(86.4)
NEURAL2	4.8	16.8	99.2	5.5	91.7	82.7
	(4.8)	(17.0)	(99.2)	(5.5)	(92.0)	(82.9)
KEENAN	4.3	15.8	87.9	4.5	86.5	83.0
	(4.3)	(16.5)	(88.3)	(4.9)	(86.8)	(83.7)
TSAY1	5.0	18.8	99.2	6.0	98.8	89.8
	(5.0)	(19.7)	(99.3)	(6.0)	(98.8)	(90.0)
TSAY2	3.6	18.4	97.1	5.6	98.8	92.4
	(3.8)	(18.9)	(97.2)	(6.1)	(98.9)	(92.8)
WHITE1	37.2	42.3	84.4	6.3	100.0	97.2
	(42.7)	(50.0)	(88.6)	(9.3)	(100.0)	(98.4)
WHITE2	22.7	34.3	81.9	6.1	100.0	97.6
	(28.0)	(41.9)	(86.2)	(8.6)	(100.0)	(98.7)
WHITE3	21.7	28.8	88.9	5.0	100.0	99.4
	(21.6)	(28.7)	(88.9)	(5.0)	(100.0)	(99.4)
MCLEOD	6.2	8.9	37.1	4.6	79.4	69.0
	(5.9)	(8.8)	(36.1)	(4.2)	(79.3)	(68.9)
RESET1	4.0	16.9	86.2	4.1	78.2	66.5
	(4.1)	(16.9)	(86.6)	(4.2)	(78.2)	(67.0)
RESET2	4.0	16.1	86.7	4.1	77.3	62.9
	(3.8)	(16.1)	(86.7)	(4.0)	(77.2)	(62.7)
BDS	(7.3)	(8.1)	(32.8)	(6.1)	(99.4)	(97.1)

[a] Power using 5% critical value simulated with Model4 (AR(2)) is shown (except for BDS test), and power using 5% asymptotic critical value is shown in parentheses. Sample size = 200, replications = 1000. The results for BDS test in Liu (1990) with embedding dimension $m = 2$ and $\varepsilon = (0.8)^6$ are reported here. The series were divided by the range of the data before applying the BDS tests.

using the 5% theoretical critical value. A great deal of variation in the power of the tests is observed. Most tests have reasonable power for the bilinear model, but the White dynamic information matrix test and McLeod–Li test are particularly successful. For the threshold autoregressive data, only the neural network test has any success and similarly for the SGN autoregressive model, where the neural network test is very powerful, the RESET test has some power, and the other tests have very little power. The particular nonlinear AR model used (NAR) is difficult to detect, as the power is low for all the tests. The bivariate cases are discussed later.

Table 8.5 shows similar power results (5% critical value, $n = 200$) for the Block2 series. To provide the simulation critical values, 6,000 simulations of Model4, an AR(2) model, were generated. 1,000 replications for each of the six models were generated, and the simulated and

Table 8.6. *Power vs. sample size for Block1 and bivariate model*[a]

	AR	BL	TAR	SGN	NAR	SQ	EXP
			NEURAL1				
$n = 50$	4.8	27.7	32.2	49.0	9.0	100.0	98.7
$n = 100$	5.6	43.0	54.3	84.1	13.8	100.0	100.0
$n = 200$	5.2	58.0	79.8	98.9	20.4	100.0	100.0
			TSAY1				
$n = 50$	4.6	25.3	9.6	17.8	12.2	100.0	99.3
$n = 100$	5.1	33.0	7.5	16.1	16.8	100.0	100.0
$n = 200$	4.7	39.3	4.2	15.0	23.8	100.0	100.0
			WHITE3				
$n = 50$	5.0	81.0	4.8	6.0	4.3	20.1	17.8
$n = 100$	4.1	98.0	4.0	8.8	5.2	47.1	32.6
$n = 200$	5.5	99.5	4.2	12.1	5.5	79.5	60.0
			RESET2				
$n = 50$	4.6	24.9	10.6	21.5	12.5	69.6	47.1
$n = 100$	5.2	33.9	8.6	26.5	18.2	84.9	57.0
$n = 200$	5.2	40.2	7.0	32.7	26.2	95.4	59.5

[a] Power using 5% simulated critical values is shown. Replications = 1000, sample size $n = 50, 100, 200$.

asymptotic 5% critical values were used to obtain estimated powers. Model1 is linear, being an MA(2), and most tests reject the null near the correct 5% rate, but the WHITE tests reject frequently, indicating dynamic misspecification, as an MA(2) is only poorly approximated by an AR(2) model. All of the tests have good power against the bilinear models and the nonlinear moving average model (Model3), but little power against the heteroskedastic MA model (Model2).

Similar tables were constructed for sample sizes 50 and 100 but are not shown in full detail. Tables 8.6 and 8.7 show power against sample size for four of the tests, NEURAL1, TSAY1, WHITE3, and RESET2. The results are generally as expected, with power increasing as sample size increases for most of the nonlinear models.

From these results and others not shown some general comments can be made:

(i) NEURAL1 and NEURAL2 are virtually the same; thus the extra work for NEURAL2 is probably not worthwhile.
(ii) TSAY1 and TSAY2 both have nuisance parameter problems; TSAY1 seems to be better.
(iii) The WHITE tests all have nuisance parameter problems; WHITE3 is generally better.
(iv) RESET1 and RESET2 are virtually identical, RESET2 being marginally better.

Table 8.7. *Power vs. sample size for Block2 models*[a]

	Model1	Model2	Model3	Model4	Model5	Model6
			NEURAL1			
$n = 50$	5.7	10.7	49.3	4.9	64.3	52.0
$n = 100$	5.2	13.2	84.5	5.5	86.2	73.1
$n = 200$	5.0	17.2	98.1	5.8	94.2	85.8
			TSAY1			
$n = 50$	6.3	10.6	51.5	4.4	74.7	56.8
$n = 100$	4.6	12.4	85.6	4.5	94.5	78.1
$n = 200$	5.0	18.8	99.2	6.0	98.8	89.8
			WHITE3			
$n = 50$	6.3	13.0	30.2	4.6	79.2	71.4
$n = 100$	10.8	18.6	58.3	5.8	99.6	95.6
$n = 200$	21.7	28.8	88.9	5.0	100.0	99.4
			RESET2			
$n = 50$	5.9	6.9	34.5	6.1	36.0	35.4
$n = 100$	3.3	11.5	60.5	6.2	56.7	49.8
$n = 200$	4.0	16.1	86.7	4.1	77.3	62.9

[a] Power using 5% simulated critical values is shown. Replications = 1000, sample size $n = 50, 100, 200$.

(v) The McLeod–Li test is generally weak compared to the alternatives.
(vi) The TSAY1 test is virtually always more powerful than the KEENAN test.
(vii) The BDS test is good with bilinear data and has average power in other cases.
(viii) No single test was uniformly superior to the others.

Table 8.8 shows the power of four tests in the bivariate case $y_t = x_t^2 + \varepsilon_t$, $\varepsilon_t \sim N(0, \sigma^2)$, where $x_t = 0.6x_{t-1} + e_t$, $e_t \sim N(0, 1)$. The three values of σ chosen were 1, 5, and 20, corresponding to approximate signal-to-noise ratios:

σ	1	5	20
var(x^2)/var(ε)	7.0	0.28	0.019

Not all situations were simulated. The NEURAL1 and TSAY1 tests are quite powerful in most situations, and have some power even with signal-to-noise ratios around 2% (corresponding to $\sigma = 20$).

Table 8.9 shows the same information for the bivariate model $y_t = \exp(x_t) + \varepsilon_t$, $\varepsilon_t \sim N(0, \sigma^2)$, where x_t is as before and the same set of σ values are used. The signal-to-noise ratios are

Table 8.8. *Power vs. sample size and noise for bivariate model (SQ)[a]*

	$\sigma = 1$	$\sigma = 5$	$\sigma = 20$
	NEURAL1		
$n = 50$	100.0		
$n = 100$	100.0		
$n = 200$	100.0	100	30
	TSAY1		
$n = 50$	100.0		
$n = 100$	100.0		
$n = 200$	100.0	100	42
	WHITE3		
$n = 50$	20.1		
$n = 100$	47.1		
$n = 200$	79.5	5	9
	RESET2		
$n = 50$	69.6		
$n = 100$	84.9		
$n = 200$	95.4	66	17

[a] Power using 5% simulated critical values is shown. 1,000 replications for $\sigma = 1$, 100 replications for $\sigma = 5, 20$. Not all situations were simulated. Sample size $n = 50, 100, 200$.

σ	1	5	20
var $(\exp(x))/\text{var}(\varepsilon)$	2.16	0.086	0.005

The results are similar to the previous case. It is encouraging that the NEURAL and TSAY tests have such good power in many cases.

6.   TESTS ON ACTUAL ECONOMIC TIME SERIES

To illustrate the behavior of the various tests for actual economic time series, five economic series were analyzed. The series were first transformed to produce stationary sequences. If z_t is the original series, $y_t = \Delta z_t$ or $y_t = \Delta \log z_t$ is fitted by $AR(p)$, where p is determined by the SIC criterion [Sawa (1978) Hannan (1980)]. Thus $X_t = (y_{t-1}, \ldots, y_{t-p})'$. For the moment, we assume the absence of ARCH effects. We discuss the consequences of ARCH below.

Table 8.10 shows asymptotic p-values for the various tests; a low p-value suggests rejection of the null. As the neural network test involves

Table 8.9. *Power vs. sample size and noise for bivariate model (EXP)*[a]

	$\sigma = 1$	$\sigma = 5$	$\sigma = 20$
	NEURAL1		
$n = 50$	98.7		
$n = 100$	100.0		
$n = 200$	100.0	99	25
	TSAY1		
$n = 50$	99.3		
$n = 100$	100.0		
$n = 200$	100.0	97	24
	WHITE3		
$n = 50$	17.8		
$n = 100$	32.6		
$n = 200$	60.0	15	4
	RESET2		
$n = 50$	47.1		
$n = 100$	57.0		
$n = 200$	59.5	24	10

[a] Power using 5% simulated critical values is shown. 1000 replications for $\sigma = 1$, 100 replications for $\sigma = 5, 20$. Not all situations were simulated. Sample size $n = 50, 100, 200$.

randomly selecting the Γ parameters, it can be repeated several times with different draws. We obtain p-values for several draws of the neural network test, but these are not independent. Despite dependence, the Bonferroni inequality provides an upper bound on the p-value. Let $P_1, \ldots, P_m$ be p-values corresponding to m test statistics, and $P_{(1)}, \ldots, P_{(m)}$ the ordered p-values. The Bonferroni inequality leads to rejection of H_0 at the α level if $P_{(1)} \leq \alpha/m$, so $\alpha = mP_{(1)}$ is the Bonferroni bound. A disadvantage of this simple procedure is that it is based only on the smallest p-value, and so may be too conservative. Holm (1979). Simes (1986), Hommel (1988, 1989), and Hochberg (1988) discuss improved Bonferroni procedures. Hochberg's modification is used here, defined by the rule 'reject H_0 at the α level if there exists a j such that $P_{(j)} \leq \alpha/(m - j + 1), j = 1, \ldots, m$'. The improved Bonferroni bound is $\alpha = \min_{j=1,\ldots,m}(m - j + 1)P_{(j)}$.

In table 10, $m = 5$ neural network tests are conducted for each series. Both simple and Hochberg Bonferroni bounds are reported. These results illustrate a cautionary feature of the neural network test, as quite different p-values are found for different draws. Thus, if one had relied on a single use of the test, quite different conclusions would be possible, just as would be true if one relied on single but different standard tests for nonlinearity. Use of Bonferroni procedures with multiple draws of

Table 8.10. *Tests on actual economic time series*[a]

Test	(1)	(2)	(3)	(4)	(5)
NEURAL	0.288	0.001	0.024	0.000	0.070
	0.277	0.001	0.024	0.000	0.975
	0.289	0.243	0.024	0.000	0.623
	0.283	0.003	0.024	0.000	0.749
	0.283	0.053	0.024	0.000	0.451
Simple Bonferroni	1.387	0.003	0.118	0.000	0.349
Hochberg Bonferroni	0.289	0.003	0.024	0.000	0.349
KEENAN	0.533	0.000	0.727	0.001	0.888
TSAY	0.532	0.000	0.726	0.001	0.066
WHITE1	0.131	0.127	0.423	0.014	0.059
WHITE2	0.116	0.134	0.423	0.015	0.061
WHITE3	0.254	0.000	0.579	0.001	0.012
MCLEOD	0.743	0.000	0.960	0.000	0.025
RESET1	0.122	0.004	0.040	0.000	0.682
RESET2	0.118	0.004	0.040	0.000	0.675
BISPEC	0.001	0.000	0.000	0.014	0.403
BDS	0.724	0.000	0.921	0.000	0.060

[a] (1) US/Japan exchange rate, $y_t = \Delta\log z_t$, AR(1), 1974:1–1990:7, monthly, 199 observations; (2) US three-month T-bill interest rate, $y_t = \Delta z_t$, AR(6); (3) US M2 money stock, $y_t = \Delta\log z_t$, AR(1); (4) US personal income, $y_t = \Delta\log z_t$, AR(1); (5) US unemployment rate, $y_t = \Delta z_t$, AR(4). Series (2), (3), (4), and (5) are monthly for 1959:1–1990:7 with 379 observations. Series (1) and (2) are not seasonally adjusted while the others are. BDS test: embedding dimension $m = 2$, $\varepsilon = (0.8)^6$.

the neural network test appears to provide useful insurance against using a single test that by chance looks in the wrong direction.

Although the results illustrate application of several tests for neglected nonlinearity to various economic time series, we must strongly emphasize that they do not by themselves provide definitive evidence of neglected nonlinearity in mean. The reason is that, unlike the situation found in our simulations, we cannot be sure that there are not other features of the series studied that lead to the observed results; in particular, the possible presence of ARCH effects cannot be ruled out.

Generally, ARCH will have one of two effects: either it will cause the size of the test to be incorrect while still resulting in a test statistic bounded in probability under the null (as for the neural network, KEENAN, TSAY, WHITE, and RESET tests), or it will directly lead (asymptotically) to rejection despite linearity in mean (as with the McLeod and Li, BDS, and Bispectrum tests). Two remedies suggest themselves: one may either (1) remove the effect of ARCH, or (2) remove ARCH. The first is relevant to tests with adversely affected size. The effect of ARCH can be removed using a heteroskedasticity-consistent covariance matrix estimator in computing the various test statistics. The approach of Wooldridge (1990) may prove especially useful. The second approach is possible whenever one is confidently able to specify the form of the ARCH effect. However, use of a misspecified ARCH model in the procedure will again adversely affect the size of the test. Furthermore, if the alternative is true, the fitted ARCH model can be expected to absorb some or perhaps even much of the neglected nonlinearity. Conceivably, this could have adverse impact on the power of the procedure. Consideration of either of these remedies raises issues that take us well beyond the scope of the present study; their investigation is left to other work.

Thus, we can take the empirical results of this section as indicating that either neglected nonlinearity or ARCH may be present in series (1)–(5), but that further investigation is needed. The results of this paper are only a first step on the way to analyzing methods capable of unambiguous detection of neglected nonlinearity in real-world settings.

7.   CONCLUSIONS

As with any Monte Carlo study, results obtained can be considerably influenced by the design of the experiment, in this case the choice of nonlinear models and choices made in constructing the test studied. Assuming that the models chosen are of general interest, we have found that several of the tests studied here have good power against a variety of alternatives, but no one of these tests dominates all others. The new neural network test considered in this paper appears to perform as well as or better than standard tests in certain contexts. Application of the tests studied here to actual economic time series suggests the possible presence of neglected nonlinearity, but further investigation is needed to separate out possible effects of ARCH.

REFERENCES

Ashley, R., D. Patterson, and M. Hinich, 1986, A diagnostic test for nonlinear serial dependence in time series fitting errors. *Journal of Time Series Analysis* 7, 165–178.

Bierens, H.J., 1987, ARMAX model specification testing, with an application to unemployment in the Netherlands, Journal of Econometrics 35, 161–190.

1990, A consistent conditional moment test of functional form, *Econometrica* 58, 1443–1458.

Bierens, H.J. and J. Hartog, 1988, Nonlinear regression with discrete explanatory variables, with an application to the earnings function, *Journal of Econometrics* 38, 269–299.

Brock, W.A., W.D. Dechert, and J.A. Scheinkman, 1986. A test for independence based on the correlation dimension, Discussion paper (Department of Economics, University of Wisconsin, Madison, WI).

Chan, W.S. and H. Tong, 1986. On tests for nonlinearity in time series analysis, *Journal of Forecasting* 5, 217–228.

Diaconis, P. and M. Shahshahani, 1984, On nonlinear functions of linear combinations, *SIAM Journal on Scientific and Statistical Computing* 5, 175–191.

Engle, R.F., 1982, Autoregressive conditional heteroskedasticity with estimates of the variance of U.K. inflations, *Econometrica* 50, 987–1007.

Friedman, J.H. and W. Stuetzle, 1981, Projection pursuit regression, *Journal of the American Statistical Association* 76, 817–823.

Gallant, A.R. and H. White, 1992, On learning the derivatives of an unknown mapping with multilayer feedforward networks, *Neural Networks* 5, 129–138.

Granger, C.W.J. and A.P. Anderson, 1978, *An introduction to bilinear time series models* (Vandenhoech und Ruprecht, Göttingen).

Hannan, E.J., 1980. The estimation of the order of an ARMA process, *Annals of Statistics* 8, 1071–1081.

Hinich, M.J., 1982. Testing for gaussianity and linearity of a stationary time series, *Journal of Time Series Analysis* 3, 169–176.

Hochberg, Y., 1988, A sharper Bonferroni procedure for multiple tests of significance, *Biometrika* 75, 800–802.

Holm, S., 1979, A simple sequentially rejective multiple test procedure, *Scandinavian Journal of Statistics* 6, 65–70.

Hommel, G., 1988, A stagewise rejective multiple test procedure based on a modified Bonferroni test, *Biometrika* 75, 383–386.

    1989, A comparison of two modified Bonferroni procedures, *Biometrika* 76, 624–625.

Hornik, K., M. Stinchcombe, and H. White, 1989, Multi-layer feedforward networks are universal approximators, *Neural Networks* 2, 359–366.

    1990, Universal approximation of an unknown mapping and its derivatives using multi-layer feedforward networks, *Neural Networks* 3, 551–560.

Huber, P., 1985, Projection pursuit, *Annals of Statistics* 13, 435–475.

Jones, L.K., 1991, A simple lemma on greedy approximation in Hilbert space and convergence rates for projection pursuit regression and neural network training. *Annals of Statistics*, forthcoming.

Keenan, D.M., 1985, A Tukey nonadditivity type test for time series nonlinearity, *Biometrika* 72, 39–44.

Lapedes, A. and R. Farber, 1987, Nonlinear signal processing using neural networks, Paper presented at the IEEE conference on neural information processing system – Natural and synthetic.

Liu, Tung, 1990, How to decide if a series is chaotic: The estimation of correlation exponent, Ph.D. thesis (University of California, San Diego, CA).

McLeod, A.I. and W.K. Li, 1983, Diagnostic checking ARMA time series models using squared residual autocorrelations, *Journal of Time Series Analysis* 4, 169–176.

Ramsey, J.B., 1969. Tests for specification errors in classical linear least squares regression analysis, *Journal of the Royal Statistical Society* B 31, 350–371.

Rumelhart, D.E., G.E. Hinton, and R.J. Williams, 1986, Learning internal representations by error propagation, in: D.E. Rumelhart and J.L. McClelland, eds., *Parallel distributed processing: Explorations in the microstructures of cognition* – 1 (MIT Press, Cambridge, MA) 318–362.

Sawa, T., 1978, Information criteria for discriminating among alternative regression models, *Econometrica* 46, 1273–1291.

Simes, R.J., 1986, An improved Bonferroni procedure for multiple tests of significance, *Biometrika* 73, 751–754.

Stinchcombe, M. and H. White, 1989, Universal approximation using feedforward networks with non-sigmoid hidden layer activation functions, in: *Proceedings of the international joint conference on neural networks, Washington, DC* (IEEE Press, New York, NY) I: 613–618.

1991, Using feedforward network to distinguish multivariate populations, Discussion paper (University of California, San Diego, CA).

Subba Rao, T. and M. Gabr, 1980. A test for linearity of stationary time series, *Journal of Time Series Analysis* 1, 145–158.

1984, An introduction to bispectral analysis and bilinear time series models, Lecture notes in statistics 24 (Springer-Verlag, New York, NY).

Tong, H., 1983. *Threshold models in nonlinear times series analysis* (Springer-Verlag, New York, NY).

Tsay, R.S., 1986. Nonlinearity tests for times series, *Biometrika* 73, 461–466.

White, Halbert, 1987, Specification testing in dynamic models, in: T.F. Bewley, ed., *Advances in econometrics, Fifth world congress* – 1 (Cambridge University Press, Cambridge) 1–58.

1989a, Some asymptotic results for learning in single hidden layer feedforward network models, *Journal of the American Statistical Association* 84, 1003–1013.

1989b, An additional hidden unit test for neglected nonlinearity in multilayer feedforward networks, in: *Proceedings of the international joint conference on neural networks, Washington, DC* (IEEE Press, New York, NY) II: 451–455.

White, Halbert, 1990, Connectionist nonparametric regression: Multilayer feedforward networks can learn arbitrary mappings. *Neural Networks* 3, 535–550.

1992, *Estimation, inference and specification analysis* (Cambridge University Press, New York, NY).

Wooldridge, J.M., 1990, A unified approach to robust, regression-based specification tests, *Econometric Theory* 6, 17–43.

CHAPTER 9

Modeling Nonlinear Relationships Between Extended-Memory Variables*

C. W. J. Granger**

Many economic variables have a persistence property which may be called extended memory and the relationship between variables may well be nonlinear. This pair of properties allow for many more types of model misspecification than encountered with stationary or short-memory variables and linear relationships, and misspecifications lead to greater modeling difficulties. Examples are given using the idea of a model being balanced.

Alternative definitions of extended memory are considered and a definition based on the properties of optimum forecasts is selected for later use. An important but not necessarily pervasive class of processes are those that are extended-memory but whose changes are short-memory. For this case, called I(1), standard cointegration ideas will apply.

Tests of linearity are discussed in both the I(1) case, where a possible group of tests is easily found, and more generally. Similarly, methods of building nonlinear models based on familiar techniques, such as neural networks and projection pursuit, are briefly considered for I(1) and the more general case. A number of areas requiring further work in this new area are emphasized.

Keywords: Extended memory, nonlinear, integrated processes, balanced equations.

1. INTRODUCTION

The objective of this paper is to relate the apparently widely held belief that relationships between economic variables are often nonlinear with the empirically observed fact that many macro-economic time series

* Econometrica, 63, 1995, 265–279.

** This paper was given as the Fisher-Schultz Lecture to the European Meeting of the Econometric Society in Uppsala, Sweden, August, 1993. The work was supported in part by NSF Grants SES 9023037 and 9308295.

have a smoothness property which, for the moment, will just be called "persistence." Economic theorists have particularly discussed nonlinear dynamic relationships, such as cost and production functions and hysterisis and boundary (full employment or capacity) effects. Econometricians have not ignored nonlinearities in their modeling procedures but have not, until recently, placed much emphasis on it. The emphasis has been on explaining major properties of series, such as trends, seasonals, and unit roots in means and, separately, possibly also in variances. When specifying a linear model, econometricians have not invariably found the theorists' models completely helpful as these theoretical models are often imprecise about features such as what lag to use and also ignore important properties of the series, such as the existence of seasonal or deterministic trend components. On some occasions the theoretical models are completely unhelpful, such as when a crucial assumption is that the variables are deterministic, which is likely to be quite contrary to the beliefs of most econometricians.

The econometrician is thus faced with the question of how to specify nonlinear models, and there are many possible approaches that have been suggested by statisticians and others, as described in Granger and Teräsvirta (1993). However, most of the well-developed techniques for testing for linearity and then modeling nonlinearity are designed for use with stationary variables. If one just tries to use them with trending or persistent variables the results can be quite unsatisfactory, for reasons that are outlined below.

This paper attempts to illustrate some of the problems that arise when persistent variables are considered, and to offer some solutions. It will be seen that many unanswered questions remain in what is a very new area. The approach taken is usually a descriptive tutorial rather than being completely rigorous so that ideas can be made as transparent as possible.

It is difficult to discuss nonlinearity without at least mentioning chaos these days, although I take the position that chaos theory is fascinating mathematics but of no practical relevance in economics (see Granger (1992, 1994)). For my purposes it will be sufficient to consider just deterministic maps of the form $X_{t+1} = f(X_t)$, $X_0 \in A$, which generate series X_t having the white noise property corr $(X_t, X_{t-k}) = 0$, $k \neq 0$, if correlation is estimated from a very long series using the standard estimate. Such processes will be called "white chaos," an example being that generated by $X_{t+1} = 4X_t(1 - X_t)$, $t > 0$, $0 < X_0 < 1$. These processes share a common property with the i.i.d. process; they each have a flat spectrum, but have many other nonshared properties. In some sciences nonlinear dynamics is almost equated with various types of chaotic processes, whereas this is not the case in econometrics, where stochastics is emphasized.

2. BALANCE OF AN EQUATION WITH SIMPLE NONLINEARITY

The situation to be considered will be when there is a single dependent variable Y_t, and an explanatory variable vector

$$\underline{W}_t = \left(Y_{t-j}, j = 1, \ldots, p, \underline{X}_{t-j}, j = 1, \ldots, p\right)$$

where the X's are the actual economic explanatory variables. Although $\underline{W}_t$ is designated as being at time t, for notational convenience, it is in fact based on an information set known at time $t - 1$. Thus, only single equation forecasting or "reduced-form" models are investigated. Considering the conditional mean

$$E[Y_t|\underline{W}_t] = \underline{\beta}'\underline{W}_t + g(\underline{W}_t),$$

the relationship between W_t and Y_t is linear in mean if $g = 0$; otherwise it is nonlinear in mean. Obvious questions that arise are how to test for linearity and, if required, how to specify and build suitable nonlinear models. These questions will be discussed later and the answers will be shown to partly depend on the properties of the series involved.

To make a number of important points it is convenient to initially consider just a pair of economic series Y_t, X_t, with conditional mean

$$E[Y_t|X_t] = g(X_t, \theta),$$

where θ is some set of parameters. For the moment, X_t is taken not to be lagged Y_t. To give a precise situation to consider, suppose one fits the regression

$$Y_t = g(X_t, \theta) + e_t \tag{2.1}$$

and estimates θ by OLS, so that it is desirable that the residuals e_t have "good" properties in some sense. To ask if (2.1) is a sensible specification it is important to consider the balance of the equation. An equation will be called balanced if the major properties of Y_t are available amongst the right-hand side explanatory variables and there are no unwanted strong properties on that side. This is easiest to explain in a linear case. Suppose that variables Y_t, X_t can have either or both of properties P_s and P_w, where P_s dominates P_w. Thus, if one variable has P_s, the other P_w, then their (weighted) sum will also have P_s; if both have P_w but not P_s, then their sum will not have P_s. Examples of strong (P_s) properties are trends in mean, strong seasonals (very high spectrum values at seasonal frequencies), unit roots, various forms of long memory (as discussed below), and strong heteroskedasticity. A trending or unit root process has a strong property compared to a stationary process, which has a relatively weak property P_w.

If the linear equation is considered,

$$Y_t = \alpha + \beta X_t + e_t,$$

then the equation is balanced if both Y_t, X_t have the same P_s or if both have just the same P_w property. As a simple example, suppose Y_t, X_t have linear trends in mean, so that

$$Y_t = b_1 t + \tilde{Y}_t,$$

$$X_t = b_2 t + \tilde{X}_t,$$

where $\tilde{Y}_t$, $\tilde{X}_t$ are both stationary; then $Y_t = \alpha + \beta X_t + e_t$ is, at least, balanced. If $b_1 \neq 0$, $b_2 = 0$, then Y_t has an important property that is not explained by the X; similarly if $b_1 = 0$, $b_2 \neq 0$, then one is trying to explain a nontrending variable (Y) by a trending one (X), and so the sensible regression result would be $\beta = 0$. The equation being balanced is just a necessary condition for a good specification and is certainly not a sufficient condition. Now consider a simple nonlinear specification involving the same trending series

$$Y_t = \alpha + \beta(X_t^2) + e_t.$$

In this case Y_t contains a linear trend t, but X_t^2 contains a quadratic trend t^2, and the equation as specified cannot be balanced.

If there are two explanatory variables, the situation becomes more complicated, and thus more interesting. Consider the linear regression

$$Y_t + \alpha + \beta_1 X_{1t} + \beta_2 X_{2t} + e_t.$$

The equation is balanced if

   (i) Y_t has P_s, one X has P_s;
   (ii) Y_t does not have P_s, neither X has P_s;
   (iii) Y_t does not have P_s, both X's have P_s but there is a linear combination $X_{1t} + A X_{2t}$ which does not have P_s. This corresponds to the cointegration and common features literature. For example, if Y_t has no trend in mean, $X_{jt} = b_j t + $ stationary, then $X_{1t} - A X_{2t}$ is stationary, with no trend if $A = b_1/b_2$.

When considering nonlinear model specification we will naturally encounter an instantaneous transformation $g(Y_t)$ of a variable Y_t. To consider the balance of equations involving such terms the question that immediately arises is, if Y_t has a property P, does $g(Y_t)$ have the same property? It is fairly easy to answer these questions if P is a trend in mean, but less easy for other properties, as will be shown.

As a simple example of the question, consider whether the square of white chaos is necessarily white chaos. For example, it is shown in Liu, Granger, and Heller (1992) that if X_t is generated by

$$X_{t+1} = 4X_t(1 - X_t),$$

then corr $(X_t, X_{t-k}) = 0$ for all $k \neq 0$ and so is white chaos, but that

$$\text{corr}\left(X_t^2, X_{t-1}^2\right) = -0.22,$$

which is (significantly) nonzero, so that X_t^2 is not white chaos. Thus, the property of whiteness has been lost when a function of the series has been taken. It follows that a relationship of the form $Y_t = g(X_t)$ where Y_t, X_t are both white chaos may not be properly specified, as both sides may not be white. The same problem would not be true if both Y_t and X_t were i.i.d., for example, provided a constant is included in the relationship.

The question of balance is related to the familiar one of misspecification. The point that will be made here, and in the next section, is that the opportunities for unbalanced equations, that is for misspecification, are greatly enhanced when one is dealing with nonlinear functions of variables having a persistence property.

One strong property that will be emphasized in this discussion is that of a unit root. Essentially, a unit root process is one that has changes that have only weak properties, such as some form of stationarity. The usual notation is that Y_t is I(1), that is integrated of order one and thus has a unit root; $\Delta Y_t \equiv X_t$ is I(0), that is integrated of order zero. Clearly the definition has no meaning unless one defines I(0) carefully. There are several different definitions, of varying degrees of practical usefulness. For the moment, just two will be considered; a third will be added later.

(i) Theoretical Definition of I(0)

X_t is I(0) if it is strictly stationary and has a spectrum bounded above and below away from zero at all frequencies. An example is an invertible moving average model of finite order with an i.i.d. input, or a stationary autoregressive model such as

$$A(B)X_t = \varepsilon_t$$

where ε_t is i.i.d. zero mean and finite variance, $A(z) = 0$ has all roots outside the unit circle, and B is the backward (lag) operator. These are linear models that are strictly stationary; many nonlinear models can also produce series with this property (although their spectral properties are less clear). The corresponding I(1) Y_t is such that $\Delta Y_t = X_t$, so that

$$Y_t = \sum_{j=1}^{t} X_{t-j} + Y_0 \tag{2.2}$$

is an equivalent representation for Y_t.

(ii) Practical Definition of I(0)

Suppose that e_t is zero mean white noise, so that $\mathrm{corr}(e_t, e_s) = 0$, $t \neq s$, and that X_t is generated by a stationary autoregressive model

$$A(B)X_t = e_t;$$

then X_t is I(0). This is a very weak form of the definition, as it just says that there is a linear filter that takes X_t to white noise (the use of autoregressive models rather than ARMA is not important here and is just for convenience). As e_t has not been assumed homoskedastic, X_t need not even be second-order stationary, according to this definition. However, it is clearly a more practical definition, as it potentially can be tested on a sample of a relevant size.

Again, it is convenient to concentrate on a special case, that of a random walk, which under the two definitions is defined as

$$\Delta Y_t = \varepsilon_t, \quad \varepsilon_t \text{ i.i.d., zero mean, and}$$

$$\Delta Y_t = e_t, \quad e_t \text{ white noise, zero mean,}$$

with starting values Y_0. From (2.2), with X_t replaced by ε_t, several properties of a "pure random walk" can be deduced, including

P$_1$: $\rho_k = \mathrm{corr}(Y_t, Y_{t-k}) \approx 1$, all k;
P$_2$: variance $Y_t = ct$, $c = $ constant;
P$_3$: Y_t has no attractor.

P$_2$ follows directly from (2.2) and P$_1$ because ρ_k is the ratio of two terms both $0(t)$. A process may be said to have an attractor if there is some mechanism that produces an inclination to return to some value – usually its mean. A random walk has no attractor. For a discussion, see Granger and Hallman (1991a). It should be noted that any unit root process, with strictly stationary differences will have properties P$_1$ to P$_3$, at least asymptotically.

If ε_t is replaced by e_t, does the corresponding random walk necessarily have these properties? The answer will be seen to be possibly not. To illustrate this, some simple examples are considered.

EXAMPLE 1 (Product of I.I.D. and Random Walk): Let

$$\theta_t = \varepsilon_t Y_t. \tag{2.3}$$

$\Delta Y_t = \eta_t$, ε_t, η_t are each i.i.d., zero mean, and are independent. Y_t starts at time $t = 0$. Then $E[\theta_t] = 0$, and $\mathrm{cov}(\theta_t, \theta_{t-k}) = \mathrm{cov}(\varepsilon_t, \varepsilon_{t-k}) \cdot \mathrm{cov}(Y_t, Y_{t-k}) = 0$, $k \neq 0$ so that θ_t is white noise, as here defined. Now define $W_t = \Sigma_{j=1}^{t-1} \theta_{t-j}$.

Then W_t is I(1) and $\Delta W_t = \theta_t$ is I(0) using the weak definition, and W_t is a form of random walk. However

$$\text{variance } W_t = \sum_j \text{var}\,\theta_{t-j} = \sigma_\varepsilon^2 \sum_j E[Y_{t-j}^2] = \sigma_\varepsilon^2 \sigma_\eta^2 \sum_{j=1}^{t}(t-j) = 0(t^2),$$

so that W_t is a random walk that does not obey property P_2.

When asking questions about the properties of $g(X_t)$ given a property of X_t, one obvious known fact is that if X_t is strictly stationary,
then so is $g(X_t)$ – to make discussion simpler, means will always be
assumed to exist. But what if X_t is merely I(0) using the weaker
definition?

Consider θ_t given by (2.3), which is white noise and so weak I(0), but
on squaring

$$\theta_t^2 = \varepsilon_t^2 Y_t^2 = \sigma_\varepsilon^2 Y_t^2 + (\varepsilon_t^2 - \sigma_\varepsilon^2)Y_t^2. \tag{2.4}$$

The second term is still white noise, but the first will be shown to be I(1),
in Example 2. Thus, a simple function of I(0) is I(1). The reason is, of
course, that θ_t is very strongly heteroskedastic and this particular function emphasizes this property.

EXAMPLE 2 (Square of a Pure Random Walk): Let $Y_t = Y_{t-1} + \varepsilon_t$, ε_t be
i.i.d., zero mean, and

$$S_t = Y_t^2 = (Y_{t-1} + \varepsilon_t)^2 = Y_{t-1}^2 + 2\varepsilon_t Y_{t-1} + \varepsilon_t^2$$

so that

$$S_t = S_{t-1} + \sigma_\varepsilon^2 + e_t$$

where

$$e_t = 2\varepsilon_t Y_{t-1} + (\varepsilon_t^2 - \sigma_\varepsilon^2).$$

Thus, e_t is white noise, in that corr$(e_t, e_s) = 0$, $t \neq s$, and so S_t is a random
walk with drift. A little algebra shows that variance (S_t) is a quadratic in
t, and so is $0(t^2)$. It is thus found that S_t has properties P_1, P_3 of a pure
random walk but not P_2.

If follows, for example, that if X_t, Y_t are each pure random walks, then
a model specification

$$Y_t = AX_t^2 + e_t$$

is not balanced, as Y_t has no drift and a variance $0(t)$ whereas X_t^2 does
have a drift and a variance of $0(t^2)$.

In Granger and Hallman (1991b) and Ermini and Granger (1993) a
number of other such examples are considered, both using statistical

theory, assuming the s_t are Gaussian and expanding functions in terms of Hermite polynomials, and by simulations. Amongst these results two that are used below are:

Logistic function $g(z) = (1 + e^{-z})^{-1}$. If Y_t is a pure random walk, then $g(Y_t)$ has properties P_1, P_3 but not P_2 as $\text{var}(g(Y_t))$ is a constant. $g(Y_t)$ can still be thought of as being I(1).

Cosine function. Cosine (Y_t) is found not to have any of the properties of a unit root process; its autocorrelations decline exponentially as lag increases, its variance is bounded, and it has a mean which is an attractor. In a Box-Jenkins analysis it would be identified as a stationary AR(1) process. In fact, $E(\cos(Y_{t+k}) \mid Y_t) = \alpha^k \cos Y_t$, some $|\alpha| < 1$.

A conclusion from these considerations is that the standard I(0), I(1) classifications are not sufficient to handle all situations when dealing with nonlinear functions. They, or the I(d) generalization including fractional differencing, may or may not be helpful in any particular case. Essentially the problem is that they are too linear in form, differencing is a linear operation, and if Y_t is I(1) it is the linear sum of I(0) components, as in (2.2). The standard tools, such as autocorrelations and linear regression coefficients are of limited usefulness, and new, more general tools are being developed. Joint normality of Y_t, Y_s is also impossible, particularly if a nonlinear relationship of the form

$$Y_t = h(Y_{t-1}) + e_t$$

is considered; e_t can be Gaussian but Y_t will not be. Obviously nonlinearity between Y_t, Y_s implies nonnormality but nonnormality does not necessarily imply nonlinearity.

In terms of balance, if

$$Y_t = g(X_t) + e_t,$$

one needs $g(X_t)$ to balance with Y_t, but the situation is complicated by the fact that $g(X_t)$ need not have the same properties as X_t. The problem is clearly seen with (2.4), if Y_t is thought to be I(1). This will put severe constraints on what functions $h(Y_{t-1})$ can be used and achieve balance. These questions of balance do not just impinge on econometricians plying their trade but also on economic theorists, who cannot ignore major properties of actual economic variables when selecting functional forms to insert into their theories, if these theories are to be used as the basis for empirical models.

3. ALTERNATIVE DEFINITIONS OF EXTENDED MEMORY

Consider a single series Y_t and an information set I_t: $Y_{t-j}, j \geq 0$, which is just the past and present of that series. Suppose that the unconditional mean of the series exists and is a constant, so that $E[Y_t] = m$. If the unconditional mean is some deterministic function of time $\mu(t)$, this will be assumed to have been subtracted from the series. Denote the condition h-step forecast in mean as

$$E[Y_{t+h}|I_t] = f_{t,h}, \quad h > 0.$$

DEFINITION 1: Y_t will be called *short memory in mean* (abbreviated as SMM) if $f_{t,h}$ tends to a constant m as h becomes large. Thus, as one forecasts into the distant future, the information available in I_t comes progressively less relevant.

More formally, using a squared norm, Y_t is SMM if

$$E\left[|f_{t,h} - m|^2\right] < c_h$$

where c_h is some sequence that tends to zero as h increases; for example, if $c_h = 0(h^{-\theta})$, $\theta > 0$, it can be said to be SMM of order θ. Such definitions are used when discussing mixingales as in McLeish (1978), Gallant and White (1988), and Davidson (1994). It might be noted, for example, that a white chaos process is SMM, as is a fractionally integrated $I(d)$ process, for $0 < d < 1$.

DEFINITION 2: If Y_t is not SMM, so that $f_{t,h}$ is a function of I_t for all h, it will be called "extended memory in mean," denoted EMM. Thus, as one forecasts into the distant future, values known at present will generally continue to be helpful. (The term "long memory in mean" might be a better one but it has a technical meaning in the time series literature, applying to processes whose spectrum tends to infinity as frequency goes to zero which essentially need not apply here and is too linear for our purposes. The designation "long memory" is usually associated with the $I(d)$, $0 < d < 1$ processes, as their autocorrelations decline with lag at a rate slower than the exponential, but they still decline. This designation has little operational significance.) For those familiar with the concept of mixing, SMM may be thought of as being equivalent to "mixing in mean" and EMM to "nonmixing in mean." EMM can be considered a nonlinear form of persistence.

A special case is if the optimum forecast turns out to be linear

$$f_{t,h} = \sum_{j=0}^{t} \beta_{h,j} Y_{t-j}$$

and the sequence $\beta_{h,j}$ does not tend to zero as h increases for all j; then Y_t can be called *linear EMM* (i.e. LEMM).

It might be noted that it is now possible to define a new form of I(1) process. Y_t might be called an extended I(1) process if ΔY_t is SMM. It should be noted that an EMM process need not be I(1), using any of the I(1) definitions. Clearly a pair of extended I(1) series can be called cointegrated if a linear combination is SMM.

There are some obvious relationships between the definitions, such as:

(i) If a process is I(1) it is necessarily LEMM.
(ii) If it is LEMM, it is not necessarily I(1).
(iii) If it is LEMM, it is EMM.
(iv) If it is EMM, it is not necessarily LEMM.

Some examples are as follows:

(i) A pure random walk, having iid inputs, is both I(1) and LEMM.
(ii) If $Y_t = \Sigma_{j=1}^{t-1}(\varepsilon_{t-j})^j + \varepsilon_t$, where ε_t is i.i.d. $N(0, 1)$ so that $E[Y_{t+h}Y_t] = \Sigma_j E[\varepsilon_{t-j}^{2j+h}] > 0$ if h is even, there will exist a linear forecasting relationship.
(iii) No example is needed as the relationship is obvious.
(iiii) No example is needed as the relationship is obvious.
(iv) If $Y_t = \varepsilon_t + \varepsilon_{t-1}\varepsilon_{t-2} + \varepsilon_{t-2}\varepsilon_{t-3}\varepsilon_{t-4} + \ldots + \Pi_{j=0}^k \varepsilon_{t-k-j} + \ldots$ which has the property $\text{corr}(Y_{t+h}, Y_t) = 0$, any $h > 0$, there are no linear relationships, but $\text{corr}(Y_{t+h}, Y_t Y_{t-h+1}) \neq 0$ so there is a nonlinear relationship (not a linear one) which can be exploited to produce forecasts.

The models in (ii), (iv) are hardly likely to be of relevance in economics, and are constructed just to illustrate possible properties of nonlinear processes.

Returning to instantaneous transformations and the effects on properties, the following rules are likely to be adequate working rules when trying to build models, although proofs of their correctness are not always available. The rules apply to $\theta_t = g(Y_t)$, and, as before, means are assumed to exist.

RULE 1: If Y_t is SMM and homoskedastic, then θ_t is SMM.

The rule is not quite correct, as an EMM component can be embedded deep in the joint distribution of the process, which is recovered by an appropriate function. It is clear that if Y_t is SMM but has strong heteroskedasticity, θ_t can be EMM, as Example 1 above showed.

If $g(z)$ is a continuous function obeying a Lipchitz condition of order one, so that essentially it increases less quickly than linear, then Kuan and White (1993) have shown that if Y_t is SMM θ_t will also be SMM regardless of homoskedasticity (they used "mixingale" instead of SMM in the statement). Examples of such functions are $\log z, z^k, k < 1$, and the logistic.

RULE 2: If Y_t is EMM and $g(z)$ is a monotone, nondecreasing function, then θ_t is EMM. Examples are: $g(z)$ is a polynomial in z or the logistic function.

RULE 3: If Y_t is EMM but $g(z)$ is not monotonic nondecreasing, then θ_t may be SMM. An example is $\theta_t = \text{cosine } (Y_t)$ where Y_t is a pure random walk, with $N(0,\sigma^2)$ innovations as $E[\cos(Y_{t+h}) \mid Y_t] = e^{-h\sigma^2} \cos Y_t \equiv f_{t,h}$ which goes to zero as h increases.

EXAMPLE 3 (Logistic Function): Let $\theta_t = \phi(Y_t)$ where Y_t is a pure random walk and $\phi(z) = (1 + e^{-z})^{-1}$ which has derivative $\phi'(z) = e^{-z}(1 + e^{-z})^{-2}$. It should be noted that $\phi(z)$ has the appearance of a probability distribution function and so is monotonic nondecreasing but bounded, and $\phi'(z)$ is shaped like a Gaussian probability density function, being positive and increasing smoothly from zero to a peak and then falling back to zero.
  Writing

$$\theta_t = \phi(Y_{t-1} + \varepsilon_t) \quad \text{where } \varepsilon_t \text{ is i.i.d. } N(0,1)$$
$$= \phi(Y_{t-1}) + \varepsilon_t \phi'(Y_{t-1} + r_t)$$

by Taylor's expansion where r_t is the residual. Thus

$$\Delta\theta_t = e_t,$$

where e_t is SMM as ϕ' (SMM) is SMM from Rule 3 and ε_t times SMM is SMM, but with a very special type of heteroskedasticity, having virtually zero variance for $|Y_{t-1}|$ large enough.
  A simple analogy of the three rules can be given if $Y_t = t$, a linear trend. Clearly a square and a logistic of this series produces "trends," that is monotonic increasing variables, whereas cosine t is oscillating and would not be considered a "trend" by most economists.

4. TESTING FOR LINEARITY

There are many tests of the null hypothesis that a relationship is linear in mean, some of which are discussed in Granger and Teräsvirta (1993) and Lee, White, and Granger (1993). The only type considered here asks if the model

$$Y_t = \mu + \underline{\beta}'\underline{W}_t + g(\underline{W}_t) + e_{1t} \tag{4.1}$$

for some specific nonlinear function $g(z)$ fits better than the linear model

$$Y_t = \mu_0 + \underline{\beta}_0'\underline{W}_t + e_{0t} \tag{4.2}$$

using again the notation $\underline{W}_t$: $(Y_{t-j}, \underline{X}_{t-j}, j = 1, \ldots, p)$.

The test consists of running the regression

$$e_{0t} = \mu_1 + \underline{\beta}_1'\underline{W}_t + g(\underline{W}_t) + \varepsilon_t \tag{4.3}$$

and then performing a Lagrange multiplier test based on nR^2 which is χ^2 for an appropriate degree of freedom under H_0, where R^2 is then determined by (4.3) and n is the sample size.

Define $f_{t-1,1} = Y_t - e_{0t}$ in (4.2) which is the one-step linear forecast; then for the Reset test of linearity

$$g(W_t) = \alpha_2 f^2 + \alpha_3 f^3 + \cdots + \alpha_q f^q \tag{4.4}$$

where $f \equiv f_{t-1,1}$. Similarly, the neural network test introduced in Lee et al. (1993) has

$$g(\underline{W}_t) = \sum_{j=1}^{q} \alpha_j \phi(\underline{\gamma}_j'\underline{W}_t) \tag{4.5}$$

where $\phi(z)$ is the logistic function and the γ terms are either estimated or chosen at random. Several other tests also can be expressed in the form (4.1) to (4.3). However, they are all based on an assumption that the series involved are stationary or in practice at least SMM. They are clearly going to work poorly, if at all, with trending, I(1) or EMM variables. As an example, suppose that Y_t and components of W_t are I(1), so that (4.2) is balanced and that e_{0t} is SMM. It follows that (4.3) will be unbalanced if the null hypothesis is not true, and $g(W_t)$ may be EMM of some form and generally will not balance with the linear component. The test will be biased against rejection of H_0. If (4.2) is not balanced, e_{0t} will be poorly estimated and the regression (4.3) will not be a standard LM test. It is clear that many of the standard tests for linearity cannot be directly applied to I(1) or EMM variables.

A solution is available in one simple case, which will be illustrated when the vector of explanatory variables $\underline{X}_t$ in $\underline{W}_t$ has just two components X_{1t}, X_{2t}. Further, suppose that Y_{t1}, X_{1t}, X_{2t} are all I(1), in that their changes are SMM, and also that Y_t is cointegrated with each of the X's, so that there exist constants A_1, A_2 such that $Z_{it} = Y_t - A_i X_{it}, i = 1,2$ are SMM. Denote by $\underline{Z}_t$ the vector having Z_{1t}, Z_{2t} as components.

Tests of linearity can now be conducted by comparing the nonlinear specification

$$\Delta Y_t = \mu + \underline{\delta}'\underline{Z}_{t-1} + \underline{\beta}'\Delta\underline{W}_t + g(\Delta\underline{W}_t, \underline{Z}_{t-1}) + e_t \tag{4.6}$$

to the linear form

$$\Delta Y_t = \mu_0 + \underline{\delta}_0'\underline{Z}_{t-1} + \underline{\beta}_0'\underline{W}_t + e_{0t} \tag{4.7}$$

by performing the regression

$$e_{0t} = \mu_t + \underline{\delta_1'}\underline{Z}_{t-1} + \underline{\beta_1'}\Delta\underline{W}_1 + g(\Delta\underline{W}_t, \underline{Z}_{t-1}) + \varepsilon_t \qquad (4.8)$$

and doing an LM test based on R^2 from (4.8). Now every component in (4.7) is SMM and, provided the functions of SMM variables are also SMM, the equations will be balanced and the residuals can be expected to have reasonable properties. It is worth noting that the Z's are not identified, as any linear combination of cointegrating relationships is also cointegrating. However, if $\underline{Z}$ enters $g()$ in a linear form, such as $\underline{\gamma}'\underline{Z}_{t-1}$ then this lack of identification is irrelevant. This occurs naturally in tests such as Reset and the neural network test, which is an advantage over some other tests. An equation such as (4.7) can be thought of as a nonlinear error-correction model. The constraints that $\underline{X}$ has just two components and there are just two cointegrations are easily removed but produce more complicated sets of possibilities that are not discussed here. The generalization to nonlinear cointegration is also possible, so that Y_t, X_t are both I(1) but $Z_t = Y_t - h(X_t)$ is SMM for some nonlinear function h, as discussed in Granger and Hallman (1991a). The analysis can proceed as above using the new Z terms and X_t replaced by $h(X_t)$.

When all variables are I(1), it is seen that presently available tests can be adapted quite easily and used with some confidence. It is not clear what happens if variables are EMM but not I(1). As before, most tests have to be adapted before they can be used. It is perhaps helpful first to consider a further example.

EXAMPLE 4: As before, let Y_t be a pure random walk, so that $Y_t = Y_{t-1} + \varepsilon_t$, i.i.d. $N(0,\sigma^2)$, and let $S_t = (Y_t + m)^2$, $R_t = (Y_t + m)^4$ where m is a constant. Some simple algebra produces

$$S_t = S_{t-1} + \text{SMM}_1 + C_1,$$

$$R_t = R_{t-1} + \sigma^2 S_t + \text{SMM}_2 + C_2,$$

where SMM denotes some SMM variable and where C_1, C_2 are constants. It follows that one can write either

$$\Delta^2 R_t = \text{SMM}$$

so that $R_t = $ I(2) or

$$R_t = f(R_{t-1}) + \text{SMM} \qquad (4.9)$$

where

$$f(R) = R + 6\sigma^2 R^{1/2}$$

so that R_t obeys essentially a nonlinear AR(1) model. As $|f(R)/R| > 1$ this NLAR model is nonstable, in fact probably explosive. For the series

R_t this suggests that the generalized differencing $R_t - f(R_{t-1})$ will produce an SMM variable, although so will second differencing.

More generally, the question naturally arises of whether such a generalized difference is available for any EMM variable. Ideally, this would be defined by

$$\Box R_t = R_t - f(R_{t-j}, j = 1, \ldots, q)$$

and q would be finite, preferably small. Although such a difference is not always available in theory, in practice there may be an adequate approximation. What is required is that if

$$E[Y_{t+1}|Y_{t-1}] = f_{t,1},$$

then $f_{t,1}$ is "near-epoch dependent," as defined in Gallant and White (1988), in that its dependence on earlier Y's is very small compared to recent ones. (Similar ideas appear in Ibragimov (1962).) Formally $|E[f_{t,1} | Y_{t-j}, j = 1, \ldots, q] - f_{t,1}|^2 < cq^{-\theta}$ for some $c, \theta > 0$. If $\Box$ exists it can be used to replace changes throughout the previous discussion, with the Z's being used as before. A generalization of cointegration can also be considered but will not be discussed.

5. NONLINEAR MODELING

Many of the lessons that were apparent from consideration of the testing question continue when one thinks about how to produce satisfactory specifications for a nonlinear model. Suppose Y_t is I(1) and it is to be explained by $\underline{X}_{t-1}$, each component of which is I(1), with $\underline{Z}_t$ the vector of cointegrations between Y_t and $\underline{X}_t$ or between the components of X_t; then define $\Delta \tilde{W}_t = (\Delta Y_{t-j}, \Delta \underline{X}_{t-j}, j = 1, \ldots, p, \underline{Z}_{t-1})$ (ΔW is here used as a notation for the vector, not as an operator on a vector). A number of important nonlinear models can then be written in the form

$$\Delta Y_t = \mu + \underline{\gamma}_0' \Delta \tilde{W}_t + \sum_{j-1}^{q} \alpha_t \phi_j \left(\underline{\gamma}_j \Delta \tilde{W}_t \right) + e_t. \tag{5.1}$$

It is seen that these models contain a linear part and also a linear sum of nonlinear functions of linear combinations of the explanatory variables. If the $\phi()$ functions are sines and cosines, one gets the so-called flexible Fourier form model; if $\phi()$ is the logistic it is a particular type of neural network model; if the $\phi_j()$ are estimated nonparametrically it produces "projection pursuit;" and if the nonlinear term is the product of a logistic function of $\underline{\delta}' \tilde{W}_t$ and a linear function $\underline{\gamma}_1 \Delta \tilde{W}_t$ one gets a regime switching model. This last model could give a different linear relationship between ΔY_t and $\Delta \tilde{W}_t$ at the peaks and troughs of the business cycles, for example. All of these models are discussed in Granger and Teräsvirta (1993).

In theory, for any particular set of parameters, the nonlinear functions of SMM variables have to be tested to check that they are SMM, but how this test is to be performed is not yet clear. Similarly, if variables are EMM but not I(1), a correct, balanced nonlinear modeling procedure still has to be determined.

The best strategy to use for nonlinear modeling of nonstationary variables is quite complicated, perhaps more difficult even than for stationary variables and certainly more difficult than for linear models, as discussed in Granger (1993). An added difficulty is that many of the nonlinear procedures, such as projection pursuit or neural network modeling, are designed to be very flexible and so data-mining may well occur. It is important both to test for linearity and to compare post-sample performances. It is recommended that heteroskedasti-crobust tests of linearity be used whenever possible. A number of methodological issues need to be considered. For example, the "general-to-simple" strategy, in which one starts with as general a specification as possible and then simplifying is after testing parameter estimates, is technically sound for linear models but is extremely difficult to implement for nonlinear ones because the range of possible models is immense. It is also unfortunately true that many of the models of form (5.1) contain many parameters or have shapes that have no economic interpretation. In most cases, these models should be thought of as approximations to some probably more complicated true generating mechanism but estimates of derivatives, partial derivatives, and elasticities can be derived from them. The regime switching models will often have a more immediate interpretation.

6. CONCLUSIONS

The success of the modeling questions discussed in this paper can only be decided from their use on realistic problems. Some interesting applications are beginning to appear, particularly a nonlinear form of the error correction model relating a pair of interest rates $R_t(i)$, $R_t(j)$ of different maturity periods. Suppose that these interest rates are each I(1), with their spread $S_t = R_t(i) - R_t(j)$ being I(0), as found in Hall, Anderson, and Granger (1992). Now consider an error-correction model, the first equation of which is

$$\Delta R_t(i) = \gamma_i(Z_{t-d})S_{t-1} + \beta_i(Z_{t-d})\Delta R_{t-1}(i) + \theta_i(Z_{t-d})\Delta R_{t-1}(i)$$
$$(+ \text{ other lagged } \Delta R(i), \Delta R(i) + e_{it})$$

where Z_t is a variable that causes the parameters of the model to change value, either suddenly if $\gamma(Z) = \bar{\gamma}$, $Z > Z_0$, $\gamma(Z) = \tilde{\gamma}$, $Z \leq Z_0$, giving a threshold switching model, or smoothly such as if $\gamma(Z)$ is a constant times a logistic function in Z, giving a smooth switching model. These models have been considered by Balke and Fomby (1992), Anderson (1992), and Kunst (1992) who found that, using $Z_{t-1} \equiv S_{t-1}$, they achieved models that both fitted data better in sample and better in forecast post-sample compared to a constant parameter model.

Dept. of Economics, University of California – San Diego, La Jolla, CA 92093, U.S.A.

REFERENCES

ANDERSON, H. M. (1992): "Nonlinearities and Shifts in Macroeconomic Regimes," Ph.D. Thesis, Economics Department, University of California, San Diego.

BALKE, N. S., AND T. B. FOMBY (1992): "Threshold Cointegration," Working Paper, Economics Department, Southern Methodist University.

DAVIDSON, J. (1994): *Stochastic Limit Theory.* Oxford: Oxford University Press.

ERMINI, L., AND C. W. J. GRANGER (1993): "Some Generalizations on the Algebra of I(1) Processes," *Journal of Econometrics*, 58, 369–384.

GALLANT, A. R., AND H. WHITE (1988): *A Unified Theory of Estimation and Inference for Nonlinear Dynamics Models.* New York: Basil Blackwell.

GRANGER, C. W. J. (1992): "Comment on Two Papers Concerning Chaos and Statistics by S. Chatterjee and M. Ylmaz and by M. Berliner," *Statistical Science*, 7, 69–122.

——— (1993): "Strategies For Modeling Non-linear Time Series Relationships," *Economic Record*, 69, 233–238.

——— (1994): "Is Chaotic Economic Theory Relevant for Economics?" to appear, *Journal of International and Comparative Economics.*

GRANGER, C. W. J., AND J. J. HALLMAN (1991a): "Long-Memory Processes With An Attractor," *Oxford Bulletin of Economics and Statistics*, 53, 11–26.

——— (1991b): "Non-Linear Transformations of Integrated Time Series," *Journal of Time Series Analysis*, 12, 207–224.

GRANGER, C. W. J., AND T. TERÄSVIRTA (1993): *Modeling Nonlinear Economic Relationships.* Oxford: Oxford University Press.

HALL, A. D., H. M. ANDERSON, AND C. W. J. GRANGER (1992): "A Cointegration Analysis of Treasury Bill Yields," *Review of Economics and Statistics*, 74, 116–126.

IDRAGIMOV, I. A. (1962): "Some Limit Theorems for Stationary Processes," *Theory of Probability and Its Applications*, 7, 349–383.

KUAN, C-M, AND H. WHITE (1993): "Adaptive Learning With Nonlinear Dynamics Driven By Dependent Processes," Working Paper, University of California, San Diego.

KUNST, R. M. (1992): "Threshold Cointegration in Interest Rates," Working Paper, Institute for Advanced Studies, Vienna.

LEE, T-W, H. WHITE, AND C. W. J. GRANGER (1993): "Testing for Neglected Nonlinearity in Time Series Models: A Comparison of Neural Network Methods and Alternative Tests," *Journal of Econometrics*, 56, 264–290.

LIU, T., C. W. J. GRANGER, AND W. P. HELLER (1992): "Using the Correlation Exponent To Decide if An Economic Series is Chaotic," *Journal of Applied Econometrics*, 75, 525–540.

MCLEISH, D. L. (1978): "A Maximal Inequality and Dependent Strong Laws," *Annals of Probability*, 3, 829–839.

CHAPTER 10

Semiparametric Estimates of the Relation Between Weather and Electricity Sales*

Robert F. Engle, C. W. J. Granger, John Rice, and Andrew Weiss**

A nonlinear relationship between electricity sales and temperature is estimated using a semiparametric regression procedure that easily allows linear transformations of the data. This accommodates introduction of covariates, timing adjustments due to the actual billing schedules, and serial correlation. The procedure is an extension of smoothing splines with the smoothness parameter estimated from minimization of the generalized cross-validation criterion introduced by Craven and Wahba (1979). Estimates are presented for residential sales for four electric utilities and are compared with models that represent the weather using only heating and cooling degree days or with piecewise linear splines.

1. INTRODUCTION

The relationship between temperature and electricity usage is highly nonlinear, because electricity consumption increases at both high and low temperatures. Estimating this relationship, however, is complicated by the need to control for many other factors such as income, price, and overall levels of economic activity and for other seasonal effects such as vacation periods and holidays. A second complicating factor is the form in which the data on sales are collected: Meter readers do not record all households on the same day and for the same period. A third factor is the possibility of unobserved changes in behavior or other causal variables that will introduce serial correlation into the disturbances.

* Journal of the American Statistical Association, 81, 1986, 310–320.
** The authors acknowledge financial support from National Science Foundation Grants SES-80-08580, SES-82-09221, MCS-79-01800, and EPRIRP1922. Much of the research for this article was carried out in collaboration with Kenneth Train and Patrice Ignelzi of Cambridge Systematics and Ahmad Farruqi of the Electric Power Research Institute. The authors are indebted to these collaborators for many helpful suggestions and contributions, but they retain responsibility for remaining errors and omissions.

This article introduces a combined parametric and nonparametric regression procedure that easily accommodates linear transformations of the data and therefore provides a convenient framework for analysis of this problem. The approach is based on smoothing splines that can be estimated in a regression context by an algorithm that looks like ridge regression or mixed regression. Shiller (1973, 1984) has used similar ideas in distributed lag models and functional form estimation. In our case, however, the smoothness parameter is estimated from the data set. Recent papers by Wahba (1984) and Green, Jennison, and Seheult (1985) are similar in spirit to this article. Ansley and Wecker (1983) and Wecker and Ansley (1983) recast the problem in a state space formulation.

The method should be contrasted with textbook econometric methodology in which the functional form is assumed to be known a priori. In conventional practice, not only the parameter values but the functional form must be estimated from the data. This involves a series of specification tests or other procedures to select the appropriate model, which is then estimated on the same data set. The method should be compared with statistical approaches to functional form estimation such as kernel estimation or its many variants with variable bandwidths [e.g., see the conference proceedings edited by Gasser and Rosenblatt (1979) and the review by Collomb (1981); these methods are invariably applied only in bivariate iid situations without the complications inherent in this application].

The problem of relating temperature and electricity sales is very important, since *weather adjusted sales* (the sales that would have occurred if the weather had been normal) are frequently used in determining electricity prices in regulatory proceedings. Similar series are often used in utility econometric models. Extreme temperatures are invariably responsible for extreme electricity demand; therefore they are critical in forecasting capacity requirements, and any nonlinearities may have great importance. In spite of the millions of dollars riding on such adjustments, the methodologies now in use are rather simplistic. For example, it is common to assume that the relationship is V shaped, with a minimum at 65° and differing high and low temperature slopes estimated as the coefficients of *cooling degree days* and *heating degree days*. This contrasts with theoretical arguments from thermodynamics, which observe that the heat loss through a barrier is proportional to the fourth power of the temperature differential, and the more practical observation that when the heater or air conditioner is operating full time, there can be no further effect of more severe weather. For a survey of the methods in use, see Electric Power Research Institute (EPRI, 1981, 1983) and Lawrence and Aigner (1979).

In Section 2 the nonparametric procedure is described and extended as required for this application. In Section 3 the data are discussed, and Section 4 gives the results. Section 5 concludes.

2. THE NONPARAMETRIC REGRESSION MODEL

To describe the nonparametric procedure, initially suppose that the data consist of the n pairs (x_i, y_i), $i = 1, \ldots, n$, generated by the simple model

$$y_i = f(x_i) + e_i, \tag{2.1}$$

where f is a function on the interval (a, b) and the residuals have the properties

$$E(e_i) = 0, \quad \text{var}(e_i) = \sigma^2, \quad E(e_i e_j) = 0, \quad i \neq j, \text{all } i. \tag{2.2}$$

Rather than considering some arbitrarily chosen parametric form, such as $f(x) = a + bx + cx^2$, the problem considered here is to estimate $f(x)$ by a nonparametric function. We consider, as an approximation to the true $f(x)$, the cubic smoothing spline $g(x)$, which solves for given $\lambda \geq 0$,

$$\min \frac{1}{n} \sum_{i=1}^{n} (y_i - g(x_i))^2 + \lambda \int_a^b [g''(u)]^2 \, du. \tag{2.3}$$

The first term penalizes lack of goodness of fit of the function to the data, and the second penalizes lack of smoothness of the approximating function. The solution to (2.3) is a unique, smooth piecewise cubic polynomial with a knot or breakpoint at every data point x_i. By varying λ, the smoothness of $g(x)$ is varied. At the extremes, when λ goes to infinity, the function is forced to be linear over the whole range of x values and is then the best least squares line through the data. When $\lambda \to 0$, y tends to be an interpolating function for the data, fitting every data point exactly.

Smoothing splines were originally proposed by Whittaker (1923), Schoenberg (1964), and Reinsch (1967); analysis of their statistical properties, when f and g are periodic, appears in Wahba (1975) and Rice and Rosenblatt (1981). An analysis of the nonperiodic case appears in Rice and Rosenblatt (1983); they also showed that the same approach can be used to estimate the derivatives of f. The important question of how λ should be chosen was discussed by Craven and Wahba (1979), Rice (1984), and Speckman (1985). This question is discussed further later.

In our application, direct observation of $f(\ ) + \varepsilon_i$ is not possible because of the presence of billing cycles, which will be explained in detail in Section 3. Rather, linear functionals of f, $l_i(f)$, are modeled (in our case, certain weighted sums from different time periods). We also wish to include other variables in the model in a parametric form. With these modifications, the model becomes

$$y_i = l_i(f) + z_i'\gamma + \varepsilon,$$

where γ is a vector of coefficients of the parametric functions. Our estimate is the g and $\hat{\gamma}$ that minimize

$$\frac{1}{n}\sum_{i=1}^{n}(y_i - l_i(g) - z_i'\hat{\gamma})^2 + \lambda\int_a^b [g''(u)]^2\, du.$$

We call this the semiparametric regression model.

The character of the function g minimizing this expression is not clear, although in the case of direct observation of f, $l_i(f) = f(t_i)$, the solution is easily seen to be a natural cubic spline. Various schemes might be tried for computing an approximation to the solution of this extremal problem; we chose to approach it in the following way: The range $[a, b]$ is discretized into a fairly large number of intervals and f is correspondingly represented by its values $\delta_1, \ldots, \delta_m$ at the midpoints of those intervals. We note that this discretization is fairly fine, so the smoothing is still being controlled through the parameter λ and not by coarse discretization. Clearly, other approximations could be used as well.

The model thus becomes in matrix form,

$$\mathbf{Y} = \mathbf{L}\delta + \mathbf{Z}\gamma + \varepsilon \tag{2.4}$$

or $\mathbf{Y} = \mathbf{X}\beta + \varepsilon$, where $\mathbf{X}$ and β are partitioned in the obvious way. The integrated squared second derivative of f is approximated by a sum of squared second-difference quotients, and our approximate solution becomes the δ and γ that minimize

$$(1/n)\|\mathbf{Y} - \mathbf{L}\delta - \mathbf{Z}\gamma\|^2 + \lambda\|\mathbf{V}\delta\|^2,$$

where $\mathbf{V}$ is the second differencing operator and each row of $\mathbf{L}$ gives the proportion of billed customer days in each temperature interval. See Section 3 for more details. Using the partitioning referred to before and letting $\mathbf{U}$ be a matrix consisting of $\mathbf{V}$ bordered by 0's, the solution is the vector β minimizing

$$(1/n)\|\mathbf{Y} - \mathbf{X}\beta\|^2 + \lambda\|\mathbf{U}\beta\|^2. \tag{2.5}$$

The disturbances in (2.4) in practice often have serial correlation, and therefore a further modification is necessary. In particular, we are interested in the case of a first-order autoregressive model for the ε_i:

$$\varepsilon_i = \rho\varepsilon_{i-1} + \eta_i.$$

The model can be easily transformed to have serially uncorrelated disturbances by quasi-differencing all of the data assuming ρ to be known. (In fact, this is also an estimation procedure, as the maximum likelihood estimate of ρ under Gaussian assumptions is simply the value that minimizes the remaining sum of squared residuals.)

The solution to (2.5) is easily shown to be

$$\hat{\beta} = (\mathbf{X}'\mathbf{X} + \lambda\mathbf{U}'\mathbf{U})^{-1}\mathbf{X}'\mathbf{Y}, \tag{2.6}$$

where $\mathbf{X}$ and $\mathbf{Y}$ are now transformed by quasi-differencing. This formula also occurs in mixed and ridge regression. Substituting (2.4) into (2.6) indicates that the estimator is biased, with the bias increasing as λ increases. The variance of the estimate conditional on particular values of λ and ρ is given by

$$\operatorname{var}(\beta) = \sigma^2 (\mathbf{X'X} + \lambda \mathbf{U'U})^{-1} \mathbf{X'X} (\mathbf{X'X} + \lambda \mathbf{U'U})^{-1}. \tag{2.7}$$

It is immediately seen that this variance decreases as λ increases. Thus there is the classical trade-off between bias and variance, and the choice of λ witl depend on the relative weights placed on these quantities.

The equivalent choice in standard econometrics is the richness of the parameterization, in terms of the number of explanatory variables included in the regression. With this analogy in mind, it is useful to consider the equivalent degrees of freedom of an estimate. Denote

$$\mathbf{A}(\lambda) = \mathbf{X}(\mathbf{X'X} + \lambda \mathbf{U'U})^{-1} \mathbf{X'} \tag{2.8}$$

so that $\hat{\mathbf{y}} = \mathbf{A}(\lambda)y$ and $\mathbf{e} = (\mathbf{I} - \mathbf{A}(\lambda))y$. The degrees of freedom in a standard parametric model would be $\operatorname{tr}(\mathbf{I} - \mathbf{A}(\lambda))$, corresponding to a regression with $\operatorname{tr}(\mathbf{A})$ regressors. We define the equivalent number of parameters by $\operatorname{tr}(\mathbf{A}(\lambda))$ and the equivalent degrees of freedom by $\operatorname{tr}(\mathbf{I} - \mathbf{A}(\lambda))$.

It can be shown that $\hat{\beta}(\lambda)$ is a consistent estimate of β under the assumptions

$$\lambda_n / n \to 0 \tag{2.9}$$

and

$$X_n^T X_n / n \to M > 0, \tag{2.10}$$

and assumption (2.10) can certainly be weakened. Furthermore, under (2.10), the value of $\lambda_n - \lambda_n^*$ say – that minimizes the mean squared error of $\hat{\beta}(\lambda)$ is of order $n^{1/2}$ and therefore satisfies (2.9).

To use (2.7) to estimate the variance of $\hat{\beta}$, an estimate is required for σ^2. Following a suggestion by Craven and Wahba (1979), the estimate used here is

$$\sigma^2 = \mathbf{e'e} / \operatorname{tr}(\mathbf{I} - \mathbf{A}(\hat{\lambda}_n)), \tag{2.11}$$

where $\hat{\lambda}$ is an estimate of λ^*, discussed at the end of this section. Given assumption (2.9) and (2.10), it can be shown that this estimate is asymptotically unbiased.

The estimate given by (2.6) is biased, and it may be instructive to examine the nature of the bias. Since

$$\beta = (\mathbf{X'X} + \lambda \mathbf{U'U})^{-1} X'Y,$$

we have

$$E\beta = (\mathbf{X'X} + \lambda \mathbf{U'U})^{-1} \mathbf{X'X}\beta = \mathbf{W}\beta, \tag{2.12}$$

say. We thus see that the expectation of $\hat{\beta}_k$ is a linear combination of the elements of β. Graphical display of the rows of W can reveal the intrinsic bandwidth induced by the choice of λ and the corresponding "window" shape. Some examples are given in Section 4. This shows that smoothing splines can be interpreted as a variable bandwidth kernel estimation method.

The final important step in the procedure is to choose the smoothing parameter λ. The basic cost function is the quadratic loss, but to minimize the expected loss, an extra penalty for parameters is required. There have been a variety of approaches in the literature to this general question; the choice of a stopping rule for fitting autoregressions and the selection of regressors when the true model is unknown are closely related problems.

An approach that is intuitively appealing is known as cross-validation (CV). The method drops one data point, estimates the model, evaluates how well the model forecasts the missing data, repeats this for all individual data points and then chooses λ to minimize the resulting sum of squares. Thus, suppose that the point (x_j, y_j) is deleted from the data. For a given λ, $\hat{\beta}_{(j)}(\lambda)$ is estimated and the term $(\hat{y}_j^{(j)}(\lambda) - y_j)^2$ is formed, where $\hat{y}_j^{(j)}(\lambda) = \hat{f}_\lambda(x_j)$. Repeating for all j gives

$$CV = \sum_{j=1}^{n} \left(\hat{y}_j^{(j)}(\lambda) - y_j \right)^2, \tag{2.13}$$

and λ is then chosen to minimize this quantity. Essentially, one is choosing λ to provide the best possible out-of-sample forecast on average.

The obvious disadvantage of this technique is that it is computationally expensive, particularly as n becomes large. For models linear in the parameters, however, the calculations can be greatly simplified by the Sherman–Morrison–Woodbury formulas given by Rao (1965).

A more direct approach is to consider criteria based on closed forms of quadratic loss with penalty functions. Some of these may be written as follows: minimize

$$[\log \mathrm{RSS}(\lambda) + m(n)\mathrm{tr}\,\mathbf{A}(\lambda)],$$

where $\mathrm{RSS}(\lambda) = \mathbf{e}'\mathbf{e}$ (RSS is residual sum of squares). For example, Akaike (1973) suggested using $m(n) = 2n^{-1}$, giving the Akaike information criterion (AIC). Schwarz (1978) suggested $m(n) = \log(n)/n$, and Hannan and Quinn (1979) suggested $m(n) = 2\log(\log n)/n$. An earlier proposal by Akaike (1969) was to minimize

$$\mathrm{FPE}(\lambda) = \mathrm{RSS}(\lambda)[1 + 2\mathrm{tr}\,\mathbf{A}(\lambda)/n],$$

where FPE is finite prediction error. Atkinson (1981) provided a useful survey of these criteria.

A further criterion, which we shall be using, was introduced by Wahba (1975), Craven and Wahba (1979), and Golub, Heath, and Wahba (1979), in the context of smoothing splines. They suggest minimizing the generalized cross-validation (GCV) criterion

$$\text{GCV}(\lambda) = \text{RSS}(\lambda)/(1 - (1/n)\text{tr}[A(\lambda)])^2. \tag{2.14}$$

To develop conditions of optimality for such a choice, we propose that it would be desirable to choose λ to minimize the expected squared prediction error

$$R(\lambda) = E\|\mu - \mathbf{A}(\lambda)Y\|^2 + n\sigma^2,$$

where $\mu = E(Y)$, which can be reexpressed in terms of the expected residual sum of squares (ERSS) as

$$R(\lambda) = \text{ERSS}(\lambda) + 2\sigma^2 \text{tr} \, A(\lambda).$$

Therefore the estimated sum of squared residuals is an underestimate of the mean squared prediction error. Approximating σ^2 by RSS/n yields a feasible estimate of the correction:

$$R(\lambda) = \text{RSS} + 2(\text{RSS}/n)\text{tr} \, A(\lambda).$$

This is the FPE criterion and the first-order term of a Taylor expansion of GCV and AIC; thus it provides some justification for their use. Ordinary cross-validation is thus interpreted as another approach to estimating $R(\lambda)$.

Further discussion of some of these criteria may be found in Rice (1984) and Shibata (1981), but more research is required to compare these and other similar methods in various situations. Teräsvirta (1985) established the asymptotic optimality of these criteria (see also Erdal 1983). In the empirical work reported later, the GCV criterion was used because of its relative simplicity and because it was shown by Craven and Wahba (1979) to be an effective method for choosing λ for ordinary smoothing splines.

3. THE DATA AND SOME MODIFICATIONS

The data for this analysis come from four utilities: Union Electric in St. Louis (STL), Georgia Electric Power in Atlanta (GE), Northeast Utilities in Hartford, Connecticut (NU), and Puget Power and Light in Seattle (PU). The data are in the form of total residential sales in megawatt hours billed in a month, which we normalized to sales per customer.

The total sales in one month are composed of the sum of sales billed in approximately 21 billing cycles. That is, the first cycle in March might cover the period from February 1 to March 1 and include n_1 customers. The second could run from February 2 to March 2 with n_2 customers. The number of customers facing the weather on any particular day and billed in March depends on which billing cycles cover this day. For example, all customers face weather on March 1 but only n_1 face weather on February 1 and n_{20} face weather on March 31. If the same average temperature occurs on several days, the number of customers in the March bills facing that temperature would be given by the sum of the number in each billing cycle covering each of the days. Thus variables can be constructed to represent the number of customer days at any particular temperature. Dividing both the total monthly bills and the customer days by the total number of customers gives a new definition of the L (and X) matrices in (2.4). The element of L corresponding to month m and the temperature interval k is given by

$$L_{mk} = \frac{1}{n_m} \sum_{\substack{c=\text{cycles} \\ \text{in month}}} \sum_{\substack{d=\text{days} \\ \text{in cycle}}} n_{c,m} I_{d,k},$$

where $I_{d,k} = 1$ if the temperature on day d was in interval k and $I = 0$ otherwise, $n_{c,m}$ is the number of customers in cycle c in month m, and $n_m = \Sigma_c n_{c,m}$. Each row of the L matrix indicates the distribution per customer over temperature for some month of the customer days, and each sums to roughly 30, since each customer is billed for about 30 days. Fortunately, for three of the utilities, the exact starting and ending dates for each cycle and the number of customers in each cycle are known. For Puget, this is approximated.

The U matrix must be adapted to the use of nonequally spaced temperature intervals, since these can be chosen by the investigator. Let the daily average temperature be x, and consider the intervals defined by the breakpoints $x_1, x_2, \ldots, x_i, x_{i+1}, \ldots, x_{k+1}$, so that there are k ordered categories. Let the corresponding midpoints be $t_1, \ldots, t_k$. Approximating the derivative by the finite difference, the second derivative at x_i can be written as

$$\frac{d^2 g}{dx^2} \approx \left(\frac{\beta_{i+1} - \beta_i}{t_{i+1} - t_i} - \frac{\beta_i - \beta_{i-1}}{t_i - t_{i-1}} \right) \Big/ \left(\frac{t_{i+1} + t_i}{2} - \frac{t_i + t_{i-1}}{2} \right)$$

$$= \frac{\beta_{i+1}}{(t_{i+1} - t_i)(t_{i+1} - t_{i-1})/2} + \frac{\beta_{i-1}}{(t_i - t_{i-1})(t_{i+1} - t_{i-1})/2}$$

$$- \frac{2\beta_i}{(t_{i+1} - t_i)(t_i - t_{i-1})}. \tag{3.1}$$

Thus the U matrix would have typical rows defined by the coefficients of β given in (3.1), which therefore depend upon the intervals chosen for the temperature categories. If the intervals are all the same, then this becomes simply the second difference of the β's as before. In practice we have made the temperature categories smaller in the middle of the distribution because the observations are much denser there, but there was little difference in the estimated shape when equal categories were used.

A series of independent variables supplied to us by the four utilities were entered linearly in the models and are labeled as z in (2.4). These data series were the same as those used in their own modeling efforts but differed slightly across utilities. For both STL and GE, the monthly price of electricity was measured as the marginal price for the average residential customer in that month, divided by the local consumer price index (CPI). As rate structures only change at most once a year, variations within the year reflect shifts in the block of the average customer, seasonality in the rate structure, and changes in the local CPI. For PU and NU the U.S. Bureau of Labor Statistics energy price indexes for Seattle and Boston are deflated by the similar comprehensive estimates of the consumer price index and used as the price variables. Generally, the prices had little effect in the estimates.

The income measures again differed slightly across utilities. STL and GE carried out their own surveys of household income, which were interpolated to monthly intervals. PU used U.S. Department of Commerce estimates of annual Seattle Standard Metropolitan Statistical Area (SMSA) personal income per household divided by the Seattle CPI, all interpolated monthly. NU used the similar Hartford SMSA personal income measure divided by the Boston CPI. In EPRI (1983) and Train, Ignelzi, Engle, Granger, and Ramanathan (1985), other measures of both income and price are examined in a parametric model with little difference in overall performance or the significance of the variables under examination.

In St. Louis, a meter-reader strike for a five-month period required estimated billing that was later corrected when the meters were again read. This effect was modeled by two strike dummy variables, each of which sums to zero.

Other factors that might affect the base or non-weather-sensitive load, such as the timing of holidays and the school year, the timing of sunrise and sunset, and other repeating phenomena, were modeled by including 11 seasonal dummy variables. The twelfth would ordinarily be included in a model with no intercept. In this model, however, the temperature variables essentially add to a constant and therefore implicitly include an intercept so that none appears explicitly in the nonparametric estimation.

The residuals in (2.4) were assumed to follow an autoregressive (AR) (1) process with zero mean and parameter ρ. As it was quite expensive to search over both λ and ρ, generally only a very rough grid search over ρ was performed. In fact, the estimates of ρ were so similar for different specifications and regions that eventually even this became unnecessary. Furthermore, the shapes of the estimated temperature response functions were surprisingly insensitive to the values of ρ.

In each case λ was determined by minimizing GCV using the MINPACK algorithm described in More, Garbow, and Hillstrom (1980),

Table 10.1. *Regression summary statistics*

	Utility			
	STL, Jan. '72– Sep. '81	GE Mar. '74– Sep. '81	PU, Jan. '74– Dec. '80	NU, Mar. '78– Sep. '81
Semiparametric				
Observations	117	90	84	43
Temperature intervals	16	25	19	17
Other regressors	14	13	13	13
Equivalent regressors	22.7	19.7	17.1	19.7
Standard error regression	.0189	.0277	.0598	.0157
GCV	.0518	.0884	.377	.0196
λ	1.8×10^5	1.3×10^5	1.0×10^6	9.6×10^4
ρ	.7	.7	.85	.85
Durbin–Watson	1.88	1.98	1.61	1.92
Parametric				
Temperature variables	3	3	3	2
Other regressors	17	14	14	14
$\hat{\sigma}$	.0196	.0291	.0589	.0150
GCV	.0542	.0940	.366	.0154

treating $\lambda/(\lambda + \lambda_0)$ as the parameter when λ_0 was chosen to be roughly the size of the final estimate. Since the optimization is only over a single parameter, a variety of methods would surely be successful.

4.   RESULTS

Table 10.1 presents summary statistics for the semiparametric estimates for the four utilities. The GCV is defined as in (2.14), and the standard error of the regression and the equivalent number of regressors are defined by (2.11) and tr($A(\lambda)$), respectively. The full results are presented in Tables 10.2–10.9.

The equivalent number of regressors associated with the weather variables varies from a high of 9 for STL to a low of 4 for PU. These numbers reflect the inherent nonlinearity in the response rather than the number of temperature intervals considered. The estimated values of λ, the smoothing parameter, are all very large; however, the actual magnitudes depend on the units of the data and therefore have no direct interpretation.

For comparison, Table 1 has summary statistics from some carefully estimated parametric models developed in EPRI (1983) for the same data sets. These models use piecewise linear splines with breakpoints at

Table 10.2. *Semiparametric Model for Union
Electric/St. Louis (total residential billing period,
Mwh sales/customer)*

Variable	Coefficient	Variable	Coefficient
–10–0°	$.936E - 02^a$	Income	$.123E - 04^a$
0–10°	$.928E - 02^a$	January	$.021^a$
10–20°	$.943E - 02^a$	February	$.011$
20–30°	$.956E - 02^a$	March	$-.007$
30–40°	$.868E - 02^a$	April	$-.017^b$
40–45°	$.843E - 02^a$	May	$-.028^b$
45–50°	$.782E - 02^a$	June	$-.024^b$
50–55°	$.706E - 02^a$	July	$.032^b$
55–60°	$.623E - 02^a$	August	$.064^a$
60–65°	$.586E - 02^a$	September	$.055^b$
65–70°	$.718E - 02^a$	October	$-.004$
70–75°	$1.120E - 02^a$	November	$-.012^b$
75–80°	$1.690E - 02^a$	Strike 1	$-.054^a$
80–85°	$2.360E - 02^a$	Strike 2	$-.141^a$
85–90°	$3.100E - 02^a$		
90–95°	$3.850E - 02^a$		

Note: The standard error is .0189; estimated λ is 182, 121.3.
[a] The t statistic is greater than 2.0.
[b] The t statistic is greater than 1.0.

Table 10.3. *Parametric Model of Residential
Electricity Use: St. Louis City (total billing period,
Mwh sales/customer)*

Variable	Coefficient	Variable	Coefficient
HDD65	$.204E - 03^a$	June	$-.085^a$
CDD65	$.917E - 03^a$	July	$-.036^b$
CDD85	$.989E - 03^a$	August	$.002$
Discomfort	$.464E - 02^a$	September	$-.011$
Price	$-.966E - 02$	October	$-.053^a$
Income	$.104E - 04^a$	November	$-.039^a$
February	$-.018^b$	December	$-.016^b$
March	$-.026^a$	Strike 1	$-.135^a$
April	$-.036^a$	Strike 2	$-.059^a$
May	$-.060^a$	Intercept	$-.102$

Note: The standard error is .0196; $\overline{R}^2 = .9712$.
[a] The t statistic is greater than 2.0.
[b] The t statistic is greater than 1.0.

Table 10.4. *Semiparametric Model for Georgia Power (total residential billing period, Mwh sales/customer)*

Variable	Coefficient	Variable	Coefficient
10–20°	$.037^a$	75–77.5°	$.023^a$
20–25°	$.032^a$	77.5–80°	$.026^a$
25–30°	$.030^a$	80–82.5°	$.029^a$
30–35°	$.027^a$	82.5–85°	$.033^a$
35–40°	$.024^a$	85–90°	$.039^a$
40–42.5°	$.022^a$	90–95°	$.046^a$
42.5–45°	$.020^a$	Income	$.217E-04^a$
45–47.5°	$.019^a$	Price	$-.013$
47.5–50°	$.017^a$	January	$-.030^b$
50–52.5°	$.016^a$	February	$-.057^a$
52.5–55°	$.015^a$	March	$.033$
55–57.5°	$.014^a$	May	$.081^b$
57.5–60°	$.013^a$	June	$.055^b$
60–62.5°	$.013^a$	July	$-.014$
62.5–65°	$.013^a$	August	$-.032^b$
65–67.5°	$.014^a$	September	$.010$
67.5–70°	$.015^a$	October	$.046^a$
70–72.5°	$.018^a$	November	$.019^b$
72.5–75°	$.020^a$		

Note: The standard error is .0277; estimated λ is 126,936.3.
[a] The *t* statistic is greater than 2.0.
[b] The *t* statistic is greater than 1.0.

Table 10.5. *Parametric Model for Georgia Power*

Variable	Coefficient	Variable	Coefficient
HDD65	$.488E-03^a$	June	$.006$
CDD65	$1.120E-03^a$	July	$-.014$
CDD75	$.222E-03$	August	$-.062^b$
Price	$-.206E-02$	September	$-.083^a$
Income	$.393E-04^a$	October	$-.045^a$
February	$-.074^a$	November	$-.036^a$
March	$-.098^a$	December	$-.064^a$
April	$-.093^b$	Intercept	$.129$
May	$-.041$		

Note: The standard error is .0291; $\overline{R}^2 = .9618$.
[a] The *t* statistic is greater than 2.0.
[b] The *t* statistic is greater than 1.0.

Table 10.6. *Semiparametric model for Puget
Sound Power and Light (total residential billing
period, kwh sales/customer)*

Variable	Coefficient	Variable	Coefficient
17–30°	39.1[a]	Income	50.2[a]
30–35°	26.7[a]	Price	−196.0
35–37°	21.9[b]	January	−223.0[a]
37–40°	18.7[b]	February	72.5[b]
40–42°	15.5[b]	March	30.7
42–45°	12.3	April	−157.0[a]
45–47°	9.2	May	−209.0[a]
47–50°	6.2	June	290.0[a]
50–52°	3.4	July	−196.0[b]
52–55°	.7	August	−215.0[b]
55–57°	−1.8	September	−171.0[b]
57–60°	−4.2	October	−244.0[a]
60–62°	−6.4	November	−161.0[a]
62–65°	−8.3		
65–67°	−10.2		
67–70°	−11.9		
70–75°	−14.4		
75–80°	−17.8[b]		
80–82°	−20.1[b]		

[a] The t statistic is greater than 2.0.
[b] The t statistic is greater than 1.0.
Note: The standard error is 59.77; estimated λ is 1,012,408.5.

Table 10.7. *Parametric model for Puget Power*

Variable	Coefficient	Variable	Coefficient
HDD65	.875*	May	−235
HDD50	.309	June	−351
HDD35	1.030	July	−301
Price	−327.0	August	−354
Income	35.0	September	−304
January	233	October	−331
February	87	November	−197
March	52	Intercept	359
April	−154		

* The t statistic is greater than 2.0.
Note: The standard error is 58.94; $\overline{R}^2 = .9712$. The mean
electric heat saturation is 39%.

Table 10.8. *Semiparametric model for Northeast Utilities/Hartford Electric (total residential billing period, Mwh sales/customer)*

Variable	Coefficient	Variable	Coefficient
3–5°	$1.110E-02^a$	Income	$.609E-02^a$
5–15°	$1.060E-02^a$	Price	$-4.140E-02$
15–20°	$.963E-02^a$	January	.009
20–25°	$.922E-02^a$	February	.010
25–30°	$.883E-02^a$	March	.041
30–35°	$.872E-02^a$	April	$.074^b$
35–40°	$.806E-02^a$	May	.039
40–45°	$.714E-02^a$	June	.030
45–50°	$.662E-02^a$	July	.025
50–55°	$.616E-02^a$	August	.002
55-60°	$.594E-02^a$	September	$-.035^a$
60–65°	$.638E-02^a$	October	$-.033^a$
65–70°	$.806E-02^a$	November	$-.017^b$
70–75°	$1.090E-02^a$		
75–80°	$1.470E-02^a$		
80–85°	$1.900E-02^a$		
85–88°	$2.240E-02^a$		

^{a} The t statistic is greater than 2.0.
^{b} The t statistic is greater than 1.0.
Note: The standard error is .0157; estimated λ is 95,888.8.

Table 10.9. *Parametric model for Northeast Utilities (total billing period, Mwh sales/customer)*

Variable	Coefficient	Variable	Coefficient
HDD65	.120E 03*	May	.016
CDD65	$.819E-03^*$	June	.011
Price	$-4.120E-02$	July	.009
Income	$.475E-02$	August	$-.009$
January	$-.009$	September	$-.036^*$
February	.001	October	$-.048^*$
March	.028	November	$-.039^*$
April	.060	Intercept	.203

* The t statistic is greater than 2.0.
Note: The standard error is .0150; $\overline{R}^2 = .9087$.

the a priori determined values of 35°, 50°, 65°, 75°, and 85°F. Thus a variable such as HDD55 is defined as

$$\sum_{\substack{\text{customer days} \\ \text{billed in month}}} \max \{55° - \text{daily average temperature, }°\}.$$

In each case a specification search suggested a basic model that included only a subset of the possible arms of the temperature function. In each case the model closest to the semiparametric one in terms of other regressors was chosen for comparison. In STL, however, the parametric models included a discomfort index and the price index, both of which were not in the semiparametric model.

As can be immediately observed, the number of temperature-related variables in the parametric specifications is far less than in the most unrestricted semiparametric model, where it is equal to the number of temperature intervals. It is also far less than the estimated equivalent number of temperature parameters in each case. Thus if the parametric models provide an adequate representation of the data, they are surely more parsimonious. A value of λ approaching infinity will lead to a linear rather than a V-shaped response, so the semiparametric models do not have the capability of achieving the parsimony of the simplest parametric versions. In fact, one modeling strategy that could be followed would be to let the semiparametric estimates guide the selection of a parametric functional form.

Nevertheless, in both STL and GE and GCV for the semiparametric model is better than (i.e., lies below) that of the parametric models. This is also true for the standard error, although such a comparison would be misleading because this criterion imposes a far smaller penalty on over-parameterization than does GCV. For PU the values of GCV are very similar, reflecting the fact that the relationship is nearly a straight line, even though the parametric model terminates this line at 65°. For NU the parametric model is substantially better. This may be attributed to the small number of observations (43) compared with the number of estimated parameters (20 for the semiparametric and 16 for the parametric). Here a priori specifications may have a particularly large benefit, since variance reduction is more valuable than bias reduction.

Turning to the plots, Figure 10.1 presents the nonparametric estimates of the weather-sensitive load for STL as the solid curve and two sets of parametric estimates as the dashed curves. The one with short dashes is the selected parametric model summarized in Table 1, whereas the longer dashes are from the model that fits all of the segments of the piecewise linear response surface. In each case the non-weather-sensitive load is defined as the load when temperature equals 65°, and therefore each of the curves is normalized to zero at that point. Although the parametric curves appear to approximate the cooling part of the curve accurately, they do not do very well in the heating region. Particularly bad is

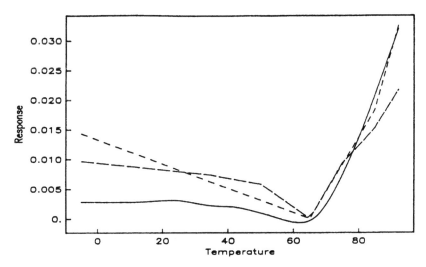

Figure 10.1. Temperature Response Function for St. Louis. The non-parametric estimate is given by the solid curve and two parametric estimates by the dashed curves.

the selected model that finds a linear relationship. In fact, the more highly parameterized model has a lower GCV as well and would be preferred on most grounds. The nearly horizontal estimated relationship is consistent with the low saturation of electrically heated homes in the city of St. Louis.

Figures 10.2, 10.3, and 10.4 show similar plots for the other three utilities. In each case there appear to be small but possibly important differences between the parametric and nonparametric curves. In STL, GE, and NU, the minimum for the nonparametric curves does not appear at 65° but at a somewhat lower temperature. In PU the parametric version truncates at 65° under the assumption that there is no air-conditioning load. It appears that electricity usage continues to fall, however, for temperatures above 65°. Several plausible explanations for such behavior can be offered. For example, even when the daily average temperature is above 65° there may be heating at night. Another possible explanation for the finding is that the service region covers two distinct areas – coastal and mountainous – but the available weather data are only from the coastal region. Thus the actual temperatures occurring in the mountain region are likely to be below those used in the model, resulting in an unusual temperature response curve in some temperature regions.

In general the nonparametric curves have a plausible shape that is free of user-defined features. The shapes are fairly well approximated by the higher-order parametric models, but even these may miss

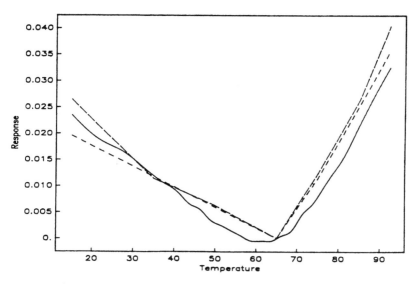

Figure 10.2. Temperature Response Function for Georgia. The non-parametric estimate is given by the solid curve and two parametric estimates by the dashed curves.

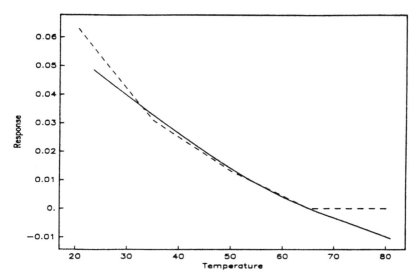

Figure 10.3. Temperature Response Functions for Puget. The solid curve is the nonparametric estimate and the dashed curve is the parametric estimate.

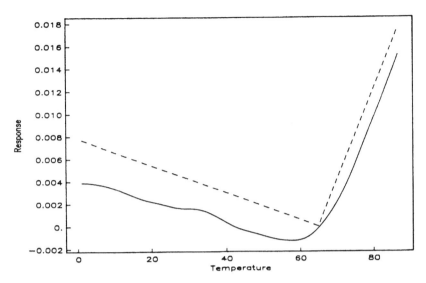

Figure 10.4. Temperature Response Functions for Northeast Utilities. The solid curve is the nonparametric estimate and the dashed curve is the parametric estimate.

key features of the data through the arbitrary choice of knots or base temperatures.

An interesting possibility that we explored empirically was the introduction of some of the parametric weather terms into the z matrix of covariates. The semiparametric procedure therefore estimated the difference between the specified parametric form and the true model. Thus, for example, heating and cooling degree days could be included with income, price, and the seasonal dummies as the standard regressors. When the approximate parametric form was well specified, the GCV estimate of λ became very large, indicating little need for extra parameters. In fact, only near $65°$ did it deviate noticeably from a straight line. When a highly inadequate parametric form was introduced, however, the optimal λ was smaller again and the curve had some shape. When this estimated shape was added to the estimated parametric shape, the result was nearly indistinguishable from those in Figures 10.1–10.4. Thus the semiparametric procedure can be viewed as a way to flexibly correct misspecified parametric models.

Figure 10.5 examines the performance of GCV in selecting the optimal degree of smoothing. Using data for GE, the upper left frame obtains estimates of the curve assuming $\lambda = 0$, so there is no smoothing. Successively higher λ's are examined until in frame d the optimal estimate is plotted. It appears that the fourth figure is simply a smoothed version of frame a but that no essential features are lost. If still

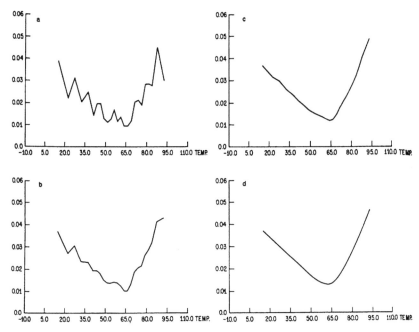

Figure 10.5. Temperature Response Functions for Georgia: (a) $\lambda = 0$ (unrestricted ordinary least squares); (b) $\lambda = 1,000$; (c) $\lambda = 10,000$; (d) $\lambda = 126,936$ (optimum).

larger values of λ were tried, the curve would eventually become a straight line.

To examine the biases in more detail, in Figures 10.6 and 10.7 we plot the weights that show how the expected value of β_i depends on the true β's. From (2.12), $E(\beta_i) = W_i\beta$ with W_i as the ith row of $\mathbf{W} = (\mathbf{X}'\mathbf{X} + \lambda\mathbf{U}'\mathbf{U})^{-1}\mathbf{X}'\mathbf{X}$. Thus the expected value of each regression coefficient is a linear combination of the true coefficients. For unbiased estimation, $\mathbf{W} = I$; but for biased estimation, the value of one coefficient will affect the bias on another. In Figure 10.6 these weights (interpolated by a cubic spline) are shown for the sixth temperature category (40°–45°) for STL to produce a kernel function that peaks near 42.5°. This figure portrays a smoothing window just as for any kernel estimator. The bandwidth of this window is implied by the estimate of λ; large values of λ imply large bandwidths. In this case the window does not appear to be symmetric, possibly because of end effects. It also has several side lobes, as do many optimal smoothers. In fact, the fixed regressors will potentially also have a weight; however, these are very small in this application.

Figure 10.7 shows the same result for the tenth temperature category (60°–65°). Here the window has a similar shape that differs in detail. The

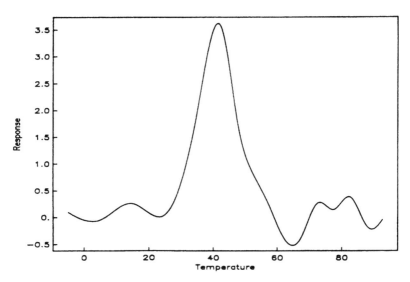

Figure 10.6. Equivalent Kernel Function for St. Louis for the Temperature Range 40°–45°.

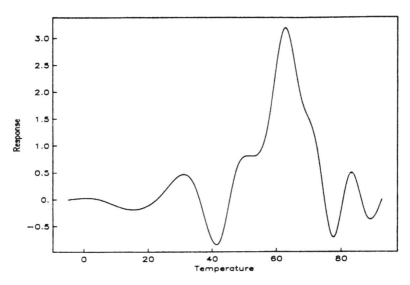

Figure 10.7. Equivalent Kernel Function for St. Louis for the Temperature Range 60°–65°.

fact that these windows are differently shaped illustrates that the smoothing does not have a constant kernel or bandwidth.

5. CONCLUSIONS

This article has extended and applied the methodology of smoothing splines to the problem of estimating the functional relationship between the weather and the sales of electricity. The extensions introduced additive parametric determinants, serial correlation of the disturbances, and a dynamic structure inherent in the data-generation process. The applications indicate the promise of the technique to produce sensible and intuitively appealing functional relationships. Frequently these reveal features in the data that a careful parametric specification search had not uncovered. The results are surprisingly robust to a variety of changes in specification.

Clearly, further experience in using this technique and further theoretical research are required. Among outstanding issues are the following: (a) A better theoretical understanding of the bias in such a mixed parametric–nonparametric model is desirable. How does the inclusion of the nonparametric component bias the estimates of the parametric components and vice versa? How does the form of the design matrix influence the bias? More generally, analysis of the local and global consistency and rates of convergence is needed. (b) There is a need for a better theoretical and practical understanding of the efficiencies of various data-driven methods for choosing the smoothing parameter λ. It was surprising and reassuring to us that the curves selected by GCV were insensitive to our specification of ρ, but the reason for this is unclear. (c) Finally, it would be desirable to develop reliable confidence bounds for the curves. This is difficult to do in the presence of bias, since the bias depends on the unknown true parameters and conventional confidence bands are built around unbiased estimates. Since our estimates are linear, their standard errors are easily computed; but confidence intervals are more difficult.

REFERENCES

Akaike, H. (1969), "Fitting Autoregressive Models for Prediction," *Annals of the Institute of Statistical Mathematics*, 21, 243–247.
——— (1973), "Information Theory and an Extension of the Maximum Likelihood Principle," in *2nd International Symposium on Information Theory*, eds. B. N. Petrov and F. Csaki, Budapest: Akadémiai Kiadó, pp. 267–281.
Ansley, Craig F., and Wecker, William (1983), "Extensions and Examples of the Signal Extraction Approach to Regression," in *Applied Time Series*

Analysis of Economic Data, ed. Arnold Zellner, Economic Research Report ER-5, Washington, DC: U.S. Bureau of the Census, pp. 181–192.

Atkinson, A. C. (1981), "Likelihood Ratios, Posterior Odds, and Information Criteria," *Journal of Econometrics*, 16, 15–20.

Collomb, G. (1981), "Estimation Non-paramétrique de la Régression: Reveu Bibliographique," *International Statistical Review*, 49, 75–93.

Craven, P., and Wahba, G. (1979), "Smoothing Noisy Data With Spline Functions," *Numerische Mathematik*, 31, 377–403.

Electric Power Research Institute (1981), "Regional Load-Curve Models: QUERI's Model Specification, Estimation, and Validation" (Vol. 2) (final report on Project 1008 by Quantitative Economic Research, Inc.), EA-1672, Palo Alto, CA: Author.

—— (1983), "Weather Normalization of Electricity Sales" (final report on Project 1922-1 by Cambridge Systematics, Inc., and Quantitative Economic Research, Inc.), EA-3143, Palo Alto, CA: Author.

Erdal, Aytul (1983), "Cross Validation for Ridge Regression and Principal Components Analysis," unpublished Ph.D. dissertation, Brown University, Division of Applied Mathematics.

Gasser, T., and Rosenblatt, M. (eds.) (1979), *Smoothing Techniques for Curve Estimation, Lecture Notes in Mathematics* (Vol. 757), Berlin: Springer-Verlag.

Golub, G., Heath, M., and Wahba, G. (1979), "Generalized Cross-Validation as a Method for Choosing a Good Ridge Parameter," *Technometrics*, 21, 215–223.

Green, Peter, Jennison, Christopher, and Seheult, Allan (1985), "Analysis of Field Experiments by Least Squares Smoothing," *Journal of the Royal Statistical Society*, Ser. B, 47, 299–315.

Hannan, E. J., and Quinn, B. G. (1979), "The Determination of the Order of an Autoregression," *Journal of the Royal Statistical Society*, Ser. B, 41, 190–195.

Lawrence, Anthony, and Aigner, Dennis (eds.) (1979). "Modeling and Forecasting Time-of-Day and Seasonal Electricity Demands," *Journal of Econometrics*, 9.

More, J. J., Garbow, B. S., and Hillstrom, K. E. (1980), *Users Guide for MINPACK-1*, Argonne, IL: Argonne National Laboratory.

Rao, C. R. (1965), *Linear Statistical Inference and Its Applications*, New York: John Wiley, p. 33.

Reinsch, C. (1967), "Smoothing by Spline Functions," *Numerische Mathematik*, 24, 383–393.

Rice, John (1984), "Bandwidth Choice for Non-Parametric Regression," *Annals of Statistics*, 12, 1215–1230.

Rice, John, and Rosenblatt, M. (1981), "Integrated Mean Square Error of a Smoothing Spline," *Journal of Approximation Theory*, 33, 353–369.

—— (1983), "Smoothing Splines: Regression, Derivatives and Deconvolution," *Annals of Statistics*, 11, 141–156.

Schoenberg, I. J. (1964), "Spline Functions and the Problem of Graduation," *Proceedings of the National Academy of Sciences of the United States of America*, 52, 947–950.

Schwarz, A. (1978), "Estimating the Dimension of a Model," *Annals of Statistics*, 6, 461–464.

Shibata, R. (1981), "An Optimal Selection of Regression Variables," *Biometrica*, 68, 45–54.

Shiller, Robert J. (1973), "A Distributed Lag Estimator Derived From Smoothness Priors," *Econometrica*, 41, 775–788.

   (1984), "Smoothness Priors and Nonlinear Regression," *Journal of the American Statistical Association*, 79, 609–615.

Speckman, P. (1985), "Spline Smoothing and Optimal Rates of Convergence in Non-Parametric Regression Models," *Annals of Statistics*, 13, 970–983.

Teräsvirta, Timo (1985), "Smoothness in Regression: Asymptotic Considerations," working paper, University of California, San Diego.

Train, Kenneth, Ignelzi, Patrice, Engle, Robert, Granger, Clive, and Ramanathan, Ramu (1984), "The Billing Cycle and Weather Variables in Models of Electricity Sales," *Energy*, 9, 1041–1047.

Wahba, G. (1975), "Smoothing Noisy Data With Spline Functions," *Numerische Mathematik*, 24, 309–317.

   (1984), "Partial Spline Models for the Semi-Parametric Estimation of Functions of Several Variables," unpublished paper presented at a conference on statistical analysis of time series.

Wecker, William, and Ansley, Craig F. (1983), "The Signal Extraction Approach to Nonlinear Regression and Spline Smoothing," *Journal of the American Statistical Association*, 78, 81–89.

Whittaker, E. (1923), "On a New Method of Graduation," *Proceedings of the Edinburgh Mathematical Society*, 41, 63–75.

PART FOUR

METHODOLOGY

CHAPTER 11

Time Series Modeling and Interpretation*
C. W. J. Granger and M. J. Morris

Summary

By considering the model generating the sum of two or more series, it is shown that the mixed *ARMA* model is the one most likely to occur. As most economic series are both aggregates and are measured with error it follows that such mixed models will often be found in practice. If such a model is found, the possibility of resolving the series into simple components is considered both theoretically and for simulated data.

Keywords: Time series; mixed autoregressive-moving average model; Aggregation; measurement error; parsimonious models

1. INTRODUCTION

THE recent publication of the book by Box and Jenkins has greatly increased interest by time series analysts and econometricians in more complicated, even if more "parsimonious", time series models. However, the intuitive interpretation of the models that arise is not always simple and an applied research worker may well ask how such a model could have arisen in practice. In this paper, the possibility that a complicated looking model could have arisen from a simpler situation is explored and some suggestions made about the possible interpretation of some models that appear to arise in practice.

The only series to be considered are those with zero means and generated by models with time-invariant parameters. Thus, possibly after an appropriate linear transformation, the series will be taken to be second-order stationary. Let X_t be such a series, so that

$$E\{X_t\} = 0, \quad \text{all } t.$$

* *Journal of the Royal Statistical Society, A*, 139, 1976, 246–257.

Initially, suppose that X_t is second-order stationary, so that the kth auto-covariance

$$\mu_k = E\{X_t X_{t-k}\} \tag{1.1}$$

is time invariant. The series will be said to be a white noise process if

$$\mu_k = 0, \text{ all } k \neq 0.$$

Use will be made of the backward operator B, defined so that

$$B^j X_t = X_{t-j}. \tag{1.2}$$

A series with the representation

$$a(B)X_t = \varepsilon_t, \tag{1.3}$$

where

$$a(B)\sum_{j=0}^{p} a_j B^j, \quad a \neq 0, \quad a_0 = 1, \tag{1.4}$$

and ε_t is white noise, will be said to be generated by an autoregressive model of order p, and denoted by $X_t \sim AR(p)$.

Suppose further that

$$a(B) = \prod_{j=1}^{p}(1 - \theta_j B) \tag{1.5}$$

so that $\theta_j^{-1}, j = 1, \ldots, p$, are the roots of the equation $a(z) = 0$. If $|\theta_j^{-1}| > 1$, all j, then X_t will be stationary. In this case

$$\mu_k = \sum_{j=1}^{p} \lambda_j \theta_j^k. \tag{1.6}$$

A series will be said to be generated by a moving average of order q if it can be represented by

$$X_t = b(B)\varepsilon_t, \tag{1.7}$$

where

$$b(B) = \sum_{j=0}^{q} b_j B^j \tag{1.8}$$

and ε_t is white noise. This is denoted by $X_t \sim MA(q)$. A necessary but not sufficient condition that such a representation is possible is

$$\mu_k = 0, \quad k > q. \tag{1.9}$$

The fact that this condition is not sufficient may be seen from the result that the maximum value of the first serial correlation coefficient $\rho_1 = \mu_1/\mu_0$ achievable from an $MA(q)$ process is

$$\rho_1(\max) = \cos\left(\frac{\pi}{q+2}\right).$$ (1.10)

It follows, for example, that if $\rho_1 = 0.8$, $\mu_k = \rho_k = 0$, all $k > 1$, then there is no corresponding $MA(1)$ process which has these values. Davies *et al.* (1974) have found more general inequalities on autocorrelations for MA processes.

A necessary and sufficient condition that there exists and $MA(q)$ model corresponding to a specific set of autocorrelation coefficients u_j, $j = 0, 1, \ldots, q$, has been given by Wold (1953, p. 154).

Let

$$u(x) = 1 + \sum_{j=1}^{q} u_j\left(x^j + x^{-j}\right).$$

Applying the transformation $z = x + x^{-1}$, let $u(x)$ be transformed into the qth order polynomial $v(z)$. The required necessary and sufficient condition is then that $v(z)$ has no zero of odd multiplicity in the interval $-2 < z_0 < 2$. Note that

$$v(2) = u(1) = f(0) \geq 0 \quad \text{and} \quad v(-2) = u(-1) = f(\pi) \geq 0,$$

where $f(w)$ is the spectrum of the moving average process. It follows that if $v(z)$ obeys the above condition, then $v(z) \geq 0$ for all z in the interval $(-2, 2)$.

An $MA(q)$ process, with $q < \infty$, is always stationary.

A stationary $AR(p)$ process can always be represented by an $MA(\infty)$ process (as can any stationary, purely non-deterministic process). If the roots of the equation $b(z) = 0$ all have absolute value greater than one, then the corresponding $MA(q)$ process may be inverted and be equally represented by an $AR(\infty)$ process.

Ever since their introduction by Yule (1921), the autoregressive and moving average models have been greatly favoured by time series analysts. It is not difficult to convince oneself that both models are intuitively reasonable and could well occur in practice. Simple expectations models or a momentum effect in a random variable can lead to AR models. Similarly, a variable in equilibrium but buffeted by a sequence of unpredictable events with a delayed or discounted effect will give MA models, for example.

A fairly obvious generalization of these models is the mixed autoregressive-moving average process generated by

$$a(B)X_t = b(B)\varepsilon_t,$$ (1.11)

where ε_t is again white noise and $a(B)$ and $b(B)$ are polynomials in B of order p and q respectively. Such a process is denoted by $X_t \sim ARMA(p, q)$ and has an autocovariance sequence given by (1.6) for $k > q$. An $ARMA(p, q)$ process can always be represented by an $MA(\infty)$ model and, with the same invertibility condition for $MA(q)$, it can also be represented in an $AR(\infty)$ form.

In practice, the $ARMA$ model is more difficult to fit to data than for example an AR model, but in other ways the $ARMA$ model may be the statistically more efficient of the two. Box and Jenkins suggest that if one fits both an $AR(p)$ model and an $ARMA(p', q')$ model, then one will generally need fewer coefficients in this second model to get a satisfactory fit, i.e. $p' + q' < p$. As there are good reasons to prefer a model with as few parameters as possible, their principle of parsimony then suggests that the $ARMA$ will often be preferable.

Although the $ARMA$ model may involve the estimation of fewer coefficients than alternative models, it is certainly more difficult to comprehend, interpret or explain how it might occur in the real world. Chatfield and Prothero (1973) comment on the difficulty in the interpretation of many Box–Jenkins models. In the following sections a number of ways are suggested in which such an $ARMA$ model can arise from simpler models. It will be concluded that a mixed model is the one that is most likely to arise in practice.

2.   THE SUM OF TWO INDEPENDENT SERIES

If X_t and Y_t are two independent, zero-mean, stationary series, then in this section statements of the following kind will be considered:

$$\text{if}\quad X_t \sim ARMA(p, m), \quad Y_t \sim ARMA(q, n)$$

$$\text{and}\quad Z_t = X_t + Y_t$$

$$\text{then}\quad Z_t \sim ARMA(x, y).$$

Such a statement will be *denoted* by

$$ARMA(p, m) + ARMA(q, n) = ARMA(x, y).$$

Lemma.

$$MA(m) + MA(n) = MA(y), \tag{2.1}$$

where

$$y \leq \max(m, n). \tag{2.2}$$

Necessity follows directly from (1.9) and the inequality from the fact that there may be an inter-reaction between the two MA processes which reduces the order of the MA process of the sum. This latter point will be discussed in greater detail below.

To prove that the sufficiency condition holds, let $v_1(z)$, $v_2(z)$ be the $v(z)$ functions for $MA(m)$ and $MA(n)$ respectively, as defined after equation (1.10). As $v_1(z)$ and $v_2(z)$ do correspond to moving averages, they will both be non-negative over the interval $-2 \leq z \leq 2$. If $v_s(z)$ is the function for $MA(m) + MA(n)$, it follows that as $v_s(z) = v_1(z) + v_2(z)$ it will also be non-negative in the interval $-2 \le z \le 2$ and so $v_s(z)$ cannot have a root of odd multiplicity in this interval, so the truth of the lemma holds. Note that if $m \ne n$ then there must be equality in (2.2).

Basic Theorem.

$$ARMA(p, m) + ARMA(q, n) = ARMA(x, y), \tag{2.3}$$

where

$$x \le p+q \quad \text{and} \quad y \le \max(p+n, q+m). \tag{2.4}$$

(This is a form of the theorem proved by Box and Jenkins in their Appendix to Chapter 4.)

Proof. Let

$$a(B)X_t = c(B)\varepsilon_t \tag{2.5}$$

and

$$b(B)Y_t = d(B)\eta_t, \tag{2.6}$$

where a, b, c, d are polynomials in B of order p, q, m, n respectively and ε_t, η_t are two independent, white noise series.

As $Z_t = X_t + Y_t$, it follows that

$$a(B)b(B)Z_t = b(B)a(B)X_t + a(B)b(B)Y_t = b(B)c(B)\varepsilon_t + a(B)d(B)\eta_t. \tag{2.7}$$

The first term on the right-hand side is $MA(q + m)$ and the second term is $MA(p + n)$ and so, from the lemma, the right-hand side is $MA(y)$ where

$$y \le \max(p+n, q+m).$$

The order of the polynomial $a(B)b(B)$ is not more than $p + q$, and so the theorem is established.

(The assumption of independence may be weakened to allow for contemporaneous correlation between the noise series. The sum would still be of the form (2.3) but the parameters of the representation would be different.)

The need for the inequalities in the expressions for x and y partly arise from the fact that the polynomials $a(B)$ and $b(B)$ may contain common roots and so part of the operator need not be applied twice. For example, if

$$(1 - \alpha_1 B)X_t = \varepsilon_t, \quad \text{i.e. } X_t \sim AR(1)$$

and

$$(1 - \alpha_1 B)(1 - \alpha_2 B)Y_t = \eta_t, \quad \text{i.e. } Y_t \sim AR(2)$$

then with $Z_t = X_t + Y_t$ we have $(1 - \alpha_1 B)(1 - \alpha_2 B)Z_t = (1 - \alpha_2 B)\varepsilon_t + \eta_t$, i.e. $Z_t \sim ARMA$ (2,1). In general, if the polynomials $a(B), b(B)$ have just k roots in common, the inequalities (2.4) become

$$x = p + q - k \quad y \le \max(p + n - k, q + m - k). \tag{2.8}$$

That the inequality for y in (2.8) is still necessary is seen from the following example. Suppose

$$(1 - \alpha B)X_t = \varepsilon_t, \quad \text{i.e. } X_t \sim AR(1)$$

$$(1 + \alpha B)Y_t = \eta_t, \quad \text{i.e. } Y_t \sim AR(1)$$

and also var (ε) = var $(\eta) = \sigma^2$.

If $Z_t = X_t + Y_t$, then $(1 - \alpha B)(1 + \alpha B)Z_t = (1 + \alpha B)\varepsilon_t + (1 - \alpha B)\eta_t$. Denote the right-hand side of the last equation by $\zeta_t = \varepsilon_t + \alpha\varepsilon_{t-1} + \eta_t - \alpha\eta_{t-1}$; then var $(\zeta_t) = 2(1 + \alpha^2)\sigma^2$ and $E\{\zeta_t\zeta_{t-k}\} = 0$, all $k > 0$, so ζ_t is a white noise process and $Z_t \sim AR(2)$ rather than $ARMA(2, 1)$ which would generally occur when two independent $AR(1)$ processes are added together. Those situations in which a simpler model arises than might generally be expected will be called "coincidental situations".

If X_t and Y_t are both stationary, then any case in which x and y in (2.4) take values less than the maximum ones might well be considered coincidental. However, a more general model proposed by Box and Jenkins for marginally non-stationary processes suggests that common roots might well be expected, this common root being unity. They suggest that many series met with in practice obey a simple kind of non-stationary model:

$$(1 - B)^f a(B)X_t = b(B)\varepsilon_t,$$

where $a(B)$ is a polynomial of order p and with all roots of $a(z) = 0$ lying outside the unit circle and $b(B)$ is of order m. In this case X_t is said to obey an integrated autoregressive-moving average model, denoted by $ARIMA(p, f, m)$. Newbold and Granger (1974) found such models fitted a large number of economic time series, although possibly with the addition of seasonal terms. If two independent series X_t and Y_t both obey such a model, i.e. $X_t \sim ARIMA(p, f_1, m)$, $Y_t \sim ARIMA(q, f_2, n)$ then their sum will be $ARIMA(x, f', y)$ where $x \le p + q$; $f' = \max(f_1, f_2)$; $y \le \max(p + n + f_1 - f_2, q + m)$, if $f_1 \ge f_2$; $y \le \max(p + n, q + m + f_2 - f_1)$, if $f_2 \ge f_1$.

Similar considerations apply to the method of taking seasonal effects into account suggested by Box and Jenkins.

Given the basic theorem there is, of course, no difficulty in generalizing it to cover the sum of any number of independent series. Using an obvious generalization of the previous notation, the theorem becomes

$$\sum_{j=1}^{N} ARMA(p_j, m_j) = ARMA(x, y),$$

where

$$x \le \sum_{j=1}^{N} p_j \quad \text{and} \quad y \le \max(x - p_j + m_j, j = 1, \ldots, N).$$

3. SERIES AGGREGATION AND OBSERVATIONAL ERROR MODELS

Two situations where series are added together are of particular inter-pretational importance. The first is where series are aggregated to form some total, and the second is where the observed series is the sum of the true process plus observational error, corresponding to the classical "signal plus noise" situation. Most macroeconomic series, such as G.N.P., unemployment or exports, are aggregates and there is no particular reason to suppose that all of the component series will obey exactly the same model. Virtually any macroeconomic series, other than certain prices or interest rates, contain important observation errors. It would be highly coincidental if the "true" series and the observational error series obeyed models having common roots, apart possibly from the root unity, or that the parameters of these models should be such that the cancelling out of terms produces a value of y in (2.4) less than the maximum possible.

It is interesting to consider a number of special cases of the basic theorem, concentrating on those situations in which coincidental reduc-tions of parameters do not occur. In the cases considered the inter-pretations given will assume that aggregates are of independent components, an assumption almost certainly not true in practice, and that the observational error is white noise and independent of the true process, an assumption of debatable reality but on which little empirical work is available from which to form an opinion.

   (i) $AR(p)$ + *white noise* = $ARMA(p, p)$
      This corresponds to an $AR(p)$ signal as true process plus a simple white noise observational error series.
  (ii) $AR(p) + AR(q) = ARMA(p + q, \max(p, q))$ *and in particular* $AR(1) + AR(1) = ARMA(2, 1)$
      This situation might correspond to a series which is aggregated from two independent AR series. A further case of possible interest is: the sum of k $AR(1)$ series is $ARMA(k, k - 1)$. Case (ii) with an $AR(p)$ signal and $AR(q)$ noise was the subject of a paper by Bailey (1965).
 (iii) $MA(p) + MA(q) = MA(\max(p, q))$ *and in particular* $MA(p)$ + *white noise* = $MA(p)$.
      Thus if a true process follows an MA model then the addition of a white noise observation error will not alter the class of model, although the parameter values will change.

(iv) $ARMA(p, m) + white\ noise = ARMA(p, p)$ if $p > m = ARMA(p, m)$ if $p < m$.

Thus the addition of an observational error may alter the order of an *ARMA* model but need not do so.

(v) $AR(p) + MA(n) = ARMA(p, p + n)$.

Again, this is possibly relevant to the aggregation case, or to the observation error case with noise not being white noise.

If one accepts the belief that time series, particularly in economics, obey either *AR* or *MA* models, both of which can be explained fairly easily in terms of the working of the economy, then the above special cases have a number of possible implications.

Cases (ii) and (v) suggest that a series that is an aggregate of several series, some of which are *AR* series, will be very likely to be an *ARMA* process, although from case (iii) an *MA* process is possible. The independence of the components can be relaxed in a realistic fashion with the same conclusion being reached. If each component consists of two parts, the first a factor common to all components representing the influence of the whole economy on them and the second a factor relating just to the particular component and independent of the economy-wide factor, then simple models can be assumed for each factor and on aggregation the more general form of the basic model involving the sum of several series will apply. Such factor models have been successfully used with series of stock market prices and firms' earnings.

The observational error or signal plus noise situation is also likely to produce an *ARMA* model, from cases (i) and (iv), although case (iii) again suggests that an *MA* model is possible.

Thus both of the realistic situations considered in this section are quite likely to produce *ARMA* models. These situations are discussed further is Sections 5 and 6. Other situations that also produce *ARMA* models are considered in the following section.

4.   TIME AGGREGATION, NON-INTEGER LAGS AND FEEDBACK MODELS

Three other situations that might occur in practice lead either exactly, or approximately, to *ARMA* models. These are:

(i) A variable that obeys a simple model such as $AR(1)$ if it were recorded at an interval of K units of time but which is actually observed at an interval of M units. Details may be found in Amemiya and Wu (1972). The variable considered has to be an accumulated one, that is of the type called a stock variable by economists.

(ii) If X_t is an instantaneously recorded variable, called a flow variable by economists, and suppose that it obeys the model

$$X_t - \alpha X_{t-b} = \varepsilon_t, \quad |\alpha| < 1,$$

where b may be a non-integer multiple or fraction of the observation period, then it is easily shown (see Granger, 1964) that this is equivalent to the $AR(\infty)$ model

$$\sum_{j=0}^{\infty} h_j X_{t-j} = \varepsilon_t,$$

where $h_j = \{\sin(j - b)\pi\}/(j - b)\pi$ and doubtless this model could well be approximated by an $ARMA$ model.

(iii) If X_t, Y_t are generated by the bivariate autoregressive scheme with feedback:

$$a(B)X_t + b(B)Y_t = \varepsilon_t, \quad c(B)X_t + d(B)Y_t = \eta_t,$$

where ε_t, η_t are uncorrelated white noise series and $b(0) = c(0) = 0$, then the model obeyed by X_t alone is found by eliminating Y_t in the equations to be

$$[a(B)d(B) - c(B)b(B)]X_t = d(B)\varepsilon_t + b(B)\eta_t$$

and so the $ARMA(p, q)$ model occurs once more, and it is easily shown that generally $p > q$.

The results of this and the previous section suggest that a number of real data situations are all likely to give rise to $ARMA$ models. Combining these situations will only reinforce this conclusion. In fact, one might well conclude that the model most likely to be found in practice is the mixed autoregressive moving-average model.

5. REALIZABILITY OF SIMPLE MODELS

Given a specific $ARMA(p, q)$ model it is interesting to ask whether or not this could have arisen from some simpler model. On occasions an answer can be found immediately: If $p < q$ then a feedback model is not appropriate, for example. To merely illustrate the problem of realizability, a few examples from Section 3 are considered. As will be seen simplifications are not always possible, as conditions on the coefficients of the $ARMA$ model need to be satisfied for a simpler model to be realizable.

(i) *Can $ARMA(1, 1) = AR(1) + white noise$?*

Suppose $(1 + aB)X_t = \varepsilon_t$ and $Y_t = \eta_t$, where both ε_t and η_t are white noise series, independent of each other, then if $Z_t = X_t + Y_t$ it was seen that Z_t is $ARMA(1, 1)$ given by

$$(1 + aB)Z_t = (1 + aB)\eta_t + \varepsilon_t. \tag{5.1}$$

Now suppose that the given $ARMA(1, 1)$ process is

$$(1 + cB)Z_t = (1 + dB)\zeta_t, \tag{5.2}$$

where ζ_t is a white noise series.

Let μ_0, μ_1 denote the variance and first autocovariance of the $MA(1)$ process on the right-hand side of (5.2). For (5.1) and (5.2) to be equivalent one needs

$$c = a, \tag{5.3(i)}$$

$$\mu_0 = (1+d^2)\sigma_\zeta^2 = (1+a^2)\sigma_\eta^2 + \sigma_\varepsilon^2, \tag{5.3(ii)}$$

$$\mu_1 = d\sigma_\zeta^2 = a\sigma_\eta^2. \tag{5.3(iii)}$$

The realizability conditions may then be written in the form

$$\frac{1}{1+c^2} > \frac{\rho_1}{c} \geq 0, \tag{5.3(iv)}$$

where

$$\rho_1 = \frac{\mu_1}{\mu_0} = \frac{d}{1+d^2},$$

the first inequality coming from (5.3(ii)) and the condition $\sigma_\varepsilon^2 > 0$, the second inequality from (5.3(iii)) and (5.3(i)).

(ii) *Can ARMA(2, 2) = AR(2) + white noise?*

Suppose $(1 + a_1 B + a_2 B^2)X_t = \varepsilon_t$ and $Y_t = \eta_t$, where both ε_t and η_t are white noise series, independent of each other; then if $Z_t = X_t + Y_t$, Z_t is $ARMA(2, 2)$ given by

$$(1+a_1 B + a_2 B^2)Z_t = (1+a_1 B + a_2 B^2)\eta_t + \varepsilon_t. \tag{5.4}$$

Now suppose that the given $ARMA(2, 2)$ process is

$$(1+c_1 B + c_2 B^2)Z_t = (1+d_1 B + d_2 B^2)\zeta_t, \tag{5.5}$$

where ζ_t is a white noise series.

Let μ_0, μ_1, μ_2 denote the variance, first and second autocovariance of the $MA(2)$ process on the right-hand side of (5.5). For (5.4) and (5.5) to be equivalent one needs

$$c_1 = a_1, \tag{5.6(i)}$$

$$c_2 = a_2, \tag{5.6(ii)}$$

$$\mu_0 = (1+d_1^2 + d_2^2)\sigma_\zeta^2 = (1+a_1^2 + a_2^2)\sigma_\eta^2 + \sigma_\varepsilon^2, \tag{5.6(iii)}$$

$$\mu_1 = d_1(1+d_2)\sigma_\zeta^2 = a_1(1+a_2)\sigma_\eta^2, \tag{5.6(iv)}$$

$$\mu_2 = d_2\sigma_\zeta^2 = a_2\sigma_\eta^2. \tag{5.6(v)}$$

These realizability conditions may be written in the form

$$\frac{1}{1+c_1^2 + c_2^2} > \frac{\rho_2}{c_2} \geq 0 \tag{5.6(vi)}$$

and

$$\frac{\rho_1}{c_1(1+c_2)} = \frac{\rho_2}{c_2}, \tag{5.6(vii)}$$

where

$$\rho_1 = \frac{\mu_1}{\mu_0} = \frac{d_1(1+d_2)}{1+d_1^2+d_2^2} \quad \text{and} \quad \rho_2 = \frac{\mu_2}{\mu_0} = \frac{d_2}{1+d_1^2+d_2^2}.$$

As an equality is involved, the realizability of the simple model may be classified as being coincidental.

(iii) *Can ARMA*(2, 2) = *ARMA*(2, 1) + *white noise?*

With the same notation as in (ii), the realizability conditions are

$$\frac{1}{1+c_1^2+c_2^2} > \frac{\rho_2}{c_2} \geq 0. \tag{5.7}$$

These examples illustrate the fact that some models are not capable of simplification and that the realizability conditions will usually be rather complicated. The conditions will also be coincidental if the number of parameters, or "degrees of freedom", are less than the parameters in the initial *ARMA* model.

The problem considered here is only of theoretical interest and is not realistic. An *ARMA* model will generally have been estimated from some data. A more realistic question, and one of considerable interpretational importance, is whether a simple model would have a level of fit that is not significantly different from that achieved by the *ARMA* model. This question is briefly considered in the next section, using simulated time series.

6. SIMULATION OF OBSERVATION ERROR MODELS

Two examples are considered:

EXAMPLE 1: Can a given *ARMA*(1, 1) be expressed as *AR*(1) + white noise?

EXAMPLE 2: Can a given *ARMA*(2, 2) be expressed as *AR*(2) + white noise?

EXAMPLE 1

Two series, each of 200 terms, are generated from *AR*(1) and white noise processes.

Series 1: $(1-0.8B)X_t = \varepsilon_t, \quad t = 1,\dots, N \quad (N = 200).$

Series 2: $Y_t = \eta_t, \quad t = 1,\dots, N \quad (N = 200).$

with $\sigma_\varepsilon^2 = 4, \sigma_\eta^2 = 1.$

The two series added together gives the series $Z_t = X_t + Y_t, t = 1, \ldots, N$, which may be regarded as being generated by the process

$$(1 - 0.8B)Z_t = (1 - 0.8B)\eta_t + \varepsilon_t$$

and this, from (5.3(i)), (5.3(ii)) and (5.3(iii)) may be written as

$$(1 - 0.8B)Z_t = (1 - 0.14B)\zeta_t \tag{6.1}$$

with $\sigma_\zeta^2 = 5.52$.

Using the maximum likelihood estimation method described in Box and Jenkins (1970) the model

$$(1 + cB)Z_t = (1 + dB)\zeta_t$$

fitted to the series $Z_t, t = 1, \ldots, N$, gives estimates $c = -0.76$, $d = -0.04$. The residual sum of squares is 1,273.0, giving an estimate of $\sigma_\zeta^2 = 6.43$. Now we take the given $ARMA(1, 1)$ series to be

$$(1 + cB)Z_t = (1 + dB)\zeta_t,$$

with

$$c = -0.76, d = -0.04, \sigma_\zeta^2 = 6.43. \tag{6.2}$$

Can this be expressed as $AR(1)$ + white noise? Realizability conditions (5.3(iv)) are satisfied since

$$\frac{1}{1 + c^2} = 0.63$$

and

$$\frac{\rho_1}{c} = \frac{d}{c(1 + d^2)} = 0.05.$$

The realizability conditions (5.3(i)), (5.3(ii)) and (5.3(iii)) may be solved to give

$$a = -0.76, \quad \sigma_\eta^2 = 0.34, \quad \sigma_\varepsilon^2 = (1 + d^2)\sigma_\zeta^2 - (1 + a^2)\sigma_\eta^2 = 5.90.$$

Thus, the series (6.2) is exactly equivalent to the series

$$(1 - 0.76B)X_t = \varepsilon_t, \quad Y_t = \eta_t, \quad Z_t = X_t + Y_t \tag{6.3}$$

with $\sigma_\eta^2 = 0.34$, $\sigma_\varepsilon^2 = 5.90$, both (6.2) and (6.3) fitting the given series equally well.

It is therefore seen that if one were given the datum Z_t, one would not know if it were generated by an $ARMA(1, 1)$ model of if it were the sum of two components, one of which is $AR(1)$ and the other is white noise. This is, of course, true of any $ARMA(1, 1)$ model for which the realizability condition holds.

EXAMPLE 2

Two series, each of 200 terms, are generated from $AR(2)$ and white noise processes.

$$\text{Series 1:} \quad (1-0.8B+0.4B^2)X_t = \varepsilon_t, \quad t=1,\dots,N \quad (N=200).$$

$$\text{Series 2:} \quad Y_t = \eta_t, \quad t=1,\dots,N \quad (N=200)$$

$$\text{with } \sigma_\varepsilon^2 = 4, \; \sigma_\eta^2 = 1.$$

The two series added together give the series $Z_t = X_t + Y_t, t = 1, \dots ,$ N which may be regarded as being generated by the process,

$$(1-0.8B+0.4B^2)Z_t = (1-0.8B+0.4B^2)\eta_t + \varepsilon_t$$

and this, from (5.6(i)) to (5.6(v)), may be written as

$$(1-0.8B+0.4B^2)Z_t = (1-0.19B+0.07B^2)\zeta_t \qquad (6.4)$$

with $\sigma_\zeta^2 = 5.59$.

The model $(1 + c_1B + c_2B^2)Z_t = (1 + d_1B + d_2B^2)\zeta_t$ fitted to the series $Z_t, t = 1, \dots , N$, gives estimates $c_1 = -1.01, c_2 = 0.59, d_1 = -0.51, d_2 = 0.12$. The residual sum of squares is 988.5 giving an estimate of $\sigma_\zeta^2 = 5.04$.

Now we take the given $ARMA(2,2)$ series to be

$$(1+c_1B+c_2B^2)Z_t = (1+d_1B+d_2B^2)\zeta_t \qquad (6.5)$$

with $c_1 = -1.01, c_2 = 0.59, d_1 = -0.51, d_2 = 0.12, \sigma_\zeta^2 = 5.04$.

Can this be expressed as $AR(2)$ + white noise? This example is more interesting than Example 1, because it involves a reduction in the number of parameters. $ARMA(2,2)$ contains five parameters, whereas $AR(2)$ and white noise contain a total of four.

The realizability conditions (5.6(vi)) and (5.6(vii)) are not both satisfied.

Equation (5.6(vi)) is satisfied because $(1 + c_1^2 + c_2^2)^{-1} = 0.42$ and

$$\frac{\rho_2}{c_2} = \frac{d_2}{c_2(1+d_1^2+d_2^2)} = 0.16$$

but the equality (5.6(vii)) is not satisfied because

$$\frac{\rho_1}{c_1(1+c_2)} = \frac{d_1(1+d_2)}{c_1(1+c_2)(1+d_1^2+d_2^2)} = 0.28.$$

It is therefore not possible to solve the equations (5.6(i))–(5.6(v)) to obtain a model of the form $AR(2)$ + white noise which is exactly equivalent to (6.5) and which fits the data equally well. However, because the given $ARMA(2,2)$ series has been constructed as the sum of $AR(2)$ and white noise, one would hope to find a model of the form $AR(2)$ + white noise which is almost as good.

We are seeking a model

$$(1+a_1B+a_2B^2)X_t=\varepsilon_t,\quad Y_t=\eta_t,\quad Z_t=X_t+Y_t$$

which may also be written as

$$(1+a_1B+a_2B^2)Z_t=(1+a_1B+a_2B^2)\eta_t+\varepsilon_t$$
$$=(1+b_1B+b_2B^2)\zeta_t,\quad\text{say}.$$

We may proceed as follows:

Let $\gamma_{Zk}=\text{cov}(Z_t,Z_{t-k})$ and $\gamma_{Xk}=\text{cov}(X_t,X_{t-k})$. Because X_t and Y_t are independent, $\gamma_{Z0}=\gamma_{X0}+\sigma_\eta^2$ and $\gamma_{Zk}=\gamma_{Xk}$, $k>0$. In particular,

$$\gamma_{Z0}=\gamma_{X1}+\sigma_\eta^2,\quad \gamma_{Z1}=\gamma_{X1},\quad \gamma_{Z2}=\gamma_{X2}.$$

The given $ARMA(2,2)$ series may be used to estimate γ_{Zk}, $k=0,1,2$, by

$$c_{Zk}=\frac{1}{N}\sum_{t=1}^{N-k}(Z_t-\overline{Z})(Z_{t+k}-\overline{Z}).$$

Then, given an estimate of σ_η^2, γ_{Xk}, $k=0,1,2$, may be estimated by

$$c_{X0}=c_{Z0}-\sigma_\eta^2,\quad c_{X1}=c_{Z1},\quad c_{X2}=c_{Z2}.$$

If $r_1=c_{X1}/x_{X0}$, $r_2=c_{X2}/c_{X0}$, the Yule–Walker equations may be solved to give estimates of a_1,a_2,

$$a_1=\frac{r_1(1-r_2)}{1-r_1^2},\quad a_2=\frac{r_1^2-r_2}{1-r_1^2}$$

and σ_ε^2 may be estimated by

$$\sigma_\varepsilon^2=c_{X0}(1+r_1a_1+r_2a_2),$$

b_1 and b_2 may then be estimated using the realizability conditions (5.6(iii))–(5.6(v)) by solving the equations

$$\frac{b_2}{b_1(1+b_2)}=\frac{a_2}{a_1(1+a_2)}$$

$$\frac{b_2}{1+b_1^2+b_2^2}=\frac{a_2\sigma_\eta^2}{(1+a_1^2+a_2^2)\sigma_\eta^2+\sigma_\varepsilon^2}.$$

These equations may be written as

$$b_1=\frac{Ab_2}{1+b_2},\tag{6.7(i)}$$

$$1+(2-C)b_2+(2-2C+A^2)b_2^2+(2-C)b_2^3+b_2^4=0,\tag{6.7(ii)}$$

where

$$A=\frac{a_1(1+a_2)}{a_2},\quad C=\frac{(1+a_1^2+a_2^2)\sigma_\eta^2+\sigma_\varepsilon^2}{a_2\sigma_\eta^2}$$

choosing the solution of (6.7(ii)) which lies between 0 and a_2 (from 5.6(v)).

The model

$$(1+a_1 B + a_2 B^2) Z_t = (1 + b_1 B + b_2 B^2) \zeta_t$$

is then fitted to the given series, and the residual sum of squares obtained.

By considering a range of values of σ_η^2 it is possible to determine the parameter values which minimize the residual sum of squares.

For the given series, these values are $a_1 = -0.91$, $a_2 = 0.60$, $b_1 = -0.40$, $b_2 = 0.20$ with $\sigma_\eta^2 = 1.62$, $\sigma_\varepsilon^2 = 2.40$. The residual sum of squares is 994.5, giving an estimate of $\sigma_\zeta^2 = 5.07$.

So the model (6.6) with $a_1 = -0.91$, $a_2 = 0.60$, $\sigma_\eta^2 = 1.62$, $\sigma_\varepsilon^2 = 2.40$ is almost as good as the $ARMA(2, 2)$ model (6.5).

It is, of course, no surprise that the particular Z_t series here considered, although it would be identified as an $ARMA(2, 2)$ process, could equally well be explained as being the sum of an $AR(2)$ plus white noise, since this is how it was generated. However, many series identified to be $ARMA(2, 2)$ might also be equally explained by the simple sum, which is more parsimonious in the sense that it involves fewer parameters to be estimated. If a series can be so decomposed into two or more components this could help with interpretation of its generating process. One might, for example, suggest that the true series might be considered as a true $AR(2)$ signal plus a white noise observation error series. If true, this decomposition would suggest the importance of the observation error measured in terms of the contribution of this error towards the variance of the optimum one-step forecasts. If this contribution is large enough it might be worth spending more to reduce observation error and thus decrease prediction error.

The technique used in our second example can easily be adapted to deal with other models and might allow the analyst to suggest the importance of the noise contribution to prediction error variance in a signal plus noise model.

REFERENCES

AMEMIYA, T. and WU, R. Y. (1972). The effect of aggregation on prediction in the autoregressive model. *J. Amer. Statist. Ass.*, 67, 628–632.

BAILEY, M. G. (1965). Prediction of an autoregressive variable subject both to disturbances and to errors of observation. *J. Amer. Statist. Ass.*, 60, 164–181.

BOX, G. E. P. and JENKINS, G. M. (1970). *Time Series Analysis*. San Francisco, Holden-Day.

CHATFIELD, C. and PROTHERO, D. L. (1973). Box–Jenkins seasonal forecasting: problems in a case study (with Discussion). *J. R. Statist. Soc.* A, 136, 295–336.

DAVIES, N., PATE, M. B. and FROST, M. G. (1974). Maximum autocorrelations for moving average processes. *Biometrika*, 61, 199–200.

GRANGER, C. W. J. and HATANAKA, M. (1964). *Spectral Analysis of Economic Time Series*. Princeton University Press.

NEWBOLD, P. and GRANGER, C. W. J. (1974). Experience with forecasting univariate time series and the combination of forecasts (with Discussion). *J. R. Statistical Soc.* A, 137, 131–164.

WOLD, H. (1953). *A Study in the Analysis of Stationary Time Series*, 2nd ed. Stockholm: Alqvist and Wiksell.

CHAPTER 12

On the Invertibility of Time Series Models*

C. W. J. Granger and Allan Andersen

A generalized definition of invertibility is proposed and applied to linear, non-linear and bilinear models. It is shown that some recently studied non-linear models are not invertible, but conditions for invertibility can be achieved for the other models.

Keywords: Time series analysis; invertibility; non-linear models; bilinear models

1. A DEFINITION OF INVERTIBILITY

Consider the univariate class of time series models which take the form

$$x_t = f(x_{t-j}, \varepsilon_{t-j}, j = 1, \ldots, P) + \varepsilon_t \tag{1}$$

where ε_t is pure white noise, so that ε_t and ε_s are independent for all $t \neq s$, and is an unobserved input to the system. If this type of model is to be used for forecasting, and provided the function $f(\ )$ does contain some $\varepsilon_{t-j}, j \geq 1$, it is necessary to be able to estimate the ε_t sequence from the observed x_t's. A natural way of doing this is to assume values for as many initial, or starting up ε's as are necessary, i.e. $\hat{\varepsilon}_{-j}, j = 0, \ldots, (P-1)$, say. Assuming now that $x_{-j}, j = 0, \ldots, (P-1)$ are also observed, then ε_1 can be estimated directly from the assumed known generating formula (1) by

$$\hat{\varepsilon}_1 = x_1 - f(x_{1-j}, \hat{\varepsilon}_{1-j}, j = 1, \ldots, P) \tag{2}$$

and then $\hat{\varepsilon}_2$ is estimated by

$$\hat{\varepsilon}_2 = x_2 - f(x_{2-j}, \hat{\varepsilon}_{2-j}, j = 1, \ldots, P)$$

and so forth. Thus, using the assumed starting up values an iterative procedure can be used to estimate all $\hat{\varepsilon}_t$, based on the observed x's and the

* *Stochastic Processes and Their Applications* 8, 1978, 87–92.

generating model. The error that will almost certainly arise from such a procedure will be denoted

$$e_t = \varepsilon_t - \hat{\varepsilon}_t.$$

We shall say that the model (1) is invertible if

$$E[e_t^2] \to 0 \quad \text{as } t \to \infty, \tag{3}$$

which assumes that the correct generating formula is known completely, both in form and the actual parameter values.

It is quite obvious from (2) that

$$\hat{\varepsilon}_t = x_t - g(x_{t-k}, k = 1, \ldots, t + P, \hat{\varepsilon}_{1-j}, j = 1, \ldots, P),$$

where $\{\hat{\varepsilon}_{1-j}\}$ are given estimates of the appropriate random variables. The condition (3) therefore implies that a model is invertible if the variance of the error involved in estimating ε_t in terms of a finite number of past and present x's tends to zero as that number tends to infinity, unconditional on the starting up values.

If the parameter values in the model are not known exactly, as would occur if they were estimated from an earlier finite length of data for instance, (3) might be replaced by

$$E[e_t^2] \to c \quad \text{as } t \to \infty, \tag{4}$$

where $c < \infty$ is some constant.

2.   LINEAR MODELS

To illustrate the definition, consider the simple first-order moving average model given by

$$x_t = \varepsilon_t + b\varepsilon_{t-1}. \tag{5}$$

If b is known, the optimum one-step forecast of x_{n+1} made at time n is just

$$f_{n,1} = b\varepsilon_n$$

but for this to be useful, ε_n must be estimated from the observed x_t. Given an assumed starting value, such as $\hat{\varepsilon}_0 = 0$, the estimated $\hat{\varepsilon}_t$ are generated by

$$\hat{\varepsilon}_t = x_t - b\,\hat{\varepsilon}_{t-1}$$

so that the error series e_t is generated by

$$e_t = \varepsilon_t - \hat{\varepsilon}_t = x_t - b\varepsilon_{t-1} - (x_t - b\hat{\varepsilon}_{t-1})$$

i.e.

$$e_t = -be_{t-1}. \tag{6}$$

(6) is a difference equation with the deterministic solution

$$e_t = (-b)^t e_0. \tag{7}$$

Clearly $e_t \to 0$ if $|b| < 1$, which is the condition given in textbooks that the MA(1) model (5) is invertible. It should be noted that the ARMA $(p, 1)$ model

$$x_t = \sum_{j=1}^{p} \alpha_j x_{t-j} + \varepsilon_t + b\varepsilon_{t-1}$$

leads to precisely the same equations (6) and (7).

If the same analysis is applied to the MA(1) model (5) but with an estimated parameter $\hat{b}$, then the difference equation (6) becomes

$$e_t = (b - \hat{b})\varepsilon_{t-1} - \hat{b}e_{t-1} \tag{8}$$

so that the error series e_t is now generated by an AR(1) process. Equation (8) has a solution in two parts, the first of which is (7) but with b replaced by $\hat{b}$ and the second is the infinite moving average representation of e_t in terms of past ε_t, i.e.

$$(b - \hat{b}) \sum_{j=1}^{t} (\hat{b})^{j-1} \varepsilon_{t-j}.$$

If $|\hat{b}| < 1$, this second component has mean zero and variance

$$V(e_t) \simeq \frac{(b - \hat{b})^2}{1 - \hat{b}^2} \text{Var}(\varepsilon_t) \tag{9}$$

for large t. Thus, the condition $|\hat{b}| < 1$ is now required to ensure both that the first component of the solution of (8) does not explode and that the second component has a finite variance. To obtain these results, it has been assumed that $\hat{b}$ is estimated once and for all and is not continually updated as extra data becomes available. It should be noted from (9) that the error series e_t can have larger variance even than ε_t, the series being estimated. There is no difficulty in extending this analysis to the case where the data is generated by an ARMA (p, q) model but an ARMA $(\hat{p}, \hat{q})$ model is estimated. It is then found that e_t obeys an ARMA $(\hat{p} + q, p + \hat{q} - 1)$ model, and will not generally have a variance that tends to zero as t becomes large, which is why the form (4) of the definition of invertibility is required.

The condition of invertibility in linear models is also used for another purpose: to help choose a unique model. For example, for the MA (1) model (5) all autocorrelations vanish except the first, which is given by

$$\rho_1 = \frac{b}{1+b^2}.$$

As ρ_1 can be easily estimated from the observed x_t, this formula can be used to estimate the coefficient b, by solving for b in terms of ρ_1. However, it is immediately obvious that there is not a unique solution for b, but it can be shown that there is always one solution corresponding to an invertible model. This becomes particularly important for MA (q) models when there are large numbers of possible solutions for the parameters, but only one corresponds to an invertible model (see, for instance, Granger and Newbold [3]).

In all of the textbooks on time-series the concept of invertibility is only discussed for linear moving average models or for the moving-average part of linear ARMA models. In these texts a moving average is said to be invertible if there is an equivalent AR (∞) model, the two models being equivalent in the sense that they both lead to identical autocovariance sequences. It is easily seen that this definition of invertibility is only relevant for linear models. The definition suggested in section 1 of this paper provides identical conditions for linear models and may also be applied to non-linear models, as will be illustrated below. It is an operational definition, as it does have indications about the ability of the model to produce useful forecasts.

For purely autoregressive models, the question of invertibility does not arise as the residual series ε_t can always be directly estimated from the observed x values, provided the parameters of the model are known. Thus, autoregressive models are always invertible.

3.   A CLASS OF NON-INVERTIBLE MODELS

A set of models which is not invertible for any non-zero values of its parameters consists of non-linear moving averages. For example, if x_t is generated by

$$x_t = \varepsilon_t + \alpha\varepsilon_{t-1}^2 \tag{10}$$

then $\hat{\varepsilon}_t$ will be solved iteratively by

$$\hat{\varepsilon}_t = x_t - \alpha\hat{\varepsilon}_{t-1}^2. \tag{11}$$

From (10), it is easily shown that x_t is second-order stationary. The solution to (11) has two components one of which is also the solution to

$$z_t = -\alpha z_{t-1}^2 \tag{12}$$

but this difference equation is not stable and its only solution, other than $z_t = 0$, is explosive. A proof may be found for example in Levy and Lessman [4] who consider the general first-order class

$$z_t = F[z_{t-1}].$$

The limit points for this system are given by

$$a = F(a)$$

and if $z_s \simeq a$ for some $s < t$, then a first approximation for z_t is

$$z_t = a + A(F'(a))^t$$

where $F'(z) = dF(z)/dz$. It is seen that a necessary condition for non-explosiveness is that $|F'(a)| < 1$ for any attainable limit point. For equation (12) the limit points are 0 and $-1/\alpha$ and for the second of these $F'(a) = 2$, so that z_t will be explosive. It follows that $\hat{\varepsilon}_t$, given by (11), will diverge from the series ε_t it is attempting to estimate and thus model (10) is not invertible and hence of no use for forecasting.

Similar difference equation considerations show that models of the form

$$x_t = \varepsilon_t + \alpha\varepsilon_{t-1}\varepsilon_{t-2} \tag{13}$$

are never invertible. These models, which have recently been considered by Robinson [5] and by Villegas [6] are possibly of analytical interest but seem to be of limited practical value.

4. BILINEAR MODELS

As a final example of the use of the invertibility definition introduced in the first section, bilinear models are considered. An example of such a model, and the only one analysed here in any detail is

$$x_t = \varepsilon_t + \alpha x_{t-1}\varepsilon_{t-1} \tag{14}$$

where ε_t is an independent, identically distributed sequence of variables. Such models have recently attracted attention by both control engineers (e.g. Bruni, di Pillo and Koch [1]) and time series analysts (Granger and Andersen [2]). The estimates of ε_t, the sequence $\hat{\varepsilon}_t$, are generated by

$$\hat{\varepsilon}_t = x_t - \alpha x_{t-1}\hat{\varepsilon}_{t-1} \tag{15}$$

and subtracting both sides from ε_t, gives

$$e_t = -\alpha x_{t-1}e_{t-1} \tag{16}$$

so that

$$e_t = (-\alpha)^t \left(\prod_1^t x_{j-1} \right) e_0 \tag{17}$$

A necessary and sufficient condition that $e_t \to 0$ in probability as $t \to \infty$ is found from (17) by squaring and taking logarithms which gives $\mathbf{E}[\log \alpha^2 x_t^2] < 0$, assuming x_t is ergodic.[1] It is very difficult to evaluate this condition as the distribution of x_t is not known, but using the inequality that the geometric mean is less than the arithmetic means provides as a sufficient condition $\mathbf{E}(\alpha^2 x_t^2) < 1$. Granger and Andersen [2] have shown that

$$E(\alpha^2 x_t^2) = \frac{\lambda^2 (2\lambda^2 + 1)}{1 - \lambda^2}$$

where $\lambda^2 = \alpha^2 \sigma_\varepsilon^2$, and $\sigma_\varepsilon^2 =$ variance (ε_t), provided $\lambda^2 < 1$. Thus, the sufficient condition is $|\lambda| < 0.606$. If $|\lambda|$ is in this region then the model will certainly be invertible. It is interesting to note that Granger and Andersen also show that the first autocorrelation for x_t generated by (14) is given by

$$\rho_1 = \frac{\lambda^2 (1 - \lambda^2)}{1 + \lambda^2 + \lambda^4} \tag{18}$$

which increases in value as $|\lambda|$ increases from zero but reaches a maximum at $|\lambda| = 0.606$. Thus, if an estimated value of ρ_1 is used in (18) and λ^2 solved for, taking a value in the region $|\lambda| < 0.606$ will ensure invertibility and also reduce the number of possible solutions for the parameters of the model, just as occurred for the MA (1) model.

5.   CONCLUSIONS

It is usual to call a moving average model invertible if it has an equiva lent autoregressive representation of infinite order. The importance of the invertibility requirement is that a non-invertible moving average model cannot be used to forecast. The invertibility condition is also used to select one of many alternative moving average models that have the same autocovariances. This definition of invertibility is not usable with more general models such as (1), so an alternative definition is proposed based on the estimatability of the white noise residual term. Using this definition, some intuitively attractive non-linear moving average models are shown to be never invertible. However, bilinear models are found to be both non-linear generalisations of ARMA models and to be sometimes invertible. It has been illustrated in [2] that some invertible bilinear models do produce superior forecasts compared to linear models

---

[1] We would like to thank Professor E. J. Hannan for pointing this out to us.

having the same autocovariances. It is also shown, for a particular case, that the invertibility condition may still be useful in helping choose between alternative estimated parameter values.

REFERENCES

C. Bruni, G. di Pillo and G. Koch, Bilinear systems in an appealing class of "nearly linear" systems in theory and applications, *IEEE Trans. on Auto Control*, AC–19 (1974) 334–348.

C. W. J. Granger and A. Andersen, *An introduction to bilinear time series models* (Vandenhoeck and Ruprecht; Göttingen, 1978).

C. W. J. Granger and P. Newbold, *Forecasting Economic Time Series* (Academic Press, New York, 1977).

H. Levy and F. Lessman, *Finite Difference Equations* (Pitman, London, 1961).

P. M. Robinson, The estimation of a non-linear moving average model, *Stoch. Process. and Appl.* 5 (1977) 81–90.

C. Villegas, On a multivariate central limit theorem for stationary bilinear processes, *Stoch. Process. and Appl.* 4 (1976) 121–133.

CHAPTER 13

Near Normality and Some Econometric Models*

C. W. J. Granger

A bivariate random variable (X, Y) with characteristic function $\phi(S_1, S_2)$ has its (p, q)th cumulant C_{pq} generated by

$$\log \phi(S_1, S_2) = \sum_{p,q=0}^{\infty} (-1)^{\frac{1}{2}(p+q)} C_{pq}(X, Y) S_1^p S_2^q$$

If (X, Y) is normally distributed, then $C_{pq} = 0$, all p, q such that $p + q > 2$.

DEFINITION: For the pair of random variables $(X_1, Y_1), (X_2, Y_2)$ with each component having zero mean and unit variance, (X_1, Y_1) will be said to be *nearer-normal than* (X_2, Y_2) if

$$|C_{pq}(X_1, Y_1)| \le |C_{pq}(X_2, Y_2)|$$

for all p, q with $p + q > 1$, provided there is at least one strict inequality. It will be assumed that all cumulants exist.

This is obviously a very stringent condition, and it cannot be applied to most pairs of random variables. A number of results have recently been discussed in the univariate case (Granger, 1977) where it is shown that the weighted sum of independent and identically distributed random variables is nearer-normal than the constituent variables. This result does not necessarily hold if the variables are not identically distributed or if they are dependent. The corresponding bivariate theorem is as follows.

THEOREM: *Consider the finite sequence of bivariate random vectors (X_i, Y_i), $i = 1, \ldots, n$, such that each vector (X_i, Y_i) has identical bivariate distribution, each component X_i and Y_i has zero mean and unit variance, and each $(X_i, Y_i)(X_j, Y_j)$ are pair-wise independent, and if*

$$W = \sum_{i=1}^{n} \alpha_i X_i, \quad Z = \sum_{i=1}^{n} \beta_i Y_i$$

* *Econometrica* 47, 1979, 781–784.

*with there being at least two non-zero α's and similarly for the β's, then
(i) $|$correlation $(W, Z)| \leq |$ correlation $(X, Y)|$, (ii)(W, Z) is nearer-
normal than (X, Y).*

PROOF: In the proof, two standard inequalities are employed: Cauchy's
inequality,

$$\left(\sum a_k b_k\right)^2 \leq \sum a_k^2 \sum b_k^2,$$

and Jensen's inequality,

$$\left(\sum |a_k|^m\right)^{1/m} \leq \left(\sum |a_k|^{m'}\right)^{1/m'}$$

if $m > m'$ with m, m' integer.
   Clearly

$$\text{variance}(W) = \sum \alpha_i^2, \quad \text{variance}(Z) = \sum \beta_i^2,$$

and

$$\text{correlation}(W, Z) = \frac{\sum \alpha_i \beta_i}{\sqrt{\sum \alpha_i^2 \cdot \sum \beta_i^2}} \cdot \text{correlation}(X, Y).$$

Section (i) of the theorem obviously holds, from Cauchy's inequality,
with strict equality occurring only if $\alpha_i = \lambda \beta_i$, all i. The situation where
this equality occurs is excluded in subsequent discussion.
   Define W', Z' to be W, Z divided by their respective standard deviations and $a_j = a_j/(\Sigma \alpha_1^2)'$, $b_j = \beta_j/(\Sigma \beta_1^2)'$.
   The characteristic function of W', Z' is immediately seen to be

$$\phi_{w'z'}(S_1, S_2) = \prod_{i=1}^{n} \phi_{XY}(a_i S_1, b_i S_2)$$

and so

$$C_{pq}(W', Z') = \left[\sum_i a_i^p b_i^q\right] C_{pq}(X, Y). \tag{1}$$

By noting that

$$\sum a_i^p b_i^q \leq \left[\sum_i a_i^{2p}\right]^{\frac{1}{2}} \left[\sum_i b_i^{2q}\right]^{\frac{1}{2}}$$

from Cauchy's inequality and that

$$\sum a_i^{2p} = \left[\frac{\left(\Sigma \alpha_i^{2p}\right)^{1/p}}{\left(\Sigma \alpha_i^2\right)}\right]^p \leq 1$$

by Jensen's inequality applied to the sequence α_i^2, and similarly for Σb_j^{2a}, it is seen that $\left|\Sigma_j a_j^p b_j^q\right| \leq 1$ and the second part of the theorem follows from taking the modulus of equation (1).

The theorem says that a bivariate vector formed by a weighted sum of bivariate vectors whose components are independent and identically distributed (i.i.d.) will generally both be nearer-normal than its constituents and the components of the vector will be nearer-uncorrelated. There is no difficulty in generalizing at least the nearer-normality part of this theorem to vectors of any order.

It should be noted that this is not necessarily a limit theorem. The sample size n can take any value from two to infinity and the results generally hold, although in the limit case, coefficients α_i, β_i can be chosen to depend on n so that no strict inequality occurs and so (W, Z) is identically distributed with all (X_i, Y_i). Such constructed cases where the theorem does not strictly hold are generally very contrived and are highly unlikely to be of any practical relevance in econometrics.

Concerning the interpretation of the nearer-normality part of the theorem, it merely says that central importance of the normal distribution found in the central limit theorem also holds true for most finite sums of i.i.d. variables. It should be noted in the theorem that the marginal distributions of each X_i and Y_i are not assumed to be equal.

Some consequences of the theorem for different situations encountered in economics are as follows:

(i) *Cross-section analysis*: Suppose that there are n micro-units, such as households, firms or districts, and that for each a pair of variables (U_i, V_i) are recorded. If there exist constants α_i, β_i such that $(X_i, Y_i) \equiv (U_i/\alpha_i, V_i/\beta_i)$ are pair-wise independent vectors with each (X_i, Y_i) having identical bivariate distribution, then any weighted average, or aggregate, of the (U_i, V_i) will be generally both nearer-normal than (X, Y) and also nearer uncorrelated. This latter property can be thought of as an aggregation bias. The result will not hold strictly for the few exceptional cases of coefficient values noted in the theorem and its proof.

(ii) *Seemingly-unrelated variables*: If a pair of stationary time series are generated by the system

$$W_t = \sum c_j W_{t-j} + \varepsilon_t,$$

$$Z_t = \sum d_j Z_{t-j} + \eta_t,$$

where (ε_t, η_t) is a vector white noise series with

$$\text{corr}(\varepsilon_t, \eta_t) = p \quad \text{and} \quad \text{corr}(\varepsilon_t, \eta_s) = 0, \quad t \neq s,$$

then (W_t, Z_t) are seemingly unrelated, to use the term introduced by Zellner (1962), with no exogenous variables involved. In a different context, such variables are said to have only instantaneous causality, see Pierce and Haugh (1977). Because of the stationarity assumption, the variables can be transformed so that W_t is a weighted sum of past and present ε_t and Z_t of past and present η_t. The theorem then suggests that, if the model is correct and provided $c_j \neq \lambda d_j$, all j, then a stronger relationship should be found between the pre-whitened series ε_t and η_t than between the unwhitened series W_t, Z_t, throwing some light on the discussion of the paper by Pierce (1977). The fact that, in practice, the reverse is often actually observed implies that the assumptions made in the theorem or the model assumed is not correct. A possibility is that the variables used in some empirical studies are not stationary, do not have finite variance and need to be differenced before correlation or regression analysis is conducted, as discussed by Granger and Newbold (1974).

(iii) *Multi-variate systems*: Consider the bivariate system.

$$W_t = \sum_{j=0}^{\infty} a_j \varepsilon_{t-j} + \sum_{j=0}^{\infty} b_j \eta_{t-j},$$

$$Z_t = \sum_{j=0}^{\infty} c_j \varepsilon_{t-j} + \sum_{j=0}^{\infty} d_j \eta_{t-j},$$

where ε_t, η_t are a pair of independent, white noise processes, with identical distributions. This is a general representation of a bivariate, stationary purely non-deterministic time series involving no exogenous variables apart from the assumption that ε_t, η_t have identical distributions. By applying the univariate version of Wald's theorem to the two series separately, they can be represented by

$$W_t = \sum_{j=0}^{\infty} f_j e_{1,t-j},$$

$$Z_t = \sum_{j=0}^{\infty} g_j e_{2,t-j},$$

where e_{1t}, e_{2t} are individually white noise series but do not necessarily form a white noise vector. e_{kt} are each sums of past and present ε_t and η_t, possibly infinite in extent, for example

$$e_{1,t} = \frac{1}{f(B)}[a(B)\varepsilon_t + b(B)\eta_t],$$

where B is the backward operator, $B^k x_t = x_{t-k}$, $f(B) = \Sigma_{i \geq 0} f_i B^i$, $a(B) = \Sigma_{i \geq 0} a_i B^i$, and $b(B) = \Sigma_{i \geq 0} b_i B^i$. By taking

$$(X_{2i}, Y_{2i}) = (\varepsilon_{t-i}, \varepsilon_{t-i}) \qquad (i = 1, 2, \ldots, \infty),$$

$$(X_{2i+1}, Y_{2i+1}) = (\eta_{t-i}, \eta_{t-i}) \qquad (i = 1, 2, \ldots, \infty),$$

it follows from the theorem that W_t is nearer-normal than e_{1t}, Z_t is nearer-normal than e_{2t}, $e_{1,t}$ is nearer-normal than ε_t or η_t, $e_{2,t}$ is nearer-normal than ε_t or η_t, (W_t, Z_t) is nearer-normal than (ε_t, η_t).

Further, if the coefficients in any model are unknown and have to be estimated, the resulting estimated residuals are nearer-normal than the actual disturbances.

Many aspects of inference and estimation in econometrics are based on an assumption of normality, of the data being used, but this assumption is rarely tested. In particular, when estimating simultaneous equation systems, it is frequently assumed that the disturbances are multivariate normally distributed. The results listed above, which easily generalize to multivariate systems, suggest that if a significance test for normality is applied, then type II errors (in which the null hypothesis of normality is accepted when it is false) are increased if individual series are used compared to pre-whitened series, but that this error is also increased if residuals from a sub-system are used compared to the residuals for a whole system. As one rarely knows the dimension of the whole system, it becomes unclear what data should be used to test for normality and not bias the result towards accepting normality.

The few tests of normality for economic data that have appeared frequently reject a null hypothesis of normality. For example, Nelson and Granger (1978) fitted ARIMA models to twenty-one economic series, both untransformed and using the Box-Cox transformation and strongly rejected normality of residuals on over two-thirds of occasions. These rejected series had coefficients of kurtosis positive and over four times the estimated standard deviation of this coefficient. Only six series appeared to have normally distributed residuals when untransformed. Thus, although the theory suggests bias in type II errors, actual tests reject the null hypothesis of normality, frequently, implying perhaps that this rejection is stronger even than standard procedures suggest. If similar results are found for a large sample of economic series, assumptions of normality linearity, and homogeneity will have to be seriously questioned, with important consequences for much of present model-building practice.

REFERENCES

GRANGER, C. W. J.: "Tendency Towards Normality of Linear Combinations of Random Variables," *Metrika*, 23 (1977), 237–248.
    and P. NEWBOLD: "Spurious Regressions in Econometrics," *Journal of Econometrics*, 2 (1974), 111–120.
NELSON, H. L., and C. W. J. GRANGER: "Experience with Using the Box-Cox Transformation when Forecasting Economic Time Series," Discussion Paper

78-1, Economics Dept., University of California, San Diego, 1978; to be published in the *Journal of Econometrics*.

PIERCE, D. A.: "Relationships – and the Lack Thereof – Between Economic Time Series, with Special Reference to Money and Interest Rates," *Journal of the American Statistical Association*, 72 (1977), 11–26.

 AND L. D. HAUGH: "Causality in Temporal Systems: Characterisations and a Survey," *Journal of Econometrics*, 5 (1977), 265–294.

ZELLNER, A.: "An Efficient Method of Estimating Seemingly Unrelated Regressions and Tests for Aggregation Bias," *Journal of the American Statistical Association*, 57 (1962), 348–368.

CHAPTER 14

The Time Series Approach to Econometric Model Building*
C. W. J. Granger and Paul Newbold**

1. TWO PHILOSOPHIES

There are currently two distinct approaches available for the analysis of economic data measured through time: the time series approach and the classical econometric model building method. These two approaches are based on quite different philosophies about what is important and how data should be approached. It is almost a tautology to say that the optimum approach should probably involve the best features of each. The object of this paper is to outline the lessons from recent advances in time series analysis, as we see them, for econometric model building. It is accepted that the ultimate aim of econometricians is to build sound models of the economy that can then be used to check hypotheses, make good forecasts, and suggest control possibilities. However, we do feel that the present methods of model construction are far from perfect and that time series techniques can be used to improve matters.

The two basic differences in approach involve the determination of the lag structure of the model and the handling of the residuals. Further differences are concerned with the treatment of trend and seasonal components. These four features of model building are not unrelated, of course. In the time series approach to modeling a great deal of attention is paid to the lag structure of variables entering the model, whereas in most econometric models a rather *ad hoc* approach is taken to the introduction of lagged variables. Consequently, time series models typically contain more lags, unless the econometric models incorporate a distributed lag approach. It could be argued that for a proper study of lags, longer series are required than are sometimes available to econometricians. The counter-argument states that econometricians can only fool themselves in believing that their models are adequate if they are built

* *New Methods in Business Cycle Research*, ed. C. Sims, 1977, Federal Reserve Bank of Minneapolis.
** This research has been conducted under National Science Foundation Grant No. SOC 74-12243, University of California, San Diego, and University of Nottingham, England.

on insufficient data, naive assumptions, and unsophisticated methods of analysis. An almost certain consequence of the use of a time series approach in econometric model building will be the introduction of more lagged variables, both endogenous and exogenous.

Residual terms are usually treated by econometricians as being mere nuisances of little real importance. Many econometric texts introduce models as a set of deterministic relationships between variables and then casually add on the "error" terms to equations to account for such things as model misspecification and variable measurement error. The very use of names such as "residuals" and "errors" implies value judgments about the importance of these terms. A better name might be "innovations," although "error" is a proper designation in a forecasting context, as will be seen. The recent tendency in time series analysis has been to model carefully the lag structure of that part of a variable unexplained by its own lagged values and by other observed variables. Suppose one has available at time n an information set I_n that is going to be used to explain, or fore-cast, X_{n+1}. I_n may contain just $X_{n-j}, j \geq 0$, or it may also contain past and present values of other variables. Let $f_{n,1}$ be the optimum one-step, least-squares forecast of X_{n+1} made at time n, then one can write

$$X_{n+1} = f_{n,1} + \varepsilon_{n+1}$$

where ε_{n+1} is necessarily a white noise series. It is seen that X_{n+1} is the sum of two components, one of which $f_{n,1}$ represents the influence of the past and present on the future and the other ε_{n+1} is the innovation series which is that part of X_{n+1} which is unexpected, or unpredictable, using I_n. Without these innovations the generating process for X_t would be deterministic, so that the series follows a smooth, perfectly predictable path, which is both a dull and a quite unrealistic situation. The actual world is clearly stochastic, and it is the innovations which keep the process going. In fact, once the relationship between X_{n+1} and I_n is known, ε_{n+1} repre-sents the only *new* information about the state of the world contained in X_{n+1}. In the above, ε_{n+1} is seen to be the one-step forecast error; and so the use of the term "error" is acceptable from a forecasting point of view, but perhaps not from a goodness-of-fit of model viewpoint unless one inherently believes the world to be deterministic. The innovation series are not directly observable, of course, and have to be estimated from the observed variables. It is worth noting that the optimum forecast is some-times more conveniently expressed in terms of these estimated innova-tions. Suppose X_t is generated by the ARMA (1,1) model

$$X_t = aX_{t-1} + \varepsilon_t + \beta\varepsilon_{t-1}, \quad |a| < 1$$

then $\quad f_{n,1} = aX_n + \beta\hat{\varepsilon}_n$

and $\quad \hat{\varepsilon}_n = X_n - f_{n-1,1}.$

Provided the process is invertible, by which we mean that ε_n can be well estimated from $X_{n-j}, j \geq 0$, it is seen that $f_{n,1}$ can be either expressed in terms of X_n and $\hat{\varepsilon}_n$ or less conveniently in terms of all $X_{n-j}, j \geq 0$. In the example, the condition for invertibility is just $|\beta| < 1$.

The casual treatment of residuals in econometric texts has perhaps led to the careless treatment of these terms in actual econometric models. The traditional approach has been first to assume the residuals to be white noise and to check this assumption by looking at the Durbin-Watson statistic, which effectively measures the first order serial correlation of the residuals. If evidence of significant first order serial correlation is found, the residuals are then assumed to be first order autoregressive. Although clearly better than just staying with the white noise assumption, the approach still has to be classified as naive. There is little reason to suppose that the correct model for the residuals is $AR(1)$; in fact, if the variables involved are aggregates and involve measurement error, an $ARMA$ model is much more likely to be correct, as indicated by Granger and Morris [41].[1] Rather than just looking at the first serial correlation coefficient, the whole correlogram for the residals should be used to identify the proper model. However, there is an important and well-known problem with this procedure, as one strictly needs to know the form of the model for the residuals before they, together with the parameters of the model, can be correctly estimated. A further advantage of looking at the whole correlogram is that the adequacy of any seasonal adjustment procedure being used can be checked. If quarterly data is being used, a significantly positive fourth order serial correlation would imply that not all of the seasonal component has been removed, and a significantly negative coefficient indicates that too much has been removed, as is found quite frequently when one is time series modeling seasonally adjusted data.

Our remarks so far have been critical of the classical econometric approach compared to time series methods. This is because econometricians pay relatively little attention to lags or the modeling of residuals. The main attention of econometricians is directed toward the simultaneity of the relationships between economic variables. The traditional viewpoint of the economy as a multitude of highly interrelated variables is one that is easily accepted by a casual glance at the data. Given just a data sample, it would be virtually impossible to find an acceptable model as there are clearly too many possibilities through which to sift. It is obviously necessary to limit severely the possible models, and this is generally done by invoking some economic theory, which indicates groups of explanatory variables and, equally important, suggests variables that can be left out of a structural form equation. The theory is rarely sufficiently precise to specify completely the lags to be used in the model, the struc-

---

[1] Numbers in [   ] correspond to the reference list, in "New Methods in Business Cycle Research," p. 219.

tural form of the residual term, or even the actual form of the economic variables that do enter the equation. The theory is thus useful in providing a basic form for the model but still leaves sufficient degrees of freedom for detailed data analysis to be worthwhile. The use of a large number of simultaneous equations in an econometric model is quite different from the traditional time series approach where just a few series are analyzed together. In fact, the vast majority of the time series literature considers only the modeling of a single series in terms of its own past. The recently popular single series Box-Jenkins approach is an obvious example. Some discussion has been directed at the case where there is a one-way causality between a pair of series, where a transfer function version of the Box-Jenkins approach is available. Only recently has attention turned to the problem of modeling a pair of series related by a two-way causality or feedback mechanism.[2] This is discussed further in a later section. There is little likelihood of extending the time series data modeling approach to a large number of series simultaneously due to the complexity of the method. The gap between the modeling of a 200-equation econometric model and the two-series time series method is a huge one and still remains. A suggestion about how this gap can be somewhat reduced is also discussed later. Other approaches have been suggested by Sims [142] and by Priestly, Rao, and Tong [123].

2. NONSENSE REGRESSIONS

It has been suggested above that there is danger in *just* looking at the Durbin-Watson statistic d when evaluating the goodness-of-fit of an equation, but of course, there is even greater danger in *not* looking at this statistic at all or in ignoring the warning signals that it may give. It is still common to find econometric models that either do not report d or have equations with apparently very high levels of fit, as measured by R^2, combined with low levels of d. It would be very easy to find many examples of equations having a d value much less than R^2, but to report them would merely embarrass the authors and would serve little other purpose. It is well known that autocorrelated residuals lead to inefficient parameter estimates, and we have shown elsewhere that the symptoms just described, high R^2 and low d, may well correspond to nothing but a nonsense regression. If the two individual variables are random walks or, more generally, are integrated or $ARIMA$ processes, then spurious "relationships" will often be "found" by using classical estimation procedures. In practice it has often been noted that the *levels* of many economic variables are best modeled as integrated processes[3] partly due to the considerable momentum in the levels of these variables.

---

[2] See Granger and Newbold [46].
[3] See Granger [39] and Newbold-Granger [107].

Examples include consumption, investment, employment, price series, and interest rates.

To further emphasize the possibility of spurious regression, that is, an "observed" relationship between two unrelated series, we present some of the results of a simulation study conducted by Newbold and Davis [106]. They generated the series

$$X_t = X_{t-1} + \varepsilon_t + b\varepsilon_{t-1}; \qquad X_0 = 100, t = 1, 2, \ldots, 50$$

$$Y_t = Y_{t-1} + \eta_t + b^*\eta_{t-1}; \quad Y_0 = 100, t = 1, 2, \ldots, 50$$

where ε_t and η_t are independent $N(0,1)$ white noise series. $IMA(1,1)$ processes were used in the study because they have been found to arise in practice and because they also have the property that a series which is the aggregate of several independent $IMA(1,1)$ series is also $IMA(1,1)$. Few models have such a stable aggregation property, as pointed out by Granger and Morris [41]. It will be seen that X_t and Y_t are independent of one another. The regression equation

$$Y_t = \beta_1 + \beta_2 X_t + \varepsilon_t$$

was fitted by ordinary least squares to 1,000 pairs of series for various values of b and b^*. Results for the usual t test of significance of $\hat{\beta}_2$ and the Durbin-Watson test are shown in Table 14.1. The main conclusion from this table is that employment of the decision procedure, "reject the null hypothesis of no relationship between the two series only if $|t|$ differs significantly from zero and d does not differ significantly from two," will generally not lead one astray (although, of course, neglect of the second condition will do so). The exception is for moderately large values of $-b^*$, with $-b$ not too large. Given this combination of circumstances, a significant regression coupled with an absence of warning signals from the Durbin-Watson statistic will be found on about 20 percent of occasions.

The relatively hopeful picture presented thus far is, however, only part of the story, for it remains to consider re-estimation of the regressions under the assumption of first order autoregressive errors. The equations were thus "corrected" for autocorrelated errors and estimated using the Cochrane-Orcutt iterative procedure. Table 2 shows the percentage of times for which significant estimates $\hat{\beta}_2$ were now obtained. The conclusion from these results is that for a wide range of wholly reasonable parameter values, the null hypothesis $\beta_2 = 0$ is rejected far too frequently.

Of course, if one knew that the error structure was $IMA(1,1)$, one should optimally estimate the regression on this basis. In the past, econometricians have shied away from moving average error structures, preferring (presumably for simplicity of computation) autoregressive processes. Hence, it should be possible to achieve a middle ground in

Table 14.1. *Percentage of times* t *and* d *statistics are significant at 5 percent level for regression of an* IMA *(1,1) series on an independent* IMA *(1,1) series*

		b = 0.0 *t*		b = -.02 *t*		b = -0.4 *t*		b = -0.6 *t*		b = -0.8 *t*	
		N.Sig	Sig	N.Sig	Sig	N.Sig	Sig	N.Sig	Sig	N.Sig	Sig
b* = 0.0 d	N.Sig	0	0	0	0	0	0	0	0	0	0
	Inconc.	0	0	0	0	0	0	0	0	0	0
	Sig	33.1	66.9	37.7	62.3	36.4	63.6	42.5	57.5	60.8	39.2
	Mean d	0.33		0.36		0.38		0.42		0.36	
	Mean$|t|$	4.07		3.70		3.50		2.98		1.87	
b* = -0.2 d	N.Sig	0	0.1	0	0.1	0	0.1	0	0	0	0
	Inconc.	0	0.2	0	0	0.1	0	0	0.1	0	0.1
	Sig	33.4	66.3	36.0	63.9	39.5	60.3	45.7	54.2	61.5	38.4
	Mean d	0.45		0.46		0.50		0.51		0.46	
	Mean$|t|$	3.70		3.65		3.41		2.81		1.90	
b* = -0.4 d	N.Sig	0.3	0.7	0.5	1.0	0.5	1.1	0.5	1.3	0.4	0.3
	Inconc.	0.5	0.6	0.2	0.8	0.1	0.6	0.4	1.6	0.2	0.2
	Sig	35.5	62.4	37.0	60.5	39.3	58.4	47.0	50.2	60.9	38.0
	Mean d	0.68		0.72		0.71		0.73		0.65	
	Mean$|t|$	3.43		3.44		3.32		2.59		1.81	
b* = -0.6 d	N.Sig	5.0	6.3	5.1	8.3	5.1	7.6	5.0	5.5	6.6	2.4
	Inconc.	2.3	2.6	2.1	2.3	2.1	3.1	2.3	1.1	2.6	1.0
	Sig	37.8	46.0	38.2	44.0	38.4	43.7	46.2	39.1	61.9	25.5
	Mean d	1.10		1.09		1.12		1.08		1.03	
	Mean$|t|$	2.89		2.72		2.78		2.27		1.52	
b* = -0.8 d	N.Sig	36.8	20.7	39.8	19.2	41.3	20.3	37.4	18.6	44.2	8.6
	Inconc.	6.2	3.2	5.8	3.9	5.7	2.7	5.3	2.6	8.0	1.8
	Sig	20.4	12.7	18.2	13.1	19.1	10.9	25.9	10.2	30.4	7.0
	Mean d	1.66		1.67		1.67		1.64		1.60	
	Mean$|t|$	1.85		1.84		1.74		1.59		1.21	

situations, where for one reason or another a solid identification of error structure is not possible. Examination of means of sample auto-correlations of $IMA(1,1)$ processes suggests that second order auto-regression might be a much better approximation than first order and that better results than those in Table 14.2 could be achieved if this error structure were used. Thus we feel that it would be of great benefit to have a test, like the Durbin-Watson, of the null hypothesis of first order autoregressive errors against the alternative of second order autoregressive errors.

Table 14.2. *Percentage of times* t *statistic is significant at 5 percent level for regression of an* IMA *(1,1) series on an independent* IMA *(1,1) series "allowing" for first order serial correlation in residuals by Cochrane-Orcutt iterative estimation technique*

	$b = 0.0$	$b = -0.2$	$b = -0.4$	$b = -0.6$	$b = -0.8$
$b^* = 0.0$	9.6	8.2	5.2	4.3	4.9
$b^* = -0.2$	15.6	10.9	10.2	7.7	6.8
$b^* = -0.4$	21.1	19.8	16.2	9.9	7.7
$b^* = -0.6$	31.3	28.7	23.4	18.7	9.5
$b^* = -0.8$	8.6	28.2	26.8	21.2	11.3

Now, in time series regressions involving the levels of economic variables, one frequently sees coefficients of multiple correlation R^2 much higher than 0.9. If these indicate anything at all, they presumably imply an extremely strong relationship between the dependent variable and the independent variables. This is extremely misleading on many occasions, as comments noting poor forecast performance which sometimes follow these equations will testify. In fact, the high R^2 values could be no more than a reflection of the fact that the dependent variable is highly autocorrelated and could easily be achieved simply by regressing this variable on its own past. Thus, in such circumstances, the value of R^2 says nothing at all about the strength of the relationship between the dependent and independent variables.

Two methods that are frequently used by econometricians to reduce the problem of low d value are to stay with levels and either introduce a lagged endogenous variable or to take the residuals to be an $AR(1)$ process. Because of estimation biases, we doubt if either of these approaches will prove successful, although both are better than doing nothing. A much sounder, simpler approach, in our opinion, is to first difference the data used; that is, use changes. As we have recently discussed[4] this whole problem and its suggested alleviation, we shall not pursue it further but merely assume that it is agreed that changes be used. An illustration of the difficulties which can arise if these points are ignored is given by Box and Newbold [10].

3. PREWHITENING

Both first differencing and seasonal adjustment, which is also frequently used, are steps toward *prewhitening* one's data, that is, producing a series having a generally flatter spectrum than the original. Evidence is now

[4] See Granger-Newbold [43].

accumulating that there may well be considerable benefits from going further and completely prewhitening the data. If two variables X_t and Y_t are linearly related, then there will always be a corresponding relationship between $F_1(X_t)$ and $F_2(Y_t)$, where F_1 and F_2 are a pair of linear filters. In theory nothing is lost in terms of the *strength* of relationships by doing this, as this strength is completely measured by the coherence function and this is unaltered by the use of filtered data. The lag relationships between the two original series will be changed if F_1 and F_2 are not identical, but the original relationship can always be recovered. It will be seen later that it is preferable to use one-sided filters. One way of doing this is to build Box-Jenkins single series models for each variable, obtaining estimates of single series innovations. Models could then be built on these innovations. As is now well known, the Box-Jenkins approach contains three distinct steps: identification of the model, estimation of its parameters, and diagnostic checking to ensure that the proper model has been chosen and estimated. If the model used fails the diagnostic check, the cycle is repeated. It is unfortunate that the word "identification" has come to have a different meaning for time series analysts and for econometricians. The former group uses the word to describe the process of choosing an appropriate lag structure for a model, whereas the latter uses the term in connection with the determination of the level of uniqueness of a multi-series model. To try to avoid confusion, we shall use the expression E-identification for the econometricians' meaning of the word.[5]

An immediate advantage in using single series innovations to estimate relationships is seen by considering the single equation

$$Y_t = a + bX_t + \varepsilon_t.$$

If the coefficients are estimated by ordinary least squares, assuming the ε_t to be white noise, and then the null hypothesis $H_0: b = 0$ is tested, the assumption and the hypothesis can only *both* be true if Y_t is white noise, something that is not generally assumed. If innovations are used for Y_t, no inconsistency occurs.

A further advantage in using single-series innovations occurs when investigating whether two series are related by a one-way causality or by a two-way causality (henceforth called feedback). The definition of causality used here is that suggested by Wiener [161], exposited by Granger [40], and applied by Sims [136] and others. If one is working within the information set $I_n: X_{n-j}, Y_{n-j}, j \geq 0$, then Y_t is said to cause X_t if X_{n+1} can be better forecast using the whole information set I_n rather than just X_{n-j}. Using a least squares criterion and linear forecasts, a testable

---

[5] It is even more unfortunate that electrical engineers use the word identification in a yet different sense, to cover all three stages of the Box-Jenkins procedure, including estimation and diagnostic checking.

Table 14.3. *Cross-correlations between changes in help wanted advertisements and changes in numbers unemployed*

k:	0	1	2	3	4	5	6	7
$\hat{\rho}_k$:	−0.74	−0.45	−0.14	0.08	0.23	0.24	0.13	0.04
k:	8	9	10	11	12	13	14	15
$\hat{\rho}_k$:	0.02	−0.14	−0.24	−0.21	−0.18	−0.04	0.07	0.06
k:		−1	−2	−3	−4	−5	−6	−7
$\hat{\rho}_k$:		−0.69	−0.49	−0.22	0.09	0.24	0.28	0.22
k:	−8	−9	−10	−11	−12	−13	−14	−15
$\hat{\rho}_k$:	−0.18	0.07	−0.11	−0.17	−0.23	−0.21	−0.09	0.04

definition of causality results. When model building, it is important to determine if there is just one-way causality (Y_t causes X_t but not vice-versa, say) or feedback (Y_t causes X_t and X_t causes Y_t) occurring. We exclude from our discussion the question of instantaneous causality for the time being. A natural diagram to look at when deciding if one has causality or feedback is the cross-correlogram, which is the plot of estimated correlation (X_t, Y_{t-k}) against k for both positive and negative k. However, even if one has one-way causality, if neither X_t nor Y_t are white noise series, the cross-correlogram will not generally be one-sided and so cannot be easily interpreted. This has been shown formally in Granger and Newbold [46]. If single-series innovations are used, derived from one-sided filters such as that corresponding to an *ARIMA* model, then it is shown in the same paper, and also by Haugh [54], that if the cross-correlogram takes insignificant values for $k > 0$, say, then one-way causality is occurring, but if the diagram has significant values for k both positive *and* negative, then feedback is present. The prewhitening has to be carried out carefully or the cross-correlogram can still be misleading. There are also interpretational problems if a two-sided filter has been used on the data to remove trend or seasonal components.

To illustrate our point about prewhitening, Table 14.3 shows cross-correlations between quarterly changes in help wanted advertisements ($Y_{1,t}$) and quarterly changes in numbers employed ($Y_{2,t}$). This United States data covers 63 changes. In the table

$$\hat{\rho}_k \equiv \hat{corr}(Y_{1,t}, Y_{2,t-k}).$$

The following univariate time series models were fitted to these series:

$$(1 - 0.82B + 0.15B^2 - 0.22B^3 + 0.40B^4)Y_{1,t} = \varepsilon_{1,t}$$
$$\quad (0.12) \quad (0.15) \quad (0.15) \quad (0.12) \quad\quad\quad (3.1)$$

Table 14.4. *Cross-correlations between residuals from (3.1) and (3.2)*

k:	0	1	2	3	4	5	6	7
$\hat{\rho}_k$:	−0.52	0.07	0.03	0.04	−0.02	−0.09	−0.11	−0.26
k:	8	9	10	11	12	13	14	15
$\hat{\rho}_k$:	0.24	−0.08	−0.17	0.02	−0.16	0.08	0.14	−0.01
k:		−1	−2	−3	−4	−5	−6	−7
$\hat{\rho}_k$:		−0.19	−0.23	−0.18	0.13	−0.07	−0.06	−0.05
k:	−8	−9	−10	−11	−12	−13	−14	−15
$\hat{\rho}_k$:	0.14	0.07	−0.00	0.02	−0.10	−0.03	−0.06	0.10

$$\left(1-0.75B+0.24B^2+0.03B^3+0.13B^4\right)Y_{2,t}=\varepsilon_{2,t}$$
$$\quad(0.13)\quad(0.14)\quad\;\;(0.15)\quad\;\;(0.13)\qquad\qquad\qquad\qquad (3.2)$$

where $\varepsilon_{1,t}$ and $\varepsilon_{2,t}$ are white noise, B is the back-shift operator such that $B_j Y_t \equiv Y_{t-j}$, and the figures in brackets beneath coefficient estimates are their estimated standard errors.

Table 4 shows the cross-correlations between the residuals from the fitted equations, with

$$\hat{\rho}_k = c\hat{o}rr\left(\hat{\varepsilon}_{1,t}, \hat{\varepsilon}_{2,t-k}\right).$$

It can be seen that the very strong indication of feedback in Table 3 is considerably muted in Table 14.4. This is because changes in the two series are very much smoother than white noise. In our opinion, any inference based on Table 14.3 would almost certainly be misleading.

If one-way causality is found, then traditional transfer function methods can be used, corresponding to the more general types of distributed lag procedures.[6] If feedback is found, then more complicated methods need to be used to model the relationship between the innovations and consequently the original series. These methods and some possible uses for them are described in the next two sections.

4. BUILDING BIVARIATE FEEDBACK MODELS

Suppose that a pair of series $Y_{1,t}$ and $Y_{2,t}$ (which may themselves be suitably differenced versions of given series $X_{1,t}$ and $X_{2,t}$) are zero mean, stationary, and exhibit feedback. A completely general model describing their relationship is

[6] See, for example, Box-Jenkins [9].

$$Y_{1,t} = \frac{\omega_1^*(B)}{\delta_1^*(B)} Y_{2,t} + \frac{\theta_1^*(B)}{\phi_1^*(B)} \eta_{1,t}^*$$

$$Y_{2,t} = \frac{\omega_2^*(B)}{\delta_2^*(B)} Y_{1,t} + \frac{\theta_2^*(B)}{\phi_2^*(B)} \eta_{2,t}^*$$

where all polynomials in B in (4.1) are of finite orders, $\eta_{1,t}^*$ and $\eta_{2,t}^*$ are mutually, stochastically uncorrelated white noise processes, and for E-identifiability, the restriction $\omega_2^*(0) \equiv 0$ is imposed.

An important first step in identifying, from given data, a model of the form (4.1) is to construct the single series *ARIMA* models

$$a_j(B)Y_{j,t} = b_j(B)\varepsilon_{j,t}; \quad j=1,2 \tag{4.2}$$

where $\varepsilon_{j,t}$ is white noise. In addition, we have found that a useful intermediate step is to build a model, linking the univariate innovations, of the form

$$\varepsilon_{1,t} = \frac{\omega_1(B)}{\delta_1(B)} \varepsilon_{2,t} + \frac{\theta_1(B)}{\phi_1(B)} \eta_{1,t}$$

$$\varepsilon_{2,t} = \frac{\omega_2(B)}{\delta_2(B)} \varepsilon_{1,t} + \frac{\theta_2(B)}{\phi_2(B)} \eta_{2,t} \tag{4.3}$$

where $\eta_{1,t}$ and $\eta_{2,t}$ are mutually, stochastically uncorrelated white noise processes and $\omega_2(0) \equiv 0$.

The model building strategy we employ, which is described and illustrated in detail in Granger and Newbold [46 and 47], proceeds in the following stages:

- Fit the single series models (4.2), where $Y_{j,t}$ may be an appropriately differenced form of a given series $X_{j,t}$, with non-zero mean subtracted if necessary.
- Calculate the cross-correlogram between the univariate model residuals, and use this to identify appropriate forms for the transfer functions $\omega_j(B)/\delta_j(B)$ in (4.3).
- Identify the error structures – that is, the forms of $\theta_j(B)/\phi_j(B)$ – in (4.3).
- Estimate the model (4.3) relating the individual innovative series.
- Check the adequacy of representation of this fitted model, and if necessary, modify and re-estimate it.
- Amalgamate the bivariate model fitted to the residuals (4.3) with the two univariate models (4.2) to suggest an appropriate structure, of the form (4.1), to describe the interrelationship between the original series.

- Estimate the model (4.1) relating the original series.
- Check the adequacy of representation of the fitted model, and if necessary, modify and re-estimate it.

In principle, the problem of building a multivariate time series model to describe the interrelationship between series $Y_1, Y_2, \ldots, Y_n$ is similar to the bivariate case. The analyst's objective should be to construct equations in such a way that the n given time series are transformed to m series which have the properties of mutually stochastically uncorrelated white noise series. However, even in the bivariate feedback situation, the practical difficulties involved are by no means simple to overcome, so that, for sample sizes likely to occur in practice, these difficulties will quickly become insurmountable as n increases.

Given a set of time series, perhaps the best strategy is to look for simplifications. For example, the series may consist of two or more disjoint groups, each group of series unrelated to the other. Again, some of the relationships may be unidirectional rather than feedback, which would greatly simplify the analysis. To assess these possibilities, one should first build univariate models of the form (4.2) and examine the cross-correlations between all pairs of estimated residuals.

It should be obvious that complicated econometric structures, of the type frequently built by macroeconomic forecasters, cannot be developed using the principles of time series analysis alone. Some sort of marriage of time series and econometric methodologies is clearly desirable.[7] For example, economic theory may be used by the time series analyst to suggest a subclass of all the possible models which accords with theory. This should greatly reduce the number of models the analyst needs to contemplate and thus should make the identification problem correspondingly simpler. A further possibility is to examine the multivariate time series properties of the residuals from structural equations of a fitted econometric model. This may suggest a more appropriate error structure than the simple forms currently assumed by model builders, who all too frequently (often in the face of overwhelming evidence to the contrary) estimate their equations under the assumption that these residuals are white noise series with zero cross-correlations everywhere except lag zero. An exception is Fair [24], who allows for the possibility of first order autoregression in the individual equation residuals.

A simpler alternative to combining time series and econometric methodologies would be to combine the forecasts produced by the two approaches, using, for example, the method of Bates and Granger [5]. An illustration, involving the combination of econometric and univariate *ARIMA* forecasts, is given by Granger and Newbold [44].

---

[7] See Wall *et al.* [156], Hendry [56], and particularly, Zellner and Palm [167] for some practical steps in this direction.

Table 14.5. *Cross-correlations between residuals from equations (4.4) and (4.5)*

k:	0	1	2	3	4	5	6	7
$\hat{\rho}_k$:	-0.16	-0.22	-0.22	-0.06	-0.13	-0.02	-0.04	0.05
k:	8	9	10	11	12	13	14	15
$\hat{\rho}_k$:	0.01	-0.06	-0.03	-0.04	0.13	0.01	0.12	0.07
k:		-1	-2	-3	-4	-5	-6	-7
$\hat{\rho}_k$:		-0.08	-0.05	-0.07	-0.09	0.04	-0.08	-0.11
k:	-8	-9	-10	-11	-12	-13	-14	-15
$\hat{\rho}_k$:	-0.07	-0.08	0.02	0.05	0.08	-0.10	0.05	-0.01

Now, by virtue of the comments of Sims [141], it is not strictly valid to use the cross-correlogram between the residuals from the univariate models to test directly for feedback against the alternative of unidirectional causality. However, this cross-correlogram should be suggestive and allow for the possibility of a fuller investigation. For example, 144 monthly observations on the number unemployed and the index of industrial production in the United States, both seasonally adjusted, were analyzed. Denoting the series by $X_{1,t}$ and $X_{2,t}$ respectively, the fitted univariate models were

$$(1+0.06B-0.21B^2-0.18B^3-0.19B^4)(1-B)X_{1,t} = \varepsilon_{1-t};$$
$$\quad (0.08) \quad (0.08) \quad (0.08) \quad (0.08)$$

$$\hat{\sigma}_{\varepsilon_1}^2 = 13617 \tag{4.4}$$

and

$$(1-0.26B)(1-B)X_{2,t} = 0.21+\varepsilon_{2,t}; \quad \hat{\sigma}_{\varepsilon_2}^2 = 0.49$$
$$\quad (0.08) \qquad\qquad (0.06) \tag{4.5}$$

where figures in brackets beneath estimated coefficients are their estimated standard errors.

The cross-correlations between the estimated residuals, denoted

$$\hat{\rho}_k = c\hat{o}rr(\varepsilon_{1,t}, \varepsilon_{2,t-k})$$

are shown in Table 14.5. To judge the magnitudes of these quantities, it should be noted that under the hypothesis of no relationship between the series, the sample cross-correlations would be approximately normally distributed with zero means and standard deviations $n^{-1/2}$, where n is the number of observations employed in their calculation.[8] In the

---

[8] See Haugh [54] and Haugh-Box [55].

Table 14.6. *Cross-correlations between residuals from (4.6) and (4.5)*

k:	0	1	2	3	4	5	6	7	8	9
$\hat{\rho}_k$:	−0.01	0.00	0.04	0.00	−0.05	−0.04	−0.03	0.04	0.01	−0.07
k:	10	11	12	13	14	15	16	17	18	19
$\hat{\rho}_k$:	−0.01	0.06	0.14	−0.00	0.12	0.10	0.04	0.14	−0.04	0.06
k:		−1	−2	−3	−4	−5	−6	−7	−8	−9
$\hat{\rho}_k$:		−0.06	−0.03	−0.04	−0.10	0.04	−0.09	−0.10	−0.05	−0.05
k:	−10	−11	−12	−13	−14	−15	−16	−17	−18	−19
$\hat{\rho}_k$:	−0.04	0.02	0.03	−0.10	−0.01	−0.01	0.03	−0.06	−0.10	0.01

present example $n = 139$, and so $n^{-1/2} = 0.085$. Based on this criteria there appears, from the top half of the table, the strong possibility that industrial production "causes" unemployment, but the second half of the table yields little or no evidence of feedback.

Denoting by $Y_{1,t}$ and $Y_{2,t}$, respectively, changes in unemployment and industrial production, the latter with mean subtracted, the model

$$
\begin{matrix}
(13.2)\ (14.2)\ \ (17.0) \\
Y_{1,t} = \dfrac{(-28.9 - 47.2B - 36.8B^2)}{(1 + 0.39B - 0.53B^2 - 0.16B^3)} Y_{2,t} \\
(0.18)\ \ \ (0.12)\ \ \ \ \ (0.12)
\end{matrix}
$$

$$
+ \frac{1}{(1 + 0.24B)}\eta_{1,t}; \quad \hat{\sigma}^2_{\eta_1^*} = 10591 \tag{4.6}
$$
$$
(0.08)
$$

was fitted. Details are given in Granger and Newbold [46]. The residuals from the fitted equation were indistinguishable, by their correlogram, from white noise. The cross-correlations

$$
\hat{\rho}_k = c\hat{o}rr\left(\eta^*_{1,t}, \varepsilon_{2,t-k}\right)
$$

between the residuals from (4.6) and (4.5) are shown in Table 6. Under the null hypothesis that $\eta^*_{1,t}$ and $\varepsilon_{2,t}$ are mutually, stochastically uncorrelated white noise series, Haugh [54] has shown that these quantities should be approximately normally distributed with zero means and standard deviations $n^{-1/2}$, if the fitted model is correct. By this criterion, none of the cross-correlations in Table 14.6 seems unusually large, and the model is hence accepted as correct. Thus, in particular, there does not appear to be any very strong evidence to suggest a feedback model might be appropriate. Thus, one "tests" unidirectional causality against feedback by doing what comes naturally to the time series analyst –

constructing a model, in this case (4.5) and (4.6), to transform the given series to mutually, stochastically uncorrelated white noise series. In this particular case it is seen that no feedback equation is required or at least that if any feedback exists it is very weak.

5. CONCLUSIONS

The techniques described in the previous section could theoretically be extended to deal with several series, although not necessarily in a unique way. However, with the length of series usually available in economics, in practice the approach soon becomes too complicated and runs into severe estimation problems as further series are added to the analysis. There are two obvious uses for the method as it now stands. The first is to build small two- or three-variable models to provide "trial horse" forecasts in helping evaluate an econometric model. Such models should prove to be more formidable opponents than the single-series Box-Jenkins models now used.[9] The second use is to perform residual analysis on the more important equations in a large-scale econometric model. The input series to the bivariate modeling technique are the estimated residuals from the pair of equations selected from the econometric model for special attention. Presumably, the econometrician will have taken account of standard economic theory when constructing the structural form, and so no restrictions remain on the model for the residuals. The resulting model should both provide superior forecasts from the econometric model and also suggest ways in which the main model should be restructured. Research along these lines is currently being undertaken.

The process of bringing together the two philosophies mentioned at the start of this paper is not altogether an easy one, although interest in it is accelerating. One may hope that, some of the worst practices of some actual model builders will soon be a thing of the past and at least a part of the time-series analyst's viewpoint will become generally accepted. It is important to emphasize that we strongly believe there is no animosity between classical econometric model builders and time series modelers. Both groups, after all, have the same eventual aim – the building of sound, large scale models. It is only the approaches that differ, and the gap between is continually narrowing, we believe, to the mutual benefit of both groups.

[9] See Granger-Newbold [42].

CHAPTER 15

Comments on the Evaluation of Policy Models*

Clive W. J. Granger and Melinda Deutsch**

Abstract

This paper examines the evaluation of models claimed to be relevant for policy making purposes. A number of tests are proposed to determine the usefulness of such models in the policy making process. These tests are applied to three empirical examples.

1. INTRODUCTION

Applied economic research produces many empirical models of various parts of the economy. The models are evaluated in a variety of ways: some will report the specification search used to reach the final model; some will employ a battery of specification tests looking at missing variables, parameter consistency or heterogeneity; some will use cross-validation or post-sample evaluation techniques; and so forth. Discussion of these procedures and some difficulties that arise can be found in the book of readings, Granger (1990). Many applied papers, as well as some theoretical ones, will end with a section on the "policy implications" of the model. These sections rarely emphasize that strictly the policy implications only follow if the model is correct and is the actual data generating mechanism, which is an unreasonably strong assumption. It is also an assumption that cannot be true if one has two competing policy models. Of course models are built for a variety of purposes, and some are fairly easy to evaluate or to compare. For example, if two models are built to provide forecasts, they can be run in real time, after the date of the construction, and the forecasts compared using some pre-agreed

* *Journal of Policy Modelling* 14, 1992, 397–416.
** This paper represents the views of the authors and should not be interpreted as reflecting the views of the Board of Governors of the Federal Reserve System or members of its staff. Partially supported by NSF grant SES 89-02950.

cost function or criterion. This approach is less easy to apply to a policy model. A complete evaluation would require some organization, such as the Federal Reserve, to use the model to decide on policy and then to see how well the policy thus achieved actually performs. It is unlikely that most models can be evaluated in such a manner, and so less ambitious methods are required.

In this paper we start with a given model that is claimed to have been built for policy purposes. We consider what the implications are of this model being used by a policy maker to try to keep a single variable of interest near to a series of target values. To do this, a policy variable has its value chosen by use of the model. As background variables change and as targets alter, so the policy variable will take a series of values. It can be argued that each different policy value represents a new "policy regime", but we would prefer to keep this phrase to indicate more momentous, less frequent events such as a change in the variable of interest (from unemployment to inflation) or of the policy variable (from interest rates to money supply) or of the policy model being utilized. In these cases the Lucas critique becomes relevant and tests of super exogeneity can be employed, as in Engle and Hendry (1993). This is an important aspect of policy model evaluation which we will not consider here, but see Hoover and Sheffrin (1992). We will not consider also the argument from the rational expectations literature that policy cannot be successful, although that argument could be used to give an interpretation to some of our results.

It has been suggested that modern policy makers do not consider specific targets and so the type of control mechanism considered here is unrealistic. As a counter-example, it may be noted that the finance ministers of the G–7 countries meet twice a year to give targets for 10 or so indicators of their economies, for use in international policy coordination; as discussed by Frankel (1990). Other examples are also available. It should be noted that the G–7 targets are not made public and so cannot be used by most economists in evaluation exercises.

In what follows we will assume that targets exist but are not known. It is also assumed that policy makers are optimizing rather than satisficing. A good discussion of alternative approaches to policy is given by van Velthoven (1990).

2.   THE CONTROL MECHANISM

Suppose that the proposed policy model takes the form

$$Y_t = a + bC_t + kX_t + e_t, \tag{1}$$

where Y_t is the variable that the decision maker is trying to influence, called the variable of interest, such as unemployment; C_t is the variable that the decision maker has available as a policy variable, such as money supply; X_t is a vector of other variables that influence Y_t; and e_t is the residual, taken to be zero-mean white noise. Equation (1) is often called the *plant equation* in the control literature. For the moment it will be assumed that the coefficients a, b, k are constant, and in particular do not change as C_t changes. Let T_t denote a *target series*, which is the desired values of Y_t. Denote $ce_t = Y_t - T_t$, the control error; and let $S(ce)$ be the cost function of the decision maker, representing the cost of an error ce.

The objective of the policy maker will be taken to be to manipulate C_{t+1} so that Y_{t+1} is as close as possible to T_{t+1} when using a one-step horizon. More precisely the policy maker will chose C_{t+1} to minimize $E_t[S(ce_{t+1})]$. It should be noted that it is generally not possible to equate Y_{t+1} with T_{t+1} because X_t and e_t are random variables that are not perfectly forecastable or controllable. The timing is also important as C_{t+1} and T_{t+1} are *determined* at time t but in a sense do not become operative until time $t + 1$. Replacing t by $t + 1$ in (1) and using a least-squares cost function suggests that the forecast of Y_{t+1} made at time t is

$$f_{t,1}^Y = a + bC_{t+1} + kf_{t,1}^X, \tag{2}$$

if C_{t+1} is known, as it is potentially for the decision maker. Here $f_{t,1}^X$ is the optimum one-step forecast of X_t using information available as time t *plus* C_{t+1}. Requiring this forecast to be equal to the target, gives

$$C_{t+1} = b^{-1}[T_{t+1} - a - kf_{t,1}^X], \tag{3}$$

and then the forecast error will be

$$ec_{t+1} = e_{t+1} + k(X_{t+1} - f_{t,1}^X).$$

Thus *if* the decision maker were using (1) to determine the policy, the values for the policy variable would be given by (3). Given a satisfactory method of forecasting X_{t+1}, everything else in (3) can be taken as known.

To an outsider things are rather different as C_{t+1} will not be known at time t and neither will be T_{t+1}. The first can be forecast but there is often little direct information about targets.

To an outsider, the best forecast of Y_{t+1} will be

$$g_{t,1}^Y = a + bg_{t,1}^C + kg_{t,1}^X,$$

according to the model (1), which is being investigated, where $g_{t,1}^X$ is the optimum one-step forecast of X_{t+1} using just information available at time t, not including C_{t+1}. The forecast error will now be

$$\varepsilon_{t+1} = Y_{t+1} - g_{t,1}^Y = ec_{t+1} + b(C_{t+1} - g_{t,1}^C) + k(f_{t,1}^X - g_{t,1}^Y).$$

As these two components will be uncorrelated if (1) is correct (as otherwise the size of ec_{t+1} could be reduced), one gets

$$E[\varepsilon_{t+1}^2] \geq E[ec_{t+1}^2] \tag{4}$$

in general. This suggests the following test for evaluating a policy model. The conditional forecast, using information in C_{t+1}, of Y_{t+1} should on average be superior to the unconditional forecast, using just information available at time t to an outsider. Note that both forecasts are constructed directly from the model that is being evaluated. Of course without this constraint, the conditional forecast should always be better than the unconditional forecast, on average, as it is based on more information. It should be noted that equality holds in (4) only if $C_{t+1} = g_{t,1}^C$, that is, the control variable C is perfectly forecastable from the information set I_t. In this case the decision maker cannot influence C and so this variable is irrelevant as a control. If the model in (1) is correct it follows from (3) that if C is perfectly forecastable, so will be the target series, T_t, and also there is no instantaneous causation from C_t to X_t. In these circumstances, the model in (1) or any other model would not be relevant for control purposes. Thus non-rejection of the null hypothesis of equality in (4) is equivalent to rejection of (1) as a control model. As this hypothesis can be rejected in many ways, it does not follow that (1) *is* useful for policy if the hypothesis is rejected. This evaluation technique is clearly relevant for a model that claims to be a policy model and is illustrated in the next section. It is also briefly discussed in Chong and Hendry (1986), reprinted as Chapter 17 of Granger (1990).

Nevertheless, (3) can be used to estimate the target series as

$$\hat{T}_{t+1} = bC_{t+1} + a + kf_{t,1}^X, \tag{5}$$

using the observed value of C_{t+1} and the forecast of X_{t+1}. If some of the estimated target values are unrealistic, such as negative unemployment or very high inflation rates, this would clearly imply that the model is inadequate. A more technical test can be used when Y_t is I(1), so that the change series ΔY_t is stationary, say. It was pointed out in Granger (1988) that if a policy control is somewhat successful, then at the very least Y_t and T_t must be cointegrated. It follows that Y_t and $\hat{T}_t$ will be cointegrated, which implies that $Y_t - bC_t - kX_t - a$ is I(0) or stationary, which can be tested using standard unit root tests. This evaluation technique is discussed in Section 4.

To summarize this discussion, there are several evaluation tests that can be applied to a model that is claimed to be relevant for policy selection, assumed to be of the form in (1).

2.1   Test 1

From the model, two (sets of) forecasts can be constructed. The "unconditional" one-step forecast of Y_{t+1} made at time t is

$$g_{t,1}^Y = a + bg_{t,1}^C + kg_{t,1}^X, \tag{6}$$

where $g_{t,1}^C$ is the optimal one-step forecast of C_{t+1} made at time t using the information set $I_t : \{X_{t-j}, C_{t-j}, j \geq 1\}$; and similarly for X. "Conditional" one-step forecasts are now made of the form

$$f_{t,1}^Y = a + bC_{t+1} + kf_{t,1}^X, \tag{7}$$

where now f^Y and f^X are the optimal one-step forecasts based on the large information set $J_t : \{I_t, C_{t+1}\}$, acting as though C_{t+1}, is known at time t, which is correct for the decision made in this framework. Forecast errors will result from the two forecasts:

$$\varepsilon_{t+1} = Y_{t+1} - g_{t,1}^Y \tag{8}$$

and

$$ec_{t+1} = Y_{t+1} - f_{t,1}^Y, \tag{9}$$

and the null hypothesis tested is equality of the mean squared errors of ε and ec. Assuming that these errors have zero means, the null hypothesis is easily tested using the procedure discussed in Chapter 9 of Granger and Newbold (1987). Define

$$D_t = \varepsilon_t - ec_t, \tag{10}$$

$$S_t = \varepsilon_t + ec_t, \tag{11}$$

and the null hypothesis is then equivalent to testing $correlation(D_t, S_t) = 0$, which follows by noting that $cov(D_t, S_t) = E[\varepsilon_t^2 - ec_t^2]$. The test employed in the next section is to regress S on a constant and D. If the coefficient of D is significantly different from zero, conclude that SSE of the conditional forecasts is significantly different from the SSE of the unconditional forecasts; otherwise conclude they are not. This is the test that is emphasized in the following section. Non-rejection of the null hypothesis is equivalent to a rejection of the usefulness of the model in (1) for policy purposes. As the forecast horizon used by the policy maker is unknown, the test was repeated for horizons, 1, 2, 3, and 4 of the observational time unit.

2.2   Test 2

If the model in (1) is correctly specified for the control variable, the conditional forecast should forecast-encompass the unconditional forecast, as discussed in Chong and Hendry (1986). This means that the poorer unconditional forecast contains no information that is helpful in improving the quality of the conditional forecast. This has to be true in theory if the forecasts are not being constructed from a given model. The test uses post-sample data to form the regression

$$Y_{t+1} = a_1 + a_2 f_{t,1}^Y + a_3 g_{t,1}^Y + residual, \tag{12}$$

and forecast encompassing occurs if $a_2 = 1$, $a_1 = a_3 = 0$, and the residual is white noise. Similar regressions can be formed for different horizon forecasts but are not reported below.

2.3   Test 3

From (5), under the assumption that the model in (1) is correctly specified, the underlying target series can be estimated. The reasonableness of these estimates can be judged by the evaluator. Clearly, this is not a formal test.

2.4   Test 4

If the target series is I(1), then Y_t will be I(0), and this can be tested by standard techniques such as augmented Dickey-Fuller tests. It will then follow that $z_t = Y_t - bC_t - kX_t - a$ is I(0), or stationary, with zero mean. Again z_t can be tested for the null of I(1) and, if this null is rejected and z_t has declining autocorrelations, one may accept its stationarity. Note that this is equivalent to testing for cointegration between Y_t, C_t, and X_t but with given coefficients, as determined by the model. If these coefficients were unconstrained and X_t included lagged Y_t, the test would be of little interest as z_t should then always be I(0).

2.5   Test 5

In the above test, it is assumed that the target series T_t is unobserved, which is usually the case. If the targets are available, C_{t+1} could be estimated from (3), giving $\hat{C}_{t+1}$, and then a regression run of the form

$$C_{t+1} = \alpha + \beta \hat{C}_{t+1} + error, \tag{13}$$

and the null hypothesis that the model is correct is tested for the joint requirements that $\alpha = 0$, $\beta = 1$, $error = $ white noise. This test is not considered in the following section.

2.6   Test 6

A further test that can be performed, but which is also not considered in the empirical sections, is to ask if some other policy variable (or its unanticipated component) is missing from the model. Thus, for example, in a model relating money supply to unemployment, unanticipated government expenditure can be considered as a possible missing variable using a Lagrange Multiplier test. If such a potential control variable is missing, the original model cannot be used as a successful policy model.

2.7   Discussion

It should be noted that these tests are not necessarily strong ones and represent only necessary conditions that a policy model should possess. The tests are for a single model and may not be helpful in comparing models. It is also assumed that C_t, or a component of it, is a potentially controllable variable. The tests are not interrelated in a simple way as they concentrate on different types of possible mis-specification of (1).

To perform Tests 1 and 2 it is necessary to form unconditional fore-casts of the control variable C_t. This will usually come from a reduced form regression of C_t on various explanatory variables, including lagged C_t. This regression can be thought of as an approximation to a reaction function for C_t. Clearly, if this equation is badly specified then this could be a reason why the null hypothesis considered in the two tests are rejected. In the empirical model considered in the next section, the control variable is taken to be the unanticipated change in money (denoted DMR), and thus its unconditional forecast will just be zero for all horizons.

There is relatively little discussion in econometrics about how to eval-uate a policy model as compared to models designed for forecasting or hypothesis testing. In other disciplines there is consideration given to policy evaluation, but it is usually nontechnical, see for example Nagel (1990).

3.   AN APPLICATION TO A MODEL OF THE UNEMPLOYMENT RATE

The first empirical example examines a model of the unemployment rate proposed by Barro and Rush (1980) which is based on the Natural Rate/Rational Expectations hypothesis. Although this model was not formulated for policy making purposes, it will be used to illustrate some of the concepts presented in this paper. The model of the unemployment rate consists of two equations: the money growth equation and the unem-ployment rate equation. The money growth equation is given by

$$DM_t = a_0 + \sum_{j=1}^{6} a_{1j} DM_{t-j} + a_2 FEDV_t + \sum_{j=1}^{3} a_{3j} UN_{t-j} + DMR_t, \quad (14)$$

where M is a quarterly average of M1, $DM_t = \log M_t - \log M_{t-1}$, $FEDV_t$ is an estimate of the deviation from the normal value of the real expenditure of the federal government, U is the quarterly average unemployment rate, and $UN_t = \log[U_t/(1 - U_t)]$. The residual, DMR_t, is the unanticipated change in the money supply, and is taken to be the control variable. Thus, for this example, the above equation is used only to estimate the control variable since it is unknown to the investigator.

The equation explaining movements in the unemployment rate is given by

$$UN_t = b_0 + \sum_{j=1}^{10} b_{1j} DMR_{t-j} + b_2 MIL_t$$

$$+ b_3 UN_{t-1} + b_4 UN_{t-2} + residual, \tag{15}$$

where MIL = military personnel/male population aged 15–44 years. This equation is the plant equation. Note that the future values of MIL_t are taken as known when forming the conditional and unconditional forecasts.

In addition, the following univariate model of the unemployment rate was used as a benchmark for comparison.

$$UN_t = a_0 + a_1 UN_{t-1} + a_2 UN_{t-2} + a_3 UN_{t-3} + residual. \tag{16}$$

The above equations were estimated using quarterly data. The estimated money growth equation was

$$DM_t = \begin{array}{l} 0.02 + 0.42\ DM_{t-1} + 0.05\ DM_{t-2} + 0.12\ DM_{t-3} \\ (3.05)\ (4.94) \qquad\quad (0.55) \qquad\qquad (1.36) \end{array}$$

$$\begin{array}{l} - 0.15\ DM_{t-4} + 0.28\ DM_{t-5} - 0.03\ DM_{t-6} \\ (1.71) \qquad\quad (3.21) \qquad\quad (0.31) \end{array}$$

$$\begin{array}{l} + 0.01\ FEDV_t + 0.01\ UN_{t-1} + 0.004\ UN_{t-2} \\ (1.45) \qquad\quad (1.15) \qquad\quad (0.21) \end{array}$$

$$\begin{array}{l} - 0.009\ UN_{t-3} + residual, \\ (0.87) \end{array} \tag{17}$$

$$T = 148[1952(1) - 1988(4)] \quad R^2 = 0.51 \quad dw = 2.00 \quad \hat\sigma = 0.00710.$$

(The moduli of t values are shown in parentheses.) The estimate of Barro's unemployment equation was

$$DM_t = \begin{array}{l} - 0.50 - 2.02\ DMR_t - 1.19\ DMR_{t-1} \\ (6.03)\ (2.87) \qquad\quad (1.64) \end{array}$$

$$\begin{array}{l} - 2.46\ DMR_{t-2} - 2.51\ DMR_{t-3} - 1.67\ DMR_{t-4} \\ (3.42) \qquad\quad (3.27) \qquad\quad (2.06) \end{array}$$

$$\begin{array}{l} - 1.71\ DMR_{t-5} - 2.14\ DMR_{t-6} - 1.16\ DMR_{t-7} \\ (2.03) \qquad\quad (2.53) \qquad\quad (1.40) \end{array}$$

$$\begin{array}{l} - 1.00\ DMR_{t-8} - 0.08\ DMR_{t-9} + 0.04\ DMR_{t-10} \\ (1.24) \qquad\quad (0.01) \qquad\quad (0.05) \end{array}$$

$$\begin{array}{l} - 0.76\ MIL_t + 1.40\ UN_{t-1} + 0.64\ UN_{t-2} + residual, \\ (5.52) \qquad\quad (19.64) \qquad\quad (9.10) \end{array} \tag{18}$$

$$T = 123[1954(3) - 1985(1)] \quad R^2 = 0.98 \quad dw = 2.06 \quad \hat\sigma = 0.04869.$$

The univariate model was estimated to be

Table 15.1. *Test 1 for Barro's model and root mean sum of squared forecast errors*

	D		Barro		
Steps ahead	Coeff.	$\|t\|$	Cond.	Uncond.	Univariate
One	−0.94	0.80	0.08	0.08	0.02
Two	0.08	0.09	0.17	0.16	0.04
Three	0.59	0.80	0.23	0.22	0.05
Four	0.26	0.44	0.27	0.22	0.07

$$UN_t = -\ 0.12 + \underset{(19.59)}{1.66}\ UN_{t-1} - \underset{(5.67)}{0.85}\ UN_{t-2}$$
$$\underset{(2.45)}{}$$
$$+ \underset{(1.65)}{0.14}\ UN_{t-3} + residual, \tag{19}$$

$$T = 138[1950(4) - 1985(1)] \quad R^2 = 0.96 \quad dw = 2.01 \quad \hat{\sigma} = 0.06545.$$

In order to test the usefulness of this model for policy making purposes the following analysis was performed. First, the conditional and unconditional forecasts were computed for the model using data from 1985(1) to 1988(4). Recall that if the model is useful for policy purposes, then the conditional forecasts should outperform the unconditional forecasts. In order to determine whether this is the case, these forecasts were compared in a number of ways. First, for Test 1, the root mean sum of squared forecast errors (RMSFE) was computed and is displayed in Table 15.1. Note that for all forecast horizons, the RMSFEs of the unconditional forecasts were smaller than the conditional forecasts.

While this suggests that the conditional forecasts do not outperform the unconditional forecasts, it is desirable to test whether the SSE are significantly different from each other.

Unfortunately, some of the assumptions necessary for the validity of this test appear to be violated in this example. In particular, the one-step ahead forecast errors appear to be autocorrelated and this serial correlation is not completely corrected for by assuming that the residuals from the relevant regression are AR(1). A similar problem seems to hold for the two-, three-, and four-step ahead forecast errors. In some of the cases, the regression results also indicate that the forecast errors are biased. If, for illustrative purposes, the apparent violation of these two key assumptions is ignored, the conclusion drawn from the test results for all forecast horizons is that the SSE of the conditional and unconditional forecasts are not significantly different.

For Test 2, the one-step regression was completely unsatisfactory, with $f_{t,1}$ having a negative coefficient (of −1.12) and the residuals containing strong serial correlation, with a Durbin-Watson statistic of 0.35. The results clearly indicate that conditions required from Test 2 for the model to be satisfactory for policy purposes are not found.

Test 4 suggests that an additional test of model adequacy should be employed if the variable that the decision maker is trying to influence, Y_t, is I(1): namely, the estimated target from the model under consideration should be cointegrated with Y_t.[1] As a first step in implementing this test, the augmented Dickey-Fuller (ADF) test with two lags and a constant term [see Granger and Newbold (1989) for a discussion of this test] was used to test for stationarity of the unemployment series. The test statistic was 2.95, thus the results are inconclusive as to whether the unemployment series is I(0) or I(1). It shall be assumed, however, for illustrative purposes, that U is I(1) so that the test for cointegration can be performed.[2] The cointegrating regression of unemployment on the estimated target from Barro's model and a constant was run, and the ADF test with two lags was used on the residuals from this regression to determine if they were I(0). The t statistic from the Dickey-Fuller test with a constant term is 19.80, indicating that unemployment and the estimated target from Barro's model are cointegrated. Thus, the unemployment model does not fail this simple test.

For Test 3, as a final test of the usefulness of the model for policy purposes, the estimated target series for the model was computed. It does not appear from Figure 15.1 that these values are unrealistic, so the model does not fail this simple test.

The above results, taken together, strongly suggest that the conditional forecasts are not superior to the unconditional forecasts and, thus, on this basis we conclude that the model is not useful for policy purposes. The error autocorrelation inter alia points to model mis-specification, and the latter may be why the forecast tests are what they are.

4.   AN APPLICATION TO TWO MODELS OF THE DEMAND FOR BORROWED RESERVES

The second example examines two models of the demand for borrowed reserves. These models are relevant to policy since the Federal Reserve targets intermediate reserves, and borrowing from the Discount Window has an obvious impact on the reserves. In addition, studies by Keir (1981)

---

[1] For this example, it should be noted that the estimated target was approximated by the in-sample fitted values from the unemployment model because the number of out-of-sample values was too small to perform the unit root test. In addition, UN and its associated target were transformed to levels because the unemployment models considered in this section estimate the I(0) variable, $UN_t = \log[U_t/(1 - U_t)]$ where U_t is the quarterly average unemployment rate.

[2] It should also be noted that the coefficients of the lagged terms in the univariate model for UN add almost to one $(1.66 - 0.85 + 0.14 = 0.95)$.

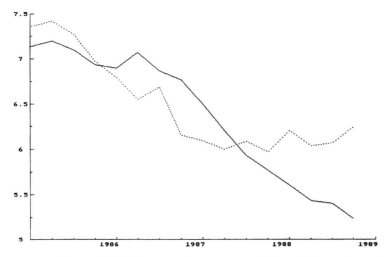

Figure 15.1. The unemployment rate (—) and the estimated target from Barro's model (...).

and others suggest that the Federal Reserve uses a version of these models. The first model was proposed by Goldfeld and Kane (1966). Briefly, a bank is assumed to have an exogenous reserve need. It can either borrow from the Federal Reserve or from an alternative source. The bank minimizes its total cost of borrowing by choosing the optimal amount of borrowing from each source. The model proposed by Goldfeld and Kane is

$$R_t^B = a_0 + a_1 K_t + a_2 R_{t-1}^B + a_3 \Delta R_t^{UB} + \varepsilon_t, \tag{20}$$

where R^B is the level of borrowing from the Discount Window, ΔR^{UB} is the change in unborrowed reserves, $K = i_D - i_S$, and i_D is the discount rate, and i_S is the interest rate of the alternative source.

Dutkowsky (1984) extended Goldfeld and Kane's model by arguing that a switching regression model gave a more accurate representation of the behavior of unborrowed reserves. The switching regression model proposed by Dutkowsky is

$$R_t^B = \begin{cases} a_0^L + a_1^L K_t + a_2^L R_{t-1}^B + a_3^L \Delta R_t^{UB} + \varepsilon_t^L & \text{if } K \leq K^* \\ a_0^U + a_1^U \log K_t + a_2^U R_{t-1}^B + a_3^U \Delta R_t^{UB} + \varepsilon_t^U & \text{if } K > K^*, \end{cases} \tag{21}$$

where K^* is an unobservable switching point that needs to be estimated. The discount rate i_D is the control variable throughout this section.

The above models were estimated using seasonally adjusted monthly data. Because of the difference in the sample period and the seasonal adjustment of the data, an additional lag of R^B was found to be significant and was included in the regression results. Goldfeld and Kane's model was estimated to be

$$R_t^B = 97.18 + 91.06\, K_t + 1.03\ R_{t-1}^B$$
$$(6.02)\ \ (6.19)\qquad (22.93)$$

$$-\ 0.24\ R_{t-3}^B - 0.12\ \Delta R_t^{UB} + residual \qquad (22)$$
$$(6.71)\qquad (4.11)$$

$$T = 198[1959(7) - 1975(12)]\quad R^2 = 0.95\quad dw = 1.89\quad \hat\sigma = 129.03.$$

For the Dutkowsky model, the unobservable switchpoint, K^*, which maximized a likelihood function, was found using a grid search and was estimated to be 0.15. Dutkowsky's estimated model was, for $K_t > 0.15$,

$$R_t^B = 225.93 + 107.35\log(K_t) + 1.06\ R_{t-1}^B$$
$$(5.78)\quad (4.86)\qquad\quad (21.70)$$

$$-\ 0.27\ R_{t-3}^B - 0.15\ \Delta R_t^{UB} + residual \qquad (23)$$
$$(6.66)\qquad (4.16)$$

and, for $K_t \le 0.15$,

$$R_t^B = 77.45 + 64.76\, K_t + 0.81\ R_{t-1}^B$$
$$(2.87)\ \ (1.92)\qquad (6.74)$$

$$-\ 0.07\ R_{t-3}^B - 0.005\,\Delta R_t^{UB} + residual \qquad (24)$$
$$(0.83)\qquad\ (0.09)$$

$$T = 192[1960(1) - 1975(12)]\quad R^2 = 0.95\quad dw = 1.91\quad \hat\sigma = 130.06.$$

The univariate model was

$$R_t^B = 48.44 + 1.28\ R_{t-1}^B - 0.16\ R_{t-2}^B$$
$$(2.86)\ \ (28.32)\qquad (1.36)$$

$$-\ 0.21\ R_{t-3}^B + residual \qquad (25)$$
$$(2.95)$$

$$T = 200[1959(5) - 1975(12)]\quad R^2 - 0.93\quad dw - 2.01\quad \hat\sigma = 164.97.$$

For Test 1 unconditional forecasts of i_D are required. As i_D is I(1), an AR(3) model for Δi_D was estimated as

$$\Delta i_{D,t} = 0.54\Delta i_{D,t-1} + 0.10\Delta i_{D,t-3} + white\ noise. \qquad (26)$$

Thus the unconditional forecast of $i_{D,t+1}$ is the unconditional forecast of $\Delta i_{D,t+1}$ plus $i_{D,t}$. Multiple-step forecasts are easily formed.

The interpretation of the results for this example proved to be less straight forward than for the first example and seemed to depend in part on the forecast horizon considered. Following the analysis above, the RMSFEs of the conditional and unconditional forecasts were computed for both models for 1976(1)–1978(12) and are displayed in Table 15.2. It can be seen that the conditional RMSFE was less than the unconditional RMSFE for some forecast horizons.

Table 15.2. *Root mean sum of squared forecast errors for two models of borrowed reserves*

	Goldfeld/Kane		Dutkowsky		
Steps ahead	Cond.	Uncond.	Cond.	Uncond.	Univariate
One	0.23	0.23	0.24	0.24	0.29
Two	0.25	0.25	0.27	0.27	0.30
Three	0.27	0.28	0.29	0.32	0.37
Four	0.31	0.32	0.35	0.34	0.45

Note: Values shown are divided by 1,000.

Table 15.3. *Test 15.1 for two models of borrowed reserves*

	D (Dutkowsky)		D (Goldfeld/Kane)	
Steps ahead	Coeff.	$|t|$	Coeff.	$|t|$
One	5.98	2.19	−3.35	0.28
Two	−0.71	0.65	−1.57	0.53
Three	−0.47	0.67	−0.04	0.02
Four	−1.21	2.76	−1.41	1.05

Further investigation was needed to determine whether these differences were statistically significant. In particular, the test involving the sum and differences of the forecast errors was employed and the results are displayed in Table 15.3.

The conclusion of Test 1 obtained for the Goldfeld and Kane model is that the conditional and unconditional forecasts are not significantly different for any of the forecast horizons. For the Dutkowsky model, the forecast errors for steps one and four were found to be significantly different, suggesting, surprisingly, that the unconditional forecasts were superior to the conditional forecasts for those forecast horizons. The significantly smaller unconditional RMSFE is prima facie evidence of model mis-specification, and the latter may be why the forecast tests are what they are.

For Test 2, as a further test of the superiority of the conditional forecasts, the conditional and unconditional forecasts were combined using the regression in (12). For a one-step horizon, the estimated parameters were as follows. The regression for Goldfeld and Kane's model is:

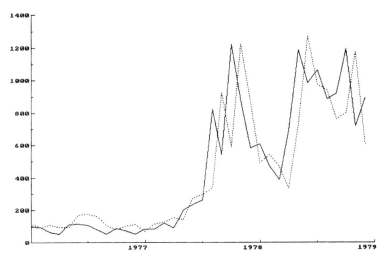

Figure 15.2. Borrowed reserves (—) and the estimated target from the Goldfeld/Kane model (...).

$$R^B_{t+1} = 46.34 - 9.41 \; f_{t,1} + 10.36 \, g_{t,1} + residual, \qquad (27)$$
$$\phantom{R^B_{t+1} = }(0.78) \;\; (1.50) \qquad\;\; (1.64)$$

$$T = 36[1976(1) - 1978(12)] \quad R^2 = 0.70 \quad dw = 2.47 \quad \hat{\sigma} = 228.39,$$

which is hardly interpretable; and the regression for Dutkowsky's model is:

$$R^B_{t+1} = 84.00 + 0.12 \; f_{t,1} + \; 0.73 \; g_{t,1} + residual, \qquad (28)$$
$$\phantom{R^B_{t+1} = }(1.37) \;\; (0.06) \qquad\; (0.09)$$

$$T = 36[1976(1) - 1978(12)] \quad R^2 = 0.66 \quad dw = 2.54 \quad \hat{\sigma} = 244.31.$$

Both of these applications of Test 2 do not support the usefulness of the models for policy purposes.

Lastly, for Test 3, the estimated target series for each model was computed. It does not appear from Figures 15.2 and 15.3 that these values are unrealistic.

Taken together, the above results indicate that neither model is useful for policy purposes as the above analysis suggests that the conditional forecasts do not appear to be superior to the unconditional forecasts.

As a final observation it is interesting to note that most of the tests described above can be used to examine the performance of a model during different regimes. For example, an investigator may believe that Dutkowsky's model is only useful for policy making purposes when $K > K^*$. Thus, the SSE of the conditional and unconditional forecasts for the

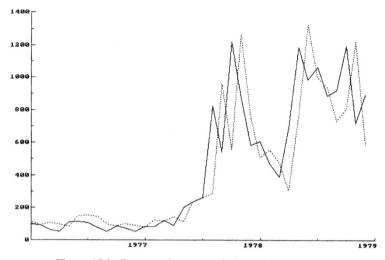

Figure 15.3. Borrowed reserves (—) and the estimated target from the Dutkowsky model (…).

Table 15.4. *Sum of squared errors for each regime in Dutkowsky's model*

Steps ahead	SSE for $K_t \leq 0.15$		SSE for $K_t > 0.15$	
	Cond.	Uncond.	Cond.	Uncond.
One	0.28	0.24	1.84	1.86
Two	0.07	0.07	2.55	2.62
Three	0.13	0.19	2.95	3.44
Four	0.18	0.24	4.12	4.03

two regimes may be calculated. The results are displayed in Table 15.4. Again, there is not clear-cut superiority of the conditional forecasts over the unconditional ones.

5. AN APPLICATION TO A MODEL FOR THE DEMAND FOR NARROW MONEY IN THE UNITED KINGDOM

The final example examines a model of the demand for narrow money in the United Kingdom. The model proposed by Hendry and Ericsson (1991) is

$$\Delta(m - p)_t = a_0 + a_1 \Delta p_t + a_2 \Delta(m - p - y)_{t-1}$$
$$+ a_3 R_t^* + a_4 (m - p - y)_{t-1} + \varepsilon_t, \tag{29}$$

Table 15.5. *Test 1 and RMSFE for Hendry and Ericsson's model*

Steps ahead	D Coeff.	$|t|$	Hendry/Ericsson Cond.	Uncond.	Univariate
One	1.34	1.58	1.22	1.52	2.47
Two	0.96	1.48	1.66	1.99	2.82
Three	0.49	1.09	1.77	2.33	3.21
Four	0.83	2.36	1.98	3.20	3.43

where $\Delta(m-p)_t$ is the growth rate of real money, Δp_t is the inflation rate, $(m-p-y)_t$ is the inverse of velocity, and R_t^* is the learning-adjusted net interest rate [see Hendry and Ericsson (1991) for a detailed description of the variables]. For the sample period 1964(1)–1985(2), the above model was estimated to be

$$\Delta(m-p)_t = \underset{(4.64)}{0.02} - \underset{(5.27)}{0.70} \Delta p_t - \underset{(2.98)}{0.19} \Delta(m-p-y)_{t-1}$$
$$- \underset{(8.24)}{0.62} R_t^{*} - \underset{(9.94)}{0.09} (m-p-y)_{t-1} + residual \qquad (30)$$

$$T = 86[1964(1)-1985(2)] \quad R^2 = 0.69 \quad dw = 2.15 \quad \hat\sigma = 0.01344.$$

The estimated univariate model was

$$\Delta(m-p)_t = \underset{(2.45)}{0.26} \Delta(m-p)_{t-1} + \underset{(2.29)}{0.25} \Delta(m-p)_{t-2} + residual, \quad (31)$$

$$T = 86[1964(1)-1985(2)] \quad R^2 = 0.16 \quad dw = 1.96 \quad \hat\sigma = 0.02170.$$

For Test 1, unconditional forecasts of R_t^* are required. A model for ΔR_t^* was estimated as

$$\Delta R_t^* = 0.01 - 0.13 R_{t-2}^* + white\ noise. \qquad (32)$$

The unconditional forecast of R_{t+1}^* is the unconditional forecast of ΔR_{t+1}^*, plus R_t^*. Multiple-step forecasts are easily formed.

Following the analysis in the first example, the RMSFEs of the conditional and unconditional forecasts were computed for both models for 1985(3)–1989(2) and are displayed in Table 15.5. It can be seen that the conditional RMSFE was less than the unconditional RMSFE for all forecast horizons.

Further investigation was needed to determine whether these differences were statistically significant. In particular, the test involving the sum and differences of the forecast errors was employed and the results are displayed in Table 15.5. The conclusion of Test 1 obtained for the

Hendry and Ericsson model is that the conditional and unconditional forecasts are not significantly different one, two, and three steps ahead but are significantly different for four steps ahead.

For Test 15.2, as a further test of the superiority of the conditional forecasts, the conditional and unconditional forecasts were combined using regression (12). For a one-step horizon, the estimated parameters were as follows:

$$\Delta(m - p)_{t+1} = 0.002 + 1.15 \; f_{t,1} - 0.31 \; g_{t,1} + residual, \qquad (33)$$
$$\phantom{\Delta(m - p)_{t+1} = } (0.26) \quad (2.65) \qquad (0.62)$$

$$T = 16[1985(3) - 1989(2)] \quad R^2 = 0.56 \quad dw = 2.32 \quad \hat{\sigma} = 0.01316.$$

Lastly, for Test 3, the estimated target series for each model was computed. The estimated target series and the observed $\Delta(m - p)$ are within one to three percentage points of each other, which is not unrealistic.

Taken together, the above results indicate that the usefulness of the above model for policy purposes may depend on the forecast horizon used by the policy maker since the above analysis suggests that the conditional forecasts do not appear to be superior to the unconditional forecasts at one, two, and three steps ahead but are superior for four steps ahead. It should be noted, however, that one interpretation of the failure of the forecast tests to reject is that they lack power because of the small sample size of the forecasts.

6. CONCLUSION

Despite the importance of reliable models used in the policy making process, there has been little consideration given to the evaluation of policy models in the econometric literature. This paper discussed a number of tests that could be used for such a purpose. While these tests provide only necessary properties that a policy model should possess, they do aid the decision maker by excluding some inadequate models.

APPENDIX. DESCRIPTION OF THE DATA

Data for Example 1

M	M1 [1950(1)–1958(12)] (Banking and Monetary Statistics: Board of Governors of the Federal Reserve System, 1976)
M	M1 [1959(1)–1988(12)] (Citibase Series FM1)
U	Unemployment rate, all workers, including resident armed forces (Citibase Series LHURR)
F	Total Federal government expenditures (Citibase Series GGFEX)
DEFLAT	Implicit price deflator: Federal government (Citibase Series GDGGF)

MALE	Male population aged 15–44 years (Sum of Citibase Series PANM4, PANM5, PANM6, PANM7, PANM8, and PANM9)
CIV	Civilian population (Citibase Series POPCIV)
POP	Total population including armed forces overseas (Citibase Series POP)

Variables for Example 1

DM_t	$\log M_t - \log M_{t-1}$
UN_t	$\log[0.01U_t/(1 - 0.01U_t)]$
FED_t	$F_t/DEFLAT_t$
$FEDV_t$	$\log FED_t - [\log FED]_t^*$
$[\log FED]_t^*$	$0.05[\log FED]_t + 0.95[\log FED]_{t-1}^*$
MIL_t	$(POP_t - CIV_t)/MALE_t$

Data for Example 2

R^B	Total borrowings at reserve banks (Citibase Series F6CMB)
i_D	Discount rate, Federal Reserve Bank of New York (Citibase Series FYGD)
i_S	Federal funds rate (Citibase Series FYFF)
R^{TOT}	Total reserves (Citibase Series FZCMRR)

Variables for Example 2

K	$i_D - i_S$
R_t^{UB}	$R_t^{TOT} - R$
ΔR_t^{UB}	$R_t^{UB} - R_{t-1}^{UB}$

Notes: For Example 1, the series listed as "data" were converted into quarterly values when appropriate and the "variables" were formed. For Example 2, the series listed as "data" were seasonally adjusted and from them the "variables" were formed.

REFERENCES

(References marked with an asterisk* are included in this volume.)

Barro, R. J., and M. Rush (1980) "Unanticipated Money and Economic Activity", in S. Fischer (ed.) *Rational Expectations and Economic Policy*, Chicago, University of Chicago Press (for the NBER).

Chong, Y. Y., and D. F. Hendry (1986) "Econometric Evaluation of Linear Macroeconomic Models", *Review of Economic Studies*, 53, 671–690. [Also, Chapter 17 of Granger (1990).]

Dutkowsky, D. (1984) "The Demand for Borrowed Reserves: A Switching Regression Model", *Journal of Finance*, 69, 2, 407–424.

Engle, R. F., and D. F. Hendry (1993) "Testing Super Exogeneity and Invariance in Regression Models", *Journal of Econometrics*, 56, 1/2, 119–139; originally cited as (1989) "Testing Super Exogeneity and Invariance", Discussion Paper No. 89-51, Economics Department, University of California at San Diego, La Jolla, California, forthcoming in *Journal of Econometrics*.

Frankel, J. A. (1990) "International Nominal Targeting: A Proposal for Overcoming Obstacles to Policy Coordination", Working Paper, Economics Department, University of California, Berkeley.

Goldfeld, S. M., and E. J. Kane (1966) "The Determinants of Member Bank Borrowing: An Econometric Study", *Journal of Finance*, 21, 499–514.

Granger, C. W. J. (1988) "Causality, Cointegration, and Control", *Journal of Economic Dynamics and Control*, 12, 551–559.

Granger, C. W. J. (ed.) (1990) *Modeling Economic Time Series: Readings in Econometric Methodology*, Oxford, Oxford University Press.

Granger, C. W. J., and P. Newbold (1987) *Forecasting Economic Time Series*, New York, Academic Press.

Hendry, D. F., and N. R. Ericsson (1991) "Modeling the Demand for Narrow Money in the United Kingdom and the United States", *European Economic Review*, 35, 4, 833–881.

Hoover, K. D., and S. M. Sheffrin (1992) "Causation, Spending, and Taxes: Sand in the Sandbox or Tax Collector for the Welfare State?", *American Economic Review*, 82, 225–248.

Keir, P. (1981) "Impact of Discount Policy Procedures on the Effectiveness of Reserve Targeting", in *New Monetary Control Procedures*, Volume 1, Federal Reserve Staff Study, Board of Governors of the Federal Reserve System, Washington, D.C.

Nagel, S. S. (1990) *Policy Theory and Policy Evaluation*, New York, Greenwood Press.

van Velthoven, B. C. J. (1990) "The Applicability of the Traditional Theory of Economic Policy", *Journal of Economic Surveys*, 4, 59–88.

CHAPTER 16

Implications of Aggregation with Common Factors*

C. W. J. Granger

Many observed macrovariables are simple aggregates over a large number of microunits. It is pointed out that the generating process of the macrovariables is largely determined by the common factors in the generating mechanisms of the microvariables, even though these factors may be very unimportant at the microlevel. It follows that macrorelationships are simpler than the complete microrelationships, but that empirical investigations of microrelationships may not catch those components, containing common factors, which will determine the macrorelationship. It is also shown that an aggregate expectation or forecast is simply the common factor component of the individual agents' expectations.

1. INTRODUCTION

Macroeconometric models have to be constructed from the data that is available rather than from ideal data. In practice, many important macrovariables are measured as unweighted sums of quantities observed for microunits, such as firms or families. Obvious examples include production of agricultural commodities, profits, employment, and consumption. One aspect of this aggregation procedure that has received little attention is the immense size of many actual economies. For example, the current U.S. economy contains over 80 million households and two and a half million corporations. These numbers are so large that various statistical limit theorems will strongly apply, so that if simplistic assumptions about the microunits are correct, there will be clear implications for macromodels relating aggregate series. The degree of explanation of one variable by another could be very high and residuals be perfectly normally distributed. If, in practice, macromodels do not have these properties, there are implications about the extent to which microvariables are related. These limitations are discussed here by supposing that the microunits, called "families," make their decisions using just two

* *Econometric Theory* 3, 1987, 208–222.

types of information, one that is available just to them individually or to a small number of families, and the other type is information available to (virtually) all families and is used by them. The two types of information produce potentially measurable variables called individual factors (IF) and common factors (CF), respectively. Throughout the analysis, the population size, N = number of families, will be assumed to be extremely large. The paper considers cross sections of stationary, zero-mean time series aggregating into macrostationary series.

The strong implications of the presence or not of these two types of factors are discussed in this section for a simple model. The object of the paper is to discuss the extent to which the correct macromodel specification can be predicted from micromodels. It is shown that for this purpose, the micromodeller should concentrate on the common factors, even if they are relatively unimportant at the microlevel.

The second section provides more rigorous definitions and a more general model is considered. It is found that a full macromodel specification is often simpler than the micromodels, after dominated terms are ignored. However, it is also seen that an incomplete micromodel will lead to unsatisfactory specification at the macrolevel. A likely source of common factors are expectations, and these are considered in the fourth section. The final section discusses whether common factors exist and, if so, what they are. An appendix contains proofs of a theorem concerning aggregation of nonlinear relationships.

The aggregation properties are made complicated but more interesting and realistic by allowing some explanatory variables to be observable, and thus usable in micro and macromodels, while other variables are unobservable and thus fall into the residual terms. It will be seen that the observability of CF's is of vital importance in measuring the degree of fit of a model, using an R^2 measure.

Many of the central issues discussed in this paper can be illustrated using the very simple model:

$$y_{jt} = a_j + x_{jt} + c_j z_t, \tag{1}$$

where y_{jt} is a value taken by some variable, such as nondurable goods consumption, for the jth microunit at time t, a_j is a family-specific constant, x_{jt} is a family specific explanatory variable, and z_t is an explanatory variable relevant to all families. Both x_{jt} and z_t have mean zero. For the present, all variables will be assumed to be stationary (and ergodic) and all x_{jt}'s are assumed to be independent of each other and of z_t. The coefficients c_j will be assumed to be drawn independently from a distribution with mean $m(c)$ and finite variance. Denoting $\bar{c} = \frac{1}{N}\Sigma_{j=1}^{N} c_j$, where N is the number of families in the economy, then the final term in equation (1) can be written as

$$c_j z_t = \bar{c} z_t + c_j' z_t, \tag{2}$$

where $c'_j = c_j - \bar{c}$. Clearly, $\bar{c}$ will closely approximate $m(c)$ if N is large. Denoting the sum of the y's by

$$S_t(y) = \sum_{j=1}^{N} y_{ji},$$

the aggregate of relationship (1) is

$$S_t(y) = S(a) + S_t(x) + S(c)z_t. \tag{3}$$

The most striking feature of this aggregation is the relative sizes of the (temporal) variances of the components. $S(x)$ is the sum of N independent components each having mean zero, and so the variance of the time series $S(x)$ is of order N, being N times the average variance of the x_{jt}'s. The final term using (2) is $N\bar{c}z_t$, which has variance $N^2(\bar{c})^2 \text{var}(z)$ and so, provided $\bar{c} \neq 0$, this term will generally dominate the term involving the x's. For N being large enough, (3) will effectively be unchanged if the second term is ignored.

Some rather startling values can be achieved by considering the simplification of

$$y_{jt} = x_{jt} + cz_t \tag{4}$$

with $\text{var}(y_j) = 1$, $\text{var}(z) = 1$, so that $\text{var}(x_j) = 1 - c^2$ and $\text{var}(S_t(y)) = N(1 - c^2) + N^2 c$. Two extreme cases will be discussed. In the first case, z_t is observed, but the x_{jt}'s are unobserved and so the macrorelationship consists of explaining $S_t(y)$ by the z_t. In the second case, the x_{jt}'s are observed and z_t is not, and the regression explains $S(y)$ by the x_{jt}. The table shows the R^2 values in the two cases if $c^2 = 0.001$ and N is one million.

	Case 1	Case 2
	z observed x_j not observed	x_j is observed z not observed
micro-R^2	0.001	0.999
macro-R^2	0.999	0.001

In the first case, the common factor is observable but would be unlikely to be found statistically significant in any regression at the microlevel. However, it becomes dominant at the macrolevel. In the second case, an empirical modeller will be very content with regressions using microdata, but the resulting model will not aggregate into anything useful at the macrolevel. Microtheory, if it is at all incomplete, will be likely to concentrate on variables that have good explanatory power at the microlevel, but if the relatively unimportant common factors are left out of the theory, then it will not be helpful in providing a macrotheory. Of course, what is important at the macrolevel must be in the microrelationships. An analogy occurs in another aggregation situation, that of summation over time. If a variable observed over a long period contains an important trend, this trend must be present but not necessarily detectable if the variable is observed over short time periods. A short-term model may well ignore this trend but will thus give a poor representation over the long term.

As a further example of the simple analysis given in this section, consider the demand for some commodity and the relationship between the aggregate demand and the prices faced by families. In the notation used above, y_{jt} is the demand for the commodity by the jth family, and p_{jt} denotes the price faced by this family, which could depend on location. Countrywide market pressures could ensure that these various price series do not move too far apart, giving

$$p_{jt} = z_t + x_{jt},$$

where z_t is the market factor linking all prices together, and x_{jt} is the difference of price in the family's location from z_t. Thus, z_t is the CF and x_{jt} the IF. The analysis shows that the aggregate price $S(p)$ will effectively equal Nz_t and the macromodel relating total demand to $S(p_t)$ really only uses z_t as an explanatory variable.

These results, and those to be presented, are concerned with the extent to which micromodels can be used to deduce the best specification of estimated macrorelationships. A complete micromodel, including all links between families, must lead to an exact specification of the macromodel. It is suggested that virtually the same specification occurs when just the common factor effects are considered at the microlevel. As has been seen, empirically derived microrelationships may miss vitally important common factors and so lead to incorrect specifications.

The aims of the paper are seen to be quite different from the concern of the majority of the aggregation literature which deals with the interpretation of macroparameters and the extent to which observed macrorelationships can suggest micromodel specifications. Generally, this literature does not consider whether factors are common or individual, particularly when relating the residuals of microrelationships. The literature typically does not consider dominance of some aggregate terms by others, so that the complete aggregate models are retained rather than the available simpler close approximation achieved by dropping relatively small quantities. However, some recent papers have specifically considered common factors, for example, Powell and Stoker [8], but the objectives of the analysis are quite different.

2. COMMON FACTORS, INDIVIDUAL FACTORS, AND MODEL SIMPLIFICATION

Consider a sequence of random variables X_j, all identically distributed with mean m and variance σ^2, both parameters being nonzero. The sequence may be said to contain a dominant common factor if the variance of the sum of the first N terms of the sequence increases proportionally to N^2, i.e., if $S_N(X) = \Sigma_{j=1}^N X_j$. Thus,

$$V_N = \text{variance}(S_N(X)) = A_1 N^2, \tag{5}$$

at least for large enough N. As was shown above, if $X_j = Z + \varepsilon_j$, where the ε_j's are all independent and also uncorrelated with Z, then V_N obeys the condition (5). Further, if one considers the coefficient of variation (CV), defined by

$$CV(X) = \frac{\text{standard deviation}(X)}{\text{mean}(X)},$$

then

$$CV(S_N(X)) = CV(X) = \frac{\sigma}{m} \quad \text{for large enough } N. \tag{6}$$

If X_j is a variable for which (5) and (6) holds for moderately sized N and larger, it will be called a common factor, denoted by CF. This is clearly a pragmatic definition, but is appropriate for this largely expository discussion. One implication of this definition is seen by considering the case

$$X_j = \beta_j Z.$$

Then,

$$S(X) = ZS(\beta)$$
$$= ZN\bar{\beta}.$$

If the mean of the distribution from which the β's are drawn is zero, then these X's will not be considered a common factor (in mean) given the above definition, but if $\bar{\beta} \neq 0$, then the X's will be a CF. One might note that if $\bar{\beta} = 0$, X_j^2 will be a CF. If the sequence X_j is such that

$$V_N = A_2 N, \tag{7}$$

for large N, it will be said to be dominated by individual factors. An example is when all the X's are uncorrelated, but some correlation may occur between X's and this condition still hold. In this case,

$$CV(S_N(X)) = \frac{1}{\sqrt{N}} CV(X), \tag{8}$$

for large enough N. Sequences obeying (7) or (8) for moderate and large N will be called individual factors (IF). It should be noted that the properties used here to define CF and IF will also hold for any large subset of the complete sequence X_j.

From these definitions there follows a natural constraint on the extent to which an IF and a CF can be related. If X is an IF, Z a CF, consider the regression

$$X_j = \alpha_j + \beta_j Z + \varepsilon_j,$$

where ε_j is an IF. Applying condition (7), it follows that $S(\beta) = 0$ and as this must hold for every substantial subset of X_j, this suggests – but does not prove – that most $\beta_j = 0$. Thus, at least the typical correlation between an IF and a CF will be zero.

The results of the previous section say that if a microvariable has a linear representation containing both CF's and IF's, then on aggregation only terms involving CF's will be of any relevance. Thus, there is a simplification of the model, in that fewer variables need to be considered when macromodeling than when completely modeling microvariables. This result can be generalized to more complicated models.

Suppose that at the microlevel there is a time-varying parameter on a common factor, so that

$$y_{jt} = (\gamma_j + \delta_j x'_{jt} + \theta_j z'_t) z_t + \text{residual}, \tag{9}$$

where x'_{jt} is an IF with zero mean. Then in the aggregate, the only terms of importance will be $S(\gamma) z_t$ and $S(\theta) z'_t z_t$. If z'_t is observed, one just has a different observed CF $z'_t z_t$, if z'_t is not observed, then z_t will still have a time-varying parameter. However, if $z'_t = 0$, so that the time-varying parameter contains no CF, the aggregate model simplifies to a constant parameter on z_t. The same result occurs with simple types of heteroskedasticity. If the residuals for y_{jt} include a common factor, with a time-varying parameter as in (9), then in the aggregate the residual will have no heteroskedasticity if this parameter has no CF. Again, in aggregation there is potential for simplification compared to the typical micromodel.

Regarding this simplification, there are two counteracting forces in operation. If the *complete* micromodel is specified, including small CF terms, the macromodel is likely to be simpler, as terms arising from individual factors may be ignored and there is a greater possibility of time-invariant parameters and homoskedasticity. However, if one starts from an incompletely specified micromodel, ignoring small CF terms, the micromodels *could* appear to have constant parameters and to be homoskedastic, but the eventual macromodel may not have these properties if, for example, the missing (but observable) CF term has a time-varying parameter involving an unobserved CF.

Now consider the case where there are no CF's as explanatory variables, either observed or not observed. If one has a model of the form

$$y_{jt} = \alpha_j + (a_j + b_j x'_{jt} + c_j z'_t) x_{jt} + \text{residual},$$

where x'_{jt} is a zero mean IF, z'_t a zero mean CF, then the regression of $S(y)$ on $S(x)$ will give

$$S(y) = S(\alpha) + (A + D z'_t) S(X) + \text{residual}$$

for some constants A, D, and one still has a time-varying parameter if $Dz_t' \neq 0$. Similarly, heteroskedasticity will be present in the macromodel if it is caused by a CF, but not otherwise. One further simplification occurs in this case of no CF. If there is a nonlinear relationship of the form

$$y_{jt} = \alpha_j + F_j(x_{jt}) + \text{residual},$$

where the x_{jt} are Gaussian IF, it is shown in the appendix that the macrorelationship between $S(y)$ and $S(x)$ will be linear to a high degree of approximation.

Naturally, if the residuals contain no CF, the aggregate residual will be highly Gaussian due to the central limit theorem.

To summarize the various cases:

(i) CF's exist and all observable.
Macrorelationships have very high R^2 values, residuals are Gaussian and constant variance.
(ii) CF's exist and all unobservable.
Very low R^2 values, residuals need not be Gaussian and may be heteroskedastic.
(iii) CF's exist, some observable, and some are not.
Any R^2 value, residuals not necessarily Gaussian, possibly time-varying parameters.
(iv) No CF's.
Linear relationship between aggregates, any R^2 value, residuals highly Gaussian, no time-varying parameters, heteroskedastic.

Note that in case (i), the high R^2 values occur for models between stationary series and not because variables, each integrated of order one, are involved in the regression. High R^2 values would be found for the changes in typical macrovariables. By considering which case arises in some applied piece of research, the presence or otherwise of common factors might be deduced. For example, if a low R^2 is found in a macromodel, it may be worth discussing what unobserved common factors could explain this finding.

3.   AN EXAMPLE: THE ARBITRAGE PRICING THEORY MODEL

Let r_{jt} be the return from the jth security in some group and suppose that there exists a common factor z_t, which enters with a lag, so that

$$r_{jt} = \alpha_j + \beta_j z_{t-1} + \varepsilon_{jt}, \tag{10}$$

where all variables are white noise and ε_{jt} contains no CF. The aggregate relation is effectively

$$S_t(r) = S(\alpha) + z_{t-1}S(\beta) \tag{11}$$

keeping just the dominant variables. Note that if z_{t-1} is unobserved, then it becomes almost perfectly observed from the aggregate relationship (11). Thus, substituting into (10) gives

$$r_{jt} = \left[\alpha_j - \beta_j \frac{S(\alpha)}{S(\beta)}\right] + \frac{\beta_j}{S(\beta)} S_t(r) + \varepsilon'_{jt}, \tag{12}$$

with the new residual ε'_{jt} being virtually the same as the original residual ε_{jt}. Rewrite (12) as

$$r_{jt} = \alpha'_j + \beta'_j R_t + \varepsilon'_{jt}, \tag{13}$$

where $R_t = \frac{1}{N} S_t(r)$ is the average return. It is seen that $S(\alpha') = 0$ and $S(\beta') = 1$, and little is lost for the micromodel by replacing the unobserved CF, z_{t-1} by R_t, but the lagged relationship is lost, and the new model (13) is now of no use in helping to specify the macromodel as it merely gives an identity on aggregation. Equation (13) is the standard form of the arbitrage pricing theory model. The analysis obviously becomes less clear-cut if r_{jt} in (10) contains several common factors.

4. EXPECTATIONS

Many theories in microeconomics use expectations as explanatory variables. In this section, the relevance of common factors in the formation of expectations is explored. It is seen that if a macromodeller assumes that all microunit expectations are based just on common factors, this generally will provide an excellent approximation of the true aggregate relationship.

Suppose that N individuals are all trying to forecast the same variable w_{t+1} using their own information sets $I_{jt}: z_{t-k}, x_{j,t-k}, k \geq 0$. z_t is a variable known to all individuals. In practice, z_t will be a vector, but this generalization is not important for what follows. It is assumed that all $x_{j,t-k}$ are independent of $x_{i,t-s}$ for $i \neq j$, and also z_{t-s}, for all s. $x_{j,t-k}$ is information available only to the jth individual and which is also orthogonal to the publicly available, common factor, information z_t. w_t will presumably be a macrovariable but need not be an aggregate. It could, for example, be a tax rate. Let U_t be the universal information set, being the union of all the individual I_{jt}, so that

$$U_t: z_{t-k}, x_{j,t-k}, \quad k \geq 0, \quad j = 1, \ldots, N.$$

Suppose also that the optimum forecast of w_{t+1}, given U_t, is

$$E_u = E[w_{t+1}|U_t] = a(B)z_t + \sum_j \beta_j(B)x_{j,t}, \tag{14}$$

where

$$a(B) = \sum a_k B^k$$
$$\beta_j(B) = \sum b_{jk} B^k$$

are lag operator polynomials. The information is seen to enter the least-squares, optimum forecast linearly. With the assumptions made, the optimum forecast, or rational expectation, of the jth person is

$$E_j = E[w_{t+1}|I_{jt}] = a(B)z_t + \beta_j(B)x_{j,t}. \tag{15}$$

If the individuals make available their individual information, then the optimum forecast is E_u given by (14). However, suppose that the individuals only realize their individual expectations E_j, then the aggregate, or average, expectation is

$$\overline{E} = \frac{1}{N}\sum_j E_j = a(B)z_t + \frac{1}{N}\sum_j \beta_j(B)x_{j,t}. \tag{16}$$

The second term in (16) will have a standard deviation $O(N^{-1/2})$ and so be negligible compared to the first. Thus, if N is large,

$$\overline{E} \approx a(B)z_t,$$

and the individual's particular information is lost in the aggregate. Note that if the x_{jt}'s do have a common factor, it would be public information and so should be included in z_t.

If expectations are used by individuals to make decisions and if the outcomes of these decisions are major components of the microvariables discussed in previous sections, then these results indicate that the common factors used in making expectations are potentially the common factors occurring in determination of macrovariables. It may be noted that E and all the E_j's are "rational," but based on different information sets; with the model as set up, every individual will outforecast the average forecast.

There is an interesting corollary to this analysis. If there exists an institution which forms a forecast based just on the common factor z_t,

$$E_0 = E[w_{t+1}|z_{t-k}, k \geq 0]$$

then now the optimum forecast is attainable, as

$$E_u = \sum E_j - (N-1)E_0. \tag{17}$$

The analysis in this section is quite different in form and purpose than that in the classical paper on the effect of aggregating forecasts by Aigner and Goldfeld [1]. They consider a very special error structure where microforecast errors add to zero and give a detailed discussion of just

Table 16.1. *Examples of coefficients of variation*[a]

Period[b]	Levels	Difference
Personal consumption, monthly		
I	0.15	0.77
II	0.20	0.47
III	0.30	0.54
Gross national product, quarterly		
I	0.14	0.15
II	0.21	0.43
III	0.29	0.54
Gross savings, quarterly		
I	0.19	11.1
II	0.21	2.3
III	0.31	1.9
Interest rates, monthly 3-month treasury bills		
I	0.41	—
II	0.33	10.0
III	0.38	8.3
Unemployment rate, monthly		
I	0.28	—
II	0.22	—
III	0.17	—

[a] All data pertain to the United States, and all series have very high first autocorrelations. If a value is not shown, the mean is small and so the coefficient of variation is not a useful statistic.
[b] I: 1951–1960; II: 1961–1970; III: 1971–1980.

the $N = 2$ case without specific consideration of the interrelationships between variables in the case of a large population size.

5. SOME PRACTICAL CONSIDERATIONS

To conclude, it is relevant to ask some practical questions, such as

1. Do CF's exist?
2. How important are they at microlevels?
3. If they exist and are observable, what are they?
4. If they exist but are not observable, what are they?

It would be easy to prove the existence of CF's by taking microdata, forming the estimated variance of the sum for a randomly selected sample of size N, and observing how this variance evolves as N increases. However, the microdata required for such a test is rarely available. The fact that coefficients of variation are not really small for macrovariables, as shown in Table 16.1, indicate that they probably come from an aggregation of CF's.

It can be argued in terms of their contribution to total variance that CF's in microequations are likely to be rather unimportant. Recall that in an aggregation of size N, the ratio of the variances from the sum of CF's to the sum of IF's is approximately N to 1. It follows that if the variances of CF's were comparable in size to the variances of the IF's in the typical microequation, then a randomly selected sample of a few thousand microunits would provide estimates of macrovariables which would closely represent the whole economy. An analogy is with the capital asset pricing model which states that one can completely diversify part of the risk by forming a portfolio over all securities, but that the majority of the diversified risk is removed by forming a portfolio over a few securities. As it seems unlikely in practice that a fairly small sample can closely approximate the whole economy, this can be taken to indicate that in practice CF's contribute a very small proportion of variance in the typical microequation. As an example, consider the consumption of durable goods by a family over a 3-month period. The consumption decision will certainly involve changes in family size, income, age and reliability of the present durable goods owned by the family, availability of bargain prices for goods, local offers and other location and family-specific variables, which may be considered IF's, as well as interest rates, which may be thought of as a CF. However, for most families, a typical, small change in the interest rate will probably be of minor importance in their decisions compared to the IF variables. An empirical study of durable goods purchased by a single family may well not detect the influence of interest rates, even though these rates are universally believed, probably correctly, to be of some relevance, at least in determining the behavior of a "marginal buyer." The family incomes considered so far to be an IF may contain a CF as a component. If one considers all of the factors that determine the income of an individual, including age, occupation, experience, education, location, health, and possibly sex and race, these are generally IF's, but the effects of labor market forces, which are inclined to keep wages of similarly endowed individuals close to each other, will add a minor CF to the long list of obviously important IF's. Of course, these arguments that CF's are the microlevel are relatively unimportant and only suggestive; they may not be completely persuasive.

A possible list of observable CF's which are variables publicly available and may be expected to enter the decision-making mechanisms of most microunits would include interest rates, tax rates (personal, corporation), previous values of macrovariables, and publicly announced forecasts or variables such as the index of leading indicators.

It was noted above that if there exist both observed and unobserved CF's, the R^2 of a macroequation can take any value. The converse also holds that if there is an observable CF and R^2 is much less than one, then there must also exist an unobserved CF. Such a CF will be some variable which is known to large number of individuals but is either unobserved or not recorded in official publications, or is known but is not used by the macromodeller. Examples would be news events or a rumor that the government is considering a tax cut, thus possibly inducing a general increase in consumption. These are widely known variables that are difficult to quantify and thus unlikely to appear in a model. A further source of the low R^2 being considered here are the very many variables which lie between the two extremes of IF and CF as discussed throughout this paper. For instance, a factor that is common to all individuals in a particular region – such as a state income tax rate – does not apply to people in other regions. There are certainly very many variables of this nature that are not strictly CF's. They are typically considered to be of minor importance but could accumulate to some relevance in the overall aggregate.

6. SUMMING UP

The dominating effects of common factors can have implications for the interpretation of micromodels. Not only are macromodels potentially simpler, to a high degree of approximation, than the complete micromodel, but low R^2 values in relationships between stationary series or non-Gaussian residuals can indicate the presence of unobserved common factors. It might be important in micromodeling to ask, "What are the unobserved CF's?"

To give a simple, final example, suppose that a macrovariable is thought to be measured with error. If this error is of any relevance, it would have to arise from an unobserved common factor. If individuals provide an estimate of some quantity, such as income, which itself contains a CF, and if their estimates are biased, then these biases will provide a CF. However, if individual estimates are unbiased, it is somewhat less clear why the individual errors can have a CF, but if they do not, the aggregate will contain no relevant measurement error.

No attempt has been made here to consider the time-series properties of aggregates of series obeying simple models. Some results in this area have been presented in Granger [4] and [5].

APPENDIX: NONLINEAR MODELS

Consider the nonlinear microrelationships

$$y_{jt} = \alpha_j + F_j(x_{j,t}) + G_j(z_t) + \varepsilon_{jt}, \tag{A.1}$$

where $x_{jt} = x'_{jt} + \delta_j \tilde{x}_t, -1 \le \delta_j \le 1, x'_{jt}$ are IF, all variables are stationary, the two common factors $\tilde{x}_t$ and z_t are assumed uncorrelated, and the ε_{jt} will be taken to have no common factor. However, it will also be assumed that $x_{jt}, \tilde{x}_t,$ and z_t are jointly normally distributed with zero mean and are uncorrelated. Further, $x_{jt}, \tilde{x}_t,$ and z_t all have unit variances.

The nonlinear functions will be assumed to have Hermite polynomial expansions

$$F_j(x) = \sum_{k=1}^{\infty} f_{jk} H_k(x),$$

$$G_j(x) = \sum_{k=1}^{\infty} g_{jk} H_k(x). \tag{A.2}$$

Virtually all continuous functions have such expansions. The sequence of Hermite polynomials are such that $H_k(x)$ is a polynomial in x of order k and have the particularly useful property that if (X, Y) are distributed normally, zero means, unit variances, and correlation p, then:

$$E[H_j(X)H_k(Y)] = 0, \quad k \neq j,$$
$$= p^k k! \quad k = j. \tag{A.3}$$

Descriptions of Hermite polynomials and their applications can be found in Erdélyi et al. [3] and Granger and Newbold [6]. The first three are $H_0 = 1$, $H_1(x) = x$, $H_2(x) = x^2 - 1$.

The observed macrovariables are $N\bar{y}_t$, $N\bar{x}_t$, and z_t, where $N\bar{y}_t = \Sigma_j y_{jt}$. $N\bar{y}_t$ is determined by

$$N\bar{y}_t = N m_1(\alpha) + \sum_j F_j(x_{jt}) + \sum_j G_j(z_t) + \sum_j \varepsilon_{jt}, \tag{A.4}$$

and a model in terms of the observable variables is considered in the form

$$N\bar{y}_t = N m_1(\alpha) + \sum_k c_k H_k(\sigma_N \bar{x}_t) + \sum_k d_k H_k(z_t) + e_t, \tag{A.5}$$

where σ_N is such that var $(\sigma_N \bar{x}_t) = 1$, so that

$$\sigma_N = \left(N^2 m_1(\delta) + N(1 - m_2(\delta)) \right)^{-1/2}.$$

In particular, if there is no common factor for the x_{jt}, so that all $\delta_1 = 0$, then $\sigma_N = 1/\sqrt{N}$.

Substituting for $G_j(x)$ from (A.2) into (A.4) and noting that x_{jt} and z_t are assumed to be independent, it follows that

$$d_k = \sum_j g_{jk} = N m_1(g_k).$$

Thus, the terms in (A.5) involving the observed common factor produce a nonlinear term that is proportional to the average micrononlinear term involving this variable. As with the previous analysis, this term will dominate the macromodel (A.5) if the x_{jt} contain no common factor, i.e., if all $\delta_j = 0$.

Considering the regression

$$\sum_j F_j(x_{jt}) = \sum_k C_k H_k(\sigma_N \bar{x}_t) + \eta_t,$$

noting that

$$\text{corr}(x_{jt}, \bar{x}_t) = \sigma_N[1 - \delta_i^2) + Nm_1(\delta)\delta_j],$$
$$\simeq \delta_j, \quad \text{if } N \text{ is large, } \tilde{x}_k m_1(\delta) \neq 0$$
$$= N^{-1/2}, \quad \text{if all } \delta_j = 0$$

and using the orthogonal properties in (A.3), it is found that if $\tilde{x}_t$ is a common factor, then

$$C_k \simeq \sum_j f_{jk}\delta_j^k = Nm_1(f_k)m_k(\delta), \tag{A.6}$$

assuming f_{jk} and δ_j are drawn independently from their distributions. If all $\delta_i = 0$, so that $\tilde{x}$ is not a common factor, it is found that

$$C_k = N^{1-k/2}m_1(f_k). \tag{A.7}$$

As $|\delta_j| \leq 1$, $m_k(\delta)$ will generally decrease as k increases, so the nonlinearity is reduced for the aggregate relationship compared to the typical microrelationship.

If the x_{jt}'s are all uncorrelated, so that $\delta_j = 0$, for all j, then the nonlinear terms in $\tilde{x}_t$ quickly decline for large N, as seen by (A.7). Effectively, $\bar{x}_t$ will only enter the aggregate equation linearly in this case. If neither common factors, $\tilde{x}_t$ or z_t, enter the microrelationships (A.1), the aggregate relationship will be linear, to a high degree of approximation for large N. If $\tilde{x}_t$ is not in (A.1) but z_t is a common factor, then the z_t terms in (A.5) will dominate those involving $\tilde{x}_t$, as in Section 1, and so the x_{jt}'s become irrelevant in the macrorelationship.

The assumption of normality is not thought to be essential for these results, but more general situations have not yet been considered.

As an example of these results, suppose that the microrelationships are all identical of the form

$$y_{jt} = ax_{jt} + bx_{jt}^2 + \varepsilon_{jt},$$

where

$$x_{jt} = \mu_t + x_{jt}'.$$

Thus, the microexplanatory variables all move together with the same mean μ_t, which is thus a common factor, but with individual independent dispersions x_{jt}', having zero mean. The only observed macrovariables are $S_t(y)$ and $S_t(x)$, the cross-section sums of the x's and y's. Clearly,

$$S(X) = N\mu_t + \sum_j x'_{jt},$$

and from the analysis of the first section, the temporal variance of the first term will dominate that of the second, for large N, so that $S(x) \simeq N\mu_t$ by ignoring the dominated term. Expanding the squared term, the aggregate relationship is

$$S(y) = aN\mu_t + aS(x') + bN\mu_t^2 + 2bN\mu_t S(x') + bS\big[(x')^2\big] + S(\varepsilon).$$

If the variance of x_{jt} is from a distribution with mean σ_2, then this mean will be a CF. Note that as these variables are positive, there must be such a CF. If $\mu_t \neq 0$, dropping dominated terms gives

$$S(y) = aN\mu_t + bN\mu_t^2 + N\sigma^2 = aS(x) + bS[(x)]^2 + N\sigma^2,$$

and so the nonlinear form is maintained at the macrolevel. However, if $\mu_t = 0$, so there is no common factor in the mean, then

$$S(y) = aS(x) + bS(x)^2 + S(\varepsilon).$$

It has been assumed that $S(x)$ is observed but that $S(x^2)$ is not observed. For example, an annual figure is available for the total consumption on savings for a state, but not the variance of these quantities across individuals. The natural question to ask is whether $S(x^2)$ can be estimated from $[S(x)]^2$. However, the correlation between these two variables is generally $O(N^{-1})$ and so is zero to a close degree of approximation. Thus, $S(x^2)$ is both unobserved and not estimable, and so goes into the residual, giving the macroregression

$$S(y) = aS(x) + S(\varepsilon) + N\sigma^2.$$

Other authors have considered the extent to which micro-nonlinear relationships are retained as macroaggregates, particularly Muellbauer [7] (described simply in Deaton and Muellbauer [2] and Stoker [9]). The analysis is quite different in method and purpose, but the use by Muellbauer of a "representative" consumer's explanatory variable effectively introduces a common factor. Stoker's elegant and general analysis can accommodate both CF's and IF's, but he does not specifically discuss the impact of these factors and the simplification of analysis achievable from their consideration.

REFERENCES

Aigner, D. J. & S. M. Goldfeld. Estimation and prediction from aggregate data, when aggregates are measured more accurately than their components, *Econometrica* 42 (1974): 113–134.

Deaton, A. & J. Muellbauer. *Economics and consumer behavior*. New York: Cambridge University Press, 1980.

Erdélyi, A., et al. *Higher trancedental functions* (Bateman Manuscript Project). New York: McGraw-Hill, 1953.

Granger, C. W. J. Long-memory relationships and the aggregation of dynamic models. *Journal of Econometrics* 14 (1980): 227–238.

Granger, C. W. J. Are economic variables really integrated of order one? In I. B. MacNeill & G. J. Umphrey (eds.). *Time series and econometric modeling*. Boston: D. Reidel, 1987.

Granger, C. W. J. & P. Newbold. Forecasting transformed series. *Journal of the Royal Statistical Society* B38 (1976): 189–203.

Muellbauell, J. Community preferences and the representative consumer. *Econometrica* 44 (1976): 979–999.

Powell, J. L. & T. M. Stoker. The estimation of complete aggregation structures. *Journal of Econometrics* 30 (1985): 317–344.

Stoker, T. M. Completeness, distribution restrictions, and the form of aggregate functions. *Econometrica* 52 (1984): 887–907.

PART FIVE

FORECASTING

CHAPTER 17

Estimating the Probability of Flooding on a Tidal River*

C. W. J. Granger, B. A.

Abstract

An estimate of the number of floods per century that can be expected at any given point of a river would obviously be an important piece of information when any expensive flood-prevention scheme is under discussion. Gumber (1958) has discussed such an estimation for a non-tidal stretch of river, and has shown how to derive estimates from existing flow data, using his method of maxima. The object of the present paper is to put forward a method of solving the intrinsically more complex problem of estimating the probability of flooding for a tidal stretch.

The mathematical theory is first briefly presented, and a general-method of finding the estimate is discussed. The final section is concerned with an application of the method to the River Trent at Gainsborough.

MATHEMATICAL THEORY

It has been found necessary to use a certain number of elementary statistical concepts in the following section, and for the convenience of readers unfamiliar with such concepts an examination of them will be found in the Appendix, p. 364.

Let T denote tide-height in feet at some fixed measuring point near the mouth of the river, and let F denote flow in cusec. at a point of the river which is effectively or actually non-tidal. If it is assumed that no important tributaries enter the river between the two measuring stations, it is seen that the water height H at any point on the tidal reaches will be dependent only upon T and F. Symbolically this may be written

$$H = b(T, F) \tag{1}$$

where $b(T, F)$ is some bivariate function of T and F.

* *Journal of the Institution of Water Engineers* 13, 1959, 165–174.

Both T and F may be considered as statistical variates, as both will contain important unpredictable elements, e.g. "surge" in T, and these variates need not be statistically independent. It is obviously possible that the meteorological factors causing a large flow may also produce an exceptional surge. Suppose they have a joint distribution function $G(x, y)$, i.e.

$$G(x, y) = \text{Probability } (T \leq x, F \leq y) \tag{2}$$

and it may certainly be assumed that $G(x, y)$ is a continuous function in both variables, and so a frequency function $g(x, y)$ may be defined by

$$g(x, y) = \frac{\partial^2 G(x, y)}{\partial x \cdot \partial y} \tag{3}$$

If flooding at a point O on the river occurs when the height at this point reaches H_o ft., say, then symbolically the probability of a flood at a given tide is

$$P_o = \iint_D g(x, y) \, dx, dy \tag{4}$$

where D is the region defined by

$$\left.\begin{array}{l} -\infty \leq x \leq \infty, -\infty \leq y \leq \infty \\ b(x, y) \geq H_o \end{array}\right\} \tag{5}$$

If the two variables T and F are independent or effectively independent in region D, and if their respective frequency functions are $t(x)$ and $f(y)$, then

$$P_o = \iint_D t(x) \cdot f(y) \, dx \, dy \tag{6}$$

where D is the same region as before.

By use of the above theory a good estimate of the required probability can be found if the functions $b(x, y)$ and $g(x, y)$ (or $t(x)$ and $f(y)$ if T and F are independent) are known, or if estimates of them are found.

It is clear that where independence of T and F does not exist, the estimation problem will be more difficult, as it is much less easy to estimate a bivariate function such as $g(x, y)$, than to estimate separately the two single functions $t(x)$ and $f(y)$. As flooding is likely to be rate, the function $g(x, y)$ will only be needed for at least one of x and y large, and so true statistical independence of variates is not required, only that $g(x, y) \backsimeq t(x) \cdot f(y)$ for either $x \geq x_o$ and/or $y \geq y_o$, and so an assumption of independence may often be a very close approximation to the truth.

Estimation of $t(x)$ and $f(y)$ may be done completely empirically if the data are sufficient, or by curve-fitting to the "tail" of the empirical distribution. In the example that follows it was found that the tide data were sufficient to use the resulting empirical distribution directory, but for the flows a curve had to be fitted.

It is doubtful if the height-function $b(x, y)$ can be estimated from past data, and the only accurate way of estimating this function would seem to be from data arising out of experiments on an accurate scale-model of the section of the river for which information is required.

PROBABILITY OF FLOODING AT GAINSBOROUGH

Introduction

The data available for considering the problem of flooding at Gainsborough was 25 years of flow volumes, and 20 years of actual bidaily maximum tide heights, together with estimates of flow occurring during floods in the last two centuries, and also some idea of the frequency of flooding in the last five or six hundred years.

The readings were those obtained by the Trent River Board, the tide in feet being measured at Keadby ($9\frac{1}{4}$ miles from the river mouth), and the flow in cusec. at Trent Bridge, Nottingham, which is on the non-tidal section of the river.

Data used in estimating the height-function came from the model of the Trent constructed by the Hydraulics Research Station of the Department of Scientific and Industrial Research (D.S.I.R.), at Wallingford, Berks.

Correlation Between Tides and Flow Over the Year

Before the method outlined on p. 358 can be used, one needs to consider the correlation between tides and flow. Figure 17.1 represents the average maximum flows and tides per month throughout the year. It can be seen that generally the period of maximum flow precedes the high spring tides, and occurs well after the high neap tides. From this may be concluded that there is no real correlation between the two, and thus the full data throughout the year may be used in the future analysis. If any one month had contained both the highest flows and tides, any flood would have probably occurred in this month, and thus the data for such a month would have been the most relevant.

Figure 17.1 does, however, show that a combination of a high tide and a high flow is most likely during February. Since it is shown later that the tide factor is relatively unimportant in causing floods, it would seem to be of little use introducing more sophistication in later sections to account for the fact that flows and tides vary in magnitude with the months.

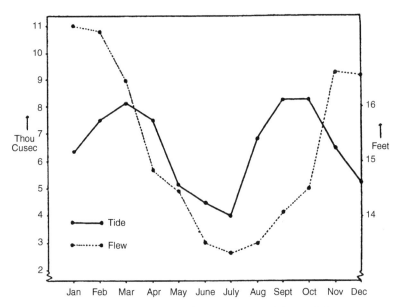

Figure 17.1. Average maximum monthly tides and flows.

It is thus seen that expression (6) may be used rather than the more complicated expression (4). Discussion of the estimation of $t(x)$ will be found below, and the estimation of $f(y)$ is discussed on pp. 170 and 171.

The Distribution of Tide Heights

To find the probability of a tide occurring above a given height, a distribution of recorded tides was computed. Data for 20 years (minus 10 months for which no records are available) showed that out of 13,272 tides, 2,685 were greater or equal to 13 ft. As it is the tides of 13 ft. or more which are most likely to combine with a moderately high flow to produce a flood, a frequency-graph of all such tides was set up as shown in Figure 17.2.

There is probably little to gain by trying to fit a theoretical curve to this empirical figure, and thus probabilities have been estimated directly from it. The probability of a tide greater or equal to X ft. ($X \geq 13.0$ ft.) may be defined as the area under the curve for tide height greater than or equal to X divided by 13,272. The diagram is plotted with tide heights in groups of two inches as x-axis, and observed frequency as y-axis. Examples of results calculated are: –

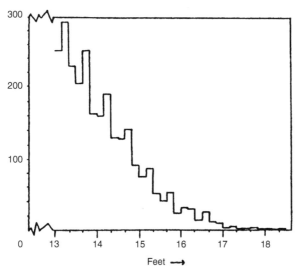

Figure 17.2. "Tail" of tide distribution.

X, ft.	Probable number of tide heights greater or equal to X in any year
13.0	147.68
13.5	105.27
14.0	71.39
14.5	45.21
15.0	25.47
15.5	13.70
16.0	7.32
16.5	3.36
17.0	0.77
17.5	0.33
18.0	0.11
18.5	0.06

Distribution of Flows

The monthly maximum flows, measured in cusec. over 25 years, were used to construct an empirical distribution to enable the probability of a certain size flow occurring in any year to be estimated. The resulting frequency graph is shown as the continuous lines in Figure 17.3. As before, estimates of the number of flows of x cusec. or more may be calculated directly, but as the data included a year (1947) of exceptional

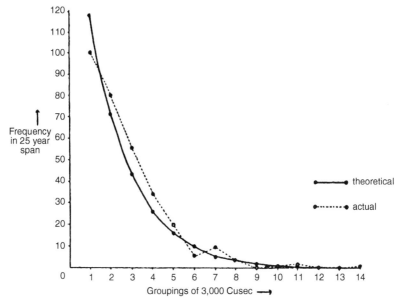

Figure 17.3. Distribution of monthly maximum flows.

flows, a theoretical distribution was fitted to the empirical distribution. This was done because an empirical distribution would indicate that a flow as large as 40,000 cusec. may be expected to occur in every period of 25 years.

Knowledge of exceptionally large flows during the last 500 years shows that the occurrence of such flows is likely to be much rarer. The significance and use of this theoretical distribution is discussed on p. 363.

Figure 17.3 is constructed from the following table: –

	Actual	Theoretical
1	100	118
2	80	71.6
3	51	43.4
4	34	26.3
5	19	16.0
6	6	9.7
7	9	5.9
8	3	3.6
9	0	2.2
10	1	1.3
11	2	0.8
12	0	0.5
13	0	negligible
14	1	"

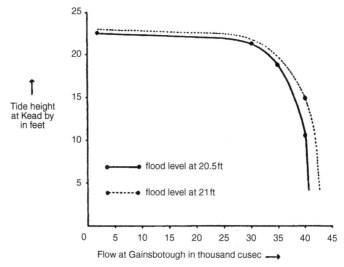

Figure 17.4. Flow/tide combinations producing flooding at Gainsborough.

where the ordinates represent flows in groups of 3,000 cusec., i.e. 1 represents 0–3,000 cusec., 2 is 3,000–6,000 cusec., etc. A statistical goodness-of-fit test, known as the chi-square test, shows that the curve fitted theoretically is a reasonably good approximation to the empirical curve.

Flood-Producing Flow/Tide Combinations

The model of the River Trent constructed by the D.S.I.R. gave sufficient data to determine those flow/tide combinations that produce a level of 20.5 ft., i.e. flood level, at Gainsborough. By extrapolation a diagram showing all such combinations may be drawn (Figure 17.4). All flow/tide combinations lying on the same side of the continuous line as the origin will not produce a height at Gainsborough as high as 20.5 ft., but all other combinations will do so.

Certain interesting aspects of this diagram can be noted. As a tide above 17 ft. is quite rare, and as the maximum tide in the period for which data are available is $18\frac{1}{2}$ ft., it is seen that the probability of a flood being produced by a moderate flow and an exceptionally high tide is negligible. A flow as large as 30,000 cusec. would require a tide of 21.2 ft. to produce a flood, i.e. 2.8 ft. above the highest recorded in the last 20 years. On the other hand, a flow of 40,000 cusec. would require only a very moderate tide of 10 ft. to produce flood conditions at Gainsborough.

It is thus concluded that the tide is relatively an unimportant factor in producing floods. The probability of a level of 20.5 ft. at Gainsborough being produced is now simply the probability of a point lying above the continuous line in Figure 17.4, i.e. the required probability is now found by applying equation (6) with $t(x)$ found from p. 360, $f(x)$ from p. 364, the double integral approximated to by double summation, and the region D determined by Figure 17.4. To reach a figure, it has been taken that (a) the probability of a tide above $18\frac{1}{2}$ ft. is zero, and (b) the probability of a high tide below 10 ft. at a period of the year when a very high flow occurs is also zero. Before any conclusion can be reached, however, a further consideration of the frequency of occurrence of really high flows at Gainsborough must be made.

The Probabilities of High Flows Occurring

Figure 17.4 shows that a flood would certainly occur if a flow of 40,000 cusec. or more reached Gainsborough. Before considering the probability of such a flow occurring, a difference between the model results and what actually happens on the river must be noted. In practice, a flow of, say, 40,000 cusec. at Nottingham would last for only a few hours, i.e. the flood waters would occur as a surge. Thus, part of this flow would be absorbed as "storage" by the river; that is, it would be used in raising the level of the river along its entire length between Nottingham and Gainsborough. It is thus seen that a flow of, say, 40,000 cusec. at Nottingham would not be of this magnitude on reaching Gainsborough.

In the following, it is assumed that 12 per cent of the Nottingham flow has been lost to storage before reaching Gainsborough. The model results were achieved using a constant flow of 40,000 cusec., and so the flow/tide combinations that would produce a flood would use the flow at Gainsborough, rather than the flow at Nottingham as provided in the basic flow data. If F_G represents flow in thousand cusec. at Gainsborough, and F_N that at Nottingham, we have

$$F_G = \frac{88}{100} F_N$$

and thus the probability of a flow at Gainsborough between F_G and F_G' may be taken as the probability of a flow at Gainsborough between

$$\frac{100}{88} = F_G \text{ and } \frac{100}{88} F_{G'}$$

As high flows are so important, it is required to find an estimate of the probability of their occurrence. Miscellaneous evidence suggests that flows at Nottingham in the order of 40,000 cusec. are rare, yet the data provided for the last 25 years contains one recorded instance of such a flow. It is thus seen that the empirical data will not by themselves provide the required probabilities, and thus these probabilities must be estimated from the theoretical curve. The curve fitted was

$$y = 300\frac{1}{2}e^{-x/2}$$

and from this it may be deduced that the probable number of flows greater than or equal to X thousand cusec. in any 25-year period is $300e^{-x/6}$. Using this formula, the following predications are made: –

(1) Probable number of flows greater than or equal to 30,000 cusec. in 100 years in 8. There have been actually 11 recorded instances of flows greater than 29,800 cusec. in the last 150 years.
(2) Probable number of flows greater than or equal to 40,000 cusec. in 75 years is 1. There are three recorded instances of such flows in the last 150 years.

It is thus seen that the fitted curve gives estimates quite consistent with known data. In the final estimate of the probability of flooding the theoretical probabilities have been used.

Final Results and Conclusion

The main results coming from this application of the general method outlined on p. 358 is that the probable number of floods at Gainsborough per century is 0.80, i.e. roughly 1 in any 125 years. Of these about 15 per cent would come from flows at Nottingham of less than 40,000 cusec. Using the theory of the binomial distribution, it follows –

Probability of no flood in any hundred years	= 0.55
Probability of one flood in any hundred years	= 0.33
Probability of two floods in any hundred years	= 0.17
Probability of three floods in any hundred years	= 0.06
Probability of four or more floods in any hundred years	= 0.01

The dotted line in Figure 17.4 shows the flow/tide combinations that would produce a flood at Gainsborough if the flood height there was 21 ft. rather than $21\frac{1}{2}$ ft. Using the method as before, the probable number of floods in any 100 years with this new level is 0.508, i.e. one every 200 years. With a flood level of $21\frac{1}{2}$ ft., the probability is 0.376, i.e. roughly 1 in every 266 years.

The author considers the results to be about as accurate as possible from the available data, but consideration of the possible errors inherent in the method leads him to the conclusion that the final probabilities will, if anything, be over-optimistic. However, he would doubt if the error would be as large as 10 per cent, i.e. probability of flood with $20\frac{1}{2}$ ft. level ought to be greater than 1 in 110 years.

It should be noted here that the final results have been presented in the more useful form of the probable number of floods per century, rather than giving a figure for P_o, as defined on p. 356, which would be the probability of there being a flood on any one day.

ACKNOWLEDGEMENTS

The author would like to thank Mr. Marshall Nixon, M.B.E., T.D., B.Sc., M.I.C.E., engineer to the Trent River Board, for suggesting the problem, providing the data, and encouraging publication of the results, and also Miss M. Sherwin for preparing the diagrams.

APPENDIX

Statistical Concepts Used in the Paper

A measurable statistical variate is one whose exact value cannot be accurately predicted at any moment, but which has associated with it the idea of a probability that its value will lie within any given range. For example, the height of the sun above the horizon can be accurately predicted for a given time on a given day, but the most accurate statement that could be made concerning the height of a man chosen at random is of the type – "there is a probability of 0.56 that his height will lie between 5 ft. 7 in. and 5 ft. 10 in."

Denoting the statistical variate by t, then an associated function $F(x)$ can be defined by

$$F(x) = \{\text{Probability that } t \leq x\}$$

$F(x)$ is called a distribution function, and its derivative $f(x)$, i.e.

$$f(x) = \frac{dF(x)}{dx}$$

is called the frequency function of t. The derivative $f(x)$ will be seen to have the property

$$f(x)dx = \text{Prob. } (x \leq t \leq x + dx).$$

Thus the probability that the variate t lies between a and b is

$$\int_a^b f(x)dx = F(b) - F(a)$$

The above remarks may be generalized to two dimensions. An object chosen at random may have two (or more) statistical variates associated with it (e.g. height and weight). Denoting these variates by t and s, a bivariate distribution function can be defined by

$$F(x, y) = \text{Prob. } (t \leq x, s \leq y),$$

e.g. the statement $F(5.75, 12.0) = 0.71$ implies that the probability of a man chosen at random being less than 5 ft. 9 in. in height and less than 12 stone in weight is 0.71. As before a frequency function may be defined by

$$f(x, y) = \frac{\partial^2 F(x, y)}{\partial x \cdot \partial y}$$

with the property that

$$f(x, y)dx \, dy = \text{Prob. } (x \leq t \leq x + dx; \ y \leq t \leq y + dy) \tag{17.A}$$

Two statistical variates are said to be "statistically independent" if their bivariate frequency function is of the form

$$f(x, y) = p(x) \cdot q(y)$$

From (A) it is seen that the probability of the variates lying in a region D of the xy-plane is given by

$$P(D) = \iint_D f(x, y) \, dx \, dy.$$

D could be, for instance, the circle $x^2 + y^2 \leq a^2$. In the special case when D is the region $x \leq a, y \leq b$, then $P(D)$ is equal to $F(a, b)$.

CHAPTER 18

Prediction with a Generalized Cost of Error Function*

C. W. J. Granger

Classical prediction theory limits itself to quadratic cost functions, and hence least-square predictors. However, the cost functions that arise in practice in economics and management situations are not likely to be quadratic in form, and frequently will be non-symmetric. It is the object of this paper to throw light on prediction in such situations and to suggest some practical implications. It is suggested that a useful, although sub-optimal, manner of taking into account generalized cost functions is to add a constant bias term to the predictor. Two theorems are proved showing that under fairly general conditions the bias term can be taken to be zero when one uses a symmetric cost function. If the cost function is a non-symmetric linear function, an expression for the bias can be simply obtained.

INTRODUCTION

Suppose that one predicts some stochastic process and that it is subsequently found that an error of size x has been made. With such an error one can usually determine the cost of having made the error and the amount of this cost will usually increase as the magnitude of the error increases. Let $g(x)$ represent the cost of error function. In both the classical theory of statistical prediction and in practice, this function is usually taken to be of the form $g(x) = cx^2$, so that least-squares predictors are considered. However, in the fields of economics and management an assumption that the cost of error function is proportional to x^2 is not particularly realistic. The actual function could, in theory at least, be estimated by standard accounting procedures and in many cases will not be symmetric. It is the object of this paper to study in a few simple cases the consequences of using a generalized cost function.

As examples of situations where non-symmetric cost functions arise, one may consider the following two cases:

* *Operational Research Quarterly* 20, 1969, 199–207.

(i) A bank intends to purchase a computer to handle its current accounts. To determine the size of computer to buy, a prediction of future business is made. If this prediction is too high, the result will be that the computer will be under-utilized and a cheaper machine could have been bought. If the prediction is too low, the result will be that part of the accounts will have to be handled by other means. There is no reason to suppose that costs will be symmetric in the two cases.

(ii) A firm is about to issue shares on a stock exchange for the first time. It approaches a bank to act as an issuing agent. The bank guarantees to buy all shares not taken by the public but is allowed to choose the price at which the shares are offered. The problem is to predict public demand for each price and then pick the best price. If too low a price is chosen, the original firm makes less money than would otherwise have been possible. If the price is too high, the issuing bank will be left with many unsold stocks and could lose more than its commission. The cost to the bank, which makes the prediction, is clearly not symmetric. The result is usually that the price chosen is subsequently shown to be too low (Merett et al. 1967).

QUADRATIC ERROR COST AND THE GAUSSIAN PROCESS

Let $\{X_t\}$ be a purely non-deterministic stationary sequence of continuous random variables. The problem to be considered is the prediction of X_{t+k} given $X_t, X_{t-1}, \ldots$. This problem is, of course, fully solved if the conditional frequency of X_{t+k} given $X_t, X_{t-1}, \ldots$ were known. However, the problem is rarely considered in this completely general form or in the form of providing confidence intervals for X_{t+k}. The usual problem considers the optimum point prediction of X_{t+k} by some function $h(X_t, X_{t-1}, \ldots)$ which is in some sense "best". If $g(x)$ is the cost of a predictive error of size x, then as $X_t, X_{t-1}, \ldots$ are known, the optimum h is that which minimizes:

$$E[g(X_{t+k} - h)|X_t, X_{t-1}, \ldots] = E_c[g(X_{t+k} - h)]$$
$$= \int_{-\infty}^{\infty} g(x - h)f_c(x)dx, \tag{1}$$

where $f_c(x)$ is the conditional frequency function of X_{t+k} given X_t, $X_{t-1}, \ldots$. One needs to assume that the integral exists, but, in practice, this is not an important limitation.

A cost function often considered is $g(x) = cx^2$ so that a least-squares predictor is found. In this case, if $M = E_c(X_{t+k})$ then as:

$$E_c\left[(X_{t+k} - h)^2\right] = E_c\left[(X_{t+k} - M)^2\right] + E_c\left[(M - h)^2\right]$$

it follows that the optimum predictor is given by:

$$h(X_t, X_{t-1}, \ldots) = M.$$

When $\{X_t\}$ is a Gaussian process, that is a process for which every finite subset of terms is normally distributed, this leads to the important result that the optimum least-squares predictor of X_{t+k} is a linear sum of X_t, $X_{t-1}, \ldots$, as $M = \sum_{j=0}^{\infty} a_j X_{t-j}$ where the a_j's are fully determined by the covariance matrix and the vector of means of the multivariate normal distribution of

$$X_{t+k}, X_t, X_{t-1}, \ldots .$$

It should also be noted in this case that $f_c(x)$ is also a normal curve with mean M and variance dependent only on the covariance matrix of the multivariate distribution, so that the values taken by X_t, $X_{t-1}, \ldots$ only affect $f_c(x)$ through M. In non-Gaussian situations M need not be a linear function of X_t, $X_{t-1}, \ldots$ and so the usual restriction of prediction theory to linear predictors is sub-optimal. However, the restriction to linear predictors does ensure considerable computational simplicity and is generally thought to be a reasonable one unless specific information is available as to the kind of non-linear form that should be used.

LINEAR COST FUNCTION

Now consider the cost function:

$$g(x) = ax, \quad x > 0, \quad a > 0,$$
$$= 0, \quad x = 0,$$
$$= bx, \quad x < 0, \quad b < 0.$$

Then:

$$E_c[g(X_{t+k} - h)] = a\int_h^{\infty} (x - h)f_c(x)dx + b\int_{-\infty}^{h} (x - h)f_c(x)dx.$$

Differentiating this with respect to h and equating to zero to find the minimum, one gets:

$$F_c(h) = \frac{a}{a - b}, \tag{2}$$

where $F_c(x)$ is the conditional cumulative distribution function of X_{t+k}. The second derivative is $(a - b)f_c(h)$ which will always be positive so that h which is found from (2) will be the optimum predictor.

In the symmetric case, $a = -b$ and so the optimum h is given by $F_c(h) = \frac{1}{2}$, i.e. $h =$ median.

The linear cost function could well arise in a number of actual situations. The prediction of the demand for some commodity provides an example, assuming that there are no stocks available at the time for which the forecast is made. As over-prediction of demand would lead to over-production and a consequent inventory cost, an under-prediction would lead to insufficient production and so to a loss in sales, and hence profits would arise. Over the range in which one hopes the forecasting error will lie, both of these costs will be approximately proportional to the size of the prediction error giving the linear cost function used above. In general the cost per unit will be quite different in the two cases of over- and under-production and so the non-symmetric function will usually be the most realistic.

If the conditional distribution is assumed to be normal, the optimal h will be of the form $M + \alpha$, where α is a constant independent of X_t, $X_{t-1}, \ldots$ and easily found from (2) and tables of the cumulative normal distribution function.

A similar procedure could be employed for any given cost function but the results are rarely of a sufficiently simple form to be useful. Thus, for example, if the cost function is taken to be:

$$g(x) = ax^2, \quad x > 0, \quad a > 0,$$
$$= 0, \quad x = 0,$$
$$= bx^2, \quad x < 0, \quad b > 0,$$

then the optimum h is found to be given by:

$$a\int_0^\infty xf_c(x+h)dx + b\int_{-\infty}^0 xf_c(x+h)dx = 0.$$

Although such results are not easy to use, by putting conditions on the form of $g(x)$ and $f_c(x)$ a number of simple theorems can be proved. These are given in the next two sections.

GENERAL SYMMETRIC COST FUNCTIONS[1]

Throughout the remainder of the paper, the class of cost functions considered are those having the properties that $g(0) = 0$, $g(x)$ is monotonic increasing (non-decreasing) for $x > 0$, monotonic decreasing (non-increasing) for $x < 0$ and differentiable at least twice almost everywhere. It follows that $g'(x) \geq 0, x > 0$ and $g'(x) \leq 0, x < 0$.

In this section the additional constraint will be used that $g(x)$ is symmetric about $x = 0$, so that $g(-x) = g(x)$. As before, $f_c(x)$ is the conditional frequency function of X_{t+k} given $X_t, X_{t-1}, \ldots$, M is the conditional mean of X_{t+k}, i.e. $E_c[X_{t+k}] = M$. $\bar{f}_c(x)$ will be used to denote the conditional distribution of $X_{t+k} - M$ given $X_t, X_{t-1}, \ldots$. The symmetry of $g(x)$ implies that $g'(-x) = -g'(x)$.

If both $g(x)$ and $\bar{f}_c(x)$ are symmetric about $x = 0$ then, with the addition of one further condition, it can be shown that the optimum

---

[1] Similar results to those proved here have been found in other contexts, such as in estimation theory with general loss function (Raiffa and Schlaifer 1967).

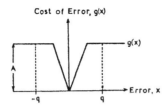

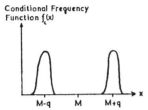

Figure 18.1. Symmetric Cost Functions.

predictor is given by $h = M$. Two theorems of this form are proved in the Appendix. In the first theorem $g'(x)$ is assumed to be strictly monotonically increasing on the whole range $-\infty < x < \infty$ and in the second theorem $\bar{f}_c(x)$ is taken to be continuous and unimodal.

These two theorems thus suggest simple conditions on $g(x)$ and $f_c(x)$ which ensure that the optimum predictor is $h = M$. The sets of conditions given by no means exhaust the possible conditions that would lead to the same result, but they do represent what seem to be the most realistic and useful sets. It is simple to show that symmetry of both $g(x)$ and $f_c(x)$ is not a sufficient condition for the optimum predictor to be equal to M. Consider the pair of functions:

The cost when $h = M$ is A but the cost when $h = M \pm q$ is only approximately $\frac{1}{2}A$ as the area under each peak of $f_c(x)$ will be $\frac{1}{2}$. Thus in this case $h = M$ is not optimum even though both $g(x)$ and $f_c(x)$ are symmetric.

NON-SYMMETRIC COST FUNCTIONS

It is easily shown that if $\{X_t\}$ is a Gaussian process then for any cost function the optimum predictor of X_{t+k} will be of the form:

$$h = \sum_{j=0}^{\infty} a_j X_{t-j} + \alpha_0,$$

where the a_j's are fully determined by the covariance matrix of the process and only α_0 is dependent upon the cost function.

As:

$$E_c[g(X_{t+k} - h)] = \int_{-\infty}^{\infty} g(x - \alpha)\bar{f}_c(x)dx, \tag{3}$$

where $h = M + \alpha$, then as $\bar{f}_c(x)$ is quite independent of $X_t, X_{t-1}, \ldots$, as pointed out in the second section, the integral and thus α_0 will also be independent of $X_t, X_{t-1}, \ldots$, $\alpha = \alpha_0$ will be chosen to minimize (3) and as M is a linear function of $X_t, X_{t-1}, \ldots$, the result follows provided that $E_c[g(X_{t+k} - h)]$ and α_0 exist.

For non-normal distributions, h can always be put in the form $h = M + \alpha$ but M will not be linear and in general α will be a function of $X_t, X_{t-1}, \ldots$.

As an illustration of the size of α for a non-symmetric cost function, consider the linear cost function introduced above:

$$g(x) = ax, \quad x > 0, \quad a > 0,$$
$$= 0, \quad x = 0,$$
$$= bx, \quad x < 0, \quad b < 0.$$

If $f_c(x)$ is normal $N(M, \sigma)$ then applying (2) the following table shows α_0 for various values of $K = a/(-b)$:

K	1	1.5	2	3	4	5	6	7
α_0	0	0.25σ	0.43σ	0.68σ	0.85σ	0.97σ	1.33σ	1.67σ

SOME PRACTICAL CONSEQUENCES OF THE RESULTS

In many actual forecasting situations a fairly precise idea should be available of the shape of the cost curve $g(x)$ but only very rarely will there be any useful information available about the conditional frequency function $f_c(x)$. It will usually be taken to be unimodal and possibly also symmetric, although a simple transformation of the data may first be necessary. It is then only a short step to assuming that $f_c(x)$ is a normal curve, thereby making a linear predictor completely relevant. The evidence for or against an assumption of normality from studies of economic and industrial data is indecisive. At present, it does seem that changes in the logarithm of price and production data are reasonably normally distributed and there are also a number of theoretical reasons for suggesting that this is so.

If a Gaussian assumption is made, the results suggest that when using a symmetric cost function, estimating the linear predictor by least squares will produce a sub-optimal but efficient and computationally simple method as it involves only covariances and the solution of a set of simultaneous linear equations. If a non-symmetric cost function is used, as should frequently be the case, a reasonable procedure would be to estimate the linear predictor $\sum_{j=0}^{m} b_j X_{t-j}$ by least squares and if this is denoted by $\hat{M}_{t+k}$, form:

$$X'_{t+k} = X_{t+k} - \hat{M}_{t+k}$$

and find α_0 by minimizing:

$$\sum g(X'_{t+k} - \alpha). \qquad (4)$$

If the resulting estimate of α_0 is $\hat{a}_0$, the predictor will then be $\hat{M}_{t+k} + \hat{a}_0$. Again this procedure will be sub-optimal but will generally be considerably simpler than finding estimates for the b_j's and α_0 by minimizing:

$$\sum_t g\left(X_{t+k} - \sum_{j=0}^{m} b_j X_{t-j} - \alpha \right).$$

In the more realistic non-Gaussian case there is no reason why a similar suboptimal procedure should not be used. Although a Gaussian assumption assures one that the prediction should be linear, such predictors can also be optimal in non-Gaussian cases (Wolfe et al. 1967). This is the case, for instance, if the data are generated by a linear autoregressive scheme with error or innovation terms that do not have a normal distribution. The parameters of the model could be estimated by least squares and then it is sensible to proceed as above to find α_0 by minimizing:

$$\sum_t g(X'_{t+k} - \alpha).$$

The linear part of the predictor could include trend and seasonal terms where necessary.

In the case of the linear cost function introduced above, the minimization is particularly simple. Suppose a linear model is fitted to the series X_t and let X'_t be the unpredicted residuals from the model, as before. Let $\hat{F}_c(x)$ be the empirical cumulative distribution function of this residual series, than α_0 is found by solving:

$$\hat{F}_c(\alpha_0) = \frac{a}{a-b},$$

which can be found directly from the plot of $\hat{F}_c(x)$ against x.

SUMMARY AND CONCLUSIONS

If one limits oneself to linear predictors, the effect of non-normality of error terms and generalized cost functions can be accounted for by adding a bias term, α_0, to the predictor. In most cases, if the distribution and the cost function are both symmetric, then α_0 may be taken to be zero. In the general case α_0 can be found by minimizing a function depending on the cost function and the observed errors. When a non-symmetric linear cost function is used α_0 is simple to find. Such a cost function will frequently prove to be a useful approximation to any actual non-symmetric cost function.

APPENDIX

Proofs of two Theorems

THEOREM 1: If $g(x)$ is symmetric about $x = 0$ and $g'(x)$ is strictly monotonically increasing on the whole range $-\infty < x \infty$ and if also $\bar{f}_c(x)$ is symmetric about $x = M$, so that $\bar{f}_c(x)$ is symmetric about $x = 0$, the optimum predictor is given by $h = M$.

Consider:

$$E_c[g(X_{t+k} - h)] = \int_{-\infty}^{\infty} g(x - h)f_c(x)dx,$$

$$= \int_{-\infty}^{\infty} g(x - a)\bar{f}_c(x)dx, \tag{5}$$

where $h = M + \alpha$.

Differentiating with respect to α and setting the derivation equal to zero, one obtains:

$$\int_{-\infty}^{\infty} g'(x - \alpha)\bar{f}_c(x)dx = 0. \tag{6}$$

As $g'(x)$ is antisymmetric about $x = 0$ and $\bar{f}_c(x)$ dx is symmetric it follows that:

$$\int_{-\infty}^{\infty} g'(x)\bar{f}_c(x)dx = 0,$$

so that $\alpha = 0$ is a solution to (6). To show that it is a unique minimum, consider:

$$\int_{-\infty}^{\infty} [g'(x - a) - g'(x)]\bar{f}_c(x)dx = 0. \tag{7}$$

As $g'(x)$ is strictly increasing:

$$g'(x - a) - g'(x) > 0 \quad \text{if } \alpha < 0$$

and:

$$g'(x - a) - g'(x) < 0 \quad \text{if } \alpha > 0.$$

As $\bar{f}_c(x)$ is positive, it follows that (7) cannot be true if either $\alpha < 0$ or $\alpha > 0$ and so $\alpha = 0$ is the only possible solution of (6). The second derivative of (5) at $\alpha = 0$ is:

$$\int_{-\infty}^{\infty} g''(x)f_c(x)dx,$$

which will always be positive under the conditions of the theorem so that $\alpha = 0$ is a minimum.

The condition that $g'(x)$ be strictly increasing can be simply relaxed to nondecreasing provided that $[g'(x - \alpha) - g'(x)]\,\bar{f}_c(x)$ is not always identically zero.

THEOREM 2: If the cost function $g(x)$ is symmetric about $x = 0$ and if $f_c(x)$ is symmetric about $x = M$, continuous and unimodal, then the optimum predictor is $h = M$.

If:

$$E_c[g(X_{t+k} - h)] = \int_{-\infty}^{\infty} g(x - \alpha)\bar{f}_c(x)dx,$$

where $h = M + \alpha$, consider:

$$I(\alpha) = \int_{-\infty}^{\infty} [g(x - \alpha) - g(x)]\bar{f}_c(x)dx,$$

where $\alpha \geq 0$. $g(x - \alpha) - g(x)$ is antisymmetric about $x = \alpha/2$, being positive when $x < \alpha/2$ and negative when $x > \alpha/2$. Thus:

$$I(\alpha) = \int_{-\infty}^{\infty} [g(x - \alpha/2) - g(x + \alpha/2)]\bar{f}_c(x)dx$$

$$+ \int_{0}^{\infty} [g(x - \alpha/2) - g(x + \alpha/2)]\bar{f}_c(x + \alpha/2)dx$$

$$= \int_{-\infty}^{0} [g(x - \alpha/2) - g(x + \alpha/2)][\bar{f}_c(x + \alpha/2) - \bar{f}_c(\alpha/2 - x)]dx. \quad (8)$$

When $\alpha > 0$ and $x \leq 0$ then $\bar{f}_c(x + \alpha/2) \geq \bar{f}_c(\alpha/2 - x)$ for unimodal $\bar{f}_c(x)$ as $\alpha/2 + x| \leq |\alpha/2 - x|$. From (8) $I(\alpha) > 0$ for $\alpha > 0$ and similarly for $\alpha < 0$. Thus $I(\alpha) > 0$ except when $\alpha = 0$ and the result follows immediately.

The proof only uses the fact that $\bar{f}_c(x)$ has the property that $f(x) > f(y)$ if $|x| < |y|$ but for a continuous function this implies that the function is symmetric about $x = 0$.

REFERENCES

A. J. MERRETT, M. HOWE and G. D. NEWBOULD (1967) *Equity Issues and the London Capital Market.* Longmans, London.
H. RAIFFA and R. SCHLAIFER (1967) *Applied Statistical Decision Theory,* Chapter 6. Harvard.
S. S. WOLFE, J. L. GASTWORTH and J. B. THOMAS (1967) Linear optimal predictors. *I.E.E.E. Trans. Information Theory* IT-13, 30.

CHAPTER 19

Some Comments on the Evaluation of Economic Forecasts*

C. W. J. Granger and P. Newbold

1. INTRODUCTION

At the present time, a good deal of effort and expenditure is being spent on the production of economic forecasts. There exists a wide range of forecasting techniques, from sophisticated regression procedures to naïve models or intuitive guesses, and it would seem essential for forecasters to attempt to assess the success or otherwise of such exercises. In this context, the two relevant questions are how good (in some sense) is a particular set of forecasts and can the forecasting procedure be modified to yield an improved performance. One element of the first question might be an enquiry as to whether or not better forecasts are being achieved by some other forecaster. Most of the available techniques for evaluating forecasts are almost entirely concerned with discovering the "best" forecasting methods from some set or, equivalently, in ranking methods. We shall argue that much of this work has little or no operational significance and that a wider viewpoint is required.

An analysis of forecast performance can be carried out at two levels. At the subjective level, one might look particularly closely at any very large forecast errors which have been made, and attempt to assess in retrospect what underlying conditions led to such errors and whether or not such conditions could have been foreseen at the time the forecasts were made. If they could, then allowance for these possibilities should be made in future forecasting exercises. There can be little doubt that subjective evaluation of this kind can be well worthwhile. However, we strongly believe that an objective evaluation of forecast performance is of the greatest importance, and feel that many of the criteria which have been employed in the past in this regard are either inappropriate or insufficiently stringent. In the remainder of this paper our intention is to expand on this assertion, and to indicate how a realistic assessment of forecast performance might be made.

* P. Newbold, *Applied Economics* 5, 1973, 35–47.

Let X_t be a univariate, discrete-time, measurable time series which is to be forecast on the basis of a specific set of information A_n, available at time n. The forecasting problem can be thought of as the formation of a predictor $P_{n,h}(A_n)$ to forecast future values X_{n+h}; $h \geq 1$, standing at time n, the predictor being based on the information set A_n. It is natural to ask how one can find the best predictor using A_n, and for this one needs a criterion by which alternative forecasts can be judged. Let $I(P, X)$ where $P = P_{n,h}$ and $X = X_{n+h}$ denote some value by which a judgment can be made. If I is considered to be a desirable feature, then P will be chosen to maximize I or, in practice, to maximize the sample estimate of I. An example would be $I = $ correlation (P, X). Alternatively, if I measures some undesirable feature, P is chosen to minimize I. If it is taken that a forecast is to be used in some decision making process and that incorrect forecasts lead to costs through sub-optimal decisions, then an approach based on cost functions seems the most reasonable. It is usual to assume that costs are a function only of the forecast error, so that $I(P, X) = I(X - P)$, which were now write as $C(e)$, where $e \equiv e_{n,h} = X_{n+h} - P_{n,h}$. We assume that $C(e) = 0$ if $e = 0$ and that $C(e) > 0$ for all $e \neq 0$. The choice of the cost function $C(e)$ is of considerable importance, and we return to a discussion of this function in Section 3 of this paper. The usual, and most mathematically tractable, cost function is, of course, $C(e) = ae^2$, where a is an arbitrary positive constant, as this leads to a least squares criterion. Some discussion on cost of error functions is given by GRANGER (1969).

The series X_t will be said to be deterministic with respect to the information set A, if there exists for every n, h a predictor $P_{n,h}(A_n)$ such that $e_{n,h} = 0$ (strictly, $\text{Prob}(e = 0) = 1$). Thus a deterministic series is completely predictable and the choice of cost function is irrelevant. A series will be called one-step deterministic if there exists a predictor $P_{n,1}(A_n)$ such that $e_{n,1} = 0$. An example of a deterministic series is $X_t = m$, where m is a constant. If A_n contains the value of m or contains X_{n-j}; $j \geq 0$ then future values X_{n+h} will be known precisely. An example of a one-step deterministic process is $X_t = Y_{t-1}$, where Y_t is a white-noise process, provided A_n contains Y_n. We strongly believe that economic time series cannot be even one-step deterministic, whatever information set A_n is used, so that forecasts will always be made with error even if all the information in the universe could be employed in making a forecast. This point is not so trivial as it may appear, since some writers seem to be suggesting evaluation procedures implying a different viewpoint, as we shall see later.

No well-defined theory of forecasting, with a general information set or arbitrary cost function, exists. The classical theory of forecasting deals with a single series; the information set A_n consists of past values of the series being forecast, $A_n = (X_{n-j}; j \geq 0)$, and the cost function is assumed to be $C(e) = ae^2$. Further, the series X_t is taken to be stationary, and only linear predictors are considered. For this situation, a number of theoretical results, a few of which are summarized in the following section, are available. Although this class of forecasts may not be of overpowering importance in practice, they can give a good deal of insight into the usefulness and relevance of possible methods of forecast evaluation.

2. UNIVARIATE TIME SERIES PREDICTION

Econometricians rarely, if ever, consider the problem of forecasting a time series in terms of its current and past values. We have suggested elsewhere (GRANGER and NEWBOLD, 1972) that if they did so, they might learn a number of valuable lessons applicable to the more sophisticated model building exercises they attempt. In this paper we shall suggest, in a similar vein, that a good deal can be learned about the evaluation of economic forecasts in terms of this simple framework.

WOLD (1938) has proved that any stationary time series X_t can effectively be decomposed into two components, one of which is deterministic and the other, called purely non-deterministic, can always be represented by an infinite moving average. Suppose, now, that X_t is just purely non-deterministic, has zero mean and is generated by an autoregressive model of the form

$$X_t = \sum_{j=1}^{P} a_j X_{t-j} + \varepsilon_t \tag{2.1}$$

where ε_t is zero mean white noise. Equation 2.1 can be written

$$(1 - a(B))X_t = \varepsilon_t \tag{2.2}$$

where

$$a(B) = \sum_{j=1}^{P} a_j B^j$$

and B is a backshift operator on the index of the time series, so that $BX_t = X_{t-1}$, $B^2 X_t = X_{t-2}$, and so on. It would be perfectly straightforward to consider the more general class of models called A.R.I.M.A. by BOX and JENKINS (1970), but as the results of this section are required only for illustrative purposes the extra complexity would be superfluous.

Using a least squares criterion, the optimum one-step ahead forecast is easily shown to be

$$P_{n,1} = a(B)X_n \tag{2.3}$$

and the optimum h-step ahead forecast to be

$$P_{n,h} = a(B)Z_{n+h-1} \tag{2.4}$$

where

$$Z_j = P_{n,j-n} \quad \text{if } j > n$$
$$= X_j \quad \text{if } j \leqslant n$$

it being presumed that the information available is $A_n = (X_{n-j}; j \geq 0)$. The one step ahead prediction errors are given by

$$e_{n,1} = X_{n+1} - P_{n,1} = \varepsilon_{n+1}$$

and so constitute a zero mean white noise process. It follows that

$$\text{Var}(X_{n+1}) = \sigma_x^2 = \text{Var}(P_{n,1}) + \sigma_\varepsilon^2 \tag{2.5}$$

where σ_ε^2 is the variance of ε_t. Hence the variance of the optimum one-step ahead predictor will be less than the variance of the series that it is predicting. The spectrum of $P_{n,1}$ will be $|a(e^{i\omega})|^2 f_x(\omega)$, where $f_x(\omega)$ is the spectrum of X_t, and hence $P_{n,1}$ will have different time series properties than the series it is predicting. The cross-spectrum between $P_{n,1}$ and X_{n+1} will be $a(e^{i\omega})f_x(\omega)$, and so coherence is unity at every frequency, but the phase-diagram will generally be complicated and not easily interpreted.

This example serves to illustrate the point that the optimal predictor generally has different distributional and time series properties than the series being predicted. Indeed, this will be the case for *any* information set, unless the series happens to be one-step deterministic for some available information set – an eventuality whose possibility, as we have said, we do not believe in for economic time series. It follows that it is pointless to compare, as many practitioners do, the distributional or time series properties of the predictor and predicted series *unless* one believes the series to be predicted is one-step deterministic. Thus we feel that DHRYMES *et al.* (1972) are wrong in saying that "cross-spectral analysis can be used to investigate the relationship between predicted and actual values". The foregoing illustration suggests, in our opinion, that rather than consider properties of predictor and actual series separately, the most fruitful approach is to consider the distributional and time series properties of the forecast error series, particularly the one-step errors $e_{n,1}$. We return to this point in later sections.

3. COST FUNCTIONS

Frequently one is in the position of wishing to compare the performance of a number of different forecasts – that is, one needs to make an *ordinal* judgment. In such a situation, the actual cost function employed may not be of overwhelming importance. To illustrate this point suppose we are dealing with a group of one-step predictors $P_n^{(j)}; j = 1, 2, \ldots, k$, and that the forecast errors produced $e_n^{(j)}$ are all zero mean white noise series, identically distributed apart from a scaling constant, i.e. $e_n^{(j)}$ has c.d.f. $F(x/S_j)$, the larger the S_j the greater the dispersion of the error series. In these circumstances, it is surely accepted that the smaller the scale factor

S_j the better is the predictor. Consider a general cost of error function $C(e)$, with $C(0) = 0$ and which monotonically increases from $e = 0$, i.e. $C(e_1) > C(e_2)$ if $e_1 > e_2 > 0$ or if $e_1 < e_2 < 0$. The expected cost of the predictor $P_n^{(j)}$ is

$$C_j = \int_{-\infty}^{\infty} C(x)\mathrm{d}F(x/S_j)$$

Now, let $P_n^{(1)}$ and $P_n^{(2)}$ be two predictors such that $S_1 > S_2$. Then

$$C_1 - C_2 = \int_{-\infty}^{\infty} C(x)\mathrm{d}F(x/S_1) - \int_{-\infty}^{\infty} C(x)\mathrm{d}F(x/S_2)$$

$$= \int_{-\infty}^{\infty} (C(xS_1) - C(xS_2))\mathrm{d}F(x)$$

Now, since $S_1 > S_2$, $C(xS_1) > C(xS_2)$, and hence $C_1 > C_2$. Thus any cost function which monotonically increases from $e = 0$ will rank the predictors in exactly the same way. This suggests that, for the making of ordinal judgments such as which method is best, the choice of cost function is not too critical. The assumption that the prediction errors all have the same type of c.d.f. is rather a strong one, but less strong than the common assumption that the errors are all normally distributed. Of course, if stronger statements than ordinal ones are required, such as a measure of the *extent* to which one forecasting method is better than another, then the actual form of the cost function becomes of clear importance.

In the remaining sections of this paper the implied cost function is the usual least squares one of $C(e) = ae^2$, where $a > 0$. We have seen that, for the purposes of ranking forecasts, this is not as critical as has sometimes been thought. We must admit that the use of the least squares criterion is dictated chiefly by convenience. However, in reality there may not exist any clearly superior alternative. If one actually goes to an accountant and asks what will be the cost of making a particular forecasting error, it is doubtful if in practice he can give a sufficiently precise answer for use in one's analysis. The potential consequences of making specific errors may be too diverse of complicated for exact costing. In such a situation, indeed, the accountant will himself be involved in a forecasting problem as costs associated with the error will almost certainly not arise immediately and it will be necessary for him to forecast future costs. If the costs take a simple form, such as ae^2, then this prediction problem is not important, as the same conclusions will be reached regardless of future a, but otherwise the problem could be either insoluble or circular in nature.

We are not seeking to under-emphasize the importance of the choice of cost function. However, with the art in its present state it is extremely difficult to carry an analysis very far unless the least squares criterion is employed.

4. RANKING FORECASTS ON A LEAST SQUARES BASIS

Let $X_t; t = 1, 2, \ldots, N$ be a time series and let $P_t; t = 1, 2, \ldots, N$ be a predictor series, available at time $t - h$; that is P_t is a forecast of X_t made h time periods previously. Denote the forecast errors by

$$e_t = X_t - P_t; t = 1, 2, \ldots, N.$$

If one is using a least-squares criterion, the obvious measure of forecast quality is the average squared forecast error

$$D_N^2 = \frac{1}{N} \sum e_t^2$$

which is an estimate of expected squared forecast error $E(e^2) = E(X - P)^2$. Indeed, the use of any statistic which is not a monotonic function of D_N^2 can yield misleading conclusions concerning the relative merits of different sets of forecasts. Consider, for example, the quantity

$$U_1 = \frac{D_N}{\left(\frac{1}{N} \sum P_t^2\right)^{1/2} + \left(\frac{1}{N} \sum X_t^2\right)^{1/2}}$$

proposed by THEIL (1958) some years ago, but which remains in current use (see, for example, KUNICHIKA, 1971 and LONNQUIST, 1971). U_1 is called the "inequality coefficient" of P and X and obeys $0 \le U_1 \le 1$. If P_t is a perfect forecast of X_t then $U_1 = 0$, but if $P_t = -bX_t, b > 0$, then $U_1 = 1$. To illustrate the difficulty in interpreting this coefficient, consider the situation where X is generated by a first order autoregressive process

$$X_t = \alpha X_{t-1} + \varepsilon_t$$

where ε_t is a zero mean white noise process. Suppose α is fixed for some $0 \le \alpha \le 1$, and consider the set of one step ahead forecasts of X_t

$$P_t = \beta X_{t-1}; 0 \le \beta \le 1.$$

We consider the limiting case, as $N \to \infty$, so that sample quantities can be replaced by their corresponding population values. Then

$$D^2 = \lim_{N \to \infty} D_N^2 = \left((1 - \alpha^2) + (\beta - \alpha)^2\right) \text{Var}(X); \quad \text{Var}(P) = \beta^2 \text{Var}(X)$$

and some simple algebra produces

$$\lim_{N \to \infty} U_1^2 = 1 - \frac{2\beta(1 + \alpha)}{(1 + \beta)^2}$$

Note that U_1^2, and thus U_1, is not a minimum for the optimal forecast $\beta = \alpha$. In fact, U_1^2 is minimized by taking $\beta = 1$, that is by maximizing the variance of the predictor series P_t, whatever the value of α. It should be quite clear, from the definition of U_1, how this arises. Thus we have shown that this statistic can fail to select the optimum forecast based on the information set $(X_{t-j}; j > 0)$ from a group of forecasts which includes it. Hence, the use of the inequality coefficient is positively dangerous. A similar criticism would apply to Somermeijer's coefficient defined by

$$S = 1 - \frac{D_N^2}{\dfrac{1}{N}\sum P_t^2 + \dfrac{1}{N}\sum X_t^2}$$

5. FORECAST EFFICIENCY

An attempt to introduce the concept of efficiency into a discussion of forecast evaluation is made by MINCER and ZARNOWITZ (1969). These authors suggest regressing actual value on predicted, that is forming the regression equation

$$X_t = \alpha + \beta P_t \tag{5.1}$$

where P_t is a predictor of X_t. A particular predictor is then called "efficient" if $\alpha = 0$ and $\beta = 1$ (or, in practice, if the sample estimates of α and β do not differ significantly from 0 and 1 respectively). This, however, hardly constitutes a definition of "efficiency" according to any acceptable interpretation of that word. To illustrate our point, consider the following example. Suppose that X_t is generated by a random walk model; that is

$$X_t = X_{t-1} + \varepsilon_t$$

where ε_t is zero mean, finite variance, white noise. Consider the group of one step predictors of X_t

$$P_t^{(j)} = X_{t-j}; j = 1, 2, 3, \ldots.$$

Now, for any $P_t^{(j)}$ the regression 5.1 will, in theory, have $\alpha = 0$ and $\beta = 1$, and so all the $P_t^{(j)}$'s will be "efficient" according to the definition of Mincer and Zarnowitz. This again illustrates the lack of success, noted in Section 2, of techniques that insist on analysing the relationship between the predictor and predicted series. The essential difference between the predictors $P_t^{(j)}$ could be brought out either by comparing average squared forecast errors or by an examination of the autocorrelations of these errors.

It would be highly desirable to have an absolute measure of the efficiency of a predictor P_n based on an information set A_n. The natural measure would be the mean squared error for the optimum predictor using A_n divided by the mean squared error for P_n; i.e.,

$$E = \frac{D_N^2 \text{ for optimum predictor using } A_n}{D_N^2 \text{ for } P_n}.$$

E would then measure the extent to which P_n differs from the optimal predictor. Unfortunately, for virtually every information set, the numerator in this expression for E will not be known. The exception is the case where $A_n = (X_{n-j}; j \geq 0)$, X_t has known spectrum $f(\omega)$ and only linear predictors are considered. Kolmogorov (1941) has shown that in this situation the minimum possible error variance is given by

$$I = 2\pi \exp \int_{-\pi}^{\pi} \log 2\pi f(\omega) d\omega$$

Generally, of course, $f(\omega)$ will not be known, but I could be estimated directly from data without model building, and this possibility has been investigated by Janacek (1973). With the exception of this particular case, the efficiency measure E seems to have little practical usefulness.

A more fruitful line of enquiry might concern an attempt to measure the relative efficiency of two predictors $P_n^{(1)}$ and $P_n^{(2)}$. Mincer and Zarnowitz suggest that it is useful to record the relative efficiency as defined by

$$RE = \frac{D_N^2 \text{ for } P_n^{(1)}}{D_N^2 \text{ for } P_n^{(2)}}.$$

However, this measure appears to us to be of little operational significance. Of course, the sign of $RE - 1$ indicates which predictor is individually superior, but the size of RE does not indicate how much better one might forecast if more effort was expended or a larger information set adopted, and yet, surely this is the all-important question. In particular, one gets no information as to whether or not the inferior predictor might contain useful information which could be incorporated into an overall forecasting procedure. It would seem to us to be foolhardy to conclude that, given a group of predictors, henceforth only the best predictor of the group will be employed and the remainder discarded, as a combination of forecasts may well outperform any individual forecast.

To illustrate the insights into forecast evaluation which can be gained from the notion of combining forecasts, we consider the combination of just two forecasts, following the discussion of BATES and GRANGER (1969). There is no particular difficulty in extending the procedures to the combination of several forecasts (see REID, 1969). Suppose that the two predictors are $P_n^{(1)}$ and $P_n^{(2)}$, producing forecast errors $e_n^{(1)}$ and $e_n^{(2)}$, and that data are available for an evaluation period $n = 1, 2, \ldots, N$. Combinations of the form

$$P_n^{(c)} = kP_n^{(1)} + (1-k)P_n^{(2)}$$

are appropriate if both $P_n^{(1)}$ and $P_n^{(2)}$ are unbiassed and the forecast errors are bivariate stationary. Let S_1^2 and S_2^2 be the sample variances of $e_n^{(1)}$ and $e_n^{(2)}$ respectively, r be the sample correlation between $e_n^{(1)}$ and $e_n^{(2)}$ and S_c^2 be the sample variance of the forecast errors using $P_n^{(c)}$. S_c^2 will be minimized by taking

$$k = \frac{S_2^2 - rS_1S_2}{S_1^2 + S_2^2 - 2rS_1S_2}$$

and, with this value of k

$$S_c^2 \leq \min(S_1^2, S_2^2).$$

If $0 \leq k \leq 1$, then k would provide a useful measure of relative efficiency, but unfortunately this restriction need not hold either in the sample or the population case. An alternative is to define 'conditional efficiency' by

$$CE(P_1/P_2) = \frac{S_c^2}{S_1^2} \quad \text{if } S_1^2 \leq S_2^2.$$

It is easy to prove that $CE = 1$ if P_1 is the optimum forecast for a given A_n. The conditional efficiency is a measure of the extra information contained in the pair of predictors rather than if just one is used. Although this definition of conditional efficiency is of some operational significance, it remains open to criticism.

In particular, the assumption of stationarity is rather restrictive. Forecasting models may change through more information becoming available or as details of technique change. The series to be forecast may well be non-stationary other than in the random-walk type sense, undoubtedly of clear relevance in economics, envisaged by BOX and JENKINS (1970). (This random-walk type non-stationarity can easily be removed by differencing.) To a certain extent, the non-stationarity problem can be taken into account by allowing the combining weights k to change through time. Bates and Granger propose a number of ways in which the weight k can be made to depend on the relative quality of the forecasting performances of the predictors in recent time periods. If the weights are allowed to change, conditional efficiency can still be measured, although the values obtained will now depend on the system of changing weights that is adopted.

Our experience with combining has indicated that it is frequently the case that a superior overall forecast can be obtained in this way, thus indicating that the inferior of two individual forecasts may nevertheless contain valuable information absent in the other and therefore should not simply be discarded. This assertion has been borne out in situations where two statistical forecasts are combined (NEWBOLD and GRANGER, 1972) and where a statistical forecast is combined with an econometric forecast (GRANGER and NEWBOLD, 1972).

6. HOW GOOD IS A PARTICULAR SET OF FORECASTS?

A typical forecasting exercise involves a great deal of expense and of effort on the part of the people involved. It is natural, then, to require some assessment of the success of the exercise in terms of the quality of the end-product – namely the forecasts generated by the exercise. The standards by which forecast quality ought to be judged should , in view of the cost of the work involved, be as stringent as possible. It is our opinion that in the past econometricians have tended to be rather lax on this point, and in this section we shall indicate rather more stringent conditions which we feel their forecasts should ideally meet.

It may well be the case that there already exist well-developed procedures for forecasting some of the quantities of interest. As a first step one can compare one's forecasts (in terms of average squared error) with those obtained by other workers. In situations where this has not been possible, econometricians have compared their forecasts with those which arise from naïve extrapolation rules such as "no change" or "same change as in previous time period". Thus the coefficient

$$U_2^2 = \frac{\frac{1}{N} \sum (X_t - P_t)^2}{\frac{1}{N} \sum X_t^2}$$

proposed by THEIL (1966) compares the performance of one's predictor with that of the "no change" forecast if X is taken to be actual change and P to be predicted change.

In recent years there has been a trend away from the use of very naïve models, in favour of more sophisticated alternatives such as autoregressive models (see, for example, COOPER, 1972) or Box-Jenkins models (see DHRYMES et al., 1972). MINCER and ZARNOWITZ (1969) propose that the most sophisticated extrapolative single series models be used, and in our experience (NEWBOLD and GRANGER, 1972) the most successful of this class are the Box-Jenkins predictors. However, if the econometric models are based on a wide information set consisting of all past and present values of various economic series, it is difficult to see the purpose of restricting the alternative forecasts to the narrower information set $A_n = (X_{n-j}; j \geq 0)$. The comparison is by no means uninteresting but it tells little about the real worth of the econometric model. If the model is based on some wide information set the only adequate alternative is a statistical forecast formed from the same information set, using a multivariate Box-Jenkins procedure (see BRAY, 1971, for a simple application to economic data) or models formed from a step-wise regression procedure, for example. The fact that the forecasting equations so achieved do not necessarily conform to economic theory need not be inhibiting, but one important problem does remain. Many econometricians use the results from their model only as a first step, and then adjust these results in the light of extraneous information, such as proposed changes in government policy or changes in the psychology of important components of the economy, that might be available. In other words, the actual information set they use to produce their final forecasts may well include non-numerical information. This type of information is very difficult to introduce into purely statistical forecasting techniques. The usefulness of the econometrician's adjustments has been discussed and illustrated by EVANS *et al.* (1972).

It is very unclear what one can achieve by comparing econometric forecasts with corresponding extrapolative forecasts. If the econometric model does not outperform extrapolative forecasts, does one conclude that the model should be rejected? If the model does outperform the extrapolative forecasts, does it follow that the model is adequate in some sense? We believe that the combining of forecasts, and the concept of conditional efficiency introduced in the previous section, have important implications for the evaluation of econometric forecasts. The model builders should not feel completely satisfied with the performance of their model simply because it predicts better than all alternatives. Rather it should obey the stronger condition that its conditional efficiency given alternative forecasting methods is insignificantly different from unity.

In summary, then, we feel that a stringent test of the adequacy of a set of forecasts from an econometric model would require that these forecasts cannot be significantly improved by combining with Box-Jenkins extrapolative forecasts or, better yet, with multivariate Box-Jenkins forecasts. If an econometric model does not meet such a requirement, then there is clearly room for improvement – possibly in terms of a more appropriate specification of lag and/or error structure.

In spite of the dangers involved, there must remain an understandable temptation to look at the relationship between predicted and actual values. Indeed, some useful information might well emerge from a critical examination of this relationship, providing that it is borne in mind that the object of the exercise is not simply to present one's forecasts in as flattering a light as possible. For example, it is common practice to graph simultaneously predicted and actual values, leading often to a very impressive picture indeed. However, it is well known (see, for example, GRANGER, 1966) that the typical time series of economic levels is a near random walk. For such a series it is a very simple matter indeed to convince oneself graphically that one has an excellent predictor of level. Indeed, the simple "no change" predictor appears very impressive in this light. Even more strikingly, BOX and NEWBOLD (1971) have demonstrated that by this graphical criterion one random walk can appear to predict another independent random walk rather well. It would be far more revealing to graph simultaneously predicted change and actual change. While the resulting picture is likely to be far less flattering to one's forecasts, it is more likely to give a meaningful representation of their effectiveness.

A second possibility arises if one considers expected squared forecast error as a function of the mean of the predictor series, its standard deviation and the correlation between predicted and actual series. One can write

$$S = E(X - P)^2 = (\mu_x - \mu_p)^2 + \sigma_x^2 + \sigma_p^2 - 2\rho\sigma_x\sigma_p$$

where μ_x and μ_p are the means of the predicted and predictor series, σ_x and σ_p are their standard deviations and ρ is the correlation between the two series. Now

$$\frac{\partial S}{\partial \mu_p} = -2(\mu_x - \mu_p)$$

$$\frac{\partial S}{\partial \sigma_p} = 2(\mu_p - \rho\sigma_x)$$

$$\frac{\partial S}{\partial \rho} = -2\sigma_x\sigma_p.$$

It follows that expected squared error is minimized by taking ρ to be as large as possible, with

$$\mu_p = \mu_x \tag{6.1}$$

and

$$\sigma_p = \rho\sigma_x \tag{6.2}$$

thus confirming our conclusion in Section 2 that the two standard deviations should optimally not be equal except for deterministic processes (those for which there exists a predictor P which is perfectly correlated with the actual series). Mincer and Zarnowitz show that this is so for predictions of changes and imply that this causes problems in forecasting changes, but fail to note that the same result holds for forecasts of levels.

Thus some measure of the quality of a set of forecasts can be obtained from the sample correlation between predictor and predicted. For reasons we have outlined above predicted changes and actual changes should be employed in this assessment. The reliability of such an exercise is far from perfect since the restrictions 6.1 and 6.2 need not necessarily hold, in which case there would exist a linear function of the predictor which was superior in terms of expected squared error. In particular, bias may well be a serious problem and its possible occurrence should not be neglected. Nevertheless, we feel that provided suitable diagnostic checks are made, the correlation between predicted change and actual change can provide a useful guide to the worth of one's forecasts.

7. DIAGNOSTIC CHECKS ON FORECAST PERFORMANCE

THEIL (1958) has observed two decompositions of average squared error, namely

$$D_N^2 = \frac{1}{N}\sum(X_t - P_t)^2 = (\overline{P} - \overline{X})^2 + (S_p - S_x)^2 + 2(1-r)S_p S_x \quad (7.1)$$

and

$$D_N^2 = (\overline{P} - \overline{X})^2 + (S_p - rS_x)^2 + (1-r^2)S_x^2 \quad (7.2)$$

where $\overline{P}$ and $\overline{X}$ are the sample means of predictor and predicted, S_p and S_x are the sample standard deviations and r is the sample correlation between the two series. The decomposition 7.1 leads to the definition of the following quantities

$$U^M = (\overline{P} - \overline{X})/D_N^2$$
$$U^S = (S_p - S_x)^2/D_N^2$$
$$U^C = 2(1-r)S_p S_x/D_N^2$$

Clearly

$$U^M + U^S + U^C = 1$$

and Theil suggests that these three quantities, which are frequently computed in evaluation exercises (see, for example, HAITOVSKY and TREYZ, 1971 and PLATT, 1971), have useful interpretations. We doubt, however, that this is so. To illustrate, we consider again the case where X is generated by the first order autoregressive process

$$X_t = \alpha X_{t-1} + \varepsilon_t \quad 0 \le \alpha \le 1$$

where ε_t is a zero-mean white noise process. The optimal one-step ahead predictor P_t of X_t based on the information set $(X_{t-j}; j \ge 1)$ is given by

$$P_t = \alpha X_{t-1}.$$

Then, in the limit as $N \to \infty$, for this predictor

$$U^M = 0; \quad U^S = \frac{1-\alpha}{1+\alpha}; \quad U^C = \frac{2}{1+\alpha}.$$

If one varies α from 0 to 1, U^S and U^C can take any values apart from the restrictions $0 \le U^S$, $U^C \le 1$, $U^S + U^C = 1$. Thus interpretation of these quantities is impossible. Again, the relevant point is that one would not expect the standard deviations of the predictor and predicted series to be equal, so that even in the limit $U^S > 0$ for any good forecast.

The decomposition 7.2 leads to the definition of the quantities

$$U^M = (\overline{P} - \overline{X})/D_N^2$$
$$U^R = (S_p - rS_x)^2/D_N^2$$
$$U^D = (1 - r^2)S_x^2/D_N^2.$$

Using the first order autoregressive process as an example, this decomposition seems to make more sense. Both U^M and U^R tend to zero for the optimum predictor and so U^D should tend to unity. The logic of this decomposition is clear in terms of the restrictions 6.1 and 6.2 which, as we have noted, should hold for any good predictor. If one forms the regression 5.1, then U^M will be zero if $\hat{\alpha} = 0$ and U^R will be zero if $\hat{\beta} = 1$. Such a test is worth performing in conjunction with the plotting of a prediction realization diagram advocated by Theil. Here predicted values are plotted against actual values and the spread of points around the "line of perfect forecasts"

$$X_t = P_t$$

may well yield information as to possible inadequacies in forecast performance. Again, it is preferable to consider predicted change and actual change.

While checks of this kind can be of some value, we feel that an examination of the forecast errors, particularly the one step ahead errors, would prove even more rewarding. One can test directly for bias, and even more importantly examine the autocorrelation properties of these errors. It should be clear that the h steps ahead forecast errors ought to have autocorrelations of orders h or greater equal to zero. In particular, the one-step ahead errors should constitute a zero-mean white noise series. Ideally, one would like to be able to do a full correlogram or spectral analysis of the error series, but it would rarely be the case that a sufficiently long series was available for this to be practicable. However, at the very least the one-step ahead errors $e_t = X_t - P_t$ should be tested for randomness. KENDALL and STUART (1966) suggest a number of non-parametric tests. An alternative test, based on the assumption of normality, against first order autocorrelation, is to compare the von Neumann ratio

$$Q = \frac{\dfrac{1}{N-1}\sum_{t=2}^{N}(e_t - e_{t-1})^2}{\dfrac{1}{N}\sum_{t=1}^{N}(e_t - \overline{e})^2}$$

with the tabulated values given by HART (1942).

8. CONCLUSIONS

Although a number of articles have been written over the years on the subject of evaluating economic forecasts, it is our feeling that current practice in this area remains deficient. In the first place, as well have shown, a number of the evaluation techniques presently employed can generate false conclusions. Perhaps more importantly, we feel that the standards which a set of economic forecasts have been required to meet are not sufficiently stringent, since the object of any evaluation exercise ought to be self-critical rather than self-laudatory.

In this paper we have examined the problem of evaluating from two viewpoints. Firstly, one would like to know how good is a particular set of forecasts. Our recommendations for possible answers to this question are set out in Section 6 of this paper. Of particular importance in this respect is the concept of conditional efficiency, introduced in Section 5. Secondly, in Section 7 we indicate a number of diagnostic checks on forecast adequacy which ought to be made. In a good deal of econometric work tests against serial correlation in the forecast errors should prove particularly useful in this context.

We have attempted throughout this paper to discuss the validity of various evaluation techniques which have been proposed in the past, and have concluded that a number of these can lead to misleading interpretations. The difficulty, as we noted in Section 2, appears to be in the fact that, for a "good" set of forecasts, the time series and distributional properties of the predictor series generally differ from these of the predicted series.

Finally, it must be admitted that the choice of cost function can be of great importance in any evaluation exercise. Throughout this paper we have employed, as dictated by mathematical convenience, the usual least squares criterion. We have shown, however, in Section 3 that if one is interested only in ordinal judgements this choice may not be too crucial.

REFERENCES

BATES, J. M. and GRANGER, C. W. J. (1969). "The combination of forcasts". *Op. Res. Q.* 20, 451-68.

BOX, G. E. P. and JENKINS, G. M. (1970). *Time Series Analysis, Forecasting and Control* San Francisco, Holden Day.

BOX, G. E. P. and NEWBOLD, P. (1971). "Some Comments on a paper of Coen, Gomme and Kendall". *J. R. Statist. Soc. A*, 134, 229–40.

COOPER, R. L. (1972). "The predictive performance of quarterly econometric models of the United States". In: *Econometric Models of Cyclical Behavior* (B. G. Hickman, ed.) New York, Columbia University Press.

DHRYMES, P. J. *et al.* (1972). "Criteria for evaluation of econometric models". *Ann. Econ. Soc. Meas.* 1, 291–324.

EVANS, M. K., HAITOVSKY, Y. and TREYZ, G. I. (1972). "An analysis of the forecasting properties of U.S. econometric models". In: *Econometric Models of Cyclical Behavior* (B. G. Hickman, ed.) New York, Columbia University Press.

GRANGER, C. W. J. (1966). "The typical spectral shape of an economic variable". *Econometrica* 34, 150–61.

GRANGER, C. W. J. (1969). "Prediction with a generalized cost of error function". *Op. Res. Q.* 20, 199–207.

GRANGER, C. W. J. and NEWBOLD, P. (1972). "Economic Forecasting – the atheist's viewpoint". Paper presented to Conference on the Modeling of the UK Economy, London Graduate School of Business Studies.

HAITOVSKY, Y. and TREYZ, G. I. (1971). "The Informational value of anticipation data in macro-econometric model forecasts". Paper presented to 10th CIRET Conference, Brussels.

HART, B. L. (1942). "Significance levels for the ratio of the mean square successive difference to the variance". *Ann. Math. Statist.* 13, 445–7.

JANACEK, G. (1972). *On Two Problems in Time Series Analysis*, Ph.D. Thesis, Nottingham University.

KENDALL, M. G. and STUART, A. (1966). *The Advanced Theory of Statistics* Vol. 3. London: Griffin.

KOLMOGOROV, A. N. (1941). "Stationary sequences in Hilbert space" (in Russian). *Bull. Math. Univ. Moscow* 2(6), 1–40.

KUNICHIKA, H. (1971). "A Note on short-term business survey – Japanese experience in improving the accuracy of business forecasts". Paper presented to 10th CIRET Conference, Brussels.

LONNQUIST, A. (1971). "The prediction power of quantitative investment forecasts as given in the Swedish investment surveys". Paper presented to 10th CIRET Conference, Brussels.

MINCER, J. and ZARNOWITZ, V. (1969). "The evaluation of economic forecasts". In: *Economic Forecasts and Expectations*, (J. Mincer, ed.). New York, National Bureau of Economic Research.

NEWBOLD, P. and GRANGER, C. W. J. (1972). "Experience with forecasting univariate time series and the combination of forecasts". Submitted for publication.

PLATT, R. B. (1971). Some measures of forecast accuracy. *Bus. Econ.* 6(3), 30–39.

REID, D. J. (1969). *A Comparative Study of Time Series Prediction Techniques on Economic Data*, Ph.D. Thesis Nottingham University.

THEIL, H. (1958). *Economic Forecasts and Policy.* Amsterdam, North Holland.

THEIL, H. (1966). *Applied Economic Forecasting.* Amsterdam, North Holland.

WOLD, H. O. A. (1938). *A Study in the Analysis of Stationary Time Series.* Stockholm, Almquist and Wicksell.

CHAPTER 20

The Combination of Forecasts*

J. M. Bates and C. W. J. Granger

Two separate sets of forecasts of airline passenger data have been combined to form a composite set of forecasts. The main conclusion is that the composite set of forecasts can yield lower mean-square error than either of the original forecasts. Past errors of each of the original forecasts are used to determine the weights to attach to these two original forecasts in forming the combined forecasts, and different methods of deriving these weights are examined.

INTRODUCTION

Our interest is in cases in which two (or more) forecasts have been made of the same event. Typically, the reaction of most statisticians and businessmen when this occurs is to attempt to discover which is the better (or best) forecast; the better forecast is then accepted and used, the other being discarded. Whilst this may have some merit where analysis is the principal objective of the exercise, this is not a wise procedure if the objective is to make as good a forecast as possible, since the discarded forecast nearly always contains some useful independent information. This independent information may be of two kinds:

(i) One forecast is based on variables or information that the other forecast has not considered.
(ii) The forecast makes a different assumption about the form of the relationship between the variables.

The second case in particular does not necessarily lead to a situation in which a combined forecast improves upon the better individual forecast, though there are occasions when it can, as is shown in Section 1 of the Appendix.

It should be noted that we impose one condition on the nature of the individual forecasts, namely that they are unbiased. A set of forecasts

* *Operational Research Quarterly* 20, 1969, 451–468.

Table 20.1. *Errors in forecasts (actual less estimated) of passenger miles flown, 1953*

Month	Brown's exponential smoothing forecast errors	Box–Jenkins adaptive forecasting errors	Combined forecast ($\frac{1}{2}$ Brown + $\frac{1}{2}$ Box–Jenkins) errors
Jan	1	−3	−1
Feb.	6	−10	−2
March	18	24	21
April	18	22	20
May	3	−9	−3
June	−17	−22	−19.5
July	−24	10	−7
Aug.	−16	2	−7
Sept.	−12	−11	−11.5
Oct.	−9	−10	−9.5
Nov.	−12	−12	−12
Dec.	−13	−7	−10
Variance of errors	196	188	150

that consistently overestimate the true values would, if combined with a set of unbiased forecasts, lead to forecasts which were biased; in all likelihood the combined forecasts would have "errors" rather larger than the unbiased forecasts. The first step therefore is to check that the individual sets of forecasts are unbiased, and if biased to correct for the average percentage (or absolute) bias.

Before the discussion of different ways in which forecasts could be combined, an empirical justification is given by making a crude combination of two forecasts. The forecasts chosen were of the international airline passenger data, for which (amongst others) Brown, and Box and Jenkins have made monthly forecasts for one period ahead. The forecasts are published in an article by Barnard (1963), who says, "the forecasting methods ... developed by Professor Box ... and Dr. (now Professor) Jenkins ... have proved ... so successful ... that we are now searching for processes ... (for which) it is possible to find alternative methods which forecast better." The combination illustrated is the arithmetic mean of the two individual forecasts, with Table 20.1 giving the details for 1953.

An enumeration of these and other forecasts of these data is made at a later stage. For the moment it may merely be noted that for the period 1951–60 the variance of errors in the three forecasts mentioned were 177.7 (Brown), 148.6 (Box–Jenkins), and 130.2 (combination with equal weights to each of the individual forecasts). Thus, even though Brown's forecasts had a larger variance than that of Box–Jenkins's forecasts, they were clearly of some value.

Work by Stone *et al.*[7] has made use of ideas rather similar to these, though their work related solely to making improved estimates of past national income figures for the U.K. and did not tackle forecasting problems.

CHOICE OF METHOD FOR DETERMINING WEIGHTS

Though the combined forecast formed by giving equal weights to each of the individual forecasts is acceptable for illustrative purposes, as evidence accumulated one would wish to give greater weight to the set of forecasts which seemed to contain the lower (mean-square) errors. The problem was how best to do this. There are many ways of determining these weights, and the aim was to choose a method which was likely to yield low errors for the combined forecasts.

Our first thought for a method was derived in the following way. It was assumed that the performance of the individual forecasts would be consistent over time in the sense that the variance of errors for the two forecasts could be denoted by σ_1^2 and σ_2^2 for all values of time, t. It was further assumed that both forecasts would be unbiased (either naturally or after a correction had been applied). The combined forecast would be obtained by a linear combination of the two sets of forecasts, giving a weight k to the first set of forecasts and a weight $(1 - k)$ to the second set, thus making the combined forecast unbiased. The variance of errors in the combined forecast, σ_c^2 can then be written:

$$\sigma_c^2 = k^2\sigma_1^2 + (1-k)^2\sigma_2^2 + 2\rho k\sigma_1(1-k)\sigma_2,$$

where k is the proportionate weight given to the first set of forecasts and ρ is the correlation coefficient between the errors in the first set of forecasts and those in the second set. The choice of k should be made so that the errors of the combined forecasts are small: more specifically, we chose to minimize the overall variance, σ_c^2. Differentiating with respect to k, and equating to zero, we get the minimum of σ_c^2 occurring when:

$$k = \frac{\sigma_2^2 - \rho\sigma_1\sigma_2}{\sigma_1^2 - \sigma_2^2 - 2\rho\sigma_1\sigma_2}. \qquad (1)$$

In the case where $\rho = 0$, this reduces to:

$$k = \sigma_2^2/(\sigma_1^2 + \sigma_2^2). \qquad (2)$$

It can be shown that if k is determined by equation (1), the value of σ_c^2 is no greater than the smaller of the two *individual* variances. The algebra demonstrating this is recorded in Section 2 of the Appendix.

The optimum value for k is not known at the commencement of combining forecasts. The value given to the weight k would change as evidence was accumulated about the relative performance of the two original forecasts. Thus the combined forecast for time period T, C_T, is more correctly written as:

$$C_T = k_T f_{1,T} + (1 - k_T) f_{2,T},$$

where $f_{1,T}$ is the forecast at time T from the first set and where $f_{2,T}$ is the forecast at time T from the second set.

Equations (1) and (2) are used as a basis for some of the methods that follow shortly. Thought, however, was given to the possibility that the performance of one of the forecasts might be changing over time (perhaps improving) and that a method based on an estimate of the error variance since the beginning of the forecasts might not therefore be appropriate. In consequence we have also constructed two methods which give more weight to recent errors than to those of the past (see methods (iii) and (iv) below).

DESIRABLE PROPERTIES OF METHODS

Good methods (defined by us as those which yield low mean-square forecast error) are likely to possess properties such as:

(a) The average weight of k should approach the optimum value, defined by (1), as the number of forecasts increased – provided that the performance of the forecasts is stationary.
(b) The weights should adapt quickly to new values if there is a lasting change in the success of one of the forecasts.
(c) The weights should vary only a little about the optimum value.

This last point is included since property (a) is not sufficient on its own. If the optimum value for k is 0.4, one may still obtain poor combined forecasts if k takes two values only, being 0 on 60 per cent of occasions and 1.0 on the remaining 40 per cent.

In addition to these properties, there has been an attempt to restrict methods to those which are moderately simple, in order that they can be of use to businessmen.

Five methods have so far been examined, and in each of them the combined forecast at time T, C_T, has been derived from giving a weight k_T to the forecast for time T from the first set and a weight $1 - k_T$ to the second forecast for time T; the weights k_T have in all cases been determined from past (known) errors of the two series denoted as

$e_{1,1}, e_{1,2}, \ldots, e_{1,T-1}$ and $e_{2,1}, e_{2,2}, \ldots, e_{2,T-1}$, except for k_1 which has been arbitrarily chosen as 0.5 for all methods.

The methods are:

(i) Let us denote $\Sigma_{t=T-v}^{T-1}(e_{2,t})^2$ by E_2, and a similar summation of the first set of forecast errors by E_1. Then:

$$k_T = \frac{E_2}{E_1 + E_2}.$$

(ii) $k_T = xk_{T-1} + (1-x)\dfrac{E_2}{E_1 + E_2},$

where x is a constant of value between zero and one.

(iii) Let us denote $\Sigma_{t=1}^{T-1} w^t(e_{2,t})$ by S_2^2. w is seen to be a weight, which for $w > 1$ gives more weight to recent error variances than to distant ones.

$$k_T = \frac{S_2^2}{S_1^2 + S_2^2}.$$

(iv) Let us denote the weighted covariance by C, where:

$$C = \sum_{t=1}^{T-1} w^t e_{1,t} e_{2,t},$$

$$k_T = \frac{S_2^2 - C}{S_1^2 + S_2^2 - 2C}.$$

(v) $k_T = xk_{T-1} + (1-x) = \dfrac{|e_{2,T-1}|}{|e_{1,T-1}| + |e_{2,T-1}|}$

The differences between methods are not the only factors, and suitable choice of the parameters, v, x and w, are also of importance. Despite this, our presentation concentrates upon the differences between the various methods, since we would expect these to be the more important.

It is pertinent to note that method (v) fails to satisfy criterion (a). It scores well on criteria (b) and (c), and for combining forecasts which are almost equally good it does very well. However, since it underestimates the weight to give to the better forecast it is to some extent an unsatisfactory method. A further disadvantage is that the weight k_T is as much affected by a given ratio arising from two small errors in the individual forecasts as it is from the ratio arising from two large errors. Thus if past errors have averaged 10, k_T will be just as much altered if $e_{1,t-1} = 0.01$ and $e_{2,t-1} = 0.02$ as if the errors were 10 and 20. None of the other methods need suffer from this disadvantage. Further, they all satisfy criterion (a), though some may not be so obviously satisfactory in respect of criterion

(b). It is perhaps easier to comment further on the methods after refer-
ring to empirical work undertaken.

PERFORMANCE OF DIFFERENT METHODS

The empirical work undertaken so far has been rather limited, in that we
have examined forecasts only of the airline passenger data referred to
above. To reach definite conclusions about most of the methods is therefore impossible. There are, however, a number of tentative conclusions
that do emerge.

Five forecasts of the airline passenger data have been examined, all
being monthly forecasts, made for one-period ahead. In addition to those
of Brown and Box–Jenkins for the years 1951–60, there are a set of forecasts prepared by P. J. Harrison for the years 1954–9 and two sets of forecasts for 1951–60 prepared by one of us. Those prepared by Harrison are
similar to the "Seatrend" ones published by him in *Applied Statistics*
(Harrison 1965), the sole difference being that the present forecasts are
based on three parameters as opposed to two for the published ones. The
two forecasts made by ourselves are referred to as the Constant Seasonal
and the Changing Seasonal forecasts. The basis of both forecasts concerns two stages, the first being the estimation of a simple seasonal component which, together with the summation of data for recent months,
is used to make a crude forecast for the next month. The second step is
to "correct" this crude forecast by utilizing information of the last
month's crude forecast error. The only difference between the two forecasts is that the Changing Seasonal forecast analyses if the seasonal components are changing over the years, and if so makes some allowance
before deriving crude forecasts. The two forecasts are described more
fully in another article (Bates 1970).

Since Brown's "exponential smoothing" and Box–Jenkins's "adaptive
forecasting" methods are fairly familiar to readers, the results of combining these two forecasts will be described first. The Brown forecasts
are obtained by analysing data from 1948 onwards, fitting a first-order
harmonic as an estimate of the seasonal, and then making estimates of
the level and trend factors in the usual exponential smoothing way. For
details consult Harrison (1965). The Box-Jenkins forecasts are derived
from forecasting 12-monthly moving sums, 11 months of which are
known. The forecast for the sum of 12 months ending in month T, F_T, is
dependent upon the forecast error in F_{T-1}, the change in error between
F_{T-2} and F_{T-1} and the sum of all past errors. For general details of the
method consult Box and Jenkins (1962).

The overall variances of the two individual forecast errors were 177.7
and 148.6; together with a correlation coefficient of 0.60, this implied that
a value of $k = 0.39$ throughout [see equation (1)] would lead to an
optimal combined forecast if the ratio of the two individual forecast error

variances were constant throughout the whole period. Equation (2), which takes no account of the correlation between the two sets of errors, gives $k = 0.46$. Using $k = 0.46$ would lead to combined forecasts not quite as good, but which might be thought to be the likely lower limit for methods (i)–(iii) and (v).

The results for combining different methods are recorded in Table 20.2, both for the absolute errors and the proportionate errors. In many ways the use of proportionate errors is a more appropriate measure, since both the mean and the absolute errors increase considerably over time, but it is to be noted that both these forecasts were prepared from an analysis based on absolute figures.[†]

It may be noted that all the methods except the fourth were capable (with appropriate choice of parameters) of yielding forecasts which were better than the ones thought to be "optimal". This is indeed surprising, since the value of the constant weights is calculated using the sum of error variances for all 10 years: in other words, the forecasts derived from the constant weights have been possible only by the use of hindsight. In contrast, each of the five methods used only past errors in making a combined forecast for any period. Why does this result occur? The absolute errors of Brown's set of forecasts were not consistently higher than Box–Jenkins's in the ratio 177.7:148.6 for all time periods. At times the Brown forecasts were good, and if the forecast error at time t was small it was likely that the error in month $t + 1$ would also be small; if, however, there was a change in trend, Brown's exponentially smoothed forecast not only failed to discern it immediately (as is inevitable), but took some time before it fully corrected for it. In consequence Brown's forecast errors are highly serially correlated, yielding a Durbin-Watson statistic of 0.83 for the period 1951–60, a value which is significant at the 1 per cent level. In addition, the seasonal model assumed by Brown fails adequately to reflect the seasonal pattern at certain times of the year. These two reasons are partly responsible for the success of the methods in yielding lower forecast errors than would have resulted from the weight k being constant throughout; they may also help to explain the success of parameters which enable the weight to be determined by the most recent error only (see, in particular, method (1) for the absolute errors). This phenomenon one would expect to be the exception rather than the rule perhaps, since an *average* of recent forecast errors would normally be regarded as a more reliable measure of "error" than the last forecast error.

The poor performance of method (iv) deserves some comment. The weighted correlation coefficient often becomes very high for high values

---

[†] In contrast it is interesting to note that a more recent set of forecasts by Box, Jenkins and Bacon are based on the logarithms of the data. The basis for deriving these forecasts is published in a book edited by Harris. The error variance of these forecasts is 160.

Table 20.2. *Overall variances of forecast errors, 1951–60*

| | Weight constant throughout | | Weights varying according to method | | | | | | | | | | | |
| | | | (i) | | (ii) | | | (iii) | | (iv) | | (v) | |
Forecasts	Wt.	Variance	v	Var.	v	x	Var.	w	Var.	w	Var.	x	Var.
Brown 178	0.39	128.6	1	125.6	1	−0.3	123.3	1	130.9	1	134.1	−0.3	125.1
Box–Jenkins 149	0.16	129.2	2	127.1	1	0	125.7	2	125.5	2	131.0	0	126.0
r = 0.60			3	129.2	1	0.6	129.2	3	125.6	3	134.2	0.6	128.7
			6	128.8	7	−0.6	122.2					1	130.2
			12	130.8	7	0	125.7						
					7	0.2	127.5						
Percentage errors:													
Brown 19.1	0.47	14.23	1	14.3	1	0	14.4	1	14.4	1	14.6	0.3	14.3
Box–Jenkins 16.7	0.42	14.19	2	14.7	1	0.25	14.2	1.5	14.1	1.5	15.0	0.3	14.18
			3	14.4	1	0.5	14.2	2	14.1	2	15.0	0.6	14.2
			6	14.16	7	0	14.1	2.5	14.2	2.5	15.2	1	14.3
			12	14.3	7	0.2	14.2						

Note: Starting values are $k_1 = 0.5$ everywhere.
For methods (i)–(iv) k_2 was usually taken as the average of k_1 and the value suggested by the strict application of the methods as described above. Reasons for this are discussed in the next section.

of w and can result in k becoming 0 or 1, thus failing to meet desired property (c) (values of k should vary only slightly about the average value). This method tends therefore to score badly when positive serial correlation of residuals is present in one of the forecast errors, since the weight w would best be high in computing $S_2^2/(S_1^2 + S_2^2)$, but is best rather lower for computing C. If the nature of forecast errors is such that serial correlation of residuals is observed or expected, then method (iv) should either not be used or be altered to something similar to:

$$k_T = \frac{S_2^2 - zC}{S_1^2 + S_2^2 - 2zC},$$

where $0 \le z \le 1$. One crude possibility might be to make $z = 1/w$.

The results for the combination of Brown and Box-Jenkins forecasts are somewhat untypical, and it is appropriate to examine the results for other combined forecasts. The principal features of the individual forecasts are given in Section 4 of the Appendix, together with the results for different combinations of forecasts (see Tables 20.A3 and 20.A4). There are five noteworthy features of these results. First, there is little to choose between the performance of the different methods of generating the weights k_t. Second, with one exception the combined forecasts have considerably lower error variance than the better of the individual forecasts used in the combination. The one exception is for the combination of the Constant and Changing forecasts, where the Changing forecast is based entirely on the same estimate of the seasonal as the Constant *except* for an allowance for a changing seasonal pattern partway through the period (1956). In all other respects these two forecasting methods are identical. Third, optimal values for the parameter x are not always found to be positive. This occurs in the combination of Brown and Changing forecasts, and also, rather surprisingly, in method (ii) for combining Box-Jenkins with both Constant and Changing. Our surprise exists because it cannot be explained by the presence of serial correlation of residuals, since none exists in any of the original series. Interestingly enough, the optimal values for x are positive for all combinations with the Harrison forecasts. Fourth, in contrast to the results obtained in combining Brown's and Box-Jenkins's forecasts, an average of a number of past errors is often a better measure of "error" than the last error only. Fifth, in methods (iii) and (iv) "high" values of w are often found to perform better than low values. Few people with experience of use of "discount" factors ($= 1/w$) would take exception to that $w \ge 2$ would perform well.

Where these oddities occur, there might be a temptation to lay the blame on the original forecasts, saying that these forecasts possess certain undesirable features, rather than attribute the oddities to characteristics of the methods. This, however, would be unconstructive. The objective is to devise robust methods for combining different forecasts. There is no reason to believe that the forecasts examined are atypically poor; quite the contrary indeed! The purpose in commenting upon the characteristics of the original forecasts is to see if it is possible to learn why the methods for combining forecasts do well or badly; analysis of, and speculation about, the reasons for the performances observed may well add useful information to that derived from a listing of the empirical results. (We hope soon to add to the empirical results by examining forecasts made for other variables.) In general, then, the objective is to discover a robust method which will combine satisfactorily the forecasts that exist, whatever their characteristics; further, it is not to be expected that the characteristics of these forecasts will always be known – hence the need for robustness.

MINOR MODIFICATIONS TO METHODS

One modification is a delay in giving full weight to methods (i) to (iv). The results given in the above section and in the Appendix use weights for time period $t = 2$ which are in most cases an arithmetic average of the weight suggested by the method and a weight of 0.5. The reason is that the methods are able to use only one error for each forecast and are therefore likely to give unreliable estimates of the errors to be expected for each series. In the third part of the Appendix is shown the distribution of:

$$\frac{\sum_t (e_{2,t})^2}{\sum_t (e_{2,t})^2 + \sum_t (e_{1,t})^2},$$

that is obtained when two sets of sample errors are taken from populations having the same variance, which itself is unchanging over time. It can be seen that the 95 per cent limits are very different from 0.5 for small sample sizes.

Though the results quoted here are for weights modified in time period 2 only, it is possible to modify the weights for a number of time periods up to time period A, say, which may be chosen arbitrarily. An appropriate formula for this might be:

$$k_T = \left(\frac{T-1}{A}\right)0.5 + \frac{A-(T-1)}{A}\hat{k}_T, \quad \text{for } T - 1 \leqslant A,$$

where $\hat{k}_T$ is the value of k_T derived from the straightforward application of the method.

A second minor modification was to restrict k_T to lie between 0 and 1. "Likely" (i.e. positive) values of the parameters would not generate values of k_t outside this range, but negative values of x have been examined in methods (ii) and (v). The restriction on the k_t's is then deemed advisable. The unfortunate effect of a negative weight for k_t is easily imagined; if two forecasts are 80 and 100 and the respective weights are -1 and $+2$ the combined forecast is 120.

COMBINING FORECASTS FROM THE OUTSET

Section 4 has given results of combining forecasts using different methods and using different values of the parameters x, w and v. In a forecasting situation, one has the problem of choosing from the outset the method by which the forecasts will be combined and the parameters of the method.

One simple way of proceeding would be the following:

(a) k_1 (the weight given to the first forecast in period 1) $= 0.5$ unless there is good reason to believe that one forecast is superior to the other.

(b) Use method (i) to determine weights for $k_2, k_3, \ldots, k_6$, summing $\sum_{t=t-v}^{t-1}(e_{2,t})^2$ and $\sum(e_{1,t})^2$ over as many terms as exist. For k_1 and beyond, sum $\sum(e_{2,t})^2$ and $\sum(e_{1,t})^2$ over the last six terms only.

The choice of the method to use is somewhat arbitrary. We have made our choice on grounds of simplicity. In so far as we have any evidence of its performance, method (i) is not obviously inferior to the others. Table A5 of the Appendix records the rankings of the performance of the different methods on combining the airline forecasts. Method (ii) also scores well, but involves the choice of an additional parameter, a choice not easy to make. The recommendation to sum over the last six terms is based partly on the performance of $v = 6$ (see Tables 20.A3 and 20.A4).

There are other possibilities which are likely to yield satisfactory results, one such being the use of method (iii) with $w = 1.5$ or 2. It is, however, doubtful whether there is much improved performance in any of these other possibilities, none of which are quite as easy to administer.

The suggestion made above must be regarded as tentative until further work has been done.

COMMENTS

It seems appropriate to emphasize what is our methodology in this work. The methods suggested utilize observed errors of the forecasts and are to this extent purely automatic; at no stage is an attempt made to analyse the reasons for errors in either set of individual forecasts, nor has any assumption been made about the underlying model of the time series. Such work is properly the responsibility of the initial forecaster(s). A moment's reflection will reveal why this is so, and why it would be fruitless to attempt to build a model of the way an economic time series is generated in order to derive the theory of how to combine forecasts. If a model of a time series can be accurately specified then it is possible to derive individual forecasts which could not be bettered. The combining of forecasts would have no part to play in such a situation. This is further commented upon at the end of Section A2 of the Appendix. Whether such a state is commonly achieved is left to the reader to judge.

There may, however, be some point in analysing certain characteristics of the initial forecast errors, since there is some suggestion that these characteristics have some effect on the relative performance of the different methods of combining, and quite considerable effect on the relative performance of different parameters within any given method. It would be unwise to base general conclusions on results only for airline passenger tickets sold, but the presence of serial correlation of residuals in one of the initial forecasts may well have implications for the choice of parameters and also may require modifications to at least one of the methods.

Finally, there may be some use in comparing individual forecasts with the combined forecast. A combined forecast with a significantly lower error variance than either individual forecast implies that the models used for the individual forecasts are capable of some improvement. One may thus obtain hints of a truer model which would be of analytic value. It should be noted, however, that this "truer model" may be of two kinds; it may be a basically different model incorporating a new variable or a different treatment of a variable, or it may be simply an acknowledgement of non-stationarity of the parameters of the model.

CONCLUSIONS

A number of methods of combining two sets of forecasts have been presented, and it is to be noted that, providing the sets of forecasts each contain some independent "information", the combined forecasts can yield improvements.

One unexpected conclusion is that, though the methods suggested for combining forecasts allow the weights to change, this can often lead to better forecasts than those that would have resulted from the application of a constant weight determined *after* noting all the individual forecast errors.

Finally, though the comments in this paper have related solely to combining two forecasts, there is every reason to combine more than two forecasts (where they exist). Work at Nottingham is now being directed towards operational ways of doing this.

Table 20.A1. *Individual forecasts of output indices for the gas, electricity and water sector*

Year	Actual index (1958 = 100)	Linear forecast	Exponential forecast
1948	58		
1949	62		
1950	67	66	66.3
1951	72	71.3	71.9
1952	74	76.5	77.4
1953	77	79.2	80.3
1954	84	81.9	83.2
1955	88	89.0	88.6
1956	92	91.6	93.7
1957	96	96.0	98.5
1958	100	100.2	103.2
1959	103	104.3	107.8
1960	110	108.1	112.1
1961	116	112.9	117.4
1962	125	118.0	123.3
1963	133	124.2	130.2
1964	137	130.9	137.8
1965	145	137.0	145.0
Sum of squared errors		263.2	84.2

APPENDIX

A1   Combining an Arithmetic and a Logarithmic Forecast

As an example of the usefulness of combining forecasts, we give below arithmetic and logarithmic forecasts of the output indices for the gas, electricity and water sector. Column 2 gives the indices, with 1958 = 100, as published in *National Income and Expenditure*, 1966. The third column records linear forecasts made in the following way. The forecast for year t is made by extrapolating the regression line formed by a least-squares fit of the actual figures for 1948 until the year $t - 1$. The fourth column records the logarithmic, or exponential, forecasts obtained from fitting equations of the form log (output) = $a + b$ (time), once again utilizing actual figures for all previous years back to 1948.

The results for combining forecasts in different ways are:

Weight constant throughout		Weights varying according to method									
		(i)		(ii)			(iii)		(iv)		(v)
Wt.	sum of squares	v	S. of sq.	v	x	S. of sq.	w	S. of sq.	w	S. of sq.	x	S. of sq.
0.16 0.5	77.3 106.6	1 2 3 6 10	44.7 55.7 76.0 101.3 97.8	1 1 1	0 0.2 0.4	44.6 50.4 60.5	1 1.5 2	101.1 74.8 64.1	1 1.5 2	101.5 69.6 58.7	0 0.2 0.5	54.7 60.3 77.5

Certain features are worthy of note. First, a constant weight of 0.16 (or indeed anything between just above zero and $\frac{1}{3}$) can yield a lower sum of squared errors than the exponential forecast on its own; despite this there is the possibility of obtaining a higher sum of squared errors as is shown by the application of the constant weight of 0.5. Second, the methods which allow the weights to vary according to recent forecast errors can yield considerable improvements upon the optimum constant weight; given the nature of the individual forecasting methods, such a result is perhaps not altogether surprising.

The example has shown that combining forecasts of linear and exponential forecast can be profitable. A word of warning is, however, necessary here. One should not assume that combining two forecasts is bound to yield an improvement upon the better of the two individual forecasts. Many of the output indices for other sectors of the economy are so clearly following an exponential trend that the best that one can achieve by a combined forecast is to give all the weight to the exponential forecast.

A2   The Relationship Between the Combined Forecast Variance and the Variances of the Original Forecast Errors

The combined forecast at time t, C_t, is derived from giving a weight k to the "first" forecast and a weight $(1 - k)$ to the "second" forecast. If the variance of errors for these two forecasts can be correctly denoted as σ_1^2 and σ_2^2 for all time periods, and if both forecasts are unbiased, then the optimum value for k is given by:

$$k = \frac{\sigma_2^2 - \rho\sigma_1\sigma_2}{\sigma_1^2 - \sigma_2^2 - 2\rho\sigma_1\sigma_2}. \tag{A2.1}$$

Under these assumptions (stationarity and unbiasedness), the variance of the combined forecast errors, σ_c^2, becomes:

$$\sigma_c^2 = \frac{\sigma_1^2\sigma_2^2(1-\rho^2)}{\sigma_1^2 + \sigma_2^2 - 2\rho\sigma_1\sigma_2}.$$

Table 20.A2. *Characteristics of the statistic $s_2^2/(s_2^2 + s_1^2)$*

Sample size n	S.E.	Confidence limits		99% Upper
		95%		
		Lower	Upper	
1	0.354	0.006	0.994	0.9998
2	0.289	0.050	0.950	0.990
3	0.250	0.097	0.903	0.967
4	0.224	0.135	0.865	0.941
5	0.204	0.165	0.835	0.916
6	0.189	0.189	0.811	0.894
7	0.177	0.209	0.791	0.875
8	0.167	0.225	0.775	0.858
12	0.139	0.271	0.729	0.806
24	0.100	0.336	0.664	0.727

These results only relate to the case in which two independent samples are taken from normal distributions: for many types of non-normal distrbution the confidence limits would be even wider. The chief point of note is the magnitude of the likelihood of getting values of the statistic close to zero or one for small samples, even when taken from populations with equal variance: for small samples a value close to zero or one is not indicative of a difference between the population error variances.

Then:

$$\sigma_c^2 - \sigma_1^2 = \frac{\sigma_1^2(\sigma_1 - \rho\sigma_2)^2}{(\sigma_1 - \rho\sigma_2)^2 + \sigma_2^2(1 - \rho^2)}. \tag{A2.2}$$

which is clearly ≥0.

Hence σ_c^2 is not less than σ_1^2, nor (by symmetry) σ_2^2.

The combined forecast yields a big improvement in all cases except where the individual forecasts are almost equally good and are highly correlated (ρ close to unity). It is only fair to note that this may well be a common occurrence.

If the larger variance is denoted by σ_2^2, then σ_2^2 can be re-written as $a \cdot \sigma_1^2$, where $a \geq 1$. It should also be noted that if $\rho = 1/\sqrt{a}$, $\sigma_c^2 = \sigma_1^2$. In particular, if σ_1^2 is the minimum variance unbiased forecast then ρ can be shown to be equal to $1/\sqrt{a}$ and hence no improvement is possible in this case by combining the individual forecasts. For details see Kendall and Stuart. There, denoting the efficiency of each forecast (i.e. the variance of each forecast relative to the minimum variance forecast) by E_1 and E_2, ρ is shown to be bounded by:

$$\sqrt{E_1 E_2} + \sqrt{(1 - E_1)(1 - E_2)}.$$

It is to be noted that $\rho > 0$ if $E_1 + E_2 > 1$.

A3   The Distribution of $\Sigma(e_{2,t}^2)/[\Sigma(e_{2,t}^2) + \Sigma(e_{1,t}^2)]$

If two samples (of errors) are taken from normally distributed populations both having zero mean and the same variance then:

$$\sum_{t=-n}^{-1} (e_{2,t}^2) \Bigg/ \left[\sum_{-n}^{-1} (e_{2,t}^2) + \sum_{-n}^{-1} (e_{1,t}^2) \right] = \frac{F}{1 + F},$$

where F is the F statistic.

If we put $X = F/(1 + F)$ then the probability that the value of X will fall in the internal $(x, x + dx)$ is given by:

$$dP = \frac{x^{\frac{1}{2}(n-2)}(1 - x)^{\frac{1}{2}(n-2)}}{B\left(\frac{1}{2}n, \frac{1}{2}n\right)} dx \qquad (A3.1)$$

Equation (3) is a beta distribution, with an expected value, or mean, of 0.5 and a standard error of $1/[2\sqrt{n + 1}]$. Recorded below are the standard errors and the 95 and 99 per cent confidence limits for the distribution for a number of different values of n.

A4   Results of Combining Forecasts of the Airline Passenger Data

The empirical work in this paper relates to combining forecasts made of the sales of airline passenger tickets. Five individual forecasts have been used: the forecasts and their principal features are:

Brown

An exponentially smoothed forecast. The residuals are serially correlated. The estimates of some of the seasonal components are subject to some error.

Box–Jenkins

No short-term serial correlation of errors. Avoids a direct estimate of the seasonal components by forecasting 12-monthly totals, thus introducing a slight negative correlation of error in month t with month $t - 12$.

Harrison

Some short-term serial correlation of errors. Good seasonal estimates; changing seasonal factors.

Table 20.A3. Overall variances of forecast errors, 1951–60

Forecasts	Weight constant throughout Wt.	Variance	(i) v	(i) Var.	(ii) v	(ii) x	(ii) Var.	Weights varying according to method (iii) w	(iii) Var.	(iv) w	(iv) Var.	(v) x	(v) Var.
Brown / Constant 178, 174	0.48	151	1	156	1	0.4	153	1	152	1	156	0	153
			3	152	1	0.6	151	1.5	153	1.5	165	0.3	151
			6	155	1	0.8	152	2	154	2	170	0.6	150
			12	154	3	0.4	152					1	151
					3	0.6	153						
r = 0.71													
Brown / Changing 178, 133	0.30	123	1	125	1	−1.5	114	1	127	1	128	−1	115
			3	127	1	0	125	1.25	123	1.25	126	0	125
			6	122	1	0.3	127	1.5	122	1.5	128	0.3	127
			12	125	7	−1	117	2	123			0.6	127
					7	0	122					1	128
r = 0.65													
Constant / Box–Jenkins 174, 149	0.32	142	1	141	1	0	141	1	144	1	146	0	142
			2	138	1	0.3	141	2	141	2	143	0.2	142
			3	142	2	0	138	3	140	3	143	0.4	143
			12	143	2	0.4	141	4	140	4	145	1	144
					1	0	123						
r = 0.79													
Changing / Box–Jenkins 133, 149	0.66	128	1	123	3	0.3	123	1	129	1	131	0	124
			3	125	6	0.6	126	2	125	2	124	0.2	124
			6	129	1	−1	128	3	124	3	125	0.4	125
			12	130	7	0	129	4	124			0.6	127
r = 0.83													
Changing / Constant 133, 174	1.00	133	1	153	1	0	153	1	143	1	135	0	149
			3	144	1	0.3	149	1.2	142	1.2	137	0.4	147
			6	141	1	0.9	144	1.5	142	1.3	138	0.8	145
			12	141	7	0	141	2	143	1.5	140	1	144
					7	0.7	141						
r = 0.88													

Table 20.A4. Overall variances, 1954–9 only

Forecasts		Weight constant throughout — Wt.	Variance	(i) v	(i) Var.	(ii) v	(ii) x	(ii) Var.	(iii) w	(iii) Var.	(iv) w	(iv) Var.	(v) x	(v) Var.
Brown	170	0.32	122	1	121	1	0	121	1	125	1	128	0	119
Harrison	130			2	113	1	0.5	113	1.2	117	1.2	113	0.4	115
				3	116	1	0.6	114	1.4	117	1.4	113	0.5	116
				6	121	2	0	113						
				12	119	2	0.6	115						
Harrison	130	0.43	106	1	118	1	0.6	110	1	107	1	110	0	113
Box–Jenkins	119			2	111	1	1	107	1.4	107	1.3	108	0.6	109
				3	106	7	0	106	1.8	107	1.6	114	1	107
				6	106	7	0.3	106						
				12	108	7	0.6	107						
r = 0.68														
Constant	152	0.42	107	1	126	1	0.3	117	1	110	1	118	0	116
Harrison	130			2	118	1	0.6	109	1.15	110	1.1	122	0.6	107
				3	112	1	0.9	106	1.3	111	1.2	125	0.9	106
				6	114	2	0.8	105						
				12	109	2	0.9	105						
r = 0.52														
Changing	116	0.59	102	1	104	1	0.3	103	1	105	1	112	0	102
Harrison	130			2	102	1	0.6	102	1.15	105	1.15	114	0.4	101
				3	103	3	1	103	1.3	106	1.3	115	0.8	102
				12	106	2	0	103						
						2	0.6	103						
r = 0.67														

Note: Columns (i)–(v) are grouped under the heading "Weights varying according to method".

Table 20.A5. *Performance rankings of methods*

Combination of forecasts	Method				
	(i)	(ii)	(iii)	(iv)	(v)
Brown and Box–Jenkins	3 (2)	2 (3)	1 (4)	5 (1)	4 (5)
Brown and Changing	1 (2 =)	2 (4)	3 (2 =)	5 (1)	4 (5)
Brown and Constant	4 (1)	2 (3)	3 (4)	5 (5)	1 (2)
Changing and Constant	3 (3)	2 (2)	4 (4)	1 (1)	5 (5)
Changing and Box–Jenkins	2 (2)	1 (1)	4 (4)	3 (3)	5 (5)
Constant and Box–Jenkins	1 = (2)	1 = (1)	3 (3)	5 (5)	4 (4)
Harrison and Brown	(3)	(2)	(5)	(1)	(4)
Harrison and Changing	(3)	(2)	(4)	(5)	(1)
Harrison and Constant	(3)	(1)	(4)	(5)	(2)
Harrison and Box–Jenkins	(2)	(1)	(3)	(5)	(4)

Constant

No short-term serial correlation. "Constant" crude seasonals fitted. Since the data exhibit definite changes in the seasonal proportions, this results in positive serial correlation of month t with month $t - 12$.

Changing

No serial correlation. Changing crude seasonal factors estimated.

Detailed results for different pairings of forecasts are given in Tables 20.A3 (1951–60) and 20.A4 (1954–9 only).

The performance of the different methods is summarized in Table 20.A5 which records their rankings as judged by the "best" choice of parameters, a rank of 1 indicating the best performance. The ranks for 1951–60 are recorded without brackets, for 1954–9 only with brackets.

It is to be noted that though the ranks for 1954–9 are often the same as for 1951–60, there are some considerable changes. The results should therefore be interpreted with some caution.

REFERENCES

G. A. BARNARD (1963) New methods of quality control. *Jl R. statist. Soc.* A 126, 255.

J. M. BATES (1970) A short-term forecasting method for seasonal data. (To be published.)

G. E. P. BOX and G. M. JENKINS (1962) Some statistical aspects of adaptive optimization and control. *Jl R. statist. Soc.* B 24, 297.

G. E. P. Box, G. M. Jenkins and D. W. Bacon (1967) Models for forecasting seasonal and non-seasonal time series. In *Spectral Analysis of Time Series*, p. 271 (Ed. B. Harris). John Wiley, New York.

P. J. Harrison (1965) Short-term sales forecasting. *Appl. Starist.* XIV, 102.

M. G. Kendall and A. Stuart (1961) *The Advanced Theory of Statistics*, Vol. II, pp. 18, 19. Griffin, London.

R. Stone, D. G. Champernowne, and J. E. Meade (1942) The precision of national income estimates. *Rev. Econ. Stud.* 9, 111.

CHAPTER 21

Invited Review
Combining Forecasts –
Twenty Years Later*
C. W. J. Granger

Abstract

The combination of forecasts is a simple, pragmatic and sensible way to possibly produce better forecasts. Simple extensions of the original idea involve the use of various available "forecasts" even if some are rather inefficient. Some unsolved questions relate to combining forecasts with horizons longer than one period. More complicated extensions are associated with "encompassing" and the combination of confidence intervals or quantiles. The relevance of information sets is emphasized in both the underlying theory and the interpretation of combinations.

Keywords: combinations, forecasts, integrated, information sets, encompassing, quantiles.

THE BEGINNINGS

In 1963 Barnard published a paper comparing forecasts made by the then-novel Box–Jenkins (BJ) modelling procedure with those from the more venerable, exponentially weighted, moving average or adaptive forecasting methods, finding BJ to be superior. Barnard might have concluded – although he did not – that the better method should be retained and the loser discarded. However, it was observed that a simple average of the two forecasts outperformed each of them. The obvious extension was to ask if a weighted combination of the forecasts would be even better. This possibility was explored by Bates and the author (henceforth, BG) in our 1969 paper, which considered the theory of how the weights should be chosen optimally and contained a practical investigation of how estimates of these and some suboptimal weights actually performed. The weights on the two forecasts were chosen to add to one,

* *Journal of Forecasting* 8, 1989, 167–173.

on the assumption that each forecast was unbiased, making the combination unbiased. As the method proposed was simple to use, completely pragmatic and appeared to often produce superior forecasts, we were confident that the combining of forecasts would quickly become standard practice. This belief was reinforced by Nelson's (1972) paper, in which he also considered the combination of forecasts, based on quite independent work. In fact, acceptance of the idea has been rather slow, although there has been a growing interest over the past six years or so. In this paper I present a completely personal viewpoint about some developments of the basic idea. I shall not attempt to survey the literature on combining, which is now voluminous and rather repetitive.

In the original BG application of combining the two forecasting techniques were based on the same (univariate) information set. For combining to produce a superior forecast, both components forecasts clearly had to be suboptimal. It is more usual for combining to produce a better forecast when the individual forecasts are based on different information sets, and each may be optimal for their particular set. Suppose that we have N forecasters, with the jth individual having information set $I_{jn}: (I_{on}, J_{jn})$ at time n, where I_{on} is the information available to everyone and J_{jn} is that available only to the jth forecaster. The contents of J_{jn} will be assumed to be independent of I_{on} and of $J_{kn}, k \neq j$. More specifically, let

$$I_{on}: z_{n-s}, s \geq 0$$

(z_t can be a vector series, but here it will be taken to be univariate for convenience) and $J_{jn}: x_{j,t-s}, s \geq 0$ and let the variables that we are to forecast be y_t. Denote the universal information set by

$$U_n: \{I_{on}, J_{in}, j = 1, \ldots, N\}$$

which consists of all the information available to all the forecasters. The optimum (linear) least-squares forecast of y_{n+1} if U_n were known is

$$
\begin{aligned}
E_u &= E[y_{n+1}|U_n] \\
&= a(B)z_n + \sum_j \beta_j(B)x_{jn}
\end{aligned}
\tag{1}
$$

where $a(B)$, $\beta_j(B)$ are lag operator polynomials. With the assumptions made, the optimum forecast of the jth person is

$$
\begin{aligned}
E_j &= E[y_{n+1}|I_{jn}] \\
&= a(B)z_n + \beta_j(B)x_{jn}
\end{aligned}
\tag{2}
$$

Forming a simple average of these individual forecasts gives

$$\bar{E} = \frac{1}{N} \sum_j E_j$$

$$= a(B)z_n + \frac{1}{N} \sum_j \beta_j(B) x_{jn} \qquad (3)$$

The second term is the sum of N independent components divided by N and so will have a standard deviation of order $N^{-1/2}$, so that if N is large

$$\bar{E} \cong a(B)z_n$$

Note that the right-hand side is the forecast made using just I_{on}. If $\bar{E}$ is formed using any other set of weights adding to one, generally a similar result will hold. Thus, E_n cannot be achieved by optimally combining the individual forecasts E_j. However, if yet another forecast enters the situation, using the information set I_{on}, producing

$$E_o = E[y_{n+1}|I_{on}] = a(B)z_n \qquad (4)$$

then it is seen immediately that the optimal forecast E_u can be achieved by

$$E_u = \sum_{j=1}^{N} E_j - (N-1)E_o \qquad (5)$$

This simple analysis illustrates a number of general points:

(1) It is seen that aggregating forecasts is not the same as aggregating information sets. $\bar{E}$ is based on all the information, but is not equal to E_u, as the information is not being used efficiently.
(2) Equal weight combinations, as in equation (3), are useful when each information set contains common and independent information components. If the quantity of shared information varies across forecasters, unequal weights will usually result.
(3) A new forecast can improve the combination even if it is not based on new, additional information (e.g. E_o).
(4) Negative weights can be useful, as in equation (5).
(5) It is useful to include as many forecasts as possible in the combination, again as in equation (5).

SIMPLE EXTENSIONS

Discussion of information is an essential feature of all forecasting situations, including combining. If we had available all the information upon which all the forecasts are based, then we would build the complete model and use this to make forecasts rather than using combining. In many cases, just the individual forecasts are available, rather than the information they are based on, and so combining is appropriate.

However, in forming the combination weight it is assumed that some past values of the y_t series is available. In the BG combinations these data were not used efficiently. For example, if $f_{n,1}$, $g_{n,1}$ are a pair of one-step forecasts of y_{n+1}, made at time n, and if the y_t series as stationary, then the unconditional mean

$$m_n = \frac{1}{n}\sum_{j=1}^{n} y_t - j$$

is also a forecast of y_{n+1} available at time n, although usually a very inefficient one. This new forecast can be included in the combination, giving

$$c_{n,1} = \alpha_1 m_n + \alpha_2 f_{n,1} + \alpha_3 g_{n,1} \tag{6}$$

at the combined forecast. The weights α_j can be obtained by regressing $c_{n,1}$ on y_{n+1} as discussed in Granger and Ramanathan (1984). Whether the weights α_j should add to one depends on whether the forecasts are unbiased and the combination is required to be unbiased. Before combining, it is usually a good idea to unbias the component forecasts. Thus, if $w_{n,1}$ is a set of one-step forecasts, run a regression

$$y_{n+1} = a + bw_{n,1} + \varepsilon_{n+1}$$

and check whether $a = 0$, $b = 1$, and if ε_n is white noise. If any of these conditions do not hold, an immediately apparently superior forecast can be achieved and these should be used in any combination.

If y_t is not a stationary series, then equation (6) is not appropriate. Suppose that y_t is integrated of order one so that changes in y_t are stationary. Then y_t does not have a mean, but an equivalent regression would have m_n replaced by y_n. This procedure is discussed by Kamstra and Hallman (1989), as well as other generalizations.

Yet other forecasts may be available for combination, such as the two-step forecasts $f_{n-1,2}$, $g_{n-1,2}$, etc. Whether using these provides a superior combination depends on how all the forecasts were made and on what information they use. In all cases, there is no reason to believe that the combination will produce the best possible forecast, given the universal information set. The use of combined forecasts is still a pragmatic attempt to produce an improved forecast, possibly to compare the components.

A more intensive use of the available data is achieved by allowing the combined weight to vary with time. A time-varying parameter regression using the Kalman filter is feasible, but a rather different method has been discussed by Engle *et al.* (1984). The usual weights were used to combine two different inflation forecasts, based on variances and covariances of forecast errors, but these second moments were modelled conditionally on previous values of the moments with the ARCH procedure (Engle, 1982). Although potentially useful, these methods diverge from the attractive simplicity of the ordinary combining techniques.

When there are many forecasts available for combination the original methods are too complicated for easy use. A pragmatic way to proceed might be to rank all the forecasts on their previous performance, measured by squared forecast error, and discard all but a few of the best. An attractive alternative method has been proposed by Figlewski (1983). The forecast error series are decomposed into parts occurring in all the errors and those found in just a particular forecast. The weights in the combination depend on the relative sizes of the variances of the two components. Using data from surveys of inflation expectations, the combined forecast was found to perform much better than an equally weighted average of the forecasts.

In all these extensions of the original combining technique, combinations have been linear, only single-step horizons are considered and the data available have been assumed to be just the various forecasts and the past data of the series being forecast. On this the last point, it is clear that other data can be introduced to produce further forecasts to add to the combinations, or Bayesian techniques could be used to help determine the weights. The fact that only linear combinations were being used was viewed as an unnecessary restriction from the earliest days, but sensible ways to remove this estimation was unclear. A procedure that had been briefly considered is to forecast $\log y_{n+1}$ (if the series is positive), to transform this into a forecast of y_{n+1}, and then to add this new forecast to the combination. Very limited experience with this procedure has not produced superior forecasts. The small amount of research into combinations of multi-step forecasts is more surprising.

Suppose that $f_{n,h}, g_{n,h}$ are alternative forecasts made at time n of y_{n+h}. Then a combination of the form

$$c_{n,h} = a_{1h} + a_{2h}f_{n,1} + a_{3h}g_{n,h}$$

could be considered. How will a_{jh} change with h? In theory, there need be no change, as the above example with information sets have common and independent components shows. However, one forecaster may produce much better longer-run forecasts than another, and so the weights can vary with h. In practice, companies may build quite different models to produce short- and long-term forecasts, and these may reproduce quite different medium-term ones. A technique to deal with this problem and to produce forecasts consistent with both models at all horizons has been suggested by Engle *et al.* (1987), based on co-integration ideas.

FURTHER EXTENSIONS

If f and g are a pair of forecasts with f historically performing better than g, and if a combination gives g a zero weight (or one statistically insignificant from zero) then f may be said to dominate g. In this case, we would be justified in disregarding the g forecasts and concentrating solely on f. This situation is related to the deeper concept of "encompassing", as discussed by Mizon (1984) and Mizon and Richard (1986).

Suppose that there exist two models, A and B, of part of the economy. For simplicity, suppose that we are interested in modelling just a single economic variable y_t. The two models may be based on different economic theories and different information sets, yet one model, say A, can dominate the other, B, in various dimensions. In particular, A can predict what B will say about characteristics of y_t, such as forecasts of its mean, variance, inter-quartile range, etc. in all circumstances. For example, A may be able to predict whether B will suggest that y will increase or decrease in the next period, regardless of the values taken by the variables in the information set used to determine B. In this case, A is said to encompass B. A necessary condition that A encompasses B is that forecasts of the mean of y_{n+1} from A dominate those from B. (For a discussion, see Chong and Hendry, 1986.) Other necessary conditions are that a forecast of some economically relevant features of y_{n+1} – such as a variance, confidence interval, quartile or moment – from A dominates the corresponding forecast from B. This is clearly a severe but interesting set of conditions.

These ideas lead naturally to the question of how we would combine estimates of quantities such as confidence intervals. The 95% confidence intervals for most economic forecasts are embarrassingly wide, and one of the most important questions facing forecasters at present is how to reduce significantly the width of these intervals. Combining different bands may provide a solution, but it is unclear how we would proceed. If we had a pair of sequences of past point and interval forecasts, how should these be combined? A related question, that has been considered is how to combine forecasts of quantiles. Let $Q_{p,n}$ be an estimate of the pth quantile $q_{p,n}$ of y_n, so that

$$\text{prob}(y_n \le q_{p,n}) = p$$

As the conditional distribution of y_n, given an information set I_{n-1}, will depend on the contents of I_{n-1}, these quantiles will then vary with n. A convenient and practical alternative to a 95% confidence interval might be the 50% interquartile range, $q_{0.75} - q_{0.25}$. A quantile estimate can be called unbiased if the proportion of y_n values that lie less than $Q_{p,n}$ tend to p as the sample size becomes large. If a quantile estimate is biased, an unbiased estimate can be found by performing a regression using a relevant cost function known as the "tick function".

Define

$$T_\theta(x) = \theta x \qquad \text{if } x > 0$$
$$= (\theta - 1)x \quad \text{if } x < 0$$

$$\text{with } 0 < \theta < 1$$

so that the two arms of $T(x)$ are straight lines rising from the origin but, generally, with different slopes. If a and b are chosen to minimize

$$\sum_t T_p(y_t - a - bQ_{p,t})$$

then $Q^*_{p,t} = \hat{a} + \hat{b}Q_{p,t}$ will be a consistent estimate of $q_{p,t}$ and so will be at least asymptotically unbiased. If $Q^A_{p,t}, Q^B_{p,t}$ are a pair of quantile estimates then appropriate combining weights can be found by minimizing

$$\sum_t T_p(y_t - a_1 - a_2 Q^Q_{p,t} - a_3 Q_{p,t})$$

as the estimated quantile. Replacing estimates by forecasts in this procedure gives a forecast quantile. A pair of such values would provide a forecast interquantile range, such as $C^*_{0.75} - C^*_{0.25}$, and this should be useful in providing an indication of the uncertainty about a median forecast, $C^*_{0.5}$, which itself may be close to the mean forecast. An example of such an analysis has been given by Granger *et al.* (1989).

Combining uncertainty measures is a step towards the larger question of how we would combine or aggregate distributions. If model A suggests that y_{n-1} will be from a conditional distribution $F^A_{n,1}(x)$, and similarly we obtain $F^B_{n,1}(x)$ from model B, possibly with these distributions based on different information sets, then there should be a way of asking whether a further distribution can be derived from these components which may be better in some sense. There is a large literature on this topic, (for example, Genest and Zidek, 1986), but a completely satisfactory combining technique has not been found.

A pragmatic method of combining distributions is the following:

(1) For each distribution function $F(x)$, derive the corresponding quantile function $Q(\theta)$, so that

$$Q(\theta) = F^{-1}(\theta)$$

As the distribution functions will vary with time, i.e. as the information set evolves, so will the quantile functions.

(2) Combine the two quantile functions for each θ using the tick function $T(\ )$. Thus functions $a_1(\theta), a_2(\theta)$ are chosen so that

$$\sum_t (T_\theta(y_t - a_1(\theta)Q^A_t(\theta) - a_2(\theta)Q^B_t(\theta))) \tag{7}$$

is minimized for each θ. In practice, some set of θ's will actually be used, spanning $(0, 1)$.

A quantile function might be called "sample unbiased" if for y_t, $t = 1, \ldots, n$, the number of $y_t \le Q_t(\theta) \cong \theta/n$. If Q^A, Q^B are both sample unbiased, then we might expect that $a_1(\theta) + a_2(\theta) \cong 1$, and this constraint could be used for simplicity. Denoting

$$Q_{ct}(\theta) = \hat{a}_1(\theta)Q^A_t(\theta) + \hat{a}_2(\theta)Q^B_t(\theta)$$

then other constraints that might be imposed when minimizing equation (7) are that $Q_{ct}(\theta)$ is sample unbiased, $\hat{a}_1(\theta)$, $\hat{a}_2(\theta)$ are smooth as θ varies (assuming $Q^A(\theta)$, $Q^B(\theta)$ are smooth) so that splines may be used, and we will certainly want to require that

$$Q_{ct}(\theta_1) > Q_{ct}(\theta_2)$$
$$\text{if } \theta_1 > \theta_2$$

so that $Q_{ct}(\theta)$ is monotonic increasing for all t. The distribution function corresponding to $Q_{ct}(\theta)$, i.e. $F_t(x) = Q_{ct}^{-1}(x)$, should provide a sensible combined function. A rather general test for the encompassing of B by A can be based on statistics such as $\int \delta(a_2(\theta))^2 d\theta$. No experience is currently available with this procedure.

CONCLUSION

It had been occasionally suggested that combining does not produce better forecasts. If that is generally true it would be very disturbing for forecasters, both time series analysts and econometricians, as it would mean that very simple methods of forecasting – based on small information sets inefficiently used – are difficult to improve upon. If true, this would have a great impact on econometrics, economic theory and the social sciences. Let us hope that it is not true.

REFERENCES

Barnard, G. A., "New methods of quality control", *Journal of the Royal Statistical Society A*, 126 (1963), 255–9.

Bates, J. M. and Granger, C. W. J., "The combination of forecasts", *Operations Research Quarterly*, 20 (1969), 319–25.

Box, G. E. P. and Jenkins, G. M. *Time Series Analysis, Forecasting and Control*, San Francisco: Holden-Day (1970).

Chong, Y. Y. and Hendry, D. F., "Econometric evaluation of linear macroeconomic models", *Review of Economic Studies*, 53 (1986), 671–90.

Engle, R. F., "Autoregressive conditional heteroscedasticity with estimates of the variance of United Kingdom inflation", *Econometrica*, 53 (1982), 995.

Engle, R. F., Granger, C. W. J. and Hallman, R. J., "Combining short- and long-run forecasts: an application of seasonal co-integration to monthly electricity sales forecasting", submitted to *Journal of Econometrics* (1987).

Engle, R. F., Granger, C. W. J. and Kraft, D., "Combining competing forecasts of inflation using a bivariate ARCH model", *Journal of Economic Dynamics of Control*, 8 (1984), 151–65.

Figlewski, S., "Optimal price forecasting using survey data", *Review of Economics and Statistics*, 65 (1983), 13–21.

Genest, C. and Zidek, J. V., "Combining probability distributions", *Statistical Science*, 1 (1986), 114–48.

Granger, C. W. J., White, H. and Kamstra, M., "Interval forecasting: an analysis based upon ARCH-quantile estimates", *Journal of Econometrics*, 40 (1989), 87–96.

Granger, C. W. J. and Ramanathan, R., "Improved methods for combining forecasts", *Journal of Forecasting*, 3 (1984), 197–204.

Kamstra, M. and Hallman, J., *Journal of Forecasting*, 8 (1989), 189–198.

Mizon, G. E., "The encompassing approach in economics", in Hendry D. F. and Wallis, K. F. (eds), *Econometrics and Quantitative Economics*, Oxford: Blackwell (1984).

Mizon, G. E. and Richard, J. F., "The encompassing principle and its application to non-nested hypotheses", *Econometrica*, 54 (1986), 657–78.

Nelson, C. R., "The prediction performance of the FRB-MIT-PENN model of the US economy", *American Economic Review*, 62 (1972), 902–17.

CHAPTER 22

The Combination of Forecasts Using Changing Weights*

Melinda Deutsch, Clive W. J. Granger, and Timo Teräsvirta**

Abstract

This paper considers the combination of forecasts using changing weights derived from switching regression models or from smooth transition regression models. The regimes associated with the switches may not be known to the forecaster and thus need to be estimated. Several approaches to this problem are considered. In two empirical examples, these time-varying combining procedures produced smaller, in some cases substantially smaller, out-of-sample squared forecast errors than those obtained using the simple linear combining model.

1. INTRODUCTION

Usually, several alternative forecasts of a given economic time series are available to an economist. Rather than choose a single forecast, Bates and Granger (1969) suggest using a combination of the alternative forecasts, since it will often outperform any of the individual forecasts. That is, suppose $f_{t,1}$ and $f_{t,2}$ are alternative one-step ahead unbiased forecasts made at time t of y_{t+1}. The combined forecast, $f_{t,c} = \beta f_{t,1} + (1 - \beta)f_{t,2}$ where $\beta \in [0, 1]$, will often have smaller out-of-sample sum of squared forecast errors than either of the original ones.

An important question is: how can one choose the combining weights so as to minimize the out-of-sample sum of squared forecast errors? One of the most common procedures used to estimate them is to perform the least squares regression

 * *International Journal of Forecasting* 10, 1994, 47–57.
** The authors wish to thank the referee for his insightful and detailed comments. The research of Clive W. J. Granger was partly supported by National Science Foundation grant SES 89-02950. The research of Timo Teräsvirta was supported by the Yrjo Jahnsson Foundation.

$$y_{t+1} = a_0 + a_1 f_{t,1} + a_2 f_{t,2} + \varepsilon_{t+1} \tag{1}$$

where a_0 is a constant term (Granger and Ramanathan, 1984). This procedure has two desirable characteristics. First, it yields a combined forecast which is often better than either of the individual forecasts. Second, the method is easy to implement. The procedure will be referred to as the simple linear combining method. Note that the weights are no longer constrained to add to one.

Many more elaborate procedures have been proposed [for a review, see Sessions and Chatterjee (1989) and LeSage and Magura (1992)]. The vast majority of these consider fixed weight linear combinations of forecasts. However, time-varying combinations may be a fruitful area of investigation. This paper considers the use of two methods, namely the combination of forecasts using switching regime models and smooth transition models. Thus, the combining weights are allowed to change immediately or gradually when there is a change in regime. In two empirical examples, these time-varying models produce substantially smaller out-of-sample squared forecast errors than those obtained using the simple linear combining model. The methods have the additional advantage that they are easy to implement and may be interpretable from economic events.

The changing weights considered here are of a special form. The weights a_1, a_2 in Eq. (1) above could be time-varying in some less-specified form, such as when using a state-space model, as in LeSage and Magura (1992) and Sessions and Chatterjee (1989). Diebold and Pauly (1987) propose a number of extensions of the standard regression-based theory of forecast combination. In numerical examples in which there was structural change in the original forecasts, they found their forecasting schemes resulted in a considerable improvement in forecasting performance. In Bates and Granger (1969), a variety of simple forms of time-varying weights were considered but were not effective in the particular example they considered.

The second section of this paper gives a brief introduction to switching regimes. Section 3 discusses the practical implementation of the use of switching models to combine forecasts. The fourth section considers combining forecasts using the more general smooth transition model. In both sections three and four an example using the US inflation rate is used. A further empirical example using the UK inflation rate is given in the fifth section. The sixth section reports the results of a comparison of the in-sample and out-of-sample performance of the alternative combining methods.

2. SWITCHING REGRESSION MODELS AND THEIR APPLICATION TO THE COMBINATION OF FORECASTS

It is usually assumed that the coefficients in a regression model are fixed. However, in some cases it is more appropriate to allow the coefficients to vary as a function of time or as a function of some relevant economic variables. The general form of such a model can be written as

$$y_t = x_t'(\beta + \lambda_t \gamma) + \varepsilon_t \quad 0 \le \lambda_t \le 1 \tag{2}$$

where $\{\lambda_t \mid t \in [1, \ldots, n]\}$ is referred to as a transition path. If $\lambda_t = 1$ when $t \in I_1$ and $\lambda_t = 0$ when $t \in I_2$, where I_1 and I_2 are two relevant regimes, then the model is referred to as a *switching regression* or *regime* model [see e.g. Quandt (1958), Goldfeld and Quandt (1972, 1973) and Granger and Teräsvirta (1993)]. The coefficients of this model take on a finite number of different values depending on the state (or regime) of the economy. If λ_t is a continuous function, then the parameters will change smoothly from one regime to another and the model is referred to as a *smooth transition model* [see e.g. Bacon and Watts (1971) and Lin and Teräsvirta (1994)].

3. COMBINING FORECASTS USING SWITCHING REGRESSION MODELS

If it is agreed that switching combining could be used, the first practical consideration is the estimation of the different regimes associated with the switching regression model when they are unknown. Several alternative approaches to this problem are considered. The first approach assumes that the lagged forecast error from the alternative forecasting models may be useful in approximating the regime. The second approach assumes that a relevant economic variable may be useful in approximating the regime. Each approach is now considered in turn.

3.1   Switching Regression Models in Which the Regime is Indicated by the Lagged Forecast Error

Consider two forecasts, $f_{t,1}$ and $f_{t,2}$ of y_{t+1}, with respective errors $z_{t,1} = y_{t+1} - f_{t,1}$ and $z_{t,2} = y_{t+1} - f_{t,2}$. Clearly, information about the forecast errors, $z_{t,1}$ and $z_{t,2}$, could aid considerably in determining the regime of the economy at any given time $t + 1$. For example, if $z_{t,1}$ is unusually large, this may indicate that the economy is in state one. Or, if $z_{t,2}$ is negative, then this may indicate that the economy is in state two. Although $z_{t,1}$ and $z_{t,2}$ are unknown at time t when the combining weights must be calculated, $z_{t-1,1}$ and $z_{t-1,2}$ may provide some information about $z_{t,1}$ and $z_{t,2}$. This suggests that switching regression models, in which the regime is indicated by the lagged forecast error from the alternative forecasting models, may be useful.

A number of functions of the lagged forecast errors were considered, in particular: (1) the sign of the lagged forecast error(s); (2) the magnitude of the lagged forecast error(s); (3) the relative size of the lagged forecast error(s). The following combination schemes were used:

$$f_{t,c} = I(t \in I_1)(a_1 f_{t,1} + a_2 f_{t,2})$$
$$+ (1 - I(t \in I_1))(a_3 f_{t,1} + a_4 f_{t,2}) \tag{3}$$

where $I(t \in I_1) = 1$ when $t \in I_1 = 0$. The particular choices of I_1 examined were

    (1) I_1 is $z_{t-1,1} \geq 0$,
    (2) I_1 is $z_{t-1,2} \geq 0$,
    (3) I_1 is $\left| z_{t-1,1} \right| \geq c \cdot magz_1$,
    (4) I_1 is $\left| z_{t-1,2} \right| \geq c \cdot magz_2$,
    (5) I_1 is $\hat{\alpha}_1 z_{t-1,1} + \hat{\alpha}_2 z_{t-2,1} + \ldots + \hat{\alpha}_n z_{t-n,1} \geq 0$
    (6) I_1 is $\hat{\beta}_1 z_{t-1,2} + \hat{\beta}_2 z_{t-2,2} + \ldots + \hat{\beta}_n z_{t-n,2} \geq 0$,

and

$$magz_1 = \sum_{t=1}^{nobs} |z_{t,1}| / nobs,$$

$$magz_2 = \sum_{t=1}^{nobs} |z_{t,2}| / nobs,$$

where $nobs$ is the number of in-sample observations, c is a constant, $\hat{\alpha}_i$, $i = 1, \ldots, n$ are the estimated coefficients of the autoregressive process $z_{t,1} = \alpha_1 z_{t-1,1} + \alpha_2 z_{t-2,1} + \ldots + \alpha_n z_{t-n,1}$ and $\hat{\beta}_i$, $i = 1, \ldots, n$ are similarly defined. The usual methods for building an autoregressive model of a time series are used to determine the order of the AR process of $z_{t,1}$ for Model 5 and of $z_{t,2}$ for Model 6. These include (1) the estimation of the correlogram and partial correlogram and (2) and estimation of an AR model and examination of the parameters of the estimated equation for significance. In this paper, for ease of computation, a maximum of two lags was considered in the empirical examples. The last two models were considered since the forecasting errors may be autocorrelated.

As a simple illustration of the usefulness of these combining methods, the above procedures were applied to two forecasts of the US inflation rate. The models used to generate the forecasts were based on two competing economic theories, namely the "monetarist" model and a "markup pricing" model, and were modifications of ones used by Engle et al. (1984). A complete description of the these models is presented in the Appendix. While the models used to generate the forecasts are not

Table 22.1. *US inflation rate: SSE for the fixed weight combination of forecasts*

Forecast	Sum of out-of-sample squared forecast errors
$f_{t,1}$	157.77
$f_{t,2}$	116.28
$f_{t,1}$ and $f_{t,2}$, linearly combined	58.54
(approximate combining weights for the simple linear model)	($a_1 = -1.1, a_2 = 1.7$)
$f_{t,1}, f_{t,2}$ and y_t, linearly combined	33.51
Simple averaging	132.84

Number of in-sample observations, 30; number of out-of sample observations, 11.

meant to be serious models of the inflation rate, they do provide an example which may be used to test the performance of the proposed combining schemes. Note that the results obtained in this paper cannot be directly compared to those of Engle et al. since the models used to generate the two forecasts $f_{t,1}$ and $f_{t,2}$ are not the same in both studies. The combining method proposed in Engle et al., is more complicated to implement than the techniques presented in this paper.

For all the combining methods, rolling regressions were employed to estimate the weights used to form the combined forecast. Specifically, the weights used to form the first combined forecast were computed using the first *nobs* observations, where *nobs* is the number of in-sample observations. For the second combined forecast, the first observation was dropped from the sample and an additional observation at time *nobs* + 1 was included at the end of the sample. This procedure was repeated until all the combined forecasts were computed. It should be noted that, while an updating procedure was used to combine the forecasts, the models used to generate the original forecasts, $f_{t,1}$ and $f_{t,2}$, were not updated.

Table 22.1 gives the sum of out-of-sample squared forecast errors of the original forecasts and the results of the linear combining procedures. The entry labelled as "$f_{t,1}, f_{t,2}$, and y_t, linearly combined" means that the forecasts $f_{t,1}, f_{t,2}$ and y_t were combined using simple linear combining to form a new forecast of y_{t+1}.

Since the forecasts $f_{t,1}$ and $f_{t,2}$ are not updated, this may introduce a bias favoring any time-varying combinations scheme over any fixed-weight combination scheme. For this reason, it is also of interest to compare the proposed combining techniques with the performance of some time-varying combination method. The out-of-sample sum of squared forecast errors (SSE) for the time-varying combining method proposed by Bates and Granger (1969) was also calculated. Bates and Granger suggest using

Table 22.2. *US inflation rate: Switching regression models in which regime is indicated by the lagged forecast error*

Model	Sum of out-of-sample squared forecast errors	Coeff.	s.e.
Model 1: $z_{t-1,1} > 0$	33.20	$0.15^{a,b}$	0.05
Model 2: $z_{t-1,2} > 0$	37.85	0.11^{a}	0.04
Model 3: $\|z_{t-1,1}\| > c \cdot mag\ z_1$	84.21	-0.10	0.11
Model 4: $\|z_{t-1,2}\| > c \cdot mag\ z_2$	25.86	$0.15^{a,b}$	0.05
Model 5: Estimated AR(2) process for $z_{t,1}$	20.56	0.26^{a}	0.05
Model 6: Estimated AR(2) process for $z_{t,2}$	35.79	0.12^{a}	0.05

[a] Coefficent of D is significant at the 5% level; [b] the constant term is significant at the 5% level.

$$f_{t,c} = k_t f_{t,1} + (1 - k_t) f_{t,2}, \text{ where } k_t = \frac{\sum z_{t-1,2}^2}{\sum z_{t-1,1}^2 + z_{t-1,2}^2}.$$ The out-of-sample

SSE for this example was 125.57, which is quite large since $f_{t,1}$ and $f_{t,2}$ are biased and the coefficients of the combining method are constrained to sum to one.

The results of the time-varying procedures proposed above are displayed in Table 22.2 and are very encouraging.

A substantial reduction in the SSE is achieved by these time-varying combination methods, with the best model yielding an approximately 65% reduction in SSE over that obtained using the simple linear combining model. It can be seen from the table that this reduction in SSE is obtained by using Model 5.

While the above results look impressive, it is of interest to test whether the reduction in SSE is significant. This can be determined using the following test [Granger and Newbold (1987), section 9.3]. Let $z_{t,lin}$ be the one-step ahead forecast error from the simple linear combining model, and let $z_{t,sw}$ be the one-step-ahead forecast error from the proposed switching regression model. Assuming that $z_{t,lin}$ and $z_{t,sw}$ are unbiased, not autocorrelated, and are from a bivariate normal distribution, the test consists of two steps: (1) form $S = z_{t,lin} + z_{t,sw}$ and $D = z_{t,lin} - z_{t,sw}$ and (2) regress S on a constant and D. If the coefficient of D is significantly different from zero, then conclude that the SSE of the switching regression model is significantly different from that of the linear combining model; otherwise conclude that it is not. Note that if the constant term in the estimated regression is significantly different from zero, then this implies that $z_{t,lin}$ and/or $z_{t,sw}$ are biased. Thus, a significant constant term indicates the violation of one of the assumptions made about the forecast errors necessary for the validity of this test. For this reason, it is important to

Table 22.3. *US inflation rate: A comparison of the out-of-sample SSE of the switching regression models with and without y_t included as an additional forecast*

Model	without y_t	with y_t
Model 1: $z_{t-1,1} > 0$	33.20	34.38
Model 2: $z_{t-1,2} > 0$	37.85	23.43

examine the significance of the constant term when interpreting the results of the test. These results are displayed in Table 22.2, with "coeff." being the estimated coefficient of D. t-statistics greater than 2.26 indicate that the coefficient of D is significant at the 5% level.

As a final observation, note the following modification of the time-varying models considered. Suppose y_{t+1} is an I(1) time series which is forecast by combining $f_{t,1}$ and $f_{t,2}$ using the simple linear combining model. Hallman and Kamstra (1989) noted that a reduction in SSE can be achieved by including an additional forecast of y_{t+1}, namely y_t, in the simple linear combining procedure. The US inflation rate is an I(1) time series and this observation is confirmed by the results in Table 1, where the out-of-sample SSE is reduced by including y_t in the simple linear combining scheme. It is of interest to determine whether the inclusion of the additional forecast y_t in the time-varying combining techniques proposed in this paper will also result in a reduction in the out-of-sample SSE. Specifically, Model 1 can be modified to be:

$$f_{t,c} = I(t \in I_1)(a_1 f_{t,1} + a_2 f_{t,2})$$
$$+ (1 - I(t \in I_1))(a_3 f_{t,1} + a_4 f_{t,2}) + a_5 y \tag{4}$$

where I_1 is $z_{t-1,1} \geq 0$. Table 22.3 above displays these results for Models 1 and 2 and indicates that including y_t in the combining scheme will sometimes improve the forecasting performance of the combined forecast.

3.2   Switching Regression Models in Which the Regime is Indicated by an Economically Relevant Variable

Economic theory may provide some guidance in approximating the regimes. In particular, the regime may be indicated by the value of a certain economic variable, denoted by W_t. For this reason, the following two models are considered:

$$f_{t,c} = I(W_t > 0)[a_1 f_{t,1} + a_2 f_{t,2}]$$
$$+ (1 - I(W_t > 0))[a_3 f_{t,1} + a_4 f_{t,2}] \tag{5}$$

$$f_{t,c} = I(|W_t| > c \cdot magW)[a_1 f_{t,1} + a_2 f_{t,2}]$$
$$+ (1 - I(|W_t| > c \cdot magW))[a_3 f_{t,1} + a_4 f_{t,2}] \qquad (6)$$

where $I(W_t > 0) = 1$ when $W_t > 0$ and $I(W_t > 0) = 0$, otherwise, $magW = \sum_{t=1}^{nobs} |W_t|/nobs$ and c is a constant.

These combination methods were again applied to the forecasts of US inflation. Stockton and Glassman (1987) provide some guidance in determining which economic variables may be appropriate for consideration. They compare the relative forecasting performance of three models of the inflation process, each based on a different economic theory, and find that the "monetarist model", in which inflation depends on changes in the money supply, does not perform well under the following two conditions: (1) when there is accelerated growth in the money supply and (2) when there is a widening gap between actual and potential GNP. Their findings suggest that a regime which depends on one of the following economic variables may be relevant for consideration: change in inflation, change in the money supply, change in wages, change in the unemployment rate, or change in real GNP.

When the regime is a function of the sign of a change in the unemployment rate (i.e. Eq. (5) with W_t = change in the unemployment rate), the out-of-sample sum of squared errors is 52.96, giving a reduction of 10% over the simple linear combination model. The other economic variables considered gave poor results and are not reported. The poor forecasting performance obtained by using these other economic variables as indicators of a regime shift may be due to the fact that these variables are already included in the two models that generated $f_{t,1}$ and $f_{t,2}$.

4. SMOOTH TRANSITION REGRESSION MODELS

In some cases, it may be more appropriate to assume a gradual change in the combining weights as the system passes from one regime to another. The more general class of smooth transition regression models allows for such a gradual change of the coefficients. A number of smooth transition regression models are considered, all of the form

$$f_{t,c} = \left(1 + e^{\gamma V_{t-1}}\right)^{-1}(a_1 f_{t,1} + a_2 f_{t,2})$$
$$+ \left(1 - \left(1 + e^{\gamma V_{t-1}}\right)^{-1}\right)(a_3 f_{t,1} + a_4 f_{t,2}) \qquad (7)$$

where V_{t-1} is some function of the lagged forecast error. The following combining schemes were considered:

(10) $V_{t-1} = z_{t-1,1}$,
(11) $V_{t-1} = z_{t-1,2}$,

Table 22.4. *US inflation rate: Smooth transition regression model*

Model	Sum of out-of-sample squared forecast errors	Coeff.	s.e.
Model 10: $V_{t-1} = z_{t-1,1}$	23.42 with $\gamma = 0.85$	−0.03	0.06
Model 11: $V_{t-1} = z_{t-1,2}$	28.04 with $\gamma = 0.01$	−0.08	0.07
Model 12: $V_{t-1} = AR(2)$ process for $z_{t,1}$	28.57 with $\gamma = 1.91$	−0.09	0.13
Model 13: $V_{t-1} = AR(2)$ process for $z_{t,2}$	25.81 with $\gamma = 0.01$	−0.05	0.10

$$(12) \quad V_{t-1} = \hat{\alpha}_1 z_{t-1,1} + \hat{\alpha}_2 z_{t-2,1} + \ldots + \hat{\alpha}_n z_{t-n,1},$$
$$(13) \quad V_{t-1} = \hat{\beta}_1 z_{t-1,2} + \hat{\beta}_2 z_{t-2,2} + \ldots + \hat{\beta}_n z_{t-n,2},$$

where $\hat{\alpha}_i$, $i = 1, \ldots, n$ are the estimated coefficients of the autoregressive process $z_{t,1} = \alpha_1 z_{t-1,1} + \alpha_2 z_{t-2,1} + \ldots + \alpha_n z_{t-n,1}$ and $\hat{\beta}_i$, $i = 1, \ldots, n$ are similarly defined. In some cases, these models performed better than the switching regression models, but they are slightly more complicated, since the value of γ that minimizes the in-sample SSE must be found by a grid search. The results for the inflation forecasts are shown in Table 22.4.

Further comparison of the alternative forecasting schemes can be made by examining Fig. 22.1. Fig. 22.1 is a graph of the US inflation rate, the original forecasts $f_{t,1}$ and $f_{t,2}$ and the combined forecast from the best time-varying model for this example, Model 5. The regimes did not switch during the out-of-sample period and the combining weights were 0.08 for the first forecast and 0.43 for the second forecast, respectively.

It is of interest to ask whether the out-of-sample SSE from the optimal switching regression method (which in this example is Model 5) is significantly different from the out-of-sample SSE from the proposed smooth transition regression methods. The results of the test of Granger and Newbold (1987) are displayed in Table 4 and suggest that the use of smooth transition combining schemes does not improve forecasting performance in this example.

5. A FURTHER EMPIRICAL EXAMPLE

This section examines an additional application of the nonlinear combining procedures discussed above. The results are again favorable, as one version of the switching model was found to result in a substantial reduction in out-of-sample forecast error.

The example combines two forecasts of the quarterly UK inflation rate from 1977:1 to 1985:2. The forecasts are obtained from two forecasting organizations which have different backgrounds: the London Business School (LBS) and the Organization for Economic

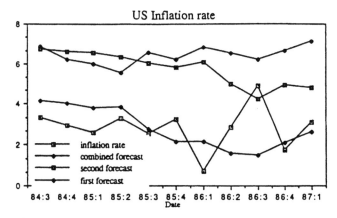

Figure 22.1. US inflation rate forecasts and combination.

Co-operation and Development (OECD). This data was published in an article by Holden and Peel (1989). The tables below display the results of combining forecasts using the methods proposed in this paper.

The out-of-sample SSE for the time-varying combining method proposed by Bates and Granger (1969) was calculated to provide a comparison of the schemes proposed in this paper with another time-varying method. The out-of-sample SSE was 7.51.

While simple linear combining does not result in a reduction in out-of-sample SSE, some of the combining schemes proposed in the paper result in improved forecasting performance, with the best model giving an almost 50% reduction in out-of-sample SSE over the OECD forecast. Models 1 and 5 yield a reduction in out-of-sample SSE over the OECD forecast. This suggests that there is some information in the forecast errors of the LBS forecasts that can be used to improve forecasting performance, since Models 1 and 5 use an estimate of the forecasting error from the LBS forecast as a "switching variable". Thus, the combining schemes proposed in the paper may suggest ways in which both the LBS and the OECD forecasting models could be improved (Table 22.5).

The plot of the combining weights for Model 5 is displayed in Fig. 22.2. It shows that, when the estimate of the LBS forecast error is positive, a weight near zero should be given to the LBS forecast. When the estimate is negative, more weight should be given. Fig. 22.3 is a graph of the UK inflation rate, the original forecasts $f_{t,1}$ and $f_{t,2}$ and the combined forecast from Model 5. Table 22.6 displays the results of the test performed by Granger and Newbold (1987, section 9.3) to determine if the out-of-sample SSE from the simple linear combining method is significantly different from the out-of-sample SSE from the proposed switching regression methods. It is also of interest to ask whether the

Table 22.5. *UK inflation rate: SSE for the fixed weight combination of forecasts*

Forecast	Sum of out-of-sample squared forecast errors
LBS forecast	13.99
OECD forecast	4.90
$f_{t,1}$ and $f_{t,2}$ linearly combined	19.56
$f_{t,1}$ $f_{t,2}$ and y_t, linearly combined	1.92
Simple averaging	7.99

Number of in-sample observations, 24; number of out-of-sample observations, 10.

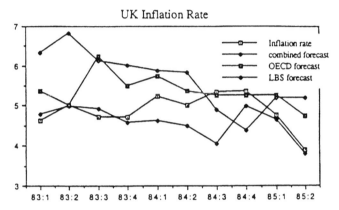

Figure 22.2. US inflation rate forecasts and combination.

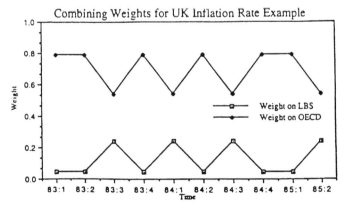

Figure 22.3. Weights associated with LBS OECD combined forecast: UK inflation rate.

Table 22.6. *UK inflation rate: Switching regression models in which the regime is indicated by the lagged forecast error*

Model	Sum of out-of-sample squared forecast errors	Coeff.	s.e.
Model 1: $z_{t-1,1} > 0$	4.41	$0.64^{a,b}$	0.22
Model 2: $z_{t-1,2} > 0$	11.24	0.35	0.61
Model 3: $\|z_{t-1,1}\| > c \cdot mag\, z_1$	5.11	$0.28^{a,b}$	0.08
Model 4: $\|z_{t-1,2}\| > c \cdot mag\, z_2$	5.51	0.33	0.58
Model 5: Estimated AR(2) process for $z_{t,1}$	2.55	$0.57^{a,b}$	0.13
Model 6: Estimated AR(2) process for $z_{t,2}$	44.59	−0.29	0.16

[a] The coefficient of D is significant at the 5% level; [b] the constant term is significant at the 5% level.

Table 22.7. *UK inflation rate: Smooth transition regression model*

Model	Sum of out-of-sample squared forecast errors	Coeff.	s.e.
Model 10: $V_{t-1} = z_{t-1,1}$	2.91 with $\gamma = 0.18$	-0.11^{b}	0.08
Model 11: $V_{t-1} = z_{t-1,2}$	5.17 with $\gamma = 0.17$	−0.25	0.14
Model 12: $V_{t-1} = $ AR(2) process for $z_{t,1}$	8.90 with $\gamma = 0.54$	$-0.44^{a,b}$	0.16
Model 13: $V_{t-1} = $ AR(2) process for $z_{t,2}$	22.06 with $\gamma = 0.21$	$-0.68^{a,b}$	0.14

[a] The coefficient of D is significant at the 5% level; [b] the constant term is significant at the 5% level.

out-of-sample SSE from the optimal switching regression method (which in this example is Model 5) is significantly different from the out-of-sample SSE from the proposed smooth transition regression methods. The results of Granger and Newbold's (1987) test are displayed in Table 22.7 and suggest that the use of smooth transition combining schemes does not improve forecasting performance in this example.

Note that, while the first example used in the paper is based on forecasts which are not updated and which may have introduced strong bias favoring any time-varying combination method used over any fixed-weight method, the LBS and the OECD forecasts are updated and there is still a considerable gain in forecasting performance.

Again, one can see from the results of Table 22.8 that a reduction in out-of-sample forecast error can be achieved by including y_t as an additional forecast in the time-varying models proposed in this paper.

The encouraging results obtained by combining the LBS and OECD demonstrate that the use of the combining schemes proposed in the paper can actually generate forecasts superior to those of sophisticated

Table 22.8. *UK inflation rate: A comparison of the out-of-sample SSE of the switching regression models with and without y_t included as an additional forecast*

Model	without y_t	with y_t
Model 1: $z_{t-1,1} > 0$	4.41	1.95
Model 2: $z_{t-1,2} > 0$	11.24	5.17

Table 22.9. *US inflation rate: In-sample and out-of-sample mean squared errors (MSE)*

Model	In-sample-MSE	Out-of-sample MSE
Model 1: $z_{t-1,1} > 0$	2.66	3.02
Model 2: $z_{t-1,2} > 0$	2.80	3.44
Model 3: $|z_{t-1,1}| > c \cdot mag \; z_1$	2.51	7.66
Model 4: $|z_{t-1,2}| > c \cdot mag \; z_2$	1.67	2.35
Model 5: Estimated AR(2) process for $z_{t,1}$	2.30	1.87
Model 6: Estimated AR(2) process for $z_{t,2}$	1.87	3.26

forecasting models and can suggest ways in which these sophisticated forecasting models can be improved.

6.   A COMPARISON OF THE IN-SAMPLE AND OUT-OF-SAMPLE PERFORMANCE OF THE ALTERNATIVE COMBINING METHODS

A number of alternative methods of combining forecasts based on switching regressions have been presented in this paper. It is of interest to ask which of these methods would perform best for a given data set. In particular, the reader may wonder whether the in-sample sum of squared forecast errors provides any information about the out-of-sample sum of squared forecast errors.

In an effort to answer this question, the in-sample mean squared forecast errors were calculated for each of the examples and compared to the out-of-sample mean squared forecast errors. It is evident from Tables 22.9 and 22.10 that the performance of the methods in-sample does provide some information about the performance of the methods out-of-sample. The results for Model 3, however, constitute an exception to this general statement. This outlier may occur because the value of the optimal value for the constant term c changes drastically over the sample

Table 22.10. *US inflation rate: In-sample and out-of-sample mean squared errors (MSE)*

Model	In-sample-MSE	Out-of-sample MSE
Model 10: $V_{t-1} = z_{t-1,1}$	2.36	2.12 with $\gamma = 0.85$
Model 11: $V_{t-1} = z_{t-1,2}$	1.74	2.55 with $\gamma = 0.01$
Model 12: $V_{t-1} = AR(2)$ process for $z_{t,1}$	1.59	2.60 with $\gamma = 1.91$
Model 13: $V_{t-1} = AR(2)$ process for $z_{t,2}$	1.10	2.58 with $\gamma = 0.01$

Table 22.11. *UK inflation rate: In-sample and out-of-sample mean squared errors (MSE)*

Model	In-sample-MSE	Out-of-sample MSE
Model 1: $z_{t-1,1} > 0$	7.03	0.44
Model 2: $z_{t-1,2} > 0$	6.29	0.11
Model 3: $\lvert z_{t-1,1} \rvert > c \cdot mag\ z_1$	4.54	0.51
Model 4: $\lvert z_{t-1,2} \rvert > c \cdot mag\ z_2$	3.94	0.55
Model 5: Estimated AR(2) process for $z_{t,1}$	7.07	0.26
Model 6: Estimated AR(2) process for $z_{t,2}$	6.29	0.45

Table 22.12. *UK inflation rate: In-sample and out-of-sample mean squared errors (MSE)*

Model	In-sample MSE	Out-of-sample MSE
Model 10: $V_{t-1} = z_{t-1,1}$	4.33	0.29 with $\gamma = 0.18$
Model 11: $V_{t-1} = z_{t-1,2}$	2.63	0.51 with $\gamma = 0.17$
Model 12: $V_{t-1} = AR(2)$ process for $z_{t,1}$	4.02	0.89 with $\gamma = 0.54$
Model 13: $V_{t-1} = AR(2)$ process for $z_{t,2}$	2.85	0.22 with $\gamma = 0.21$

period. The results for the UK inflation rate are shown in Tables 22.11 and 22.12. These results are not in accordance with the previous example, in that the in-sample SSE does not provide information about the out-of-sample performance.

7. CONCLUSION

Preliminary results from these time-varying combination methods seem very encouraging. The time-varying methods considered in this paper are very easy to implement and can result in a substantial reduction in sum of squared forecast errors. The results from the empirical examples demonstrate that the combining schemes proposed in the paper can actually generate forecasts superior to those of sophisticated forecasting models, which would suggest that there are ways in which these sophisticated forecasting models can be improved.

APPENDIX

The two forecasts of the inflation rate are generated by two models which are slight modifications of those in Engle et al. (1984). The first model relates inflation to the growth in the stock of money. The estimated equation for the first model is:

$$\dot{p}_t = 2.22 + 0.26\dot{p}_{t-4} + 0.33\dot{M}_{t-1} - 1.41D1_t + 2.50D2_t + \text{residual}$$
$$\quad\ \ (1.36)\ (1.96)\quad\ \ (1.59)\quad\quad (1.93)\quad\ \ (3.20)$$
$$R^2 = 0.63 \quad D.W. = 1.97 \quad \sigma^2_{residual} = 2.36 \tag{A1}$$

(the moduli of t-values are shown in parentheses),
where P is the implicit price deflator for GNP, M is the monetary base and $D1$ and $D2$ are dummy variables included to account for the effects of wage and price controls in the early 1970s. Growth rates are 400 times the log differences. The sample period for the two models is 1969:3 to 1976:4. The second model is a version of the markup pricing model. The estimated forecasting equation for the second model is:

$$\dot{p}_t = 5.35 + 0.24\dot{p}_{t-1} + 0.03\dot{v}_{t-1} - 8.81(p - v)_{t-4} + \text{residual}$$
$$\quad\ \ (4.03)\ (1.31)\quad\ \ (1.67)\quad\ \ (2.80)$$
$$R^2 = 0.48 \quad D.W. = 1.76 \quad \sigma^2_{residual} = 3.04 \tag{A2}$$

where V is the factor price for crude materials. The above equations are used to generate forecasts from 1977:1 to 1987:1.

REFERENCES

Bacon, D. W. and D. G. Watts, 1971, Estimating the transition between two intersecting straight lines, *Biometrika*, 58, 525–534.

Bates, J. M. and C. W. J. Granger, 1969, The combination of forecasts, *Operations Research Quarterly*, 20, 451–468.

Diebold, F. X. and P. Pauly, 1987, Structural change and the combination of forecasts, *Journal of Forecasting*, 6 (1), 21–40

Engle, R. F., C. W. J. Granger and D. Kraft, 1984, Combining competing forecasts of inflation using a bivariate ARCH model, *Journal of Economic Dynamics and Control*, 8, 151–165.

Goldfeld, S. M. and R. E. Quandt, 1972, Nonlinear Methods in Econometrics (North-Holland, Amsterdam).

1973, A Markov model for switching regressions, *Journal of Econometrics*, 1, 3–16.

Granger, C. W. J. and P. Newbold, 1987, *Forecasting Economic Time Series* (Academic Press, New York).

Granger, C. W. J. and R. Ramanathan, 1984, Improved methods of combining forecasts, *Journal of Forecasting*, 3, 197–204.

Granger, C. W. J. and T. Teräsvirta, 1993, *Modeling Dynamic Nonlinear Relationships* (Oxford University Press, Oxford).

Hallman, J. and M. Kamstra, 1989, Combining algorithms based on robust estimation techniques and co-integration restrictions, *Journal of Forecasting*, 8, 189–198.

Holden, K. and D. A. Peel, 1989, Unbiasedness, Efficiency and the combination of economic forecasts, *Journal of Forecasting*, 8, 175–188.

LeSage, J. P. and M. Magura, 1992, A mixture-model approach to combining forecasts, *Journal of Business Economics and Statistics*, 10 (4), 445–452.

Lin, C. J. and T. Teräsvirta, 1994, Testing the constancy of regression parameters against continuous structural change, *Journal of Econometrics*, forthcoming.

Quandt, R. E., 1958, The estimation of the parameters of a linear regression system obeying two separate regimes, *Journal of the American Statistical Association*, 53, 873–880.

Sessions, D. N. and S. Chatterjee, 1989, The combining of forecasts using recursive techniques with non-stationary weights, *Journal of Forecasting*, 8 (3), 239–251.

Stockton, D. J. and J. E. Glassman, 1987, An evaluation of the forecasting performance of alternative models of inflation, *The Review of Economics and Statistics*, 108–117.

CHAPTER 23

Forecasting Transformed Series*
C. W. J. Granger and P. Newbold

Summary

Suppose that a forecasting model is available for the process X_t but that interest centres on the instantaneous transformation $Y_t = T(X_t)$. On the assumption that X_t is Gaussian and stationary, or can be reduced to stationarity by differencing, this paper examines the autocovariance structure of and methods for forecasting the transformed series. The development employs the Hermite polynomial expansion, thus allowing results to be derived for a very general class of instantaneous transformations.

Keywords: time series; forecasting; transformed variables; non-linear forecasts; hermite polynomials.

1. INTRODUCTION

Suppose that a time series analyst has derived a model for a series X_t, and thus can forecast this series, but then finds that he requires forecasts not of X_t but of an instantaneously transformed version

$$Y_t = T(X_t),$$

where $T(\ )$ is some well-behaved function. How should forecasts of Y_t be formed? This situation occurs frequently and may arise, for example:

(a) If an econometrician has built a model to explain price movement but, for reasons of his own, has used the logarithms of the basic variables in the model. This model will then provide forecasts of log prices, whereas the required end product is forecasts of prices, so that $X_t = \log \text{Price}_t$ and $Y_t = \exp (X_t)$. Recent econometric models also involve other transformations of the data, particularly for exogenous variables.

* *The Journal of the Royal Statistical Society* B 38, 1976, 189–203.

(b) If, to get data which are nearer Gaussian, the analyst first transforms his original data Y_t by using a Box and Cox (1964) transformation of the form

$$X_t = (Y_t - m)^\Theta.$$

The use of such transformations is mentioned, for example, in Box and Jenkins (1970), by Zarembka (1968) and by Wilson in the discussion on Chatfield and Prothero (1973).

Under the assumption that $\{X_t\}$ is a stationary Gaussian series and that the function $T(\ )$ can be expanded in a series of Hermite polynomials, Section 2 of this paper derives the auto-covariance properties of Y_t and several examples are given whereby the model obeyed by Y_t is derived from that for X_t. In Section 3, the stationarity assumption is somewhat relaxed by allowing X_t to be generated by an integrated mixed autoregressive moving average model. Section 4 considers the forecasting problem and four alternative methods of forecasting are considered and expressions obtained for the loss involved in not using the optimum forecast. The final section draws conclusions and suggests various generalizations.

The use of Hermite polynomials in tackling such problems was originated by Barrett and Lampard (1955) and has more recently been considered by Donelson and Maltz (1972) for a particular, continuous time, situation. The clear advantage of this method is the remarkable generality of the results that can be achieved, although it is very dependent on a Gaussian assumption for the X_t series.

For the convenience of readers unfamiliar with the properties of Hermite polynomials, the most important of these are listed in the Appendix together with a brief discussion of expansion of functions in a series of these polynomials.

2. AUTOCORRELATION PROPERTIES OF TRANSFORMED SERIES: THE STATIONARY CASE

Let X_t be a stationary Gaussian time series with mean μ, variance σ^2 and autocorrelation structure $\text{corr}(X_t, X_{t-\tau}) = \rho_\tau$. Let us set

$$Z_t = \frac{X_t - \mu}{\sigma} \text{ for all } t.$$

Then Z_t and $Z_{t-\tau}$ will be jointly distributed as bivariate Normal with zero means, unit variance and correlation ρ_τ.

Consider, now, an instantaneous transformation of the form $Y_t = T(Z_t)$ with expansion $T(Z) = \Sigma_{j=0}^{M} \alpha_j H_j(Z)$. Then

$$E(Y_{t-\tau}) = E\left\{\sum_{j=0}^{M}\alpha_j H_j(Z_{t-\tau})\right\} = \alpha_0 \qquad (2.1)$$

by (A.2), and hence the transformed series has mean α_0. Further, using (A.4)

$$E(Z_t Y_{t-\tau}) = E\left\{H_1(Z_t)\sum_{j=0}^{M}\alpha_j H_j(Z_{t-\tau})\right\} = \alpha_1 \rho_\tau \qquad (2.2)$$

and so the covariance between the transformed and original series is $\mathrm{cov}(X_t Y_{t-\tau}) = \alpha_1 \rho_\tau \sigma$.

Using (2.1), the autocovariance sequence of the transformed series is given by

$$C_{Y,\tau} = \mathrm{cov}(Y_t Y_{t-\tau}) = E\left\{\sum_{j=1}^{M}\alpha_j H_j(Z_t)\sum_{i=1}^{M}\alpha_i H_i(Z_{t-\tau})\right\} = \sum_{j=1}^{M}\alpha_j^2 j!\,\rho_\tau^j$$
$$(2.3)$$

by (A.1). In particular, setting $\tau = 0$ in this expression yields

$$\mathrm{var}(Y_t) = \sum_{j=1}^{M}\alpha_j^2 j!.$$

Thus the autocorrelation sequence of the transformed series is

$$\rho_{Y,\tau} = \sum_{j=1}^{M}\alpha_j^2 j!\,\rho_\tau^j \Bigg/ \sum_{j=1}^{M}\alpha_j^2 j!.$$

Hence, if $\rho_\tau \neq 0$ for some $\tau \neq 0$, it follows that

$$|\rho_{Y,\tau}| < |\rho_\tau| \text{ for } M > 1.$$

Thus, in a sense, the transformed series will be closer to white noise than the original series. We shall expand on this point in Section 4.

We now consider some specific examples of instantaneous transformations.

EXAMPLE 1: *Quadratic transformations*
    Consider first the transformation

$$Y_t = a + bX_t + cX_t^2 = a + b(\sigma Z_t + \mu) + c(\sigma Z_t + \mu)^2$$
$$= a + b\mu + c\mu^2 + (b + 2c\mu)\sigma Z_t + c\sigma^2 Z_t^2.$$

This can be written as

$$Y_t = T(Z_t) = \alpha_0 H_0(Z_t) + \alpha_1 H_1(Z_t) + \alpha_2 H_2(Z_t)$$
$$= \alpha_0 + \alpha_1 Z_t + \alpha_2(Z_t^2 - 1),$$

where

$$\alpha_0 = a + b\mu + c(\mu^2 + \sigma^2), \quad \alpha_1 = (b + 2c\mu)\sigma, \quad \alpha_2 = c\sigma^2. \tag{2.4}$$

It follows from (2.3) that the autocovariance sequence for the transformed series is

$$C_{Y,\tau} = \alpha_1^2 \rho_\tau + 2\alpha_2^2 \rho_\tau^2, \tag{2.5}$$

where α_1 and α_2 are given in (2.4). As we have seen in (2.4), the mean of the transformed series is α_0.

EXAMPLE 2: *Quadratic transformation of pth-order autoregressive process*

Suppose, now, that the original series X_t follows a pth-order autoregressive process. Then we can write

$$\rho_\tau = \sum_{j=1}^{p} a_j G_j^\tau, \quad |G_j| < 1 \quad \text{for } j = 1, 2, \ldots, p.$$

Thus

$$\rho_\tau^2 = \sum_{j=1}^{p} a_j^2 G_j^{2\tau} + 2\sum_{j<k} a_j a_k (G_j G_k)^\tau$$

and it follows from (2.5) that we can write, in general,

$$C_{Y\tau} = \sum_{j=1}^{p'} b_j F_j^\tau,$$

where $p' = p + \frac{1}{2}p(p + 1) = \frac{1}{2}p(p + 3)$. Thus, in general, the transformed series will have the same autocovariance structure as the sum of $\frac{1}{2}p(p + 3)$ independent first-order A.R. processes; i.e. it will in general be a mixed ARMA $\{\frac{1}{2}p(p + 3), \frac{1}{2}p(p + 1)\}$ process.

EXAMPLE 3: *The square of a first-order autoregressive process*

We now specialize Examples 1 and 2 to consider the case where X_t is a first-order auto-regressive process $\dot{X}_t - \phi \dot{X}_{t-1} = \varepsilon_t$, where $\dot{X}_t = X_t - \mu$ and ε_t is a white noise process with variance σ_ε^2. Hence $\rho_\tau = \phi^\tau$ and $\sigma^2 = \sigma_\varepsilon^2/(1 - \phi^2)$. We consider the transformation $Y_t = X_t^2$.

From (2.4) of Example 1, we see that this can be written as

$$Y_t = T(Z_t) = \alpha_0 H_0(Z_t) + \alpha_1 H_1(Z_t) + \alpha_2 H_2(Z_t),$$

where $\alpha_0 = \mu^2 - \sigma^2$, $\alpha_1 = 2\mu\sigma$, $\alpha_2 = \sigma^2$. Hence, from (2.1), we see that the transformed series has mean $\mu^2 + \sigma^2$ and from (2.5) that its autocovariance structure is given by

$$C_{Y,\tau} = \alpha_1^2 \rho_\tau + 2\alpha_2^2 \rho_\tau^2 = \sigma^2 (4\mu^2 \phi^\tau + 2\sigma^2 \phi^{2\tau}). \tag{2.6}$$

Thus Y_t will have the same autocovariance structure as $Y_{1,t} + Y_{2,t}$, where $Y_{1,t} - \phi Y_{1,t-1} = e_{1,t}$, $Y_{2,t} - \phi^2 Y_{2,t-1} = e_{2,t}$; $e_{1,t}$ and $e_{2,t}$ are independent white noise process with variances $4\mu^2\sigma^2(1 - \phi^2)$ and $2\sigma^4(1 - \phi^4)$ respectively. Hence Y_t has the autocovariance properties of the series

$$(1 - \phi B)(1 - \phi^2 B)Y_t = (1 - \phi^2 B)e_{1,t} + (1 - \phi B)e_{2,t},$$

where B is a back-shift operator on the index of the time series. As is well known, this model can be written in general as

$$(1 - \phi B)(1 - \phi^2 B)Y_t = (1 - \Theta B)e_t.$$

Note that if the mean μ is very large compared to σ, then the behaviour of the transformed series will approximate first-order autoregressive, as is clear from (2.6).

EXAMPLE 4: *Transformations of moving average processes*

Suppose, now, that X_t follows a moving average process of order q, i.e. $\rho_\tau = 0$ for $\tau > q$. It follows immediately from (2.3) that $C_{Y,\tau} = 0$ for $\tau > q$, and hence that for transformations of the type considered here, Y_t will have the autocovariance structure of a qth-order moving average process. In fact, more correctly, we should say that the transformed series is moving average of order at most q. Consider, for example, a quadratic transformation of a first-order moving average process. It follows from (2.5) that the resulting process will be white noise if

$$\rho_1 = -\alpha_1^2/2\alpha_2^2.$$

Perhaps at this stage we should re-emphasize the importance of our assumption of normality. Let us suppose

$$X_t = \varepsilon_t Z_t, \tag{2.7}$$

where ε_t is independent of ε_s for $t \neq s$, Z_t is a non-white noise sequence and the series ε_t and Z_t are mutually stochastically independent. Then it is straightforward to show that, while the series X_t is white noise, the series X_t^2 is not. However, X_t cannot be of the form (2.7) if it is Gaussian, since such an assumption would require X_t and X_s to be independent – not merely uncorrelated – for $t \neq s$.

EXAMPLE 5: *The exponential transformation*

Consider, finally, the transformation

$$Y_t = \exp(X_t) = \exp\left(\mu + \frac{1}{2}\sigma^2\right)\sum_{j=0}^{\infty}\frac{\sigma^j}{j!}H_j(Z_t)$$

since we can write $Y_t = \exp(\mu + \sigma Z_t)$. Hence, from (2.1), the means of the transformed series is

$$E(Y_t) = \exp\left(\mu + \frac{1}{2}\sigma^2\right) \tag{2.8}$$

and from (2.3) its autocovariance sequence is given by

$$C_{Y,\tau} = \exp(2\mu + \sigma^2) \sum_{j=1}^{\infty} \frac{(\sigma^2 \rho_\tau)^j}{j!}.$$

Thus

$$C_{Y,\tau} = \exp(2\mu + \sigma^2)\{\exp(\sigma^2 \rho_\tau) - 1\}. \tag{2.9}$$

Our purpose in this section has been to relate the autocovariance properties of a particular time series to those of certain instantaneous transformations of that series. We feel that this is important since power transformations of the Box-Cox (1964) type are in current use in univariate time series analysis. In building time series models, Box and Jenkins (1970) have devised an iterative strategy of model identification, estimation and diagnostic checking. The identification stage of their model building cycle relies on the recognition of typical patterns of behaviour in the sample autocorrelation function (and its transform, the partial auto-correlation function). Our results indicate that if the series to be fitted is subjected to instantaneous transformation, it can be the case (except for moving average processes) that the autocorrelation function of the transformed series exhibits markedly different behaviour patterns from that of the original series.

3. AUTOCORRELATION PROPERTIES OF TRANSFORMED SERIES: INTEGRATED PROCESSES

In this section we go on to examine the application of methods of the previous section to time series which require first differencing to produce stationarity. (That is, in the notation of Box and Jenkins (1970), we are considering ARIMA $(p,1,q)$ processes.) As has been noted by Newbold and Granger (1974), such series seem to occur very frequently in economics.

Let X_t be a time series such that

$$\nabla X_t = u_t, \tag{3.1}$$

where u_t is a stationary Gaussian time series with mean zero and variance σ_u^2. We consider (3.1) to have been generated by a model of the form

$$X_t = \mu + \sum_{j=1}^{t} u_j, \tag{3.2}$$

i.e. to have started at time $t = 0$ with $X_0 = \mu$. Let us write

$$C_{t,t'} = E\left(\sum_{j=1}^{t} u_j \sum_{i=1}^{t'} u_i\right). \tag{3.3}$$

Then from (3.2) and (3.3) X_t is Normally distributed with mean μ and variance $C_{t,t}$. Now, set $Z_t = (X_t - \mu)/\sqrt{C_{t,t}}$. Then Z_t and $Z_{t-\tau}$ will be jointly distributed as bivariate Normal with zero means, unit variances and correlation $\rho_{t,t-\tau} = C_{t,t-\tau}/\sqrt{(C_{t,t}C_{t-\tau,t-\tau})}$.

We consider an instantaneous transformation of the form

$$Y_t = T(Z_t) = \sum_{j=0}^{M} \alpha_j^{(t)} H_j(Z_t). \tag{3.4}$$

(Note that in (3.4), for reasons which will become clear later, $\alpha_j^{(t)}$ depends on t.) Using the arguments of the previous section, it follows immediately that

$$E(Y_t) = \alpha_0^{(t)}. \tag{3.5}$$

Further, an argument exactly analogous to that of the previous section yields

$$\text{cov}(Y_t, Y_{t-\tau}) = \sum_{j=1}^{M} \alpha_j^{(t)} \alpha_j^{(t-\tau)} j! \, \rho_{t,t-\tau}^j$$

and hence

$$E(Y_t Y_{t-\tau}) = \sum_{j=1}^{M} \alpha_j^{(t)} \alpha_j^{(t-\tau)} j! \, \rho_{t,t-\tau}^j + \alpha_0^{(t)} \alpha_0^{(t-\tau)}. \tag{3.6}$$

Now, typically, our interest will be in ∇Y_t rather than Y_t, and it follows immediately from (3.5) and (3.6) that

$$E(\nabla Y_t) = \alpha_0^{(t)} - \alpha_0^{(t-1)} \tag{3.7}$$

and

$$\text{cov}(\nabla Y_t, \nabla Y_{t-\tau}) = \sum_{j=1}^{M} \alpha_j^{(t)} \alpha_j^{(t-\tau)} j! \, \rho_{t,t-\tau}^j + \sum_{j=1}^{M} \alpha_j^{(t-1)} \alpha_j^{(t-\tau-1)} j! \, \rho_{t-1,t-\tau-1}^j$$
$$- \sum_{j=1}^{M} \alpha_j^{(t)} \alpha_j^{(t-\tau-1)} j! \, \rho_{t,t-\tau-1}^j - \sum_{j=1}^{M} \alpha_j^{(t-1)} \alpha_j^{(t-\tau)} j! \, \rho_{t-1,t-\tau}^j. \tag{3.8}$$

The results (3.7) and (3.8) are completely general, although it should be noted that the variances about the expectations in (3.8) are explosive. We shall consider two specific examples.

EXAMPLE 1: *Quadratic transformations*

Let us examine again the transformation $Y_t = a + bX_t + cX_t^2$. This can be written as $Y_t = T(Z_t) = \alpha_0^{(t)} + \alpha_1^{(t)} Z_t + \alpha_2^{(t)}(Z_t^2 - 1)$, where

$$\alpha_0^{(t)} = a + b\mu + c(\mu^2 + C_{t,t}), \quad \alpha_1^{(t)} = (b + 2c\mu)C_{t,t}^{\frac{1}{2}}, \quad \alpha_2^{(t)} = cC_{t,t}. \tag{3.9}$$

It follows from (3.7) that the mean of ∇Y_t is given by

$$E(\nabla Y_t) = c(C_{t,t} - C_{t-1,t-1}) = cE\left(u_t^2 + 2u_t \sum_{j=1}^{t-1} u_j\right). \tag{3.10}$$

We note that for large t, that is for a series assumed to have started up in the remote past ($t = 1$ in (3.2)), $E(\nabla Y_t)$ is very nearly constant if u_t constitutes a stationary process. (In fact it is exactly constant for all $t > q$ if u_t is a qth order moving average process.) Substituting $M = 2$ and (3.9) into (3.8), the autocovariances are obtained as

$$\text{cov}(\nabla Y_t \nabla Y_{t-\tau}) = (b + 2c\mu)^2 (C_{t,t-\tau} + C_{t-1,t-\tau-1} - C_{t,t-\tau-1} - C_{t-1,t-\tau})$$
$$+ c^2 (C_{t,t-\tau}^2 + C_{t-1,t-\tau-1}^2 - C_{t,t-\tau-1}^2 - C_{t-1,t-\tau}^2). \tag{3.11}$$

Thus, in particular, if $Y_t = X_t^2$ we have on substituting $b = 0$ and $c = 1$ in (3.10) and (3.11)

$$E(\nabla Y_t) = E\left(u_t^2 + 2u_t \sum_{j=1}^{t-1} u_j\right) \tag{3.12}$$

and

$$\text{cov}(\nabla Y_t \nabla Y_{t-\tau}) = 4\mu^2 (C_{t,t-\tau} + C_{t-1,t-\tau-1} - C_{t,t-\tau-1} - C_{t-1,t-\tau})$$
$$+ 2(C_{t,t-\tau}^2 + C_{t-1,t-\tau-1}^2 - C_{t,t-\tau-1}^2 - C_{t-1,t-\tau}^2). \tag{3.13}$$

EXAMPLE 2: *The square of an* ARIMA (1,1,0) *process*
Next we consider the case where u_t is generated by a first-order autoregressive process $u_t - \phi u_{t-1} = \varepsilon_t$ so that X_t follows the ARIMA (1,1,0) process $\nabla X_t - \phi \nabla X_{t-1} = \varepsilon_t$.
It follows from (3.12) that

$$E(\nabla Y_t) = C_{t,t} - C_{t-1,t-1} = \sigma_u^2 + 2\sigma_u^2 \sum_{j=1}^{t-1} \phi^j = \sigma_u^2 \left\{1 + \frac{2\phi(1 - \phi^{t-1})}{1 - \phi}\right\}.$$

Now, if we make the assumption that the series started up in the remote past, so that t is large and ϕ^t negligible, we have $E(\nabla Y_t) = C_{t,t} - C_{t-1,t-1} \simeq \sigma_u^2(1 + \phi)/(1 - \phi)$. Clearly, then, $C_{t,t} - C_{t-\tau,t-\tau} \simeq \tau \sigma_u^2(1 + \phi)/(1 - \phi)$. It then follows, from the definition (3.3), that

$$C_{t-j,t-j-\tau} = \frac{\sigma_u^2 \phi(1 - \phi^{t-j-\tau})(1 - \phi^\tau)}{1 - \phi^2} + C_{t,t} - \frac{(\tau + j)\sigma_u^2(1 + \phi)}{1 - \phi}$$

for all $j, \tau \geq 0$,

or, approximately, for large t,

$$C_{t-j,t-j-\tau} = \frac{\sigma_u^2 \phi}{1 - \phi^2}(1 - \phi^\tau) + C_{t,t} - \frac{(\tau + j)\sigma_u^2(1 + \phi)}{1 - \phi} \quad \text{for all } j, \tau \geq 0.$$

Further, from (3.3), $C_{t-j-\tau,t-j} = C_{t-j,t-j-\tau}$. Some straightforward, but tedious, algebra then produces from (3.13) the result $\text{cov}(\nabla Y_t, \nabla Y_{t-\tau}) = A(\tau) + B\phi^\tau + C\phi^{2\tau}$, where $A(\tau) = 0$ for all $\tau \neq 0$, $A(0) > 0$.

Thus ∇Y_t will have the same autocovariance structure as $\nabla Y_{1,t} + \nabla Y_{2,t} + \nabla Y_{3,t}$, where

$$\nabla Y_{1,t} + \phi \nabla Y_{1,t-1} = e_{1,t}, \ \nabla Y_{2,t} - \phi^2 \nabla Y_{2,t-1} = e_{2,t}, \ \nabla Y_{3,t} = e_{3,t},$$

where $e_{1,t}$, $e_{2,t}$, and $e_{3,t}$ are independent white noise processes. Hence ∇Y_t has the autocovariance properties of the model

$$(1 - \phi B)(1 - \phi^2 B)\nabla Y_t = (1 - \phi^2 B)e_{1,t} + (1 - \phi B)e_{2,t}$$
$$+ (1 - \phi B)(1 - \phi^2 B)e_{3,t}.$$

This model can be written, in general, as

$$(1 - \phi B)(1 - \phi^2 B)\nabla Y_t = (1 - \theta_1 B - \theta_2 B^2)e_t,$$

where e_t is a white noise process. Thus, in general, ∇Y_t has the same auto-covariance properties as an ARMA (2.2) process.

We have shown in this section that there is, in principle, no difficulty in applying the methods for analysing instantaneous transformations, developed in the previous section, to those time series which require first differencing to induce stationarity. Very general results can easily be obtained for a wide class of instantaneous transformations applied to time series of this kind – in particular we have derived formulae for the mean and autocovariance sequence of changes in the transformed series. As we have noted in some specific examples, the auto-covariance of the differenced series is not generally invariant under transformations.

4. FORECASTING TRANSFORMED VARIABLES

In this section we consider the situation where, standing at time n, one has a forecast $f_{n,h}$ of X_{n+h} which is optimum in the sense of quadratic loss, given an information set I_n (i.e. $f_{n,h} = E(X_{n+h} | I_n)$). In the formulation of forecasting models information from a wide variety of sources is typically taken into account. The information set should always include current and past values of the series to be forecast – a point which, while obvious to time series analysts, appears on occasion to be overlooked by economic forecasters. In addition, the information set will often include current and past values of related time series. Finally, non-quantitative considerations may be taken into account – thus economic forecasts derived from quantitative models are frequently modified judgmentally. The treatment which follows is not completely general in that we need to assume that the optimum forecast $f_{n,h}$ is Normally distributed. We assume that X_{n+h} has mean μ and variance σ^2 (the integrated process can be treated by employing the formulation (3.2), along the lines of Section 3), and in most of what follows it will be further assumed that X_t is a Gaussian process. Consider, now, an instantaneous transformation of the form $Y_{n+h} = T(Z_{n+h})$, where

$$Z_{n+h} = \frac{X_{n+h} - \mu}{\sigma}. \tag{4.1}$$

We consider four forecasts of Y_{n+h}:

(i) The optimal quadratic loss forecast of Y_{n+h} given the information set I_n. We denote this as $g_{n,h}^{(1)}$.

(ii) The naive forecast

$$g_{n,h}^{(2)} = T\{(f_{n,h} - \mu)/\sigma\}.$$

(iii) The forecast $g_{n,h}^{(3)}$ of Y_{n+h} which is optimal in the quadratic loss sense in the class of forecasts that are linear in $X_{n-j}; j \geq 0$.

(iv) The forecast $g_{n,h}^{(4)}$ of Y_{n+h} which is similarly optimal in the class of forecasts that are linear in $Y_{n-j}, j \geq 0$.

The forecast $g_{n,h}^{(1)}$

Let us write

$$X_{n+h} = f_{n,h} + e_{n,h},$$

i.e. $e_{n,h}$ is the h step ahead forecast error when X_{n+h} is optimally forecast on the basis of the information set I_n. Then, given the assumption of Normality, it follows that the conditional distribution of X_{n+h} given the available data is Normal with mean $f_{n,h}$ and variance $S^2(h)$, where $S^2(h) = \text{var}(e_{n,h})$. Let us write

$$W_{n+h} = \frac{X_{n+h} - f_{n,h}}{S(h)} \quad \text{and} \quad Y_{n+h} = \sum_{i=0}^{M} \gamma_i H_i(W_{n+h}).$$

This is an instantaneous transformation, since $f_{n,h}$ and $S(h)$ are here regarded as constant, so that in general the γ_i's will be functions of $f_{n,h}$ and $S(h)$. Then, since W_{n+h} is conditionally distributed as a standard Normal variate, it follows that the optimal quadratic loss forecast, i.e. the conditional expectation of $Y_{n,h}$, is by (2.1)

$$g_{n,h}^{(1)} = \gamma_0. \tag{4.2}$$

In evaluating the expected squared error of this and subsequent forecasts, two quantities are of interest – the conditional expectation given the data and the unconditional expectation which is simply the average of the first quantity over all possible realizations of the data set. It follows immediately from (2.3) that the expected squared forecast error, given the data, is

$$V_c^{(1)}(h) = \sum_{j=1}^{M} \gamma_j^2 \, j!. \tag{4.3}$$

The unconditional expected squared error can be found by writing

$$Y_{n+h} = \sum_{i=0}^{M} \alpha_i H_i(Z_{n+h}),$$

where Z_{n+h} is given by (4.1). In this formulation we can write

$$g_{n,h}^{(1)} = \sum_{j=0}^{M} \alpha_j A^j H_j(P),$$

where $A = \{1 - S^2(h)/\sigma^2\}^{\frac{1}{2}}$, $P = (f_{n,h} - \mu)/\{\sigma^2 - S^2(h)\}^{\frac{1}{2}}$. A little algebra then yields, using (A.5), the unconditional expected squared forecast error as

$$V^{(1)}(h) = \sum_{j=1}^{M} \alpha_j^2 \, j! (1 - A^{2j}). \tag{4.4}$$

In subsequent discussion of sub-optimal forecasts, the conditional expected squared error can be used to provide a measure of the loss in efficiency for a specific data set, while the unconditional quantity can be used to give a measure of expected loss.

Let us define, as a measure of the forecastability of a series from the given information set, the quantity

$$R_{h,Y}^2 = \frac{\mathrm{var}\left(g_{n,h}^{(1)}\right)}{\mathrm{var}(Y_{n+h})},$$

where $g_{n,h}^{(1)}$ is the optimum forecast of Y_{n+h} from the given information set, and $\mathrm{var}(Y_{n+h})$ is the unconditional variance. If the error of forecast is $\eta_{n,h}^{(1)}$, then

$$\mathrm{var}(Y_{n+h}) = \mathrm{var}\left(g_{n,h}^{(1)}\right) + \mathrm{var}\left(\eta_{n,h}^{(1)}\right)$$

and hence from (4.4)

$$R_{h,Y}^2 = \sum_{j=1}^{M} \alpha_j^2 \, j! \, A^{2j} \Big/ \sum_{j=1}^{M} \alpha_j^2 \, j!.$$

Then, since $0 < A^2 < 1$, and $R_{h,X}^2 = A^2$, it follows that $R_{h,Y}^2 < R_{h,X}^2$, for $M > 1$. Thus the transformed series Y is always less forecastable than the original series X, and in this sense is "nearer white noise".

We now illustrate the above results with two simple examples.

EXAMPLE 1

We consider first the transformation

$$Y_{n+h} = \exp(X_{n+h}).$$

This is of great importance, since frequently time series are analysed in logarithmic form, although inference concerning the original series is of primary concern. Now, we can write

$$Y_{n+h} = \exp\{f_{n,h} + S(h)W_{n+h}\}$$

$$= \exp\left\{f_{n,h} + \frac{1}{2}S^2(h)\right\}\sum_{j=0}^{\infty}\frac{S^j(h)}{j!}H_j(W_{n+h}).$$

Hence, by (4.2), the optimal forecast is

$$g_{n,h}^{(1)} = \exp\left\{f_{n,h} + \frac{1}{2}S^2(h)\right\}.$$

It follows from (4.3) that the conditional expected squared error is

$$V_c^{(1)}(h) = \exp\{2f_{n,h} + S^2(h)\}\sum_{j=1}^{\infty}\frac{S^{2j}(h)}{(j!)^2}j!$$

and hence $V_c^{(1)}(h) = \exp\{2f_{n,h} + S^2(h)\}[\exp\{S^2(h)\} - 1]$. Finally, writing from (4.1)

$$Y_{n+h} = \exp(\mu + \sigma Z_{n+h}),$$

it is straightforward to show that the unconditional variance (4.4) is

$$V^{(1)}(h) = \exp\{2(\mu + \sigma^2)\}[1 - \exp\{-S^2(h)\}]. \tag{4.5}$$

EXAMPLE 2

As a second example, we consider again the transformation $Y_{n+h} = X_{n+h}^2$ which may be written $Y_{n+h} = \gamma_0 + \gamma_1 H_1(W_{n+h}) + \gamma_2 H_2(W_{n+h})$, where

$$\gamma_0 = f_{n,h}^2 + S^2(h), \quad \gamma_1 = 2f_{n,h}S(h), \quad \gamma_2 = S^2(h).$$

Then, from (4.2), the optimal forecast is $g_{n,h}^{(1)} = f_{n,h}^{(2)} + S^2(h)$ and by (4.3) the conditional expected squared error is $V_c^{(1)}(h) = 4f_{n,h}^2 S^2(h) + 2S^4(h)$. Writing the polynomial expansion in terms of the Z_{n+h} of (4.1), it follows from (4.4) that the unconditional expected squared forecast error is

$$V^{(1)}(h) = 4(\mu^2 + \sigma^2)S^2(h) - 2S^4(h). \tag{4.6}$$

The forecast $g_{n,h}^{(2)}$

We now consider the naive forecast of Y_{n+h}, obtained by substituting $f_{n,h}$ for X_{n+h} in the transformation function $g_{n,h}^{(2)} = T\{(f_{n,h} - \mu)/\sigma\}$. The conditional expected squared forecast error is then simply the conditional mean of $(Y_{n+h} - g_{n,h}^{(2)})^2 = \{(Y_{n+h} - g_{n,h}^{(1)}) + (g_{n,h}^{(1)} - g_{n,h}^{(2)})\}^2$ and hence

$$V_c^{(2)}(h) = \sum_{j=1}^{M}\gamma_j^2 j! + (g_{n,h}^{(1)} - g_{n,h}^{(2)})^2.$$

Writing

$$g_{n,h}^{(2)} = \sum_{j=0}^{M} \alpha_j H_j \{(f_{n,h} - \mu)/\sigma\}$$

some straightforward but tedious algebra yields, using (A.5),

$$V^{(2)}(h) = \sum_{j=1}^{M} \alpha_j^2 j! (1 - A^{2j})$$

$$+ \sum_{j=0}^{M} A^{2j} (j!)^{-1} \left\{ \sum_{k=1}^{\left[\frac{1}{2}(M-j)\right]} \alpha_{j+2k} \frac{(j+2k)!}{k!} \left(-\frac{1}{2} B^2\right)^k \right\}^2, \quad (4.7)$$

where A is defined as in (4.4) and $B^2 = 1 - A^2$. The first term in this expression is simply $V^{(1)}(h)$ given in (4.4). The second term thus represents the average amount lost in squared error through use of the naive predictor. To illustrate, we return to our two examples.

EXAMPLE 1
   Consider again, the transformation

$$Y_{n,h} = \exp(X_{n,h}) = \exp(\mu + \sigma Z_{n,h}) = \exp\left(\mu + \frac{1}{2}\sigma^2\right) \sum_{j=0}^{\infty} \frac{\sigma^j}{j!} H_j(Z_{n,h}).$$

The first term in (4.7) is given by $V^{(1)}(h)$ in (4.5). To evaluate the second term we have

$$\sum_{j=0}^{M} A^{2j} (j!)^{-1} \left\{ \sum_{k=1}^{\left[\frac{1}{2}(M-j)\right]} \alpha_{j+2k} \frac{(j+2k)!}{k!} \left(-\frac{1}{2} B^2\right)^k \right\}^2$$

$$= \exp(2\mu + \sigma^2) \sum_{j=0}^{M} (A^2 \sigma^2)^j (j!)^{-1} \left\{ \sum_{k=1}^{\left[\frac{1}{2}(M-j)\right]} \left(-\frac{1}{2} B^2 \sigma^2\right)^k (k!)^{-1} \right\}^2$$

and as M tends to infinity, this expression tends to

$$\exp(2\mu + \sigma^2) \exp(\sigma^2 A^2) \left\{ 1 - \exp\left(-\frac{1}{2}\sigma^2\right)(1 - A^2)\right\}$$

or since $\sigma^2 A^2 = \sigma^2 - S^2(h)$, this term is given by

$$\exp\{2(\mu + \sigma^2)\} \left[\exp\left\{-\frac{1}{2} S^2(h)\right\} - \exp\{-S^2(h)\} \right]^2.$$

Thus, from (4.5), the expected squared error of the naive forecast is

$$V^{(2)}(h) = \exp\{2(\mu + \sigma^2)\}$$

$$\left(1 - \exp\{-S^2(h)\} + \left[\exp\left\{-\frac{1}{2} S^2(h)\right\} - \exp\{-S^2(h)\} \right]^2 \right).$$

We see, then, that use of the naive predictor leads to the proportionate increase in expected squared forecast error

$$\frac{V^{(2)}(h) - V^{(1)}(h)}{V^{(1)}(h)} = \frac{\left[\exp\left\{ -\frac{1}{2} S^2(h) \right\} - \exp\left\{ -S^2(h) \right\} \right]^2}{1 - \exp\left\{ -S^2(h) \right\}}.$$

EXAMPLE 2

We again consider the transformation,

$$Y_{n+h} = X_{n+h}^2 = \alpha_0 + \alpha_1 H_1(Z_{n+h}) + \alpha_2 H_2(Z_{n+h}).$$

In the second term of (4.7) only the value at $j = 0$ is different from zero. This term is then

$$\sum_{j=0}^{M} A^{2j} (j!)^{-1} \left\{ \sum_{k=1}^{\left[\frac{1}{2}(M-j) \right]} \alpha_{j+2k} \frac{(j+2k)!}{k!} \left(-\frac{1}{2} B^2 \right)^k \right\}^2 = \alpha_2^2 B^4$$

$$= \sigma^4 B^4 = S^4(h).$$

Thus, from (4.6), the expected squared error of the naive forecast is

$$V^{(2)}(h) = 4(\mu^2 + \sigma^2) S^2(h) - S^4(h).$$

Thus we see that use of the naive predictor leads to the proportionate increase in expected squared forecast error

$$\frac{V^{(2)}(h) - V^{(1)}(h)}{V^{(1)}(h)} = \frac{S^2(h)}{4(\mu^2 + \sigma^2) - 2S^2(h)}.$$

Up to this point we have been discussing only optimality with respect to quadratic loss functions. In fact it may in some situations be desirable to employ alternative loss functions, perhaps the most popular of which is to assume that loss is proportional to the absolute value of the forecast error. If this loss function is employed then it is well known (see, for example, Granger, 1969) that the optimal forecast of Y_{n+h} is the median of the conditional density function of Y_{n+h} given the information set I_n. It is straightforward to verify that this median is in fact the naive forecast $g_{n,h}^{(2)}$, provided the transformation from X to Y is bijective.

The forecast $g_{n,h}^{(3)}$

We now assume that the available information set consists only of current and past values of the series X, that is

$$I_n = (X_{n-j}, j \geq 0). \tag{4.8}$$

We consider forecasting the transformed variable as a linear combination of the members of this information set. Now, the covariance between

X_t and $Y_{t-\tau}$ follows from (2.2). Hence, the cross-spectrum between X_t and Y_t will be a constant times the spectrum of X_t, and from classical Kolmogorov theory of forecasting (see, for example, Whittle, 1963) it follows that the quadratic loss optimal forecast of Y_{n+h} which is linear in the members of I_n is

$$g_{n,h}^{(3)} = \alpha_0 + \alpha_1\left(\frac{f_{n,h} - \mu}{\sigma}\right).$$

The forecast error is then

$$\eta_{n,h}^{(3)} = Y_{n+h} - g_{n,h}^{(3)} = \sum_{j=0}^{M} \alpha_j H_j\left(\frac{X_{n+h} - \mu}{\sigma}\right) - \left\{\alpha_0 - \alpha_1\left(\frac{f_{n,h} - \mu}{\sigma}\right)\right\}.$$

It is then straightforward to verify that the unconditional expected squared forecast error is

$$V^{(3)}(h) = E\left\{\left(\eta_{n,h}^{(3)}\right)^2\right\} = \sum_{j=2}^{M} \alpha_j^2 j! + \alpha_1^2 S^2(h)/\sigma^2.$$

Of course, the conditional expected squared error is simply

$$V_c^{(3)}(h) = V_c^{(1)}(h) + \left(g_{n,h}^{(1)} - g_{n,h}^{(3)}\right)^2.$$

The forecast $g_{n,h}^{(4)}$

We again assume that the available information set is (4.8), and now consider the problem of forecasting Y_{n+h} as a linear combination of Y_{n-j}; $j \geq 0$. Now, the mean and autocovariance structure of the transformed series are given in (2.1) and (2.3), and corresponding results for integrated processes in (3.7) and (3.8). Thus, in principle, the problem of optimal linear forecasting is solved.

In practice, the solution is greatly facilitated in those cases where one can readily find a linear stochastic model possessing the appropriate autocovariance structure. To illustrate, we consider only the stationary case. Let us assume that an appropriate model is of the form

$$\phi(B)(Y_t - \alpha_0) = \theta(B)e_t, \tag{4.9}$$

where $\phi(B) = 1 - \phi_1 B - \phi_2 B^2 - \ldots - \phi_p B^p$, $\theta(B) = 1 - \theta_1 B - \theta_2 B^2 - \ldots - \theta_q B^q$, and e_t is a white noise process. The mean α_0 is subtracted, as indicated by (2.1). Then optimal forecasts may be derived from (4.9) in the usual fashion (see, for example, Box and Jenkins, 1970). Further, the variance of the optimal linear forecast is given by

$$V^{(4)}(h) = \sigma_e^2(1 + \psi_1^2 + \ldots + \psi_{h-1}^2), \tag{4.10}$$

where σ_e^2 is the variance of e_t and $\phi(B)(1 + \psi_1 B + \psi_2 B^2 + \ldots) = \theta(B)$.

Of course, it may not always be straightforward to discover a linear model with the given autocovariance structure. However, a stationary process can always be written as an infinite order moving average, and for some sufficiently large integer Q this process can be terminated with very little loss of information. That is, we can write approximately

$$Y_t - \alpha_0 = (1 + \psi_1 B + \psi_2 B^2 + \ldots + \psi_Q B^Q) e_t.$$

Wilson (1969) gives an algorithm for obtaining the ψ_j's and σ_e^2 from a given set of auto-covariances, and Q can be chosen so that subsequent values of $\psi_j; j > Q$ are negligibly small. The variance of the optimal linear forecast is again given by (4.10).

We illustrate these results with a single simple example. Suppose X_t is generated by the first order moving average process

$$X_t - \mu = \varepsilon_t + 0.5\varepsilon_{t-1}. \tag{4.11}$$

We assume, as usual, that X_t has variance σ^2, so that ε_t has variance $0.8\sigma^2$. the auto-correlations of the X_t process are then

$$\rho_1 = 0.4, \quad \rho_\tau = 0, \quad \tau > 1. \tag{4.12}$$

We consider again the transformation $Y_t = \exp(X_t)$. The mean and auto-covariance sequence of the transformed series are given in (2.8) and (2.9) respectively. Hence the variance is

$$C_{Y,0} = \exp(2\mu + \sigma^2)\{\exp(\sigma^2) - 1\} \tag{4.13}$$

and the autocorrelations are

$$\rho_{Y,\tau} = \{\exp(\sigma^2 \rho_\tau) - 1\} / \{\exp(\sigma^2) - 1\}.$$

Thus from (4.12) we have

$$\rho_{Y,1} = \{\exp(0.4\sigma^2) - 1\} / \{\exp(\sigma^2) - 1\}, \quad \rho_{Y,\tau} = 0, \quad \tau > 1. \tag{4.14}$$

It follows from (4.14) that the transformed process is a first order moving average. To consider a specific example, let us assume that σ^2 is unity. Then $\rho_{Y,1} = 0.286$. Thus, using (2.8), Y_t follows the process

$$Y_t - \exp\left(\mu + \frac{1}{2}\right) = e_t + 0.31 e_{t-1}, \tag{4.15}$$

where $\sigma_e^2 = \{1 + (0.31)^2\}^{-1} C_{Y,0}$. Hence, $\sigma_e^2 = 4.26 \exp(2\mu)$. Thus, from (4.15), the variance of the forecast errors is

$$V^{(4)}(1) = 4.26 \exp(2\mu), \quad V^{(4)}(h) = 4.67 \exp(2\mu), \quad h \geq 1.$$

This may be compared with the expected squared error of the optimum forecast, which is given in (4.5). From (4.11) it follows that $S^2(1) = 0.8$, $S^2(h) = 1$, $h \geq 1$. Substituting in (4.5) we than find that $V^{(1)}(1) = 4.07 \exp(2\mu)$, $V^{(1)}(h) = 4.67 \exp(2\mu)$, $h \geq 1$. Thus we see, as expected, that there is no loss in using the linear model for forecasting more than one step ahead. For-one-step ahead forecasts, the proportionate increase in mean squared error from use of the linear model is

$$\{V^{(4)}(1) - V^{(1)}(1)\}\{V^{(1)}(1)\}^{-1} = 0.047.$$

In those cases where a simple linear model cannot be found that corresponds exactly to the autocovariance sequence of the Y's, one can in theory at least, turn to purely analytical methods to find the forecast error variances. Let the spectrum of X_t be $f(\omega)$ and denote by $C[f(\omega), g(\omega)]$ the convolution of the two functions $f(\omega)$ and $g(\omega)$, so that

$$C\{f(\omega), g(\omega)\} = \int_{-\pi}^{\pi} f(\omega - \lambda) g(\lambda) d\lambda$$

and let $C[\{f(\omega)\}^{\kappa}]$ be the κ-fold convolution of $f(\omega)$ on itself, so that

$$C\left[\{f(\omega)\}^{\kappa}\right] = C\left(f(\omega), C\left[\{f(\omega)\}^{\kappa-1}\right]\right);$$

then the Fourier transform of the sequence ρ_t^j is just $C[\{f(\omega)\}^j]$. Thus, from (2.3), the spectrum of Y_t, $f_Y(\omega)$, is given by

$$f_Y(\omega)\sigma_Y^2 = \sum_{j=1}^{m} \alpha_j^2 j! C\left[\{f(\omega)\}^j\right].$$

The minimum one-step error variance achievable from a linear forecast based on present and past Y_t's is then given by

$$V^{(4)}(1) = \exp \frac{1}{2\pi} \int_{-\pi}^{\pi} \log 2\pi f_Y(\omega) d\omega$$

and, for any given sequence ρ_τ, this value can be found by numerical integration. Similar, but more complicated expressions exist for $V^{(4)}(h)$.

In practice, when one is given just data in the first place, it will always be possible to find a linear model that will have a spectrum that well approximates $f_Y(\omega)$. Intuition, as well as the Box-Jenkins principle of parsimony, suggests that a mixed autoregressive, moving average model will generally provide the best approximation. Once this model has been identified and estimated, forecasts can be generated in the standard way.

5.   CONCLUSIONS

If one is faced with the task of forming the forecast of a transformed variable given a model for X_t, our results suggest that one can frequently do very much better than using $g_{n,h}^{(2)}$, the naive forecast, in which the optimum forecast of X_{n+h} is inserted into the transforming function. For many of the models and transformations met in practice, it is possible to find the optimum forecast for Y_{n+h} and this is to be recommended. However, some extra effort is required to do this and for speed one could either use the naive forecast or the linear forecast of Y_{n+h} based on X_{n-j}, $j \geq 0$, i.e. $g_{(3)}^{n,h}$. Neither is necessarily near to the optimal forecast and one is not clearly always superior to the other, but both are easily obtained. A better compromise might be to combine these two simple forecasts, as suggested by Bates and Granger (1969) and investigated by Newbold and Granger (1974), but no exercise is yet available on combining this particular pair of forecasts. The methods given in this paper enable a very wide class of transformations and models to be considered, although in some cases the amount of algebraic manipulation required to find the optimum forecast, or the loss from using a sub-optimal one, is rather large.

Although the paper has considered just instantaneous transformations of the form $Y_t = T(X_t)$ there is no difficulty in extending the results to cover transformations of the form

$$Y_t = T(\Sigma_j X_{t-j}), \quad Y_t = \sum_{j=0}^{Q} T_j(X_{t-j}).$$

Further, if one's original data are of the form $X_t = X'_t + \mu_t$, where X'_t is a Gaussian, stationary process and μ_t is some deterministic component, such as a trend or a seasonal factor, then the methods derived above can be applied to $X_t - \mu_t$, but the coefficients α_j in the expansion of $T(x)$ in terms of Hermite polynomials will in general now depend on μ_t, and hence will no longer be time invariant. As was suggested in Section 3, this presents no great extra difficulty.

The theory outlined above cannot be directly applied to multiple functions, such as $T(X_t, X_{t-j})$ or $T(X_t^{(1)}, X_t^{(2)})$. The case of this type that arises frequently in practice, particularly in econometrics, is where the series are used in product or ratio form. It is hoped to consider these structures in a later paper. The theory also cannot be applied to the types of non-linear iterative models considered by Nelson and Van Ness (1973), as the resulting series will not be Gaussian. The formation of optimal h-step forecasts from such models appears to be a formidable problem and was not considered by Nelson and Van Ness.

APPENDIX

Properties of Hermite Polynomials

The system of Hermite polynomials $H_n(x)$ is defined in terms of the standard Normal distribution as

$$H_n(x) = \exp(x^2/2)\left(\frac{-d}{dx}\right)^n \exp(-x^2/2) \quad \text{or}$$

$$H_n(x) = (-1)^n \phi^{(n)}(x)/\phi(x),$$

where ϕ is the standard Normal p.d.f. Explicitly, we can write

$$H_n(x) = n! \sum_{m=0}^{[n/2]} (-1)^m \{2^m \, m! (n-2m)!\}^{-1} x^{n-2m},$$

where $[N]$ is the largest integer less than or equal to N. Thus, one has

$$H_0(x) = 1, \quad H_1(x) = x, \quad H_2(x) = x^2 - 1,$$
$$H_3(x) = x^3 - 3x, \quad H_4(x) = x^4 - 6x^2 + 3, \quad H_5(x) = x^5 - 10x^3 + 15x$$

and so on.

We define expectation operators E_0 and E such that

$$E_0\{\psi(x)\} = (2\pi)^{-\frac{1}{2}} \int_{-\infty}^{\infty} \psi(x) \exp(-x^2/2) dx,$$

$$E\{\psi(x)\} = (2\pi\sigma^2)^{-\frac{1}{2}} \int_{-\infty}^{\infty} \psi(x) \exp\{-(x-\mu)^2/2\sigma^2\} dx.$$

The Hermite polynomials constitute an orthogonal system with respect to the standard Normal p.d.f., so that

$$E_0\{H_n(x)H_k(x)\} = \begin{cases} 0, & n \neq k, \\ n!, & n = k, \end{cases} \tag{A.1}$$

and since $H_0(x) = 1$, it follows that

$$E_0\{H_n(x)\} = 0, \quad n > 0. \tag{A.2}$$

The polynomials obey the recursion formula $H_{n+1}(x) - xH_n(x) + nH_{n-1}(x) = 0$ and have as a generating function

$$\exp(tx - t^2/2) = \sum_{n=0}^{\infty} H_n(x) t^n / n!. \tag{A.3}$$

A particularly important result is that the bivariate Normal p.d.f. for variables with the same variance may be written

$$f(x_1, x_2) = \frac{(1-\rho^2)^{-\frac{1}{2}}}{2\pi\sigma^2} \exp\left\{ -\frac{1}{2} \frac{x_1^2 + x_2^2 - 2\rho x_1 x_2}{\sigma^2(1-\rho^2)} \right\}$$

$$= \frac{1}{2\pi\sigma^2} \exp\left\{ \frac{-1}{2\sigma^2}(x_1^2 + x_2^2) \right\} \sum_{n=0}^{\infty} \frac{\rho^n H_n(x_1/\sigma) H_n(x_2/\sigma)}{n!},$$

a formula due to Mehler. It than follows that if X and Y are distributed as bivariate Normal with zero means, unit variances and correlation coefficient ρ

$$E\{H_n(X)|Y = y\} = \rho^n H_n(y)$$

and

$$E\{H_n(X)H_k(Y)\} = \begin{cases} 0, & n \neq k, \\ \rho^n n!, & n = k. \end{cases} \tag{A.4}$$

A further useful result is the summation formula

$$H_n(Ax + By) = \sum_{k=0}^{n} {}_nC_k A^k B^{n-k} H_k(x)H_{n-k}(y), \quad \text{for } A^2 + B^2 = 1. \tag{A.5}$$

A general method for obtaining the Hermite polynomial expansion for a function $T(x)$ follows by noting that if

$$\sum_{j=0}^{\infty} \alpha_j H_j(x) = T(x)$$

then $\alpha_n = E_0\{(d/dx)^n T(x)\}/n!$. If $T(x)$ is any function such that $E_0\{T(x)\} < \infty$, then there always exists an asymptotic expansion of the form $T(x) = \lim S_N(x)$ as $N \to \infty$, where

$$S_N(x) = \sum_{j=0}^{N} \alpha_j H_j(x)$$

and such that $\lim E_0[\{T(x) - S_N(x)\}^2] = 0$ as $N \to \infty$. Some particular expansions are

$$|x|^{\lambda} = \alpha_0 + \alpha_0 \sum_{m=1}^{\infty} \left\{ \prod_{V=0}^{m-1} (\lambda - 2V) \right\} H_{2m}(x)/(2m)!, \quad \lambda + 1 > 0,$$

where

$$\alpha_0 = 2^{\lambda/2} \Gamma\left\{ \frac{1}{2}(\lambda + 1) \right\} \Big/ \Gamma\left(\frac{1}{2} \right),$$

and

$$|x|^{\lambda+1} \operatorname{sign} x = (\lambda + 1)\alpha_0 \left\{ H_1(x) + \sum_{m=1}^{\infty} \prod_{V=0}^{m-1} (\lambda - 2V) H_{2m+1}(x)/(2m+1)! \right\},$$

$$\lambda + 2 > 0.$$

The expansion for $\exp(tx)$ is obtained from the generating function (A.3).

A comprehensive account of the properties of Hermite polynomials and indications of proofs of some of the above results may be found in Erdélyi *et al.* (1953, Vol. 2, Chapter 10), although care must be taken over notational differences.

ACKNOWLEDGEMENT

We wish to thank the referee for suggestions which improved both the content and presentation of this paper.

REFERENCES

BARRETT, J. F. and LAMPARD, D. G. (1955). An expansion for some second order probability distributions and its application to noise problems. *I.R.E. Trans. PGIT*, IT-1, 10–15.

BATES, J. M. and GRANGER, C. W. J. (1969). The combination of forecasts. *Oper. Res. Q.*, 20, 451–468.

BOX, G. E. P. and COX, D. R. (1964). An analysis of transformations. *J. R. Statist. Soc.* B, 26, 211–243.

BOX, G. E. P. and JENKINS, G. M. (1970). *Times Series Analysis, Forecasting and Control*. San Francisco: Holden-Day.

CHATFIELD, C. and PROTHERO, D. L. (1973). Box-Jenkins seasonal forecasting: problems in a case study. *J. R. Statist. Soc.* A, 136, 295–336.

DONELSON, J. and MALTZ, F. (1972). A comparison of linear versus non-linear prediction for polynomial functions of the Ornstein–Uhlenbeck process. *J. Appl. Prob.*, 9, 725–744.

ERDÉLYI, A. *et al.* (1953). *Higher Transcendental Functions*. Bateman Manuscript Project. New York: McGraw-Hill.

GRANGER, C. W. J. (1969). Prediction with a generalized cost of error function. *Oper. Res. Q.*, 20, 199–207.

NELSON, J. Z. and VAN NESS, J. W. (1973). Choosing a non-linear predictor. *Technometrics*, 15, 219–231.

NEWBOLD, P. and GRANGER, C. W. J. (1974). Experience with forecasting univariate time series and the combination of forecasts. *J. R. Statist. Soc.* A, 137, 131–146.

WHITTLE, P. (1963). *Prediction and Regulation*. London: English Universities Press.

WILSON, G. T. (1969). Factorization of the generating function of a pure moving average process. *SIAM J. Numer. Analysis*, 6, 1–7.

ZAREMBKA, P. (1968). Functional form in the demand for money. *J. Amer. Statist. Assoc.*, 63, 502–511.

CHAPTER 24

Forecasting White Noise*

C. W. J. Granger**

1. INTRODUCTION

It is well known that if x_t is a time series and that if one attempts to forecast x_{n+1} using a least-squares criterion and information set $I_n = \{\underline{z}_{n-k},\ k \geq 0\}$ where $\underline{z}_t$ is a vector of time series including x_t as a component, then the optimum forecast is $f_{n,1} = E[x_{n+1} | I_n]$ and the resulting forecast error, $e_{n,1} = x_{n+1} - f_{n,1}$, is white noise. This fact is doubtless the reason why a number of eminent time series analysts have made statements which might be summarized as: "The objective of time series analysis is to find a filter which, when applied to the series being considered, results in white noise." This statement applies to both univariate and multivariate series. Presumably this position is justified because a white noise cannot be forecast so that once white noise is achieved no further modeling needs to be considered. It will be shown in this paper that such a position is over simplistic. One can achieve white noise, but it may not be the best one available, so that better models and improved forecasts can be achieved. Three types of white noise will be considered:

1. A time series x_t will be called white noise (w.n.) if

$$\text{correlation}\ (x_t, x_{t-k}) = 0, \quad \text{all } k \neq 0$$

2. x_t will be called pure white noise (p.w.n.) if x_t, x_{t-k} are independent for all $t, k \neq 0$. Clearly, if x_t is Gaussian and white noise, then it will be pure white noise, but pure white noise need not be Gaussian. In all cases, it will be assumed that $E[x_t]$ is zero and variance (x_t) is finite.

* *Proceedings of the Conference on Applied Time Series Analysis of Economic Data*, October 1981, edited by A. Zellner, U.S. Department of Commerce, Bureau of the Census, Government Printing Office, 1983, 308–314.

** The author would like to thank Robert Engle and Ian Domowitz for helpful discussions and John Conlisk for most of the material in section 5. This work was supported by NSF grants SES 80-04414 and SES 80-08580.

3. x_t will be called empirical white noise if

$$\bar{x}_n = \frac{1}{n}\sum_{t=1}^{n} x_t$$

and

$$\lim_{n\to\infty}\frac{1}{n-k}\sum_{t=k}^{t=n}(x_t-\bar{x}_n)(x_{t-k}-\bar{x}_n)=0,\quad \text{all } k\neq 0$$

Thus, the estimated autocorrelogram will, in the limit, be the same as that of white noise.

In this paper, a variety of models will be considered which produce series that are at least empirical white noise but which are somewhat forecastable. The measure of the usefulness of a forecasting model that is used is

$$R^2 = 1-\frac{\text{var}(e_{n,1})}{\text{var}(x_n)}$$

where $e_{n,1}$ is the one-step forecast error resulting from the forecast. If any of the components of R^2 are not time invariant, they will be replaced by their average values.

2.   CAUSAL VARIABLES

It might be though that a pure white noise is inherently unforecastable, but a simple example shows this not to be true, as if $x_t = y_{t-1} + e_t$ where y_t, e_t are independent, pure white noise series, then if y_t is observable, x_t will be p.w.n. but forecastable, with

$$R^2 = 1-\frac{\text{var } e_t}{\text{var } x_t}$$

which can take any value between 0 and 1. Thus, x_t is not forecastable just from its own past but becomes forecastable when past values of y_t are added to the information set.

More general cases where the introduction of a new variable produces useful forecasts include

$$a(B)x_t = b(B)y_t + e_t \tag{2.1}$$

and

$$x_t = \beta(B)y_t + \gamma(B)e_t \tag{2.2}$$

where x_t, y_t, and e_t are all zero-mean white noise series and $a(B)$, etc., are polynomials in the backward operator B. As it is necessary that the spectra of both sides of the equation are equal, it follows that $a(B)$ and

$b(B)$ are polynomials of the same order, and similarly for $\beta(B)$ and $\gamma(B)$, and the following conditions hold

$$|a(z)|^2 \sigma_x^2 = |b(z)|^2 \sigma_y^2 + \sigma_e^2 \quad \text{(all } z)$$

and

$$\sigma_x^2 = |\beta(z)|^2 \sigma_y^2 + |\gamma(z)|^2 \sigma_e^2 \quad \text{(all } z)$$

where $z = e^{-i\omega}$. It is interesting to note that if more than one lagged y_t is involved, it is necessary to use lagged x's, either directly or when estimating lagged e's. It should also be noted that x_t given by (2.2) can be pure white noise if it is Gaussian.

These models indicate that quite complicated temporal structures can lead to white noise. It is interesting to ask, if the autocorrelations of the two components in (2.2) increase in magnitude, will the forecastability of x_t decrease? In at least one simple case, this does seem to occur. Consider the model

$$x_t = \beta_0 y_{t-1} + \beta_1 y_{t-2} + \varepsilon_t + b\varepsilon_{t-1}$$

in the special form

$$x_t = \beta_0 [\mu y_{t-1} + (1-\mu) y_{t-2}] + \varepsilon_t + b\varepsilon_{t-1}$$

As μ varies the distribution of the weights between the two lagged y's varies. If one denotes

$$Z_t = \mu y_{t-1} + (1-\mu) y_{t-2}$$

then as μ increases from 0 to $\frac{1}{2}$, the first-order autocorrelation of Z_t, ρ_1^z, rises to a maximum and similarly R_x^2 falls to minimum. Then as μ increases from $\frac{1}{2}$ to 1, ρ_1^z falls back to zero and R_x^2 increases once again. Thus, the forecastability of x_t does depend on the extent of the autocorrelations of the components of x_t.

A practical application of the search for causal variables may be found in Ashley and Granger (1979). Although regression techniques may be used to find useful causal variables, an optimum procedure to be used when the series to be explained is known to be white noise is difficult to obtain because of the nonlinear and complicated constraints on the parameters involved. Further research seems to be required on this topic.

3. INSTANTANEOUS TRANSFORMATIONS

If x_t is a Gaussian series and $w_t = g(x_t)$ is an instantaneously $(1-1)$ transformed series, then using optimum forecasts based on the univariate information set $l_t: \{x_{t-k}, k \geq 0\}$ or equivalently, $\{w_{t-k}\}$, it was shown in Granger and Newbold (1976) that

$$R_x^2 \geq R_W^2$$

Thus, x_t is always more forecastable than the transformed series. The question arises, can a forecastable series be transformed into white noise? It is shown in Granger and Newbold (1976) that if x_t is Gaussian and has zero mean unit variance and $g(x)$ can be expanded in terms of Hermite polynomials as

$$g(x) = \sum_{j=0}^{M} \alpha_j H_j(x)$$

then the τth autocorrelations of x_t, w_t, denoted by ρ_τ and $\rho_{w,\tau}$, are related by

$$\rho_{w,\tau} = \sum_{j=1}^{M} \alpha_j^2 \, j! \, \rho^{\tau j} \bigg/ \sum_{j=1}^{M} \alpha_j^2 \, j!$$

It follows that if any ρ_τ is positive, then the corresponding $\rho_{w,\tau}$ will also be positive, so w_t cannot be white noise. Thus, for example, no AR(1) model can be transformed to white noise, as $\rho_2 > 0$.

However, consider the MA(1) model series

$$x_t = \varepsilon_t + b\varepsilon_{t-1}$$

and if

$$w_t = \alpha_1 x_t + \alpha_2(x_t^2 - 1)$$

then if

$$\frac{\alpha_1^2}{2\alpha_2^2} = \frac{-b}{1+b^2}$$

so that b must be negative, it follows that

$$\rho_{w,\tau} = 0 \quad \text{all } \tau > 0$$

Thus, it is possible that a series cannot be forecast linearly from its own past (w_t here), whereas there is a transformed series that is forecastable (x_t). In fact, if x_t is known, then w_t can be forecast from it.

It is unclear how one would ever detect such hidden nonlinear forecastability. The assumption of normality is critical to the theory given above, and if one's data, w_t, is nonnormal, it may be worthwhile to search for an instantaneous transformation that produces a series x_t that is Gaussian. However, note that the sequence $x_t, t = 1, \ldots, n$ has to be multivariate normal, and marginal normality is not sufficient. Finding such a transformation may be very difficult, and it is doubtful if the Box-Cox transformations are general enough to be useful.

4.   BILINEAR MODELS

A simple, single-term bilinear model is of the form

$$x_t = \beta x_{t-j}\varepsilon_{t-k} + \varepsilon_t$$

It is shown in Granger and Andersen (1978a) that the superdiagonal form of this model, for which $j > k$, is white noise, is stable if $\beta\sigma_\varepsilon < 1$ and can be invertible so that for some value of $\beta\sigma_\varepsilon$, the ε_t series can be estimated from the model x_t. In particular, for the model

$$x_t = \beta x_{t-2}\varepsilon_{t-1} + \varepsilon_t \tag{4.1}$$

the model is invertible if $\beta\sigma_\varepsilon < 0.707$ and one finds $R^2 = \beta^2\sigma_\varepsilon^2$. Thus R^2 varies between 0 and 0.5 for models that are stable, appear to be white noise, but are forecastable (nonlinearly) from the past of the series.

There are many other bilinear models with similar properties. For example, the diagonal bilinear model (extended by adding MA(1) terms) of the form

$$x_t = \beta x_{t-1}\varepsilon_{t-1} + \varepsilon_t + b\varepsilon_{t-1}$$

is easily shown to be white noise, provided $b = -\beta^2\sigma_\varepsilon^2$ and R^2 ranges between 0 and 0.667 for invertible forms of the model. It is interesting to note that simple bilinear models cannot be extended by AR(1) terms, such as

$$x_t = \alpha x_{t-1} + \beta x_{t-1}\varepsilon_{t-k} + \varepsilon_t$$

and become white noise unless $\alpha = 0$.

A broader class of models that are not forecastable linearly, even with a wider information set, was noted by Granger and Andersen (1978a). Suppose that y_t and u_t are both Gaussian white noise series and that x_t is generated by

$$x_t = \beta y_{t-1}x_{t-1} + u_t$$

then

$$\text{corr}(x_t, x_{t-k}) = 0 \quad (\text{all } k \neq 0)$$

and

$$\text{corr}(x_t, y_{t-k}) = 0, \quad (\text{all } k)$$

so that the bivariate series (x_t, y_t) is white noise, and yet x_t is forecastable (nonlinearly) from knowledge of past x_t and y_t. More complicated cases, possibly involving feedback, are easily found.

The Lagrange multiplier test (see Engle 1979, for instance) to distinguish between the bilinear model (4.1) and white noise suggests use of an estimate of $E[x_t x_{t-1} x_{t-2}]$ as an appropriate statistic. If (4.1) is the correct model, this quantity has value $\beta \sigma_\varepsilon^2 \mathrm{var}(x_t)$, so the appropriate test seems to be to regress x_t on x_{t-1}, x_{t-2} and see if the regression coefficient is significantly different from zero. It might be noted that the residual is white noise for this regression under both the null and the alternative hypothesis and so the standard test will be efficient. Appropriate tests for other bilinear models are also easily devised.

An alternative test procedure, suggested and used in Granger and Andersen (1978a), is to look at the serial correlations of x_t^2 which will be those corresponding to white noise if x_t is pure white noise but not if x_t is generated by a bilinear model.

5. NORMED MARKOV CHAINS

Consider a series x_t that can only take values $x(k), k = 1, 2, \ldots, N$. If $x_t = x(k)$, it will be said to be in state k at time t. Suppose further that the probability that x_t is in state k depends only on its state at time $t - 1$ and not on states at previous times, so that

$$\mathrm{Prob}\,(x_t = x(j) | \, x_{t-1} = x(i), x_{t-2} = x(k), x_{t-3}$$
$$= x(m)\ldots) = \mathrm{Prob}\,(x_t = x(j) | \, x_{t-1} = x(i)) = P_{ij}$$

Thus, P_{ij} is the transition probability from state i to state j, and the matrix $\underline{P} = \{P_{ij}\}$, is the transition probability matrix. Thus, x_t becomes a normed Markov chain. The columns of $\underline{P}$ add to 1,

$$\sum_i P_{ji} = 1, \quad \text{each } j$$

The equilibrium marginal probabilities π_j are defined by

$$\pi_j = \lim_{t \to \infty} \mathrm{Prob}\,(x_t = x(j))$$

and, from the usual Markov chain theory, are given by

$$\underline{\pi} = \underline{P}\underline{\pi}$$

where

$$\underline{\pi}' = (\pi_1, \pi_2, \ldots \pi_N)$$

Define $\underline{\Pi}$ to be the $N \times N$ matrix with π_j in the jth diagonal position and zeros everywhere else. The mean and variance of the marginal distribution are given by

$$\text{mean} = \underline{\Pi}' \underline{x}$$

and

$$\text{variance} = \underline{x}' \underline{\Pi} \underline{x}.$$

where $\underline{x}' = (x(1), x(2), \ldots, x(N))$. For simplicity, $\underline{x}$ will be assumed to be normalized so the mean is zero and the variance is one. With these assumptions, the mth serial correlation is given by

$$\rho_m = \underline{x}' P^m \Pi \underline{x} \qquad (5.1)$$

The conditional forecasts are

$$E[x_{t+1} \,|\, x_t = x(i)] = \sum_j \rho_{ij} x_j = E_i$$

Provided these quantities are not all equal, the series is forecastable with average forecast error variance $1 - \sum_j \pi_i E_i^2$.

Lai (1976) has pointed out that an N-state Markov chain can have a correlogram which corresponds to an AR(1) series, but there are also various ways in which such a chain can be white noise. For instance, if for given $\underline{x}$ there is a P such that

$$P\Pi_x = 0 \qquad (5.2)$$

it follows immediately that $\rho_m = 0$, all $m > 0$, but there is no reason to suppose that all the E_i are identical. For example, if

$$P = \begin{bmatrix} 0.8 & 0 & 0.8 \\ 0.1 & 0 & 0.1 \\ 0.1 & 1 & 0.1 \end{bmatrix}, \underline{x} = \begin{bmatrix} -\dfrac{\alpha}{4} \\ 0 \\ \alpha \end{bmatrix}$$

where $\alpha = \sqrt{5/22} = 0.4767$, then $\underline{\pi}' = (8/11, 1/11, 2/11)$ so that the mean $= M \underline{\pi}'x = 0$, and the variance is one. With these values, $\underline{PPx} = 0$ so that $\rho_m = 0$, $m > 0$. Nevertheless

$$\begin{bmatrix} E_1 \\ E_2 \\ E_3 \end{bmatrix} = \underline{x}' \underline{P} = \begin{bmatrix} -0.1\alpha \\ \alpha \\ -0.1\alpha \end{bmatrix}$$

so that the optimal forecast of the next x value, using a least-squares criterion, is approximately -0.05 if the previous x takes either of the values -0.2 or 0.48, but the optimal forecast is 0.48 if the previous x is zero. In this case, R^2 is only 0.023, so the series is not exactly highly forecastable. Nevertheless, the possibility of forecasting does exist and, doubtless, better examples can be found. In fact, the results of the next section suggests that there may be no upper bound to R^2 other than unity.

Normed Markov chains may be thought of as discrete approximations to nonlinear AR(1) models of the form

$$x_t = f(x_{t-1}) + e_t$$

where e_t is white noise. For such a model to produce nonexplosive series, it is necessary that $|f(x)| \le |x|$ except for a few exceptional distributions for the e_t. The requirement that the x_t have a discrete distribution is not particularly important, as actual data could be thought of as being measured with error, the error having a continuous distribution. In any case, many economic variables do have, in practice, discrete distributions: for example, prices, interest rates, automobile production and employment. The restriction to a Markov series is more serious and can only be overcome with a considerable increase in complexity.

An appropriate test for a Markov chain can be based on estimates of the E_i, that is, classify x_{t-1} into M regions and form average x_t conditionally on each. However, such methods may require substantial amounts of data and may be efficient, but less general procedures can be devised by regressing x_t on $f(x_{t-1})$ for some appropriate f function such as $f(x) = x^2$.

6. TRULY CHAOTIC MODELS

There has recently been considerable interest in a class of deterministic difference equations that, in a sense, behave like stochastic generating equations (see, for example, May 1974, Li and Yorke 1975, and Bunow and Weiss 1979). Such models occur in physics, meteorology, and mathematical biology. Three examples are

$$\text{logistic } x_t = 4x_{t-1}(1 - x_{t-1}) \tag{6.1}$$

$$\text{triangular } x_t = 1 - 2|x_{t-1} - 1/2| \tag{6.2}$$

and

$$\text{cubic } x_t = x_{t-1} + 4x_{t-1}(x_{t-1}^2 - 1) \tag{6.3}$$

It has been found that each equation produces a sequence for most values that is empirical white noise, which is why the term "chaotic" has been applied to these models. The sequences all lie in the region 0 to 1 and have a pair of nonstable equilibrium points, that is, values such that $x_t = x_{t-1}$, these being 0 and 3/4 for (6.1), 0 and 2/3 for (6.2) and 0 and 1 for (6.3). The triangular model is particularly interesting as it produces a sequence which is apparently rectangularly distributed over 0 and 1. The examples given are of the form $x_t = f(x_{t-1})$, but more general examples are available. At the moment, it appears not to be understood what properties $f(x)$ has to have to produce a chaotic series (see Oona and Osikawa 1980.)

A particularly simple model claimed in Lorenz (1980) to be chaotic is

$$x_t = x_{t-1}^2 - 2$$

with $2 < x_0 < 2$. The equilibrium points are 2 and -1. If $x_0 \neq 2$, this first equilibrium point is never reached, but there will be a set of starting-up values l_n such that $x_n = -1$; for example, $l_2 = (-\sqrt{3}, \sqrt{3}, -1)$, and as n increases l_n will include more points. Thus, some care has to be taken in selecting x_0 so that an equilibrium point is never reached.

For this particular process, the x_t and x_t^2 processes will be white noise, but naturally a regression of x_t on x_{t-1}^2 will give perfect forecastability. To test for the possibility of such models occuring in practice, the procedures suggested at the end of the previous section are appropriate.

The worrying aspect of chaotic models, that is, nonlinear deterministic series, that are white noise is that it will be quite impossible to test for all possible forms of such models. Thus, one can never know if one's white noise is in fact perfectly forecastable, having been generated by an unknown chaotic model. The importance of having a reliable theory to suggest appropriate functional forms is immediately obvious.

7.   NONLINEAR MOVING AVERAGE MODELS

Consider the generating model

$$x_t = \beta \varepsilon_{t-1} \varepsilon_{t-2} + \varepsilon_t \tag{7.1}$$

where ε_t is taken to be Gaussian white noise. Also, x_t will be zero-mean white noise. It is shown in Granger and Andersen (1978b) that the model is not invertible, that it is given a guess of ε_0, say $\hat{\varepsilon}_0 = 0$, then the sequence ε_t cannot be estimated from the observed x_t sequence. In fact, $\hat{\varepsilon}_t$ diverges from the true ε_t for any nonzero value of β unless true ε_0 is equal to $\hat{\varepsilon}_0$. In practice, one never knows ε_0 without error, so that ε_t cannot be estimated and thus optimum forecasts, based on the model, cannot be formed. Robinson (1977) has discussed a method of moments estimate for the parameter β of this and similar nonlinear moving average models.

It does not follow from these remarks that one cannot forecast series generated by (7.1). The Lagrange multiplier test statistic to test $\beta = 0$ in (7.1), is $E[x_t, x_{t-1}, x_{t-1}]$, and this suggests considering regressing x_t on x_{t-1}, x_{t-2}, that is

$$x_t = \lambda x_{t-1} x_{t-2} + e_t \tag{7.2}$$

Some algebra shows that

$$E[x_t, x_{t-1}, x_{t-2}] = \beta \sigma_\varepsilon^4$$

$$\lambda = \frac{\beta}{[1 + 4\gamma + 3\gamma^2]}$$

where $\gamma = \beta^2 \sigma^2$, and

$$R^2 = \frac{\gamma}{(1 + 4\gamma + 3\gamma^2)(1 + \gamma)}$$

for equation (7.2). The R^2 takes a maximum value of 0.093 at $\gamma = 1/3$. At this value of γ, the true R^2, based on equation (7.1) is 0.25, indicating how much forecastability is lost by using (7.2) compared with what could be achieved if (7.1) were invertible. It is, of course, not clear that the forecast based on (7.2) is the best achievable, but it has been shown that the series generated by (7.1) is white noise, yet is somewhat forecastable.

Doubtless, there are plenty of other nonlinear moving average models with similar properties. An example would be

$$x_t = \varepsilon_t + \beta(\varepsilon_{t-1})\varepsilon_{t-1} \tag{7.3}$$

where $\beta(x)$ is an odd function, with $\beta(-x) = -\beta(x)$, provided the model is invertible. Wecker (1981) has considered the case

$$\beta(x) = \beta, x \text{ positive}$$
$$= -\beta, x \text{ negative}$$

He shows that the model is invertible if $|\beta| < 1$, considers the estimation problem and applies it to real data. His proof of invertibility can be adapted to prove that a sufficient condition for invertibility of (7.3) is just $|\beta(x)| < 1$ for all x.

8.   TIME-VARYING PARAMETER MODELS

One might expect that if the parameters of a model change sufficiently dramatically through time, then any temporal structure might become so mixed up that the resulting series becomes empirical white noise. As an example of this occuring, consider the nonstationary MA(1) model

$$x_t = \varepsilon_t + b(t)\varepsilon_1 \tag{8.1}$$

where ε_t is zero-mean white noise. Taking the mean of x_t as known to be zero, an estimate of the average variance, that is, the variance estimated as if x_t were stationary, is then

$$V_n = \frac{1}{n}\sum_{t=1}^{n} x_t^2$$

which has expected value $\sigma_\varepsilon^2\left[1+\dfrac{1}{n}\sum_{t=1}^{n}x_t^2\right]$. Similarly, the estimate of

the average list autocovariance is

$$C_n = \frac{1}{n}\sum_{t-2}^{n}x_t x_{t-1}$$

which has expected value $\sigma_\varepsilon^2\displaystyle\sum_{t-2}^{n}\dfrac{b(t)}{n}$. It is thus seen that if the estimated

mean value of $b(t)$ is zero, the series will be empirical white noise, as the
expected value of C_n will be zero as n tends to infinity.

All other autocovariances are obviously zero, as x_t is MA(1). Examples would be $b(t) = Z_{t-1}$, where Z_t is some zero-mean observable variable, or $b(t)$ is a periodic function of period k, so that $b(t) = b(t-k)$, with

$$\sum_{t=1}^{k-1}b(t) = 0 \cdot$$ If $b(t)$ is known or is forecastable without error, which is true

for the two examples just given, the model is invertible provided

$$\lim_{n\to\infty} E\left[\prod_{t=1}^{n}b^2(t)\right] = 0$$

(See Granger and Andersen 1978b). In this case, ε_n can be estimated from
the observed x's and, combined with the known $b(n)$, it follows that x_{n+1}
can be forecast in a linear, time-varying fashion.

Consider now the other extreme, when $b(t)$ is entirely unknown, except
that the sequence $b(t)$ is not white noise and changes smoothly in some
sense. Presumably some adaptive filtering procedure, similar to the
Kalman filter, can be used, provided the question of invertibility is not
ignored. However, for the purpose of this paper, it is sufficient to find some
forecasting procedure, even though it is not optimal. By noting that

$$E[x_{t-1}x_{t-2}] = \sigma_\varepsilon^2 b(t-1)$$

and that ε_{t-1} and x_{t-1} will be correlated, a possible forecasting method
might use an equation of the form

$$x_t = \gamma x_{t-1}^2 x_{t-2} + e_t \tag{8.2}$$

Since

$$E[x_t x_{t-1}^2, x_{t-2}] = 2b(t)b(t-1)\sigma_\varepsilon^2$$

which on the average will not be zero if

$$\lim_{n\to\infty}\frac{1}{n}\sum_{t=2}^{n}b(t)b(t-1)$$

is nonzero, which could follow from the assumption that $b(t)$ changes slowly. It follows that γ will not be zero and thus (8.2) will provide forecasts that, on average, have some forecasting ability. As the forecasts have no time-varying parameters, they can doubtless be improved.

Higher order moving average models with time-varying parameters that generate white noises can be constructed, but the conditions on the parameters become rather complicated and will not be considered in any detail.

Surprisingly, it is much more difficult, and may be impossible, to get empirical white noise from time-varying parameter autoregressive models. These difficulties are easily demonstrated by considering the extreme case

$$x_t = (-1)^t \alpha x_{t-1} + \varepsilon_t, \quad |\alpha| < 1$$

so that the relationship between x_t and x_{t-1} reverses in sign for each change in t. Note that

$$x_t = \alpha^2 x_{t-2} + \varepsilon_t + (-1)^t \alpha \varepsilon_{t-1}$$

so the second autocorrelation must be positive. The class of autoregressive models with periodic coefficients, known as cyclostationary, is attractive, but none of them appear to result in empirical white noise.

9.   NUMERICAL ILLUSTRATIONS

In connection with this conference, the Bureau of the Census sent authors data for 13 miscellaneous, individual time series. To illustrate the possibility of modeling white noise, single series, Box-Jenkins models were formed for nine of these series. After the residuals passed the usual diagnostic checks, simple tests were performed on them to see if any of the models mentioned above might be appropriate. Illustrations of the results obtained are –

(1) Currency component of M-1A money supply, monthly 1968–80.
    After the 1st and 12th differencing, the resulting series, denoted x_t, was modeled by

$$x_t = 53.035 + \varepsilon_t + 0.436\varepsilon_{t-1}$$

based on 142 observations. Both the constant and moving average parameter had t-values greater than 4. Adding further terms to the model did not improve it significantly. The first 60 estimated autocorrelations of the estimated residuals, $\hat{\varepsilon}_t$, were all in the region ±0.20 with the largest (in magnitude) values at lags 4 ($\hat{\rho}_4 = -0.20$), 13 (-0.19), 23 (0.19), 27 (-0.20) and 60 (0.20). The model passed the Box-Pierce statistics test, adjusted for downward bias. However, the regression

$$\hat{\varepsilon}_t = \alpha_0 + \alpha_1 \hat{\varepsilon}_{t-1}\hat{\varepsilon}_{t-2} + \text{residual}$$

produced an insignificant $\hat{\alpha}_0$, but $\hat{\alpha}_1 = -0.001$ with a t-value of 2.45 and an R^2 of 0.04.

(2) Steel, value of shipments from blast furnaces, and steel mills, monthly 1950 to 1980.

After differencing, the model fitted was

$$x_t = 0.267x_{t-1} + \varepsilon_t - 0.239\varepsilon_{t-12}$$

based on 277 data points, both estimated parameters being clearly significant. The estimated residuals had autocorrelations no greater than 0.08 in magnitude for the first 23 lags, except at lag 14 ($\hat{\rho}_{14} = -0.16$), but significant positive autocorrelations did occur at lags 24 (0.19) and 36 (0.23), suggesting that seasonal effects still remained. The model was not corrected to take these into account. The regression

$$\varepsilon_t = \alpha_0 = \alpha_1 \hat{\varepsilon}_{t-1}\hat{\varepsilon}_{t-2} + \text{residual}$$

produced an insignificant value for $\hat{\alpha}_0(t = 0.04)$, but $\hat{\alpha}_1 = -0.000347$ with $t = 3.49$, $R^2 = 0.04$. Further, the regression

$$(\hat{\varepsilon}_t)^2 = \alpha_1\beta_0 + \beta_1(\varepsilon_{t-1})^2 + \beta_2(\varepsilon_{t-2})^2$$
$$+\beta_3(\varepsilon_{t-3})^2 + \beta_4(\varepsilon_{t-4})^2 + \text{residual}$$

produced a significant $\hat{\beta}_0(t = 3.01)$, $\beta_1 = 0.304$ ($t = 4.99$), and $\hat{\beta}_4 = 0.140$ ($t = 2.28$), $R^2 = 0.12$.

(3) Unfilled orders, radio and TV, monthly 1958–80.

If x_t is the raw data, the model fitted was

$$(1 - B^{12})(1 - a_1B - a_2B^2)x_t = \varepsilon_t + b_1\varepsilon_{t-1} + b_2\varepsilon_{t-12}$$

with $a_1 = 0.66$, $a_2 = 0.22$, $b_1 = -0.156$, $b_2 = 0.755$ and all highly significant, with 262 data. The autocorrelations of the estimated residuals only had two values greater than 0.10 in magnitude, with values -0.11 at lag 2 and -0.14 at lag 18. Some evidence of nonwhite noiseness is evident from the regressions

$$\hat{\varepsilon}_t = \underset{(0.81)}{2.8} \underset{(3.05)}{-0.96E-03}\hat{\varepsilon}_{t-1}^2 + \text{residual} \quad R^2 = 0.035$$

$$\hat{\varepsilon}_t = \underset{(0.97)}{3.35} -0.112E-02\varepsilon_{t-2}^2 + \text{residual} \quad R^2 = 0.05$$

and

$$(\hat{\varepsilon}_t)^2 = \underset{(3.27)}{0.231E04} + \underset{(3.31)}{0.204}(\hat{\varepsilon}_{t-1})^2 \quad R^3 = 0.06$$

with *t*-values shown in parentheses.

Somewhat similar results were found for some of the other series. Although generally the amount of forecastability found was not exciting in these examples, there is clear evidence that some of the residual series were not pure white noise and were possibly forecastable. As it is currently unclear how to distinguish between some of the models presented in earlier parts of the paper, no attempt was made to estimate such models.

10.   CONCLUSIONS

A number of models have been listed that provide at least empirical white noise yet are, in fact, forecastable, sometimes just from their own past. It seems incorrect to stop once white noise is achieved, but rather a wider class of models needs to be considered. A new set of identification procedures needs to be developed that is more general than the usual linear autocorrelations, partial correlations, and spectrum. For the simple models considered in this paper, the third moments $E[x_t x_{t-k} x_{t-j}]$ seem to be of potential value, but they are not sufficient for all possibilities.

One clear conclusion that can be reached is that one can never be sure that a white noise is not forecastable, either from some nonlinear or time-varying model or from the use of a wider information set, so one should never stop trying to find superior models.

REFERENCES

ASHLEY, R. A., and GRANGER, C. W. J. (1979), "Time Series Analysis of Residuals From the St. Louis Model," *Journal of Macroeconomics* 1, 373–394.

BUNOW, B., and WEISS, G. H. (1979), "How Chaotic is Chaos?" *Mathematical Biosciences* 47, 221–237.

ENGLE, R. (1979), "A General Approach to the Construction of Model Diagnostics Based on the Lagrange Multiplier Principle," LSE Discussion Paper.

GRANGER, C. W. J., and ANDERSEN, A. P. (1978a), *An Introduction to Bilinear Time Series Models*, Gottingen: Vanderhueck and Ruprecht.

(1978b), "On the Invertibility of Time Series Models," *Stochastic Processes and Their Applications* 8, 87–92.

GRANGER, C. W. J., and NEWBOLD, Paul (1976), *Forecasting Economic Time Series*, New York: Academic Press.

LAI, C. D. (1976), "First-Order Autoregressive Markov Processes," *Stochastic Processes and Their Applications* 7, 65–72.

LI, T.-Y., and YORKE, J. A. (1975), "Period Three Implies Chaos," *Amer. Math. Monthly* 85, 985–992.

LORENZ, E. N. (1980), "Nonlinear Weather Prediction," paper presented to WMO Symposium on Probabilistic and Statistical Methods in Weather Forecasting, Nice, France.

MAY, R. H. (1974), "Biological Populations With Nonoverlapping Generations, Stable Points, Limit Cycles and Chaos," *Science* 186, 645–647.

OONO, Y., and OSIKAWA, M. (1980), "Chaos in Difference Equations, I," *Progress in Theoretical Physics* 64, 54–67.

ROBINSON, P. M. (1979), "The Estimation of a Nonlinear Moving Average Model," *Stochastic Processes and Their Applications* 5, 81–90.

WECKER, W. (1981), "Asymmetric Time Series Models," *Journal of American Statistical Association* 76, 16–21.

CHAPTER 25

Can We Improve the Perceived Quality of Economic Forecasts?*

Clive W. J. Granger

"*Economic predictions are fallible and advice is highly variable*",
President Jimmy Carter, Camp David Summit, Summer 1979, quoted by Klein (1981)

Summary

A number of topics are discussed concerning how economic forecasts can be improved in quality or at least in presentation. These include the following: using 50% uncertainty intervals rather than 95%; noting that even though forecasters use many different techniques, they are all occasionally incorrect in the same direction; that there is a tendency to underestimate changes; that some expectations and recently available data are used insufficiently; lagged forecasts errors can help compensate for structural breaks; series that are more forecastable could be emphasized and that present methods of evaluating forecasts do not capture the useful properties of some methods compared to alternatives.

1. CRITICISMS OF FORECASTS

It is easy to find criticisms of economic forecasts, both of their perceived quality and of the methods used in their construction. Some of the criticism is from academics, such as by Keating (1985), and more appear in the business press. Examples of the latter are Robert Chote (*New Scientist*, 31 October 1992), "Why the chancellor is always wrong," with sub-head "No one takes the governments forecasts of economic upturns seriously. The problem lies with the Treasury's computer model," and by Robert Samuelson (*Newsweek*, 13 February 1995), "Soothsayers on the

* *Journal of Applied Econometrics* 11, 1996, 455–473.

decline", "Economists know less than they – or most Americans – think." A great deal of this criticism is probably deserved. Much of the purely academic writing on forecasts, for example, seems to be simplistic, inflexible, too conservative and insufficiently concerned with presentation. The initial objectives of this paper are to ask if some of the points made by the critics are helpful, if a substantial rethinking of standard practices is worth attempting and if this will produce a noticeable improvement in forecasts.

No forecast can be properly evaluated in isolation and so it is worth noting that 1995 is the silver anniversary of the publication of the famous book by George Box and Gwilym Jenkins (1970) whose univariate models, at least, provide substantial opponents in any forecasting competition. This paper is dedicated to their path-breaking work.

So that attention is paid to realistic situations, it is worth starting by looking at some actual forecasts. The 3 December 1994 issue of *The Economist* included British Treasury forecasts for 1995 and 1996 (first half) as shown in Table 25.1.

Exports and imports are for goods and services, inflation excludes mortgage-interest payments. "Deficit" is properly known as the public sector borrowing requirement (PSBR). In fact the Treasury provides forecasts of PSBR annually to 1999. There is no shortage of such forecasts produced either by various official agencies or by other economists using many alternative techniques of various degrees of statistical and economic sophistication. What do we learn from such forecasts?

1. The forecast horizon can be at least six quarters ahead and sometimes several years.

Table 25.1. *Examples of forecasts for the U.K. economy*

	Forecasts			
% Change on year earlier	1993	1994	1995	1996
GDP	2	4	$3\frac{1}{4}$	3
Consumer spending	$2\frac{1}{2}$	$2\frac{1}{2}$	$2\frac{1}{2}$	$3\frac{1}{4}$
Investment	$\frac{1}{4}$	$3\frac{3}{4}$	$5\frac{3}{4}$	$6\frac{3}{4}$
Exports	3	$8\frac{1}{4}$	7	$6\frac{1}{4}$
Imports	$2\frac{3}{4}$	$4\frac{3}{4}$	$5\frac{1}{4}$	$5\frac{3}{4}$
Inflation Q4 (RPI)	$2\frac{3}{4}$	2	$2\frac{1}{2}$	$2\frac{1}{2}$ (2Q)
Billion pounds				
Current account	$-10\frac{1}{2}$	-4	$3\frac{1}{2}$	$3\frac{1}{2}$
Govt deficit, fiscal year	$45\frac{1}{2}$	$34\frac{1}{2}$	$21\frac{1}{2}$	13
(as % of GDP)	7	5	3	$1\frac{3}{4}$

2. Usually there is no indication of the level of uncertainty associated with the forecasts, such as a confidence or probability interval (although HM Treasury does publish mean absolute deviations).
3. It is not clear if these are unconditional forecasts or if they are conditional on the current conditions continuing. If the forecasts are issued by a government agency it is not clear if they are actually forecasts or really "plans" or expectations. This question is particularly pertinent for variables that the government is attempting to control or influence.
4. Some of the variables being forecast, and whose forecasts are emphasized in the press, are difficult to forecast, particularly with a horizon of several quarters. Further, several of these variables are inherently difficult to estimate. This may be because of definitional problems, such as GNP and unemployment, and so they will involve substantial measurement errors, be subject to large revisions and also be slow in appearing. Some will also be involved with seasonal adjustments which will induce further errors. For many important variables there is an estimate of the actual value in some period, the "outcome", and then a sequence of revisions of this value. It is unclear if the forecasts are of the initial estimate or of the final revised value, which can be quite different for a variable such as imports.
5. Forecasts are often provided with no indication of the forecasting techniques used, the assumptions made or the information set that was available. It is therefore not possible to replicate the forecast or to check their robustness to the use of alternative conditioning assumptions or to ask the effect of M1 being replaced by M2 or one interest rate being replaced by another. The forecasting group has to be judged just by the quality of the output, the actual forecasts, which is probably the correct emphasis.

Several of these topics will be discussed below. The widespread interest in macro forecasts suggests that they are found to be useful by government and applied economists and by investors. The relevance to this last group is well illustrated by the story in *Newsweek*, 19 December 1994, about the Orange County (Government) Investment Pool which was worth $8 billion, which borrowed a further $12 billion and "bet heavily on lower interest rates", perhaps based on a forecast, resulting in a loss of $1.5 billion. (The actual figures have changed since the story appeared but the magnitudes are similar.) The importance of a superior forecast in this case is obvious.

To illustrate the quality of the forecasts being achieved by a variety of economists an article by Zarnowitz and Braun (1993) is extremely helpful, as it surveys the experience of 22 years of the NBER-ASA Quarterly Economic Outlook Surveys and then compares these forecasts with several alternative techniques. Table 25.2 shows ME (mean error, where error = Predicted – Actual), MEA (mean absolute error), RMSE (root mean squared error) for three forecast methods and three variables (two growth rates and inflation) over five different spans measured in quarters, plus the mean (M) and standard deviation (SD) of the actual values taken by the variables. Columns are also given for "ratio" defined as 100 MAE/RMSE for each forecast method. The forecasts summarized are the individual forecasts given to the NBER-ASA survey, those resulting from the Michigan economic model and a Bayesian vector autoregressive (BVAR) model. Further examples of US forecast uncertainty are provided by McNees (1992).

To expand the examples of forecast uncertainty, Table 25.3 shows mean absolute errors for forecasts of ten UK variables with four- and eight-quarter horizons, made by the National Institute of Economic Research for the period 1981 to 1992. The "error range" shown is the smallest absolute error to the largest absolute error over this period. The final column is the average actual values taken by the variable, most of which are one-year growth rates. On average, the MAE for the eight-quarter span is about 50% larger than the MAE over four quarters. Where comparisons are possible, for real GDP and inflation, the MAE figures for the US and UK forecasts are similar in size, even though different time periods and forecasting techniques are used.

Zarnowitz and Braun (1993) (henceforth ZB) often indicate variability of forecast errors by providing MAE and RMSE values in their tables. However, it is surprising how little information is provided by having both statistics rather than just one of them, as seen by the relative constancy of the ratio MAE/RMSE shown in Table II. The ratio generally lies just below 0.8 and even though it is not quite true in every case, for all the cases ZB give, frequently this ratio is remarkably close to 0.77. A possible explanation comes from considering a variable X which has a mixed distribution, being $N(0, 1)$ with probability $(1 - p)$ and $N(0, \sigma^2)$ with probability p. If $\sigma^2 \gg 1$, the second element may be thought of as a distribution of outliers. A simple calculation then gives a population value for the ratio of

$$\text{ratio} = \sqrt{\frac{2}{\pi}} \left[\frac{1 - p + p\sigma}{\left((1 - p) + p\sigma^2\right)^{1/2}} \right]$$

If $p = 0$, so there are no outliers, this ratio = 0.798; but if $\sigma^2 = 10$ then the ratio = 0.78 if $p = 0.01$ and 0.73 if $p = 0.05$. ZB find that the errors are usually not normally distributed, having skewness and kurtosis values

Table 25.2. *Forecasts of growth in normal nominal and real GNP and in inflation*

Span	Survey of individual forecasts				Michigan forecast				BVAR				Actual	
	ME	MAE	RMSE	Ratio	ME	MAE	RMSE	Ratio	ME	MAE	RMSE	Ratio	M	SD
GNP														
0–1	−0.09	0.62	0.81	77	−0.09	0.80	1.08	74	0.07	0.84	1.11	76	1.98	0.96
0–2	−0.11	1.12	1.45	77	0.13	1.24	1.60	78	0.18	1.45	1.92	77	4.00	1.00
0–3	−0.11	1.60	2.07	77	−0.34	1.45	1.91	76	0.26	2.08	2.73	76	6.07	2.14
0–4	−0.14	1.99	2.58	77	0.51	1.81	2.38	76	0.33	2.59	3.45	75	8.20	2.63
0–5	−0.30	2.48	3.20	75	0.97	2.15	2.95	73	0.38	3.23	4.23	76	10.38	3.12
Real GNP														
0–1	−0.01	0.64	0.85	75	0.01	0.77	1.02	75	0.08	0.78	1.00	78	0.61	1.03
0–2	0.09	1.09	1.44	76	0.25	1.09	1.49	74	0.20	1.09	1.51	72	1.23	1.77
0–3	0.25	1.56	2.08	75	0.46	1.34	1.77	76	0.28	1.53	2.03	75	1.86	2.40
0–4	0.45	2.00	2.74	73	0.77	1.58	2.18	73	0.35	1.76	2.34	75	2.50	2.95
0–5	0.48	2.47	3.38	73	1.20	1.96	2.88	68	0.39	2.05	2.04	78	3.15	3.45
Implicit price deflation														
0–1	−0.07	0.42	0.54	78	−0.10	0.39	0.51	77	0.05	0.37	0.48	77	1.36	0.65
0–2	−0.19	0.77	0.99	78	−0.14	0.72	0.87	83	0.11	0.76	0.97	78	2.74	1.25
0–3	−0.36	1.16	1.50	77	−0.15	1.00	1.32	76	0.17	1.18	1.53	77	4.16	1.84
0–4	−0.57	1.63	2.10	78	−0.27	1.40	1.98	71	0.23	1.65	2.18	76	5.60	2.43
0–5	0.65	2.14	2.79	77	−0.28	1.78	2.42	74	0.28	2.19	2.94	74	7.08	3.03

Table 25.3. *Average absolute errors, NIESR February forecasts (all figures per cent unless otherwise stated)*

	Four-quarter forecast		Eight-quarter forecast		Average outturn 1982–91
	Absolute average error	Min–Max absolute error range	Absolute average error	Min–Max absolute error range	
Real GDP growth	1.21	0.2–2.3	2.06	1.5–4.7	2.45
Domestic demand growth	1.52	0.2–3.9	2.75	0.8–6.3	3.05
Consumers' expenditure growth	1.94	0.1–5.2	2.74	0.0–5.5	3.24
Investment growth	3.72	0.3–9.0	6.37	1.0–13.8	4.33
Export volume growth	2.57	0.5–6.4	2.24	0.1–5.1	3.45
Import volume growth	2.33	0.1–4.6	4.29	0.1–9.3	5.61
Real personal disposable income growth	1.72	0.4–4.0	2.20	0.9–4.2	2.88
Retail price inflation (Q4/Q4)	1.40	0.1–3.2	2.30	0.4–5.1	5.73
Current account (£ billion)	3.59	0.1–12.0	4.99	0.6–15.3	−5.25
Public sector borrowing requirement (£ billion)	6.62	0.5–12.1	9.91	2.0–23.0	2.52

Source: National Institute of Economic Research Review, January 1993.

that seem too large (although formal tests are not given). Thus, the ratio values observed in practice are consistent with normally distributed errors mixed with a few outliers, although other distributions would give similar ratio values. If one accepts the outlier interpretation, it is interesting to ask why the error distribution is long-tailed; that is, why do forecasters do so badly on occasions? An obvious response is that the economy occasionally experiences unexpected structural shifts. This possibility is discussed further below.

Even though economic forecasts are far from perfect they may be no worse than those made by other prognosticators such as political pundits, sports writers and book, theatre, film and music critics who often predict the success or not of activities in their regions but rarely have their predictions evaluated. David Hendry in a recent letter to a national British newspaper noted an interesting non-symmetry of action by the British government. When the official weather forecasting service missed correctly forecasting a particularly damaging storm the response was to buy larger computers for the forecasters; when the economic forecasters failed to predict a major economic event it was decided to substantially reduce support for research in our area.

A problem in trying to take a wide perspective about forecasts is that there are many different techniques employed, so that generalizations become difficult. It is also well understood that the economy is a very complex mechanism, at all levels of aggregation, which makes forecasting it such an interesting challenge. It is difficult to appreciate and interpret the data summarizing an economy, even ignoring data error problems. By listing the properties of forecasts of the economy made by a very wide variety of techniques based on quite different viewpoints and information sets, it is possible that we will understand some of the properties of the economy. The fact that a wide variety of techniques is used is an advantage in this situation. It is a further objective of the paper to see what properties can be suggested about the economies from the properties of forecasts of it.

2.   REPRESENTING FORECAST UNCERTAINTY

By itself a point forecast is of limited use and should have associated with it an indication of uncertainty. This was certainly emphasized in Box and Jenkins (1970) and in most forecasting textbooks since but the impact in published forecasts has been minimal. The tests discuss interval forecasts, sometimes called confidence intervals or probability limits (Box and Jenkins) or prediction intervals (PIs) (Chatfield, 1993). These intervals are usually estimated by forming the root mean squared prediction error produced in the past by the forecasting method, assuming that these errors are normally distributed and the well-known properties of this distribution to get the limits. It is interesting to note that Box and Jenkins (1970) state "These limits may be calculated for any convenient set of probabilities, for example 50% and 95%." Academic writers have concentrated almost exclusively on 95% intervals, whereas more practical, hands-on forecasters, if intervals are used, seem to prefer 50% intervals, or something similar which statisticians would interpret as a preference for the inter-quartile range. The most frequently seen bands are $\pm\hat{\sigma}$ or $\pm$MAE which, if errors are Gaussian, correspond to 68% and 58% probability intervals, respectively. The 50% interval corresponds to $\pm0.675\sigma$. The obvious difficulty with these intervals are that they are based on the two assumptions of normality and constancy of variance through time, neither of which are likely to be correct in practice. There does appear to be some advantages of using a 50% type interval, as it is more robust to the distributional assumption and is less affected by outliers, for example. It can also be checked on a past history of forecasts, at least to see if roughly a half of the errors lie inside the 50% interval and a half outside.

A useful discussion of PIs has recently been provided by Chatfield (1993), who concentrates on 95% intervals and most of the basic points made there need not be repeated here. A problem with 95% PI is that it will often be embarrassingly wide. To be told that a model gave a point forecast of the US unemployment rate of 6% with a 95% interval (0.86–11.14%) would surely be too uncertain to be plausible. The figures came from the discussion of Chatfield and the actual unemployment rate for the period was 10.53%. Intervals of 50% are less likely to be unbelievable and figures well outside them can be interpreted as possible evidence of a structural break starting or of an outlier or some exceptional event. It might be worth considering using 50% and 80% intervals, say, to provide "warning" and "action" signals that the model is breaking down as in standard quality-control charts. Whether or not such warning signals from a number of forecasters provide a great deal more information has to be determined.

Using typical figures in Zarnowitz and Braun (1993) for figures of unemployment rate one-year forecasts in the period 1968–90, a point forecast would have a 50% range of 5.46–6.54% and a 95% range would be 4.4–7.6 per cent. Thus, for the wider range, the amount of uncertainty is roughly half the level of the forecast. In human terms the range is 3 million jobs, which translates into considerable social disutility or personal suffering, unless one really believes that unemployment is a desire for leisure. A side-benefit from improved forecasts should be narrower probability intervals. What is perhaps worrying is that even though the bands are wide, Chatfield (1993) has a section entitled "Why are PIs too narrow?" He notes that the usual Gaussian, constant variance technique for estimating 95% bands produces a range such that over 5% of errors lie outside it.

Of course, economists are not the only scientists who are concerned about levels of uncertainty: cosmologists in early 1994 gave the age of the universe from 7 to 20 billion years (and recent discoveries have increased the range) and in the same year UN demographers gave a point forecast of world population in 2050 AD of 9.8 billion with a range of 7.9–11.9 billion. The uncertainty of 4 billion is two-thirds the present world population.

It is surprising how little discussion there is in practice of the use of conditional interval forecasts, perhaps based on ARCH specifications, around most forecasts, except in financial areas. Either heteroscedasticity is not present for macro economic forecasts, for example, or practitioners have not looked for it. A generally held belief is that forecasts based on misspecified models will produce heteroscedastic errors, it follows that if the errors are homoscedastic then there will be implications about, and limitations to, the misspecification that is inevitable in reality. It should be noted that this is one aspect of the fact that finding forecast intervals is itself a forecasting problem.

If a major component of the variance of errors comes from exceptional events, or outliers, as suggested in the previous section, there would clearly be considerable benefit in improving forecasts of these events.

3. ALL SWING TOGETHER

If an economy goes through a period when it is relatively easy to forecast, resulting in narrow probability intervals, a group of competent forecasters of comparable quality should be in agreement, but if the economy is difficult to forecast you can expect less agreement between forecasters, unless they collaborate. An interesting discussion of the relationship between consensus and uncertainty for forecasts is given by Zarnowitz and Lambros (1987).

Unfortunately, there does seem to be a tendency for forecasts to congregate on one side of the actual value rafter than to straddle it. For example, the 18 December 1994 issue of the (London) *Sunday Times* discussed the performance of 45 forecasting groups, including consultants, banks, investment firms, academics and governmental, for four UK economic variables for 1994. When the article appeared only initial estimates of the outcomes were available and these had to be used as "actual". The figures are summarized in Table 25.4.

It is seen that there is a strong tendency for the forecasts to cluster around the Treasury forecast as knowledge of it is available early, and, at least on this occasion, not to straddle the actual very much. Many forecasters presumably using a wide variety of techniques consistently underestimated the strong recovery of the UK economy in 1994. A few years earlier most had misforecast a similar downturn. It might be noted that

Table 25.4. *Properties of forecasts of growth of U.K. economy, December 1994*

GDP Growth (%)			
Mean forecast:	2.48	Mean absolute dev.	0.26
Median forecast:	2.5	Standard deviation (σ)	0.37
Range:	1.5–3.2	Mean ± ab. dev.	2.24–2.76
UK Treasury forecast:	2.5	Mean ± σ	2.13–2.87
		Mean ± 2σ	1.76–3.24
Actual growth:	4.0		
Every forecast was less than	4.0		
Inflation (%)			
Mean forecast:	3.17	Mean absolute dev.	0.49
Median forecast:	3.2	Standard deviation (σ)	0.63
Range:	1.8–4.6	Mean ± ab. dev.	2.8–3.7
UK Treasury forecast:	3.25	Mean ± σ	2.6–3.8
		Mean ± 2σ	2.0–4.4
Actual Inflation:	2.3		
Two forecasts were less than actual, 43 greater			
Unemployed (jobless) (millions)			
Mean forecast:	2.71	Mean absolute dev.	0.093
Median forecast:	2.72	Standard deviation (σ)	0.18
Range:	2.34–3.01	Mean ± ab. dev.	2.62–2.80
UK Treasury forecasts:	2.75	Mean ± σ	2.53–2.89
		Mean ± 2σ	2.35–3.09
Actual Unemployed:	2.47		
One forecast was less than actual, 44 were greater			
Current account (government deficit) (billion pounds)			
Mean forecast:	−10.76	Mean absolute dev.	2.49
Median forecast:	−11.0	Standard deviation (σ)	3.31
Range:	−16.5 to −3.1	Mean ± ab. dev.	−13.25 to −8.27
UK Treasury forecasts:	−9.5	Mean ± σ	−14.07 to −7.45
		Mean ± 2σ	−17.38–4.14
Actual:	−4.0		
One forecast was greater than actual, 44 less			

the same survey for 1995, published in *The Sunday Times*, 24 December 1995, found that of 41 forecasts, only one was *less* that the actual annual growth rate in GDP of 2.7%, with 40 forecasting higher values.

Similarly evidence is given in Hallman, Porter and Small (1991) in which ten to twelve forecasts of inflation are presented each year from 1971 to 1989. In eleven of these nineteen years either all the forecasts or all but one are too low (8 years) or too high (3 years). Zarnowitz and Braun (1993) show time-series plots of the ASA-NBER group mean forecasts plus one standard deviation (across forecasts) bands for real and nominal GNP growth rates and inflation for three horizons. Although most of the time the actual value of the variable lay within the band, on a few occasions the actual outcomes lie substantially outside these bands. The occasions mostly correspond to sudden, large changes in value of the variable.

The results might imply that occasionally the economy undergoes substantial changes that are very difficult to forecast by (virtually) any of the techniques currently used to forecast economic variables. These changes could last for a very short time spans, "outliers", somewhat longer periods, "bubbles" or much longer when they would be classified as "structural breaks." It is not easy for a single forecaster to know when these changes start; it will just show as an actual outcome outside a wide probability interval. However, as a group, the forecasters appear to have a powerful tool. If many forecasters using a variety of techniques all produce probability intervals which do not include the outcome, or if very few do, there is an indication of a change. Of course, if there is close collaboration between the forecasters, or if they all follow the same leader, such as the Treasury's forecasts, this advantage is largely lost.

The results presented here could be interpreted as saying that current macro forecasting techniques do not forecast well the major business cycle turns, which, if this were so, would amount to a substantial criticism, I am not, in fact, giving that interpretation.

It does seem that it would be worth while to find when the majority of economic forecasts failed to forecast a change in the economy and then to analyse if there is any way of forecasting when these "exceptional" periods occur.

4. UNDERESTIMATING CHANGE

Table 1A.5 of Zarnowitz and Braun (1993) shows summary statistics for individual forecasts in the NBER-ASA survey for five other macro variables for five horizons. All the variables are percentage changes. A feature of this table is that all twenty-five means of forecast errors are negative, as are the medians (throughout the paper, error is defined as forecast – actual). This feature is not pervasive; elsewhere in the paper for seven variables, five horizons and between one and five forecasting methods, 65% of mean errors were negative when the variables were changes and 51% were negative when the variables were levels. The results indicate that there is a tendency to underestimate changes.

If such a problem does exist, it is not a new one. Theil (1960) has a section 5.1 entitled "Why are Changes Generally Underestimated?" in which he gives a number of examples. He states: "This phenomenon, which amounts to an underestimation of the levels of the variables to be predicted in times of rises and to an overestimation of this level in times of falls, is not entirely unknown; but its general occurrence is not sufficiently realized! If forecasts of changes are inclined to be downwardly biased, this needs to be investigated and corrected whenever possible." This comment concerns a possible bias in the mean change forecast and is not related to the fact that the variance of the optimum forecast is always less than the variance of the variable being forecast An optimum forecast would not be biased. If we take the numerical values above at their face value, one has $E[\Delta e_t | I_{t-1}] < 0$ but $E[e_t | I_{t-1}] = 0$. However, as the first of these terms is just the second minus e_{t-1}, and thus e_t, has a non-symmetric distribution, with $Prob(e_t > \frac{1}{2})$. If this is a feature of actual forecasts it needs further examination, but in practical terms one just needs to check that the implied bias in forecasting changes is not occurring.

5. HOW FAR AHEAD CAN WE FORECAST[1]

Many published macro forecasts are for one and two years ahead but longer horizons do occur. McNees (1992) notes that some of the leading US forecasting organizations such as DRI, the UCLA Business School and Wharton Econometrics may provide forecasts of a thousand or more variables typically with horizons up to 12 quarters. A further example is forecasts made by the National Institute of Economic and Social Research in London, published in November 1994, and giving annual forecasts out to 1997 plus an average value for 1998 to 2002. In particular, oil prices (in $ per barrel) go from 15.8 in 1993 to 14.5 in 1997 to an average of 16.2 for 1998 to 2002. A further example has been the New Zealand Institute of Economic Research forecasting in 1994 the demand for hotel rooms in Auckland in 2005. Many of these longer horizon forecasts are made using simple random walks, possibly with a linear drift or exponential growth models, so that detailed fluctuations are not forecast and small misspecifications or misestimation of parameters lead to substantially different long-term forecasts.

In some sciences there seem to be a horizon beyond which useful forecasting is not possible; in weather forecasting there seems to be four or five days, for example. It is unclear if economics has similar boundaries as variables differ in their forecastability. Stock market daily returns are forecastable over very short horizons, if at all, whereas the absolute values or the squares of their returns appear to be linearly forecastable over long horizons. There certainly seems to be a widely held belief that the economy can be forecast over the business cycle. It also seems possible that the length of time between turning points in these cycles

---

[1] I would like to thank Paul Newbold for suggesting this topic.

is forecastable (see article in *Newsweek*, 5 December 1994, p. 33) which suggests economic growth will continue into 1996 or 1997).

A feature that will provide limits to how far ahead one can forecast is when the (forecastable) signal gets lost in the (unforcastable) noise. A very perceptive and readable account of this question is given by Lawrence Klein (1981). He notes that Paul Samuelson (1975) said "I feel almost as if there is a Heisenberg Indeterminacy principle dogging us, which will limit the asymptotic accuracy of forecasting we shall be able to attain." Klein takes this to mean that if the measurement error of GNP is 10% then there can never be less than a 10% forecasting error, on average. Of course, this argument applies to all horizons but dominates in the longer run for stationary series, such as growth rates. In practice we know little about the size, or properties, of the measurement errors for most macro variables, and this situation seems to have improved little over the past 25 years. It is interesting to quote Klein's (1981) estimates of the ultimate error bands for a few US variables:

> 1.5% for change in real GNP.
> 2% for inflation.
> $\frac{1}{2}$ percentage point for unemployment.
> 150 basis points for short-term interest rates.

He adds, "We might aspire to be within these bands two-thirds of the time," and so they can perhaps be considered as $\pm\sigma$ bands. Compared to the figures given in Zarnowitz and Braun (1993) it seems that Klein's value for real GNP growth is close to that achieved by forecasters, but the inflation band is too wide and the unemployment band is too narrow. There is a great more that could be said on this topic, particularly relating the apparent finding of unit roots in economic series to structural breaks and possibly also fractionally integrated or types of long-memory processes.

6.   TOO MUCH EMPHASIS ON OLD DATA?

The strongest criticism of the models used to produce economic forecasts is aimed at the fact that they are constructed from old data and thus are more backward- than forward-looking. As a journalist writes "Another big problem is that econometric models are reliable only to the extent that history repeats itself – models can only be estimated using historical data" (*Times Higher Educational Supplement*, 25 November 1994, p. 6). Estimation may not be the problem but models just using lagged variables may seem to be, but the criticism appears to be irrelevant. Surely the basic axiom of forecasting is that a forecast can only be based on information that is available at the time the forecast is made. If we have an information set $I_n : X_{n-j} \, j \geq 0$ of values of variables known publicly at time n, the forecasts of some variable at time $n + h, h > 0$ made at time n can only be based on I_n. However, the obvious question arises, who knows what and when and what is made public? For the forecaster, the question becomes the perennial one of what variables to include in the information set. In this and in later sections various suggestions are made about what variables should be considered for inclusion. At a prosaic level, it is important to include variables whose estimates appear quickly; for example, rather than use employment (issued with a 2-month delay in the UK) one could use unemployment, available monthly with a 12-day delay; or instead of using official aggregate import figures, available quarterly with a delay of over 2 months, some customs figures may be reasonable substitutes, available monthly and which appear quite rapidly.

Expectations or planned expenditures should also be considered for inclusion in information sets. The two obvious examples are the manufacturing investment intention surveys conducted in various countries and the planned or forecast government expenditures issued by government agencies. The UK Treasury gives such forecasts for a 3-year horizon in a budget in November each year. Even though the quality of these forecasts does not appear to be exceptional, the values given seem to be taken seriously by the financial press. There are a number of ways these forecasts could be used. A simple model relating a variable (Y_t) to current government expenditure (G_t) by

$$Y_t = a + bG_t + e_t \tag{1}$$

assuming e_t is white noise for ease, obviously gives forecasts

$$f_{t,1}^Y = a + bf_{t,1}^G \tag{2}$$

However, this assumes the forecasts are unbiased and efficient. A better procedure is to run a regression

$$Y_{t+1} = \alpha + \beta f_{t,1}^G + \varepsilon_t$$

giving forecast

$$f_{t,1}^Y = \alpha + \beta f_{t,1}^G$$

This still ignores the information in the other two forecasts issued by treasury. A better initial regression would be

$$Y_{t+1} = \alpha_1 + \sum_j \beta_j f_{tj} + e_t$$

giving the obvious forecast after insignificant coefficients are put to zero.

In passing, it might be noted that an equation such as (1) might fit very well, according to R^2, but this gives little indication of its usefulness as a forecasting equation. This will be determined by the forecastability of G_t, as seen by equation (2).

This section has emphasized the advantages of using expectations and planned expenditures in information sets. The next two sections suggest further variables that should be considered for inclusion.

7.   THE USE OF FORECAST ERRORS

It is generally accepted that occasionally the economy undergoes structural changes, generated either internally or externally, and that these changes can persist. If a forecaster is using some form of structural model, such as a traditional econometric model with simultaneity or even a VAR in levels or an error-correction model, then the model can become misspecified after the change, which will affect some parameter values. If the structural break corresponds to a policy regime shift, then some parameter values can be expected to alter according to the well-known Lucas critique, for example. The consequence is that if the old model is still used after a structural change, biased forecasts may result. There is, of course, an old technology from the days of exponential smoothing forecasts which kept track of such possible biases, as suggested by Trigg (1964) and discussed by Gilchrist (1976, Chapter 16). An estimate of the recent mean error $\tilde{e}_t$ is given by

$$\tilde{e}_t = (1-b)e_t + b\tilde{e}_{t-1}$$

where b is near to but less than one, and e_t is the most recent error. Immediately after a known break b could be put near zero and then it should be quickly increased to 0.75 or 0.9 as information accumulates.

More recently, Hendry and Clements (1994), Clements and Hendry (1996) suggest allowing for biases in structural model forecasts after breaks. This is clearly a good idea if done carefully. $\tilde{e}_t$ could be added to the forecast, with the appropriate sign to reduce any bias, or it could be added if it becomes large enough according to some criterion.

The correction of a possible bias is just one use of past forecast errors as a source of useful information that could improve forecasts. Of course, moving-average terms, which can be thought of as weighted sums of previous forecast errors, are emphasized in the models discussed by Box and Jenkins (1970) and the multivariate generalizations, such as vector ARMA models have been widely discussed, as in Granger and Newbold (1987) and Lütkepohl (1991). As usual, some of these models suffer from the problem of having too many parameters and being not parsimonious. Nevertheless, it might be worth including at least one lag of all the forecast errors from other variables in each equation. In the theory of optimum linear forecasts, the forecast errors are the essential new information entering the system each period and should be treated accordingly. I am told that practical model-based forecasters already use recent residuals in setting their adjustments and that this information often does appear to improve their forecasts.

If one is modeling a vector $\mathbf{Y}_t$ of variables jointly denote the one-step forecast errors $\mathbf{e}_{t,1}$ when forecasting $\mathbf{Y}_{t+1}$ at time t. Suppose that there is a further, non-overlapping, vector $\mathbf{W}_t$ of variables, producing corresponding one-step errors $\mathbf{e}_{t,1}^W$. Suppose also that all variables are $I(1)$ and that the first set of variables have cointegrating vectors $\mathbf{Z}_{1t}$, and the second set $\mathbf{Z}_{2t}$. A standard error-correction model for $\mathbf{Y}_t$ would be of the form

$$\Delta \mathbf{Y}_t = \gamma_1 \mathbf{Z}_{1,t-1} + \text{lags}\,\Delta \mathbf{Y}_t + \mathbf{e}_{t-1,1}^Y$$

but experiences suggests that a parsimonious and often superior specification is

$$\Delta \mathbf{Y}_t = \gamma_1 \mathbf{Z}_{1,t-1} + \gamma_2 \mathbf{Z}_{2,t-1} + \text{lags}\,\Delta \mathbf{Y}_t + \tilde{e}_{t-1,1}^Y$$

Thus, bringing in the "disequilibrium errors" Z_{2t} from another system is a simple and efficient way of gaining information from another part to the economy to the part, involving $\mathbf{Y}_t$, that is under study. This is easier to do than trying to model the whole joint system $(\mathbf{Y}_t, \mathbf{W}_t)$ and considering just the equations involving the Y variables. It is thus suggested that if an error-correction model is being used to form forecasts, the linear combinations of Zs from other parts of the economy be considered for inclusion in the model.

By analogy, forecast errors from other parts of the economy could also be helpful is used in the information set. An analogy that can be employed is with early forms of weather forecasting, when there were outlying recording stations surrounding the core part of the country. The weather reaching these stations from various directions was used as a leading indicator for the main area. Some sections or parts of the economy could act as leading indicators of important incoming exogenous shocks to the major economy.

There is increasing evidence that it is useful to consider error-correction models with Z terms entering lagged but non-linearly. A discussion can be found in Granger and Swanson (1996).

8. CHOOSING WHAT WE FORECAST – USING LEADING INDICATORS

The usual situation is that the forecaster is told what variable to forecast – there is no choice. This could be why economic forecasters are perceived to be so unsuccessful. Perhaps we are only asked to forecast the series that are very difficult to forecast but not those for which good-quality forecasts are possible. It might be worth ranking important variables in their order of apparent forecastability and then making sure that values are issued publicly of some of the more forecastables to counteract those that are less successful. For example, if those who explore constituent variables for leading, coincident and lagging indices have any abilities then variables in a leading index should be difficult to forecast but those in a lagging index should be easy. According to Stock and Watson (1993), variables that seem to be helpful in forecasting business cycles are: manufacturing and trade sales, capacity utilization rate, unemployed (less than five weeks), personal consumption expenditures, contracts and orders for plant and equipment and various inventories. A sensible forecaster may be reluctant to be judged on the ability to forecast *just* these series, as now it is rare to see forecasts of series such as the index of consumer expectations, purchasing manager new orders index, interest rate spreads or a stock market index, all of which are generally viewed as satisfactory leading indicators. Some lagging indicators, according to Franklin (1994) are average duration of unemployment, labour cost per unit of output in manufacturing, commercial and industrial bank loans outstanding, and the consumer price index for services. Of course, one has to consider whether or not such leading indicators are reliable after a structural break has occurred.

Once one gets into the business of choosing what to forecast, presumably from sensible lists of economic variables, more possibilities arise. Box and Tiao (1977) use canonical analysis to rank series from most to least forecastable on a least-squared criterion. A simpler form of their procedure can be applied directly to the residuals of an error-correction or VAR model with m variables so that $\mathbf{Y}_t = \mathbf{u} + f_{t-1,1} + \mathbf{e}_t$ in level form with $E[\mathbf{e}_t] = 0$, $\text{cov}[\mathbf{e}_t, \mathbf{e}_t'] = \Omega$. Applying a canonical analysis to the residuals, one can write $\Omega = \mathbf{PDP}'$ where $\mathbf{PP}' = \mathbf{I}$ and $\mathbf{D}$ is diagonal. The values on the diagonal of $\mathbf{D}$ are all positive and assume that they are ranked from the largest λ_1 to the smallest λ_m. It follows that there will be a linear combination (with $\mathbf{p}_m\mathbf{p}_m' = 1$)

$$w_t^{(m)} = \mathbf{P}_m'(\mathbf{Y}_t - \mathbf{u} - f_{t-1,1}) \tag{3}$$

having a variance λ_m which should be substantially less than that of the forecast errors for any one of the individual variables. For example, two vector error-correction models were constructed using the variables investigated in King, Ploser, Stock and Watson (KPSW) (1991). The first used just the logs of three variables GDP, Consumption and Investment with two cointegrating relationships imposed $(-1, 1, 0)$ and $(-1, 0, 1)$ and six lags were used in the model. The residuals from the three equations had the following standard deviations:

RG = residual GNP	0.00979
RC = residual Cons	0.00629
RI = residual Inv	0.01958

Using a principal component analysis, the combination with the smallest eigenvalue was $PC_3 = 0.5375 \times RG - 0.8413 \times RC - 0.0573RI$ which has a standard deviation 0.00429. (Note that the sum of the square of these coefficients is one.) Thus, there is a linear combination of the original variables which is essentially 0.54GNP – 0.84Consumption, which is easier to forecast than any of the three component variables, having errors with a 32% smaller standard deviation.

Using all six of the variables in KPSW gives residuals for those variables with standard deviations ranging from 0.00550 (for Consumption) to 0.01659 (Investment). The principal component with weights 0.573 on GNP, –0.784 on Consumption and 0.217 on M2 gives a residual with a standard deviation 0.00344. Thus, again, this particular combination of the original variables, with coefficients whose squares add to one to normalize, is more forecastable than any individual variable, by about 37%. A post-sample evaluation of these results has not yet been conducted. The transformations being considered are just on the forecast errors, which are a white-noise vector, and have no consequence on the dynamics of the model, such as cointegration. I do not know of an interesting statistical interpretation of the vector of the original variables which is the most or least forecastable, but it would be suggestive if these variables had important economic interpretations in a particular application.

There has been some discussion of how alternative forecasts of a variable should be evaluated (see Clements and Hendry, 1993, and the discussion and references given there) but there seems to have been little consideration of the question of how to compare variables on their forecastability. The obvious criterion to use is to compare mean squared errors, as above in Box and Tiao (1977) and the results using principal components. However, this may not be enough to rank variables on forecastability. Consider a pair of series

$$Y_t = aX_{t-1} + bY_{t-1} + e_t \tag{4}$$

$$X_t = \rho X_{t-1} + \varepsilon_t \tag{5}$$

with $|b| < 1$, $|\rho| < 1$, e_t, ε_t iid, mean zero series with unit variances and independent of each other, so that the series are stationary with zero means. If $a \neq 0$, X_t leads Y_t, but there is no feedback, so X_t can be considered a leading indicator. Figures 25.1–3 show two extreme cases, plotting Y_{n+1} against its optimum forecast $f_{n,1}$, in the first case $a = 0$, $b = 1$ and in the second, $a = 1$, $b = 0$, $\rho = 1$. Obviously virtually the same diagrams would have occurred if b and ρ had been near to, but just less than, one. Under the assumptions made, forecast error variances will be the same in each case, but in (i) the optimum forecast lags behind the series being forecast; in (ii) there is very little lag. In case (ii) movements and terms in Y_{n+1} are forecast earlier than in case (I) because of the existence of a leading indicator. In a more realistic case, where both a and b lie between 0 and 1 and are not near either of these boundaries then the forecast can be lagged between zero and one. It is not easy to show statistically the existence of this lag. The lag statistics derived from the cross-spectrum

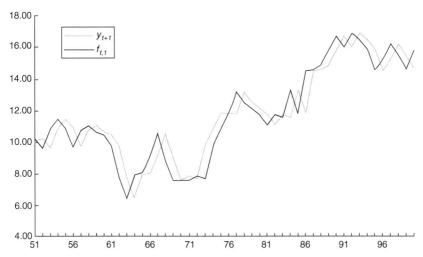

Figure 25.1. $y(t+1)$ and the one-step-ahead forecasts of $y(t+1)$, $a = 0$, $b = 1$, $\rho = 1$.

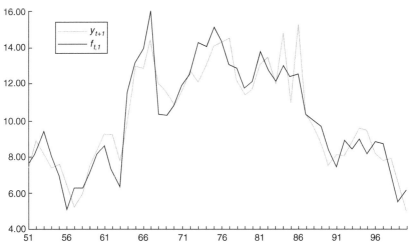

Figure 25.2. $y(t+1)$ and the one-step-ahead forecasts of $y(t+1)$, $a = 1$, $b = 0$, $\rho = 1$.

as discussed in Granger and Hatanka (1964, Chapter 5) cannot be interpreted if there is feedback between the series, which there will be generally for a series and its forecast if that forecast includes lagged terms of the series. A simple way of indicating these lag differences between the variable and its forecast is to consider two covariances

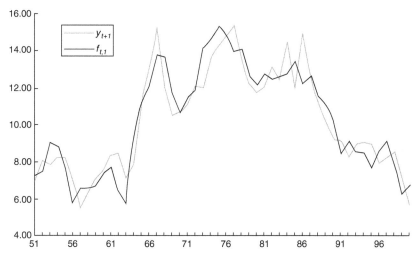

Figure 25.3. $y(t + 1)$ and the one-step-ahead forecasts of $y(t + 1)$, $a = 0.5$, $b = 0.5$, $\rho = 1$.

$$C_0 = \text{cov}(Y_t, f_{t-1,1})$$

and

$$C_1 = \text{cov}(Y_{t-1}, f_{t-1,1}).$$

For the simple system (4) and (5) shown above, some algebra gives

$$C_0 - C = D\left[(1 - \rho)a^2 V_x - (1 - b\rho)b V_E\right] \tag{6}$$

where $D_{-1} = (1 + b)(1 - \rho b)$, $V_x \equiv \text{var } X$, $V_\varepsilon \equiv \text{var } \varepsilon$. It is clear that C_0 can be larger or less than C_1, and that if ρ and b are both near one then $C_0 - C_1$ can become small. If $a = 0$, so there is no leading indicator, $C_1 > C_0$, but as the leading indicator becomes more important, the inequality direction changes. It is thus suggested that if two variables have the same MSE values, which equate to the same C_0 values, you might prefer to forecast the one with the lowest C_1.

9. CONDITIONAL OR UNCONDITIONAL FORECASTS?

The perception of economic forecasts would improve if a more careful distinction were made between conditional and unconditional forecasts. Many of the criticisms of the quality of economic forecasts confuse forecasting with the policy implications, the quotation from President Carter at the top of the paper provides an example. McCloskey (1990) criticized much of economics and manages to confuse conditional and unconditional forecasts and also point and interval forecasts. Policy should strictly be connected with conditional forecasts – if interest rates are R_1 then unemployment will be EM_1, if interest rates are R_2 then unemployment will be EM_2 and so forth. If the policy maker has a target unemployment rate in mind, interest rate will be selected so that the conditionally forecast unemployment is as close to the target as possible. If such policy making occurs, where does this leave the forecasts? Macro forecasts would be both more interesting and potentially more relevant for policy considerations if they were stated specifically as being based on a certain set of assumptions that is conditional on different major government policy variables, such as interest rates, money supply or government expenditure. Presumably, tighter forecast intervals would apply around these conditional forecasts, compared to unconditional ones. If a government can – or believes it can – manipulate inflation by changing interest rates, then it makes little sense to produce individual forecasts of inflation and interest rates (or no forecast at all of interest rates, as in the UK); rather, a joint forecast should be provided. This could either be a forecast of the most likely pair of values, of several conditional forecasts, or inflational levels for given interest rates, say.

These remarks take us to the edge of a much larger and very important question of how to evaluate policy models and statements, an area to which econometricians are now starting to pay some attention (see Ericsson and Irons, 1994). To ask that the underlying assumptions being made by forecasters be stated is not really enough. For policy evaluation one really needs to know the target values that the controllers were attempting to achieve, as observed in Wallis's letter to *The Economist*, 2 September 1995.

10. FORECASTING DURING A STRUCTURAL BREAK

Tests exist for a structural break but they are hardly required; it is usually clear at the break that it is occurring, although its importance could be overestimated. Suppose that there is a high probability the economy is currently undergoing a structural break – the country is entering a new economic alliance (such as joining the European Community), there has been a major political change (as in Eastern Europe and in South Africa recently), or there has been a large exogenous shock (such as the first oil price increase in 1973/4). How should the forecaster react? One has to have an enormous belief in the super-exogeneity of one's model to keep producing forecasts in the same way as before. Model specifications will probably change and certain coefficient values will change around the break; in fact, to an econometrician, that is almost the definition of a break. If the same model is used, it will produce a sequence of large forecast errors. At the break a large error is almost inevitable, except by luck, but immediately afterwards a structural model will continue having problems whereas an adaptive model, such as a random walk or $\text{ARMA}(p, 1, q)$ will quickly learn and produce relatively more satisfactory errors. An example is given in Granger and Ashley (1979) who compared the performance of the St Louis Federal Reserve model with a simple, univariate Box–Jenkins model around the first oil shock period. A reasonable strategy seems to be to switch to an adaptive model at a break and then return to one's usual model once enough post-break data have accumulated so that new parameter values can be estimated. A more formal regime-switching and time-varying parameter, Kalman filter format can also be adapted. If one superimposes the problems discussed in the previous two sections, so that a structural break occurs because of a policy regime shift or if an unconditional forecast induces a policy maker to change a policy variable, one inevitably gets a difficult forecasting situation, which needs further discussion in the literature.

11.   CAN WE DO BETTER IN THE FUTURE?

The conclusions from the paper can be gathered into three categories:

Suggestions to Improve Forecasts

In one's information set I_n, upon which forecasts $f_{n,h}$ are to be based, use the most up-to-data values of variables as possible or, if necessary, proxies for them; use past forecast errors – both linearly and non-linearly – from the variable being forecast and also other variables, to help correct possible biases in the forecast. Use lagged error-correction terms – both linearly and possibly non-linearly – from the cointegrating system including the variable to be forecast and also from other cointegrating systems. Further, include leading indicators in I_n when searching for possible forecasting models; also expectational variables such as planned expenditures, but make better use of these variables than previously. Check if there is tendency to under-forecast changes and, if so, allow for this bias.

If several different forecasting techniques produce interval forecasts that do not include the actual outcome, consider this as evidence that there has been, or there is occurring, a structural break. If there is a structural break or one believes one is occurring currently, switch from a structural model (that is, one containing "equilibrium constraints") to a completely adaptive one such as a random walk or $\text{ARI}(p, 1)$. One can return to a revised structural model as data accumulate after the break about possible parameter value changes.

Suggestions to Improve the Perceived Quality of Forecasts

Other than improving the actual quality, one cannot pretend we can forecast further ahead than we really are able to; we can make sure that our lists of publicly announced forecasts include variables that can be well forecast (e.g. lagging indicators?). We could perhaps find linear combinations of our main variables that are relatively well forecasted and, if they have a sensible interpretation, issue forecasts of them. It would help if forecasts could be stated as being conditional or unconditional. If the former and if based on assumptions about future government policy, these assumptions should be stated. Possibly alternative forecasts could also be issued conditional on other assumptions.

Probability intervals could be at a 50% range and based on a conditional analysis if there is any evidence of heteroscedasticity.

What Do We Learn about the Economy?

Forecast errors, through time and across forecasters seem not to be Gaussian but rather to be Gaussian with a heavy-tailed mixture. There occur occasions when the macro economy moves in a manner that is unexpected by virtually all forecasters, using a wide variety of techniques and information sets. Together, these facts suggests that there are unexpected "structural breaks" in the economy on occasions or perhaps there are expected breaks with unexpected consequences, such as a financial deregulation. Clearly, forecasters have to be aware of the possibility and have a strategy to use when breaks occur, as suggested above. It seems that research into forecasting the timing of real or apparent structural breaks either through the non-linear structure of the dynamics of the economy or by appropriate leading indicators will be an interesting research topic for the future, comparable to the effort spent in the past or forecasting turning points in the business cycle.

NOTE

This paper should be considered as a document to encourage discussion on a number of topics rather than a definitive account of these topics.

ACKNOWLEDGEMENTS

I would like to thank Antonio Espasa, Ken Wallis, David Hendry and Paul Newbold for helpful discussion while preparing this paper and also the very useful comments by the editors and referees. The paper was partially supported by NSF Grant SBR 93-08295. I would also like to thank Norman Morin for the figures and calculations in Section 8.

REFERENCES

Box, G. E. P. and G. M. Jenkins (1970), *Time Series Analysis, Forecasting and Control*, Holden-Day, San Francisco.

Box, G. E. P. and G. C. Tiao (1977), "A canonical analysis of multiple time series," *Biometrika*, 64, 355–365.

Chatfield, C. (1993), "Calculating interval forecasts", *Journal of Business and Economic Statistics*, 11, 121–135.

Clements, M. P. and D. F. Hendry (1993), "On the limitations of comparing mean square forecast errors", *Journal of Forecasting*, 12, 617–676 (with discussion).

Clements, M. P. and D. F. Hendry (1996), *Economic Forecasting*, Cambridge University Press, Cambridge.

Ericsson, N. R. and J. S. Irons (1994), *Testing Exogeneity*, Oxford University Press, Oxford.

Franklin, N. (1994), *Guide To Economic Indicators*, 2nd edition, M. E. Sharpe, Armont, New York.

Gilchrist, W. (1976), *Statistical Forecasting*, Wiley, Chichester.

Granger, C. W. J. and R. Ashley (1979), "Time series analysis of residual from the St. Louis model", *Journal of Macroeconomics* 1, 373–394.

Granger, C. W. J. and M. Hatanaka (1964), *Spectral Analysis of Economic Time Series*, Princeton University Press, Princeton N.J.

Granger, C. W. J. and P. Newbold (1987), *Forecasting Economic Time Series*, Academic Press, San Francisco.

Granger, C. W. J. and N. Swanson (1996), "Further developments in the study of cointegrated variables", *Oxford Bulletin of Economics and Statistics* 58, 537–554.

Hallman, J. J., R. D. Porter, and D. H. Small (1991), "Is the price level tied to the M2 monetary aggregate in the long run?" *American Economic Review* 81, 841–858.

Hendry, D. F. and M. P. Clements (1994), "Can econometrics improve economic forecasting?" *Swiss Journal of Economics and Statistics*, 130, 267–298.

Keating, G. (1985), *The Production and Use of Economic Forecasts*, McKuen, London.

King, R. G., C. I. Plosser, J. H. Stock, and M. W. Watson (1991), "Stochastic trends and economic fluctuations", *American Economic Review*, 81, 819–840.

Klein, L. R. (1981), *Econometric Models and Guides for Decision Making*, Free Press, New York.

Lütkepohl, H. (1991), *Introduction to Multiple Time Series Analysis*, Springer-Verlag, Berlin.

McCloskey, D. N. (1990), *If You're So Smart*, University of Chicago Press, Chicago.

McNees, S. K. (1992), "How large are economic forecast errors?" *New England Economic Review*, July/August, 25–42.

Samuelson, P. A. (1975), "The art and science of macromodels over 50 years", *The Brooking Model*, G. Fromm and L. R. Klein (eds), North Holland, Amsterdam.

Stock, J. H. and M. Watson (1993a), "A procedure for predicting recessions with leading indicators: econometrics issues and recent experience", in J. H. Stock and M. Watson (eds), *Business cycles, Indicators and Forecasting*, University of Chicago Press, Chicago.

Theil, H. (1961), *Economic Forecasts and Policy*, 2nd edition, North-Holland, Amsterdam.

Trigg, D. W. (1964), "Monitoring a forecasting system", *Operational Research Quarterly*, 15, 271–274.

Zarnowitz, V. and P. Braun (1993), "Twenty-two years of the NBER-ASE Quarterly Economic Outlook surveys", in J. H. Stock and M. Watson (eds), *Business Cycles, Indicators and Forecasting*, University of Chicago Press, Chicago.

Zarnowitz, V. and L. A. Lambros (1987), "Consensus and uncertainty in economic prediction", *Journal of Political Economy*, 95, 591–621.

CHAPTER 26

Short-run Forecasts of Electricity Loads and Peaks*

Ramu Ramanathan, Robert Engle, Clive W. J. Granger, Farshid Vahid-Araghi, and Casey Brace

Abstract

This paper reports on the design and implementation of a short-run fore-casting model of hourly system loads and an evaluation of the forecast performance. The model was applied to historical data for the Puget Sound Power and Light Company, who did a comparative evaluation of various approaches to forecasting hourly loads, for two years in a row. The results of that evaluation are also presented here. The approach is a multiple regression model, one for each hour of the day (with week-ends modelled separately), with a dynamic error structure as well as adaptive adjustments to correct for forecast errors of previous hours. The results show that it has performed extremely well in tightly controlled experiments against a wide range of alternative models. Even when the participants were allowed to revise their models after the first year, many of their models were still unable to equal the performance of the authors' models. © 1997 Elsevier Science B.V.

Keywords: comparative methods; energy forecasting; forecasting competitions; regression methods; exponential smoothing.

1. INTRODUCTION

Electric utilities have always forecast the hourly system loads as well as peak loads to schedule generator maintenance and to choose an optimal mix of on-line capacity. As some facilities are less efficient than others, it is natural to bring them into service only during hours when the load is predicted to be high. Nowadays however, the need for accurate hourly load forecasts is even greater. There are several reasons for this that reflect the newer technologies available for generation and transmission of power. As utilities add smaller generating equipment, it becomes

* *International Journal of Forecasting* 13, 1997, 161–174.

easier to adjust capacity flexibly in response to demand. Furthermore, utilities are now able to adjust capacity and demand through short term purchases and sales of power. Today and increasingly in the future, excess power can be sold and shortfalls can be made up by purchases. A careful calculation of the expected demand and supply can lead to contracts that enhance the profitability of the utility. All these lead to still more reliance on very short-run forecasts.

This paper reports on the design and implementation of a short-run forecasting model of hourly system loads and an evaluation of the forecast performance. The methodology was applied to historical data for the Puget Sound Power and Light Company, but the approach is more general and can be adapted to any utility. Puget Power did a comparative evaluation of various approaches to modeling hourly loads and those results are also presented here but without identifying the participants except by coded labels. Because of space limitations, many of the details (especially tables and charts) are omitted. For a copy of a more detailed paper, contact Professor Ramu Ramanathan at the Department of Economics, University of California, San Diego, La Jolla, CA 92093-0508, U.S.A.

2. METHODOLOGIES

There have been a number of approaches to modeling hourly loads [see Bunn and Farmer (1985); Electric Power Research Institute (1977) for a collection of several papers on the topic]. Ackerman (1985) compared three alternative models; (a) a twenty-fourth-order differencing of the raw data modeled as a first-order autoregressive (AR) process, (b) consecutive differencing modeled as AR(24) combined with a moving average (MA) of the first order, and (c) a simple AR model on a different data set that eliminated the input of the load dispatcher. They found the third specification to be more robust than the others across different data sets. Gupta (1985) proposed a model that not only took into account historical data and weather information but was adaptive in nature. Thus, model parameters were automatically corrected in response to changing load conditions. Schneider et al. (1985) formulated the total system load in terms of four components; basic load, weather sensitive load, error component, and a bias correction. The basic load is modeled by sine and cosine functions. Temperature effects were captured by a nonlinear function. The bias in forecasts from these terms is used to construct a bias correction that is added to the forecast to obtain a revised forecast. The authors found that the approach worked quite well for data from the San Diego Gas and Electricity Company. The approach adopted by Ramanathan et al. (1985) is a two-step method. First, a short-run model is formulated for a three month period that relates the hourly load to quickly changing variables such as the temperature, time of day, day of the week, and so on. The parameters of this model are then related in a second stage to slowly changing variables such as income, electricity price, demographic and industrial structure, and so on. The authors applied this technique to two very different data sets (a cross section of households observed over a full year and 30 regions of the United States observed for a 14 year period) and found the approach to approximate historical load shapes quite well. However, this is a load-shape model and does not forecast very easily.

3. DESCRIPTION OF THE PRESENT PROJECT

The main goal of the present project was to develop a number of models to produce very short run forecasts of hourly system loads. Several teams of researchers were invited to participate in a real-time forecasting competition (labeled the "shoot-out") using historical data from the Puget Sound Power and Light Company (Puget) which acted as the host utility. This paper presents a detailed specification of the models developed by Engle, Granger, Ramanathan, and Vahid–Arraghi (EGRV) whose study was sponsored by the Electric Power Research Institute (EPRI), and a comparative evaluation of the forecast performance of the various models. The EGRV study also modeled the distributions around the forecast values so that a measure of error could be ascribed to each forecast, but those results are presented elsewhere [see the EPRI project final report Electric Power Research Institute (1993)] and were not part of the shoot-out.

At Puget, the daily forecasts were made at 8:00 A.M. by Mr. Casey Brace. Forecasts were produced for the entire next day, starting at midnight and through the following midnight and hence they were made from 16 to 40 hours into the future. On Friday, he forecast the entire weekend as well as Monday (16 to 88 hours). Before holidays, he forecast until the next working day. At the time the forecasts are produced, the information available are the weather service forecasts of temperatures at each hour as well as current and past weather and load information.

In order to formulate a statistical model to carry out the same task, Puget developed a data base of hourly observations for the fall and winter months from 1983–1990. Included with the data set were the hourly loads and the hourly weather observations. Each potential forecasting method was coded into a software program that would run on a PC. At 8:00 A.M. the program would be run and the requested data on past weather, past loads, and weather service forecasts would be entered. The official experiment began on November 1, 1990, and continued for five months, through to March 31, 1991. Altogether ten participants entered one or more forecasting models for this comparison. These included two EGRV models, several neural network models, several state space models, two pattern recognition models, a naive model, and most importantly, a model by Puget Power's expert Mr. Lloyd Reed. Because the models are proprietary, we do not have permission to describe in detail the forecasting models used by the other researchers. However, Harvey and Koopman (1993) have published one model using time-varying splines. Also, Brace et al. (1993) presented a paper at the Second International Forum on the Applications of Neural Networks of Power Systems. The techniques used range from the fairly conventional to very modern approaches. The results are interesting and are discussed below. Because of the importance of the problem and the enthusiasm of the participants, the experiment was continued for a second year, from 1991–1992. In this case, the participants were somewhat different and all model builders were given information on the other models and on the forecast results of the previous year. The second time around, the models were therefore more sophisticated than the first time.

4.   THE EGRV MODEL

4.1   The Basic Strategy

All the models discussed in Section 2 used the data set as a single consecutive series, that is, they were arranged chronologically. After considerable research investigating several different approaches to hourly load forecasting, we decided on an hour by hour modeling strategy. In preliminary tests, this strategy proved superior in both fitting the data within the sample period and in forecasting 1989–90 without using this data in the analysis. We thereby rejected approaches using nonlinear and nonparametric models, time-varying parameter models, and general dynamic regression models. The basic strategy of the hour by hour model is very simple. In fact, it is the simplest strategy we considered. The forecasting problem of each hour is treated separately. That is, we estimate the load for the first hour of the day with one equation and the load for the second hour of the day from a different equation, and so on. Since we are forecasting for a full day, we have 24 separate forecasting equations. Furthermore, weekends and weekdays are separated so that there are actually 48 separate models. Each of these equations is very similar and is based only on information known at 8:00 A.M. on the day the forecast is made. In each case, there are four types of variables: deterministic, temperature, load, and past errors. A generic equation for HOUR1 can be written as

$$
\begin{aligned}
\text{HOUR1} = {}& a\text{DETERMINISTIC} \\
& + b\text{TEMPERATURE} + c\text{LOAD} \\
& + d\text{PASTERRORS} + e
\end{aligned}
\tag{1}
$$

DETERMINISTIC refers to variables that are perfectly predictable, such as the day of the week, the month of the year, and the year. In most cases, these effects are modeled by dummy variables. The monthly binary variables are important because the load changes over the winter, not simply because the temperature changes. There are other annual patterns which must be picked up. The year variables are important because they model any long term growth in the regional economy and its demand for electricity. Although these could be modeled by binary variables, that would give no ability to forecast into the future. Instead, we use two trends; one is linear with the year and the other is its reciprocal. Clearly, an economic forecast of the regional economy could be much more accurate. The temperature variables are very important in modeling the short-run fluctuations in demand. Perhaps unsurprisingly, this is the most complex part of the model. Since the weather service forecasts temperature for each hour of the next day, the forecasting model can be estimated with the actual temperature even though it would not be known by the forecaster. The forecast is constructed simply by inserting the forecast of the weather into the model. The most important variable is the current temperature. Since Puget Power used the model only in the winter, there is no cooling load, so the relation between temperature and load is monotonic. The higher the temperature, the lower the demand. However, the relation is slightly nonlinear as the square of the temperature is also useful, giving a quadratic relation which has a steeper slope at very low temperatures. The temperature effect is not constant across months either. For many of the hours, an interaction between the monthly binary variables and the temperature is significant. In addition to the temperature at the hour for which the load is being forecast, the daily maximum temperature is important for both the forecast day and the previous day. Both the level and the square of this temperature are used. Finally, a seven-day moving average of past-midnight temperatures is used to allow for the effects of long cold spells which appear to have very significant augmenting effects on the loads. Altogether, there are twelve variables that depend upon temperature. These allow a rich specification of the weather component of the model. The variable LOAD is simply the load at 8:00 A.M. This is measuring the state of the system at the time of the forecast. The higher the load is at 8, the higher it is expected to be a day later. The size of this coefficient is, however, only about 10% so that most of the forecast is due to other factors. One naive model would be to forecast that the load tomorrow would be what it was today so that this coefficient would be close to 1 at least for HOUR8. Our results clearly reject this model. The load is allowed to have different impacts after a weekend or after a holiday. The lagged errors are an innovative feature of the model. At 8:00 A.M. it is known how accurate were the previous day's predictions of the model for the first 8 hours. It is also known how accurate were the predictions two days ago for all 24 hours. A wise judgemental forecaster would surely look at these and consider adjusting the forecast somewhat as a result. We approach this problem statistically by introducing the last five lagged errors into the model. We would generally expect that a positive coefficient would be appropriate, as factors which were missed yesterday would be expected to be partially recurring today. The fifth lag corresponds to the error from the same day the previous week since weekends are ignored in the weekday model. The coefficients of the most recent error vary from a high of 50% to a low of about 20%. Because the errors are partly caused by errors in the temperature forecast, which should not be corrected by the utility (unless they are trying to beat the weather service at its own forecast), the residuals to be used must be based upon the model forecast errors using the true temperatures. This feature of the model allows it to recover relatively quickly from short lived changes in the load shape.

A criticism of the EGRV approach is that it is "only" a multiple regression model and, in particular, one with numerous correlated variables. The model aims to capture the very short-run dynamics of household behavior as the hours of the day change and as the household behavior interacts with temperature. People get up, go to school or work, return home, and so forth, and at each time different appliances are used. The model is not built using basic economic theory that suggests including the price of electricity and appliances or the stock of appliances because, in the very short run, these do not change. Thus, slowly changing variables such as increases in population, industrial growth, global warming, and so on are of little or no relevance in a model that is attempting to forecast from one day to the next. An adaptive model, introduced below, will adjust for any biases that result from the exclusion of these variables. We see from the results discussed later that the regression model with dynamic error structure has outperformed most of the complicated models. Utilities typically have personnel who can carry out the kind of analysis performed by EGRV. As for the second objection, it should be noted this is a forecasting model and hence we are not particularly interested in interpreting the signs of individual coefficients. It is well known that multicolinearity does not seriously jeopardize the forecasting ability of a model and often enhances it.

4.2   An Example for HOUR1

Explanatory variables for HOUR1 include binary variables for the day of the week, month of the year, and yearly trends. They also include 1 A.M. temperatures, temperature squared, max of the day and max of the previous day and their squares, seven day average, and interactions of temperature and monthly binary variables. Finally they include the previous day's 8 A.M. load and its interactions with Monday and the day after a holiday. This model is estimated by ordinary least squares with a fifth-order Cochrane–Orcutt autoregressive error structure. Any version of such a Generalized Least Squares program will do and probably a simple iterative procedure would be adequate. Such an iteration would first estimate the model by OLS and then introduce the lagged residuals into the equation and re-estimate it by OLS again. The general model specified above has 31 coefficients and about 1,000 observations. Such a model is not obviously overparameterized, especially since many of the variables are orthogonal to each other. However, it is sensible to set to zero coefficients which are insignificant and then respecify the model in order to improve the precision of the remaining coefficients and to increase the powers of hypothesis tests. In the present case, 13 variables were eliminated. The final model estimated for 1983–1990 and used for the Fall/Winter 1990–91 forecast comparison is:

$$
\begin{aligned}
\text{HOUR1} = {} & 1678.9 + 40.6\text{YEAR} + 32.4\text{DEC} + 0.5\text{FEB} \\
& + 71.7\text{MAR} - 193.9\text{MONDAY} \\
& + 223.9\text{DAYAFTERHOLIDAY} - 2.86\text{TEMP} \\
& + 0.39\text{TEMP}^2 - 7.68\text{SEVENDAYAVGMIDTEMP} \\
& - 3.62\text{YESTERDAYMAXTEMP} \\
& + 0.08\text{LOAD8A.M.} \\
& + 0.07\text{MONDAY*LOAD8A.M.} \\
& + 0.10\text{DAYAFTERHOLIDAY*LOAD8A.M.} \\
& + 0.52e[t-1] + 0.15e[t-2] + 0.07e[t-3] \\
& + 0.14e[t-5] \qquad\qquad\qquad\qquad\qquad\qquad (2)
\end{aligned}
$$

This model shows the typical form of all of the equations. Temperature, the seven day average of temperature, previous day's and maximum temperature are all negative reflecting the heating load. The lagged load contributes 8% to the forecast except on Mondays when it is $0.08 + 0.07 - 0.10$ or 5%, and after holidays when it is -2%, indicating a drop in load at 1 A.M. after a holiday. When the model was re-estimated for the 1991–92 forecasting experiment with the addition of the data from 1990–91, the same specification was used but the coefficients turned out to be slightly different. Generally the changes are small enough so that the model properties are unaltered.

4.3   Models Across the Hours

We have examined the forecasting model for HOUR1 in detail. A similar process is carried out for all 24 hours. Although the same variables are considered in each case to begin with, different variables finally remain in the model as the significance varies. This, in fact, is quite sensible. Some portions of the load curve may vary more over the year than others and consequently the monthly binary variables are important for modeling them. At some times of the day weather sensitive loads are more important than at others and at some times of the year the load may be more responsive to temperature than at others. We did, however, carry out a SUR estimation with common variables, but the differences in forecasts were negligible. We therefore chose to omit insignificant variables in order to improve efficiency. Most of the variables which are dropped in the equations are the monthly binary variables and their interactions with temperature. Overall, the final number of variables in each equation goes from a low of 14 to a high of 20 with an average of 16. Table 26.1 gives the estimated values for three representative hours (1 A.M., 8 A.M., and 5 A.M.) using 1990–91 data. It is particularly interesting to examine the effect of one variable across the hours. For example, the temperature coefficient for HOUR1 is –2.86 while for HOUR8 it is –25.03, or almost ten times larger. The effect of the heating load is expected to be much more important at 8 in the morning than at midnight. Presumably many customers have set-back thermostats which are relatively unresponsive to external temperatures until the morning. The general impression from examining the coefficients is that they do vary across hours in a rather systematic fashion. This observation confirms our earlier conclusion that building a separate model for each hour was far superior to assuming that the same model could be used for all hours. It is natural to try to estimate one very complicated model rather than 24 simpler ones. However, there are 393 coefficients in the 24 hourly models and it seems unlikely that a very effective approximation can be found which is sufficiently parsimonious to allow estimation, testing, and forecasting. A general impression of the success of this approach can best be achieved by examining a series of plots of the daily forecasts. In Appendix D of the EPRI report the actual and fitted values are plotted for each day from November 1, 1990 through to March 3, 1991. The fits are generally impressive. Analysis of the worst fitting episodes indicates that large components of the load forecast errors are due to errors in the weather forecasts.

4.4   Statistical Analysis

It is worth discussing the statistical theory behind this model in order to understand better why it works. Clearly, it seems surprising that the best forecast of HOUR1 and HOUR2 should be estimated separately from different data sets. This discussion shows why this procedure is not only statistically sound but has led to a very natural parameterization.

Each equation can be formulated as a regression with its own coefficients and error terms:

$$y_{ht} = x_{ht}\beta_h + u_{ht} \tag{3}$$

Table 26.1. *Model A coefficients at selected hours*

Deterministic components	1 A.M.	8 A.M.	5 P.M.
Constant	1,678.9	3,586.4	2,904.5
Year	40.6	95.3	88.3
Year inverse	0.0	151.9	0.0
October	0.0	−157.2	0.0
November	0.0	−118.0	0.0
December	32.4	−128.7	0.0
February	70.5	0.0	247.6
March	71.7	0.0	344.6
Monday	−193.9	0.0	0.0
Day after holiday (including Monday)	223.9	196.8	0.0
Friday	0.0	31.3	−53.6
Temperature components			
Temperature	−2.86	−25.03	0.00
October × temperature	0.00	0.00	0.00
November × temperature	0.00	0.00	0.00
December × temperature	0.00	0.00	0.00
February × temperature	0.00	0.00	−6.33
March × temperature	0.00	0.00	−8.30
Temperature squared	0.39	0.13	0.34
Moving AVG of last 7 days midnight temps	−7.68	−8.60	−5.44
Maximum temperature	0.00	0.00	−12.99
Yesterday's maximum temperature	−3.62	−2.90	−1.83
Maximum temperature squared	0.00	0.00	0.00
Yesterday's max. temp. squared	0.00	0.00	0.00
Lag load components			
Load at 8:00 A.M. yesterday	0.08	0.13	0.07
Monday load at 8 yesterday	0.07	0.00	0.00
After holiday load at 8 yesterday	−0.10	−0.08	0.00
Autoregressive parameters			
Lag 1	0.52	0.40	0.00
Lag 2	0.15	0.18	0.37
Lag 3	0.07	0.00	0.29
Lag 4	0.00	0.00	0.10
Lag 5	0.14	0.00	0.12

where h refers to the hour, t refers to the day and there are k variables in this regression. Some of these variables are deterministic, some are weather variables and some are lagged load variables. Many are interacted with binary variables. The error terms are assumed to follow an autoregression in days so that

$$u_{ht} = \rho_{h1}u_{ht-1} + \rho_{h2}u_{ht-2} + \ldots + \rho_{h5}u_{ht-5} + v_{ht} \tag{4}$$

The same model is more conveniently written as a panel model where each hour has its own equation. This is exactly the form of the hour by hour model. By grouping the variables we can write this as:

$$Y = X\beta + U \text{ and } E(uu') = \Omega \tag{5}$$

Eq. (5) is the well-known system of seemingly unrelated regressions or a SUR system. It is typically assumed that each row of U, which in our case corresponds to one day of hourly residuals, is contemporaneously correlated but not correlated over time. This assumption is reasonably accurate for this example except for two cases. The first has already been mentioned. There is correlation across days which is being modeled by Eq. (4). Thus, if the daily autocorrelation is taken into account in the x variables by including lagged errors, then the longer lagged correlations will not be present. Secondly, although the correlation between hours which are far apart can reasonably be taken as small, the correlation between hour 1 and hour 24 on the previous day may be large. Thus, the assumption of only contemporaneous correlation will not be strictly true for the first and last few hours. The beauty of the SUR model is that estimation of the system by Maximum Likelihood is accomplished by estimating each equation by ordinary least squares as long as the same variables enter each equation. This is discussed in any econometrics textbook; see for example Theil (1971) for an elegant proof. In our application, the same variables are considered for each equation, so this theorem applies exactly at the beginning of the specification search. Since insignificant variables are dropped from each equation, the final variables are different for different equations. This means that a slight improvement could be achieved by system estimation but it is presumably smaller than the gain from parsimoniously estimating each equation. This result explains why estimating each equation separately is a sensible procedure. It does not however say that forecasting from each separately is sensible, so we must now consider this question. The forecast from system (5) or system (3) has two components; the first is the systematic part and the second is the error forecast. This can be expressed as:

$$E_t(y_{ht+1}) = E_t(x_{ht+1})\beta_h + E_t(u_{ht+1})$$
$$\text{for } h = 1, 2, \ldots, 24 \tag{6}$$

where the estimated value of β_h would be used with the weather service forecast of x_{ht+1} for the systematic part. The error forecast is generated from Eq. (4) as

$$E_t(u_{ht=1}) = \rho_{h1}u_{ht} + \ldots + \rho_{h5}u_{ht-4}$$
$$+ E_t(v_{ht=1}) \text{ for } h = 1, \ldots, 24 \tag{7}$$

assuming that u_{ht} is observed by the time the forecast is made. Since for some hours it is not, then the second lag is used both for estimation and forecasting. Because the v_{ht+1} are correlated across hours, there is a possibility of forecasting the last term in Eq. (7). Suppose

$$E(v_{ht+1}|v_{h-1,t+1}) = \theta_{h-1}v_{h-1} \quad h = 1, \dots, 24 \tag{8}$$

then

$$E_t(v_{ht+1}) = (\theta_{h-1}\theta_{h-2} \dots \theta_8)v_{8t} \tag{9}$$

Since v_{8t}, the 8 A.M. error, is the most recent error observed when forecasting, and all the forecasts are at least 16 hours in the future, the products are always products of at least 16 terms. Even if the θ's are rather close to one, the product of so many terms is likely to be very small so that there is little gain from forecasting this component. Thus forecasting each equation separately is also very close to optimal in this comparison. Improvements would be possible primarily if shorter horizon forecasts were required. Thus, with the parameterization in Eq. (3) there is little cost to the very simple procedure of estimating and forecasting each equation separately. The remaining question is whether the equations in (3) are correctly specified. In particular, do they have a similarity which may be exploited in joint estimation? For example, suppose it was believed that some or all of the β's were the same for all hours. In this case, system estimation, possibly using a relation such as Eq. (5) would allow this constraint. Practically all of the other models estimated by both EGRV and the other participants in this experiment constrained many of the coefficients to be the same across hours. Various hypothesis tests of Eq. (5) continually revealed that the coefficients were not constant across periods. Consequently new x variables were introduced which interacted the old x's with dummy variables representing particular hours. Thus the number of β's in Eq. (3) became very large. It is our general impression that in this application, the real benefit comes from allowing the β's to differ across equations. Nevertheless, it remains possible that only a subset of the β's truly change over the hours or at least that the changes should be more smooth. Thus a compromise between completely free coefficients and some cross equation constraints could prove even better.

5. ADAPTIVE MODELS

To allow for learning, we used a second, adaptive version of the models described above. The model is designed to adjust the forecasts for a persistent error (this is in addition to the presence of lagged errors in the model). It is certainly possible that the economic environment changes in ways not known by the model builders during the year. A judgemental forecaster will slowly change his methods to compensate for systematic errors. The adaptive version of the model is designed to do just this, but using statistical analysis. This benefit must be offset by a loss of accuracy in the situation where the model structure remains constant. The adjustment used in this model is simply an exponential smoothing of the forecast errors of each hour using the following rule [See Ramanathan (1995), pp. 607–611 for a discussion of exponential smoothing] which is readily seen as a linear combination of forecast and adjustment errors.

$$\bar{y}_{t+1} - \hat{y}_{t+1} = \phi(y_t - \hat{y}_t) + (1 - \phi)(\bar{y}_t - \hat{y}_t)$$

where $\hat{y}_t$ is the hour by hour model forecast and $\bar{y}_t$ is the adaptive version. Expanding this and rearranging terms, we obtain the following equation:

$$\tilde{y}_{t+1} - \hat{y}_{t+1} = \tilde{y}_t - \hat{y}_t + \phi(y_t - \tilde{y}_t) \tag{10}$$

Thus, a preliminary forecast $\hat{y}_{t+1}$ is first made. It is then adjusted, using Eq. (10), to generate the exponentially smoothed forecast $\tilde{y}_{t+1}$. A slow adjustment will alter forecasts only after errors become very persistent, while a faster adjustment will pick up errors more quickly but will also respond to pure noise some of the time. Because the model was estimated and specified over a fixed sample period, the specification used is effectively constant over this period. Hence the optimal smoothing appeared to be zero from our first experiments. We chose a parameter 0.02 which corresponds to a half-life of about 50 days. As can be seen in the forecast comparison discussed below, this constant lead the two models to be very similar. Consequently, in the 1991–92 comparison, the constant was increased to 0.05 which corresponds roughly to a 20 day half-life. The benefits of this process were particularly apparent in the weekend model where the adaptive version performed much better than the original model.

6.   RESULTS

As mentioned earlier, the official forecast period was November 1 through to March 31 of the following year. This section presents a comparative evaluation of the various models used in the two competitions. The comparative statistics were compiled by Mr. Casey Brace of Puget Power and we summarize them here.

6.1   The 1990–91 Forecast Results

In the 1990–91 competition, 11 models were entered and these are as labeled below. However, to preserve the confidentiality of the other teams, who are well respected in the area of forecasting, only codes were supplied to us with brief descriptions of the approach (provided below). Our models are called A and B.

A.	ANN2
B.	STAT
C.	FS
D.	L

E.   NAIVE
F.   OH2
G.   OH3
H.   A (our basic hour by hour model)
I.   B (the adaptive version of A)
I.   REG
J.   SHELF

ANN2 used recurrent neural networks, L refers to the judgemental forecast produced by Puget Power's own personnel, OH models are multilayered perceptron artificial neural networks, and SHELF used time-varying splines [see Harvey and Koopman (1993)]. Details about other models are not available to us but might be obtainable from Puget Power Company.

The criterion used by Puget Power to compare forecasts is the mean absolute percentage error (MAPE) for each hour, plus the A.M. peak period (7 to 9 A.M.) and the P.M. peak period (4 to 7 P.M.). Table 26.2 shows which forecasting method won each cell, with weekdays summarized separately from weekends. It is seen that one or the other of the EGRV models (labeled A and B) wins 82 of 120 weekday hours (that is, 68%), 13 of the 48 weekend hours (that is, 27%), 5 out of 7 A.M. peaks (71%), 4 of the 7 P.M. peak periods (57%), and 4 of the 7 totals. Table 26.3 shows the mean absolute percentage error (MAPE) for the A forecasts. It finds MAPE values for the daily average over 5 only for Saturday, Sunday, and Monday.

Puget Power received its forecasts of hourly temperatures from a local weather service and we were provided with these forecasts for the periods we were forecasting. Table 26.4 shows the MAPEs for the temperature forecasts and it indicates that Saturday, Sunday, and Monday's temperatures are forecast less well than other days. The Sunday and Monday forecast of temperatures are both issued on Friday and are for longer horizons than the other days, and so forecast errors are expected to be higher, with Monday worse than Sunday, as observed. However, why Saturday's temperature forecast should be worse than the other weekdays is a mystery, unless less effort is made to produce this forecast. As all the models relied heavily on temperature forecasts, the quality of our forecasts will decrease as the temperature forecasts get poorer, which possibly explains why the EGRV models do less well on Saturday, Sunday, and Monday.

There were two distinct cold snaps during the 1990–91 forecasting competition. In each the MAPE of the EGRV models increased and our overall rankings dropped – to second in the first cold snap (19–23 December 1990) and to fifth in a brief second snap (28–30 December 1990). A detailed analysis of the MAPEs for the A model around and including the first cold snap shows that some large biases occur and

Table 26.2. *Best forecast (lowest MAPE) for each cell*

Time	Mon	Tue	Wed	Thur	Fri	Sat	Sun
1 A.M.	B	A	A	A	FS	SHELF	SHELF
2 A.M.	STAT	STAT	A	A	FS	L	STAT
3 A.M.	FS	STAT	B	SHELF	FS	A	FS
4 A.M.	FS	B	B	B	FS	A	SHELF
5 A.M.	STAT	B	B	B	SHELF	SHELF	SHELF
6 A.M.	B	FS	B	B	FS	B	B
7 A.M.	A	FS	B	B	FS	FS	B
8 A.M.	A	FS	A	B	FS	FS	B
9 A.M.	STAT	FS	A	A	FS	B	B
10 A.M.	STAT	FS	A	B	B	A	STAT
11 A.M.	FS	FS	A	A	A	B	L
NOON	FS	B	A	A	A	L	L
1 P.M.	L	B	A	A	A	L	L
2 P.M.	B	FS	B	B	B	L	B
3 P.M.	B	B	B	A	A	L	L
4 P.M.	A	A	B	B	B	L	A
5 P.M.	A	B	B	B	B	L	L
6 P.M.	L	A	B	B	B	L	FS
7 P.M.	FS	A	A	A	A	FS	L
8 P.M.	L	B	A	A	A	L	FS
9 P.M.	FS	B	A	B	A	L	L
10 P.M.	FS	B	B	B	A	L	L
11 P.M.	FS	A	A	B	L	SHELF	ANN2
MIDNIGHT	FS	L	B	A	A	SHELF	B
A.M. PEAK	A	FS	B	B	FS	B	B
P.M. PEAK	L	A	B	B	B	L	FS

"A" is our basic model, "B" is our adaptive model, and "SHELF" used time-varying splines. Details about other models are unavailable to us, but might be obtainable from Puget Power.

MAPE values are generally higher. However, the temperature forecasts for this period are also worse than usual. If the local service is unable to forecast cold spells, this implies that models such as EGRV's that rely on these forecasts will produce less satisfactory forecasts of load during such spells. It would be useful, however, to investigate why some of the other models (which also were faced with poor weather forecasts) did considerably better than the EGRV models.

6.2   The 1991–92 Forecast Results

Based on the above experience, we made a number of improvements in the model specifications. In the 1991–92 winter competition, all the models were respecified to some extent and several new models were

Table 26.3. *Mean percentage absolute forecast error for Model A*

Time	Mon	Tues	Wed	Thurs	Fri	Sat	Sun	Hourly Avg
1 A.M.	4.53	3.97	3.24	3.64	3.81	4.77	4.65	4.08
2 A.M.	4.67	4.51	3.14	4.47	4.54	4.26	5.50	4.44
3 A.M.	4.62	5.04	3.74	5.74	4.70	4.25	5.81	4.84
4 A.M.	5.10	5.08	3.75	5.74	5.01	4.54	5.96	5.03
5 A.M.	5.90	5.26	4.29	5.87	4.97	5.38	6.61	5.47
6 A.M.	5.59	5.54	4.39	4.94	5.35	6.11	7.70	5.66
7 A.M.	5.47	5.12	4.13	4.64	5.33	6.62	6.66	5.43
8 A.M.	4.89	4.47	3.21	3.89	4.45	6.49	5.90	4.76
9 A.M.	4.69	4.18	2.64	3.36	4.07	5.20	5.44	4.22
7–9 A.M.	5.02	4.59	3.32	3.96	4.61	6.10	6.00	4.80
10 A.M.	4.53	3.75	2.93	2.81	3.93	4.02	4.96	3.84
11 A.M.	5.12	3.42	3.29	3.28	3.65	4.31	5.21	4.04
12 P.M.	4.81	3.08	3.20	4.09	3.50	4.64	5.51	4.12
1 P.M.	5.31	3.13	3.55	4.43	3.80	5.47	6.16	4.55
2 P.M.	5.60	3.87	3.67	4.34	4.44	6.09	7.10	5.02
3 P.M.	5.17	4.08	4.21	4.36	6.37	6.22	6.73	5.31
4 P.M.	4.63	4.01	4.59	5.56	6.15	6.95	6.00	5.43
5 P.M.	5.11	4.10	4.48	5.21	5.92	6.77	5.88	5.36
6 P.M.	5.43	4.21	4.53	4.97	4.94	5.27	5.22	4.94
7 P.M.	5.23	3.53	3.51	3.90	3.84	4.34	4.99	4.19
4–7 P.M.	5.10	3.96	4.28	4.91	5.21	5.83	5.52	4.98
8 P.M.	5.73	5.53	2.99	3.99	3.65	4.43	5.79	4.30
9 P.M.	5.83	3.84	3.05	3.98	3.97	4.54	5.75	4.42
10 P.M.	5.33	4.06	2.75	4.16	4.38	4.43	5.77	4.40
11 P.M.	5.06	4.76	3.27	4.61	4.34	4.81	5.17	4.57
12 A.M.	4.43	5.44	5.06	4.68	4.59	5.31	5.73	5.04
Day Avg	5.12	4.25	3.65	4.44	4.57	5.22	5.84	4.73

added. Altogether now 14 models were compared. These are as labeled below:

A. ANN2
B. GJP
C. L
D. OH
E. A (EGRV's basic hour by hour model)
F. B (the adaptive version of A)
G. RAHMAN
H. SHELF
I. SMU1
J. SMU2
K. SMU3
L. SMU4
M. SMUA
N. SMUB

Table 26.4. *Mean absolute percentage error in forecast temperatures*

Time	Mon	Tues	Wed	Thurs	Fri	Sat	Sun	Hourly Av
1 A.M.	9.23	6.25	4.77	7.18	6.14	8.18	7.58	7.04
2 A.M.	10.03	6.39	4.64	7.93	7.23	7.31	8.31	7.39
3 A.M.	10.26	6.72	6.10	8.72	5.00	8.96	8.46	7.73
4 A.M.	11.09	6.42	5.54	7.51	5.63	8.78	7.78	7.52
5 A.M.	11.38	6.81	6.74	7.76	5.32	9.08	8.58	7.94
6 A.M.	12.12	7.50	6.81	7.79	5.46	10.64	8.87	8.44
7 A.M.	10.53	6.88	6.53	6.68	5.54	9.70	7.31	7.58
8 A.M.	10.14	6.04	6.01	7.70	5.41	10.89	8.01	7.74
9 A.M.	9.77	5.68	6.41	7.63	5.29	10.38	7.68	7.54
7–9 A.M.	10.15	6.20	6.32	7.33	5.41	10.32	7.67	7.62
10 A.M.	8.98	4.86	6.34	5.44	5.60	9.50	8.86	6.94
11 A.M.	8.55	5.78	6.83	6.53	7.05	9.52	7.61	7.41
12 P.M.	8.46	5.30	7.46	7.12	7.86	9.30	6.78	7.33
1 P.M.	8.62	6.01	6.20	7.09	8.03	7.03	6.04	7.00
2 P.M.	10.51	6.67	5.71	7.36	9.49	7.10	8.25	7.86
3 P.M.	9.85	7.24	6.33	7.27	9.46	8.05	7.55	7.96
4 P.M.	9.86	6.14	6.08	7.32	8.78	8.56	7.76	7.78
5 P.M.	9.37	7.07	6.28	6.82	7.81	8.08	9.54	7.85
6 P.M.	8.50	5.78	5.62	6.10	7.26	8.86	9.89	7.43
7 P.M.	9.11	6.70	6.77	6.61	7.95	7.63	10.67	7.92
4–7 P.M.	9.21	6.42	6.19	6.71	7.95	8.28	9.47	7.57
8 P.M.	9.26	8.63	7.04	8.20	8.34	8.48	10.01	8.56
9 P.M.	9.20	8.71	8.68	8.18	7.48	9.67	9.81	8.82
10 P.M.	9.85	10.18	8.46	8.37	8.03	9.63	9.52	9.14
11 P.M.	10.47	11.04	9.51	9.15	9.15	8.29	8.68	9.46
12 A.M.	10.11	10.94	9.88	8.85	7.88	8.56	8.64	9.25
Day Av	9.80	7.07	6.70	7.47	7.13	8.80	8.38	7.90

GJP used the Box–Jenkins transfer function intervention-noise methodology. SMU models are based on adaptive multi-layered feed-forward neural networks trained with back-propagation [see Brace, et al. (1993) for more details on these and on RAHMAN). The forecasts are tabulated separately for Tues–Fri, Monday and weekends. In each case the morning peak, afternoon peak and daily mean absolute percentage errors (MAPE) are computed and tabulated by Puget Power in Table 26.5. Of the six weekday tabulations, F (our adaptive Model B) was the best model for the four peak periods and was beaten only by E (our basic Model A) for the Tues–Fri daily average. Several models did slightly better for the Monday average. Our basic Model A (E in Table 26.5) was the second best model for each of the peak periods.

On weekends the results are also good but not overwhelming. The adaptive model B (F in Table 26.5) is best for weekend afternoons and the basic Model A (E in Table 26.5) falls slightly into third behind L. For

Table 26.5. *Mean absolute percentage error (MAPE) for 1991–92*

	A	B	C	D	E	F	G	H	I	J	K	L	M	N
Tue–Fri														
A.M.	3.70	4.22	3.40	4.40	3.32	**3.18**	4.05	3.86	4.83	4.65	4.18	4.09	3.86	4.09
P.M.	4.00	4.25	3.57	5.13	3.29	**3.28**	3.67	4.04	4.77	4.55	4.35	3.89	5.53	5.53
Daily	2.77	3.28	2.73	3.59	**2.45**	2.55	2.68	2.87	2.91	3.06	2.57	2.65	2.88	2.85
Weekend														
A.M.	NA	6.05	5.68	NA	7.86	6.38	5.69	5.59	5.71	5.71	5.71	**4.66**	5.71	
P.M.	NA	4.73	4.10	NA	4.13	**3.82**	4.67	4.65	4.21	4.21	4.21	4.21	6.35	6.35
Daily	NA	3.47	3.56	NA	4.15	3.53	3.66	3.80	3.64	3.64	3.64	3.64	3.42	**3.30**
Monday														
A.M.	6.71	6.36	6.05	6.92	5.99	**5.75**	7.83	6.34	6.32	6.45	6.38	6.19	6.21	6.19
P.M.	5.11	5.62	4.94	6.54	4.74	**4.64**	6.53	5.70	5.60	5.86	5.39	5.59	7.70	7.70
Daily	5.81	4.60	5.26	6.40	4.97	4.63	5.75	5.24	4.61	4.85	**4.49**	4.51	5.19	4.95

Entries in bold type refer to the best model for that period.

weekend mornings SMU4 (labelled L in Table 5) was the best, and for overall average, model N, SMUB is the best. However, it is also the worst for weekend afternoons, so there is some instability there.

In order to understand further the strengths and weaknesses of the EGRV models, we did our own decomposition of MAPE by hour for each model and mean percentage error (not presented here). The latter measure does not take absolute values and therefore can be positive or negative. If the forecasts are biased then the MPE will exhibit the bias. Both models have particular biases on Monday from hours 1 through to 7. These show up in high MAPE and in the much higher Monday averages. By the time of the peak hours, the biases are over so that the weaker performance on Mondays than other days can basically be attributed to these hours. Since the problem shows up in a bias it should be possible to correct it through respecification of these equations. A similar set of biases occur, particularly in A on Sunday and to some extent on Saturday mornings. These however, extend over into the peak period resulting in inferior peak performance.

Thus, the overall analysis of the forecast errors indicates that the weaknesses of these models are in the very early mornings of Saturday, Sunday, and Monday. If a model is to be inaccurate somewhere, this seems as good a place as anywhere. The overall impression especially in comparison with the other models is of extraordinarily good performance which could possibly be improved even a little more. Although a detailed analysis of cold snaps was not carried out with the 1991–92 data, preliminary study indicates that the days when the model does not do well also coincide with days when the weather service forecasts were not very accurate. This was the pattern noticed earlier in the 1990–91 data.

7.   CONCLUSIONS

We have developed a simple and flexible set of models for hourly load forecasting and probabilistic forecasting. These have performed extremely well in tightly controlled experiments against a wide range of alternative models. When the participants were able to revise their models along the lines of our successes of 1990–91, they still were unable to equal the performance of the hour by hour model presented here. Although the model has many parameters, the estimation method is very simple; just ordinary least squares with general order serial correlation. It should be possible for other utilities to adapt this approach for their use. An econometrician familiar with the use of least squares software should be capable of handling general order autoregressive errors. Data handling and forecasting can be done using spreadsheet software, although more user-friendly code can be written directly.

A useful extension to the present project would be to use optimum combination techniques that are likely to be superior to individual forecasts. Another useful extension would be to use "switching-regime" techniques, especially during cold-snaps. Thus, when forecasts are going badly during abnormally cold spells a different model will "kick-in" that, hopefully, will yield better forecasts. This approach has been investigated by Deutsch et al. (1994).

ACKNOWLEDGEMENTS

We are grateful for the financial support of the Electric Power Research Institute (Project No. RP2919-04) and to its project manager Phillip Hummel. Thanks are also due to Peter Cleary, former manager of the project for EPRI, for his encouragement and enthusiastic support of the project, and to Allan Mitchem of the Virginia Electric Power Company for sharing the details of their hour by hour model. We also acknowledge the invaluable help of our research assistants Chor Yiu Sin, Megan Werner, and Diana Weinhold. Finally, thanks are also due to the referees of this paper.

REFERENCES

Ackerman, G. (1985), Short-term load prediction for electric-utility control of generating units, in: D. W. Bunn and E. D. Farmer, eds., *Comparative Models for Electrical Load Forecasting*, Wiley, New York.

Brace, M. C., V. Bui–Nguyen and J. Schmidt (1993), Another look at forecast accuracy of neural networks, Paper presented to the Second International Forum on the Applications of Neural Networks to Power Systems, April 19–22, 1993, at the Meji University, Yokohama, Japan.

Bunn, D. W. and E. D. Farmer, 1985, Comparative Models for Electrical Load Forecasting (Wiley, New York).

Deutsch, M., C. W. J. Granger, and T. Teräsvita (1994), The combination of forecasts using changing weights. *International J. of Forecasting* 10, 47–57.

Electric Power Research Institute (1977), Forecasting and Modeling Time-of-day and Seasonal Electricity Demands, EPRI EA-578-SR, Palo Alto, California.

Electric Power Research Institute (1993), Probabilistic Methods in Forecasting Hourly Loads EPRI TR-101902, Palo Alto, California.

Gupta, P. C. (1985), Adaptive short-term forecasting of hourly loads using weather information, in: D. W. Bunn and E. D. Farmer, eds., *Comparative Models for Electrical Load Forecasting*, Wiley, New York.

Harvey, A. and S. J. Koopman (1993), Forecasting hourly electricity demand using time-varying splines. *J. Amer. Stat. Assoc.* 88, 1228–1237.

Ramanathan, R., C. W. J. Granger and R. Engle (1985), Two-Step Modeling for Short-Term Forecasting, in: D. W. Bunn and E. D. Farmer, eds., *Comparative Models for Electrical Load Forecasting*, Wiley, New York.

Ramanathan, R. (1995), Introductory Econometrics with Applications, Third Edition, (The Dryden Press, Forth Worth, Texas).

Schneider, A. M., T. Takenawa and D. A. Schiffman (1985), 24-hour electric utility load forecasting, in: D. W. Bunn and E. D. Farmer, eds., *Comparative Models for Electrical Load Forecasting*, Wiley, New York.

Theil, H. (1971), *Principles of Econometrics*, John Wiley, New York.

Index

For EU product safety concerns, contact us at Calle de José Abascal, 56–1°,
28003 Madrid, Spain or eugpsr@cambridge.org.

www.ingramcontent.com/pod-product-compliance
Ingram Content Group UK Ltd.
Pitfield, Milton Keynes, MK11 3LW, UK
UKHW012155180425
457623UK00007B/49